Public Order Offences

Public Order Offences

John Marston, LLB, Solicitor
Principal Lecturer in the Department of Law,
De Montfort University, Leicester

Paul Tain, BA, MJUR
Stipendiary Magistrate

LAW & TAX

ISBN 0752 001124

Published by
FT Law & Tax
21–27 Lamb's Conduit Street
London WC1N 3NJ

A Division of Pearson Professional Limited

Associated offices
Australia, Belgium, Canada, Hong Kong, India, Japan, Luxembourg, Singapore, Spain, USA

First published 1995

A CIP catalogue record for this book is available from the British Library.

Printed in Great Britain by Hartnolls Ltd, Bodmin, Cornwall

Contents

Preface

Our intention has been to provide a useful examination of the major public order offences and powers. The text is directed at those involved in the criminal justice system including solicitors, barristers, clerks to the justices, the police and so on. We examine in detail chiefly the Public Order Act 1986 and the Criminal Justice and Public Order Act 1994 and, in doing so, have been able to draw upon the solid base of two earlier books written in response to these major legislative provisions. We have sought to broaden the treatment to include analysis of a number of other offences and the common law preventive powers, which retain remarkable vitality.

The authors acknowledge that what should or should not fall within the scope of 'public order law' admits of no ready definition, indeed much of the current legislation tends to confuse rather than enlighten the debate as to what should properly be included. Much of the core material is easily identifiable and would be agreed by most interested parties as representing public order offences and powers. Thereafter the level of disagreement will rise. Of course, what may be included will be dependent upon available space. Thus, bearing in mind relevant factors, in our estimation there is no place for the mass of legislation in relation to activities on the highway, or offences contrary to public morality or decency, or criminal libel or blasphemy, nor offences against national security.

Tempting as it might have been to delve into every interesting nook and cranny, we have tried to identify offences commonly associated with public disorder and to examine these in such a way as to be useful to those involved in the criminal justice system. We have focused on the criminal law aspects and have been unable to include analysis of the private law implications, important though these undoubtedly are.

We do not claim to be encyclopaedic; but we hope that we have been able to address those matters selected in a way which will provide ready answers to commonly encountered problems. That there is always scope for further research is the lot of all lawyers. We apologise if we have omitted topics which others would have included or have included those which others would have omitted.

Our families have displayed understanding and forbearance and we thank them for this. Our publishers have shown encouragement and skill, not the least in the preparation of the table of cases and index, for which we are grateful. Errors and omissions are to be laid at our door. We have attempted to state the law as we understand it at 1 September 1995.

John Marston
Paul Tain

October 1995

List of Abbreviations

CDA 1971	Criminal Damage Act 1971
CJA 1972	Criminal Justice Act 1972
CJA 1988	Criminal Justice Act 1988
CJPOA	Criminal Justice and Public Order Act 1994
CLA 1967	Criminal Law Act 1967
CLA 1977	Criminal Law Act 1977
ECHR	European Convention on Human Rights
PACE	Police and Criminal Evidence Act 1984
POA 1936	Public Order Act 1936
POA 1986	Public Order Act 1986
TULR(C)A 1992	Trade Union and Labour Relations (Consolidation) Act 1992

Table of Cases

Table of Statutes

Table of Statutory Instruments

Table of European Provisions

Chapter 1

Introduction

This book covers criminal law relating to public order. It does not focus on civil law, although there are references to civil law matters where they directly affect particular aspects of the criminal law. Nor does it go into the psychology or sociology of group action in public disorder, or examine the methods used by public authorities to police protest. Nevertheless where such matters are directly relevant to the criminal law context, they are reviewed to that extent.

1.1 History

The report of Lord Scarman (or Sir Leslie Scarman, as he then was) into the Red Lion Square disorders (a violent assault on a police cordon leading to a riot on 15 June 1974) (Cmnd 5919) began in the following terms:

> There is a case—some would think a strong case—for codifying our law as to public order so as to ensure that the fundamental human rights set out in the United Nations Declaration of 1948 and the European Convention of 1951 are protected by statute . . . the real issue is . . . whether our law confers upon those whose duty it is to maintain public order sufficient powers without endangering the right of peaceful protest.

Twenty years later substantial changes were made to public order law in the Criminal Justice and Public Order Act 1994 (CJPOA), leaving the same central questions unresolved.

Lord Scarman went on to define the historic requirements of the common law in relation to public order:

> There must be disorder or the threat of disorder before police powers may be used: but when they are needed the powers exist, and are strong. Moreover it is a policeman's duty to use them . . . The law requires of the citizen as the necessary condition for the exercise of his rights that he respects the rights of others, even though he may fundamentally disagree with them and totally disapprove of their policies.

He then set out the public order dilemma arising from the question of protest in a passage cited in the Green Paper issued prior to the Public Order Act 1986 (Cmnd 7891).

> Civilised living collapses—it is obvious—if public protest becomes violent protest or public order degenerates into the quietism imposed by a successful oppression. The fact that those who at any one time are concerned to secure the tranquillity of the streets are likely to be the majority must not lead us to deny the protestors their opportunity to march: the fact that the protestors are desperately sincere and are exercising a fundamental human right must not lead us to overlook the rights of the majority.

The focus of Lord Scarman was protest and demonstration. Yet the law upon which he and the legislature concentrates has wider implications, incorporating individual acts of small-scale criminality as well as the definition of complex issues relating to the right or freedom to protest and the right of peaceful passage.

Until 1986 the serious offences affecting public order were the common law offences of riot, rout, affray and unlawful assembly. They were complex and archaic, out of touch with developing society. Covering the lower end of the scale of public order matters, s 5 of the Public Order Act 1936 had relied upon breach of the peace, rendering the Act less effective than was required as regards powers in relation to processions. The main aim of the 1936 Act had been to counteract the growth of political violence associated with quasi-military groups. The Public Order Act (POA) 1986 placed in statutory form the serious public order offences and removed the reliance on breach of the peace for the less serious offences. It left in force the preventive powers of the police and the powers of the lower courts in relation to binding over to be of good behaviour or to keep the peace. Both of these are reviewed in Chapter 2. The 1986 Act regulated processions, certain assemblies, aspects of racial hatred and violence at sporting events.

The CJPOA 1994, in so far as it concerned public order, dealt with a range of public order issues which had developed since the 1986 Act. The principal themes were that lawful activity should be protected and interference with it penalised and similarly that quiet enjoyment of property should be protected and interference with it penalised. Another theme was that legal provision for assemblies and processions should be developed to reflect current circumstances. In relation to protest it modified the position between the majority and the minority of sincere protestors that Lord Scarman had referred to by increasing the extent to which regulation impinged on ill-defined rights to protest, both in the area of processions and assemblies, and in relation to protestors such as hunt saboteurs who had taken their protest to the hunting field.

1.2 Dilemmas of public order law

While it may be necessary to have a body of law dealing with public order, there are inherent difficulties in the UK in resolving precisely where public order law fits into the system. If public order is isolated from all else, it is difficult to relate the preventive powers which enable interventions by individual members of the community to the statutory offences of riot and violent disorder which have precise requirements and definitions. These ancient preventive powers lie alongside serious offences recently defined by statute. There is no all embracing statutory code placing each aspect of public order law in context with the rest of the subject.

In a legal system where the majority of public order offences are statutory, it is odd that the lower courts should still have the special power to bind over despite the Law Commission's recommendation that the power should be abolished and not replaced (see 2.12.10). Given that laws should be comprehensible to the community, the recurrent difficulty of identifying acceptable public order conduct against a background of clear regulation suggests that significant changes are still needed.

The statutory offences embrace such a wide range of conduct that the Acts deal with different classes of behaviour. At the higher end of the scale are offences involving serious community disruption. At their worst, these offences strike at the root of the proper organisation of the community. At the lower end is conduct by an individual which is essentially nothing more than disorderly.

If a man threatens another with unlawful violence it is an offence. That conduct has the elements of involving conduct by one person, aimed at another, which will be clearly wrong to most observers. It does not matter that the offence is governed by a public order law statute as opposed to a statute dealing with offences against the person. It is something that most people understand as unlawful. Much more difficult to comprehend are the more serious group public order offences where an individual may appear to do nothing, yet by his presence and defined participation he may be committing an offence. This risks offending the public who may not be able to identify that the person is acting unlawfully. Indeed the public may believe that inappropriate legal assumptions of complicity are being made to the detriment of an individual accidentally in the wrong place at the wrong time. Or, conversely, the public may regard presence as being tantamount to participation and sufficient to condemn even an accidental presence at the scene of disorder. Moreover, perceptions of public disorder are likely to depend on an individual's view of the particular group involved in the protest or demonstration.

This diversity of legal provision affects both those charged with policing the community and the community itself. The responsible authorities have to determine what approach to take in varying circumstances and where to draw the line between permitted and proscribed conduct. Decisions as to when to impose conditions on processions or assemblies and when to impose an order prohibiting processions or trespassory assemblies are not necessarily perceived as objective assessments of public safety and other appropriate considerations. The use of the statutory powers will inevitably be regarded by some of those affected as abuse. If the authorities pitch their interventions at a level that the community dislikes, they risk falling into disrepute with sections of the public, and the statutory scheme becomes less effective. It is in the use of discretions to set boundaries for protest, movement and assembly that the greatest risk to public faith in the system of laws lies. In a time when television cameras are everywhere and news is often broadcast live, the importance of ensuring that the policing of public order is appropriate to the context cannot be overstated.

1.3 Perception of rights

Although the UK has no bill of rights, there is a view that such an assertion of rights would be helpful to the community. Many people believe that they have readily ascertainable rights in relation to protest, assembly, movement and speech. In reality the position in the UK is that the individual is generally permitted to do that which is not proscribed by statute or common law. What a person is permitted to do is not set out and he may test the interpretation of the legal provisions to see if he is straying into something which is contrary to law. If it is not, he may do whatever it is, but if he is wrong then he commits an offence. Establishing what can and cannot be done is a matter of trial and error. Taking, for example, the public right to pass along a public right of way, if the person uses the right of way for any purpose other than passage, he becomes a trespasser (*Harrison v Rutland* (1893)). If he stands and protests, he becomes a trespasser in civil law. A hundred years after that decision, however, the public at large are unlikely to be conscious of these legal refinements.

Restrictions which prevent a person being hit or his goods being taken are easily understood, but the restrictions which keep peace between neighbours and prevent large gatherings are much less easily understood, particularly by the innocent neighbour or the member of the large gathering with an honourable motive. If a bill of rights were created, it would not only set out the rights of the individual, as an individual and as part of a group, but also the legitimate restrictions on the specified individual freedoms. If the European Convention on Human Rights or the Canadian Bill of Rights were taken as guidelines for a UK bill of rights, the statement of general rights and restrictions would convey little to an average lay person, and the US position even less.

Lord Scarman intimated that a right to protest existed in English law and Lord Denning has spoken of 'a right to demonstrate and the right to protest on matters of public concern. These are rights which it is in the public interest that individuals should possess; and indeed they should exercise without impediment so long as no wrongful act is done' (*Hubbard v Pitt* (1975)). This was repeated in *R v Coventry City Council ex p Phoenix Aviation* (1995): 'Some protest is lawful; some alas is not. The precise point at which the right of public demonstration ends and the criminal offence of public nuisance begins may be difficult to detect' (Simon Browne LJ). These expressions of principle fit uneasily, however, with the judgement in *Duncan v Jones* (1936), which held that 'the right of assembly . . . is nothing more than a view taken by the court of the individual liberty of the subject'.

In 1949 Sir Alfred (later Lord) Denning, sought to define freedom in his Hamlyn Trust lectures: 'By personal freedom I mean the freedom of every law abiding citizen to think what he will, to say what he will, and to go where he will on his lawful occasions without let or hindrance from any other persons'. Even in 1949 freedoms or rights were subject to community disciplines for the protection of individuals, and the potential for the improper exercise of discretions was also reviewed by Lord Denning with a formula which some might view differently now. He stated that 'the police are not regarded here as the strong arm of the executive, but as the friends of the people . . . and no one is inclined to resist the authority of the police, because it can be safely assumed to be lawfully used'. Today, when policemen are called upon to police public order in all its myriad forms, these words might be accepted less universally. They express what was to become a crucial problem for police forces, that of appearing to be the strong arm of the executive.

The willingness of the courts to preserve rights or balance freedoms is a vital ingredient in public order law. As the *Phoenix Aviation* case demonstrates, the touchstone for the courts tends to be the rule of law; see also *Bennett v Horseferry Road Magistrates' Court* (1993), albeit in a different context. The judicial control over discretions exercised by the police or the executive must be real in order to preserve the confidence of the community. Although significant cases are generally dealt with by the higher courts, it is the lower courts, in particular magistrates' courts, who face the difficult task of questioning the discretions of individual police officers (see *Piddington v Baker* (1960)).

1.4 European Convention on Human Rights

The European Convention on Human Rights was ratified in 1951 and came into force in 1953. It has not been incorporated into UK domestic law and operates as a treaty under international law. It cannot be enforced *directly* in the UK. The effectiveness of the convention in the UK is dependent upon the extent to which the government is prepared to comply with decisions of the European Court when non-compliance with the convention is proved. There are no domestic legal sanctions which can be invoked against a government not complying with a European Court decision. Generally, however, the UK government has complied with such decisions, usually by way of legislative changes.

Although the convention is not directly enforceable in the UK, it has become part of the currency of dialogue about rights and freedoms as European ties develop. Article 11 provides for freedom of assembly and association with others:

> 1. Everyone has the right to freedom of peaceful assembly and to freedom of association with others, including the right to form and to join trade unions for the protection of his interests.
> 2. No restriction shall be placed on the exercise of these rights other than such as are prescribed by law and are necessary in a democratic society, for the prevention of disorder or crime for the protection of health or morals or for the protection of the rights and freedoms of others. This Article shall not prevent the imposition of lawful restrictions on the exercise of these rights by members of the armed forces, of the police or of the administration of the State.

The Standing Advisory Commission on Human Rights considered the arguments for and against a bill of rights for the UK (Cmnd 7009). Amongst eight arguments in favour were the following:

> 4. A Bill of Rights would encourage a more actively and socially responsive judicial role in protecting basic rights and freedoms: it would alter the judicial method of law making so as to enable the courts to recognise the fundamental importance of certain values and the relationship between them.
> 5. The enactment of a Bill of Rights in this country would enable the UK to be manifestly in conformity with its international obligations and would also enable the citizen to obtain redress from UK courts without needing, except in the last resort, to have recourse to the European Commission in Strasbourg.

The Commission also set out the arguments against a bill of rights. Amongst eight arguments was the following:

> 2. A Bill of Rights would create expectations which could not be satisfied in practice. It would be regarded as a panacea for all grievances

> whereas its real value (if any) would be only a limited one. It would be least effective when it was most needed: ie to protect fundamental rights and freedoms against powerful currents of intolerance, passion, usurpation and tyranny.

Whether the European Convention will in due course be incorporated into domestic law as a form of bill of rights is a matter for continuing speculation.

1.5 Aspects of group disorder

There has been considerable analysis of the freedoms of individual citizens and the responses of groups as they exercise these freedoms.

> There might be relevance to the present day in studies of the response of the authorities to potential trouble. Where these were inept, shortsighted or limited by the absence of appropriate means of enforcing order the result could be disastrous. For many incidents it is possible to trace how protest turned into violence or an attack on property became a bloody battle as a consequence of the readily available policing force. . . It was the local yeomanry who turned the Manchester reform meeting in the St Peter's fields at which all the leaders had called for a respectable and peaceful occasion into the bloody incident of 'Peterloo' (Norman Tutt, *Violence*, DHSS Social Work Development Group, 1976, p 43).

The policing of protests has a historic dimension. Crowd problems are hardly new either:

> Although collective behaviour in crowds is usually sensible and inconspicuous, the potential stupidity, irrationality and childlike behaviour of the crowd have been noted by many observers . . . In such situations a mob is itself dehumanised but at the same time dehumanises others so that remorseless violence can occur without shame or guilt feelings (Tutt, p 187).

Public order may be prejudiced by the individual, but it is group activity that is the primary concern and has the greatest potential for short-term damage and long-term disruption to community security. The way in which groups respond has been analysed:

> The explanation rests on the premise that, where social strains are present and conditions are structurally conducive, a 'generalised hostile belief' among the disaffected and thence a 'hostile outburst' occur. Structural conduciveness is characterised by (1) the presence of an agency to which the blame for an unsatisfactory state of affairs may be attached; (2) the absence or failure of grievance channels; and (3) the possibility of effective communication among the aggrieved (D Waddington, *Contemporary Issues in Public Disorder*, Routledge, 1992, p 12).

Significant group disorders have immediate as well as longer-term causes. The violence on the Broadwater Farm estate in London in 1985, for example, was triggered in the short term by the death of illegal immigrant Mrs Jarrett, whatever the longer-term background (Waddington, p 91).

1.6 Policing

Police powers and the criminal law tend to follow particular problems. They are often the government's response to problems, eg the provisions of the 1986 Public Order Act relating to disorderly behaviour, tampering with goods and illegal encampments followed a spate of incidents. Statutory powers for the police in relation to demonstrations, processions, assemblies and other gatheringss have widened over recent years. The very existence of powers has been sufficient to cause objection. A variety of groups have opposed the CJPOA, on the grounds that it interferes with the freedom of movement of new age travellers, or that it revokes the right of silence, or that it prevents the activities of hunt protestors. All these groups voiced anxiety about the encroachment of state powers on the individual's freedom. When those powers are essentially discretionary, much depends on the way they are used in practice and controlled by the courts, as well as on the developing culture of the community. The widespread use of video surveillance at football matches and criminal cases has in the event created little visible anxiety that the cameras are reducing individual freedom. Instead they are seen as protective. This is very much a matter of how they are described and perceived:

> London demonstrations are routinely monitored by sixty cameras placed at symbolic locations, enabling an area of 200 square miles to be covered by the Scotland Yard operation room . . . The resolution of these cameras is good enough to pick out number plates or the faces of individual demonstrators (Waddington, p 184).

The right to express dissent at Hyde Park, which has existed since 1872 and is perceived as inalienable, has evolved and the police now see a need to use video cameras to monitor the expression of dissent. This follows complaints about the extremist and threatening nature of some of the speeches and comments of various groups using the Hyde Park forum.

Lord Scarman expressed the view that 'the sombre lesson of recent British history is that the balance between public order and individual liberty . . . is in its operation the business of the police' (*Papers of 7th Commonwealth Law Conference*, 1983). Community policing was one method recommended by Lord Scarman. As the maintenance of public order depends on the relationship between the community and those who police it, the use of 'beat officers' and significant community liaison were seen as a way of improving community and police relationships to the advantage of public order. The extent to which they have worked is a matter for conjecture, as there has subsequently been a variety of substantial public order difficulties.

A single violent demonstration without public support has the power to rally public support behind what might otherwise be seen as too restrictive legislation:

> the few unpopular and highly inconvenient demonstrations have already produced, in recent months, demands for tighter legal control and these in turn threaten to force the hand of the law to the detriment of the freedom of expression (VT Bevan, 'Protest and Public Order', [1979] PL 163).

1.7 Developing police roles

Whether or not police officers prefer a wide discretion or clear and specific offences, their discretions appear to be widening progressively from their common law preventive powers, through the POA 1986 and the CJPOA. Police discretion has developed since 1986 when the police were given powers to condition marches and assemblies in order to avoid serious disruption, through to the 1994 Act which gives them powers to direct people away from specified open air parties, the revised powers of search and the power to place a cordon sanitaire around ancient monuments to prevent gatherings. All of these features show the police being required to make judgments about events before they have happened. Since these judgments may reflect a particular view of society and impinge on groups or individuals who take a different view, the police risk being seen in a political role supportive of one point of view as opposed to another.

The issue of fox hunting imposes on the police an unenviable role. On the one hand, the law acknowledges a 'right' of protest, on the other, the protection of the exercise of lawful rights is the foundation of the aggravated trespass provisions in the 1994 Act. Caught between the two extremes are the police, attempting to find a balance. Their position has always been difficult in that they may be seen as an arm of the executive when part of their function is to help preserve the individual's rights by the proper exercise of discretion in relation to matters of civil liberty. Their dilemma has not changed; it was described in the Canadian case *R v Zwicker* (1938):

> The well known saying from Gilbert and Sullivan that 'A policeman's lot is not a happy one' is true—at times, but is also true with regard to public officials. They must expect more or less so called abuse. . . In this country a

> policeman is a peace officer, and his duty is not only to the public generally but to every individual citizen, and to protect that citizen, and to protect him as far as possible, even against his own weakness and not to hail him before the magistrate for every foolish thing he does.

The danger of police officers misapplying their discretion is reviewed in Home Office Research Study 135, *Policing Low Level Disorder: Police Use of s 5 Public Order Act 1986*. This study of the use of s 5 was designed to consider fears that the section was 'used where the police rather than vulnerable members of the public were the victims; and its use in a wide variety of situations prompted concern that the provision might fall into disrepute in the way that the former "sus" laws had done by their disproportionate use against ethnic minorites'.

There is a potential for problems arising from the use of police discretions in this arena and the summary of the study identifies the police as commonly using s 5 as a mechanism for enforcing respect for the police as opposed to using it to protect the vulnerable in the community:

> In conclusion, the report raises the questions about the extent of police intervention in incidents of low level disorder and whether it is always appropriate to use section 5 to make arrests. First, although the behaviour leading to section 5 arrests is often genuinely offensive, judged by any standard, it is for consideration whether in some cases the conduct described is serious enough to cause real offence to those members of the public present or the police themselves. . . There is a danger that undiscriminating use of section 5 will bring it into disrepute. The section 5 provision will be most efficacious if it is reserved for precisely those cases for which it is intended: in which vulnerable members of the public are genuinely likely to, or do, suffer from offensive behaviour.

1.8 The future

Public order law is not codified and indeed is probably incapable of codification. Nor is it comprehensible to the community at large. Some see the adoption of a bill of rights as the essential means of clarifying the right to demonstrate and assemble and redressing the current imbalance between the rights of the individual or groups and the state. The opposite view, however, is taken by others who support the uniquely British way of dealing with rights and freedoms, which was argued by Dicey:

> the principles of private law have with us been so extended as to determine the position of the Crown and of its servants; thus the constitution is the result of the ordinary law of the land (AV Dicey, *An Introduction to the Study of the Law of the Constitution*, 10th edn, Macmillan, 1959, p 203).

Supporters of a bill of rights would claim that this approach has manifestly failed for the past 100 years and was probably always a failure.

Our law is constantly changing as society changes. What was perfectly tolerable 50 or 100 years ago may be perceived differently now, in the field of public order law as much as any other area of law.

Chapter 2

Common Law Preventive Powers and Duties

2.1 Introduction

The Public Order Act 1986 and the Criminal Justice and Public Order Act 1994 do not constitute a comprehensive code on the law relating to public order. While certain common law offences have been abolished and certain statutory provisions have been repealed or amended, much of the pre-existing law remains intact. In this respect it is particularly important to note that the common law powers to deal with or prevent breaches of the peace are unaffected by either Act, and indeed specifically preserved by the 1986 Act (see s 40(4)). This approach is in line with that taken in ss 17, 24 and 26 of the Police and Criminal Evidence Act 1984; powers to arrest for breaches of the peace are unaffected and powers to enter premises to deal with breaches of the peace are expressly preserved. Consequently, it is necessary to review the common law powers to prevent or deal with breaches of the peace.

2.2 Preventive powers: general

It will often be the case that the common law preventive powers arise in the context of an offence under s 51 of the Police Act 1964 (assault or wilful obstruction of a constable acting in the execution of his duty), or in an action for damages for trespass to the person. Whether a police officer is acting in the execution of his duty will often be answered by asking whether or not he is acting to control a breach of the peace; that this elementary point is often overlooked can be seen in the House of Lords decision in *Lavin v Albert* (1982).

The preventive powers are available to ordinary citizens and the police, and reasonable force may be used in support of those powers. A constable who is acting within this preventive capacity is within the execution of his duty for the purposes of s 51(1) and (3) of the Police Act

1964 (assaulting and wilfully obstructing a constable in the execution of his duty). Assault or wilful obstruction of a citizen assisting a police officer will also be an offence contrary to s 51.

In circumstances where a constable is doing something which at law he is not compelled to do, he may still be acting in the execution of his duty, all the more so if he anticipates a breach of the peace: see *Coffin v Smith* (1980) (police officers attending a youth club whose leader was ejecting youths were acting in the execution of their duty), doubting *R v Prebble* (1858) (police officer clearing licensed premises not acting in execution of his duty where there had been no actual or threatened breach of the peace). Steps taken in performance of the preventive duty will constitute a defence to any civil action which may be brought against the constable or citizen.

Ordinarily, where the legality of police intervention will be justified by direct evidence, but where a serious disturbance involving breaches of the peace is taking place, the court may draw the inference that an attempted arrest by an unidentified police officer is lawful and accordingly interference with that arrest by another person amounts to an offence contrary to s 51 of the Police Act 1964 (*Plowden v DPP* (1991)). Such inferences may not be drawn where police officers involved are readily identifiable and direct evidence to support the legality of the original arrest is available (*Riley v DPP* (1990); see also *Chapman v DPP* (1989)).

2.3 Powers and duties in connection with a breach of the peace

Section 40(4) of the 1986 Act is clear:

> Nothing in this Act affects the common law powers in England and Wales to deal with or prevent a breach of the peace.

The full range of preventive powers based upon actual or apprehended breaches of the peace is thus preserved. It is important to note that despite the development of wider powers of arrest in the Police and Criminal Evidence Act 1984, both the arrest powers and the preventive powers in connection with actual or apprehended breaches of the peace will continue to play an important role in the policing of public disorder.

The common law imposes a duty on all citizens to suppress actual breaches of the peace. This duty is of ancient origin and is illustrated by clear and uncompromising statements in the *Bristol Riots* case (1832), *R v Pinney* (1832) and *R v Kennett* (1781). The authoritative modern statement of the duty in respect of both actual and apprehended breaches of the peace is found in Lord Diplock's speech in *Lavin v Albert* (1982):

> . . . every citizen in whose presence a breach of the peace is being, or reasonably appears to be about to be, committed has the right to take reasonable steps to make the person who is breaking or threatening to break the peace refrain from doing so; and those reasonable steps in appropriate cases will include detaining him against his will. At common law this is not only the right of every citizen, it is also his duty, although, except in the case of a citizen who is a constable, it is a duty of imperfect obligation.

In *R v Pinney* the court considered the obligations of a public officer, but more general observations were made:

> The King's subjects are bound to be assistant to them [magistrates] in suppressing the riot, when reasonably warned.

And, in the *Charge to the Bristol Grand Jury* (1832) it was said that

> by common law every person may lawfully endeavour of his own authority and without any warrant or sanction of the magistrate, to suppress a riot by every means in his power . . . it is his bounden duty of a good subject . . . to perform this to the utmost of his ability. If the riot be general and dangerous he may arm himself against evil doers to keep the peace.

In the light of modern policing methods, the wider comments in the older cases as to the duty of the citizens to suppress riots may now be otiose, but the importance of the duty to deal with breaches of the peace is that it is placed upon every citizen and that in so acting to suppress breaches of the peace police officers, and others, will be acting lawfully.

2.4 Duty to assist a constable

It is an offence at common law for a citizen to fail to come to the assistance of a constable when that constable sees a breach of the peace and there is reasonable necessity for calling on the citizen to assist. The offence is an extension of the duty to deal with or prevent breaches of the peace. In *R v Brown* (1841) the court said that 'It is no unimportant matter that the Queen's subject should assist the officers of the law, when duly required to do so, in preserving the public peace . . .' and that 'every man is bound to set a good example to others by doing his duty in preserving the public peace'.

It seems likely that the offence will extend to occasions where the constable apprehends an imminent breach of the peace. The appropriate *mens rea* is unclear. There is a defence of physical impossibility or lawful excuse, although the scope of the defence is uncertain. See *R v Brown* (1841), *R v Sherlock* (1886), *R v Waugh* (1876). The Royal Commission on Criminal Procedure (Cmnd 8092) indicated that there have been prosecutions for this offence in modern times and cited one example from

Gwent where a police officer was attacked by a group whilst arresting another person for being drunk and disorderly. The constable called upon a passer-by to come to his assistance but he failed to do so. The passer-by was fined £50 in respect of the offence. Where a person is assisting a constable acting in the execution of his duty, then the offences under s 51 of the Police Act 1964 are relevant.

2.5 Definition of a breach of the peace

One leading writer, Brownlie, has commented that 'Rather oddly it may seem, the creation of a breach of peace is probably not a substantive crime . . . Problems of definition exist' (*Brownlie's Laws of Public Order and National Security*, 2nd edn, Butterworths, 1981). Professor Glanville Williams observed ([1954]) Crim LR 578) the 'surprising lack of authoritative definition of what one would suppose to be a fundamental concept in criminal law'. He also called it (146 JPN 199) 'A notion . . . of immense historical significance and . . .the foundation of modern rules of law. Nevertheless, the courts have failed to resolve precisely what they mean by it, largely because they are constantly under the temptation to make it do far too much work'.

In his report on the Red Lion Square disorders of 15 June 1974 (Cmnd 5919), Lord Scarman noted with apparent approval the view expressed in *Moriarty's Police Law* (1972, 21st edn) that 'The "Queen's Peace" or shortly "the peace" is the normal state of society, and any interruption of that peace and good order which ought to prevail in a civilised country is a breach of the peace'. Although as a view this may reflect the tranquillity which is generally desirable, its emphasis on mere breaches of tranquillity as amounting to breaches of the peace is too broad to be sustained. Breach of the peace was referred to by the draftsman of the Draft Criminal Code as 'a somewhat vague notion' and the suggested formulation, which was based on *R v Howell below*, was

> (4) A breach of the peace occurs when, by unlawful violence, harm is done to a person, or in his presence his property, or a person fears on reasonable grounds that unlawful violence likely to cause such harm is imminent.

The 1986 Act departed from the 1936 Public Order Act and based its principal offences on the concept of 'unlawful violence', rather than on breach of the peace. However, the common law continues to depend upon this ill-defined but useful concept. In England and Wales breach of the peace is not a substantive offence, unlike in Scotland where the law recognises it as a crime.

Although the courts have consistently refused to provide a definition of breach of the peace, the Court of Appeal in *R v Howell* considered that:

> . . . there is a breach of the peace whenever harm is actually done or is likely to be done to a person or in his presence to his property or a person is in fear of being so harmed through an assault, an affray, a riot, unlawful assembly or other disturbance.

A disturbance not involving violence or the fear of violence will not itself amount to a breach of the peace, and mere noise and disturbance will be insufficient (see *R v Howell*, *Wooding v Oxley* (1839), *Hardy v Murphy* (1795), *Green v Bartram* (1830), *Jordan v Gibbon* (1863)). Noise and disturbance may provide a constable with evidence from which he may conclude that an imminent breach of the peace is likely. In the same way, a mere trespass will not amount to a breach of the peace, although there may be additional circumstances from which it might reasonably be apprehended that a breach of the peace was likely as a natural consequence of the trespass, eg continued incursions into property in the face of clearly expressed threats to use violence to resist the trespass (see *Percy v DPP* (1995)).

The statement in *R v Howell* was approved, by the Court of Appeal, in *Parkin v Norman* (1982) where it was preferred to the dictum of Lord Denning MR in *R v Chief Constable for Devon and Cornwall ex p Central Electricity Generating Board* (1982), whose observations are too wide for general application:

> There is a breach of the peace whenever a person who is lawfully carrying out his work is unlawfully and physically prevented by another from doing it . . . if anyone unlawfully and physically obstructs the workers, by lying down or chaining himself to a rig or the like, he is guilty of a breach of the peace.

Although there is scope for accepting the first part of Lord Denning's dictum where the physical obstruction involves actual or threatened personal violence, passive obstruction cannot of itself be a breach of the peace. Of course, such action may well give rise to a reasonable belief that there may be an imminent breach of the peace, eg where there is an attempt to force a passage and there is a belief that the physical but passive obstruction may take a more violent course. Although the remaining members of the Court of Appeal in *R v Chief Constable of Devon and Exeter ex p CEGB* did not join in with Lord Denning's dictum, there was disagreement about the exact point at which police might intervene to deal with the demonstrators in that case.

The analysis in *R v Howell* has been doubted in *Lewis v Chief Constable of Manchester* (1991) where the Court of Appeal, in a civil action, considered that an act which places a person in fear of harm is not of itself a breach of the peace but is merely the ground upon which the power of arrest is activated. The actual infliction of harm is necessary to constitute a breach of the peace. The court drew a distinction between the conditions justifying arrest and the definition of a breach of the peace, although the court acknowledged the distinction made little practical difference, and the decision may do no more than reflect the attempt in *R v Howell* to provide a distillation of relevant factors drawn from the earlier cases.

Accordingly, there is currently a close correlation between 'violence' as defined in s 8 of the 1986 Act and breach of the peace, although the latter may be more flexible in its application. For example the type of disturbance in the older cases such as *Howell v Jackson* (1834), *Ingle v Bell* (1836), *Cohen v Huskisson* (1837), *Webster v Watts* (1847) (where the breach of the peace was seen to arise from the gathering of a crowd which because of its size and general manner threatened the peace) would not readily fall within ss 1–4 of the 1986 Act in the absence of actual threats or use of violence. Certainly, since the earlier cases tend to turn on the pleadings, caution is needed when reliance is placed on the older cases, and in *R v Howell* Watkins LJ observed that 'the older cases are of considerable interest but they are not a sure guide to what the term is understood to mean today'.

The meaning of breach of the peace for the purposes of the law relating to binding over follows the same principles set out above (*Percy v DPP* (1955)). The equation, in *Everett v Ribbands* (1952), of breach of the peace with any breach of law has been disapproved (*Percy v DPP*).

2.6 Breach of the peace in a private place

A breach of the peace may occur on private premises even though no member of the general public is likely to come into the vicinity of the disturbance amounting to a breach of the peace. The point was not taken in *Wilson v Skeock* (1949) *Robson v Hallett* (1967), or in *R v Chief Constable of Devon and Exeter ex p CEGB*, where the conduct amounting to breach of the peace occurred on private property; the point was decided in *McConnell v Chief Constable of Greater Manchester* (1990). The nature of the property or the presence of the public are matters which go to the question of whether or not a breach of the peace is likely to occur as a result of a particular course of conduct (*McConnell v Chief Constable of Greater Manchester*).

2.7 Lawful action as a breach of the peace

The question of whether lawful action may constitute a breach of the peace should not be confused with the other and distinct issue of whether or not a constable may restrict or terminate a lawful activity when he reasonably apprehends an imminent breach of the peace. Lord Denning in *R v Chief Constable of Devon and Exeter ex p CEGB* seemed to suggest that lawfulness is irrelevant to the issue of whether or not a breach of the peace exists: 'But in deciding whether there is a breach of the peace . . . the law does not go into the rights and wrongs of the matter, or whether it is justified by self help or not'.

Despite this dictum, which was unsupported by the other members of the Court of Appeal, it is suggested that in the absence of unlawful violence (or threat thereof) no breach of the peace can be said to occur. In normal circumstances any exchange of violence will inevitably involve a breach of the peace, even if one of the parties is acting lawfully. In deciding whether or not there is a breach of the peace the courts are not concerned with allocating responsibility, there need only be some unlawful activity involving violence or threat thereof. Responsibility is an issue which needs to be considered only at the stage of deciding that action is reasonable and appropriate..

In *Marsh v Arscott* (1982), a struggle occurred when an individual attempted to eject police officers from his property. McCullough J remarked:

> . . . the police officers, having been told to leave, were acting unlawfully in remaining. If the defendant was using no more force than was reasonably necessary to evict them he was acting lawfully, and in arresting him the police were acting unlawfully. This violent incident amounted to a breach of the peace but it was one for which the police officers were responsible and not the defendant himself . . . Suppose . . . that the defendant's threats and use of force towards the police had been unlawful, once again there would have been a breach of the peace. In this event the defendant would have been responsible for breaching the peace. Thus, regardless of who was acting lawfully and who was acting unlawfully there was at the time of the incident a breach of the peace.

This approach can also be seen in *Joyce v Hertfordshire Constabulary* (1984). The court decided that one police officer could intervene in a struggle between the appellant and another police officer and need not be certain that there had been a lawful arrest. The court observed that 'What was going on was in fact a struggle and a breach of the peace and the rights and wrongs do not matter'. In *McBean v Parker* (1983) Dunn LJ said, of the requirement in *R v Howell* of the need for 'harm', that it seemed to him that '. . . the harm done or likely to be done must be unlawful harm'.

The problem with Lord Denning's approach is that it is difficult to see why a lawful action should be classified as a breach of the peace and therefore be susceptible to intervention. Will the ejection of a trespasser, under the common law power of self-help, be a breach of the peace where the trespasser does not struggle and reasonable force is employed? To label this a breach of the peace, and thereby excuse the intervention of police officers, is to extend inappropriately the range of breach of the peace.

Of course, this is not to say that the removal of demonstrators may not, in appropriate circumstances, give rise to a reasonable anticipation that a breach of the peace will occur. Whether it does or not was discussed somewhat inconclusively by the Court of Appeal in the *CEGB* case.

2.8 Reasonably apprehended breaches of the peace

Action may be taken not only in relation to breaches of the peace which are actually occurring but also in respect of reasonably apprehended imminent breaches of the peace. The difficulties of identifying the risk of breaches of the peace can be seen from the disparate views of the court in the *CEGB* case. Lord Denning accepted the possibility that the simplest obstruction of the Board's employees might give rise to a reasonable apprehension of a breach of the peace. But Lawton LJ did not see any risk of a breach of the peace in mere removal of the protestors:

> . . . police officers . . . cannot act unless they see a breach of the peace or have reasonable cause for suspecting that there is a real imminent risk of one occurring . . . If those obstructing do allow themselves to be removed without struggling or causing an uproar (which seems to me unlikely . . .) the police will have no reason for taking action, nor should they.

On the other hand, Templeman LJ took the view that:

> An obstructor who will not leave the site unless he is forcibly removed presents a threat and danger of a breach of the peace even if he disclaims any intention of causing a breach of the peace.

In any event, he went on to say:

> . . . the police will be entitled to intervene if an obstructor resists being carried away from the site or runs to another part of the site or tries to return to the site, thus obliging the board's representatives to seize him so that he may be permanently excluded. Such conduct by an obstructor . . . will create an imminent and serious danger of a breach of the peace for which the obstructor will be responsible and liable to arrest or removal by the police.

Whether a breach of the peace is reasonably apprehended as imminent is a question of fact, and the belief as to the imminence of the breach of the peace must not only be honest but also be founded on reasonable grounds. The courts have been reluctant to interfere with decisions of magistrates on this point: see *Piddington v Bates* (1960), *Kavanagh v Hiscock* (1974) and *Tynan v Balmer* (1966).

There must be grounds for the constable's reasonable belief. A mere statement by the constable that he anticipated a breach of the peace will be insufficient (*Piddington v Bates*). There must be a real and not merely a remote possibility of a breach of the peace (see *Piddington v Bates*). In *R v Chief Constable of Devon and Exeter ex p CEGB*, Lawton and Templeman LJJ both refer to the need for a 'real and imminent risk' or 'imminent and serious danger' of a breach of the peace. It has also been said that 'The possibility of a breach must be real to justify any preventive action. The imminence of immediacy of the threat to the peace determines what action is reasonable' (see *Moss v McLachlan* (1985)).

2.9 Arrest in respect of breach of the peace

The leading authority is *R v Howell* where Watkins J drew together many of the older authorities and remarked:

> . . . there is a power of arrest for breach of the peace where (1) a breach of the peace is committed in the presence of the person making the arrest, or (2) the arrestor reasonably believes that such a breach will be committed in the immediate future by the person arrested although he has not yet committed any breach, or (3) where a breach has been committed and it is reasonably believed that a renewal of it has been threatened.

There is also a power to arrest in fresh pursuit of someone who has committed a breach of the peace (see *R v Light* (1857), *R v Walker* (1854) and *R v Marsden* (1868)).

Arrest may be with a view to taking a person before a magistrate to be bound over or as a preliminary to a charge on a substantive offence, eg assault. A statement that the arrest is for a breach of the peace will be sufficient in either instance and will satisfy the requirements of s 28 of the Police and Criminal Evidence Act 1984 (see *R v Howell*).

Once a breach of the peace has ended and there is no danger of recurrence, the power of arrest will lapse. Arrest in such an instance is not permissible under s 25(1) of the Police and Criminal Evidence Act 1984 since breach of the peace is not of itself an offence, although the facts giving rise to the breach of the peace may reveal another offence for which arrest may be permissible under s 25 of the Police and Criminal Evidence Act 1984, or other provision.

2.9.1 Other action

The general proposition is that the citizen may take reasonable steps to deal with or prevent actual or reasonably apprehended imminent breaches of the peace. See *Lavin v Albert* where it was held that:

> . . . every citizen in whose presence a breach of the peace is being, or reasonably appears to be about to be, committed has the right to take reasonable steps to make the person who is breaking or threatening to break the peace refrain from doing so; and those reasonable steps in appropriate cases will include detaining him against his will. At common law this is not only the right of every citizen, it is also his duty, although, except in the case of a citizen who is a constable, it is a duty of imperfect obligation.

Accordingly, police officers have been held to be entitled to act in a wide variety of ways which would normally involve serious interference with the liberty of the individual. The same powers may apply where a breach of the peace is likely to be renewed (see *Price v Seeley* (1843), *Baynes v Brewster* (1841), *Timothy v Simpson* (1835)); or where there is fresh pursuit (see *R v Marsden*).

The statements in certain of the earlier cases that the preventive action should be a matter of last resort or necessity appear not to have been relied upon in more recent authorities where the reasonableness of the action appears to be the major consideration in deciding the lawfulness of the action.

2.9.2 Detention

It is permissible to restrain someone and detain him for as long as reasonable to prevent the breach of the peace or its recurrence (see *Lavin v Albert* (1982)). It seems that the person detained need not be the person seeking to use violence (*Lavin v Albert, Humphries v Connor* (1864)).

2.9.3 Entry

In connection with entry to premises, the general common law powers were abolished by s 17(5) of the Police and Criminal Evidence Act 1984, but the common law powers of entry without warrant to deal with or prevent breaches of the peace were expressly preserved by s 17(6). It is clear that there is power to enter premises to deal with breaches of the peace actually occurring: see *Robson v Hallett*. Where a constable is *unlawfully* on premises and apprehends an actual or threatened breach of the peace on the premises then that constable need not leave the premises only to re-enter lawfully (see *Robson v Hallett, Lamb v DPP* (1990)).

Where a breach of the peace is not actually occurring but is apprehended as likely to occur, there is power to enter and remain on premises of any description, whether private or public (see *McLeod v Commissioner of Police of the Metropolis* (1994), *Thomas v Sawkins* (1935), *McGowan v Chief Constable of Hull*). Although the point was not specifically in issue in *McLeod v Commissioner of Police of the Metropolis* (1994), it seems now that the power to enter and remain on premises extends to public meetings on private premises and to private meetings on private premises. The narrowest realistic view of the ambiguous and unsatisfactory decision in *Thomas v Sawkins* was that the power to enter private premises in anticipation of a breach of the peace was restricted to public meetings. The widest view of *Thomas v Sawkins* was that it extended the anticipatory power of entry to premises of all descriptions. In *McLeod v Metropolitan Police Commissioner*, Neill LJ delivering the judgment of the Court of Appeal held that the power of entry in anticipation of a breach of the peace should not be dependent upon the nature of the premises or upon the nature of any invitation offered to the public:

> . . . I am satisfied that Parliament in s 17(6) has now recognised that there is a power to enter premises to prevent a breach of the peace as a form of preventive justice. I can see no satisfactory basis for restricting that power to particular classes of premises such as those where public meetings are held. If the police reasonably believe that a breach of the peace is likely to take place on private premises, they have power to enter those premises to prevent it. The apprehension must, of course, be genuine and it must relate to the near future. . .
>
> It seems to me it is important that when exercising his power to prevent a breach of the peace a police officer should act with great care and discretion; this will be particularly important where the exercise of his power involves entering on private premises contrary to the wishes of the owners or occupiers. The officer must satisfy himself that there is a real and imminent risk of a breach of the peace, because, if the matter has to be tested in court thereafter there may be scrutiny not only of his belief at the time but also of the grounds for his belief.
>
> It may be necessary in some future case to consider how far in advance of a possible breach of the peace the right to enter arises. It will depend on the facts of the case, and on the nature and scale of the apprehended breach.

Although in the case of breaches of the peace actually occurring forced entry will be permitted, it is not clear that force may be used to compel entry in the case of the anticipatory preventive power. In the event of a constable being invited on to premises by someone with authority (see *McGowan v Chief Constable of Hull, R v Thornley*), then the constable may remain despite the revocation of that permission where there in reasonable anticipation of an imminent breach of the peace or an actual breach of the peace, and may not be ejected forcibly (*Thomas v Sawkins*).

2.9.4 Dispersal of a meeting

In *Duncan v Jones* (1935) the holding of a meeting on the highway (although not alleged to have been an obstruction of the highway) was reasonably apprehended as likely to lead to breaches of the peace. Refusal to comply with the request of the police officer to disperse amounted to a wilful obstruction of that constable (see also *O'Kelly v Harvey* (1883)). In *Duncan v Jones* it was said:

> . . . the respondent reasonably apprehended a breach of the peace. It then . . . became his duty to prevent anything which in his view would cause that breach of the peace. While he was taking steps so to prevent a reasonably apprehended breach of the peace he was wilfully obstructed by the appellant.

The use of preventive powers is frequently seen in the policing of pickets. The Code of Practice on picketing, issued under the Employment Act 1980, observes:

> 26. . . . The law gives the police discretion to take whatever measures may reasonably be considered necessary to ensure that picketing remains peaceful and orderly.
>
> 28. It is for the police to decide, taking into account all the circumstances, whether the number of pickets at any particular place is likely to lead to a breach of the peace. If a picket does not leave the picket line when asked to do so by the police, he is liable to be arrested for obstruction either of the highway or of a police officer in the execution of his duty if the obstruction is such as to cause, or be likely to cause, a breach of the peace.

For examples of cases demonstrating the application of the common law principles underlying the Code of Practice, see also *Piddington v Bates* (where the power was used to limit the number of pickets), *Kavanagh v Hiscock* (preventing pickets from approaching vehicles) and *Tynan v Balmer*, a case on public nuisance; see also *Smith v Reynolds* (1986) and *Riding v Long*.

Most recently, in the miners' strike of 1984, the anticipatory preventive powers of the police were held to extend to preventing pickets from journeying to the site of certain coal mines. At what precise stage such actions are unjustifiable will be a matter of fact. There may be some distinction between such directions being given 105 miles from a site and those given five miles from a site. In *Moss v McLachlan*, the road check was one and a half miles from two collieries and four miles from two other collieries. The road checks were lawful because of the reasonable apprehension of a breach of the peace. The police had reason to believe that striking miners stopped at road checks were on their way to picket *en masse* at one or more of the collieries and that there would be a breach of the peace should they be allowed to continue. The miners refused to obey a direction to turn back and were arrested for obstructing the police in the execution of their duty. The appellants were held to have been properly convicted since the direction had been properly given by the police acting in the execution of their duty.

2.9.5 Seizure of items

When appropriate, the discretion of constables may extend to the removal of articles designed or likely to lead to breaches of peace. In *Humphries v Connor*, the seizure of an orange lily, symbolic of a particular political persuasion and deeply provocative to a crowd of a different political view, was held to be justified because of the reasonable anticipation of a breach of the peace by the crowd. Placards, banners, flags, emblems and similar objects might be seized on this basis or directions given as to their use; see, for example, *Minto v Police* (1987) which concerned the use of a loud hailer. Breach of these directions would amount to wilful obstruction of a constable in the execution of his duty contrary to s 51(3) of the Police Act 1964.

2.10 Party against whom action may be taken

The courts appear to expect that the police will take action against the party 'responsible' when that person can clearly be identified. For example, in the *CEGB* case, Lord Denning MR and the other members of the Court of Appeal clearly had it in mind that the police would operate only against the obstructors as the party 'responsible'. As a matter of discretion this may well be so, but it should be noted that in the exercise of their preventive powers, the police are not restricted to action only against those 'responsible'; they may take action against anyone who is acting otherwise lawfully (see *Humphries v Connor*). Whether such action is reasonable will depend upon all the circumstances.

In *McBean v Parker* a police officer intervened to stop a struggle between the appellant and his colleague who was attempting to carry out an unlawful search of the appellant. The police officer was present throughout the stop and attempted search and could not be said to have been acting in the execution of his duty to prevent a breach of the peace since he knew that the initial detention had been unlawful. Dunn LJ said that:

> . . . in a situation of this kind where two officers are involved and all that was needed was for the appellant to be told the reason for the search to make what was done lawful, it follows that if, thereafter, the person who is apprehended uses reasonable force to repel a search by one officer he is doing nothing unlawful. The other officer . . . cannot be said to be acting in the execution of his duty if he then attempts to restrain him . . . I will limit my decision to those facts.

But if a police officer comes across a struggle between an individual and another police officer, he can intervene, since there is a breach of the peace. In *Joyce v Hertfordshire Constabulary*, at a football match, the police officer responsible for the initial detention of the defendant, with whom he then had a struggle, could not be identified. Another constable saw the struggle as part of a general and violent disturbance involving a group of fans, and intervened to seize the defendant who then resisted. The defendant was charged with conduct contrary to s 5 of the 1936 Act. The defence suggested that since the initial struggle was a result of an unlawful detention, the defendant had simply been using reasonable force to escape and the second officer should not have intervened.

The divisional court saw no merit in this view and made two points: (1) the court had been entitled to assume that the first detention was lawful; (2) even if it had been unlawful, there was still a breach of the peace and the officer to whose attention it came was obliged to intervene: 'What was going on was in fact a struggle and a breach of the peace and the rights and wrongs do not matter'. In intervening, the officer was acting in the execution of his duty and further struggles by the individual amounted to threatening behaviour and to offences contrary to s 51 of the Police Act 1964.

An individual who is in fact freeing himself from an unlawful detention may well find himself in difficulties vis-à-vis all but that constable and any other who may be tainted with the illegality of his colleague. A constable who comes across a general mêlée, in which it is possible that some of the parties will be acting in self-defence, need not assess who is responsible and may proceed against all concerned since there is a breach of the peace; see *Timothy v Simpson*:

> If no-one could be restrained of his liberty in cases of mutual conflict, except the party who did the first wrong, and the bystanders acted at their peril in this respect, there would be very little chance of the public peace being preserved by the interference of private individuals . . . [or] of peace officers. . . .

The possibility of abuse of the preventive power was noted in *Humphries v Connor*. Fitzgerald J was reluctant to agree with his colleague because he thought that the police ought not to act against those who are carrying out lawful acts which others find displeasing and use as an excuse to break the peace. Rather, the police should act against those who threaten to, or who actually break the peace. To do otherwise would, in his view, make 'the law of the mob supreme'. O'Brien J perceived that there was a risk and specifically excluded abuse of power from the scope of his decision:

> Our decision would not be applicable to a state of facts where the power was abused; and . . . it would not protect any constable from any unnecessary, excessive, or improper exercise of such power in other cases.

The same issues may arise in relation to binding over to keep the peace; see *R v Inner London Crown Court ex p Benjamin* (1986) where the decision to imprison the respondent for refusing to be bound over was upheld despite the absence of any threat of violence on his part. The risk to the peace came from those who objected to his persistent sounding of a conch shell in a crowded market. See also *R v Morpeth Ward JJ ex Ward* (1992) and *Percy v DPP* (1995).

2.11 Hostile audience

The dilemma facing police officers, and others, in controlling public behaviour is often summed up in debate as 'the hostile audience problem'. At the simplest of levels, where the lawful activity of a person or group is met by unlawful action or threats by opponents, then the police officer is faced with a dilemma. Should the lawful activity be curtailed, or should the unlawful activity be dealt with and the lawful activity protected? The risk of creating a 'heckler's veto' is apparent, and interference in response to threats by opponents was described in *Humphries v Connor* 'as making, not the law of the land but the law of the mob supreme'.

The same issue arises in the context of the justices' power to bind over; for recent illustrations see *R v Inner London Crown Court ex p Benjamin* (1986) and *R v Morpeth Ward JJ ex p Ward* (1992).

In *Beatty v Gillbanks* (1882), the lawful activity of the Salvation Army marchers was violently opposed by the Skeleton Army, a group which had often engaged in violence to thwart the aims of the Salvationists. At the time, in order to bind over, there had to be established an actual or apprehended crime, in that instance the offence of unlawful assembly. The binding over order imposed on the leader of the Salvationists' procession was quashed on the basis that there had been no intention on his part to cause the disturbance, and, by implication, that the disturbance was not the natural and necessary consequence of his action.

The principle in that case receives support from *R v Londonderry JJ*

(1891) but has received little support elsewhere; see *O'Kelly v Harvey* (1883), *Duncan v Jones* (1935), *Humphries v Connor* (1864) and particularly in *Wise v Dunning* (1902) where the court was prepared to sanction a more realistic view of the natural consequences of the use of insulting and abusive behaviour.

In the absence of a formally guaranteed right of assembly or protest, the matter ultimately resides with the discretion of the police officer, albeit that the courts exercise control to a limited extent. Dicta in a range of cases (see for example, most recently *R v Coventry City Council ex p Phoenix Aviation* (1995) indicate the view of the higher courts that the rule of law must prevail and that, save in exceptional circumstances, any discretion should favour the continuance of the lawful activity including freedom of peaceful assembly, procession and speech.

Nonetheless, the statutory formulae for the offences contrary to ss 4, 4A and 5 of the 1986 Act, among others, and the grant of wide executive powers to control processions and assemblies, do reflect a line drawn by Parliament. This is implicit acceptance that there may be restrictions on speech or activity imposed in response to a hostile or potentially hostile audience. As far as the common law is concerned, the scope for the exercise of police discretion is at least as wide as that in the 1986 Act, and the criteria are a good deal more flexible.

2.12 Binding over

The powers of justices to bind over are of ancient origin and apparently predate the Justice of Peace Act 1361. For the history, see generally *Lansbury v Riley* (1914) and Law Commission Working Paper No 103. The powers have been the subject of extensive review by the Law Commission (see 2.12.10) and considerable adverse criticism which throws their future into some doubt. Such criticism is not novel and there have been several attempts to repeal the Justices of the Peace Act 1361, albeit without government support.

The extensive powers to bind over to keep the peace or be of good behaviour are derived from the Justice of Peace Act 1361 or common law and the Magistrates' Courts Act 1980 which have been unaffected by recent legislative changes to the substantive law. As with the powers of the police in connection with breaches of the peace, the powers are preventive in nature (*Veater v Glennon* (1981). The common law has long been concerned with preventive justice which '. . . consists in restraining a man from committing a crime he may commit but has not yet committed, or of doing some act injurious to members of the community which he may do but has not yet done . . .' (*R v Halliday* (1889)).

As Blackstone said:

> This preventive justice consists in obliging those persons, whom there is probable ground to suspect of future misbehaviour, to stipulate with and to give full assurance to the public, that such offence as is apprehended shall not happen; by finding pledges or securities for keeping the peace, or for their good behaviour.

It has been said that the justices' jurisdiction to bind over 'rests on the maxim or principle "*salus populi suprema lex*" in pursuance of which it sometimes happens that individual liberty may be sacrificed or abridged in the public good' (*Lansbury v Riley* (1914)).

2.12.1 Powers in general

Justices of the peace may require any person before the court to enter into a recognisance, with or without sureties, to keep the peace or be of good behaviour, or both, for a specified period. Research by the Law Commission, conducted before the introduction of the Crown Prosecution Service and the 1986 Public Order Act, suggests that 79 per cent of binding over orders were made both to keep the peace and be of good behaviour; 12 per cent to keep the peace and 9 per cent to be of good behaviour.

Good behaviour encompasses keeping the peace, and is thus the more extensive of the two; see *Hughes v Holley* (1987) where it extended to behaviour *contra bonos mores*, contrary to a good way of life or 'offensive and contrary to standards of generally accepted decent behaviour'. Breach of the peace bears the same meaning as for the common law preventive powers of the police.

Failure to consent may result in imprisonment. Breach of the recognisance may result in forfeiture of the whole or part of the sum but is not punishable by imprisonment (*R v Finch* (1962)). A binding over order is neither a conviction nor a punishment.

The powers to bind over to come up for judgment and to bind over a parent or guardian to enter into a recognisance to take proper care of a child or young person lie outside the scope of this book.

2.12.2 Statutory complaints procedure

The statutory complaints procedure originated in the old commissions of the peace and was codified in s 25 of the Summary Jurisdiction Act 1879. It was restated in s 91 of the Magistrates' Courts Act 1952 and currently is provided for under s 115 of the Magistrates' Courts Act 1980:

> The power of the magistrates' court on the complaint of any person to enter into a recognisance, with or without sureties, to keep the peace or be of good behaviour towards the complainant shall be exercised by order on complaint.

Although this procedure has as its objective the binding over of the respondent, the justices' other powers to bind over may be employed in the course of a hearing by way of complaint. Despite the wording of s 115(1), the order may be either to keep the peace generally or to be of good behaviour towards the actual complainant.

The power to bind over on complaint resides in a magistrates' court and not individual justices; see ss 115, 121 and 148 of the Magistrates' Court Act 1980. Any person may obtain the issue of a summons under s 51 of the Magistrates' Courts Act 1980 to bring the respondent before the magistrates' court to seek an order binding over the respondent to keep the peace or be of good behaviour towards the complainant.

The order sought under the statutory complaints procedure may not be made until the conclusion of the proceedings and after the court has heard sworn evidence (see *R v Aubrey-Fletcher ex p Thompson* (1969)). The court must be satisfied that the allegations have been proved beyond reasonable doubt.

2.12.3 Other procedures

A person may be arrested in respect of a breach of the peace and brought before a court (for the powers of arrest see 2.9). An order may be made only upon conclusion of the case but is not dependent upon a finding that a breach of the peace had actually occurred (*R v Morpeth Ward JJ ex p Ward* (1992)).

The powers of justices survived intact the statutory changes in the Summary Jurisdiction Act 1879, and similar powers are enjoyed by the Crown Court and judges of the Court of Appeal. Under s 1(7) of the Justices of the Peace Act 1968:

> It is hereby declared that any court of record having a criminal jurisdiction has, as ancillary to that jurisdiction, the power to bind over to be of good behaviour, a person who or whose case is before the court, by requiring him to enter into his own recognisances or to find sureties or both, and committing him to prison if he does not comply.

2.12.4 Conditions and failure to consent

No other penalty may be added and no conditions may be imposed on the order (see *Goodland v Chief Constable of South Yorkshire* (1979), *Lister v Morgan* (1978), *R v Randall* (1987), *R v Ayu* (1959)). The order may name the person protected by the order (*Wilson v Skeock* (1949)).

In the event of failure to comply with the order to enter into a recognisance, the respondent may be committed to custody for up to six months. Such refusal to enter into a recognisance is not itself contempt of court and cannot be dealt with under s 12(1) of the Contempt of Court Act 1981 but it may (particularly if repeated), be a kindred offence for the purposes of s 9(1)(c) of the Criminal Justice Act 1982. This may have important consequences, eg in *Howley v Oxford* (1985) and *Chief Constable of Surrey v Ridley* (1985) as regards the imposition of imprisonment on a person aged between 17 and 21; and see also *Veater v Glennon*. As regards binding over juveniles with their consent, see *Conlan v Oxford* (1984).

2.12.5 Subject of the order

Any of the following participants in proceedings may be bound over without proof of any offence and at any stage of the proceedings including upon acquittal or conviction, upon withdrawal of the prosecution case or a decision to offer no evidence, or upon adjournment: complainant, prosecutor or witness (*R v Hendon JJ ex p Gorchein* (1973), *R v Wilkins* (1907), *Sheldon v Bromfield JJ* (1964), *R v Sidhu* (1976)), except a witness not called upon to give evidence (*R v Swindon Crown Court ex p Pawittar Singh* (1984), *R v Lincoln Crown Court ex p Jones* (1989), *R v Kingston upon Thames Crown Court ex p Guarino* (1986)); respondent, defendant whether convicted or acquitted (*Wilson v Skeock* (1949), *R v Inner London Crown Court ex p Benjamin* (1987), *R v Woking JJ ex p Gossage* (1973)).

In any instance where the binding over is imposed prior to conviction there is no power to impose any other penalty, such as a fine.

2.12.6 Nature of the proceedings: criminal or civil

When acting pursuant to the statutory complaint procedure, justices of the peace exercise what is technically their civil jurisdiction but is effectively a quasi-criminal jurisdiction (see *Everett v Ribbands* (1952) and *R v Bolton JJ ex p Graeme* (1986)). It is unclear whether the criminal or civil standard of proof is to be employed, nor need the facts be proved by admissible evidence. In *Percy v DPP* (1995) the Queen's Bench Division favoured the criminal standard in the light of *R v Bolton JJ ex p Graeme* and the consequences and circumstances of the proceedings, applying *Re Bramblevale Ltd* (1970) where it was held that, to establish a civil contempt, proof beyond reasonable doubt was required.

Proceedings for forfeiture of a recognisance are civil and require the civil standard of proof (*R v Southampton JJ ex p Green* (1976) and *R v Marlow JJ ex p Sullivan* (1984)), although that point was doubted, *obiter*, in *Percy v DPP*.

2.12.7 Need for evidence

The power to bind over requires evidence that there might be a future breach of the peace occasioned by the person concerned (*R v Aubrey Fletcher ex p Thompson* (1969)), and this is so even where the person concerned consents, (*R v Marylebone Metropolitan Stipendiary Magistrate ex p Okunnu* (1987)). The magistrates must direct themselves properly as to the meaning of breach of the peace and the likelihood of its occurrence, and must be satisfied that there is a real risk of the conduct continuing and that a breach of the peace may occur.

The evidence need not be sworn evidence but has 'to be such as, when considered carefully and not capriciously, it justified a conclusion that there was a risk of a breach of the peace unless action was taken to prevent it' (*R v South West London Magistrate's Court ex p Brown* (1974)). In the absence of any such evidence the power to bind over does not arise, although it seems that the violence which is anticipated may stem from the activities of others, provoked or encouraged by the acts of the person bound over (see *Wise v Dunning* (1902), *R v Morpeth Ward JJ ex p Ward* (1992) and *R v Inner London Crown Court ex p Benjamin* (1987)). To prove a danger to the peace it is sufficient that the natural consequence of the behaviour persisted in would be enough to provoke others to violence (*Wise v Dunning* (1902), *R v Morpeth Ward JJ ex p Ward* (1992) and *R v Inner London Crown Court ex p Benjamin*).

The same general principles apply to the power to bind over to be of good behaviour (*R v South Molton JJ ex p Ankerson* (1988)), including where the person's behaviour was unlawful and where it was felt by justices to be *contra bonos mores* (*Hughes v Holley* (1987)) and a repetition is feared (*R v Sandbach JJ ex p Williams* (1935), *Hughes v Holley*).

2.12.8 Procedural safeguards

There are a number of procedural safeguards.

Good practice in court
In more recent times the higher courts have tended to indicate more effective procedural safeguards, although such as do exist have been frequently criticised. It now seems clear that defendants, whether acquitted or not, complainants, witnesses or others who are before the court ought

to be told when the court is considering a bind over and the reasons for it and they should be given the opportunity to make representations (see *R v South Molton JJ ex p Ankerson, R v Hendon JJ ex p Gorchein* (1974), *Sheldon v Bromfield JJ* (1964)). Such good practice does not extend to misconduct in the face of the court (*R v North London Metropolitan Magistrate, ex p Haywood* (1973)).

Enquiry into means

There must be an enquiry into means (*R v Nottingham Crown Court ex p Brace* (1990), *R v Central Criminal Court ex p Boulding* (1984), *R v South Molton JJ ex p Ankerson* (1988)), although perhaps not where the sum proposed is an obviously nominal amount. The sum fixed must be reasonable but need not be restricted to the maximum penalty available for the offence in respect of which the person appears before the court, if relevant.

Not subject to conditions

The order itself cannot be made subject to conditions (see 2.12.4).

Finite period

The order must be for a finite period (*R v South Molton JJ ex p Ankerson* (1988)), although the period is a matter of discretion (*R v Edgar* (1913)). It should not be used in order to circumvent restrictions on imposing bail conditions (*R v South Molton JJ ex p Ankerson* (1988)).

Consent to the order

There must be consent to the order; an order may not be imposed. The consent element is of course unrealistic in the light of the sanction of imprisonment. Imprisonment is not available in the event of a breach of the recognisance.

2.12.9 Other matters

Appeals against binding orders are governed by the Magistrates' Courts (Appeals from Binding Over Orders) Act 1956 by way of a re-hearing in the Crown Court.

Forfeiture of recognisance is governed by s 120 of the Magistrates' Courts Act 1980.

2.12.10 Future of binding over

Criticism of the scheme of preventive justice is not new, but in the light of the adverse criticisms voiced by the Law Commission, the long-term future of the justices' powers to bind over may be in some doubt.

On consultation, the Law Commission found there was a clear preponderance of support for the continuance of a power to bind over despite the objections of principle identified. Support for binding over was largely directed at what were regarded as the considerable practical advantages of the present system, and the perceived lacuna which would exist should the system be abolished. Practical matters such as the ability of the courts to defuse situations without conferring the stigma of conviction, but with a warning as to future conduct, the saving of court time and money, and the additional sentencing option, all influenced those in favour of retention of the powers.

The arguments relied upon by the Law Commission related to the unconstitutionality of the powers and process arising from (1) the unsatisfactory nature of the current practice and procedure, regarded as irredeemable breaches of principles of natural justice; (2) the wide range of criminal sanctions and cautioning practices currently available; and (3) the impracticability of designing a satisfactory and new form of judicial warning system.

The unsatisfactory nature of the current practice and procedure were addressed on both an academic and a practical level and related to (1) the vagueness of the meaning of breach of the peace and good behaviour and the consequent difficulty of those bound over in knowing precisely what they might or might not do; (2) the absence of any power to impose conditions which would clarify the conduct to be avoided; (3) the unrealistic requirement for consent and the power to punish for refusal (but not for breach of the recognisance); (4) the absence of any limit to the duration or amount of the recognisance; and (5) the likelihood that in many material respects the practice relating to binding over would breach the European Convention on Human Rights (supported by the rejection in the United States of binding over as a violation of the constitutionally protected right of due process).

The Law Commission concluded that the powers of binding over to keep the peace and be of good behaviour under the Justices of the Peace Act and at common law and in related legislation should be abolished without replacement.

There are no current plans to introduce legislation to take on board these criticisms and implement the proposal of the Law Commission. It is not unusual for Law Commission proposals, even those couched in such strong terms, to lay dormant, although a successful challenge to the powers in the forum of the European Court of Human Rights might prove a catalyst to reform or abolition.

Chapter 3

Riot, Violent Disorder and Affray

3.1 Statutory provisions

3.1.1 Public Order Act 1986

The Public Order Act 1986 provides for the most serious public order offences:

> 1.—(1) Where 12 or more persons who are present together use or threaten unlawful violence for a common purpose and the conduct of them (taken together) is such as would cause a person of reasonable firmness present at the scene to fear for his personal safety, each of the persons using unlawful violence for the common purpose is guilty of riot.
>
> (2) It is immaterial whether or not the 12 or more use or threaten unlawful violence simultaneously.
>
> (3) The common purpose may be inferred from conduct.
>
> (4) No person of reasonable firmness need actually be, or be likely to be, present at the scene.
>
> (5) Riot may be committed in private as well as in public places.
>
> (6) A person guilty of riot is liable on conviction on indictment to imprisonment for a term not exceeding ten years or a fine or both.

> 2.—(1) Where 3 or more persons who are present together use or threaten unlawful violence and the conduct of them (taken together) is such as would cause a person of reasonable firmness present at the scene to fear for his personal safety, each of the persons using or threatening unlawful violence is guilty of violent disorder.
>
> (2) It is immaterial whether or not the 3 or more use or threaten unlawful violence simultaneously.
>
> (3) No person of reasonable firmness need actually be, or be likely to be, present at the scene.
>
> (4) Violent disorder may be committed in private as well as in public places.
>
> (5) A person guilty of violent disorder is liable on conviction on indictment to imprisonment for a term not exceeding five years or a fine or both, or on summary conviction to imprisonment for a term not exceeding six months or a fine not exceeding the statutory maximum or both.

3.—(1) A person is guilty of affray is he uses or threatens unlawful violence towards another and his conduct is such as would cause a person of reasonable firmness present at the scene to fear for his personal safety.

(2) Where two or more persons use or threaten the unlawful violence, it is the conduct of them taken together that must be considered for the purposes of subsection (1).

(3) For the purposes of this section a threat cannot be made by the use of words alone.

(4) No person of reasonable firmness need actually be, or be likely to be, present at the scene.

(5) Affray may be committed in private as well as in public places.

(6) A constable may arrest without warrant anyone he reasonably suspects is committing affray.

(7) A person guilty of affray is liable on conviction on indictment to imprisonment for a term not exceeding three years or a fine or both, or on summary conviction to imprisonment for a term not exceeding six months or a fine not exceeding the statutory maximum or both.

6.—(1) A person is guilty of riot only if he intends to use violence or is aware that his conduct may be violent.

(2) A person is guilty of violent disorder or affray only if he intends to use or threaten violence or is aware that his conduct may be violent or threaten violence. . .

(5) For the purposes of this section a person whose awareness is impaired by intoxication shall be taken to be aware of that of which he would be aware if not intoxicated, unless he shows either that his intoxication was not self-induced or that it was caused solely by the taking or administration of a substance in the course of medical treatment.

(6) In subsection (5) 'intoxication' means any intoxication, whether caused by drink, drugs or other means, or by a combination of means.

(7) Subsections (1) and (2) do not affect the determination for the purposes of riot or violent disorder of the number of persons who use or threaten violence.

7.—(1) No prosecution for an offence of riot or incitement to riot may be instituted except by or with the consent of the Director of Public Prosecutions.

(2) For the purposes of the rules against charging more than one offence in the same count or information, each of sections 1 to 5 creates one offence.

(3) If on the trial on indictment of a person charged with violent disorder or affray the jury find him not guilty of the offence charged, they may (without prejudice to section 6(3) of the Criminal Law Act 1967) find him guilty of an offence under section 4.

(4) The Crown Court has the same powers and duties in relation to a person who is by virtue of subsection (3) convicted before it of an offence under section 4 as a magistrates' court would have on convicting him of the offence.

8.—In this part—

'dwelling' means any structure or part of a structure occupied as a person's home or as other living accommodation (whether the occupation is separate or shared with others) but does not include any part not so occupied, and for this purpose 'structure' includes a tent, caravan, vehicle, vessel or other temporary or movable structure;

'violence' means any violent conduct, so that—

(a) except in the context of affray, it includes violent conduct towards property as well as violent conduct towards persons, and

(b) it is not restricted to conduct causing or intended to cause injury or damage but includes any other violent conduct (for example, throwing at or towards a person a missile of a kind capable of causing injury which does not hit or falls short).

9.—(1) The common law offences of riot, rout, unlawful assembly and affray are abolished . . .

10.—(1) In the Riot (Damages) Act 1886 and in section 515 of the Merchant Shipping Act 1894 (compensation for riot damage) 'riotous' and 'riotously' shall be construed in accordance with section 1 above.

(2) In Schedule 1 to the Marine Insurance Act 1906 (form and rules for the construction of certain insurance policies) 'rioters' in rule 8 and 'riot' in rule 10 shall, in the application of the rules to any policy taking effect on or after the coming into force of this section, be construed in accordance with section 1 above unless a different intention appears.

(3) 'Riot' and cognate expressions in any enactment in force before the coming into force of this section (other than the enactments mentioned in subsections (1) and (2) above) shall be construed in accordance with section 1 above if they would have been construed in accordance with the common law offence of riot apart from this Part.

(4) Subject to subsections (1) to (3) above and unless a different intention appears, nothing in this Part affects the meaning of 'riot' or any cognate expression in any enactment in force, or other instrument taking effect, before the coming into force of this section.

3.1.2 Common concepts

Riot (s 1), violent disorder (s 2) and affray (s 3) replaced the common law offences of riot, rout, unlawful assembly and affray, which were abolished by s 9(1) of the 1986 Act. There are overlaps between offences but two features are common to each of the serious offences. The first is unlawful violence, and the second is the degree of that violence judged from the standpoint of a hypothetical bystander, 'a person of reasonable firmness present at the scene'.

3.2 Violence

In defining the conduct which will satisfy the *actus reus* of these serious offences, and the lesser offence in s 4, the 1986 Act does not rely upon the concept of breach of the peace but upon unlawful violence. It should be noted that any conduct which amounts to violence may also amount to a breach of the peace (*R v Howell* (1839)) and, if so, will activate the common law powers dealt with previously (see 2.9). The use or threat of unlawful violence may also amount to other offences such as criminal damage or one of the range of assaults.

3.2.1 Definition

'Violence' is defined in s 8 of the Act as:

> any violent conduct, so that—
> (a) except in the context of affray, it includes violent conduct towards property as well as violent conduct towards persons, and
> (b) it is not restricted to conduct causing or intended to cause injury or damage but includes any other violent conduct (for example, throwing at or towards a person a missile of a kind capable of causing injury which does not hit or falls short).

The partial definition, adopted in s 8, was that offered by the Law Commission but is not satisfactory since it includes the word it is attempting to explain. The Law Commission wished to avoid a definition based upon specific offences against the person or property taking the view that where such offences are committed then they may properly be charged, although in many instances of disorder it may be difficult to prove the requisite intent of the individual, the result of his action or the identity of the victim. Accordingly the Law Commission at para 5.33 of their report *Criminal Law—Offences Relating to Public Order* (Report 123) observed:

> The definition . . . emphasises the nature of violent conduct rather than its consequences . . . [V]iolence is not limited to physical damage or injury . . . and . . . it must in some way be violence towards persons or property; and the example is given of the throwing of a missile towards a person, capable of causing injury (a paper dart would thus not qualify) whether that missile falls short or wide of the mark. Many other examples of violence will amount to violent conduct upon these criteria, such as the wielding of a lethal instrument or the discharge of a firearm in the direction of another. The example is given because it explains the concept without the difficulties of a detailed list or extended definition. The conduct must be such that it can be regarded as violence towards persons or property and the jury must be sure that it was of such a character.

Statutory definitions of violence elsewhere are rare although since 'violence' is an ordinary word of the English language it ought to be interpreted in such a way as to be given its ordinary meaning; thus an ordinary sensible man will know violence when he sees or hears it (see *Brutus v Cozens* (1972)).

Support for this approach is found in *R v Criminal Injuries Compensation Board ex p Warner, Webb, and Others* (1985). In deciding whether a crime was a 'crime of violence' for the purpose of the criminal injuries compensation scheme, the court imposed no special construction; since the words were ordinary words it took the view that 'the ordinary or generally understood meaning of the words must prevail'. This approach was approved by the Court of Appeal in that case. And in *Dino Services Ltd v Prudential Assurance Co Ltd* (1989), in the context of the interpretation of 'violent' in an insurance policy, Kerr LJ observed that:

> The word 'violent' is an ordinary English word, which here appears in a common commercial document. It seems to me that there is no reason why its meaning should be in any way different from what an ordinary person would understand.

See also the definition of 'violent offence' within s 31 of the Criminal Justice Act 1991, 'an offence which leads or is intended or likely to lead, to a person's death or to physical injury to a person'. This definition, which is narrower than in the 1986 Act has been considered in *R v Palin* (1995), *R v Touriq Khan* (1995), *R v Cochrane* (1993), and calls for the definition to be amended have been made by the Court of Appeal in *R v Richart* (1995) and *R v Ragg* (1995).

In the Law Commission Report No 76 (*Conspiracy and Criminal Law Reform*), it was said that 'violence will cover any application of force to the person, but carries a somewhat restricted meaning in relation to property'. In relation to s 2(6) of the Criminal Law Act 1967, force, in the context of entry to premises, was said to be the application of energy to an object with a view to moving it (*Swales v Cox* (1981)). In the context of the serious public order offences it seems possible to argue that whereas force may be involved in violent conduct, the converse is not true, ie not every use of force involves violence, and violent conduct would suggest a substantial degree of force whether applied to the person or property and deriving the tenor of violence from all the surrounding circumstances. Some assistance for this approach is to be found in the interpretation of insurance policies where a distinction is often drawn between an entry which is merely forced and an entry where violence was used (see *Dino Services Ltd v Prudential Assurance Co Ltd* (1989)).

In any event, there will be occasions where violence does not involve contact either with the person or property. As the Law Commission explained, it would be wrong to restrict violence to cases where force is actually applied, a punch thrown but which misses its target is just as much the use of violence as a punch which finds its target. Waving a weapon so as to cause a person fear of injury or concern may properly be described as violent conduct; see s 8: '. . . it is not restricted to conduct . . . intended to cause injury . . .'.

The fact that damage or injury results should not be a decisive factor in deciding if violence was used. Throwing a rotten tomato at a politician may well be described as the use of violence, but that emerges from the throwing rather than the fact that it happens to hit and necessitates clothing to be cleaned. By contrast, daubing a politician's clothing with paint may be criminal damage and assault but probably will not be violent behaviour.

3.2.2 Unlawful violence

During the early stages of the passage of the 1986 Act, the definition of violence included 'violence not justified by law, for example, the law relating to self-defence or the prevention of crime or disorder'. At a late stage the epithet 'unlawful' was adopted in ss 1, 2, 3 and 4 and the above definition was omitted. Commentators have suggested that the word 'unlawful' is superfluous, and that it might safely be ignored since Parliament could not be taken to have intended to exclude the application of the general defences to criminal charges (for examples of mere surplusage see *McMonagle v Westminster City Council* (1990) and *R v R* (1991)).

Certainly, the word violence tends to be employed in a perjorative fashion and is used to describe behaviour of which the speaker disapproves. Force is more often used to describe behaviour in a more neutral or even approving fashion. Thus, the Police and Criminal Evidence Act 1984, s 117 legitimises the use of reasonable force by a constable where necessary in carrying out a power granted by that Act, and that presumably would include conduct which in another context might be described as violence, for example the breaking down of a door using a sledge-hammer.

It could be argued that the use of the word 'force' in s 3 of the Criminal Law Act 1967, might suggest that 'violence' should be read as only extending to unreasonable force, but this view would fail to give sufficient weight to the epithet 'unlawful'. In the instance of conduct such as the use by police of riot shields and truncheons in the suppression of a riot, there is a natural reluctance to describe it as violence, and the term force is often substituted. Equally, in such an instance, where it is sought to criticise the deployment of that tactic or the degree of force employed, there may well be a tendency to describe the force used as violence.

The view of the Court of Appeal is that 'unlawful' must have some meaning, and accordingly the general law will apply and the use of violence justified by law will not be an offence under ss 1, 2, 3 and 4. In *R v Rothwell & Barton* (1993) the recorder had directed the jury that self-defence, reasonable defence of a friend and force used to prevent a breach of the peace were not defences to a charge of violent disorder. It was held that the prosecution had to demonstrate the unlawfulness of the violence used or threatened, and the Court of Appeal quashed the verdict.

In *R v Bane* (1994), the Court of Appeal held that, no matter how weak the defence, a defendant is entitled to have the matter considered by the jury, and that self-defence was a defence to a charge of affray. See also *R v Key* (1993) where the judge failed properly to deal adequately with the meaning of unlawful violence, and *R v Pulham and Pulham* (1995) where the judge failed to leave the issue of self-defence to the jury.

For the effect of a misdirection on the issue see 3.8.

It will be a matter for the prosecution to satisfy the jury (or magistrates in the case of violent disorder or affray tried summarily) that the force used by the defendant was unlawful, although the defence will be under an evidential burden of raising that as an issue (*R v Rothwell & Barton* (1993)).

Commonly the issue of the unlawfulness of force will arise in the context of the use of reasonable force in self-defence or defence of others or of property, and the issue will be decided by applying the ususal principles. Given the difficulties inherent in self-defence it has been said in a case of affray that when self-defence is an issue, it is desirable that the judge should follow the words of Lord Morris in *R v Palmer* (1971) when addressing the jury, and that a summing up which omitted those or similar words would be defective (*R v Rivolta* (1994)).

Any person may use reasonable force in the prevention of crime, or in arresting or assisting in the arrest of an offender or suspected offender (Criminal Law Act 1967, s 3(1)).

Where the alleged offence occurs in the context of an exercise by the police of their powers, eg arrest or entry to premises, there may be difficult questions of both fact and law relating to the legality of police conduct.

Violence may be used in the prevention of actual or apprehended breaches of the peace. On other occasions violence may be justified by way of self-help, for example, to bring to an end or prevent an unlawful detention, or the removal of demonstrators from a site, or trespassers from property (although the trespassory conduct may now be caught by other provisions of the 1986 Act, as amended). Note also the strict constraints placed upon self-help in the civil context of the law of nuisance in *Burton v Winters* (1993), and in *Lloyd v DPP* (1992) where in the context of a charge of criminal damage for the removal of a wheel clamp the court observed that 'self help involving the use of force can only be contemplated where there is no reasonable alternative'.

There may be other examples of lawful violence, eg s 5 of the Criminal Damage Act 1971 provides a specific defence. Duress and necessity may provide defences in appropriate cases.

3.3 Threats of unlawful violence

In violent disorder and affray both those who threaten unlawful violence and those who use unlawful violence are guilty (s 2(1), s 3(1)). For the purposes of riot, only those who use unlawful violence are guilty (s 1(1)), those who threaten unlawful violence are not guilty, except perhaps of incitement or as secondary parties. For the purposes of riot and violent disorder those who threaten unlawful violence, whether by verbal or other means, are included when assessing the required number of participants.

Threats of any description may also fall within s 4, s 4A or s 5, or if of a racial character within ss 18 or 19 (see Chapter 4).

At times there may be doubt whether conduct constitutes violence or the threat of violence. For example, X waves a fist in the air in the direction of V. That behaviour may be described as violence since it is violent conduct towards a person and is not prejudiced by virtue of the fact that it neither caused injury nor was intended to cause injury. On the other hand it may be better described as a threat of violence. In any event unless the necessary degree of apprehension is engendered (see 3.4) it may be better to proceed under either s 4 or s 5 of the 1986 Act.

As regards conduct which will amount to a threat of violence there is still some scope for doubt. In the context of mass picketing or a disturbance during a march or assembly, it is not clear whether large numbers alone may constitute a threat of violence, although it seems unlikely.

Will a chanting crowd be said to be using violence? See the comments in *Thomas v NUM* at 5.1.10. The emphasis in s 8 is on violent *conduct* and it seems reasonably clear that verbal threats alone, whether oral or written, cannot fall within the meaning of 'violence' as explained by s 8.

Since violence is said to be 'any violent *conduct*' it is difficult to accept that oral or written threats unaccompanied by separate acts could fall within the meaning of conduct. This is especially so as the Act, like its predecessor, draws a distinction elsewhere between words and behaviour. The distinction in ss 1,2 and 3 between those who threaten violence and those who use violence would militate against a contrary view. Thus, a purely verbal threat, unaccompanied by any other activity, is unlikely to fall within the meaning of violence but may amount to a threat of violence for the purposes of ss 1–3.

For the purposes of ss 1, 2, 4, 4A and 5, a threat may be made by words alone; but for the purposes of affray, 'a threat cannot be made by the use of words alone' (s 3(3)). Section 3(3) has been examined on two occasions, in *R v Robinson* and *R v Dixon* (see 3.7.4).

3.4 Person of reasonable firmness present at the scene

In the case of the serious offences (ss 1, 2 and 3) the standard by which the violence or threats of violence are to be judged is that of the person of reasonable firmness present at the scene. It need not be shown that such a person either was present or was likely to have come on to the scene. This person may conveniently be described as the hypothetical bystander. The hypothetical bystander will not be regarded as fearing for the safety of others, whether male or female, aged or infant, and is a hypothetical and objectively assessed individual; this corresponds to the approach taken in connection with the common law in *R v Plastow* (1989).

Proof of the degree of fear does not appear to have caused juries any problems. The feelings of anyone actually involved either as victim or as participant or as bystander cannot be used as the relevant measure of the required level of fear, although evidence from them will of course tend to be employed to establish the nature of the fear which would have been engendered in the hypothetical bystander.

3.4.1 Present at the scene

The violence must be of such a degree as would have put the hypothetical bystander in fear of his personal safety had he been there. It need not be shown that such a person was actually there or would have been likely to have come on to the scene, for riot (s 1(4)), for violent disorder (s 2(3)), and for affray (s 3(4)). This is so even where the offence is committed in a private place to which the public do not have access. Use of the word 'would' rather than 'might' indicates that the question is one of probability rather than possibility.

The common law also relied on the concept of bystander in the context of affray. In *Attorney-General's Reference (No 3 of 1983)* (1985), it was said:

> We have employed the word 'bystander' . . . as a convenient abbreviation and in deference to what seems to have become common usage. The word has however connotations which make it not altogether apt. We use it in the sense of 'innocent members of the public within sight or earshot of the fighting'. We reject as impracticable the distinction which counsel . . . seeks to draw between persons who are the intended victims of those unlawfully fighting on the one hand and those on the other hand who are . . . 'merely sucked into the mêlée'.

In *R v Davison* (1992) the Court of Appeal had regard to the Law Commission's explanation of 'present at the scene' (at para 3.38):

> As regards 'presence at the scene', there may be some degree of uncertainty as to what is meant by 'presence', but we doubt whether it is possible or desirable to be more specific as to how far away from or how near to the disturbance the hypothetical person must be. Every case will to this extent depend on its circumstances, but we believe that a jury will sufficiently understand what is meant by 'present at the scene', that is anyone who would have been in real danger of becoming involved in the disturbance.

The advantage of this approach is to demonstrate that the entirety of the circumstances must be taken into account by the magistrates or jury for the purposes of evaluating the degree of violence involved. Most important will be type of conduct. The use of weapons, the numbers of participants and the nature of the premises will all be relevant. For example, where conduct occurs in a confined space it may well be that a relatively slight degree of violence will suffice to render the hypothetical bystander fearful for personal safety given that he would be unable to manoeuvre himself to a place of safety; yet were that same degree of violence to be employed in the open then the relevant standard would not be satisfied.

3.4.2 Actual bystanders or participants

There may be instances, probably relatively few, where the surrounding circumstances are such as to persuade the arbiters of fact that violence, for example a fight, was limited to those involved and that others, perhaps close by, were not affected by what happened. Direct evidence of the inactivity of actual bystanders might then lead the arbiters of fact to conclude that objectively a hypothetical bystander would equally not have been affected.

In *DPP v Cotcher* (1992) magistrates took the view that the defendants 'assaulted three persons clinically and no other persons were involved or likely to be involved in violence'. As the Court of Appeal pointed out, such a case will be rare. The inactivity or passivity of actual bystanders will simply be one factor to assist the arbiters of fact in deciding the objective criterion, in the same way as the excitability or fear will not be decisive of the objective question. Actual bystanders may well exhibit no apprehension simply because they have been cowed into that state, or they may well have become accustomed to the exhibition of violence and it no longer concerns them.

DPP v Gormley is another case where magistrates were held to have applied the law correctly in concluding that in the circumstances of that case (including evidence that the actual bystanders, two women in a car who intervened to deter the fighters, were not afraid), a hypothetical bystander would not have been caused to fear for his personal safety.

3.4.3 Victims as bystanders

In *DPP v Gormley* the divisional court adverted to the problem, stemming from the common law, whether or not the victim of violence was capable of being a bystander (see *Attorney-General's Reference (No 3 of 1983)* (1985)). Although that point may have been a matter of some relevance to the common law, for the purposes of the statutory offence of affray as drawn by the 1986 Act, actual bystanders, whether or not participants, are not required and the question left open at common law is irrelevant to the statutory offences of riot, violent disorder and affray. The only question for the court is whether, on the facts, a person of reasonable firmness would have been caused to fear for his personal safety, and that is a question for all the circumstances including consideration of the victim, if there is such a person.

3.5 Riot

The common law offence of riot was hedged about with uncertainties and was rarely used. The definition was generally accepted as being reflected in the following extract from *Field v Receiver of the Metropolitan Police*:

> (1) number of persons three at least; (2) common purpose; (3) execution or inception of the common purpose; (4) an attempt to help one another by force if necessary against a person who may oppose them in the execution of their common purpose; (5) force or violence . . . displayed in such a manner as to alarm at least one person of reasonable firmness and courage.

The 1986 Act retains many of the features of the common law offence. Section 1(1) provides:

> Where 12 or more persons who are present together use or threaten unlawful violence for a common purpose and the conduct of them (taken together) is such as would cause a person of reasonable firmness present at the scene to fear for his personal safety, each of the persons using unlawful violence for the common purpose is guilty of riot.

The following indictment approved by the Court of Appeal (see *R v Tyler* (1992), and *R v Jefferson*) is to be found in *Blackstone's Criminal Practice* (Blackstone Press, 1993), para B11.19:

> . . . on or about the . . . day of . . . , being one of 12 or more persons present together at . . . and using [or threatening] unlawful violence for a common purpose, namely . . . , used unlawful violence for the said common purpose by assaulting members of the public, the conduct of the 12 or more persons aforesaid, taken together, being such as would cause a person of reasonable firmness present at the scene to fear for his personal safety.

In the past, proof of common purpose often turned out to be a serious stumbling block to the successful prosecution of the more serious public order offences. No doubt this will continue to demand careful consideration before prosecutions are launched.

3.5.1 Use or threat of unlawful violence

Generally, see 3.2–3.3 above. Section 1 of the 1986 Act has been judicially described as consisting of two parts (*R v Tyler, R v Jefferson, R v Mandair* (1994)). The first part indicates the context of the offence and comprises 12 or more persons present together using or threatening unlawful violence for a common purpose and which would have an appropriate effect on the mind of a hypothetical bystander. It should be noted that those who use or threaten violence are counted in for the purposes of establishing the required number of participants (see 3.6.2).

The second part specifies the precise offence which comprehends only the use of violence; threats of violence are not an alternative. A person using unlawful violence, but not a person threatening it, may be convicted of riot, subject to the law relating to secondary parties (*R v Tyler* (1982) and *R v Jefferson* (1994)).

An indictment which alleges that the defendant used or threatened unlawful violence will be flawed but may be amended during the course of trial. In *R v Tyler* Farquharson LJ said:

> The statement of offence clearly and accurately referred to riot. The particulars disclosed the correct offence but widened its ambit to include 'threaten' as well as the 'use' of violence. In our judgment, that is not in the same category as alleging an offence which does not exist, as in *Gaston*. It gives an imperfect description of one that does. In those circumstances, the defect is capable of amendment on the basis laid down in *McVitie*.

In *R v Jefferson* the Court of Appeal applied the principle in *R v Tyler* to a similarly badly framed indictment. Even though there had been no amendment, the prosecution case and the judge's directions had made it clear that the case against the defendants was that they had encouraged and intended to encourage, and thereby aided and abetted, those who had used unlawful violence.

Those who threaten unlawful violence (as well as those who encourage it by other means) may, in appropriate instances, be guilty of aiding and abetting or inciting riot (or be guilty of other offences under ss 2–5). The 1986 Act contains nothing to exclude the application of the normal common law principles (*R v Jefferson*, see 3.5.14).

3.5.2 Common purpose

There must be a purpose common among the alleged participants. The retention of this (and its exclusion from violent disorder and affray) marks the special seriousness of behaviour committed collectively by a group. And, prior to the 1986 Act it was remarked that riot is an offence 'which derives its great gravity from the simple fact that the persons concerned were acting in numbers and using those numbers to achieve their purpose' (*R v Caird* (1970)).

Individual motives are irrelevant to the proof of the offence. Prior agreement or planning is not necessary. Common purpose may be shown by admissions of the defendant, by evidence of planning, or by the circumstances as a whole, eg the object of the attack or the presence of banners; see s 1(3), 'the common purpose may be inferred from conduct'.

The common purpose will often be an unlawful purpose, but it seems it may also be a lawful purpose. What renders the activity open to condemnation is the use of violence during the course of or in order to achieve the common purpose. The purpose must be shown to be common to at least the minimum number of participants (ie 12). An accurate assessment of the activity upon which the defendant and others were engaged is all that need be shown and such activity may be stated as the common purpose, eg that they were attempting to prevent the police from gaining access to a particular place, or to use unlawful violence to celebrate a football victory (*R v Jefferson*).

Although it may be preferable to state the common purpose in the indictment, the Court of Appeal has upheld a conviction for riot where the prosecution case establishing the common purpose was clear from the outset, and where the judge summed up on the basis of the alleged common purpose (*R v Jefferson*).

3.5.3 Twelve or more persons present together

The minimum number of persons who must be present together has been increased to 12 from the common law requirement of 3. Despite the historical significance in this figure (the Riot Act 1714), it remains somewhat arbitrary, although the large number does indicate the gravity attached to the offence.

The meaning of 'present together' will be a question of fact for the jury. There must be violence, or the threat of violence, from each of the 12, although the violence or threats need not be simultaneous (s 1(2)). Where there is sporadic disorder it may be difficult to establish that there were 12 persons present together at the specific time violence was used or threatened. Where there is doubt as to the number of participants or whether they are present together, a charge of violent disorder might be appropriate (provided that three or more can be shown to be present together), or affray, or threatening behaviour contrary to s 4.

Where there are only 12 defendants and it is not alleged that there were any more participants then, in the unlikely event of a prosecution, the acquittal of one should inevitably lead to the acquittal of the remainder on the riot charges if the evidence was that there had been exactly 12 participants in the riot and that they were all before the court. Most commonly, the allegation will be that some of the participants only were being prosecuted and that others who participated are not before the court.

Where it is alleged that there were more than 12 participants, then the acquittal of one defendant will not be fatal if the jury is satisfied that the overall number involved amounted to 12 or more. This was explored in *R v Beach and Morris* (1909), a case on the common law. The computation of the number of participants has proved difficult in several reported cases on violent disorder and the principles identified in those cases will apply equally to the offence of riot (see 3.6.3).

As far as the computation of numbers involved is concerned, the *mens rea* required for the offence is not taken into account in the computation of the 12 required (s 6(7)); the prosecution need only show the use or threat of unlawful violence by the other participants.

3.5.4 Public or private place

There is no restriction on the location in which the ingredients of a riot may occur. This affirms the common law approach; see, for example, *Pitchers v Surrey County Council* (1923), where the riot occurred in an army camp.

3.5.5 *Mens rea*

Section 6 states the *mens rea* required for all the offences under Part I of the Act. For the purposes of riot, s 6(1) is relevant. Section 6(5) and (6) are common to all the offences. For application of s 6(7), see 3.6.3. According to the Law Commission's explanatory note to its draft Bill, the effect of s 6(7) is that:

> when a person is charged with an offence where proof of a number of participants is required . . . the mental element . . . requires to be proved only in relation to that person: the mental element of the other participants . . . is irrelevant.

It follows that the self-induced intoxication of the others is also irrelevant for the purposes of calculating the number present. However, where intoxication is alleged there may be difficulties in establishing a common purpose.

It must be shown that the defendant intended to use violence or that he was aware that his conduct may have been violent. While stressing that *mens rea* is relatively unimportant from a practical point of view, the Law Commission deliberately effected a move away from the view of recklessness as applied in *R v Caldwell* (1982) and preferred the approach taken in the case of *R v Cunningham* (1982). The *mens rea* is therefore either an intention to do the harm or foresight of the type of harm and a decision to take the risk.

Generally, where awareness is impaired by intoxication, then the defendant will be taken to have been aware of that of which he would have been aware if he had not been intoxicated (s 6(5)). Where the defendant alleges that the intoxication was not self-induced or was as a result of medical treatment, then the burden will be upon the defendant to prove this on the balance of probabilities.

Where the defendant is so intoxicated that he cannot form the common purpose necessary, then he is entitled to be acquitted since according to the Law Commission, para 6.28:

> the element of common purpose . . . amounts in substance to a further mental element of intent . . . [I]f there were sufficient evidence to indicate that a defendant accused of riot was too intoxicated to have the common purpose, he could not be found guilty of riot.

In such a case the defendant could, however, be found guilty of violent disorder which does not rely upon any element of common purpose.

3.5.6 Arrest

Riot is an arrestable offence (by virtue of the possible term of imprisonment) and the provisions of the Police and Criminal Evidence Act 1984 apply; see s 24 (arrest without warrant for an arrestable offence) and s 28 (statement of reasons). A statement that arrest is for rioting may be preferable, but an indication that the arrest is for using violence may suffice since it indicates the nature of the offence. In any event, the power at common law to arrest for breach of the peace exists and a statement that the arrest is for breach of the peace would serve for the time being, although a full statement of reasons and arrest on the charge of riot would have to follow in accordance with the 1984 Act.

3.5.7 Consent to prosecutions

Prosecutions for riot or incitement to riot must be by, or with the consent of, the DPP (s 7(1)). Consent is now governed by ss 25 and 26 of the Prosecution of Offences Act 1985 and is effectively that of the Crown Prosecution Service. Consent need only be lodged at the court of trial with the clerk and need not be proved (see *R v Dexter* (1899) and now s 25 of the 1985 Act). A consent in broad terms, eg where the charge is not specified, is nonetheless sound, see *R v Cain* (1975) where the consent read:

> In pursuance of my powers under the . . . Act I hereby consent to the prosecution of name of address for an offence or offences contrary to the provisions of the said Act.

In *R v Pearce* (1981) consent in the above form sufficed for a prosecution under s 5A of the 1936 Act but it did not provide consent to prosecution for conspiracy to commit s 5A offences since it did not refer to any Act but the 1936 Act (as amended).

3.5.8 Trial

The offence is triable only on indictment. The maximum sentence is ten years' imprisonment or a fine or both (s 1(6)).

3.5.9 Alternative verdicts

Section 7(3) applies only to violent disorder and affray, and conviction for s 4 as an alternative to riot is not available. Conviction for violent disorder or affray as an alternative to riot may be available in an appropriate case under s 6 of the Criminal Law Act 1967 (see further 3.8).

3.5.10 Duplicity

Section 1 is to be treated as creating one offence only (see s 7(2)).

3.5.11 Dispersal of rioters

The powers and duties to disperse rioters have already been dealt with (see breach of the peace powers, Chapter 2). At various times there have been calls for the return of the Riot Act 1714. The former Act, repealed in 1967, had long fallen into obsolescence and was a draconian mechanism developed in a time of great emergency, mainly for the purpose of increasing the penalty on conviction for riot to death and granting an indemnity to peace officers in respect of the use of lethal force in the dispersal of rioters. A specific power to compel dispersal was not created in the 1986 Act, in part because of the practical difficulties in making an appropriate announcement. In the light of the power to make directions under ss 12 and 14 it may be doubted whether this justification alone merits the exclusion of a power to order dispersal.

3.5.12 Riot by involvement in other offences

In *R v Sharp and Johnson* Lord Goddard remarked that:

> The term riot is a term of art and, contrary to popular belief, a riot may involve no noise or disturbance of the neighbours though there must be some force or violence. For instance if three men enter a shop and forcibly or by threats steal goods therein technically they are guilty not only of larceny or robbery but also of riot.

In *J W Dwyer Ltd v Metropolitan Police District Receiver* (1967), a case on the Riot (Damages) Act 1886, where four hooded men armed with iron bars raided a jeweller's shop and robbed the owner, it was held that there had been a riot.

Under the terms of the 1986 Act, provided there are sufficient participants, there is no reason why this result should not follow, eg a large gang raid on a warehouse or security van. Violent disorder might also be charged, but with a relatively low maximum penalty, this may not be appropriate.

3.5.13 Secondary parties

The general law of aiding and abetting and incitement applies to the offences in ss 1–5 of the Public Order Act 1986 (see *R v Jefferson*). In that case, the Court of Appeal considered that their conclusion, that the ordinary law relating to aiding and abetting was unaffected by the 1986 Act, was supported by the preparatory material for the 1986 Act, ie the Law Commission Report and the White Paper.

Mere presence at the scene will not suffice for conviction as a secondary party. There must be a sufficient degree of participation or active encouragement (for an extreme example in the public order context see *Devlin v Armstrong* (1972)) or promotion by words, signs or other actions, supported by an intention to do so. For the application of the relevant law in other public order cases, see *Allen v Ireland* (1984), a case on s 4 of the 1986 Act.

3.5.14 Riot in other legislation (s 10)

Riot and cognate expressions occur in numerous statutes. The effect of s 10 is clear with regard to the Acts specified, ie the Riot Damages Act 1886, Merchant Shipping Act 1894 and Marine Insurance Act 1906. Thus in the first two Acts the words 'riotous' and 'riotously' will be construed in accordance with s 1. In the third Act, policies will be construed in accordance with s 1 unless the contrary intention appears. In marine insurance policies, the word riot bears the meaning given to it by the common law so that the provisions of s 1 are now appropriate. In *The Andreas Lemos* (1983) Staughten J construed the word 'riot' in an insurance policy, according to the common law. Thus, a clandestine theft was not a riot and 'nobody but a Sloane Ranger would say . . . "it was a riot"'.

The effect on other legislation is less clear. It appears that most legislation is construed in accordance with the common law view of riot and will therefore now be interpreted in the light of s 1. Examples would be the Licensing Act 1964, the Representation of the People Act 1983 and the Ecclesiastical Courts Jurisdiction Act 1860.

The Riot (Damages) Act 1886 provides a scheme for compensation in respect of damage to property flowing from riots. In the case of personal injury a claim might be made under the Criminal Injuries Compensation scheme. The 1886 Act replaced earlier Acts which had themselves consolidated and amended the laws relating to remedies against 'the hundred'. The Act deals only with injury to property, ie 'house, shop or building' and property therein. Motor cars in the street would not be within the scope of the Act.

To fall within the terms of the Act of 1886, the assembly must be not only riotous but also tumultuous. A crime of stealth will not be covered: *J W Dwyer Ltd v Metropolitan Police District Receiver* (1967), referred to in *D H Edmonds Ltd V East Sussex Police Authority* (1988), as 'an instance of a quiet riot'. According to *Dwyer*, there must be rioters who are 'in such numbers and in such a state of agitated commotion and . . . generally so acting, that the forces of law and order should have been well aware of the threat which existed . . .'.

'Riotous' and 'tumultuous' are not the same thing. Although not spelled out by the court in the *Edmonds* case, there must be substantial noise, a substantial number of participants (inherent now in the definition of riot), an open and not secret gathering, an assembly over a considerable period of time and widespread commotion from those involved in the riot.

The Act provides for a form of contributory negligence. Where the applicant provoked or contributed to the riot or his own loss, the compensation may be reduced. The procedures for claim are governed by regulation (see Riot (Damages) (Amendment) Regulations, SI 1986 No 36) and the claim will be made to the relevant police authority or the receiver in the Metropolitan Police District.

3.6 Violent disorder (s 2)

Violent disorder is the successor to the common law offence of unlawful assembly. The offence of unlawful assembly was generally regarded as being made out where there was 'an assembly of three or more persons with a common purpose either to commit a crime of violence or to achieve any other object, lawful or not, in such a way as to cause a reasonable man to apprehend a breach of the peace'.

When considering the replacement of unlawful assembly, the government chose not to follow the recommendation of the Law Commission for the creation of two offences one of which (using violence) would be triable on indictment, the other of which (threatening violence) would be triable summarily. Under the Act both those who use and those who threaten unlawful violence may be tried for the same offence and jointly. It is upon sentence that distinctions may be drawn between levels and manner of involvement.

3.6.1 Elements of violent disorder

Section 2(1) states:

> Where 3 or more persons who are present together use or threaten unlawful violence and the conduct of them (taken together) is such as would cause a person of reasonable firmness present at the scene to fear for his personal safety, each of the persons using or threatening unlawful violence is guilty of violent disorder.

The new offence differs from the common law in one important respect: it lacks the element of common purpose. It relies on the fear of an individual for his personal safety where that fear is induced by actual use or threats of violence. An assembly of individuals who intend either to commit a crime by open force or to further a common purpose by methods which would cause apprehension of breaches of the peace will not commit an offence of violent disorder. Previously such an assembly would have been an unlawful assembly. This may be of importance where there is evidence of an assembly at which is planned a series of attacks on different targets one after another, and where the participants are prevented by arrest from carrying out any or all of these attacks, the assembly will not constitute the offence of violent disorder.

An allegation of violent disorder will commonly amount to an allegation of affray where the assertion is that the violence was used or threatened towards another person and the threats are not made by words alone.

3.6.2 At least three persons

There must be at least three persons present together. There is no need to establish a common purpose, although it must be possible to say that the participants were 'present together'. This seems to be a requirement of at least knowledge of each other's presence but it is not a requirement that they should be acting in concert. In most cases there will be no difficulty in establishing that the participants are present together, eg a gang of youths on a street corner hurling missiles at a police car or bus. In some cases the facts may not allow of such easy interpretation, eg sporadic violence or threats from a few people in a large crowd. In such instances charges of threatening behaviour contrary to s 4 would be appropriate or, in extreme instances, affray contrary to s 3. As to difficulties of computation, see 3.6.3.

The use or threats of violence need not be simultaneous (s 2(2)) but there must presumably be something more than sporadic or infrequent acts or threats of violence. Sporadic acts or threats of violence are unlikely to generate the degree of fear necessary to establish the offence.

Unlike riot both those who threaten and those who use unlawful violence are guilty of violent disorder.

3.6.3 Computation of the number involved

For the purposes of riot and violent behaviour the mental element required by s 6(1) and s 6(2) of the 1986 Act respectively, 'does not affect the determination for the purposes of riot or violent disorder of the number of persons who use or threaten unlawful violence' (s 6(7)). It may be possible to envisage circumstances where a participant, whether or not he is also a defendant, uses or threatens violence but does not have the relevant mental element of intending to use violence or of being aware that his conduct may be violent. In such a case, that person may be counted in for the purposes of riot and violent disorder, but as defendant he could not be convicted, subject to the provisions of s 6(5) and (6), which deal with the effect of intoxication.

Given the unlikelihood of this situation, it will be appreciated readily that the more frequent suggestion will be that among the participants some were using or threatening not unlawful but lawful violence, eg in self-defence, and were intending to do so. If such an account is accepted then this will reduce the numbers who may be counted in, and in a marginal case may well reduce the number below the relevant threshold.

There have been a number of cases dealing with this difficult issue. In *R v Mahroof* (1989) the particulars in the indictment read:

> EB, AM and TS on the 29th day of June 1987 being present together did use or threaten unlawful violence and the conduct of them was such as would cause a person of reasonable firmness present at the scene to fear for his personal safety.

Both EB and TS were acquitted of violent disorder and the jury did not convict on s 4 (see s 7(3)). Evidence was given during the trial that two unnamed individuals had also been present at the scene and had participated. The judge directed the jury that they had to consider each defendant separately but at the same time to bear in mind the need to convict only if they were satisfied that there had been three persons using or threatening unlawful violence.

The Court of Appeal concluded that, subject to two important qualifications, the indictment contained a sufficient allegation despite the omission of any reference to the involvement of others. The qualifications were that there should be evidence of the involvement of others in the unlawful violence, and that the defence should be properly informed of any allegations which they would have to meet. In *R v Mahroof* the second qualification had not been met. The Court of Appeal observed that the most obvious way to inform the defence is to make the allegation clear in the indictment.

In *R v Fleming and Robinson* (1989) the allegation was that only four persons had been involved in a fight. Two were convicted, one was acquitted and in respect of the remaining one the jury failed to agree. The Court of Appeal concluded that, subject to very rare instances of someone being present using or threatening unlawful violence but not having the relevant *mens rea*, the conviction could not stand. There was no one else present who could be counted in as the necessary third person. The Court of Appeal observed that:

> On a charge under s 2 of the Public Order Act 1986, where the only persons against whom there is evidence of using or threatening unlawful violence are those named in the indictment, the jury should be specifically directed that if it cannot be sure that three or more of the defendants were using or threatening violence, then it should acquit every defendant even if satisfied that one or more particular defendants were unlawfully fighting.

R v Mahroof and *R v Fleming and Robinson* were applied in *R v Worton* (1990). In this case there was evidence of participation in violence by a large number. Of the four charged with violent disorder only three were tried, and of these one was acquitted. The evidence of participation by others meant that *R v Fleming and Robinson* could be distinguished and that the first qualification in *R v Mahroof* was satisfied. The second qualification in *R v Mahroof* was satisfied since the defence had been apprised by the way the evidence was led of the allegation that others were involved. The Court of Appeal upheld the appeal against conviction on the basis that in the circumstances the trial judge misdirected the jury. He had to do more than describe the offence in general terms, he had to:

> . . . go on and warn the jury specifically that if any of the three defendants should be acquitted of violent disorder, then they must necessarily acquit the other two, unless satisfied that some other person not charged was taking part in the violent disorder.

In *R v McGuigan* (1991) the Court of Appeal made it clear that a direction from the judge that aiders and abetters might be counted in for the purposes of violent disorder, amounted to a misdirection. Before a person can be guilty of aiding and abetting, the prosecution must show that the substantive offence has been committed, and that requires at least three independent participants using or threatening unlawful violence. If two persons use or threaten unlawful violence, a third person cannot by aiding and abetting them render them guilty of violent disorder.

3.6.4 Unlawful violence

This has the meaning attributed to it in s 8, and is discussed in greater depth at 3.2. For the purposes of violent disorder violence will include violent conduct towards property as well as the person. Violent conduct will not necessarily involve injury or damage, and throwing a missile will suffice.

3.6.5 Person of reasonable firmness present at the scene

This has been discussed generally at 3.4. No such person need actually be on the scene or likely to come on the scene. The 'hypothetical bystander' is simply the standard by which the relevant degree of violence is to be established.

3.6.6 Private or public places

As with riot and affray, the offence may be committed in either a public or a private place (s 2(4)), eg a public house, a road, a private party. There is no reason why the offence should not be committed in a dwelling house, although careful consideration will be needed of occasions where it will be proper to charge violent disorder in a purely domestic situation occurring within a dwelling house. By way of contrast, it should be noted that offences contrary to ss 4 and 5 do not normally extend to conduct occurring in a dwelling house.

3.6.7 *Mens rea*

See generally 3.5.6. For violent disorder the *mens rea* requirement is:

> 6(2) A person is guilty of violent disorder or affray only if he intends to use or threaten violence or is aware that his conduct may be violent or threaten violence.
>
> 6(5) For the purposes of this section a person whose awareness is impaired by intoxication shall be taken to be aware of that of which he would be aware if not intoxicated, unless he shows either that his intoxication was not self-induced or that it was caused solely by the taking or administration of a substance in the course of medical treatment.
>
> 6(6) In subsection (5) 'intoxication' means any intoxication, whether caused by drink, drugs or other means, or by a combination of means.

3.6.8 Secondary parties

See 3.5.14.

3.6.9 Continuing offence

Unlawful assembly was a continuing offence and the offending activity might have been one event or a series of acts taking place over different locations, provided always that the common intention was not lost. In *R v Jones* (1974) it was suggested that a count in an indictment disclosed more than one offence since it, and further particulars, referred to several sites at which similar incidents of violence occurred on the same day. The defence suggested that the incidents at each site were isolated and separated from each other by journeys and meal breaks during which no violence took place. The court rejected this:

> . . . The ingredients of the offence are (i) the *actus reus* of coming together and (ii) the *mens rea* involved in the intention of fulfilling a common purpose in such a manner as to endanger the public peace. These ingredients have to be co-existent. There is nothing . . . which indicates that, at any time between the arrival at Shrewsbury and the departure from Telford, those charged with the offence ceased to be an assembly or ceased to have the intent of making an unlawful assembly.

With the statutory relaxation of the common law requirement of assembly for a common purpose, a different conclusion would now be reached. Separate counts for each such incident would have to be preferred in cases like *R v Jones* since each of the incidents would be separated by a period of inactivity during which no bystander would be put in fear.

3.6.10 Arrest

Violent disorder is an arrestable offence by virtue of the possible sentence (see s 2(5)) and the powers to arrest without warrant under s 24 of the Police and Criminal Evidence Act 1984 apply. The appropriate statement of reasons required by s 28 of the Police and Criminal Evidence Act 1984 should refer to violent disorder, although it may be that the use of the word 'violence' would adequately indicate to the defendant the reasons for the arrest. Since the offence contains the elements of a breach of the peace, an arrest or other preventive action made in that respect would be permissible.

3.6.11 Duplicity

Although s 2 may be read as creating two offences, s 7(2) provides that for relevant purposes it is to be treated as creating one offence only.

3.6.12 Trial and alternative verdicts on indictment

Violent disorder is triable on indictment (maximum of five years' imprisonment) or summarily (maximum six months' imprisonment or fine or both) (s 2(5)). As to mode of trial the *Practice Note* [1990] 3 All ER 979, which provides guidance, not direction, to magistrates deciding on mode of trial for offences triable either way, concludes that cases of violent disorder should generally be committed for trial.

The *National Mode of Trial Guidelines* were produced in 1990 and updated in 1994 to reflect case law developments. Essentially, until 1994, mode of trial had been important in the sense that if a case was retained in the magistrates' court, it could not subsequently be sent to the Crown

Court for sentence under s 38 of the Magistrates' Courts Act 1980 unless the character and antecedents of the defendant made it necessary to impose a greater sentence than the magistrates had power to impose. The problem arose in those cases where at mode of trial the magistrates underestimated the gravity of the case, kept it in the magistrates' court and then after trial realised its true seriousness. In such a case, where the defendant had no previous convictions the court could not commit to the Crown Court for sentence.

The 1995 guidelines reflect the terms of s 25 of the Criminal Justice Act 1991 in relation to commitals for sentence (see *R v Sheffield Crown Court & Sheffield Stipendiary Magistrate ex p DPP* (1994), *R v North Sefton Magistrates' Court ex p Marsh* and *R v Dover Magistrates' Court ex p Pamment* (1993)). It is now established that there is no need to review the character of the defendant before committing for sentence. It is sufficient if at any time the magistrates feel the offence is so serious that their sentencing powers are inadequate. Essentially, now, if an error has been made on determination of mode of trial, the court will be able to remedy it by committing a convicted defendant to the Crown Court for sentence.

A person tried on indictment may, if found not guilty, be found guilty of an offence under s 4 (s 7(3)) and may be punished accordingly (s 7(4)). Section 6(3) of the Criminal Law Act 1967, which also allows for alternative verdicts, is unaffected by s 7. See further 3.8.

3.6.13 Policy behind s 2

Both the Law Commission and the Government in its White Paper indicated their view of prosecution policy and in the light of the large degree of overlap between the offences in ss 2–5, the comments remain significant:

> Of course, not every case in which three or more people participate in the specified conduct will necessarily be regarded as appropriate to be dealt with under this offence. Prosecutors may well feel that some cases are not sufficiently serious to warrant proceedings for a 'combination' offence and that this offence will be appropriate for use only when the extra gravity of the circumstances of the group's conduct is such as to justify prosecution for such an offence. (Law Commission, para 5.29)
>
> Like the Law Commission, the Government anticipates that it will be used in the future as the normal charge for serious outbreaks of public disorder. But it will be capable of being applied over a wide spectrum of situations ranging from major public disorder to minor group disturbances involving some violence. The proposal to make it triable either way will give it a useful degree of flexibility for dealing with lesser outbreaks of group violence, such as those commonly associated with football hooliganism. (White Paper, para 3.13)

3.7 Affray

3.7.1 Introduction

The common law offence of affray consisted of unlawful fighting or display of force in such a manner that a person of reasonably firm character might be likely to be terrified. Although the offence had fallen into disuse, it enjoyed a rejuvenation in the 1950s. The Law Commission observed:

> Affray is typically charged in cases of pitched street battles between rival gangs, spontaneous fights in public houses, clubs and at seaside resorts, and revenge attacks on individuals. It is sometimes charged on its own, but is often accompanied by charges of one or more offences, most of them falling within the general rubric of offences against the person.

The higher courts emphasised that there should be a high degree of fear and that this requirement should not be watered down. The retention of an offence of affray which reflects much of the common law marks the seriousness of the offence not so much for the extent of the injuries inflicted but rather because of the nature of the offence, ie the participation in acts of violence causing alarm and terror to the public. The government were able to accept the recommendations of the Law Commission and to give effect to them in the Act.

Although affray is said to be essentially an offence against public order and not an offence against the person, it is capable of being employed as a species of the latter. Unless the governing factor of the violence needed to threaten a hypothetical bystander is rigorously and realistically applied, then the offence will certainly lose its character of an offence against public order.

3.7.2 Elements of affray

Section 3(1) states:

> A person is guilty of affray if he uses or threatens unlawful violence towards another and his conduct is such as would cause a person of reasonable firmness present at the scene to fear for his personal safety.

3.7.3 Unlawful violence

A person must use or threaten unlawful violence (s 3(1)), see 3.2 and 3.5.1. For the purposes of affray, the word 'violence' does not include violence to property (s 8). In *Cobb v DPP* (1992) an information alleging affray referred to the threat or use of violence 'by causing damage to property, fighting and assaulting C'. The reference to causing damage to property was irrelevant and immaterial to the charge of affray, and did not vitiate the charge.

The unlawful violence must be used or threatened 'towards another'; violence offered to passers-by generally would be sufficient. There must be a victim, ie a person towards whom violence has been used or threatened, but another participant would suffice. The phrase 'towards another' is found in s 4 and it suggests that the defendant must be at least aware of the presence of the other person. Any fear actually induced in the victim does not replace the fear of the hypothetical bystander as the gauge of the violence but will be one of those matters to be taken into account in assessing the likely impact upon the hypothetical bystander (see 3.4).

The brandishing of a weapon whether or not accompanied by words, would suffice. Such conduct would also fall within ss 4 and 5 of the Act and s 1 of the Prevention of Crimes Act 1953.

3.7.4 Threats by word alone

Threats of unlawful violence cannot be made by words alone s 3(3)—'a threat cannot be made by words alone'. This reflects the approach view of the common law (*R v Sharp and Johnson* (1957), *Taylor v DPP* (1973)). Care must be taken in summing up to avoid inadvertent suggestions that words alone might be sufficient to constitute the offence; for example in *R v Robinson* (1993), a reference to spoken words alone being *probably* not enough amounted to a misdirection.

In *R v Cullen* (1984) the defendant was alleged to have thrown a coin at a police officer causing injury, and to have shouted abuse. The jury acquitted of assault occasioning actual bodily harm but convicted of affray. The judge had directed the jury to the effect that the '... throwing of a coin, if that is proved, and any words used by the defendant would cause a person ... to fear for his safety'. It was held by the Court of Appeal that, bearing in mind the inconsistent verdicts, the direction had indicated to the jury that it was open to them to convict on the basis of words alone.

In *R v Robinson* (1993), there was no evidence of anything other than the use of words alone even where the context was that the manner in which they were spoken was aggressive and the atmosphere tense, and the events occurred in the middle of the night.

In *R v Dixon* (1993) two police officers cornered the defendant and his alsatian dog on the driveway of a house. The dog was in an excitable state, barking and snarling. The defendant told the dog 'go on, go on' repeatedly. The dog bit the police officers and returned to the defendant who said 'go on, kill', whereupon the police officers retired to a safe distance to await assistance. The defendant denied affray on the basis, *inter alia*, that the threat was verbal only and that there was no evidence that the dog had responded to his words or had been trained to respond. The prosecution case was based on events leading up to but excluding the biting of the police officers.

The Court of Appeal held that the defendant had been properly convicted of affray. It was not the prosecution case that the dog had responded to the words but that the words constituting the threats had been issued while the dog was in an excitable state and as a means of using the dog to create fear. Even on this view, it is not easy to see what the defendant did except for speaking words. It seems possible that the case may be viewed as an example of the use of violence, where the use of violence derives from the context as a whole.

3.7.5 Involvement in a group

Where a group is involved, an individual defendant will still be guilty of affray even if his own actions taken alone would not amount to an offence, eg by not causing the necessary degree of terror. It is the conduct of the group as a whole which must be considered and the terror which is induced by that conduct. Section 3(2) states that 'Where 2 or more persons use or threaten the unlawful violence, it is the conduct of them taken together that must be considered for the purposes of subsection (1)'.

3.7.6 Secondary parties

See 3.5.13.

3.7.7 Private and public places

The offence may be committed in public and in private, according to s 3(5) which reflects the common law.

3.7.8 Person of reasonable firmness present at the scene

See 3.4. Neither the actual nor the likely presence of a person of reasonable firmness need be shown (s 3(4)). This confirms the approach of the common law to attacks in public places (see *Attorney General's Reference (No 3 of 1983)*) although it is wider than the common law approach to violence in a private place where it had to be shown that a person was likely to come across the violence.

Since the offence may be committed by one person only it would bc possible to convict of affray in a wide variety of instances, eg an attack by a youth on his parents in the home. Whether it would be proper to bring a charge of affray on such an occasion is another issue. The Law Commission remarked:

> . . . it seems unlikely . . . that a personal quarrel between two people involving mutual assaults without the danger of the involvement of others . . . would fall within the offence . . . such incidents can hardly be said to give rise to the serious disturbance to public order with which the offence is intended to deal (para 3.38).

3.7.9 *Mens rea*

The Act states in s 6(2)(5)(6):

> 6.—(2) A person is guilty of violent disorder or affray only if he intends to use or threaten violence or is aware that his conduct may be violent or threaten violence.
> (5) For the purposes of this section a person whose awareness is impaired by intoxication shall be taken to be aware of that of which he would be aware if not intoxicated, unless he shows either that his intoxication was not self-induced or that it was caused solely by the taking or administration of a substance in the course of medical treatment.
> (6) In subsection (5) 'intoxication' means any intoxication, whether caused by drink, drugs or other means, or by a combination of means.

See 3.5.6.

3.7.10 Arrest

Affray is not an arrestable offence since it does not fall with the criteria in s 24 of the Police and Criminal Evidence Act 1984. There is, however, a power for a constable to arrest without warrant (s 3(6)), which power is expressed in limited terms. It is restricted to arrest on reasonable suspicion that the person is committing the offence. Where the activity has terminated there is no power to arrest without warrant unless the general arrest conditions in s 25 of the Police and Criminal Evidence Act 1984 apply, as they might do in cases where there is a need to prevent further violence or damage. A statement of reasons using the word affray or violence or threat of violence would be sufficient to explain the ground for the arrest.

The common law power to arrest or restrain to prevent apprehended breaches of the peace would be available in appropriate circumstances, eg if a renewal was feared (see 2.9).

3.7.11 Trial

Affray is triable either way with a maximum sentence on trial on indictment of three years or a fine or both (s 3(7)). As to mode of trial, see the *Practice Note* which concludes that cases of affray should be committed for trial at the Crown Court only where they involve (1) organised violence or use of weapons; (2) significant injury or substantial damage; (3) the offence has clear racial motivations; or (4) an attack on police officers, ambulancemen, firemen and the like.

The list is not exhaustive and is subject to the general proviso that the courts' sentencing powers are felt to be insufficient. Additional factors which may influence the mode of trial decision might be cases where the evidence is complex, where the trial may take a substantial period, where the number of defendants is large, where issues of self-defence may be raised, where violence is extreme or premeditated or not spontaneous. In these cases trial on indictment may be appropriate (see also *R v Crimlis* (1976)). In other cases summary trial may be appropriate.

The possibility of summary trial will enable the prosecution both to indicate the nature of the violence and to draw a clear distinction between that conduct and conduct within s 4. There is a large degree of overlap between ss 4 and 3 and in some instances a charge under s 3 will be appropriate. At the same time, a trial on indictment might be felt to be too heavy handed and yet a charge under s 4 might not be felt to represent the degree of criminality of the participants. In this instance a charge under s 3 and summary trial would be appropriate.

Where it is desired to commit for sentence after conviction for affray, the general considerations at 3.6.12 are relevant.

3.7.12 Duplicity

Section 3 might be read as creating two offences. To avoid doubt or difficulties, s 7(2) provides that for relevant purposes it creates only one offence. Once the fighting ceases then the offence terminates. Should fighting recommence, then a new offence starts. Should the fighting spill from one place to another without ceasing, then one offence only is committed (see *R v Woodrow* (1959)).

3.8 Alternative verdicts for riot, violent disorder or affray

A person tried on indictment for an offence of violent disorder or affray, may, if found not guilty, be found guilty of an offence under s 4 (Public

Order Act 1986, s 7(3)) and may be punished accordingly (s 7(4)). For s 4 see 4.2. There are material differences between the serious offences and the offence in s 4. In particular, for the purposes of s 4 there is no test employing the (hypothetical) reasonably firm person present at the scene. And, although the serious offences may be committed in any place, public or private, including a dwelling house, the offence in s 4 cannot be committed in a dwelling house.

Section 7(3) is expressed to be without prejudice to s 6(3) of the Criminal Law Act 1967. On trials on indictment, except murder and treason, where the accused is found not guilty by a jury, s 6(3) of the 1967 Act permits the jury to find the accused guilty of an alternative offence which is within the jurisdiction of the trial court (see *R v Collison* (1980)). The allegations in the indictment must 'amount to or include (expressly or by implication) an allegation of' the alternative offence (see also *R v Wilson, R v Jenkins* (1984)).

It has been held that s 6(3) of the 1967 Act is unaffected by s 7 (*R v O'Brien* (1993)). Section 6(3) continues to be relevant to the serious public order offences since in appropriate circumstances it will permit someone charged with riot or violent disorder to be found guilty in the alternative of affray (see *R v Fleming and Robinson* even where the jury were not specifically directed on the alternative charge), or someone charged with riot to be found guilty in the alternative of violent disorder. The Court of Appeal on an appeal against conviction may substitute an offence under s 3 for that of which the jury convicted under s 2 (see *R v Fleming and Robinson*).

When applying the general law to the serious public order cases in particular, there may be instances where it would not be possible to substitute a conviction on one serious offence for another. In *R v McGuigan and Cameron* (1995), the defendant was acquitted on a charge of violent disorder but the conviction was overturned on appeal on the basis that there had not been three or more persons involved (see 3.6.2). A conviction for affray could not be substituted because the circumstances of the violence included violence directed at property. Accordingly, it would have been wrong to conclude that the jury must have been satisfied that the appellant had used or threatened violence to the person. For the same reason conviction for the lesser offence contrary to s 4 could not be substituted under s 7(3) of the Public Order Act 1986.

The importance of s 7(3) is that it permits the summary offence under s 4 of the 1986 Act to be dealt with by a court trying a charge on indictment, contrary to the expectation in s 6(3) of the 1967 Act. Section 7(3) applies whether the defendant has been found not guilty by the jury of its own volition having considered the evidence or where it has been directed by the judge to acquit (*R v Carson* (1990)).

Where a defendant on arraignment, without pleading to the indictment alleging affray or violent disorder, has tendered a plea of guilty to a s 4 offence, that plea may be accepted under s 6(1) of the Criminal Law Act 1967 and there is no need for a jury to be arraigned (*R v O'Brien* (1992)). If the plea is unacceptable to the prosecution, then it is deemed to have been withdrawn (*R v Hazeltine* (1967), *R v Notman* (1994)). Where the plea of guilty has been withdrawn, as in *R v Notman*, then a jury which acquits of the offence contrary to s 2, or s 3, can only convict of an offence contrary to s 4 either where they have been directed as to the elements of s 4 and told that it was open to them to convict, or where there has been a formal admission of an offence contrary to s 4 by a defendant who was in charge of the jury (*R v Notman*).

A direction to a jury on an indictment alleging violent disorder, which properly dealt with the issue of the unlawfulness of violence in respect of violent disorder and affray as an alternative verdict, but which failed to emphasise unlawfulness in respect of the violence necessary to support the alternative of threatening behaviour, was a material misdirection. Accordingly, a conviction for the alternative of threatening behaviour was quashed (*R v Afzal* (1993)). On the other hand, a failure to direct the jury properly on the issue of the intent required in order to convict of threatening behaviour as an alternative to affray, but where the direction on affray was correct, was not a material irregularity and appeal against conviction was dismissed (*R v Stanley and Knight* (1993)). The jury had been properly told to consider the alternative only if they acquitted of affray.

Where the offence in respect of which there has been an acquittal or in respect of which an appeal is upheld, involves violence to property, it may not always be possible to substitute a conviction under s 7(3) since the offence under s 4 involves using towards another person threatening abusive or insulting words or behaviour (*R v McGuigan and Cameron*).

Alternative verdicts are not available within magistrates' courts, although it is permissible within the guidelines laid down by the House of Lords in *Chief Constable of Norfolk v Clayton* (1983), for a magistrates' court to try two or more informations charging different offences.

3.9 Sentencing for serious offences

Athough the cases on sentencing for the common law offences are not a useful guide to sentencing under the new statutory offences, nonetheless there are comments in earlier cases which will no doubt continue to be of importance, especially *R v Caird* where it was remarked that riot, and presumably now also violent disorder, '. . . derives its great gravity from the simple fact that the persons concerned were acting in numbers and using those numbers to achieve their purpose'.

The extent of involvement is not a factor which will reduce sentence or alleviate the seriousness of the offence. As the cases on the common law indicate, the court has to have regard to the overall level of violence used and the scale of the disorder. The acts of individuals must not be viewed in isolation; it is the totality of the violence which is the aggravating factor. See generally *R v Caird*, *R v Muryani* (1986) and *R v Pilgrim* (1983). Cases on the current law which make the same point include *R v Pass* (1995) and *R v Sallis* (1994), a case on the sentencing of a prisoner involved in a riot where the Court of Appeal approved the words of the trial judge that:

> When a large number of persons participate in a riot or violent disorder, the gravity of the offence is encompassed by the totality of the violence used, and each offender . . . must bear his full responsibility, irrespective of the precise participation.

Instances of serious public disorder, in particular group disorder, will frequently involve difficulties in identifying the roles played by a particular defendant. As with other sentencing contexts, the factual basis on which sentencing takes place should be clear, and in the absence of an unequivocal acceptance of the prosecution case generally the sentencer will be expected to reach a conclusion as to the particular facts he accepts. *Newton* hearings are as applicable to public order cases as any other context and should be held where the factual basis is material to sentencing, although given the views expressed in *R v Caird* this will not always be necessary in the case of serious group violence. On the other hand if the sentencer indicates that the sentence is based on a view as to the facts which is at variance with the defendant's account then on appeal the sentence is likely to be quashed (*R v Cotter and Farrell* (1989) and *R v Jackson Crisp* (1989)).

Where a *Newton* hearing takes place then the sentencer should direct himself properly as to the admissibility of identification evidence and the principle in *R v Turnbull* (1976) (see *R v Gandy* (1989)).

As to compensation orders, there has to be a causal link between the participation of the defendant in the affray or violent disorder and the injury sustained by the victim, although strict concepts of causation applied in tort or contract are not appropriate (*R v Taylor* (1993) and *R v Geurtjens* (1993)). In *R v Darby* (1990) it was permissible to isolate the series of events in order to demonstrate that the event which caused the injury was the independent act of another defendant or individual.

The definition of 'violent offence' within s 31 of the Criminal Justice Act 1991, 'an offence which leads or is intended or likely to lead, to a person's death or to physical injury to a person' is likely to encompass the sort of offences involving serious public disorder.

3.9.1 Violent disorder

Section 2(5) of the Public Order Act 1986 states:

> A person guilty of violent disorder is liable on conviction on indictment to imprisonment for a term not exceeding 5 years or a fine or both, or on summary conviction to imprisonment for a term not exceeding 6 months or a fine not exceeding the statutory maximum or both.

The guidelines issued by the Magistrates' Association indicate that seriousness factors particularly relevant to violent disorder are that the offence (1) occurred in a busy public place; (2) involved a large group; (3) put people in fear; and (4) involved vulnerable victims. The entry point for the offence is a custodial sentence.

Relevant cases on the appropriate sentence for violent disorder are:

- *R v Greene* (1993): the statutory maximum term of imprisonment was not appropriate where the defendant had pleaded guilty to violent disorder, even in a case exhibiting serious characteristics such as the use of weapons and a revenge attack. Sentence reduced to three years' imprisonment.
- *R v Charles Andrew Watson* (1990): a sentence of 18 months' imprisonment was not excessive for an offence involving a revenge attack and extensive violence, even where the participants were of previous good character and the precipitating factor was the fatal stabbing of a colleague. The sentence should seek not only to punish but to deter others.
- *R v Betts* (1995) applying *R v Watson*: a sentence of 15 months' imprisonment for a retaliatory attack involving weapons including a lethal weapon, was not excessive.
- *R v Vanes and Vanes* (1989): sentences of 12 months, for a defendant of good character, and 24 months, for a defendant with previous convictions for violence, upheld in respect of a pre-arranged fight between two feuding families, 'People cannot form into factions and do battle with one another . . . without expecting to lose their liberty'.
- *R v Rawlins* (1993): three years' imprisonment for a defendant of previous good character, convicted of involvement in a concerted and widespread attack on police officers in a successful attempt to effect the release of a person under arrest, upheld.

- *R v Coote* (1993): a sentence of 12 months' imprisonment on a defendant pleading guilty to an attack on a police officer attempting to arrest someone and bring a violent event to an end, upheld.
- *R v Frayling* (1993): a sentence of nine months' imprisonment on a defendant of previous good character pleading guilty to involvement in a violent incident in a public house and involving the use of weapons, reduced to a term of six months. But the court indicated that an immediate and substantial term of imprisonment should be expected for anyone identified as using a weapon or causing actual damage, particularly in a public house which was a type of property particularly vulnerable to such attacks.
- For cases on sentencing prisoners convicted of riot and violent disorder, see *R v Sallis* (1994) and *R v Mahoney* (1993).

3.9.2 Affray

Section 3(7) states:

> A person guilty of affray is liable on conviction on indictment to imprisonment for a term not exceeding 3 years or a fine or both, or on summary conviction to imprisonment for a term not exceeding 6 months or a fine not exceeding the statutory maximum or both.

In the case of affray many of the features which relate to the mode of trial decision will also be relevant to the sentence. The guidelines issued by the Magistrates' Association indicate that seriousness factors particularly relevant to affray are that the offence (1) occurred in a busy public place; (2) involved a group action; (3) put people in fear; (4) involved vulnerable victims. A factor reducing seriousness is that the defendant acted alone. The entry point for the offence in the magistrates' court is a community penalty.

Relevant cases on the appropriate sentence for violent disorder are:

- *R v Gilliver* (1991): a sentence of six months' imprisonment on a defendant, with previous convictions for violence, pleading guilty to affray occurring between two rival groups in a public house, upheld.
- *R v Crosdale and Crosdale* (1993): a sentence of three years' imprisonment (the maximum) imposed on a defendant who pleaded not guilty was upheld. The incident had involved forced entry to a flat, actual violence and the use of sawn-off shot-guns to threaten the victims. The short duration of the incident was far outweighed by the exceptional degree of terror.
- *R v Whalley and Vincent* (1989): a sentence of 24 months' imprisonment for affray involving racially abusive behaviour and threats with a knife

against waiters in a restaurant was reduced to 12 months' imprisonment.

- *R v Alderson* (1989): a sentence of 30 months' imprisonment on a defendant pleading guilty to affray upheld. The incident consisted of physical attacks on foreign students in a café and damage to property. The incident was preceded by racially abusive remarks, and occurred in a closely confined space where there were old people and children present.
- *R v Grzybowski and Grzybowski* (1994): sentences of 12 months' detention in a young offender institution and 18 months' imprisonment were upheld in respect of defendants pleading guilty. The affray involved the defendants and others going armed with pieces of wood to the home of a man and challenging him to a fight. Windows were broken with a scaffold board but there was no attempt to enter the building. The man and his wife and three children were inside the house throughout.

Chapter 4

Summary Offences and Racial Hatred

4.1 Introduction

4.1.1 Résumé of provisions discussed

This chapter deals with ss 4, 4A and 5 of the Public Order Act 1986 and provisions relating to racial hatred. Attempts made in 1994 to incorporate a specific new summary offence involving racial harassment failed, and the new s 4A offence enacted by the Criminal Justice and Public Order Act 1994 has no specific race component. In simple terms s 4A appears to increase the penalty range for what would previously have been a s 5 POA offence, when committed with intent. This has created the danger that in cases where intent is demonstrated, the original non-imprisonable s 5 will fall into disuse in favour of the imprisonable s 4A of the POA 1986.

4.1.2 The choice of s 4 or s 5

Sections 4 and 5 are different in type; they are not points on a sliding scale of seriousness. Prosecutors must pitch prosecutions correctly. In closing, defence advocates must tell magistrates if and why the wrong charge has been brought. Magistrates do not want to convict merely because something untoward has happened, and if it is the wrong count they will acquit.

The majority of public order cases are dealt with in the magistrates' courts as summary only matters under s 4 or s 5 of the POA 1986. However, there is often an overlap between the statutory provisions, making it difficult for the courts to determine whether a particular case is an offence at all, a serious s 5 case or more accurately a s 4 case. These are real problems for the courts, advocates and ultimately defendants because the charge controls the sentence range. They also create the dilemma facing a court which finds facts which amount to a s 5 case but has no power to make an alternative finding of guilt if the wrong charge has been brought. The choice available to both police and prosecutors is significant in that their interpretation of a set of facts which may fit all of the three provisions equally well determines which penalty range the court will have to consider. To that extent they exercise a discretion which it is difficult to challenge save by negotiating an alternative plea or resolving the case in court by showing that the wrong alternative has been chosen.

4.1.3 Section 5 research

In a recent study (Brown and Ellis, *Policing Low Level Disorder*, Home Office Research Study 135, 1994) into the use of s 5 charges in six police forces, it emerged that s 5 was used in a quarter of cases to deal with insults solely directed at the police and not, as the Government had intended, to deal with rowdy youngsters disturbing the public. Brown and Ellis conclude that, 'from many of the cases of the section 5 cases and from interviews with arresting officers, the impression comes across very strongly that what is at issue in many of the cases is the enforcement of respect for the police'.

Although the study showed that one-fifth of all s 5 cases ended in the defendant agreeing to be bound over, in cases where the police were the target, the usual outcome was conviction followed by a fine:

> . . . in the absence of authoritative guidance, local police have gone their different ways—a clear managerial failure to structure discretion; about the speed with which s 5 came to be used frequently for a purpose for which it was not intended ie as a resource for the police to use in order to maintain respect when their authority is challenged.

Given the above analysis, it would also be interesting to compare the use of ss 4, 4A and 5 and see how far they have been implemented in accordance with the expressed intentions of Parliament. (See also 1.5 and 1.6 on group disorder and policing.)

4.1.4 Reasons for the provisions

The rationale of these provisions should be remembered. It may not always be proper to adduce information as to background in court but when it is, magistrates ought to be receptive to indications that the allegation goes beyond what was intended by Parliament, and the s 5 research undertaken by Brown and Ellis may be used to significant effect in court argument alongside the following.

The Law Commission and the government identified in *Offences Relating to Public Order*, Law Commission Report 123, the following points from the case law on s 5 of the 1936 Act, highlighting the difficulties inherent in summary public order matters:

(a) the need, in so far as practicable, to maintain the principle in *Beatty v Gillbanks* (1882), that provided a person's conduct is not threatening, abusive or insulting he will commit no offence even if it provokes others to violence;

(b) the need to avoid the use of the concept of 'breach of the peace';

(c) theoretical difficulties which arose from the issue of causation in s 5 of the 1936 Act, including the need to protect those who are disinclined to react to threatening, abusive or insulting conduct by themselves having recourse to violence (*Parkin v Norman* (1982), *Marsh v Arscott* (1982)). Section 5 of the 1936 Act was concerned with cause and effect and the necessary effect was a breach of the peace; it was not enough that the conduct of the defendant should itself amount to a breach of the peace;

(d) the offence was restricted to public places and there was a major need to avert difficulties apparently encountered at major public disorder incidents, and in other cases (eg *Marsh v Arscott*, *R v Edwards and Roberts* (1978)) where the offending activity occurred on private premises to which the public did not have access;

(e) s 5 of the 1936 Act was not designed to deal with minor acts of hooliganism either falling short of the criteria of threatening, abusive or insulting or which engendered not fear of violence but a more generalised sense of unease or apprehension.

4.1.5 Aid and abet

It is possible to aid, abet, counsel or procure an offence under the POA 1986, even though the words 'only if he intends' appear in s 6. In *R v Jefferson and Others* (1991) the court analysed whether anything in the 1986 POA excluded the general common law principles of aiding and abetting:

> In our judgement, the offences created by the 1986 Act may be committed by aiders and abettors as well as by principals . . . In our view s 6 is concerned only with identifying . . . the requisite *mens rea* . . . It does not exclude or cut down in relation to any of those offences the liability of an aider or abettor (*per* Auld J).

4.2 Fear or provocation of violence (POA 1986, ss 4 and 6)

4.2.1 Checklist

- No victim required but conduct must be directed at person present
- section covers both public or private place
- no offence committed if both people are inside a dwelling (or one of them is in another dwelling)
- 'intent' has a complex meaning, covering four states of affairs (see ss 4 and 6(3))
- 'such violence' means immediate unlawful violence
- 'threatening' has its ordinary meaning
- display includes tee-shirt

Section 4 of the Public Order Act 1986 states:

> 4.—(1) A person is guilty of an offence if he—
> (a) uses towards another person threatening, abusive or insulting words or behaviour, or
> (b) distributes or displays to another person any writing, sign or other visible representation which is threatening, abusive or insulting,
>
> with intent to cause that person to believe that immediate unlawful violence will be used against him or another by any person, or to provoke the immediate use of unlawful violence by that person or another, or whereby that person is likely to believe that such violence will be used or it is likely that such violence be provoked.
>
> (2) An offence under this section may be committed in a public or a private place, except that no offence is committed where the words or behaviour are used, or the writing, sign or other visible representation is distributed or displayed, by a person inside a dwelling and the other person is also inside that or another dwelling.
>
> (3) A constable may arrest without warrant anyone he reasonably suspects is committing an offence under this section.
>
> (4) A person guilty of an offence under this section is liable on summary conviction to imprisonment for a term not exceeding six months or a fine not exceeding level 5 on the standard scale or both.

The offence is punishable with imprisonment up to six months or a fine to level 5 (s 4(4)). There is a power of arrest where a constable reasonably suspects that a person is committing an offence under the section (s 4(3)). The offence is summary only although in certain cases it may be an alternative verdict in the Crown Court (ss 4(4)) and 7(3)).

4.2.2 Where the offence is committed

The scope of s 4 is not restricted to public places and the offence may, with one exception, be committed anywhere. There is no need to decide whether a place is a public or a private place, although the authorities on 'public place' may be helpful (see POA 1986 s 57(1); *Anderson v Miller* (1977); *Knox v Anderson* (1983)).

The only restriction is where the conduct occurs in a dwelling (s 4(2)). Dwelling is defined in s 8 of the POA 1986. Where the conduct occurs in a garden or on a driveway or a staircase of a block of flats, then the offence may be committed. The communal landing of a block of self-contained flats does not form part of 'a person's home' as defined in s 8 and therefore the offence may be committed there (*Rukwira v DPP* (1993)). Where a person inside a dwelling uses threatening, abusive or insulting conduct towards someone outside, eg in the street, at the front door or in the garden of that or another house, then the offence may be committed (*R v Va Ku Haw* (1990) and see *Atkin v DPP*).

In *Atkin v DPP* (1989) an appellant had been convicted of a s 4(1)(a) offence when customs officers had gone to his farm. The bailiff stayed outside the farmhouse while the customs officers went inside to speak to the appellant. The appellant said that the bailiff would be a 'dead un' if he came in. As he had a gun in the room, his statement was taken seriously. A customs officer went out and told the bailiff who naturally felt threatened. The justices held that the appellant intended the threat to be conveyed to the bailiff outside and convicted. The divisional court, in allowing the appeal, held that the words 'uses towards another person' in the section meant 'uses in the presence of and in the direction of another person directly'. It follows that for a s 4 offence to be proved, the words must be addressed towards a person present. Since the relevant persons were inside the dwelling house, no offence contrary to s 4 had been committed (s 4(2)). The court in *Atkin v DPP* did not have to address the issues of what view they would have taken if the conversation had occurred in a different part of the farm buildings.

The trespassing hooligan no longer has a defence (*R v Edwards and Roberts*), provided he is not in a dwelling house. A person who posts offensive literature through a letter box will be guilty of an offence since the distribution does not occur in a dwelling (see also *Chappell v DPP* (1989) and the Malicious Communications Act 1988).

4.2.3 Words, behaviour, distribution, display

The prohibited conduct consists of the use of words or behaviour, or the distribution or display of any writing, sign or other visible representation.

The display of a flag, badge, emblem, armband or tee-shirt may be caught, depending on the context. The words 'display' and 'distribute' are not defined for the purposes of s 4 and are to be given their ordinary meaning. Whether the orange lily in *Humphries v Connor* (1964) would be caught by the words 'writing, sign or other visible representation' provision is debatable.

The word 'distribute' in the POA 1986, Part III dealing with racial hatred, is restricted to distribution to the public or a section of the public. This qualification is omitted from s 4 and any distribution will suffice for offences under that section, whether to the public or an individual or group of people. Distribution has been held to include leaving pamphlets in the front porch of an MP's house, which was to an individual, not to a section of the public (*R v Britton* (1967)).

4.2.4 Threatening, abusive, insulting

To constitute the offence, the conduct must be threatening, or abusive or insulting. These words have a long statutory history, going back to s 5 of the POA 1936, and their interpretation is largely governed by cases following that Act. Synonymous expressions, such as: 'behaviour evidencing a disrespect or contempt for the rights of others' do not define the words of the section. Conduct which is annoying is not enough (*Brutus v Cozens* (1972)) and it must be more than disgusting or offensive behaviour (*Parkin v Norman* (1982)). The words were described as 'very strong words' in *Jordan v Burgoyne* (1963). *Brutus v Cozens* is the leading case on the interpretation of the words and the House of Lords declined to define them:

> ... an ordinary sensible man knows an insult when he sees one ... Parliament has given no indication that the word is to be given any unusual meaning. Insulting means insulting and nothing else (*per* Lord Reid).

The essential element of *Brutus v Cozens* is that it is for the tribunal of fact to determine whether given behaviour is insulting.

4.2.5 No victim required

There is no requirement that any person should actually feel insulted or threatened or abused. In *Parkin v Norman* McCullough J remarked that

> ... if the conduct in question is of this character it does not, in our judgement matter whether anyone feels himself to have been threatened abused or insulted. Insulting behaviour does not lose its insulting character simply because no one who witnessed it was insulted...

In *Parkin v Norman*, the activity had not and would not have been witnessed by anyone who would have been insulted; nonetheless it could be classed as 'potentially insulting'. That potentiality gave it the necessary character of insulting but this referred only to the capacity of words to be insulting and does not deal with the other requirements of s 4 of the POA 1986.

The approach of the court in *Brutus v Cozens* and *Parkin v Norman* was of general application and has been applied to the meaning of 'threatening' (*Ewart v Rogers* (1985), where the need for an element of menace in order to constitute a threat was recognised). The judgment in *Parkin v Norman* also gave useful observations upon the nature of an insult. This approach should be applied equally to threats and abuse:

> One cannot insult nothing. The word presupposes a subject and an object and, in this day and age, a human object. An insult is perceived by someone who feels insulted. It is given by someone who is directing his words or behaviour to another person or persons.

4.2.6 Directed towards someone

The above dictum in *Parkin v Norman* introduced the idea that for there to be an insult, the conduct had to be directed at a specific person or persons. In *R v Newham JJ ex p Sadiku* (1985), the divisional court took this approach and concluded that urinating on the public highway could not be said to be 'insulting' in the circumstances of that case: 'There was no question here of the behaviour being in any way directed at the persons who were present'.

Parkin v Norman has been explained on the basis that:

> what the . . . passage must be understood to mean is that words or behaviour cannot be insulting if there is not a human target which they strike, whether they are intended to strike that target or not. . . . The magistrates were perfectly entitled to infer that the two appellants must have known that other people would be likely to be present . . . Their conduct . . . if in the ordinary sense it was capable of being insulting, would be likely to make some impact on anybody who was nearby. . . .[I]t can properly be said that the conduct could be insulting albeit it was not deliberately aimed at a particular person (*Masterson v Holden* (1986)).

The significance of the words 'directed towards' or 'aimed at' can now be seen in the opening phrase of s 4(1)(a). In practice the criteria may not have been applied strictly. The decisions indicate that the issue is one of fact and the divisional court will not interfere with findings of fact unless no court properly directing itself could have reached that conclusion.

4.2.7 Intention or awareness

A difficulty inherent in s 4 is that there are two separate mental elements. The first is that in s 6(3) which requires proof by the prosecution of a mental element as to the description and character of the behaviour. The second is in the description of the offence itself, ie the intention to provoke violence or cause fear. The first is always required. The second is required only where the prosecution seek to establish it rather than the objective likelihood of provocation or fear.

The question of intent in s 4 allegations is dealt with both in s 4 itself and also in s 6(3) which provides that the defendant must have intended the conduct described to have the proscribed character, or be aware that it was likely to have such a character. He must intend his words, behaviour or the writing, sign or representation to be threatening, abusive or insulting or be aware that it may be any of those things. The issue of the defendant's intent is a matter for finding by the magistrates. By incorporating awareness into the provision, the intention was that the court should be able to determine whether there were obvious consequences to follow from a defendant's conduct, which he should have been aware of, independently of his actual intent.

In *Kelleher v DPP* (1994) it was argued that the necessary intent could not be attributed to a defendant shouting threats at another man if that other man was surrounded by policemen. Obviously, it was said, that man would not feel threatened in fact because of the protection provided by the policemen. The court determined that by analysing the defendant's mind at the time it was clear that in this case his intention was to make the man feel threatened and therefore that the intent element of the offence was made out whether the man did feel threatened or not.

In *DPP v Wilmot and Another* (1991) a magistrates' court dealing with a s 4 allegation had formulated the view that under s 6(3) they could not be satisfied beyond reasonable doubt that the defendants had intended their words to be threatening and therefore dismissed the allegation. The context involved two men running into premises shouting 'get him' and then chasing the man. The defendants had said the meeting was spontaneous and the words may have been provocative and frightening to others in the premises but that was not their intention. The magistrates also felt that the defendants were not aware of the threatening nature of the behaviour. The divisional court found as follows:

> it is impossible to conclude that either defendant can have been unaware that his conduct might have been threatening, abusive or insulting. For words like these to be shouted and for a law abiding citizen to be chased through a shop and out into the street speaks for itself (*per* Hodgson J).

While this conduct 'spoke for itself' in the view of the High Court, it had not said the same thing to the magistrates who perhaps tried to delve too deeply into the actual thought processes of the defendants rather than applying ordinary meaning to the expression 'is aware that it may be threatening'.

Prior to the POA 1986, various observations about intent were canvassed. They remain of interest as a demonstration of the higher courts analysing the interpretation of words still forming part of the public order law, but since 1986 the statutory position has been clear. Either intent or awareness is required, and these words have not led to significant numbers of requests to the higher courts to define their meaning.

4.2.8 Uses . . . towards another person

Section 4 only arises if the conduct is specifically used towards another person. These words were not found in the 1936 Act, nor are they found in s 5 of the 1986 Act. They are reminiscent of McCullough J's comment in *Parkin v Norman* that '. . the defendant's conduct was aimed at one person and one person only'.

The use of the words in s 4(1)(a) introduced a requirement that the defendant must be shown to have deliberately directed his conduct at a specific person or persons and must therefore be shown to have been aware of their presence. It must then be shown that the conduct falls within one of the three categories proscribed by the Act. The person towards whom the conduct is directed must be present in the sense that he must be in earshot for this element of the offence to be made out, as set out in *Atkin v DPP* (see discussion at 4.2.2) but there remains the possibility that the conduct need not be threatening, abusive or insulting to that other person (or persons) specifically, even though this will usually be the case. The other person will usually be a victim, but this will not always be the case. In some cases the other person will in fact be an associate of the defendant and the threat, abuse or insult will have been directed to him with a view to encouraging him to violence against another. If the intended or likely effect of the conduct is to encourage any person to indulge in violence, then the offence will be made out.

Suppose that on a picket line one picket uses threatening behaviour towards a person passing through the picket line on a bus. The picket may be convicted of a s 4 offence either if the likelihood is that the worker will believe that immediate violence will be used (eg throwing stones or banging on the side of the bus), or if the threats are likely to provoke violence. Such violence will not necessarily be by the person towards whom the threats were made but will be by other persons present at the scene who are likely to be provoked to violence. A man who makes threats to a person about another person who is present but does not hear the threats is caught by the provision because he uses the threats to the first person intending to provoke violence towards him by another person who may be provoked by the words used.

4.2.9 Components of intention or likelihood/causing fear or provocation of unlawful violence

At 4.2.7 the issues of intent are set out. Section 4 of the POA 1986 is concerned with conduct which is intended or likely to cause fear or to provoke unlawful violence. It should be kept in mind that the word 'fear' does not appear in the section itself, only in the marginal note. Terror is not an ingredient of the section; belief that violence will be used is. It is not concerned with conduct which is itself violent unless that conduct is supported by the necessary intention or likelihood. Nor is s 4 concerned with the actual effect of the behaviour; its intended or likely consequences are what matter. It must now be shown either that the person at whom the conduct had been aimed, was intended, or likely, to be made to believe that unlawful violence would be inflicted on him or another, or that the person at whom the conduct had been aimed, or someone else, was intended or likely to be provoked to unlawful violence. One of four alternative states of affairs must be shown (*Kelleher v DPP*):

> That the defendant intended to cause the person at whom he directed the conduct to believe that immediate unlawful violence would be used against him or another person by any person, ie by the defendant or anyone else. Or
>
> That the defendant intended to provoke the person at whom he directed the conduct or any other person to use immediate unlawful violence. Or
>
> That it was likely that the person at whom he directed the conduct would be likely to believe that immediate unlawful violence would be used (presumably against him or any other person). Or
>
> That it was likely that immediate unlawful violence by the person at whom he directed the conduct or by any other person, would be provoked.

4.2.10 Likelihood test

Although intention will frequently be inferred from the nature of the conduct, on occasions it may well be difficult to prove. It may be easier on occasions to prove the likelihood of the conduct either causing the other person to believe that violence will be used or provoking violence, whether on the part of that person or some other person. In neither case is there any need to demonstrate actual belief that violence would occur or actual provocation to violence.

The Act uses the word 'likely'. Regard must always be had to the circumstances. 'Likelihood' is a higher burden to overcome than 'liable' (*Parkin v Norman* (1982)). Police officers are not 'likely' to react by using unlawful violence but they are likely to believe that unlawful violence will be used against them. Whether or not conduct has the necessary character is decided by the ordinary man who may take into account the actual audience or victim or participants. It is not decided by asking whether the audience or victim was threatened. But the likelihood of fear or provocation of violence can only be assessed by reference to the actual audience or victim or participants. The speaker who uses what are objectively assessed as threats to an audience which has special susceptibilities or even a predisposition to violence must take that audience as he finds them. He cannot plead for his actions to be tested against a 'reasonable audience' (*Jordan v Burgoyne*). Nor is it possible to argue that conduct should be tested against a 'reasonably firm bystander'. The section is intended to protect both the public peace and the timid citizen.

4.2.11 Belief test

The belief of the person towards whom the conduct is directed need not be reasonable; it may be entirely unreasonable or irrational. The user of such conduct must take his victim as he finds him. If, given the character of the victim, it is likely that he will anticipate the infliction of violence, then that is an end of the matter. There need not actually be such a belief, intention to cause such a belief is sufficient, as is likelihood that such belief will be caused.

In *Marsh v Arscott* (1982) the charge failed on two grounds:

(a) the carpark in question was not a public place;
(b) even though the behaviour may have been threatening, abusive or insulting, it was not likely to occasion a breach of the peace since the only people who witnessed it were police officers. Police officers could not be said to be likely to react in such a way as to occasion breaches of the peace.

Under s 4 a conviction would have followed since:

(a) the offence can be committed on private property; and
(b) the person towards whom the conduct had been directed, the police officer, might be likely to believe that unlawful violence would be used against him (*DPP v Orum* (1988)).

4.2.12 Conduct affecting non-victim

Where the conduct is intended, or likely, to encourage persons other than the 'victim' to react violently, then the offence will be made out. In

Simcock v Rhodes (1977) an abusive remark by one youth to a police officer was not likely to cause the police officer to react by causing a breach of the peace. However, there were present at the scene other youths and it was likely that they would be encouraged to breaches of the peace. In terms of s 4, abusive language had been used towards another person (the police officer), whereby it was likely that unlawful violence would be provoked (by the youths). The defendant had also used towards another person (the police officer) abusive language whereby he was likely to believe that violence on the part of any of those present would be used against him. That case also demonstrates the difficulties inherent in the formulation 'uses towards another person'. It could be said that the language had been used towards everyone present and not simply the police officer.

4.2.13 Intent where PC not in execution of duty

In *Woodhouse and Others v DPP* (1991) the court was required to establish whether the necessary intent could be shown in a case where the policeman was acting otherwise than in the execution of his duty. At a railway station two youths were seen to headbutt a barrier. They did not show their tickets (which they did have). Officers approached them but the men declined to stop and an officer prevented one from moving away while he made enquiry. This led to the men and their appellant friends becoming threatening towards the officers and an arrest for threatening behaviour occurred. The question was whether the officer had the right to prevent the men from walking away. If not, could the threatening behaviour be threatening or was it merely a permitted use of force? In the event the court were able to sidestep the issue because they found the threatening behaviour was from a point in time effectively preceding the issue of the lawfulness of the stop, but they did permit of the possibility in an appropriate case of the threats being negatived by preceding unlawful conduct. The court did not analyse the prospective significance of the threat of lawful violence because on the particular facts it was not required. Nevertheless intemperate language, even in the context of the use of lawful violence might be expected to lead a court to the view that unlawful violence by others would be provoked.

The unwillingness of the higher courts to extend the scope of conduct, whether violent or insulting, to be defined as reasonable and therefore not an offence is shown in the unreported case on s 5, *Lewis v DPP* (1995) where Keene J said: 'That would lead to situations where the more extreme were the opinions of the defendant, the more readily would his conduct be regarded as reasonable'. Nevertheless in *Woodhouse and*

Others v DPP Watkins LJ set out the general principle that '. . . the citizen who is wrongly treated by the officer is entitled to go to the extent of using force, if need be, to resist what it is the officer does to him'.

In *Collins v Wilcock* (1984) it was held that except when exercising his power of arrest or some other statutory power, the policeman had no greater right that any other citizen to restrain another. Thus, if he used more than normal force to attract the attention of a person to whom he wished to speak, then he committed a battery which would take him outside the execution of his duty. The question of the extent to which a policeman using degrees of force may be acting outside his duty has been reviewed in other cases (see *Bentley v Brudzinski* (1982), *Kenlin v Gardiner* (1967) and Chapter 7).

It remains likely that the issue of intent will continue to give rise to this category of defence to s 4 allegations despite the principle that the law should not readily recognise new claims to justify the use of force and that reasonable excuse is given a restricted meaning in the interests of policy (*R v Ball* (1990)).

4.2.14 Immediate unlawful violence

The use of the word 'immediate' was taken by the Law Commission in its report and Working Paper to correspond closely to the concept of 'imminence' in the common law breach of the peace preventive powers (cf *Moss v McLachlan* (1984)) although in the usual case there will be no real difficulty in establishing the immediacy of the violence. The divisional court has been asked to analyse the word 'immediate'.

In *R v Horseferry Rd Metropolitan Stipendiary Magistrate ex p Siadatan* (1991), the divisional court reviewed a decision by a magistrate to refuse to issue a summons against Penguin Viking, the publishers of *The Satanic Verses* by Salman Rushdie, on the basis that this was the distribution of abusive and insulting writing whereby it was likely that unlawful violence would be provoked contrary to s 4 of the POA 1986. The magistrate had refused to issue the summons because the 'such violence' referred to had to be 'immediate'. The applicant contended that the prospective violence need not be immediate but only unlawful and where violence was likely to be provoked, the section provided: 'or whereby that person is likely to believe that such violence will be used or it is likely that such violence will be provoked' (POA 1986, s 4). His claim was that because the drafting of the provision did not incorporate the word 'immediate' into the second limb of the provision, the violence need not be immediate. The court took the view that the two expressions, 'immediate unlawful violence' and 'immediate use of unlawful violence' meant the same thing and that 'such violence' meant immediate unlawful violence. The *Criminal Law Review* commentary questioned the court's interpretation:

> There is much force in the applicant's argument that the proper grammatical meaning of the section is that the phrase 'such violence' refers back to the most proximate previous use of the word 'violence' and that is in the phrase 'unlawful violence' not 'immediate unlawful violence' ([1990] *Criminal Law Review* 599).

Where one group of football supporters aims threats or insults at an opposing group on the other side of the ground, it is easy to envisage the belief in, or provocation of, immediate violence. The threat might be as to post-match violence, which might still have the quality of imminence in the sense of proximity in time and space.

4.2.15 Distant threatened group

A more difficult case might be where threats are aimed at a religious or ethnic group, who live predominantly on the oppposite side of a town. That other group might be intended or likely to anticipate unlawful violence, but it might not be easy to establish that the violence they would anticipate could properly be termed immediate. That might be regarded as an application consistent with the decision in *Siadatan*.

In *R v Ambrose* (1973) the appellant addressed to a girl aged 12 words which did not fall within the Act, being at worst rude and offensive. The girl reported the words to her father who, together with another man, became very angry and indicated that they felt like assaulting the appellant. Because of the finding on the language, the court felt that there was no need to enquire further into the question whether insulting words are likely to cause a breach of the peace if the breach of the peace is likely to occur some time later and in different circumstances. In this sort of case where the victim is not likely or intended to be caused to fear the infliction of violence, no offence will be made out since the violence likely to be provoked could not be described as immediate.

In *R v Richmond Magistrates' Court ex p White* (1989) the court was asked to review a magistrates' decision not to issue a summons against the publishers of *The Satanic Verses* by Salman Rushdie. The court analysed the process whereby the magistrate had reached his decision and reviewed the law: 'He came to the conclusion . . . that he was not satisfied that the distribution in the area for which he was responsible . . . was such as to be likely to give rise to violence' (Kennedy J). The court acknowledged that another view might have been taken by others. Clearly the prospect of violence had to be sufficiently proximate and likely, to enable proceedings to issue. The magistrate had formed the view that it 'was anyone's guess' as to whether the publication would lead to violence (see also *R v Horseferry Rd Metropolitan Stipendiary Magistrate ex p Siadatan*).

4.2.16 Duplicity

Section 7(2) provides that s 4 creates one offence only. This was the position under s 5 of the 1936 Act.

4.2.17 Arrest

The issue of whether there was genuine and reasonable suspicion that a person was committing an offence may be challenged in court but it has to be kept in mind that public order cases demand instant decisions by policemen faced with difficult individuals and groups and an obligation to protect the peace. In that context, while it may be right to challenge the reasonableness of the suspicion leading to the arrest, courts will make allowances for the emergency nature of the circumstances and in practice it may be difficult to persuade courts, except in obvious cases, that reasonable suspicion did not exist (*G v Superintendent of Police* (1988)) (see also Chapter 7).

4.3 Public Order Act 1986, s4A

4.3.1 Checklist

- Under s 4A offending conduct must be aimed at a person
- a person must be harassed, alarmed or distressed
- intent only requires intent to cause harassment, etc
- harassment, alarm and distress have their ordinary meaning
- no offence where both accused and harassed person in same dwelling
- accused may offer defence that he was inside a house and had no reason to believe he could be seen or heard outside

Although there is no reference to race in the new provision, it is designed to increase the penalties available for a range of offending which often has a racial motive. If the power is aimed at that particular category of offender, it may function as the Government anticipated. If, however, the new s 4A is commonly used as an alternative to 'ordinary' s 5 cases with the increased penalty, then all s 4A will have done is to have increased the likely penalty for relatively minor public order law breaches and the risk of the law failing to achieve the proper balance between limiting individual rights and protecting the public peace. It will not be playing a key role in the fight against racial harassment.

In the Home Office guide to the Criminal Justice and Public Order Act 1994 the provision is described as being 'designed to deal more effectively with cases of serious racial harassment, particularly where the behaviour is persistent'. While that may be the intention, there is nothing in the provision which directs its focus to racial cases. Its operation in practice will depend upon the view taken by the prosecuting authorities and the police, and the research findings are not especially hopeful.

4.3.2 Provisions

Section 4A provides:

> 40—(1) A person is guilty of an offence if, with intent to cause a person harassment alarm or distress, he—
> (a) uses threatening, abusive or insulting words or behaviour, or disorderly behaviour, or
> (b) displays any writing sign or other visible representation which is threatening abusive or insulting, thereby causing that or another person harassment, alarm or distress.
> (2) An offence under this section may be committed in a public or private place except that no offence is committed when the words or behaviour are used, or the writing sign or visible representation is displayed, by a person inside a dwelling, and the person who is harassed alarmed or distressed is also inside that dwelling.

4.3.3 Venue

The trend in the POA 1986 is continued. This offence may be committed in a public or a private place. A private place is only exempted if it is a dwelling and the victim is in that dwelling as well as the alleged perpetrator. A person who affixes posters to his window or dwelling which are capable of being seen by passers by or neighbours is capable of committing the offence subject to compliance with the other requirements.

4.3.4 Victim

This new offence is only committed if the intention is to cause 'a person' harassment, alarm or distress and the conduct actually causes 'that or another person' harassment, alarm or distress. This offence is therefore quite different from s 5. Section 5 merely requires the conduct to be in the hearing or sight of a person likely to be caused harassment, alarm or distress thereby. In the new provision, the conduct must be aimed at a person who must be capable of identification. That person or another who is actually caused harassment, alarm or distress must also be identified. It may be difficult to say that a person has been caused distress by the particular conduct unless they give evidence to that effect. Mere evidence of distress may not link the distress to the particular conduct. However, if the evidence of distress is sufficiently compelling it might well be that the court would be able to draw the inference that the conduct caused the distress. A set of remarks directed at a person followed by that person being reduced to floods of tears might well lead a court to the obvious inference that the tears were the consequence of the particular remarks or behaviour. Conduct aimed at one person who remains unaffected by it is still an offence if it affects a third party against whom it is not directed, whether or not there is any connection between the intended victim and the third party. The new s 4A is also different in this respect from s 4 which focuses on conduct towards an individual with the exception of provocation which can have the effect on 'that or another person'.

4.3.5 Intent

The specific intent in s 4A is less complex than the four components of intent in s 4. All the defendant has to intend is 'to cause a person harassment, alarm or distress'. In most cases the intention will be obvious and deliberate. In other cases it will be for the court to draw proper inferences from the circumstances surrounding the case. It is only a positive intention on his part which will render him guilty. To that extent, proving the case will be that much more difficult, which is perhaps surprising given that s 4 and s 4A make the same penalty range available to the court. Although the decision in *Wilmott and Another v DPP* (1991) related primarily to the s 6(3) finding, it was made clear that intention speaks for itself where the conduct is clear so the category of cases where the difficulty over the application of s 6(3) arises may be small. It is possible to behave in a threatening way without intending it to cause a person harassment, alarm or distress, particularly if the behaviour occurs on an occasion when the defendant is able to persuade a court that he did not think there was anybody there, but the most likely route for the resolution of this issue is that courts will hold to the view that the intent is made out by the nature of the conduct in question.

It is important to note that s 6(3) of the POA 1986 appears not to apply to s 4A because s 4A is inserted into the Act after s 4 and not within it. If this somewhat inconsistent position is confirmed as being correct, it means that being aware that his conduct 'may be threatening, abusive or insulting' will not suffice to make out the offence. An alternative view is that s 4A is part of s 4 and therefore subject to s 6(3) and (4) in the same way as the balance of the section. This is a matter which may in due course be resolved on appeal.

4.3.6 Harassment, alarm or distress, threatening, abusive or insulting, disorderly

These words are not defined in the statute and should be given their ordinary meaning. They are strong words indicating a level of extreme concern, going beyond 'annoyance', 'disturbance' or 'aggravation' (*Brutus v Cozens*). A policeman may be harassed, alarmed or distressed although whether he was will be a question of fact (*DPP v Orum* (1988)).

'Threatening, abusive or insulting' are defined in relation to s 4 at 4.2.4. In so far as they relate to writing, signs or other visible representation, it is only the display that is caught by the provision. There is no reference to distribution in the terms contained in s 4. It might also be argued that distribution may involve a display in certain contexts depending on all the surrounding circumstances and precisely how the distribution took place. In an appropriate case, given that s 4 is expressed in wider terms, it might be that distribution would be caught by that provision.

'Disorderly' is examined below in relation to s 5 and has been the subject of a number of references to the higher courts, although not generally in relation to the 1986 Act. For the purposes of s 4A it will have the same meaning as in s 5.

4.3.7 Defences

The offence is not committed by one person to another inside the same dwelling (s 4A(2)). The definition of dwelling is set out in s 8 of the POA 1986. It is a defence for the accused to prove that he was inside a dwelling and had no reason to believe the words or behaviour used or the writing, sign or other visible representation displayed would be heard or seen by a person outside that or any other dwelling. The burden is on the defence which must satisfy the court to the civil test, ie on a balance of probabilities. The defence is not made out by simply showing his state of mind and that he genuinely did not believe his conduct would be heard or seen outside the dwelling. The test is objective. Was there reason for him to believe that it would not be heard or seen? As seen in *DPP v Wilmott and Another* (1991) *above*, courts are expected to take a common sense view of events that speak for themselves. The reference in this defence to 'outside that or any other dwelling' may appear to be surplusage, given that s 4A(2) excludes an offence by a person in one dwelling to a person in another dwelling, but it is not. If a defendant phoned a victim and harassed him or her over the phone in the belief that the victim was in the house answering the phone but the victim was in fact outside using a cordless phone, then the potential for an offence exists. This will be a matter for analysis on the particular facts in any given case. The defence that his conduct was reasonable (s 4(3)(b)) is analysed in relation to s 5 below at 4.4.17. Reference to the Convention rights and history of rights of protest is set out at 1.1 and 1.4 (see also 1.3).

4.3.8 Arrest

A constable may arrest without warrant a person he reasonably suspects is committing the offence. For the occasions when the policeman is not the observer he will utilise s 25 of the Police and Criminal Evidence Act 1984 (PACE). It should be noted that the extra requirements of s 5, at s 5(4), that the policeman should warn the person to stop prior to arresting him in connection with continuing offensive conduct are not repeated in relation to the new s 4A.

4.3.9 Duplicity

Section 7(2) provides that s 4A creates only one offence to avoid duplicity, despite the multiplicity of elements in the section.

4.4 Offensive conduct (POA 1986, s 5)

4.4.1 Checklist

- Focus of section was originally minor hooliganism
- conduct must be in presence of person affected
- a person must be likely to be caused harassment, alarm or distress
- a policeman may be harassed
- HO research shows police widespread use of s 5 to deal with insults directed at police themselves (4.1.3)
- what accused aware of may be a matter of common sense
- displaying true photograph may amount to insulting or abusive behaviour
- section 5 arrest must be after warning and the arrest itself must be by the warning officer
- where s 5 is charged after arrest for other offence, warning not needed
- defence of reasonable conduct

Section 5 is a widely expressed catch-all provision designed to provide the prosecuting authorities and the police in particular with the means to deal with a wide range of the less serious public order disturbances. After the appropriate warning has been given, if the misbehaviour continues then the police may arrest. This enables the policeman to intervene relatively promptly to prevent a difficult situation becoming worse.

The apparent generality of the offence, which may contradict the principles of due process, was tempered at one stage by the requirement that someone should actually have been harassed, alarmed or distressed to a substantial degree, but this dual requirement was not enacted despite anxiety that the threshold of criminality was being lowered by the provision. This requirement has been incorporated in s 4A of the 1986 Act to the extent that the behaviour must be intended to cause a person harassment, alarm or distress and must actually do so. In practice the section has been reviewed in the higher courts, but it seems not to have proved the problem in enforcement that was envisaged in 1986.

The intention was to provide an offence suitable to encompass minor acts of hooliganism not otherwise falling within the scope of s 4 of the Act. The White Paper described the mischief:

> 3.22 . . . Instances of such behaviour might include: hooligans on housing estates causing disturbances in the common parts of blocks of flats, blockading entrances, throwing things down the stairs, banging on doors, peering in at windows, and knocking over dustbins; groups of youth persistently shouting abuse and obscenities or pestering people waiting to catch public transport or to enter a hall or cinema.

4.4.2 Elements of the offence

Section 5(1) provides:

> 5.—(1) A person is guilty of an offence if he—
> (a) uses threatening, abusive or insulting words or behaviour, or disorderly behaviour, or
> (b) displays any writing, sign or other visible representation which is threatening, abusive, or insulting,
>
> within the hearing or sight of a person likely to be caused harassment, alarm or distress thereby.

Although there are clear similarities between s 4 and s 5 (eg the criteria of threatening, abusive or insulting and the venue) there are important distinctions:

(a) the criteria in s 5 are extended by the addition of 'disorderly' to the list of prohibited behaviour (but not words);

(b) fear or provocation of violence in s 4 is replaced by likelihood of harassment, alarm or distress in s 5;
(c) the words 'towards another person' in s 4 are omitted from s 5;
(d) section 5 extends only to the display and not distribution of writing, sign etc. Thus it does not extend to letters, eg poison pen letters, or the posting of leaflets through a door.

4.4.3 Victim

It is tempting to say that there is no victim for a s 5 offence but it is not an offence which can occur *in vacuo*. It is simply required that the proscribed conduct occurs within the hearing or sight of a person who is likely to be caused harassment, alarm or distress by the conduct (s 5(1)(b)). That person would normally be perceived as the victim. There is no requirement that the conduct should be directed towards that or any other person in particular. In *DPP v Orum* it was made clear that a policeman could be harassed, alarmed or distressed by particular conduct. Glidewell J said:

> I find nothing in the context of the 1986 Act to persuade me that a policeman may not be a person who is caused harassment, alarm or distress by the various kinds of words and conduct to which s 5(1) applies . . . However . . . it is not to say that every police officer in this situation is to be assumed to be a person who is caused harassment. Very frequently, words and behaviour with which police officers will be wearily familiar will have little emotional impact on them save that of boredom.

Each case depends on its own facts and is a matter for the finding of the tribunal of fact. In *R v Ball (Simon Leonard)* (1990), the Court of Appeal looked at a case where a policeman had arrested for s 5 in circumstances where he was the only person present and had not been harassed, alarmed or distressed. The case established that a policeman was capable of being 'likely to be' harassed, alarmed or distressed and that it was a matter of fact in each particular case as to whether he would have been likely to be so affected.

4.4.4 Requisite intent

In *DPP v Clarke and Others* (1991) a group of people opposed to abortion had gathered outside an abortion clinic carrying a picture of an aborted foetus and refused to stop displaying the pictures when requested to by the police. They were charged with an offence contrary to s 5(1)(b) of the POA 1986. The justices found that the display was abusive or insulting; that it was in the sight of someone likely to be caused harassment, alarm or distress by it, namely one of the policemen. Applying an objective test to s 5(3) they found the behaviour unreasonable. They then applied a subjective test to s 6(4) and concluded on a balance of probabilities that the defendants did not intend nor were they aware that the display might be threatening, abusive or insulting. They therefore dismissed the charges.

On appeal the divisional court found that the component parts of s 5(1) were to be distinguished and that the intent or awareness requirement in s 6(4) did not relate to the 'within the sight' part of s 5(1). Dealing with the defence, the divisional court found that the s 5(3)(a) defence had to be proved by the defence on a balance of probabilities and that the s 6(4) intent, being part of the offence, had to be proved by the prosecution beyond reasonable doubt:

> So far as the defence provided by s 5(3) is concerned, the section makes it clear that the burden of proof rests upon the defendant . . . the standard of proof is the balance of probabilities. So far as s 6 is concerned, the burden of proving that the defendant had the requisite mental element rests upon the prosecution . . . the standard required is proof beyond reasonable doubt. The section plays an important role in the protection of freedom of speech (*per* Nolan LJ).

While the *DPP v Clarke* case sets out the position in relation to intent and the related defences in a case where the court upheld justices who acquitted, *Wilmott and Another v DPP* (1991) should be borne in mind. In that case the court made the point that what a person is aware of is a matter of common sense. So provided some evidence is called by the prosecution, it would be a case for the court to draw proper inferences as to the defendant's 'awareness' from the evidence before them.

In *Lewis v DPP* (1995) the court were again called upon to deal with issues relating to abortion clinics. In that case a placard held aloft showing a baby lying in a pool of blood and titled '21 weeks abortion' was held to be abusive and insulting. The issue of awareness and intent was more readily resolved against the defendant because others had put down the placard on being requested to do so by the police. He had picked it up and continued to display it when asked again not to. It therefore followed that he intended the placard to be abusive and insulting and was aware that the representation on the placard was abusive or insulting.

One of the issues reviewed by the divisional court was whether the placard was abusive or insulting and in that context, the court's comment on the capacity of a truthful representation to be abusive is instructive. It is probably also a logical development of the common sense approach to awareness determined in *Wilmott and Another v DPP*:

> The point taken is that the photograph on the placard was an accurate representation of the result of abortion, and that what is truthful cannot be abusive or insulting . . . A patient may be abused in having the activities (lawful activities in this case) depicted in the way they were on that placard (*per* Pill LJ).

4.4.5 Arrest

An arrest under s 5 may be made where the person has engaged in offensive conduct, been warned by the officer as to his conduct and then engaged in further offensive conduct, either immediately afterwards or shortly after the warning. The arrest may only be by the officer who gave the warning. An arresting officer, other than the one who administered the warning, is acting other than in the execution of his duty. In *DPP v Hancock and Tuttle* (1995) justices dismissed allegations of resisting two constables and assaulting a constable. The appeal was dismissed because the power of arrest in s 5(4) was only exercisable by the officer who had personally given the warning required by s 5. An officer who had not given the warning acted otherwise than in execution of his duty in effecting arrest under s 5.

It should be noted that in the case of a person arrested for an offence other than s 5, eg common assault or breach of the peace, but who is subsequently charged with an offence contrary to s 5, the position is different. In that case the warning and requirement for arrest by the warning officer do not apply, as the arrest is not for s 5. In that case only the elements of s 5 and the intent in s 6 need be made out.

In any event, whether or not the arrest under s 5 is lawful has no bearing on whether the offence under s 5 is made out. The s 5 behaviour precedes the arrest and an invalid arrest cannot retrospectively affect the criminality of the behaviour. In *DPP v Hancock and Tuttle* the offence charged was the more technical s 51 and which related to behaviour during the arrest.

In *Groom v DPP* (1991) the divisional court reviewed how courts should deal with the warnings required in s 5. In that case, following an incident of racial abuse outside the town hall, a police officer followed the abuser into the building and an exchange took place during which the officer told the person that he had harassed the person outside and that he should apologise. The appellant said 'Or else you'll nick me?' She replied 'Yes'. The appellant continued his agressive manner and told her to get stuffed, whereupon she arrested him for an offence contrary to s 5. The question was whether her words constituted the required warning or not. Bingham LJ, in supporting the view that she had given sufficient warning, said:

> It is also a salutary principle that in analysing the effects of what people say and do in confused and violent, or potentially violent, situations, tribunals of fact should concentrate in a common sense way on the substance of what was said and done and not indulge in a nice analysis more appropriate to academic debate than to the crude realities of life.

It would appear that it is the substance of the warning and not its form that is essential.

4.4.6 Venue

Section 5 penalises conduct which occurs in private or public places subject to the same restriction in the case of dwellings as now appears in s 4A (see 4.3.3). It is no offence if the 'other person' is inside the same dwelling as the offender or in another dwelling.

> A person yelling or gesturing to persons in the street . . . would not commit an offence vis-à-vis another person within his own house or a neighbouring house across the street (*Chappell v DPP* (1989)).

4.4.7 Nature of the conduct

There must be either the use of threatening, abusive or insulting words (s 5(1)(a)) or threatening, abusive or insulting or disorderly behaviour (s 5(1)(a)) or the display of any writing, sign or visible representation which is threatening, abusive or insulting (s 5(1)(b)). In this book such conduct is referred to as 'offensive behaviour', a description which is not used in s 5 except in the context of arrest for the offence (s 5(4)). Display only is prohibited, not distribution. The distribution of literature might be dealt with under s 4. It might also be argued that the distribution of offensive literature might amount to disorderly conduct.

4.4.8 Threatening, abusive or insulting

These words have been considered earlier, but in the context of s 5 allegations, in *Herrington v DPP* (1992), the court went through the definittions contained in *Brutus v Cozens* to analyse what 'threatening' meant. In the *Herrington* case the divisional court upheld magistrates who had found that a man who had 'gone down the garden, turned and stared for a period of time at the lady's kitchen window when standing nude and facing his genitals towards her' was engaging in threatening behaviour within the meaning of s 5. See also *Lewis v DPP* (4.4.4) where the showing of a placard with a picture of a foetus in a pool of blood and wording was held to be abusive or insulting.

4.4.9 Disorderly

'Disorderly' has been used to describe different types of conduct and in *Martin v Yorkshire Imperial Metals Ltd* (1978) it was referred to as 'rather a weasel word; it might mean disorderly in the sense of riotous or the sort of conduct which is inferred in the well known phrase "disorderly house"; or it might mean . . . any conduct which is contrary to orders'. It is best known in the offence of 'drunk and disorderly' (Criminal Justice Act 1967, s 91) which is of ancient origin. Much of the conduct which falls within s 91 may also fall within s 5. The meaning of disorderly will be derived from its context, ie its relationship to the remainder of the list (threatening, abusive and insulting) and the impact upon people who witness it, ie there must be conduct which is conducive to creating extreme concern in victims. It is an ordinary English word and needs no definition (see *Brutus v Cozens*). Regard must be had to the circumstances in which conduct occurs in order to determine whether or not it merits the appellation 'disorderly'. The conduct of a football crowd would be disorderly if it were to be repeated in a theatre during a performance. While the list of words in ss 4 and 5 are often taken to represent a descending order of seriousness, they are really no more than different types of conduct which are penalised because of their likely or intended impact upon others, ie the threat of violence or harassment.

In *Chambers and Another v DPP* (1995) the divisional court looked at aspects of the word disorderly. In that case during 1993 the defendant interfered with a land engineer by standing in front of his theodolite, preventing him from taking measurements. He kept his hand in front of the machine when warned by the police that his conduct was disorderly and was causing harassment, alarm or distress. The defendants were convicted by magistrates. They appealed to the Crown Court where they were again convicted. The Crown Court found among other things that they had been disorderly. The divisional court applied the *Brutus v Cozens* principle that disorderly is a word whose ordinary meaning should be used and left to the tribunal of fact:

> For my part, I can see no reason why one should conclude that the word 'disorderly' is being used in some unusual or narrower sense than normal in the context of s 5(1) . . . whether behaviour on any occasion is characterised as disorderly is a question of fact for the trial court to determine. That decision can be upset if the trial court has misdirected itself or has reached a decision which no reasonable tribunal could properly reach (*per* Keene J).

4.4.10 Disorderly behaviour: New Zealand cases

Some guidance as to the meaning of 'disorderly' may be obtained from New Zealand case law where it was used in s 3D of the Police Offences

Amendment Act No 2 1960 (see now s 4(1)(a) of the Summary Offences Act 1981):

> Every person commits an offence . . . who . . . behaves in a riotous, offensive, threatening, insulting or disorderly manner. . .

The leading authority on disorderly conduct in relation to that offence is the New Zealand Court of Appeal case of *Melser and Others v Police* (1967). The following useful comments were made and although caution has to be exercised when considering a statutory provision with a different history it is a useful indicator of matters which may be considered in English courts. The additional factor in s 5 is that there must be a likelihood of harassment, alarm or distress:

> not only must the behaviour seriously offend against those values of orderly conduct which are recognised by right-thinking members of the public but it must at least be of a character which is likely to cause annoyance to others who are present. . .
>
> . . . the collation of the words show that they are directed to conduct which at least is likely to cause a disturbance or annoyance to others. To lay down a wider test would, I think, be contrary to the public interest and might unduly restrict the actions of citizens who, for one reason or another, do not accept the values of orderly conduct which at the time are recognised by other members of the public. In short, there must be reasonable room for change in habits and behaviour (*per* North P).

4.4.11 Disorderly behaviour: Scots cases

Disorderly behaviour has been considered in Scotland. In *Campbell v Adair* (1945) a bus inspector investigated a complaint that a woman had boarded a bus improperly. He upbraided the woman and interviewed her in a bullying fashion despite the fact that she was badly shaken after a fall from the bus. The inspector was found guilty of disorderly behaviour under the Glasgow Police Act 1866 (riotous, disorderly or indecent behaviour).

4.4.12 Disorderly behaviour: 1936 POA cases

Conduct which may fall within s 5 can be seen in many cases where prosecutions occurred under the 1936 Act. For example in *Ewart v Rogers* (1985) a group of youths disturbed a householder by banging on the front windows and door and smashing milk bottles. In *R v Newham JJ ex p Sadiku*, urinating in public might have been classed as disorderly. In *R v Venna* (1975) the conduct of youths in shouting and singing and dancing in the street and banging dustbin lids was described by the court as unruly and disgraceful and anti-social. It might equally have been described as disorderly.

4.4.13 Noisy parties

Whether the offence can be used to deal with noisy parties is not clear. If the only people likely to suffer harassment, alarm or distress are people within their houses then the offence will not be made out. Equally it may be difficult to class such parties as disorderly. This was the view of the government during debate in the *House of Commons Hansard, Parliamentary Debates*, vol 96, No 104, para 967. In practice it appears that s 5 has not been used as a means of dealing with noisy parties which were still the subject of debate and indeed legislation in the CJPOA.

4.4.14 Within the sight or hearing of

The conduct must occur within the hearing or sight of a person likely to be caused harassment, alarm or distress. There is no requirement that a victim should give evidence or that someone need be shown to have been harassed, alarmed or distressed. It must be shown that the conduct did in fact occur within the sight or hearing of a person and that the person was likely to be caused harassment, alarm or distress by such conduct. The offence is based upon likely consequences, not intended or actual consequences. Should there be witnesses who can relate their feelings, then the task of the prosecution will be easier. Even if such witnesses cannot be found or are unwilling to give evidence, the prosecution may still succeed although the difficulties inherent in this are apparent. The absence of a requirement to produce a victim who was actually harassed, alarmed or distressed was a deliberate step to avoid cases where a victim would be too nervous or frail to give evidence. The Minister of State at the Home Office observed that:

> The prosecution will not necessarily have to produce the victim in court, but it will have to identify in each case who it was who was likely to be alarmed . . . The court's mind will be concentrated upon the impact or likely impact of the defendant's behaviour on those who were around at that time. (HC Deb, vol 96, No 104, col 964).

That the offensive conduct was within the sight or hearing of such a person is an inference which may be drawn from the facts as a whole, eg offensive conduct in a shopping precinct where it is likely that a police officer will be able to relate only that there were shoppers who hurried away apparently upset or annoyed. Where there is noise late at night in the vicinity of an old people's home, then the burden of showing that a person is likely to be harassed, alarmed or distressed will be relatively simple to discharge.

In *Lodge v Andrews* (1988), the divisional court analysed a number of the issues relating to 'within the sight or hearing'. In this case a young man who had just engaged in a minor confrontation with two police officers chose to walk down the middle of a road towards a bridge over which a car was about to come in circumstances which might be expected to give rise to a risk of accident. Two issues were canvassed. Could the car driver be a person within whose sight or hearing the misconduct occurred? And could the policeman suffer harassment, alarm or distress save by reference to his own personal position, ie not on behalf of either the motorist or the disorderly young man who might be at risk? The divisional court took the view that the car driver was likely to have been alarmed by the disorderly young man in the middle of the road. In relation to the policeman, having considered *DPP v Orum*, the court went on to say that the apprehension he feels need not relate to himself or a close relative. By way of example the court raised the possibility of disorderly behaviour adjacent to a child. They would expect such conduct to distress or alarm an observing policeman.

The defendant would appear to have to take his victims as he finds them and if they are especially timid and easily harassed, etc then, upon proof of this fact (which may involve them having to give evidence, for example where a person would not normally be adversely affected), the defendant can properly be convicted. He may be able, however, to maintain a defence under s 5(3)(a) of the POA 1986.

4.4.15 Harassment, alarm or distress

Harassment, alarm and distress are not defined. Since they are ordinary words of the English language and are not intended to have any special meaning they should be given their ordinary meaning (see *Brutus v Cozens*). They are strong words and should not be equated with 'annoyance' or 'disturbance' or 'aggravation'; they indicate a level of extreme concern. It is worth reiterating that just as a police officer may fear the use of unlawful violence, so too may he be likely to be harassed, alarmed or distressed. But the level of tolerance which may be expected of a police officer may be rather higher than that of the ordinary citizen (*DPP v Orum*).

4.4.16 Defence to s 5: no reason to believe

Each of the three defences set out in s 5(3) of the POA 1986 must be established by the defendant on the balance of probabilities. Each defence applies to all offences under s 5. The first possible defence is that the defendant 'had no reason to believe that there was any person within hearing or sight who was likely to be caused harassment, alarm or distress' (s 5(3)(a)). Not only must the absence of belief be genuine but the defendant must also, objectively, have had no reasonable grounds for the belief. Of the need to provide this sort of defence Mr Giles Shaw, Minister of State, remarked in the committee stage of the Bill:

> We wanted to provide a defence for the defendant who is not aware and has no reason to be aware that his behaviour is likely to cause alarm, harassment or distress, and we wanted to bring within the offence people whose behaviour would be unlikely to harass a normal victim but who used their knowledge of the victim's weakness to make life miserable for a vulnerable person (HC, SC G, col 236).

In *Masterson v Holden* the activity occurred in the presence of people who were distressed and roused to anger. It might be a defence to s 5 to demonstrate that the couple had no reason to believe that there was anyone in the vicinity who was likely to be harassed, eg because of the cosmopolitan nature of the particular district. In the absence of an authority on the express defence point, it is difficult to be sure because of the changing view of society. This illustrates an important difference between s 4 and s 5. In s 4 conduct must be used towards another person. In s 5 these words are not used and the conduct need not be aimed at anyone; having no reason to believe that a person who will be affected is present will provide a defence.

It will also be remembered that the prosecution must establish an intention to use offensive behaviour, and the proximity of other people may also be relevant to that point.

4.4.17 Defence to s 5: inside dwelling and no reason to believe

Again, this must be proved on a balance of probabilities by the defence and is available in all s 5 cases. The section provides that it is a defence if 'he was inside a dwelling and had no reason to believe that the offensive conduct would be heard or seen by a person outside that or any other house' (s 5(3)(b)). This defence is likely to be of limited application since the offence will rarely be committed when the defendant is inside a dwelling.

4.4.18 Defence to s 5: reasonable conduct

Again this defence must be proved on a balance of probabilities by the defence and is available to all s 5 charges. The section provides that it is a defence: 'that his conduct is reasonable' (s 5(3)(c)). The circumstances will indicate when conduct can be said in the first place to be offensive, and if it can be said to be offensive then it is at the same time difficult to see how it can be reasonable. The scope of this particular defence is uncertain, not least because for the prosecution to succeed it will have to have established an intention to use offensive conduct (s 5(4)) but the relationship between this provision and the 'right to protest' (see 1.1, 1.4) in demonstration cases should be kept in mind. It may not be possible on particular facts to use the defence, but there may be conduct which is arguably reasonable in the general context of lawful protest. It should not be discarded as a possibility.

Little guidance was given during the passage of the bill as to the likely scope of this defence. In committee it was said that the defence was intended as 'a general safety net'. There was some suggestion that high jinks might 'induce a modest level of offence' and that it would be wrong to use the offence for that type of activity. Unfortunately no examples were given which might explain these ambiguous observations. In addition it was suggested that there were examples of behaviour which might be reasonable on the basis that they came close to lawful authority, eg 'if firemen or police officers use strong language when they want people to get out of the way, that may be deemed unreasonable to some but in the context would probably be acceptable'. The practical nature of the examples may be doubted. More to the point might be cases where offensive behaviour is used by an occupier in an attempt to rid himself of trespassers. Will the use of offensive conduct be 'reasonable'? Would it make any difference if the trespassers were police officers (compare the behaviour in *Marsh v Arscott*)? To what extent will the abuse which is commonly hurled at those who cross picket lines be reasonable, eg the shouts of 'scab' or 'blackleg'?

In *Lewis v DPP* (1995) the divisional court also analysed the defence of reasonableness. In this case, discussed earlier in 4.4.4, the defendant stood outside an abortion clinic holding a placard depicting a baby in a pool of blood. It was argued on his behalf that while the test of reasonableness of conduct can only be answered by reference to an objective standard of reasonableness in accordance with the decision in *Clarke v DPP* (see again 4.4.4), in a s 5 case, the test should be applied to the facts as the particular defendant knew them. An analogy was drawn on behalf of the defendant with the notion of honest belief as a defence to a rape charge. This was rejected by the divisional court:

> The analogy is not sound . . . In this case the appellant's belief as to what was happening in the clinic accords with the actual state of affairs . . . he is not entitled to have his conduct judged only on the basis of his own moral stance or beliefs (*per* Pill LJ).

The court went on to review whether the particular defendant had acted reasonably:

> In considering whether the defendant had established that he had acted reasonably, the Court was entitled to take into account that he persisted in his conduct after being asked to desist . . . the appellant, unlike the women who were not prosecuted, persisted in displaying the placard (*per* Pill LJ).

The court went on with their review of reasonableness:

> It cannot be right that a trial court should have to adopt the same approach in judging the issue of reasonable conduct and view the matter entirely through the eyes of the defendant . . . That would lead to situations where the more extreme were the opinions of a defendant, the more readily would his conduct be regarded as reasonable (*per* Keene J).

The case of *DDP v Lewis* therefore follows *DPP v Clarke*, pointing out problems which may arise in the event of defendants attempting to find an alternative approach to the s 5 defence of reasonableness.

4.4.19 Prevention of crime as a defence

A common defence to s 5 allegations is that the defendant was doing what he regarded as necessary to prevent the offending behaviour of some other person. In *R v Ball* (1990) Ball grabbed a policeman from behind to prevent his brother being arrested for a s 5 offence. Ball claimed that he was acting in reasonable defence of his brother and that the officer was acting unlawfully, there being no reasonable grounds for suspecting him of having committed an offence. The court did not agree that the arrest was unlawful and reviewed issues relating to honest belief. It was held that:

> honest belief on reasonable grounds in the unlawfulness of an arrest was not a defence to assault (*R v Fennell* (1970)) and it was logical that a similar belief in excessive force by the police in executing a lawful arrest would also not afford a defence.

The reality is that s 3 of the Criminal Law Act 1967 (CLA) entitles a person to do that which is reasonable in the prevention of crime. Some public order cases, including s 5 cases, will require the court to establish as a question of fact whether the defendant was engaged in lawful conduct to prevent crime. This defence cannot be used as a means of justifying action where the alleged crime being prevented is in fact a lawful activity to which the particular defendant takes exception. The abortion clinic cases of *Clarke v DPP* and *Lewis v DPP* are not the only examples of protest against lawful activity being the subject of judicial analysis. Protestors against live animal export may regard the treatment of the animals during the transportation as a crime. In reality that is a moral judgment and the export is both legal and lawful. Action to prevent it cannot therefore be protected by the notion of preventing crime. In *Morrow v DPP*(1993) the issue again related to protests over abortion clinics. In that case the appellants had entered an abortion clinic and created difficulties once inside. They had been charged with s 5 offences and relied upon the statutory defence that their conduct was reasonable and also that their conduct was lawful under the provision of s 3(1) of the CLA 1967. The court held that the defence under s 3 was not apt to the situation which arose in this case where an aggressive demonstration was being held. The appellants were described by the court as being involved in preventing people from exercising their lawful rights and therefore it was difficult to see the relevance of the s 3 defence. The court made the point that the s 3 defence was not created to protect people who plan a demonstration which involved aggressive behaviour when on the premises of others and disrupting perfectly proper conduct of people. This case should also be seen alongside the decision made in relation to the attempt by public authorities to prevent trade in live animals through their ports. Where protest and lawful activity meet, the courts see the protection of lawful activity as being a matter of fundamental importance (*R v Coventry City Council ex p Phoenix Aviation*):

> English law is unsurprisingly replete with examples of ringing dicta vindicating the rule of law ... One thread runs consistently throughout all the case law: the recognition that public authorities must beware of surrendering to the dictates of unlawful pressure groups (*per* Simon Brown LJ).

4.4.20 Interface of ss 4 and 5

Section 4 is specifically designed to deal with activities which are likely to lead to fear of or provocation to violence. Section 5 is specifically designed to deal with activities which lead to a serious degree of discomfort. This is not to say that in appropriate instances conduct which falls squarely within s 4 may not be dealt with under s 5. Rather, conduct which does not fall within a 'lesser' category should not be made to fit within a more serious category (see 4.1.2 for research on use of s 5 and Chapter 1 for material relevant to any cases of public disorder).

4.4.21 Arrest

A constable, in uniform or not, may arrest without warrant in the circumstances set out in s 5(4)(5). The first reference in s 5(4) to 'he engages' may be read as meaning is engaged in and not 'is or has been engaged in'. By the nature of the offence it will be unusual for a constable to be able to witness the actual conduct and to issue a warning while it is continuing. If this interpretation is correct, then the power of arrest will be exercised on few occasions. However, the power of arrest under s 25 of the Police and Criminal Evidence Act will, of course, be available if any of the general arrest conditions in that Act are satisfied (see 1.6 and 1.7 on policing).

The meaning of shortly or immediately is a question of fact for each case. Immediately would appear to be superfluous since any activity which occurs immediately can be said to have occurred shortly.

4.4.22 Duplicity

Section 7 precludes the risk of duplicity by saying that the section creates only one offence.

4.4.23 Sentence

The offence carries a maximum penalty of a fine to level 3.

4.5 Racial hatred

4.5.1 Checklist

- Behaviour includes gestures
- display does not have restricted meaning
- conduct in dwelling not caught unless seen from outside
- private meetings outside dwellings are caught
- intent to stir up or likely to stir up racial hatred
- publish/distribute offences now arrestable offences
- Race Relations Act 1976 protects any racial group in Great Britain—wide definition

The common law provided little protection for racial groups against incitement to hatred. Such incitement may have been sedition and the gravity of incitement to racial hatred as an offence is shown by the decided cases. In *R v Relf* (1979) a sentence of 15 months was reduced to nine months on a man who had distributed leaflets which were derogatory towards West Indians. In *R v Edwards* (1983) a comic strip designed to prejudice children against Jews and Asians led to a sentence of 12 months. The creation of the new s 4A of the POA 1986 with an expressed purpose of being available for cases of serious racial harassment further reinforces the legislative position that offences with a racial element are penalised with particular seriousness when that racial element can be identified. In so far as the new offence is used by those who prosecute and the courts dealing with race-related offences, the availability of the six months' custodial sentence reflects the need for a custodial sentence for racial harassment. Historically the custodial sentences mentioned above were upheld on the basis that each ethnic or religious group was entitled to protection from such incitement under the Queen's peace. Section 5 of the 1936 Act could be used in appropriate circumstances although reliance on breach of the peace restricted its usefulness and it was ineffective against more insidious forms of incitement or incitements which occurred privately. Section 6 of the Race Relations Act 1965 was the first statutory provision to attempt to deal with the mischief but that too suffered from restrictive provisions, eg the need to prove both an intention to incite racial hatred and a likelihood of racial hatred being stirred up. Section 70 of the Race Relations Act 1976 introduced s 5A into the 1936 Act. This was substantially the same as s 6 of the Race Relations Act although the need to prove intent was removed and the likelihood of racial hatred being stirred up became the sole test. The section remained limited in its application. It did not contain a power of arrest; publication and distribution were defined restrictively, not dealing with distribution of material to members of a club or organisation. There were provisions in other Acts dealing with incitements to racial hatred. The Cable and Broadcasting Act 1984 and the Theatres Act 1968, together with s 5A, were repealed by Sched 3 to the POA 1986 and six new offences were created in ss 18–23.

4.5.2 Racial Hatred (s 17)

The hatred to be stirred up must be 'against a racial group in Great Britain'. The definition of racial group (s 17) was adapted from the Race Relations Act 1976. The definition is wide enough to cover Jews (*Seide v Gillette*) and Sikhs (*Mandla v Dowell Lee*) as well as many other groups such as gypsies. The meaning of 'ethnic origins' was considered in *Mandla v Dowell Lee* where the House of Lords provided guidelines as to the criteria for deciding whether a group might be classed as having ethnic origins. See also *Commission for Racial Equality v Dutton* (1989).

4.5.3 Words, behaviour and display of written material (s 18)

It is an offence (a) to use threatening, abusive or insulting words or behaviour, or (b) to display threatening, abusive or insulting written material, either where the defendant intends racial hatred to be stirred up by such use, or where, having regard to all the circumstances, racial hatred is likely to be stirred up by such use. 'Gestures' is not a word used within the section. They will be included in behaviour. In certain circumstances, a Nazi-style salute falls within the section, as might a clenched fist salute. Certain words or behaviour are not included (see s 18(6) and s 22(1)). Written material is defined in s 29. 'Display' is not restricted to display to the public or a section of it.

4.5.4 Venue

The Act prohibits conduct generally in public and private places. Where the offending words or behaviour are used in a private place, eg at a private meeting, an offence may still be made out. The only restriction is that there is no offence where the prohibited conduct occurs in a dwelling (which is defined in s 29) and is observed only by people inside that or any other house. If it is observed outside a dwelling house then there will still be a defence for the defendant who is able to show on the balance of probabilities that he was inside a dwelling house and had no reason to believe that the conduct would be observed by a person outside that house and not in another dwelling (s 18(4)). Where the conduct occurs in any other place, eg a factory, club or private meeting, the defence will not apply.

4.5.5 Threatening, abusive or insulting

These words are interpreted as for ss 4 and 5. The difficulty is that while blatant propaganda can be brought within the scope of the Act, more sophisticated propaganda may not. Such propaganda may sufficiently obfuscate the issues as to ensure that the 'ordinary person' could not perceive them as falling within the appropriate categories, eg if the matter purports to have an 'educational' flavour. Brownlie observes that the formula is not very helpful and 'at least superfluous' and 'likely to have a restrictive effect' (*Brownlie's Law of Public Order and National Security*, 2nd edn, Butterworths, 1981). Where spoken words or behaviour are used, a prosecution under s 18 may be sustained but before a mixed audience (ie not composed of like-minded people) offences contrary to ss 4 or 5 may be easier to establish. Where a person is not shown to have intended to stir up racial hatred (ie where the prosecution are able to prove likelihood), it will be necessary for the prosecution to establish that a person did intend his words or behaviour to be threatening, abusive and insulting or was reckless as to that (s 18(5)).

4.5.6 Intention or likelihood

All the offences now adopt the alternative of either intent to stir up racial hatred or the likelihood of racial hatred being stirred up. Section 5A of the 1936 Act relied on likelihood alone. The material may indicate the intention of the defendant. If this cannot be shown, it will be necessary to demonstrate the likelihood of racial hatred being stirred up. The words 'in all the circumstances' indicate that regard should be had to the facts surrounding each event. Words or gestures which are threatening, abusive or insulting and which might be likely to stir up racial hatred in some circumstances might not be likely to do so in other circumstances. There is the world of difference between threatening, abusive or insulting material displayed during a respectable seminar discussing problems of racial harassment and such display at a meeting to promote the views of a particular organisation.

4.5.7 Arrest

A constable, in uniform or not, may arrest without warrant a person he reasonably suspects is committing an offence (s 18(3)). Where this is not applicable, eg because the conduct has stopped, then recourse may be had to s 25 of the Police and Criminal Evidence Act 1984. See 1.7 for some of the dilemmas facing police officers.

4.5.8 Publication/distribution of racially inflammatory written matter (s 19)

It is an offence to publish or distribute threatening, abusive or insulting written material either with intent to stir up racial hatred or whereby it is likely that racial hatred will be stirred up (s 19(1)(a)(b)). Where a person is not shown to have intended to stir up racial hatred but the prosecution are able to prove likelihood, it will be a defence for the defendant to prove that he was not aware of the content of the material and did not suspect or have reason to suspect that it was threatening (s 19(2)). Written material is defined in s 29 as including any sign or other visible representation. 'Writing' includes typing, printing and photography but does not extend to videos or films; but see in this respect ss 21 and 22.

'Publishes' and 'distributes' are restricted by s 19(3) to distribution or publication to the public or a section of the public, and the meaning of publish or distribute is not otherwise defined.

Distribution or publication to the members of an association to which the defendant belonged was not an offence under the amended 1936 Act.

Since the 1986 Act it is an offence. Thus the private circulation of material within an association is an offence provided (a) it can be said to be publication or distribution to 'the public or a section of it' and (b) there is the necessary intention or likelihood.

The meaning of 'section of the public' is not entirely clear. While it is clear that the intention of Parliament was to include members of an association within the definition, it is not clear whether members of a club will also be within the scope of the Act. Although it dealt with an earlier Act, *Charter v Race Relations Board* (1973) appears to be persuasive of the point that a genuine club exercising strict membership restrictions would not be a section of the public for the purposes of the Act. However, since that case concerned the supply of goods or services, such result may not follow for the purposes of the offences under the Act.

For an example of the judicial approach to the meaning of distribution or publication see *R v Britton* (1967) where the court took a pragmatic view of distribution and publication. Leaving pamphlets in the front porch of an MP's house was capable of being a distribution. Had the pamphlets been visible from the road, there might also have been a publication. However, in that case the distribution had not been to a 'section of the public'. Posting a bill on a wall or daubing a slogan might be said to be both publication and display for the purposes of s 4.

4.5.9 Arrest

Section 155 of the CJPOA amends s 24(2) of the Police and Criminal Evidence Act to make offences contrary to s 19 of the POA 1986 arrestable offences. Publishing material intended to or likely to stir up racial hatred is now arrestable.

4.5.10 Possession of racially inflammatory written matter or recordings (s 23)

A person commits an offence if:

(a) he has in his possession threatening, abusive or insulting written material or a recording of visual images or sounds,
(b) with a view to the purposes specified in s 23(1)(a) and (b) provided,
(c) he intends racial hatred to be stirred up or if it is likely to be stirred up.

'Written material' and other terms of s 23 are explained in s 29. Section 23 does not extend to possession for certain purposes outlined in s 23(4). The purposes in s 23(1)(a) and (b) include publication, distribution, showing or playing, and these must be to the public or a section of the public (see ss 29, 19(3) and 21(2)). Display is also included but is not so restricted. It must be a display for the purposes of s 18.

Possession of a video recording or film is within s 23. It is complementary to s 21 which prohibits the distribution, showing or playing of, *inter alia*, video recordings. A person who receives a video recording or film for editing purposes or as part of a chain of distribution will be in possession of the recording even though the actual distribution may be by another person. In so far as written material is concerned, s 23 is complementary to ss 18 (display) and 19 (distribution or publication). Both the physical element of possession and the required mental element are dealt with in the reported cases dealing with such things as the unlawful possession of drugs (see *DPP v Brookes* (1974); *Warner v Metropolitan Police Commissioner* (1969); *R v Wright* (1962); *R v Ashton-Rickhardt* (1965); *R v Lewis* (1987)). The offence is not 'knowingly possess'; the defendant need only know that he has some written matter or recording. Accordingly, there is a defence of innocent possession in s 23(3) which may be of assistance to anyone who is not shown to have intended to stir up racial hatred. This may apply to a firm which delivers to a printer in an envelope proofs of an offending article or delivers a bundle of leaflets to an address of a political party (provided this can be said to be possession within the Act).

The defence must prove the relevant matters upon the balance of probabilities.

A journalist who has collected racially inflammatory material for research purposes will not possess it for the purposes of s 23 if he intends only to use it as background material. If he intends that it should be published in whole or in part then, if he has an intention that racial hatred should be stirred up, he may be convicted. If this is not his intention, regard should be had to the circumstances of the proposed publication etc in deciding whether or not racial hatred is likely to be stirred up, eg publication in a respectable social science journal or as part of a genuine educational programme (s 23(2)). There is no power of arrest attached to s 23. The power of arrest under s 25 of the Police and Criminal Evidence Act 1984 is available in appropriate circumstances.

There is power for a justice of the peace to issue a search warrant to search for material falling within ss 23 and 24. For procedures in connection with search warrants and their execution, see Police and Criminal Evidence Act 1984 and the Code of Practice.

4.5.11 Plays, recordings, broadcasts and cable programmes

It is an offence to present or direct a public performance of a play which involves the use of threatening, abusive or insulting words or behaviour with the intention thereby to stir up racial hatred or whereby in all the circumstances racial hatred is likely to be stirred up (s 20). These provisions replace those in the Theatres Act 1968 which dealt with incitement to racial hatred.

It is an offence for a person to distribute, show or play a recording of visual images or sounds which are threatening, abusive or insulting if he intends thereby to stir up racial hatred or where racial hatred is likely to be stirred up (s 21). This offence is intended to deal with the use of video or other recordings which are used to promote racially inflammatory propaganda. There is evidence of the growth of video recordings for this purpose. The offence is not restricted to particular venues and may be committed in both public and private places, eg private meetings. The distribution must be to the public or a section of the public (ss 29 and 21(2)) and in some instances there may be some doubt as to what is a section of the public for this purpose (see *Charter v Race Relations Board*).

Certain persons identified in s 22(2) may be guilty of an offence if a programme involving threatening, abusive or insulting visual images or sounds is broadcast or is included in a cable programme service. There must be either the usual intent or likelihood of racial hatred being stirred up. The offences do not extend to certain broadcasts or cable programmes (s 22(7)). Section 29 explains the terms used in s 23. Certain minor changes are made to the Cable and Broadcasting Act 1984; the amendments are clearly set out in Sched 2, para 5.

There are no powers of arrest attached to any of these offences, and the provisions of s 25 of the Police and Criminal Evidence Act 1984 apply.

4.5.12 Miscellaneous matters which apply to Part III

Section 26 protects certain reports of court and parliamentary proceedings. A court must order forfeiture upon conviction where it convicts for an offence contrary to either s 18 and the offence relates to written material, or ss 19, 21 or 23. The court must order forfeiture of all written materials or recordings produced to it and shown to be materials or recordings to which those offences apply.

Where offences are committed by bodies corporate, s 28 provides that certain other people, eg directors, may also be prosecuted if it can be shown that they connived at or consented to the offence.

The consent of the Attorney-General is required to all prosecutions or he must himself bring the action (s 27(1)). The offences are triable summarily or on indictment (s 27(2)) and are punishable by two years' imprisonment or a fine or both upon conviction on indictment or to imprisonment for six months or a fine or both upon summary conviction. For cases on sentencing see *R v Edwards*, *R v Pearce*, *R v Relf*.

4.5.13 Duplicity

Each of ss 18–23 creates one offence (s 27(3)).

Chapter 5

Processions and Assemblies

5.1 Processions

5.1.1 Checklist

- Statutory powers cover processions in any public place
- procession must be moving—not necessarily on foot
- whether procession or not is question of fact
- written notice required unless not reasonably practicable
- spontaneous processions do not, by their nature, require advance notice
- no notice required for customary or common processions and funerals
- organisers and participants may commit offences
- conditions may be imposed before or during processions
- serious disruption to life of community hard to define
- power to prohibit to prevent serious public disorder (POA 1986, s 13)

There are important statutory preventive powers relating to public processions in ss 11–13 of the Public Order Act 1986 which have not been modified by the Criminal Justice and Public Order Act 1994. The objective of these powers is to provide a means of identifying public processions and arranging for them to be subjected to the conditions necessary to prevent them from leading to certain consequences specified in the Act or to enable application to be made in appropriate cases to prevent all public processions for a period of time to avoid the risk of serious public disorder. The law relating to processions does not incorporate an express right to protest or to march, subject to the proviso that the highway is dedicated for passage and repassage. To that extent, processions are *prima facie* lawful. These rights, in so far as they exist at all, are inextricably enmeshed in the rights of the individual and are more fully developed in Chapter 1. In *Duncan v Jones* (1936) Lord Hewitt said 'The right of assembly. . . . is nothing more than a view taken by the court of the individual liberty of the subject'.

Essentially the individual may do anything which is not proscribed by either statute or the common law. Groups of individuals should be presumed to be entitled to process as a matter of UK law, subject to the statutory provisions. The legislation has taken account of the European Convention on Human Rights and Fundamental Freedoms (ECHR) by acknowledging in the White Paper (*Review of Public Order Law*, Cmnd 9510) prior to the 1986 Act that the right to peaceful protest and the right to march existed. Nevertheless, given that the ECHR is not part of UK law, it is an uneasy acknowledgment although the ECHR provisions are subject to restraints 'necessary in a democratic society in the interests of public safety . . . or the prevention of disorder'.

5.1.2 Definition of public procession

Section 16 of the POA 1986 defines a public procession as being a procession which takes place in a public place. A public place is defined as:

(a) any highway, or in Scotland any road within the meaning of the Roads (Scotland) Act 1984, and
(b) any place to which at the material time the public or any section of the public has access, on payment or otherwise, as of right or by virtue of express or implied permission.

The Oxford English Dictionary defines 'procession' as the 'action of a body of persons going or marching along in orderly succession in a formal or ceremonial way . . . a body of persons marching in this way'.

In *Flockhart v Robinson* (1950) procession is defined as follows: 'A procession is not a mere body of persons; it is a body of persons moving along a route'. In that case the problem arose when a lawful procession in the City of London broke up to disperse. Unfortunately a group had moved into an area where processions were prohibited. They were in a loose formation and not in ranks, and in the form of a rabble not a compact body. It was held that at some stage the group had become a procession spontaneously by adopting an orderly formation, even though there was no prior arrangement.

Lord Denning observed in *Kent v Metropolitan Police Commissioner* (1981): 'A public procession is the act of a body of persons marching along in orderly succession—see the Oxford English Dictionary. All kinds of processions take place every day up and down the country—carnivals, weddings, funerals, processions, to the Houses of Parliament, marches to Trafalgar Square and so forth'.

Whether a particular group is a procession or not is a question of fact on each occasion. A group of rugby supporters disgorged from a coach en route to the match may not be a procession despite their numbers because their progress may be disorganised. If they are marshalled carefully they may take on the nature of a procession, as may a crocodile of school children organised by the teachers albeit that they are not caught by the statutory provisions.

The procession need not be people on foot. The dictionary definition incorporates the word 'going' in addition to the word 'marching'. A procession comprising exclusively driven vehicles would be caught. Thus a lord mayor's parade or a student rag parade would be caught by the definition.

An individual walking a given route, whether in a formal or ceremonial way, would not be a procession. The element of the 'body' of people would be missing. In certain instances an individual doing that could create public disorder as rival groups gathered to egg him on or to prevent his passage. He would have to be monitored in relation to other provisions to prevent disorder. An example of such a disruptive walk by an individual was the walk by Martin Webster, a member of a far right party, along the route of a proscribed procession through Manchester. His walk, albeit not a procession, attracted both supporters and counter-demonstrators and the police were obliged to keep the groups apart.

Given that the s 16 definition includes any place to which the public has access, public processions are not restricted to the highway and will include parades preceding rallies held in arenas even if they are innocuous as a boy scout or girl guide rally. They will also include an Easter parade around the grounds of a church. It is important to note that many such parades will be excluded from statutory control as common or customary processions (s 11(2)).

5.1.3 Advance notice of public processions

Section 11 of the POA 1986 sets out to avoid the potential difficulties which might be expected to arise if the police were unaware of public processions by requiring written notice in advance to be provided to the police in particular contexts. The failure to give notice does not vitiate the validity or legality of the procession itself.

Section 11(1) provides that:

> (1) Written notice shall be given in accordance with this section of any proposal to hold a public procession intended—
> (a) to demonstrate support for or opposition to the views or actions of any person or body of persons,
> (b) to publicise a cause or campaign, or
> (c) to mark or commemorate an event,
> unless it is not reasonably practicable to give any advance notice of the procession.

Inevitably many processions will fall to be defined as belonging to more than one of these categories. In particular processions relating to terms of employment might fall into both the category of opposing a body's view and being designed to publicise a cause. Political processions are invariably going to require advance notice to be given under the section, as are processions designed to express grief for a person who has died in a context which has caused public anxiety, except where it is a funeral procession within s 11(2).

A difficulty arises in relation to a procession organised at very short notice. The statutory mechanism for written notice assumes at least six days' notice (s 11(5) and (6)) or if that is not reasonably practicable then as soon as is reasonably practicable (s 11(6)). Section 11(1) appears to envisage a circumstance where it is not practicable to give any advance notice by using the formula 'unless it is not reasonably practicable to give any advance notice'. Most processions requiring advance notice will have to give either the full six-day notice or a shorter written notice. If they do not they will commit an offence (s 11(7)). Occasionally the procession will be incapable of notice, being entirely spontaneous. Where a factory closure announcement is made and the employees stop work to march to the company headquarters or where a group of neighbours respond to the death or injury of a child in a road accident to march on their local council to protest at the unsafe nature of a road or where in the course of an election supporters spontaneously decide to march in solidarity with their chosen candidate, it is possible that as a question of fact the organisers could be held not to be required to give advance notice because it would not be reasonably practicable to do so. Given that the reference to 'any advance notice' at the end of s 11(1) does not incorporate the word 'written', it might be thought that there is a category of case where oral notice would suffice. This cannot be the case. 'Any advance notice' must relate back to the last usage of 'notice', which is 'written notice' used in the first words of s 1(1) and there is therefore no provision for oral notice. However, in the event of prosecution, a defendant may be assisted in proving on a balance of probabilities that it was not reasonably practicable to give the statutory written notice if he has in any event given oral notice to the police even though this was a procession of a type which required spontaneous action to respond to an immediate and unforeseeable matter, such as waste spills or unexpected visits by foreign political leaders. It should be kept in mind that the fact that it was not reasonably practicable is a matter for the defendant to prove. There will be very few cases where a delay of a few hours will render a procession meaningless, apart from a procession following a sporting success, which might be rendered meaningless within 24 hours. (In practice such processions are generally planned in advance on a contingency basis anyway.) Such a delay would, however, enable the police to be notified so as to take precautions as appropriate, and reduce the risk of prosecution and conviction for the organiser.

Certain processions are excluded from the requirements for advance notice. Section 11(2) provides that notice is not required 'where the procession is one which is commonly or customarily held in the police area (or areas) in which it is proposed to be held or is a funeral procession organised by a funeral director acting in the normal course of his business'.

Sometimes there will be an issue as to whether a given procession is common or customary. In such cases it might be better to give the notice anyway to avoid the risk of prosecution. Many cases will be straightforward. Remembrance Day parades, university rag parades, Easter parades and other religious parades may be clear to all concerned, but even they may still require notice if they move from area to area and that arrangement is not protected by custom or common practice. Sometimes issues of custom and common usage will raise wider constitutional issues relevant to processions. Parades in Northern Ireland are a case in point where custom comes into conflict with current public order requirements.

5.1.4 Form of advance notice

The advance notice to the police must comply with the following:

- it must be in writing (s 11(1));
- it must be delivered to any police station in the police force area where the procession is intended to start; or in the case of a procession which will start in Scotland and cross into England, notice should be given to a police station in the first police area in England on the proposed route (s 11(4)(a)(b));
- it must be delivered either by hand not less than six days before the date of the procession or by recorded delivery post provided actual delivery takes place not less than six clear days before the procession's intended date (s 11(5)); there is no presumption of service;
- if six days' notice cannot be given, then notice must be given in writing by hand as soon as delivery is reasonably practicable (s 11(6)); the notice must specify the intended start time, route and the name and address of at least one of the organisers (s 11(3)).

This is subject to the proviso for cases where no notice is possible. In most cases the police will have prescribed forms of notice incorporating provision for much more information than this to enable them to police the event adequately from the point of view of both public safety and traffic management and also to determine whether they need to impose conditions under the terms of s 12 of the POA 1986.

5.1.5 Offences relating to notice

There are two statutory offences in relation to notice of public processions and they can only be committed by an organiser. They are:

- failure to satisfy the notice requirements (s 11(7)(a));
- non-adherence to the date, time or route specified in the notice (s 11(7)(b)).

These offences can only be committed by the people organising the procession and their liability exists whether they take part in the procession or not.

Two statutory defences are available to an organiser who may prove on the balance of probabilities that:

- he did not know of and did not suspect or have reason to suspect the failure to give notice;
- the failure arose from something beyond his control and from the agreement or direction of a policeman (s 11(9)).

These offences are triable only summarily and punishable by fines up to level 3 (s 11(10)). The burden of proof of the defence is on the organiser to the civil standard. Given the wording of the provision, anyone who organises a procession without due diligence is likely to be unable to prove the defence requirements in the event of a non-compliance.

5.1.6 The Organiser

The word 'organiser' is central to the provision, but it is not defined in the statute. It therefore should be accorded its ordinary meaning. The case of *Flockhart v Robinson* sets out two points of view in the majority decision and the dissenting judgment of Finnemore J:

> 'Organised' is not a term of art. When a person organises a procession, what does he do? A procession is not a mere body of persons: it is a body of persons moving along a route. Therefore the person who organises the route is the person who organises the procession . . . (*per* Goddard CJ).

This assessment of the position appears to be too all-embracing. To give the word 'organise' its ordinary meaning implies an element of preparation prior to the event which would exclude mere stewards. This statutory provision envisages an organiser as a person who gives the advance notice and is therefore involved from before the start of the procession. Given that this was a case on the POA 1936, perhaps the words of

Goddard CJ do not control the definition and an analysis nearer to today's position is set out in the dissenting judgment where Finnemore J said:

> The mere fact that a person takes part in a procession would not of itself be enough. I do not think that the fact the defendant was the leading person in the procession would by itself be enough, although it might be some evidence to be considered . . . I think organising a procession means something in the nature of arranging or planning a procession . . .

In *DPP v Baillie* (1995) the divisional court looked at a more modern aspect of the definition of 'organiser' in the context of assembly, but it is also applicable to the procession provisions. The respondent distributed news sheets with free festival information; he operated an incoming telephone calls and answering machine service. Believing that a particular festival was to take place, the police served a notice of conditions (relating to assembly) on the respondent, whom they treated as an organiser. The relevant notice began 'Re proposed festival on 12 June *et sequentes*' and referred to 'this event or any similar event'. The vagueness of the notice was adversely commented on by the court.

There were three questions to resolve:

(1) Was he an organiser merely by disseminating information?
(2) Had the police had regard to the time or place of the event given that they did not have any details of it?
(3) Could an offence be committed if he was arrested before the event and still had time to comply with the conditions?

The divisional court did not deal with the third question, but decided that the police were not operating within the terms of s 14(1) because they did not know the time or place of the festival. In other words they could not have made their decisions taking into account the time or place because they did not know either. Such information would also be necessary for a procession prosecution under s 12. The court did not give a comprehensive definition of who would be caught by the word 'organiser' but felt that there was just sufficient evidence to support the magistrates' decision that the defendant was an 'organiser'. What weighed with the court was the absence of a public announcement relating to the event, thus elevating the defendant's role as a purveyor of information.

5.1.7 Conditions on processions

The power to impose conditions on processions is contained in s 12 of the POA 1986. The power to impose conditions does not circumscribe either the preventive powers of the police (Chapter 2) or their other common law and statutory powers and duties in connection with public order. The power to impose conditions does not restrict the civil liabilities of the organisers or the participants in the procession. The mere fact that notice has been duly served and conditions duly imposed by the relevant police officer does not preclude the possibility of an interested party seeking injunctive remedy to prevent a given procession. Section 12 applies to any public procession of any character even if it is a procession outside the terms of s 11 as to notice.

Conditions may be imposed either before or during a procession by the senior police officer. For the period before the procession, the senior police officer will be the chief police officer for the relevant area (s 12(2)(b)), subject to the power to delegate (s 15). The conditions imposed must be in writing (s 12(3)). For the duration of the procession or during the time participants are assembling for an intended procession, the senior police officer is the most senior ranking officer at the scene (s 12(2)(a)). During the procession or the assembly period the conditions need not be given in writing.

The conditions may be imposed on either the organisers or the participants and they are described as being directions containing conditions (s 12(1)). For directions imposed before the start of the assembly of participants, the conditions must be in writing but once the assembly has begun, there is no requirement for the conditions to be imposed in writing.

The criteria for the imposing of conditions are set out in s 12(1) of the POA 1986. The senior officer must have regard to:

(a) the intended or actual time or place of the procession . . .; and
(b) the circumstances in which it will be held; and
(c) its route.

He may impose conditions if he reasonably believes (ie actually believes on objective grounds) that the procession . . . may result in serious public disorder, serious damage to property or serious disruption to the life of the community (s 12(1)(a)) or that the purpose of the organisers is to intimidate others (s 12(1)(b)). The reasonableness of the belief is objectively ascertainable, as is any other reasonable belief or suspicion upon normal principles.

5.1.8 Serious

There is a view that 'serious' does not take the definition of public disorder or damage any further. That is a curious approach both to statutory interpretation and to the clear fact that public disorder is graded through the POA 1986 by particular aspects of definition contained in each provision and by level of seriousness. The requirement is that the senior police officer present has to carry out an assessment of the procession, taking account of the available information. If that leads to the belief that there may be disorder, but falling short of serious public disorder, then conditions cannot be imposed. If they are, then quite apart from the fact that any prosecution would fail (notionally in the case of a procession in course and actually in the case of an intended procession), the organisers or any interested party might seek judicial review of the decision made to impose conditions. Whether the courts would be able to make the distinction between 'serious' and other public disorder, and whether the courts would generally substitute their view for the view of a senior officer on the ground is open to doubt but each exercise of power is open to review in accordance with the principles in the *Wednesbury Corporation* case (see *Holgate-Mohammed v Duke* (1984)).

5.1.9 Serious disruption

Serious disruption to the life of the community is undefined in the Act and probably incapable of definition. By their nature, processions might be said to disrupt the community, if only to the extent of reducing the progress of traffic through towns and cities. This might lead to conditions being imposed to reduce the impact of the procession on the community, even though some would hold that processing is not disruptive to normal life, but a part of everybody's normal life. It is arguable that such conditions are imposed for reasons not included in the Act. Slowing traffic down might not be regarded as a serious disruption to the life of the community. It is difficult to envisage a procession seriously disrupting local life in the same way that an assembly might. The large gatherings of people in the pickets at the Grunwick factory and the Wapping newspaper premises had an impact on the local community which a procession could not be expected to match. Perhaps a 24-hour procession circulating in a limited area might mean that shops could not function, and to that extent it was a serious disruption. Generally, however, serious disruption would arise from serious public disorder and does not develop the impact of the provision. 'Community' is not defined and so has its ordinary meaning. In many locations 'community' has more than one meaning. In a busy shopping street in London, there is the community of shopkeepers, the community of local residents and the wider community of London as a whole. The serious disruption could be to any of those communities. When London black cab drivers block the streets of London by driving extremely slowly to demonstrate a particular viewpoint, it could be argued that they are part of the wider London community; it could be argued that they are not part of the community where the demonstration takes place. They are clearly capable of causing disruption to the community. It is a question of fact whether they cause serious disruption to the life of the community.

5.1.10 Intention to intimidate

Whether the intention is to intimidate is a question of fact in each case. The notion that interference with the lawful activities of other members of the community should be prevented by the criminal law is central to parts of both the POA 1986 and the CJPOA (see, for example, s 68 on aggravated trespass). The provision is based on s 7 Conspiracy and Protection of Property Act 1875 which is referred to in Sched 2 POA 1986 with the addition of a power of arrest by a constable on reasonable suspicion that an offence is being committed under s 7, without warrant. In the White Paper before the 1986 Act, the provision was described as 'a libertarian safeguard designed to prevent demonstrations whose overt purpose is to persuade people from being used as a cloak by those whose real purpose is to intimidate or coerce'.

Given that processions are commonly designed to persuade—politicians, workers or the authorities generally—the risk that persuasion may be misconstrued as coercion requires a delicacy of touch from those enforcing the provision. The police will always be vulnerable to allegations of an inappropriately heavy-handed approach to conditions for processions. They will be accused of interfering with the liberty of the subject and his right to protest and process.

Intimidation was defined to a degree in *R v Jones* (1974) pursuant to the Conspiracy and Protection of Property Act 1875: '"intimidate" in this section includes putting persons in fear by the exhibition of force or violence or the threat of force or violence; and there is no limitation restricting the meaning to cases of violence or threats of violence to the person'.

A procession precedent to an industrial picket could fall within the definition of s 12 and be subjected to conditions through directions from the senior officer.

One of the many difficulties facing the police in relation to processions is the foundation for the 'reasonable belief' as to the purpose of the procession. It will not be uncommon for there to be more than one purpose. While it may be obvious in the context of mass picketing that the purpose is intimidatory (albeit that mass picketing is a species of assembly rather than a procession), there will be cases where the purpose is not clear. In *Thomas v NUM* (1985) Scott J said:

> . . . counsel for the . . . defendants submitted that mass picketing (by which I understand to be meant picketing so as by sheer weight of numbers to block the entrance to premises or to prevent the entry thereto of vehicles or people) was not *per se* tortious or criminal. In my judgement, mass picketing is clearly both common law nuisance and an offence under s 7 of the 1875 Act.

In non-industrial cases the question of purpose is more of a problem. Persuading a firm to discontinue animal experiments may not be obviously intimidatory. An implied threat to embargo the company's goods would not be intimidatory. Threats of violence towards customers or employees would and in the context of assembly, blocking the premises' entrance in numbers would fall foul of the judgment in *Thomas v NUM*.

In *DPP v Fidler and Moran* (1991) two separate groups, one in favour of abortion, the other opposed to abortion were stationed outside an abortion clinc. Opponents of abortion were charged with watching and besetting contrary to s 7 of the Conspiracy and Protection of Property Act. It was held that although their intention was to prevent abortions from being carried out, their chosen method was to dissuade by means of graphic photographs, models and verbal persuasion. The court held that to establish s 7, it would be necessary to prove that the purpose of the defendants was to compel relevant parties to cease performing abortions. It was not sufficient to create the offence merely to seek to dissuade. This case contrasts with other cases involving abortion clinics where the allegation has been of conduct contrary to s 4 or s 5 of the POA 1986.

5.1.11 Relevance of conditions

The conditions must be such as appear to the relevant police officer necessary to prevent the apprehended disorder, damage, disruption or intimidation. Despite the absence of the word 'reasonably' from the relevant part of s 12 ('such conditions as appear to him necessary'), there must be a correlation between the anticipated problem and the conditions imposed. (Some of the dilemmas facing police officers are set out at 1.6 and 1.7.) The conditions specifically referred to in the section relate to the rerouting of the procession and preventing the procession from going to specified public places—no go areas. Inevitably the police are going to use their experience to prevent political extremists from entering areas where opposing views are held in circumstances which might lead to disorder. Racially sensitive areas will be vetoed in appropriate cases. A dilemma which the police find difficult to resolve is that the very existence of a procession by one group will lead to an apparently impromptu gathering to demonstrate protest against the processors. The best example of this is processions which can be excluded from racially sensitive areas; their opponents, however, will always gather to protest at the procession wherever it may be. Whatever conditions are imposed, there is a high likelihood of public disorder at their processions.

Notwithstanding the areas of conflict, the majority of conditions will be consensual and obvious. These conditions would routinely cover:

- place and time of assembly prior to start;
- time of departure, route and duration;
- carrying of flags, banners and emblems;
- loudhailers;
- stewarding;
- use of vehicles;
- numbers in line abreast on the route;
- medical provision.

5.1.12 Offences

It is an offence for an organiser knowingly to fail to comply with a condition imposed under s 12. The condition must be properly imposed. Whether he is an organiser is a question of fact (*Flockhart v Robinson*). 'Knowingly' requires *mens rea*, including deliberately closing one's mind or deliberately not making enquiries.

It is a defence for an organiser to show on a balance of probabilities that the failure arose from circumstances beyond his control. Thus if a participant uses a loudhailer against a condition, it will not be an organiser offence if the organiser knew nothing of it and had taken precautions to make the condition known.

A non-organiser participant offends if he knowingly fails to comply with a condition unless he can show it arose from circumstances beyond his control. The participant with the proscribed loudhailer will have a defence if he uses it because he had seen no warnings but if he continues to use it in the face of advice then he will offend. A processor who is swept by a crowd into a proscribed area by weight of numbers may well have a defence.

A police officer in uniform may arrest without warrant anyone he reasonably suspects of committing an offence (s 12(7)). If the offence has already occurred, he will use the power in s 25 of the PACE Act 1984. It should also be noted that incitement to commit an offence is an offence (s 14(6)).

5.1.13 Prohibition of public processions

The power to prohibit public processions is set out in s 13 of the POA 1986 and has not been amended by the CJPOA. The Act distinguishes between the roles of the Commissioner of Police for the City of London and the Commissioner of Police for the Metropolis on the one hand and chief officers of police on the other. In the two London areas, the chief officer may, with consent from the Secretary of State, prohibit by order the holding of all public processions, or any specified class of public procession in the whole of his area or part of his area (s 13(4)).

In the areas outside London, a different procedure applies. In those areas, in the qualifying circumstances the chief officer must apply to the district council for an order prohibiting all public processions or a specified class of public processions in the district as a whole or in part of the district (s 3(1)). It should be noted that in the case of the non-London areas the provision is directive on the chief officer to apply, although the council's decision in response to the application is discretionary. In London it is the chief officer's decision that is discretionary, because local authorities play no part. In both areas the order may relate to part only of the relevant area.

5.1.14 Criterion for prohibition

The only criterion for imposing the prohibition or requesting it from the council is the reasonable belief by the chief officer that serious public disorder cannot be prevented by the exercise of the condition-making power in s 12. It should be noted that disruption to the community and intimidation are not included as grounds for the prohibition or application, although the view will no doubt be that both of those things are capable of giving rise to the anticipation of serious public disorder. The chief officer's belief must be reasonable and will be based on his assessment of the prevailing circumstances. If a counter-rally is to be held, and the area concerned is small and the procession risks swamping it, if there have been recent disturbances or if it is an area with high local tension, then any of these things might lead to a reasonable belief that the serious public disorder might occur. Because it is the exercise of a statutory discretion, it is susceptible to judicial review in accordance with the well-known principles in *Associated Provincial Picture Houses* v *Wednesbury Corporation* (1948). In the case of the district council acting with the consent of the Secretary of State, their response is discretionary and may therefore be reviewed in the court in the same way. In *Kent v Metropolitan Police Commissioner* an application for judicial review was made in respect of the chief officer's decision to impose a blanket prohibition. It was claimed that he had not directed his mind properly to the matters to be considered and in particular that the ban would affect a large number of processions over a large area. The Court of Appeal view was that:

> a climate of activity . . . hooligans and others were attacking the police, who were simply doing their duty . . . they might attack the peaceful procession itself . . . This is a matter for the judgement of the Commissioner himself 'There is such a risk of public disorder—even from the most peaceful demonstration being attacked by hooligans—that a ban must be imposed'.

In this case the evidence of the Commissioner was described as meagre but it is clear that in the absence of evidence of bad faith the courts will be extremely slow to intervene.

In relation to blanket bans, it was said:

> . . . a class or group of classes of processions can be as well identified by expressly excluding certain classes as it can by listing all the classes which are not excluded.

5.1.15 Timescale for prohibition

The permitted timescale of a prohibition order is up to three months but may well be as short as 24 hours. The evidence of banning orders made in the 1980s is that periods beyond 30 days are the exception and generally the preferred ban has been the blanket ban for a given area. A blanket ban is a ban on all processions subject to exceptions within certain classes. Such bans may be revoked or varied by a subsequent prohibition (s 13(5)). In 1961 the following prohibition was made: 'Any public procession organised by the body of persons known as the Committee of 100 or any such public procession organised by any person or persons acting on behalf of the said committee'.

In 1974 'any public procession in connection with the death of James McDade', one of the IRA hunger strikers, was prohibited.

5.1.16 Prohibition offences

The organiser, participant or person who incites participation or organisation of a prohibited procession commits an offence (s 13(7)(8) and (9)) if he acts knowingly. The penalty range varies according to the particular offence. An organiser is liable to a fine up to level 4 or imprisonment up to three months. A participant is liable to a fine up to level 3 and the inciter is liable to imprisonment up to three months or a fine up to level 4 (s 13(11)(12) and (13)).

Such a person may be arrested without warrant by a constable in uniform on reasonable suspicion that he is committing the offence (s 13(10)). A person who organises a prohibited procession which in the end does not occur commits an offence. This provision is not the same as the organiser offence in relation to a condition breach where the offence only arises if the procession takes place.

5.2 Assemblies

5.2.1 Checklist

- An assembly is made up of 20 or more
- includes pickets, vigils and queues
- conditions may be imposed before or during assembly
- conditions only on place, duration and numbers

The statutory law relating to the control of public assemblies has been developing since 1986. Prior to that Act there were no general statutory provisions for their control. The innovation made then has since been developed further with the provisions contained in ss 70 and 71 of the CJPOA dealing with trespassory assemblies and their prohibition and the power to stop people en route to a prohibited assembly. The 1994 developments had their genesis in anxiety at the assemblies at such places as Stonehenge and their association with risks of damage to such historic monuments. Wider powers to control assemblies by advance notice requirements were not actually sought by the police or recommended by the House of Commons Home Affairs Committee Report.

5.2.2 Definition

Section 16 of the POA 1986 defines 'public assembly' as 'an assembly of 20 or more persons in a public place which is wholly or partly open to the air'. The Oxford English Dictionary describes an 'assembly' as: 'gathering together, meeting, the state of being collected or gathered. The coming together of persons or things. A gathering of persons, a number of people met together'. While it is clear from both the statutory and also the dictionary definitions that a procession would generally be an assembly as well, subject to numbers, it is clear that the intention is that they should have different provisions to deal with the relatively static assembly on the one hand and the moving procession on the other.

'Assembly' is a broad description incorporating pickets, lobbying groups, vigils, festivals, some queues, groups drinking in pub gardens and football crowds. The statutory definition is sufficiently wide to require the application of the ordinary meaning of the words used. The higher courts will regard that as an issue of fact for the fact-finding tribunal and will not generally interfere in the absence of a bizarre analysis.

'Public place' is analysed above. It is sufficiently wide to include the factory entrance where a picket line might be stationed. The concept of 'partly open to the air' means that a closed building with its door open is not caught, but a Dutch barn or football stadium is caught.

Prior to 1986 the definition of 'public place' had been reviewed in *Cawley v Frost* (1976) and it describes an approach which is appropriate to the expression 'open to the air' as well. Lord Widgery said:

> where you have an establishment which is set up to provide for the public, such as Halifax Town football club or Wembley Stadium, one ought to approach it on the basis that is a public place in its entirety . . . *Prima facie* you look at the whole of the establishment and you are not . . . deterred from doing that merely by finding that certain portions of the establishment have been denied to the public for one reason or another.

'Open to the air' is an expression reminiscent of the definition in the 1936 Act prior to its amendment by the Criminal Justice Act 1972. This created a category of open space but did not, for example, include a railway platform since that was integral to a building (*Cooper v Shield* (1971)). Open to the air must not be *de minimis*. A roof with no walls or walls with no roof would be open to the air whereas a building with wide open doors would not.

One practical problem which may arise in relation to 'public places' is the extent of the relevant place. It may be that conduct beyond the boundary of a relevant place will not be caught and so the definition will be crucial. At an assembly in a marquee in the grounds of a school, it will be necessary to determine whether the 'place' is the marquee or the school grounds, even assuming that the marquee is partly in the open air. Again this will be a question of fact to be analysed in accordance with the *Cawley v Frost* approach above.

5.2.3 Conditions on assemblies

Essentially the powers to impose conditions on assemblies reflect those to impose conditions on processions and are found in s 14 of the POA 1986, albeit that the conditions are more limited. Conditions may be imposed by the senior police officer either before the assembly or during its course (s 14(2) and (3)).

Conditions may be imposed on organisers or on those taking part and the police officer must have regard to the intended or actual time or place of the assembly, and the circumstances in which it will be held. He may impose conditions if he believes reasonably that the assembly may result in serious public disorder, serious damage to property or serious disruption to the life of the community, or if the purpose of the organisers is to intimidate others.

The analysis of the definitions of the various expressions is set out at 5.1.7 and remains the same in relation to assemblies.

The conditions he may impose must be such as appear necessary to prevent the apprehended disorder, damage or disruption or intimidation.

For the purpose of assemblies the conditions may only relate to the place at which the assembly may or may continue to be held, its maximum duration and the maximum number of persons (assuming that number to be greater than 20). The existence of conditions does not prevent the police from using their other powers, including those in relation to obstruction. A negative condition may be used as to place, ie not within 200 yards of a particular location. By the same token, if part of an assembly remains after the time limit, it will be a question of fact whether the assembly is then in breach of the condition. Simply changing the personnel of the assembly will not enable organisers or participants to avoid breach. It will suffice to reduce the number of participants below 20 but moving location may well leave the assembly in breach of the location condition depending on the expressions used in it.

The following conditions appeared in *DPP v Baillie* (1994):

(1) Any event must be licensed in accordance with the Local Government (Miscellaneous) Provisions Act 1982 in respect of public entertainment and environmental health.

(2) The place will be subject to advance agreement with the police to ensure the life of the community is not disrupted by noise nuisance from whatever source associated with the event.

(3) The maximum duration will be subject to advance agreement with the police to ensure there is no public disorder or disruption to the life of the community caused by noise or unsociable hours.

(4) The maximum number of persons who constitute the assembly will be subject to advance agreement with the police to ensure:
   (a) there is no public disorder caused by overcrowding and/or inadequate lighting;
   (b) there is no damage caused to roadside verges and neighbouring property resulting from inadequate arrangements for off-street parking;
   (c) there is no damage or disruption to the life of the community resulting from inadequate sanitary arrangements;
   (d) there is no disruption to the life of the community resulting from too great a volume of traffic for the access and egress routes to and from the assembly.

Although the matter was not contested before the court, it is arguable that the second, third and fourth conditions are too vague and amount not to conditions but a requirement for advance notice of an assembly. No doubt the conditions were drawn thus because of the secrecy of the event and the problems the police had in knowing when or where the event would be held, or whether it would be held in a public place. Absence of reliable information does not excuse the imposition of such a direction in advance.

It is also possible that the first condition was invalid. Section 14 refers to the imposition of a condition 'as to the place at which the assembly may be (or continued to be) held'. The licensing requirement clearly relates to the use to which the place is put, and as such can be said to relate to the place, but that is not what was intended by the Act. It is arguable that s 14 should be narrowly construed so as to permit the police only to decide where the assembly may be held. As drawn the condition is an attempt to enforce a different Act.

Directions containing conditions given in relation to assemblies which are intended but are not yet under way must be given in writing. Once the assembly is under way, there is no requirement for the directions imposing conditions to be in writing (s 13(3)).

The offences in relation to conditions imposed on assemblies and the penalties are as for processions. The right to seek judicial review of such conditions is also the same.

5.2.4 Checklist for prohibiting trespassory assemblies

- Application may only be made for intended assemblies
- existing assemblies are excluded
- serious disruption or significant damage
- no prohibition if occupier permits assembly
- knowingly organising, participating or inciting are offences
- stop en route power within five mile radius

In response to the perceived need both to protect public monuments from the ravages of large assemblies purportedly exercising historic rights and to protect ordinary members of the community from the consequences of trespassory assembly, a new s 14A of the POA 1986 was created in the CJPOA. The provision goes beyond the powers contained in the 1986 Act and reflects a view different from that expressed in the *Review of Public Order Law* (Cmnd 9510) which was to the effect that a banning power in relation to such assemblies ran the risk of proving too great an infringement of the rights of free speech and assembly. Quite what the logical relationship between that position and the power to ban processions was is not clear.

Section 14A goes further than the common law power to prevent a reasonably anticipated breach of the peace, although it should be kept in mind that the common law power remains and can be applied to prevent a meeting and therefore an assembly (*Duncan v Jones* (1936)).

The provision continues the distinction between the Metropolitan and City areas of London and the rest of England and Wales and Scotland in that the prohibition mechanism in London permits the chief officer of police to make the order with the consent of the Secretary of State (POA 1986, s 14A(4)). In the district council areas the chief officer may apply to the relevant district council. In England and Wales the district council may with the consent of the Secretary of State grant the prohibition applied for or grant it subject to modifications approved by the Secretary of State.

5.2.5 Trespassory assembly problems

The problem of trespassory assembly is demonstrated by *R v Historic Buildings and Ancient Monuments Commission for England (aka English Heritage) ex p Firsoff* (1991). The case related to processions and the exercise of discretion by English Heritage in response to a request from the chief constable to support his ban on processions under s 13 of the 1986 Act in relation to difficulties which had occurred at Stonehenge. The issue was whether it was a proper exercise of discretion to keep Stonehenge closed at the summer solstice so as to prevent a peaceable and lawful person from exercising his right to have free access to the site in accordance with the terms of the gift of Stonehenge to the nation. The dilemma facing English Heritage had been that as a result of serious disturbances on previous occasions, it had been felt necessary to close Stonehenge during the solstice period. The court analysed the position carefully on the basis that English Heritage decisions were capable of being judicially reviewed and looking at Mr Firsoff's arguments that because his conduct would be proper in every sense, barring him with everybody else could not be a proper exercise of the discretion. The court found:

> It is satisfactory to the court to know that English Heritage recognises its continuing duty to keep the matter under review. It may be that, although several alternative methods of coping with the problem have been tried in the past, some combination of an all ticket event and an order under s 13 is the sort of arrangement to which it would be worthwhile giving further consideration (*per* Nourse LJ).

The chief officer may apply at any time for an order prohibiting for a specified period all trespassory assemblies in the district or part of it. He may only apply if he

> reasonably believes that an assembly is intended to be held in any district at a place on land to which the public has no right of access or only a limited right of access and that the assembly—

(a) is likely to be held without the permission of the occupier of the land or to conduct itself in such a way as to exceed the limits of any permission of his or the limits of the public's right of access, and
(b) may result—
  (i) in serious disruption to the life of the community, or
  (ii) where the land or a building or monument on it, is of historical, architectural, archaeological or scientific importance, in significant damage to the land, building or monument (POA, 1986, s 14A(1) inserted by the CJPOA).

5.2.6 Assembly in course

The police officer's application is in respect of an intended assembly. In the event of an assembly in course, these new rights do not apply and he will be dependent upon his common law powers to prevent a breach of the peace. Not all trespassory assemblies will give rise to risk of breach of the peace and to that extent the police officer's power may be limited. The difficulties this will create for the police are demonstrated by *DPP v Baillie* (see 5.2.3). The police are dependent upon advance knowledge of what is planned. This may be well known in the case of the summer solstice at Stonehenge, but might be less well known in other cases, particularly where relatively covert tactics are adopted by organisers.

The police officer must have 'reasonable belief' that the assembly is intended and this may be tested on normal principles.

Trespassory assembly is not restricted to a public assembly and has a specific focus to permit application for prohibition. It must be on land in the open air. There must be no public right of access or a limited public right of access. Even then the prohibition is only available if the assembly is without permission or exceeds any limited permission which may exist and in addition to that either the serious disruption provision applies or the significant damage provision applies in the case of the special category of land. The police officer need only have reasonable belief that serious disruption or serious damage may result. This is a lower requirement of belief than that required in the case of the trespass which is not expressed in the conditional.

'Serious disruption' is discussed at 5.1.9. This formula could include the creation of traffic difficulties, the consequences of large numbers not having toilet facilities, noise pollution, thefts on a large scale from the local community or damage in the sense of local woodland being used for firewood, ie an assault on local amenity, but all of these things must be serious and must be disruptive. The Act does not help define the expression at all and it will be a matter for the judgment of the police officer in deciding whether to make application.

'Significant damage' is not defined by the section and is a change from the 'serious damage' formula used in ss 13 and 14. It may be that 'significant' means something different from serious and in the context of monuments may be expected to fall short of 'serious' given its ordinary meaning. The Act does not help as to what is of historical, architectural, archaeological or scientific importance. It is a question of fact in each case, but the fact that a building is listed or a monument scheduled will inevitably be conclusive. Difficulties might arise in relation to property of lesser significance.

While the provision has the potential to cover lawful trade union picketing in the form of peaceful persuasion of workers not to work (s 220 of the Trade Union and Labour Relations (Consolidation) Act 1992), the reality is that such conduct will not be caught because there will generally be no basis for reasonably believing that either serious disruption or (if relevant) significant damage may be the result of such an assembly of people.

5.2.7 Limits of prohibition

The prohibition notice only prohibits the proscribed assembly if it takes place without the permission of the occupier or so as to exceed the limits of any permission or the limits of any public right of access. 'Limited' in this context is defined at s 14A(9) and means their use of it is restricted to a particular purpose or restricted in some other way.

In the first place, therefore, the proscription cannot be applied to a permitted gathering, so long as the permission is given by the occupier. The target is only a trespassory assembly. The disruptive consequences of a meeting held with permission are not targeted by these particular provisions.

Whether the average citizen understands the restrictions on his right to use land may be open to question. In *Harrison v Duke of Rutland* (1893) it was established that in relation to a right of way, if a person does something other than walk along the right of way, or something incidental to passage, then he is a trespasser. In that case he waved his umbrella as a deliberate act, to interfere with a pheasant shoot. He was a trespasser because he had exceeded his right in relation to the right of way and had done more than merely pass and repass. In *Hickman v Maisey* (1900) the limitations on a person's rights in relation to the highway were even more starkly related. In that case a racing tout used the highway to spy upon horses in training. It was held that his use of the highway was beyond passing and repassing and therefore he trespassed to the subsoil. Each of these examples show the ease with which a person may 'exceed the limits of any permission of his or the public's right of access' and therefore the ease with which the basis for reasonable belief could be made out.

The use of a right of way across a historic monument will exceed the limited right if it is then used to assemble.

It should be noted that s 14A refers to an assembly and not 'public assembly'. Section 14(A)(9) defines an assembly as 20 or more persons. It also defines land as meaning in the open air. There are restrictions on the prohibition which may be imposed. It cannot last for more than four days and cannot exceed an area comprising of a circle of radius more than five miles from a specific centre. The prohibition will therefore always be centred on a specific monument, building or place.

The police officer must apply for an order banning all trespassory assemblies within the area defined. He cannot elect to ban one or a class of such assemblies. Whether this limitation has any practical significance is hard to assess, given that its focus is trespassory assemblies, which by their nature ought not to be happening anyway.

5.2.8 Trespassory assembly offences

The offences arising from trespassory assemblies are set out at the new s 14B of the POA 1986 (CJPOA, s 70). They reflect the offences arising from the public assembly provisions. It is an offence knowingly to organise a prohibited assembly, knowingly to participate in a prohibited assembly or to incite the commission of either of those offences in England or Wales (s 14B (1)(2) and (3)). It will be noted that the offences require *mens rea*, yet there are no specific requirements for notice of the decision to be served on organisers or participants. The offences carry imprisonment or a fine up to level 4 for the organising offence, a fine up to level 3 for the participation offence, and imprisonment for up to three months and a fine up to level 4 for the incitement offence (s 14B(5)(6) and (7)). Special provision is made in relation to incitement in Scotland (s 14B(8)).

A constable in uniform may arrest on reasonable suspicion that an offence is being committed.

In the event of the proscribed assembly being rendered non-trespassory by virtue of occupier permission being given, then it is no longer a proscribed assembly (s 14A(5)).

The difficulties which may arise in relation to the definition of an organiser were considered in *DPP v Baillie* (see 5.1.6 and 5.2.3).

5.2.9 Stop power relating to unlawful assembly

Section 71 of the CJPOA creates a new s 14C to the POA 1986. This new section gives the police the power to stop people en route to an unlawful trespassory assembly and direct them not to proceed in the direction of the assembly. The section provides that if a constable in uniform reasonably believes that a person is on his way to a proscribed assembly in an area to which a s 4A order relates, he may stop the person and direct him not to proceed in the direction of the assembly (s 14C(1)(a) and (b)). This power may only be exercised within the area to which the order applies, ie within five miles of the specified location.

Non-compliance with a direction which a person knows has been given is an offence and a constable in uniform may arrest without a warrant, on reasonable suspicion that a person is committing the offence (s 14C(2)(3) and (4)). This offence carries a penalty of up to a fine on level 3 (s 14C(5)).

This is perceived as an important power to control developing situations before the crowds reach the proposed site of the assembly. As such, it has been seen as an assault on fundamental rights. Conversely the power has been seen as a proper means of protecting both communities and also ancient monuments and historic buildings. Television scenes of confrontations at Stonehenge indicated a need to intervene before the participants reached their target. The Government were clear about their objectives: '1,000 lager louts may decide to pile into a little village' (HC SCB, 10/2/94, col 643). 'It is up to the chief officer of police . . . to consider the law . . . There could be hundreds of different cases, and thousands of hypothetical ones and it is up to the chief officers and the council to decide what they think will happen' (HC SCB, 10/2/94, col 645). The intention was to protect the lawful occupation and use of land, with or without monuments or buildings. One of the themes of the CJPOA was to preserve the rights of lawful land users from interference by those without rights. Nevertheless, in its creation of a body of opposition, the Act provided an ample demonstration of the risk of public order legislation being perceived as an attack on fundamental and historic rights, even when those notional rights had not previously existed and earlier judgments had emphasised the need to protect the lawful occupation of land.

Chapter 6

Trespass and Raves

6.1 Trespass and disorder

The relationship between trespass, protest and public disorder has been long recognised. Television pictures of the removal of new age travellers and road scheme protestors alongside documented policing difficulties arising from large-scale unlicensed open air gatherings have led to various statutory interventions. In general terms these have involved the power to direct trespassers to leave, and the creation of offences in the event of non-compliance with such a direction. Section 39 of the POA 1986, which dealt with mass trespass, was repealed by CJPOA 1994 (Sched 11). Aspects of offending related to trespass were redefined in Part V of the CJPOA 1994. A number of controversial provisions to do with the unlawful use of land were introduced by this part of the CJPOA 1994. In particular the Act created powers to remove trespassers from land and to divert people from proceeding to particular sites, and those organising or attending raves. The offence of aggravated trespass was created to meet the behaviour of individuals such as hunt saboteurs. In relation to squatters, interim possession orders for the recovery of possession of premises were provided with penalties for false statements made in support. The obligation, formerly contained in Part 2 of the Caravan Sites Act 1968, on local authorities to provide sites for gypsies was removed and local authorities acquired the power to remove persons and vehicles unlawfully on land.

6.2 Removal of trespassers on land

6.2.1 Checklist

- Two or more people trespassing on land may be directed to leave
- senior police officer must reasonably believe they have a common purpose to reside
- steps must have been taken by or for the occupier to ask them to leave

- removal permitted if one person has caused damage, or
- there are more than six vehicles

Over the years preceding the 1994 Act, a particular problem became apparent. Despite previous statutory interventions, the courts were unable to provide a speedy and effective remedy for local communities affected by hippy convoys and large groups of travellers taking up residence in a particular area or trespassing on farmland, common land or other sites. The identification of the problems had taken time. Section 39 of the POA 1986 had been implemented to deal with specific problems during the early 1980s, particularly mass trespass by hippies or hell's angels. The modifications made by ss 61 and 62 of the CJPOA were intended to provide more effective measures than those in the previous s 39. Although s 39 of the POA 1986 was not for use against gypsies (Association of Chief Police Officers *Good Practice Guidelines* 24 and 32), there is no doubt that ss 61 and 62 may be applicable to certain gypsy trespasses, assuming that chief constables are prepared to contemplate their use against gypsies. Prior to the 1994 Act, there appeared to be consensus that there was a problem to resolve. Reservations about the 1994 Act concern the dangers that the provisions could affect other groups to an inappropriate degree in a liberal democracy.

The government view was that the proposed provisions would not be capable of misapplication because of the limiting terms in which the provisions were drafted and the discretion of the police in their implementation. The objective was to provide a quick and fair remedy to remove disruptive trespasssers or significant groups of trespassers.

There was concern that the provisions would conflict with fundamental human rights as to movement and assembly and the rights set out in the European Convention on Human Rights and the International Covenant of Civil and Political Rights. These provisions ensure that everyone has the right to a guarantee of respect for privacy and family life, home and correspondence. Freedom from discrimination is also guaranteed. However, during the passage of the bill through Parliament, it was stated that 'None of the clauses in this part of the Bill aims to criminalise trespass. We want to deal with specific problems involving aggravated trespass, whether with intimidation or mass invasion with vehicles, with which clause 45 deals' (Mr Maclean, HC SCB, 8/2/94, col 531).

6.2.2 Direction

The senior policeman present may direct all members or any member of a group to leave land and remove vehicles or other property if he reasonably believes that:

- there are two or more people;
- they are trespassing on land;
- they have a common purpose to reside there for any period;
- reasonable steps have been taken by or on behalf of the occupier to ask them to leave;
- and *either* that one or more person has damaged land or property on the land or used threatening, abusive or insulting words or behaviour towards the occupier, a member of his family or his employee or agent;
- *or* that they have six or more vehicles on the land (s 61(1)).

The direction to leave is not defined by the Act. It will therefore be accorded its ordinary meaning. The direction may be given to persons who, while not originally trespassers, have since become trespassers (see 6.2.10). It will have to be a direction capable of being heard by the recipient and its form will therefore depend to a degree upon the size of the gathering. Section 61(3) provides for a constable other than the directing constable to communicate the direction to the person directed. Loudhailers and even helicopter loudhailers may sometimes be the only way to give the direction. Unlike s 63(4) (raves), 'reasonable steps . . . to bring it to their attention' will not be sufficient to make a direction valid for s 61(3). While the formula of the Act does not allow for a conditional direction as to the route to take, the sequence of departures and so on, it might well be that conditions could be imposed to avoid the risk of breach of the peace or threat to the safety of the public (see 2.9). Therefore failure to comply with a route or sequence condition might be wilful obstruction of a constable acting in the execution of his duty (Police Act 1964, s 51).

The associated detailed directions need to be kept in mind. In the case of challenge in the magistrates' court an advocate will seek proof that the particular direction claimed was given. If no definitive record has been maintained, this might be a problem which could be exploited by a defendant. If the directing officer has not kept a detailed record of the precise direction he gave, then the court might find that no definable direction had been given and therefore that no offence was committed by not moving on.

If the communication of the direction differs from the actual direction in detail, the court will have to determine whether it had to be communicated verbatim or in substance only.

6.2.3 Reasonable belief

These powers depend upon the existence of reasonable belief. The validity of the direction is unaffected by the fact that the reasonable belief may turn out to be a mistaken belief. On the other hand it would be a defence to an allegation of non-compliance with a direction that there was no trespass.

6.2.4 Two or more persons

Where the persons present are there with the occupier's consent, this section has no application, whatever the implications of their presence for local people. Trespass means as against the occupier of the land and the police officer must reasonably believe that such a trespass exists. The initial entry on to the land need not have been trespassory, nor need the trespassers have arrived at the same time, so long as the occupation is trespassory or reasonably believed to be so by the directing constable at the time he gives the direction. The possibility of esoteric argument as to the precise status of a particular notional trespasser may be dissuasive as far as constables are concerned, thereby effectively confining the provision to the large-scale trespasses against which the sections were directed.

6.2.5 Land

Land does not include buildings apart from agricultural buildings and scheduled ancient monuments. The occupation of factories, universities or a house would not be dealt with by this provision.

Land is not defined in the Act as to its geographical extent. Thus a constable could notionally issue a direction to leave a very substantial area so long as it was in the same occupation. Generally the land would be circumscribed by reference to adjacent fields or possibly to a particular farm. A direction would be meaningless if it could not be understood by the recipients.

Land does include common land. It does not include highways except for footpaths, bridleways or byways open to all traffic or roads used as public paths.

6.2.6 Common purpose to reside

'Reside' has its ordinary meaning and therefore involves living regularly at a particular location. It does not necessarily mean sleeping in that location each and every night. The persons concerned may have a multiplicity of reasons for trespass but it will be sufficient that the constable reasonably believes that one of those reasons is the common purpose to reside. It may be a purpose formulated after the initial decision to stop but it must be common to the persons. If only one has the intention to reside, then the element is missing. The section is aimed at persons who might ordinarily be expected to have mobile homes or other accommodation with them. There is a residual risk of argument over the purpose to reside, particularly if the direction is being given very quickly after the trespass commences.

A person may have a purpose to reside even though he has a home elsewhere. The position of children in groups trespassing will be of importance. A child with an adult will enable the common purpose to be made out in that there will be two people together and if they intend to stay they will have a common purpose to reside.

6.2.7 Request to leave

The constable must also reasonably believe that reasonable steps have been taken by or on behalf of the occupier to ask the trespasser to leave (see 6.2.14). The constable will need to note the basis of his belief about the steps taken. Whether the steps taken are reasonable depends upon the circumstances of the case. Posting notices, shouting from a parked car, visiting and speaking to persons all may be appropriate but the steps can only be reasonable if there has been a real prospect of the request coming to the attention of the persons addressed.

6.2.8 Damage or threats

This provision does not make criminal damage a prerequisite. Any damage, however small and however caused, suffices and the word is not defined by the section save to the extent that it includes the deposit of any substance capable of polluting the land (s 61(9)). On damage to property see *Morphitus v Salmon* (1990). If it suffers temporary or permanent physical harm or impairment of use or value, then property is damaged. It is arguable therefore that chopping firewood, causing grass to be crushed and causing ruts would be damage. It matters not that the damage is caused by only one person of the group, or that the abusive words are said by only one person. The provision is triggered for the group as a whole. Nor do the threats, abuse or insults require a specific intent. It is sufficient if such words are used.

6.2.9 Vehicle

The definition of a vehicle is set out at s 61(9). It should be kept in mind that a car and a caravan constitute two vehicles not one. The vehicles need not actually have been brought on to the land by the trespassers so long as they have control of them. This precludes the trespasser from using the fact that a particular vehicle belongs to somebody else to exclude the operation of the section.

6.2.10 Person not originally trespasser

Where persons were not originally trespassers but have become such, the same power arises so long as the qualifying criteria arise after they became trespassers and not before (s 61(2)).

6.2.11 Offences

An offence is made out if a person knows that a direction as above applies to him and fails to leave the land as soon as reasonably practicable or if he returns to the land as a trespasser within three months of the date on which the direction was given.

The offence is summary and the maximum penalty is either three months' imprisonment or a fine up to level 4 or both (s 61(4)). A constable in uniform may arrest without warrant on reasonable suspicion that an offence is being committed (s 61(5)). The general arrest provisions would also apply (PACE, s 25).

It may be that police officers will find it difficult to decide whether or when to use the power, even assuming that they view it differently from s 39 of the POA 1986. The police role was discussed in Parliament:

> A landowner may want the police to chuck people off his land, but if the police reasonably conclude that those people do not have 'the common purpose of residing there for a period' or that they are not causing damage, have not been abusive or do not have six vehicles, the police will use their discretion . . . the police know the situations for which they need the power (Mr Maclean, HC SCB, col 539).

As is commonly the case with public order provisions, the powers appear draconian and an assault on individual freedoms by the state through the government. The reality of the provision will only be capable of analysis once it is clear how it will be enforced by police, given their reluctance to use s 39 of the POA 1986 and by the courts subsequent to that.

6.2.12 As soon as reasonably practicable

As soon as reasonably practicable does not mean as quickly as a reasonable police officer requires but rather, what is practicable for the trespasser (*Krumpa v DPP* (1989)):

> It will be up to the police to determine that in each circumstance. If it is true that there are no spark plugs—not that they have been deliberately removed—or if the trespassers need parts from a garage and it is Christmas day, I understand that it will be difficult to leave within minutes . . . The norm will be that when the direction is given, people will have to leave sooner rather than later and, in the vast majority of cases, much earlier than 24 hours (Mr Maclean, HC SCB, col 550).

6.2.13 Direction or arrest

It will be a matter for the policeman present to decide whether to arrest a person under the POA 1986 or the Criminal Damage Act 1971 (CDA) or to give a direction under this Act (assuming he is the senior officer present) if he attends the scene and actually sees conduct described by both Acts. If he arrests under the POA 1986 or CDA 1971, then the directive powers may well have to be given at the same time as the arrest. That will be a problem if the arresting officer is not the senior officer present.

6.2.14 Reasonable steps by the occupier

Reasonable belief that reasonable steps have been taken by the occupier to ask trespassers to leave will be made out by the officer being told the position by a person apparently telling the truth (see 6.2.7). There will therefore be no delaying factors in the formulation of the basis for the direction. It should, however, be kept in mind that this power to direct only arises once the apparent trespass exists. If the occupier wishes to prevent an anticipated trespass, then he must avail himself of his civil injunctive remedies, assuming he can identify defendants adequately. If the police wish to prevent, then it is a question of using their preventive powers if appropriate or determining whether to seek a trespassory assembly ban.

6.2.15 Defences

There is a statutory defence if the accused can show either:

(a) he was not trespassing; or
(b) he had a reasonable excuse for failing to leave the land as soon as reasonably practicable or for re-entering the land (s 61(6)).

6.2.16 Seizure

Section 62(1) of the CJPOA states that:

> If a direction has been given under section 61 and a constable reasonably suspects that any person to whom the direction applies has, without reasonable excuse—

(a) failed to remove any vehicle which appears to the officer to belong to him or to be in his possession or under his control; or
(b) entered the land as a trespasser within the period of three months beginning with the day on which the direction was given, the constable may seize and remove that vehicle.

This provision only relates to vehicles and not other property. The objective is to end the trespass and the inconvenience caused by it. To that end the vehicles are the focus.

6.3 Open air loud music at night (raves)

The powers in relation to raves are set out in ss 63–67 of the CJPOA and are discussed below.

6.3.1 Checklist

- Only superintendent or above may give direction to leave
- must be event for 100 or more
- amplified music at night includes repetitive beats
- open air includes venue partly open to the air
- the occupier cannot commit offence
- power to stop people en route to a rave
- power to order forfeiture of goods

The provisions contained in the 1994 Act enable the police to give directions if a rave is taking place or being prepared (s 63). The provisions create offences if the directions are not complied with (s 63(6)), the power to seize property (s 64) and the power to stop people making their way to raves (s 65). There is a power for the court to forfeit sound equipment (s 66) and for charges to be incurred in respect of the storing of seized property (s 67).

These provisions were aimed at loud music played at high volume through modern sound systems at gatherings lasting many hours and sometimes many days, to the considerable annoyance of neighbours and the community at large:

> . . . a case where people in 11 vehicles formed a bridgehead and in a few days 4,000 to 5,000 people had turned up. That is a typical example of the rave we are trying to get at (Mr Maclean, HC SCB, col 591).

Much publicity focused on large-scale outdoor raves involving several thousand participants descending by car on the venue. Noise levels were enormous and the noise went on all night without remission. The gatherings were highly profitable and there was a perceived link to the unlawful use of drugs.

This was not the only category of commercial party organisation which functioned all night to the serious detriment of neighbours. During Commons committee the question of indoor urban parties in tower blocks was raised as meriting the same approach, but the essential response of the government was that indoor events required a licence if they were commercial and that they should be dealt with via the licensing provisions. This view did not take account of the difficulty of demonstrating that a party in a flat or series of flats is not truly private, but it was the view that prevailed and the narrow focus of these provisions remained. It remains a matter for local authorities to serve notices under the Control of Pollution Act to deal with noisy indoor parties. The police can then be called upon to assist if the notice is breached. Only unlicensed events in the open air are caught by the provisions.

6.3.2 Police officer

A police officer of at least the rank of superintendent may direct people to leave land and remove vehicles or other property from that land if he reasonably believes that:

(a) two or more people are on the land in the open air preparing for a defined gathering;
(b) ten or more are waiting for such a gathering to start; or attending such a gathering in progress;
(c) ten or more persons are attending such a gathering.

There appear to be problems with the specified numbers. While it may be possible to say two people are preparing for a gathering of 100 (s 63(2)(a)) or that ten are waiting for such an event (s 63(2)(b)), it is simply impossible to say that ten people are attending a gathering of 100 (s 63(2)(c)), unless the intention is to catch the ten people left at what was previously a gathering of 100. Even if that is the intention it does not work; it is either a gathering of ten or of 100 at the moment the policeman formulates his belief. It cannot be both.

6.3.3 Event

At the event there must be:

(a) 100 or more people on land in the open air;
(b) amplified music played during the night with or without intermission;
(c) music likely to cause serious distress to the inhabitants of the locality because of its loudness, duration and the time at which it is played.

6.3.4 Target

The target of these powers is narrow. The section itself does not refer to the rave. It is referred to in the headnote to ss 63–66 and the marginal note to ss 63 and 65.

6.3.5 Open air

The open air rave is the specific focus, but s 63(10) sets out that that includes 'a place partly open to the air'. Anything taking place in an aircraft hangar will escape as will anything taking place in a closed building. A Dutch barn may be caught; an ordinary barn will not:

> A tent or a marquee can be in the open air. A Dutch barn is not enclosed and is therefore in the open air. An aircraft hangar without doors is in the open air. The interpretation must be left to the officers at the scene (Mr Maclean, HC SCB, col 592).

This political quotation describes the police discretion as to interpretation. That may well be circumscribed in due course by the judiciary whose job it is to determine the proper interpretation of statutory words according to strict rules of interpretation.

6.3.6 A hundred persons

The choice of the number 100 as the trigger figure is clearly deliberate to keep the focus on the bigger events, but the organiser figure of ten people on land setting up the event might delay police intervention if steps are being sought to circumvent the provisions. All the organisers need to do is to use nine people instead of ten.

6.3.7 Night

It is essential that the amplified music occurs during the night to create the offending rave (s 63(1)). It does not have to be continuous and the absence of music during the daytime will not prevent the gathering being caught. It will be for the courts to define 'night' in due course. Whether it will mean the hours of darkness by reference to notions of dawn and dusk, or whether it means between specific hours is not defined. The reality is that it probably does not matter. A rave goes on all night and does not simply exist in the twilight times which might be difficult to fit into the section. To make money, raves are 'all nighters' and that is the focus of the section.

6.3.8 Intermissions

The gathering is deemed to continue during intermissions. When it lasts several days, it is only the night time element which qualifies. Music includes repetitive beats (s 63(1)(b)). Gathering does not include licensed gathering (s 63(9)(a)).

6.3.9 Direction

The direction to leave or remove property must be communicated to the people concerned but it may be the constable at the scene who tells them (s 63(3)) and it will be deemed given if reasonable steps have been taken to let them know (s 63(4)). This contrasts with the basis of communication in s 61(3) where there is no reference to 'reasonable steps'. Reasonable steps in the context of a rave might include using the PA system to make an announcement. It might be sufficient to switch off the PA and to reduce the lighting, especially strobe lighting. That done the crowd would be aware that the event was over.

6.3.10 Offence

An offence is created for a person who fails without reasonable excuse to leave as soon as reasonably practicable or, having left, returns within seven days without reasonable excuse. The offence carries imprisonment up to three months or a fine up to level 4 or both and on reasonable belief that the offence is being committed, a constable may arrest without a warrant (s 63(6)–(8)).

6.3.11 Exemption from the section

The occupier, his family, his employee or agent or any person whose home is situated on the land is exempted from direction under this section (s 63(5) and (10)).

6.3.12 Land

Land in the open air includes land partly in the open air (s 63(10)).

6.3.13 Superintendent's power to investigate

If a superintendent reasonably believes that a direction would be justified he may authorise a constable (who need not be in uniform) to enter land without warrant to:

(a) ascertain if the direction would be justified;
(b) exercise any powers in s 63; or
(c) if the direction has been given, seize and remove vehicles or sound equipment on the land, belonging to or under the control of the person given the direction.

Albeit there is no express provision for the use of force, the act of seizure itself is permitted. Anybody seeking to prevent that might be liable to arrest for obstructing a police officer in the execution of his duty.

6.3.14 Seizure

The power to seize only applies if the directed person has:
(a) failed to leave;
(b) been arrested under the section; or
(c) failed to remove property or vehicle in accordance with the direction.

The property of exempted people cannot be seized (s 64(5)).

6.3.15 Stopping people en route

Once a direction has been given a constable in uniform has various powers. Within five miles of the boundary of the land in respect of which the direction has been given, he can stop any person he reasonably believes is en route to the gathering and direct them not to proceed in the direction of the gathering. He cannot give the direction to those in the exempted class (s 65). There may be problems arising from the proper interpretation of the five-mile radius in the case of barns in large fields. Where is the measurement taken from, the barn or the boundary of the field? The police officer will have to be clear in giving the direction in the first place. In the event of non-compliance with such a direction he may arrest a person he believes is committing an offence under the section, namely failing to comply with a direction not to proceed in the direction of the gathering (s 65(5)). In an appropriate case, s 25 of PACE will apply.

6.3.16 Forfeiture

A person convicted of non-compliance with a direction under s 63 may be ordered to forfeit goods seized from him, provided they were in his possession or under his control at the time (s 64(4)). The court is obliged to take the value of such items, and the effect on the offender of forfeiture into account before making an order (s 66(3)). Any person seeking to reclaim property seized will need to apply within six months, under the Police (Property) Act 1897, showing that he had not consented to the offender having the item or had not known, and had no reason to suspect, that it was likely to be used at a relevant gathering (s 67(7)).

Vehicles and sound equipment seized may be retained until the end of the case against the person from whom it was seized. There is power to charge for storage and the power to retain pending payment of the storage charges (s 67).

6.3.17 Rave organiser reaction

It is likely that organisers will move away from the type of event targeted because of the potential for substantial losses created by the seizure provisions. The noise requirements, both as to volume and time period, are ill-defined by the Act and are left to the court to resolve. Serious distress may well be a higher level of requirement than the government anticipated. The serious distress may arise from daytime music rather than the music during the night. Therefore, even if the organisers turn the music down at night, they will be caught by the provision. Where the borderline between distress and serious distress falls is difficult to determine. The expression will fall to be defined in accordance with the principles in *Brutus v Cozens* (1972). No offence is created for non-compliance with a direction to remove vehicles or other property. Although it was not debated, this is presumably because the seizure provisions will be triggered.

The objective of these provisions is to put at serious risk the expensive equipment required for such occasions. The impact may be dented if organisers choose to hire the equipment under a contract which excludes its use for events defined by s 63, since such contractual provision would protect the hirer from loss generally and he would recover his equipment. This would be a substantial risk, because s 65(5) requires the owner of the equipment to apply to the magistrates for the return of the equipment if he wants it back. The section permits the magistrates to order the return of the equipment, it does not require them to so order. There is therefore a continuing risk to the owner that they will not make the order and that their exercise of discretion will be upheld if appealed. The question remains as to whether the operation will be viable with equipment held pending court decision on the offence. Sound equipment is very expensive and to provide an adequate return on its cost it needs to be in regular use. If it remains unused because it is subject to argument in court, then organisers are not making money. Only the organisers of the gatherings will be able to make that calculation from their profit and loss account. It is likely that the web of statutory provisions here may end unlicensed outdoor gatherings of this type and that the Government will need to turn its attention to the consequences of the unlicensed indoor variety.

The police will not be able to seize from the exempted category of person including the land occupier's agent. There is a risk in certain cases that the definition will apply to those setting up the gathering and to the equipment in so far as the organiser may be operating in part as the agent of the occupier of the land. This will be a matter for argument in the court if organisers are prepared to take the very substantial risk of losing their equipment.

Although the court must consider the consequences of forfeiting items seized, they will do so in the context of weighing the loss to the offender against the benefits generally of depriving an offender of the means of his offence.

6.4 Aggravated trespass

The offence of aggravated trepass and police powers to remove offenders are set out in ss 68 and 69 of the CJPOA and are discussed below.

6.4.1 Checklist

- Adjoining land hard to define in aggravated trespass
- intent to intimidate, obstruct or disrupt required
- only the senior policeman present may direct to leave
- direction must be specific, otherwise non-compliance may be hard to prove

The 1994 Act deals with trespassers who, while trespassing on land in the open air, either disrupt lawful activity there or on adjacent land, obstruct such activity or intimidate persons engaged in such lawful activity (s 68). An offence is created and power is given to the police to remove people engaged in aggravated trespass (s 69).

The aggravated trespass provisions are designed to deal with trespassers who disrupt lawful activity on land. The most obvious example of the target group is the hunt saboteurs. The provisions have been criticised because of their potential for application to situations never envisaged by the government and to that extent exemplify the problem of public order law. It has the potential of wider application than was intended, creating the risk of greater state intervention in individual rights than the community will tolerate and thereby jeopardising public order, rather than protecting it. As always it will depend on the application of the provisions in practice. A demonstration on the town hall steps might be caught because the demonstrators would be trespassing (or possibly so) and their intention might well be to disrupt, however well behaved they were; the circumstances might be caught by the open air element of the provision. By the same token it was thought that legitimate motorway protestors might be penalised in an inappropriate way. The government view was that the discretion would be sparingly exercised. This will remain to be seen but reliance on discretion creates vagueness and uncertainty which places an undue burden on police officers and may bring the law into even greater disrespect (see 1.6, 1.7).

6.4.2 Arrest and penalty

Aggravated trespass is an offence and a policeman in uniform may arrest a person without warrant on reasonable suspicion that he is committing an offence (s 68(4)). The penalty for the offence is up to three months in prison or a fine up to level 4 or both (s 68(3)).

6.4.3 Offence

Aggravated trespass is committed if:

> A person . . . trespasses on land in the open air and, in relation to any lawful activity which persons are engaging in or are about to engage in on that or adjoining land in the open air does there anything which is intended by him to have the effect—
> (a) of intimidating those persons or any of them so as to deter them or any of them from engaging in that activity,
> (b) of obstructing that activity, or
> (c) of disrupting the activity (s 68(1)).

Trespass may arise after a lawful entry to the land has lasted beyond the licence to be there. Trespass also occurs where a person lawfully on particular land proceeds to engage in conduct going beyond his permission (*Harrison v Duke of Rutland* (1893)). Trespassers will not be able to plead necessity as a defence in cases where the necessity is to prevent cruelty to animals. *London Borough of Southwark v Williams* (1971) effectively rejects necessity save in the narrowest circumstances. Unlike s 61, aggravated trespass under s 68 applies only in the open air. Partly open buildings, such as Dutch barns, will not be covered by the provision although the conduct en route to the Dutch barn might well be caught.

6.4.4 Lawful activity

Activity is lawful if it can be undertaken without committing an offence (s 68(2)). The lawful activity must be being engaged in or about to be engaged in and it must be on that or adjoining land. There may be some interpretive difficulty over the meaning of 'about to'. How proximate to the activity must it be? If hunt saboteurs attend a field and prepare to disrupt a hunt that in fact will not visit that field, are they attempting to commit an offence contrary to the section?

There may be difficulty over the use of the word 'adjoining'. If land, in the context of this section, means land in one ownership, then adjoining land will mean neighbour's land lying next to the land in question. This may be as difficult for protestors to resolve as it will be for policemen. If land means an identifiable parcel of land, the adjoining land may be a separate field in the same ownership but lying next to the one being trespassed on initially.

There may also be difficulty over 'engaged in'. A farmer is engaged in farming even though he may not be in a given field. A protestor who conducts himself in a way calculated to disrupt the farming operation even though the farmer is not present will be caught.

6.4.5 Intention

The intention has to be that the conduct will intimidate, obstruct or disrupt. If the intention is not any of these then no offence is committed. It will be a question of fact for the police officer considering giving a direction to leave, or the court when dealing with an allegation in court, to determine what the intention of the person was. In most cases it might be obvious, but engaging in peaceful persuasion of huntsmen would not fall within the section.

6.4.6 Land

Land does not include land forming part of the highway unless the particular highway is a bridleway, footpath or byway. Thus protest on the highway is not precluded by this section, although such protest will often raise the problem of defining the relationship between tolerated protest in the community and wilful obstruction of the highway contrary to s 137 of the Highways Act 1980. Protest on a footpath, bridleway or byway may well constitute an offence under this section assuming the other elements are present to create the offence.

6.4.7 Does there anything

Although it may be argued that this part of the section requires positive action to create the offence, that need not necessarily be the case. A person or group who are doing nothing other than stand in a given location may be doing something within the terms of the Act if they, as trespassers, stand and thereby obstruct the lawful activity of the other persons. Generally it will be more positive conduct which is caught, but not necessarily always. In *Fagan v MPC* (1968) the court was divided over the question of whether declining to remove a car from a policeman's foot constituted assault.

6.4.8 Direction to leave

The senior policeman present on land may direct a person or people to leave land if he reasonably believes that a person is committing, will commit or has committed the offence of aggravated trespass or that two or more are trespassing with common purpose of intimidating people to deter them from engaging in a lawful activity or of obstructing or disrupting the lawful activity (s 69(1)).

The difficulty in court may relate to the extent to which the direction has to be recorded and the terms of the direction given. If the timescale, specific land and date are not properly dealt with, then in court it may prove difficult to prove non-compliance. Most cases, however, will simply involve the policeman saying to the trespasser, 'Get out of this field now', and courts should have little problem with that.

6.4.9 Offence and penalty

An offence is created if, having been given a direction and knowing it has been given, a person fails to leave the land as soon as practicable or if he returns to the land within seven days once he has left it. The penalty is up to three months' imprisonment or a fine to level 4 or both. Arrest does not require a warrant (s 69(5)).

It is a defence if the person can show that at the time of arrest for breach of the direction he was not trespassing or that he had a reasonable excuse for not leaving or for returning (s 69(4)).

6.4.10 Comment

These provisions protect lawful activity on land from interference by trespassers intent upon intimidating, obstructing or disrupting it. Hunting is lawful and the government view is that people should be able to go about their lawful operations even if they are distasteful to other members of the community. This view has also been developed in the abortion clinic cases and in the cases relating to the export of live animals for slaughter where the right of the exporter to be protected in his lawful trade has been protected by the courts (the *Phoenix Aviation* case). Any person who is trespassing and while doing so is blowing a horn or shouts or lays false trails on adjacent land will fall foul of the provisions. He will then be liable to a direction to leave or to arrest or both. The only steps that appear to remain permitted to a hunt saboteur are to operate from places where he is not *prima facie* a trespasser, ie footpaths, bridleways and highways. This is unlikely to enable them to function as they have in the past. They will need to review their tactics if they are to avoid breaking the law.

On a practical basis, some of the hunt saboteur incidents occur on footpaths and there may be a difficulty over whether the saboteur is trespassing or not. If he is not, he commits no offence. It is worth noting that as the hunt saboteur makes his way quietly from one place to another by trespassing across land doing nothing intimidating, obstructive or disruptive, then he commits no offence. If he then makes his protest from a footpath, he may well become a trespasser and render himself liable under the section. In *Harrison v Duke of Rutland* the protestor waved his umbrella from the perceived security of a public footpath to disrupt a pheasant shoot on the Duke's land. The question was whether he was protected by being on the footpath or whether he was in fact a trespasser as against the Duke who owned the land over which the footpath ran. The court decided that because he used the footpath for a purpose other than the passing and repassing for which a footpath existed, he was a trespasser. Thus a protestor on a footpath might easily be a trespasser in relation to the footpath. Indeed in certain cases the footpath would constitute part of the land rather than being adjacent to it. Section 68(5) adopts the same definition of highways and roads as land for the purposes of this provision as that set out in s 61(9)(b).

6.5 Possession of premises

Sections 72–76 of the CJPOA tackle the issue of squatting.

6.5.1 Introduction

The 1994 Act deals with the consequences of not complying with an interim possession order in summary proceedings and the offences of obtaining such an order by false statements (ss 75–76). They also deal with arrangements to improve the position of displaced residential occupiers and intending occupiers (ss 72 and 74) and residential squatting (s 73).

> The existing remedy for removing squatters from property has clearly been inadequate for some time . . . it is much too expensive and too slow. It should not be solely the province of the exceptionally wealthy . . . The law must be accessible to those of modest or little means who suddenly find their property occupied (Mr Maclean, HC SCB, col 663).

The provisions are consistent with the Government's developing theory of protecting all categories of lawful occupants of land. The full extent of squatting as a problem appears relatively uncertain, but there was some measure of agreement in committee that some steps were necessary. The anxiety was that in addressing the problem, the proposals might have the capacity to be abused by unscrupulous landlords to the disadvantage of vulnerable tenants.

The government view was that the problems of squatting should be addressed. In essence the squatter was the one acting unlawfully and that as the law stood he was overprotected:

> . . . it will be for a civil court to decide whether to order the squatters to leave, as a form of interim relief. That power will be subject to the safeguard that, having left, the alleged squatters will be entitled to a full hearing of the case in the usual way and to recover costs and damages as well as reinstatement in the property, if it is found that they had lawful entitlement to possession. (Mr Maclean, HC SCB, 664).

6.5.2 Interim possession order

An interim possession order is an order made under rules of court for the bringing of summary proceedings for possession of premises occupied by trespassers. There is a new procedure for obtaining an interim possession order (County Court Rules, Part 2, Ord 24). This new procedure which is an alternative to the procedure set out at Part 1 of Ord 24, applies to premises as defined in s 12 of the Criminal Law Act 1977, a building or part of a building under separate occupation, any land ancillary to a building or buildings with any land ancillary thereto. The definition includes any immovable structure and any moveable structure designed or adapted for residential purposes. This includes caravans and houseboats. It is not an order which is available in the case of trespassers on land which is not ancillary to a building. Rules provide for notice of the proceedings to be served on the alleged squatters, and for a hearing *ex parte* on application except in the case of residential premises where the occupier may file an affidavit if he believes he has a right to occupy. In certain instances this may lead to a hearing at which he may attend. If the applicant satisfies the court on a balance of probabilities that he is entitled to occupation, then an interim possession order will be made which will require the squatters to leave the premises within 24 hours. Generally this notice will have to be served within 48 hours and lodged with the local police station within 24 hours of service. In due course a final hearing will take place at which the court will consider making a final order of possession or any applications from the squatter who claims a right of occupation.

The 1994 Act makes it an offence punishable with six months' imprisonment or a fine on level 5 for a person either not to leave the premises within 24 hours of service of the order or to return within a year (s 76(2)) of the service of the order. The section also applies to any trespasser who occupies during the currency of the interim possession order. Thus a person who takes over from an original squatter is caught by the provision. A constable in uniform may arrest without warrant on reasonable suspicion (s 76(7)).

To protect occupiers from unscrupulous abuse of the new provision, it is made an offence triable either way, punishable on indictment with two years' imprisonment or a fine or both, and summarily with six months or a fine not exceeding the statutory maximum, to make a statement to obtain an interim possession order, knowing it to be or being reckless as to its being, false or misleading in a material particular (s 75):

> The maximum penalty under s 56 has deliberately been made the same as that in the Protection from Eviction Act 1977 for the offences of unlawfully depriving a residential occupier of his premises . . . There is a tremendous discrepancy between the penalty which squatters may suffer and that for owners who knowingly or recklessly seek an interim possession order (Mr Maclean, HC SCB, col 672).

6.5.3 Displaced residential occupiers

Under CLA 1977, s 7 it is an offence punishable with six months' imprisonment or a fine on level 5 on the standard scale for a squatter to fail to leave premises when ordered to do so by a displaced residential occupier of the premises. The Act adds to CLA 1977 a new s 12A which redefines 'displaced residential occupier' and under which there will be three categories:

(a) a person with a freehold interest or a leasehold interest with at least two years to run;
(b) a person with a tenancy or a licence to occupy granted by a person in the first category;
(c) a person with a tenancy granted by an 'authority' as defined in the subsection;

excluded by a trespasser as defined, and holding a certificate signed by him and a JP or commissioner of oaths specifying his interest and the fact that he requires the premises as a residence for himself. It is a defence to proceedings under CLA 1977, s 7 to show that no certificate was produced at the time the squatter was required to leave (s 12A(9)). It is an offence punishable with six months' imprisonment or a fine on level 5 or both (except in the case of an authority tenant) to make a false or reckless statement (s 12A(8)).

The provisions of CLA 1977, s 6 have been amended by the addition of a new subs 6(1A) (by s 72 the Act) excluding displaced residential occupiers from liability for violent entry.

6.5.4 Reasons for the change

The main element of this part of the Act is the set of requirements dealing with the interim possession order. It is an attempt to make proceedings against squatters quicker, more effective and less expensive. The civil court decides whether the squatter goes but once the decision is made, then if he stays he commits an offence. To ensure that removal of non-squatters is not achieved by the unscrupulous, the penalties for misinforming the court include imprisonment for matters falling short of perjury.

For residential occupiers facing the squatter problem, the law is changed. They will no longer be criminals if they use force to gain entry to their property. It could be argued that this endangers public order by permitting force in these confrontations. The government view was that people should be able to use reasonable force to effect an entry to their own property.

6.5.5 Certificate

By the use of a relatively straightforward procedure of obtaining a certificate signed both by them and a JP or commissioner of oaths, with the relevant information in it, the displaced residential occupier will be entitled to the assistance of the police in obtaining occupancy of their premises. The squatter will be committing an offence if he does not vacate and therefore will be liable to arrest. The procedure will be to obtain the certificate and then attend the premises with a policeman who will in effect enforce the removal of the squatter (CLA 1977, s 12A).

6.6 Unauthorised campers and gypsy sites

The powers to remove unauthorised campers are set out in ss 77–79 of the CJPOA and are discussed below.

6.6.1 Checklist

- Local authority must avoid breach of Children Act 1989
- DoE Circular 18/94 requires council to act in a humane and compassionate way
- notice to leave when residing on highway or unoccupied land
- generally no specific names required on notice to leave
- definition of vehicle wide—includes body without wheels
- home elsewhere is no defence
- provisions affect all nomadic people, whether gypsy or not

Another plank of the government's policy of protecting the lawful possession of property, this part of the Act was designed to deal with persons camping on land without authority. Although it does not criminalise trespass, it certainly criminalises non-compliance with a direction to move and has been seen as a *de facto* criminalisation of alternative lifestyles. The provisions do not distinguish between different categories of travellers. It has the capacity to place the government in conflict with international conventions (see 6.6.10).

The obligation on local authorities under the Caravan Sites Act 1968 to provide gypsy sites has been revoked (s 80) as had been mooted in the DoE Circular, Reform of Caravan Sites Act 1968. They may provide such sites but there will be no government funding involved and local opposition and the tightening of planning controls will commonly prevent effective provision of sites. The definition of the term gypsy has been amended to include any person of a nomadic lifestyle. This new definition may be affected by the decision in *South Hams DC v Gibbs* (1994) which makes it clear that 'nomadic habit of life' implies an identifiable connection between the nomadic life and the means of making a living. It excludes groups such as new age travellers whose nomadic life is not related to their income generation. Local authorities have been empowered to require unauthorised campers to move on (s 77). It is now an offence not to comply and on complaint, a magistrates' court may order vehicles or property to be removed if present in contravention of a direction (s 78), permitting the local authority to make the arrangements. Special provisions (s 79) deal with the problem of service of the direction on unnamed persons.

6.6.2 Background

During the early 1990s the government view was that the policy of requiring local authorities to provide sites for gypsies was not working and that the more provided, the more people were attracted to the itinerant life:

> As more sites have been provided, more people have taken to the lifestyle. I believe that genuine gypsies have been disadvantaged as more and more people who could not be considered as genuine gypsies get on the band-wagon. Genuine gypsies are forced out of their traditional haunts . . . by others who do not deserve the same protection (Mr Maclean, HC SCB, col 695).

The provisions were clearly related to the other trespass provisions in that they permit control of unauthorised use of land for residence, in this case by local authorities. The counter-view was that prior to the implementation of the 1968 Act there had been an impossible position with travellers constantly moved from one illegal site to another with nowhere legitimate to go. These provisions would have the effect of returning the community to that position. Under the 1968 Act, a local authority with designation because of their sufficiency of sites could move promptly to remove illegal campers from unofficial sites. The risk to caravan dwelling children was developed by the opposition as one of the primary negative consequences of the provisions:

> With the repeal of the 1968 Act the proposal will be inefficient and ineffective, will undermine child care and education and will work to the detriment of local communities. Campers will arrive . . . and be moved around in the unproductive way of the past which was damaging to travellers, and, above all, to local communities (Mr Michael HC SCB, col 691).

This view of developments is already being followed through in the court system with the Public Law Project having been given leave to seek judicial review of a decision to 'direct to move' made in respect of a group of travellers by the Wealden District Council. Part of the argument is that the council is required by DoE Circular 18/94 to act in a humane and compassionate way which they failed to do, and to comply with the obligations contained in the Children Act 1989 with regard to the children among the travellers. It is worth keeping in mind the terms of DoE Circular 18/94:

> Where gypsies are camped unlawfully on council land and are not causing a level of nuisance which cannot be effectively controlled, an immediate forced eviction might result in unauthorised camping in the area which could give rise to greater nuisance. Accordingly, authorities should consider tolerating gypsies' presence on the land for short periods and could examine ways of minimising the level of nuisance on such tolerated sites, for example, by providing basic services for gypsies . . .

The divisional court have now ruled that the local authority 'adopted the wrong approach to the case and omitted entirely to inform itself of potentially relevant matters both before giving a removal direction and before seeking a removal order' Sedley J made it clear that the local authority had a duty to think about those encamped and also local residents and to balance their conflicting needs. These considerations had to be kept in mind at the time of the decision to give the removal notice and only applied to the people encamped. New arrivals would have to be considered anew and new notices made and served if appropriate. The government view relied upon the gypsies' own capacity to provide sites for themselves so long as they were treated favourably from the point of view of planning and assisted by local authorities.

> A new approach is needed and we hope to bring it about by encouraging the ever-growing trend for gypsies to make provision for sites (Mr Maclean, HC SCB, col 692).

This view failed to take account of DoE Circular 1/94 which withdrew advice in favour of granting permission for caravan sites in green belt areas on a special case basis. The circular makes it less likely that gypsies will get permission because the policy is no longer expressed positively. The government also emphasised the inappropriateness of having two sets of rules for the local authorities, depending upon whether they were designated or not.

The restriction of the local authorities' powers to gypsies was also seen as anomalous. The intention was to provide a universal set of remedies for local authorities to deal with all unauthorised camping by whomsoever.

6.6.3 Direction

Local authorities may give direction to leave land and remove vehicles and any other property if it appears that persons are residing in a vehicle or vehicles on land forming part of the highway, any unoccupied land or any occupied land without the permission of the occupier (s 77(1)).

6.6.4 Notice

A notice of the direction must be served. That notice will suffice if it identifies the land and is addressed to the occupants of the vehicles on the land. A specific name is only required if there is only one person named in the direction (s 77(2)).

6.6.5 Offence

It is an offence carrying the penalty of a fine on level 3 not to comply with such a notice (s 77(3)). The offence is committed if a person served fails to leave the land as soon as practicable (or fails to move the vehicle or property). It is also an offence to return to the land in a vehicle within three months from the day of the direction.

6.6.6 Defence

It is a defence if the reason for non-departure, non-removal of property or re-entry was due to illness, mechanical breakdown or other immediate emergency (s 77(5)).

6.6.7 Vehicle

'Vehicle' is widely interpreted to include any vehicle whether or not it is in a fit state for use on the roads, and includes any body, with or without wheels, appearing to have formed part of such a vehicle, and any load carried by, and anything attached to such a vehicle; and a caravan as defined in s 29(1) of the Caravan Sites and Control of Development Act 1960.

6.6.8 Home elsewhere

A home elsewhere is not a defence to the allegation of residence.

6.6.9 Magistrates' order

If satisfied that there is a direction and continuing residence, then the magistrates' court may on complaint make an order that vehicles, property and people residing in them be removed (s 77(6)(a)). The court order enables the local authority to take reasonable steps to ensure the order is complied with, including entering on land and doing what is necessary to enter the vehicles and make ready for removal. It is an offence to obstruct anyone doing so and the penalty that may be imposed is a fine up to level 3.

The summons following the complaint may be served on the occupant of a particular vehicle or to all occupants of vehicles on specified land. There is no power to arrest for non-attendance at court. Good service is effected by attaching the document to a prominent place on all the vehicles concerned (s 79(2)). It must also be displayed prominently on the land concerned and copied to the owner or occupier of the land unless upon reasonable enquiry the owner or occupier cannot be ascertained (s 79(4)).

6.6.10 Focus

The focus of the Act is not gypsy people but nomadic people of any sort. The provisions are not complicated and enable local authorities to require unauthorised campers to move on. Whether this power will be more effective than the pre-1968 regime is difficult to assess. The decision has been made that it is essential to remove promptly all categories of trespasser, and nomadic people will frequently be trespassers. The government view is that the 1994 Act does not discriminate because it uses an expression 'nomadic habit of life'. It may prove difficult to relate that to the provisions of the ECHR. The convention has been discussed in Chapter 1, but in the context of gypsies it should be kept in mind that respect for privacy and family life, home and correspondence are all guaranteed. The UN Convention on the Rights of the Child specifically acknowledges the right of gypsy children to enjoy their own culture and to preserve their own identity without interference. If their culture depends upon a nomadic habit of life and that lifestyle is as unprotected as it appears to be by these provisions, then UK law will be in conflict with international conventions.

Chapter 7

Obstruction Offences

A wide range of offences involve obstruction. The offences commonly encountered are those involving assault or wilful obstruction of a constable acting in the execution of his duty (see 7.1), and wilful obstruction of the highway (see 7.2). Both offences will be applicable to a wide range of activities which may fall outside the scope of public order, eg warning a driver of an imminent speed trap, or allowing a stall or supermarket trollies to encroach on the highway. Nonetheless the principles which emerge from the cases are equally applicable to activities which do relate to public order.

7.1 Assault or wilful obstruction of a constable acting in the execution of his duty (Police Act 1964, s 51)

Section 51 of the Police Act 1964 deals with assault or wilful obstruction of a constable in the execution of his duty. The section states:

(1) Any person who assaults a constable in the execution of his duty, or a person assisting a constable in the execution of his duty, shall be guilty of an offence and liable on summary conviction to imprisonment for a term not exceeding six months or to a fine not exceeding level 5 on the standard scale or both.

(2) Section 17(2) of the Firearms Act 1968 (additional penalty for possession of firearms when committing certain offences) shall apply to offences under subsection (1) of this section.

(3) Any person who resists or wilfully obstructs a constable in the execution of his duty, or a person assisting a constable in the execution of his duty, shall be guilty of an offence and liable on summary conviction to imprisonment for a term not exceeding one month or to a fine not exceeding level 3 on the standard scale or both.

7.1.1 Common element of execution of duty

There is no strict correlation between duty and power, although no doubt many instances of duty are accompanied by an appropriate power. Thus, although there is a general police duty to detect crime, the common law does not furnish the police with whatever powers are necessary to achieve that end, nor does the common law accept that what is done officially is done lawfully.

The offences in s 51 are wider than assaulting or wilfully obstructing a constable in the execution of a power, and there are instances where an offence will be committed even though the police constable is not executing a power and where the offence involves refusal to co-operate with the police, although precisely when this will be so remains unclear.

It is insufficient to establish that the police officer was 'on duty' when the assault or obstruction occurred; nor is it a defence to show that the police officer was doing something he was not obliged by law to do. In *Coffin v Smith* (1990), police officers who attended a youth club whose leader was ejecting youths were acting in the execution of their duty. The court preferred not to follow the decision in *R v Prebble* (1858) where a police officer clearing licensed premises was held not to have been acting in the execution of his duty where there had been no actual or threatened breach of the peace.

Execution of duty involves a twofold consideration. The first is whether or not the police officer is doing anything which falls within the range of activities which might be said to be a police officer's duties. The second is whether or not the police officer has committed any act which requires justification at law.

The offence is not concerned with the good faith of the police officer concerned, and a police officer acting in good faith may be acting outside the execution of his duty.

7.1.2 General police duties

The courts have never sought to develop an approach to police duties which required them to specify precisely the nature and scope of these duties. Such a precise and inflexible approach would run counter to the general approach of the common law even though the development of police duties almost inevitably creates extensions of police powers, as in *Chief Constable of Kent v V* (1983).

In *Johnson v Phillips* (1976) it was said of police duties that:

> The first function of a constable has for centuries been the preservation of the peace. His powers and obligations derive from the common law and from statute . . . The powers and obligations of a constable under the common law have never been exhaustively defined and no attempt to do so has ever been made . . .

And in *R v Waterfield and Lynn* (1964) Ashworth J observed that '. . . it would be difficult . . . to reduce within specific limits the general terms in which the duties of police constables have been expressed'.

If the courts are able to find a duty in the police in certain respects, then disobedience of a citizen to orders given in pursuance of that duty may in some instances be an offence; in other instances it may not. See *Johnson v Phillips* where a motorist refused to obey a constable's instruction to reverse down a one-way street in contravention of road traffic law. That refusal amounted to wilful obstruction of a constable in the execution of his duty:

> The law protects the liberty of the subject, but it must recognise that in certain circumstances . . . a constable may oblige persons to disobey a traffic regulation and not only in those cases that are explicitly dealt with by Parliament . . . a constable would be entitled, and indeed under a duty, to give such an instruction if it were reasonably necessary for the protection of life or property.

7.1.3 More specific application of duty

The courts do not go so far as to say that whenever a police officer is acting in pursuance of some police objective or general duty, he will be said to be acting in the execution of his duty for the purposes of s 51. The better approach is revealed by Ashworth J in *R v Waterfield and Lynn* (1964):

> In most cases it is probably more convenient to consider what the police constable was actually doing and in particular whether such conduct was *prima facie* an unlawful interference with a person's liberty or property. If so, it is then relevant to consider whether (a) such conduct falls within the general scope of any duty imposed by statute or recognised at common law and (b) whether such conduct, albeit within the general scope of such a duty, involved an unjustifiable use of powers associated with the duty.

Thus, whenever a police officer interferes with the rights or liberties of a citizen he must be able to point to the proper exercise of power, and the focus shifts to the justification for interference. A constable who is acting unlawfully cannot at the same time be acting in the execution of his duty.

7.1.4 Justification for interference

Justification for interference with the rights or liberties of the individual will usually be found in statute. The residual common law powers of importance concern breaches of the peace.

7.1.5 Breaches of the peace

Commonly in instances of disorder the justification for interferences with the citizen's liberty or property will be the common law powers to deal with breaches of the peace. The powers of the police in connection with breaches of the peace have already been examined in Chapter 2. Failure properly to exercise these powers will result in the constable being taken beyond the execution of his duty.

7.1.6 Public safety

As has been seen the emphasis in *Johnson v Phillips* was on the role of the police in ensuring public safety. The court there observed that:

> It is his general duty to protect life and property: see *Glasbrook Brothers Ltd v Glamorgan County Council* [1925] A.C. 270 where Viscount Finlay said: 'There is no doubt that it is the duty of the police to give adequate protection to all persons and their property.' Stemming from that duty is his duty to control traffic on public roads.

The principle which underpins *Johnson v Phillips* is sufficiently broad to apply to directions given by a police officer to a citizen on foot to move clear of an area or follow a particular route in the interests of public safety, and disobedience to such an order would be a wilful obstruction of the police officer acting in the execution of his duty, or wilful obstruction of the highway (*Samuelson v Bagnall* (1985)).

7.1.7 Entry to premises with consent

A police officer who enters premises with consent, express or implied, must leave expeditiously when requested to do so by the owner or someone acting with authority. Failure to leave will make him a trespasser and take him outside the execution of his duty (*Davis v Lisle* (1936), *Robson v Hallett* (1967), *McArdle v Wallace* (1964).

Whether or not a constable will have implied licence to enter premises will depend upon the application of the general law, but it is reasonably clear that approaching a front door of a house, or entering the public areas of business premises will be within the scope of implied licence (*Robson v Hallett*, *Davis v Lisle*, *Halliday v Nevill* (1984)). Leaving a front door open in the knowledge that a police officer is standing there may constitute implied licence by conduct (*Faulkner v Willets* (1982)).

The activation of a burglar alarm connected to a police station gives implied authority to the police to enter the premises to investigate the alarm (*Kay v Hibbert* (1977)), and an attack, even by the occupier, before a reasonable time has elapsed will be a s 51 assault. It seems that this will be the case even where the occupier purports to revoke the licence but refuses to co-operate with the police so that his identity may be confirmed (*Kay v Hibbert*). *Kay v Hibbert* was applied in *Ledger v DPP* (1991) to an entry to premises under implied licence and a purported revocation by the occupier who refused to identify himself to the police. The wilful obstruction which subsequently occurred was an offence within s 51(3).

Revocation of implied or express licence must be in clear and unequivocal terms; mere vulgar abuse may be insufficient (*Gilham v Breidenbach* (1982), *Snook v Mannion* (1982) and may in some instances constitute an offence contrary to s 5 of the Public Order Act 1986 (see *DPP v Orum*, 4.2.11). A failure expressly to countermand an earlier licence to enter cannot be taken to be revocation (*Riley v DPP* (1990)).

A police officer, whose consent to enter or remain on premises has been terminated, may nonetheless remain on the premises if he reasonably anticipates an actual or imminent breach of the peace, and he need not vacate the premises and return (*Robson v Hallet*, *Lamb v DPP* (1990)).

A police officer invited on to premises by a co-occupier, such as a spouse or partner of the other co-occupier, is acting lawfully in remaining, despite a request from the co-occupier that he should leave. The licence continues either until withdrawn by the party extending it or until the police officer satisfies himself that the spouse or partner (and presumably any children) is safe (*R v Thornley* (1981)). This principle seems to extend even to non-owning co-occupiers (*R v Thornley*, *McGowan v Chief Constable of Hull* (1967)).

A police officer may be invited into premises at which a party is taking place by a party-goer, and will be there lawfully until proper revocation of licence by the occupier or someone with authority (*Jones and Jones v Lloyd* (1981)). Knowledge or awareness of the existence of the authority is irrelevant to the question whether or not the police officer is acting in the execution of his duty.

7.1.8 Questioning and detention without arrest

A police officer may address questions to a citizen and in doing so will be in the execution of his duty. It will be otherwise if he detains the citizen with a view to asking the questions or pursuing enquiries of another (see *Bentley v Brudzinski* (1982), *Ludlow v Burgess* (1971), *Kenlin v Gardiner* (1967)). In *Kenlin v Gardner*, the detention by police officers of two schoolboys was held to be unlawful since the police officers had not been attempting to arrest the boys, they had simply wanted to detain them to help with their enquiries. It is not sufficient to possess a power to arrest or stop-search, there must be a purported use of any such power.

Whether or not a police officer has committed a battery or false imprisonment, and thereby taken himself outside the execution of his duty, will often be a difficult issue of fact but the law is reasonably clear and emerges from *Collins v Wilcock* (1984). The same principles apply equally to police officers as to other citizens.

Any touching of another person, however slight, may amount to a battery, subject to specific exceptions such as powers of arrest. There is also a broader general exception allowing for the exigencies of everyday life. Although many of the physical contacts of ordinary life are not actionable because they are impliedly consented to, the courts prefer to treat them as falling within a general exception embracing all physical contact which is generally acceptable in the ordinary conduct of daily life.

Among such forms of conduct is touching a person, even more than once if appropriate, for the purpose of engaging his attention, though using no greater degree of physical contact than is reasonably necessary in the circumstances (see *Wiffin v Kincard* (1807)). But a distinction is drawn between a touch to draw a man's attention, which is generally acceptable, and a physical restraint, which is not (see *Rawlings v Till* (1837)).

If a police officer's use of physical contact in the face of non-co-operation persists beyond generally acceptable standards of conduct, his action will become unlawful. And if a police officer restrains a man, then his action will be unlawful, unless he is lawfully exercising a power.

It has been said that not every trivial interference with the citizen will amount to a course of conduct which takes a police officer outside the execution of his duty (*Donnelly v Jackman* (1970)). That case was itself a highly unusual decision which has not generally found judicial favour (see *Collins v Wilcock*) and involved a police officer repeatedly tapping a defendant on the shoulder even though he had already indicated that he did not wish to speak to the police officer. The defendant, who struck the constable during the altercation, was convicted of assaulting the constable in the execution of his duty.

A police officer who reinforces his request with the threat, actual or implicit, to use force if the other person does not comply will be acting unlawfully.

It is apparent from *Rice v Connolly* (1966) that the concept of helping police with their enquiries is not something recognised at common law as a separate and distinct offence. In *R v Lemsatef* (1977) the court stated that

> First, it must be clearly understood that neither customs officers nor police officers have any right to detain somebody for the purposes of getting them to help with their enquiries. Police either arrest for an offence or they do not arrest at all . . . arrest can[not] be carried out without the accused person being told the offence for which he is being arrested. There is no such thing as helping the police with their enquiries.

The vice for police officers to guard against is detaining an individual without authority. Any decision to arrest should be communicated to the suspect and the necessary formalities carried out (Police and Criminal Evidence Act 1984, ss 28 and 31), and failure to do so will take the police officer outside the execution of his duty (*R v Inwood* (1973)).

7.1.9 Statutory powers of the police

Although the range of police powers is outside the scope of this book, it is axiomatic that powers should be exercised correctly; failure to do so will take the police officer outside the execution of his duty. A failure by a police officer to exercise powers under the Public Order Act 1986 or the Criminal Justice and Public Order Act 1994 correctly will take him outside the execution of his duty and any disobedience to an order made pursuant to a power will not be wilful obstruction.

As to arrest see *DPP v Hawkins* (1988), *Lewis v Chief Constable of South Wales* (1991), *Nicholas v Parsonage* (1987), *Edwards v DPP* (1993). As to entry see *Kynaston v DPP* (1987), *Chapman v DPP* (1989), *Swales v Cox* (1981), *D'Souza v DPP* (1992), *Hart v Chief Constable of Kent* (1983). As to stop-search powers see *McBean v Parker* (1983), *Brazil v Chief Constable of Surrey* (1983), *Pedro v Diss* (1981). As to motoring powers see *Lodwick v Sanders* (1985), *Sanders v DPP* (1988).

7.1.10 Establishing the legality of police action

Ordinarily, the legality of police intervention must be justified by direct evidence. And where the legality of action depends upon a chain of events, then the legality of police action must be demonstrated throughout the chain of events. An inference of legality may not be drawn where police officers involved are readily identifiable and direct evidence to support the legality of the original arrest is available: *McBean v Parker* (1983) (legality of prior stop-search has to be established), *Riley v DPP* (1990), *Griffiths v DPP* (1992), *Edwards v DPP* (1993) (legality of the arrest of a third party must be established in order to convict the defendant of obstructing a constable by interfering with a lawful arrest), *Chapman v DPP* (1989) (legality of entry to premises must be established in order to convict the defendant of interfering with the entry or search). A police officer's reasonable and genuine belief as to a particular state of affairs will be insufficient (*Kerr v DPP* (1994)).

But where there has been a serious disturbance involving breaches of the peace, the court may draw the inference from the circumstantial evidence that an attempted arrest by an unidentified police officer is lawful and accordingly interference with that arrest by another person amounts to an offence contrary to s 51 of the Police Act 1964 (*Plowden v DPP* (1991)).

7.1.11 Assault

Assault includes battery, and requires the intentional or reckless application of unlawful force to the person, or threat causing another to fear the application of unlawful force, knowing it to be unlawful. Usually the assault will involve a positive act but in certain instances an omission may suffice (see *Fagan v Metropolitan Police Commissioner* (1968)).

In the light of the public policy issues in giving police officers special protection (see *Blackburn v Bowering* (1994)), knowledge of or recklessness as to the fact that the person assaulted is a constable is not required, nor need the prosecution establish that the defendant knew that the police officer was acting in the execution of his duty (*R v Forbes and Webb* (1865), *R v Maxwell and Clanchy* (1909), *McBride v Turnock* (1964), *R v Brightling* (1991)). There is thus an element of strict liability, mitigated only by the impact a genuine belief (even if unreasonable) that the other is not a police officer may have on the defence of self-defence.

A defendant who, in self-defence or defence of others, assaults a police officer, knowing that he is a police officer, in the genuine and reasonable belief that a police officer is acting outside the execution of his duty, when he is within it, will not have a defence (*R v Bentley* (1850), *R v Fennell* (1971)), and see also *R v Ball* (1990) as to the consequence of a belief that police were using excessive force during an arrest. This amounts to a mistake of law and will not excuse the defendant. A defendant who, knowing that another is a police officer, intervenes either in defence of others or himself will only be entitled to be acquitted where the police officer is in law acting outside the execution of his duty. In such a case, the use of excessive force would lead to a charge of assault *simpliciter* rather than the more technically demanding s 51 offence.

A defendant who defends himself or another against the actions of a police officer, and who uses reasonable force in the circumstances, will not be guilty of s 51 assault where he mistakenly believes that the police officer is not a police officer. Such a belief must be genuine but need not be reasonable (see *R v Williams* (1987), *Beckford v R* (1987) and *Blackburn v Bowering* (1994)). This is a mistake of fact and the defendant must be judged by the facts as he mistakenly took them to be. The reasonableness of the belief is relevant only to the issue of its genuineness.

7.1.12 Wilful

'Wilful' has caused difficulties in a wide range of statutory contexts and has no fixed meaning. Within s 51, wilful connotes something which is done intentionally. It must be shown that the defendant was aware that the person obstructed was a police officer (*Ostler v Elliott* (1980)). A reasonable belief that the other is not a police officer will provide a sound defence.

The requirements in *Willmott v Atack* (1977) that the act of the defendant should be hostile, and in *Hills v Ellis* (1983), that the action should be aimed at the police, have been taken to be largely without substance, since motive and emotion are irrelevant in criminal law. Wilful requires no more than an intention to obstruct (*Lewis v Cox* (1985)). This in itself was said in *Lewis v Cox* to require something which is done deliberately and with the knowledge and intention that it should have an obstructive effect. There must be deliberate acts with the intention of bringing about a state of affairs which, objectively viewed amount to an obstruction, *Moore v Green* (1983).

Interfering with a lawful arrest in the belief that it is unlawful will be a wilful obstruction (*Hills v Ellis*, *Lewis v Cox*, where the defendants were warned that their actions were making the police's task harder).

7.1.13 Resist and obstruct

'Resist' has received no attention from the English courts in the reported cases, although there are several Australian decisions relating to similar provisions.

'Obstruction' has received its widest description in *Hinchcliffe v Sheldon* (1955) where it was said to mean making it more difficult for the police to carry out their duties. The scope of that dictum has meant that obstruction may be by physical means (*Hinchcliffe v Sheldon*, *Lewis v Cox*), or by other means, including omissions such as a refusal to co-operate (*Ledger v DPP* (1991), *Lunt v DPP* (1993)).

In *Rice v Connolly* the divisional court regarded wilful as connoting something intentional and without lawful excuse. The reference to the absence of lawful excuse belongs more properly to an analysis of the *actus reus* of the offence rather than to the *mens rea*, and the proposition advanced by the court serves only to confuse. In that case the obstruction consisted of a refusal to answer police enquiries or to accompany the police to a police box so that further enquiries might be made. The lawful excuse was the absence of any legal duty to do so.

Following *Rice v Connolly*, it is not possible to maintain that obstruction cannot comprise omissions, even if there is taken to be a distinction between refusals or failures to act, and allowing the continuation of a state of affairs such as occurred in *Fagan v Metropolitan Police Commissioner* and *Duncan v Jones*. In *Johnson v Phillips* (1976) a refusal to reverse down a one-way street was held to be an obstruction and to be wilful.

Despite dicta to that effect in *Dibble v Ingleton* (1972), it is not entirely convincing to say that a passive obstruction by omission is not an obstruction unless the law imposes an obligation to act, given the difficulty of forecasting in advance when such an obligation will arise. Nonetheless *Dibble v Ingleton* has been applied in *Lunt v DPP* with the result that a failure to open a door to the police who had a power to enter was a wilful obstruction.

There will be situations where, in response to a power being properly exercised by the police (or others such as Customs and Excise), the law will impose a positive duty on the citizen to act, and where failure to do so will be taken to be a wilful obstruction. In other instances the law may simply impose a duty on the citizen in the absence of a police power. For example a motorist, when requested to stop by a police officer in uniform exercising the power in s 163 of the Road Traffic Act 1988, must keep his vehicle at a standstill while the police officer has an opportunity to carry out his statutory enquiries, even though the Act does not confer a power on the constable to keep the vehicle there (*Lodwick v Sanders* (1985), *Sanders v DPP* (1988)).

A positive act of obstruction need not be independently unlawful in order to amount to an obstruction for the purposes of the Act; this is inherent in the offence and was expressly accepted in *Dibble v Ingleton* where it was held to be a wilful obstruction to drink whisky before a breath test and after a request for the breath test.

Generally, refusal to answer questions will not be a wilful obstruction (*Rice v Connolly*); doing so in abusive terms may be (*Ricketts v Cox*) although in such an instance it is possible that a charge under s 5 of the Public Order Act 1986 would be more appropriate. *Ricketts v Cox* was applied in *Ledger v DPP* to a verbally aggressive, vulgar and generally unhelpful refusal to co-operate with the police. Advising someone of their right to remain silent will not be wilful obstruction (*Green v DPP* (1991)), subject presumably to the manner in which that advice is proffered.

7.1.14 Arrest for s 51 offences

There is no specific power of arrest in s 51, nor are the offences in s 51 arrestable offences. The offence under s 51(1) (assault) will involve a breach of the peace and accordingly the common law power of arrest arises. The general power of arrest in s 25 of the Police and Criminal Evidence Act 1984 will also apply. The offence in s 51(3) will not necessarily involve a breach of the peace and the common law power of arrest does not arise as a matter of course. According to *Wershoff v Metropolitan Police Commissioner* (1978), a police officer

> may only arrest without warrant anyone who wilfully obstructs him in the execution of his duty if the nature of that obstruction is such that he actually causes, or is likely to cause, a breach of the peace, or is calculated to prevent the lawful arrest or detention of another.

See also *Riley v DPP* (1990) and *Gelberg v Miller* (1961) where the point was described as one of 'grave constitutional importance' and was the subject of an express acceptance by the Attorney-General as to the absence of any such power, subject only to the power to arrest for breach of the peace.

7.2 Obstruction of the highway

The proposition which underpins the use of the highway is that the highway is for passage and repassage, and for purposes reasonably incidental thereto. Generally, it is an offence both at common law and contrary to statute to obstruct the highway; obstruction of the highway is also capable of amounting to the common law offence of public nuisance. The principles underpinning each are broadly similar and the authorities on the topic appear to be drawn freely from the range of offences.

There are many other provisions relating more generally to activities permitted on or near the highway or the use of the public highway (for example the Highways Act 1980, the Sexual Offences Act 1985, s 1, kerb-crawling, Control of Pollution Act 1974, s 62, noise in streets from loudspeakers), or other locations, either nationally or locally (for example the Trafalgar Square Regulations) and whether public or private (for example the Military Lands Acts 1892–1903).

7.2.1 Highways Act 1980, s 137

Section 137 of the Highways Act 1980 states:

> (1) If a person, without lawful authority or excuse, in any way wilfully obstructs the free passage along a highway he shall be guilty of an offence and liable to a fine not exceeding level 3 on the standard scale.

The meaning of highway ascribed by the Act is to be found in s 328 and it 'means the whole or a part of a highway other than a ferry or waterway'. Highway is a common law concept which involves a way over which all members of the public are entitled to pass and repass, and includes footpaths and bridleways as well as carriageways. This offence is frequently deployed in many instances of disorder, for example in respect of pickets, those who distribute leaflets, 'sit-down demonstrators', and those who otherwise assemble on the highway.

7.2.2 Elements of the offence

For there to be an unlawful obstruction of the highway the prosecution must demonstrate:

(a) the fact of obstruction;
(b) that it was wilful; and
(c) the absence of lawful excuse.

Magistrates must consider all of the elements (see *Hirst and Agu v Chief Constable of West Yorkshire* (1986)).

7.2.3 Obstruction

Except where the obstruction is so slight as to fall within the *de minimis* principle, any stopping on the highway will be an obstruction (see *Hertfordshire County Council v Bolden* (1987), *Seekings v Clarke* (1961), *Wolverton UDC v Willis* (1962) and *Hinchon v Briggs* (1963), the latter two cases under other legislation, on the *de minimis* principle).

It is sufficient if there is an occupation of a part of the road, thereby interfering with people having the use of the road as a whole. Even a single individual standing on the highway is capable of amounting to an obstruction (see *Scarfe v Wood* (1969)). A slight obstruction created while addressing a crowd is an obstruction even though there remains ample room for pedestrians to pass unaffected by the obstruction (*Homer v Cadman* (1886), *Arrowsmith v Jenkins* (1963)). Evidence that others were or were not inconvenienced by an obstruction will serve only to illuminate the issue of whether or not the use of the highway was unreasonable; it will not be relevant to the issue of whether or not there was an obstruction.

Activities both on and off the highway may give rise to a charge under the section. For example conducting a business on premises adjacent to the highway in such a way as to encourage a crowd to develop on the highway, but not if the business is carried on in an ordinary way, is capable of amounting to an unreasonable use of the highway and an offence under statute or at common law. The cases commonly cited in this context are *Fabbri v Morris* (1947) and *Dwyer v Mansfield* (1946), a civil case. See also *Pugh v Pigden and Powley* (1986) where the court considered that it was material to consider that the stall in question had been situated in the same place for many years and that the respondents had used their best efforts to prevent the queue encroaching on the street.

Conduct which will fall within the section ranges from the commonplace to the absurd; thus it will be an obstruction to collect trolleys on the highway outside a supermarket (*Devon CC v Gateway Food Markets Ltd* (1990)) or to trade from a vehicle parked on the highway (*Nagy v Weston* (1965), *Pitcher v Lockett* (1966), or to juggle with firesticks in a pedestrian precinct (*Waite v Taylor* (1985)).

Picketing, even when conducted within relevant legislation, confers no immunity from the criminal law nor any lawful authority on the participants, who will run the risk of obstructing the highway should they try to compel individuals to stop (*Broome v DPP* (1974), *Kavanagh v Hiscock* (1974)). The right to communicate peacefully does not exist alongside an obligation on others to stop and listen (*Broome v DPP*) and a picket may be compared with a hitchhiker standing alongside a road (*Broome v DPP per* Lord Reid). Pushing through a police cordon at a picket line in order to stop a vehicle will be a wilful obstruction of a constable acting in the execution of his duty (*Kavanagh v Hiscock*).

The same general principles apply to non-industrial picketing; see *Tynan v Balmer* (1967) and *Hubbard v Pitt* (1976) for a view of the propriety of non-industrial picketing. It seems unlikely that the imposition of conditions upon an assembly in accordance with s 14 will provide a lawful excuse, although it may be some evidence of reasonable user.

A club tout who approached groups of pedestrians to engage them briefly in conversation, thereby causing other pedestrians to walk off the narrow pavement and into the roadway committed an obstruction (*Cooper v Metropolitan Police Commissioner* (1986)). Distributing leaflets or assembling with banners is capable of amounting to an obstruction (*Hirst and Agu v Chief Constable of West Yorkshire*).

7.2.4 Wilful

It is sufficient if the obstruction is deliberate; see *Arrowsmith v Jenkins* (1963) where wilful was held to mean of one's own free will. In *Fearnley v Ormsby* (1879) it was said that wilful means 'purposely': 'It amounts to this, that he knows what he is doing, and intends to do what he is doing, and is a free agent'. There is no need for there to be an intention to obstruct.

7.2.5 Lawful authority or excuse

Lawful authority relates to matters such as permits or licences granted under statutory authority. A reasonable and honestly held belief as to lawful authority is no defence (*Arrowsmith v Jenkins*), nor will the previous practice of a local authority or the police in relation to a particular activity (*Redbridge London Borough v Jacques* (1971), *Pugh v Pigden and Powley*).

On the other hand, lawful excuse will frequently turn upon the reasonableness of the user, and excuse and reasonableness have been equated (*Nagy v Weston*). The classic description of reasonable user is found in *Nagy v Weston*. This was approved by Lord Denning in *Hubbard v Pitt* (1975), by the Court of Appeal in *Hipperson v Newbury Electoral Officer* (1985), and applied in *Hirst and Agu v Chief Constable of West Yorkshire*:

> Whether or not the use amounting to an obstruction is or is not an unreasonable use of the highway is a question of fact. It depends upon all the circumstances, including the length of time the obstruction continues, the place where it occurs, the purpose for which it is done, and, of course, whether it does in fact cause an actual obstruction as opposed to a potential obstruction.

There have been attempts in *Waite v Taylor* (1985) and *Jones v Bescoby* (1987) to impose a stricter test. That test was to the effect that where the obstruction did not flow from the use of the highway for passage or repassage, or for purposes reasonably incidental thereto, then there would be an unreasonable obstruction of the highway (see also *Pitcher v Lockett* (1966)). Thus, juggling with firesticks (*Waite v Taylor*) or stopping vehicles at a picket line (*Jones v Bescoby*) could not be said to be use of the highway for passage and were automatically unreasonable.

This departure from the test in *Nagy v Weston* was rejected in *Hirst and Agu v Chief Constable of West Yorkshire*. The question 'unreasonable use or not?' may relate either to matters associated with passage or to matters unassociated with passage. The unreasonableness of the use is distinct from the question whether or not there is an obstruction, and it is for the prosecution to demonstrate the unreasonableness of the use rather than for the defence to establish its reasonableness.

The activity complained of must be inherently lawful, and, for example, unlawful picketing cannot be said to be an activity for which there is a lawful excuse (*Hirst and Agu v Chief Constable of West Yorkshire*). The appropriate approach for the court to adopt is first to consider whether or not there was an obstruction. The second is to consider whether or not it was wilful. The third question is whether the prosecution proved it was without lawful authority or without lawful excuse.

The importance of freedom of speech and protest were recognised by Lord Denning in *Hubbard v Pitt* (a civil case relating to the grant of an interlocutory injunction) and *Hirst and Agu v Chief Constable of West Yorkshire* where the words of Lord Denning were expressly applied to the offence under the Highways Act:

> [The courts] should not interfere by interlocutory injunction with the right to demonstrate and to protest any more than they interfere with the right of free speech; provided that everything is done peaceably and in good order.

7.2.6 Arrest

There is no longer a specific power to arrest for obstruction of the highway, although unlawful obstruction of the highway is one of the general arrest conditions in s 25 of the Police and Criminal Evidence Act 1984:

> (1) Where a constable has reasonable grounds for suspecting that any offence which is not an arrestable offence has been committed or attempted, or is being committed or attempted, he may arrest the relevant person if it appears to him that service of a summons is impracticable or inappropriate because any of the general arrest conditions is satisfied.
> (2) In this section 'the relevant person' means any person whom the constable has reasonable grounds to suspect of having committed or having attempted to commit the offence or of being in the course of committing or attempting to commit it.
> (3) The general arrest conditions are—
> (d) that the constable has reasonable grounds for believing that arrest is necessary to prevent the relevant person—
>
> . . .
>
> (v) causing an unlawful obstruction of the highway.

7.2.7 Conclusion

The conclusion which seems to flow from the nature of the test propounded in *Nagy v Weston* is that the question whether or not there has been an offence effectively resides in the magistrates, in whose judgment in particular cases robust pleas of freedom of speech, rights of protest and general liberties may have more, or less, success.

The offence itself is quite capable of employment as a tool both of practical preventive justice and censorship, in the hands of the police and magistracy. The threat to move on or be arrested will often deprive a protest of its efficacy, and a conviction subject to suitable penalty such as conditional discharge or binding over may provide a potent disincentive to a defendant.

In connection with processions and assemblies the offence under s 137 provides a useful additional power which may well bypass the provisions of the 1986 Act. In particular, the absence of rights of assembly or protest (see Chapter 1) and the use of police discretion ensure the continuing importance of the offence.

7.3 Metropolitan Police Act 1839, s 52 and City of London Police Act 1839, s 22

Under s 52 of the Metropolitan Police Act 1839 and s 22 of the City of London Police Act 1839, the Commissioner of Police may make regulations and give directions to prevent the obstruction of streets in the Metropolitan Police District, eg by assemblies or processions which are capable of giving rise to obstruction of the streets or to disorder or annoyance of a kind likely to lead to breaches of the peace. For the construction of the provision, see *Papworth v Coventry* (1967). These regulations and directions provide a useful form of prior control over processions and assemblies and have been used to counter novel types of disorder such as in connection with the 'Stop the City' demonstrations in 1983–84.

7.4 Town Police Clauses Act 1847 and other legislation

The Town Police Clauses Act 1847, s 21 is of similar effect and applies in certain areas outside the metropolitan police district. The local authority has power in limited instances to make orders as to the routes vehicles should follow in order to prevent obstructions. The instances are 'in all times of public processions, rejoicings, or illuminations, and in any case when the streets are thronged or liable to be obstructed'. The phrase 'in any case' is to be construed *eiusdem generis* with public processions, etc (see *Brownsea Haven Properties v Poole Corporation* (1958)).

Both s 28 of the Town Police Clauses Act 1847 and s 54 of the Metropolitan Police Act 1839 create summary offences of obstruction to the footpaths or thoroughfares. Obstruction in this legislation has received a more restricted meaning than in the 1980 Act and requires actual obstruction.

The sessional orders of the House of Commons require police constables to prevent obstruction of the streets leading to the House. Where the police act in connection with these measures, then obstruction of the police will be an offence contrary to s 51 of the Police Act 1964 (see *Pankhurst v Jarvis* (1909) and *Despard v Wilcox* (1910)).

7.5 Public nuisance

Public nuisance is a crime at common law but is remediable by injunction at the instance of the Attorney-General in a relator action brought by an affected party, or at the instance of a local authority exercising its rights under s 222 of the Local Government Act 1972 to protect the local community (see generally *Attorney-General v PYA Quarries* (1957)). Equally, where an individual suffers particular damage above and beyond that suffered by the community as a whole, that individual will be able to maintain an action in tort. It is perhaps in the civil context rather than in the criminal context that public nuisance is most commonly encountered as a means of controlling public assemblies or activities on or nearby the highway.

The offence is so broadly defined and versatile and the conduct which has been held to fall within the offence is of such diversity as to defy categorisation; it ranges from public order matters to public health matters, from matters of public decency to matters of public safety. Recently in *R v Coventry City Council ex p Phoenix Aviation* (1995), a judicial review decision, Simon Brown LJ said that:

> The precise point at which the right of public demonstration ends and the criminal offence of public nuisance begins may be difficult to detect. But not only is all violent conduct unlawful; so too is any activity which substantially inconveniences the public at large and disrupts the rights of others to go about their lawful business.

Public nuisance is sufficiently broad to encompass many activities of modern life which affect the public at large, and its use in these circumstances is the modern application of longstanding principles. The offence has been considered in the context of bomb hoaxes (*R v Madden* (1975)), acid house parties (*R v Shorrock* (1993) fine of £2,500 imposed on owner of a field let for an acid house party; *R v Ruffell* (1992) 12 months' imprisonment suspended on the organiser of an acid house party; *R v Taylor* (1992), £5,000 fine on organiser of an acid house party), joy riders (*R v Mason* (1995), 30 months' imprisonment on a joy rider whose activities attracted large crowds of onlookers antagonistic to the police).

In so far as public order matters are concerned, much of what falls within the crime of public nuisance may also be found provided for in bye-laws, eg relating to the making of noise or the playing of instruments.

7.5.1 Definition

Stephen's Digest of the Criminal Law (9th edn, 1950) defines public nuisance as 'an act not warranted by law or an omission to carry out a legal duty, which act or omission obstructs or causes inconvenience or damage to the public in the exercise of rights common to all His Majesty's subjects'.

In *Blackstone's Commentaries* (3 BL COM (1st edn, 1768)) it is said that:

> Nuisance . . . signifies any thing that works hurt, inconvenience, or damage. And nuisances are of two kinds; public and common nuisances, which affect the public, and are an annoyance to all the king's subjects; for which reason we must refer them to the class of public wrongs, or crimes and misdemeanours; and private nuisances . . .

In *Gillingham Borough Council v Medway (Chatham) Dock Co Ltd* (1992), Buckley J in the High Court considered that contrary to the definition in *Stephen's Digest* it was not necessary that public nuisance should involve an otherwise unlawful activity. In so far as the use of the highway is concerned, this point does not matter since misuse of the highway will be unlawful.

7.5.2 Range of the effects of the activity

The range of the activity must be such as to affect the neighbourhood. In *Attorney-General v PYA Quarries* it was said that:

> any nuisance is 'public' which materially affects the reasonable comfort and convenience of life of a class of Her Majesty's subjects. The sphere of the nuisance may be described generally as 'the neighbourhood'; but the question whether the local community within that sphere comprises a sufficient number of persons to constitute a class of the public is a question of fact in every case. It is not necessary, in our judgment, to prove that every member of the class has been injuriously affected; it is sufficient to show that a representative cross-section of the class has been so affected for an injunction to issue.

In *Soltau v De Held* (1851) Kindersley VC, said:

> I conceive that, to constitute a public nuisance, the thing must be such as, in its nature or its consequences, is a nuisance—an injury or a damage, to all persons who come within the sphere of its operation, though it may be so in a greater degree to some than it is to others.

In *R v Lloyd* (1802) an indictment for a nuisance by noise was preferred by the Society of Clifford's Inn, but since the noise complained of affected only three houses in the Inn the indictment could not be sustained.

7.5.3 Highway

It is generally accepted that it is only unreasonable use of the highway which will amount to a public nuisance (*R v Train* (1862)). See *Jacobs v London County Council* (1950) where public nuisance was said to be 'Any wrongful act or omission upon or near a highway, whereby the public is prevented from freely, safely and conveniently passing along it'. And in *Lowdens v Keaveney* (1903) it was said that 'Where the use of the highway is unreasonable and excessive, that is a nuisance, irrespective of any guilty or wrongful intent'.

In *Tynan v Balmer* (1966) pickets moving in a circle on the highway outside a factory were told by police to stop and when they did not do so they were arrested and charged with s 51(3) wilful obstruction. It was held that the circling amounted to an unreasonable use of the highway and that the police were acting in the execution of their duty.

Demonstrations, pickets and other assemblies, usually occurring on or about the highway, may amount to the common law offence of public nuisance (see *R v Clark* (1963), *R v Moule* (1964), *R v Adler* (1964) and *Hubbard v Pitt*, a civil case). Although picketing will not necessarily constitute the offence (but see *Tynan v Balmer*), mass picketing will. In *Thomas v NUM* Scott J remarked:

> . . . if picketing . . . is peacefully and responsibly conducted . . . I can see no reason at all why it should be regarded *per se* as a common law nuisance . . . In my judgment, mass picketing is clearly . . . common law nuisance . . .

As is the case with the Highways Act 1980, activities on premises adjacent to the highway are capable of amounting to public nuisances, for example the exhibition of certain items in a window which attract a large crowd, thereby blocking the highway, as in *R v Carlile* (1834) (an anti-clerical protest involving the display of effigies of bishops) and adopting an unreasonable method of running a shop adjacent to the highway, eg *Lyons, Sons & Co v Gulliver* (1914), a theatre queue, *Wagstaff v Edison Bell Phonograph Corpn Ltd* (1893), *R v Moore* (1832).

7.5.4 *Mens rea*

Until recently the *mens rea* of the offence had received little consideration, although the position has now been clarified in *R v Shorrock*, drawing support from *R v Moore*. There the defendant let his field for a weekend to three individuals who held an acid house party which caused great disturbance over a wide area. Although he denied specific knowledge of the purposes of the licensees, he was convicted. On the question of the judge's direction on *mens rea*, the conviction was upheld, the Court of Appeal holding that, *per* Rattee J:

> . . . the appellant was guilty of the offence . . . if either he knew or ought to have known, in the sense that the means of knowledge were available to him, that there was a real risk that the consequences of the licence granted by him in respect of his field would be to create the sort of nuisance that in fact occurred . . .

In reaching its decision on the relevant *mens rea*, the court concluded that the basis of liability in both criminal and civil jurisdictions was the same.

Chapter 8

Blades, Offensive Weapons and Explosives

8.1 Blade or pointed article

8.1.1 Checklist

- No *mens rea* needed for s 139 offence to exist
- section applies to blade or sharply pointed instrument
- lock knife always caught
- folding pocketknife only caught if blade over 3 inches
- fruit peeling not defence for blade over 3 inches
- defences of national costume, religious reason and use at work

Section 139 of the Criminal Justice Act 1988 provides:

> (1) Subject to subsections (4) and (5) below, any person who has an article to which this section applies with him in a public place shall be guilty of an offence.
> (2) Subject to subsection (3) below, this section applies to any article which has a blade or is sharply pointed except a folding pocketknife.
> (3) This section applies to a folding pocketknife if the cutting edge of its blade exceeds 3 inches.
> (4) It shall be a defence for a person charged with an offence under this section to prove that he had good reason or lawful excuse for having the article with him in a public place.
> (5) Without prejudice to the generality of subsection (4) above, it shall be a defence for a person charged with an offence under this section to prove that he had the article with him—
> (a) for use at work;
> (b) for religious reasons; or
> (c) as part of any national costume.
> (6) A person guilty of an offence under subsection (1) shall be liable on conviction to a fine not exceeding level 3 on the standard scale.
> (7) In this section 'public' place includes any place to which at the material time the public have or are permitted access, whether on payment or otherwise.

8.1.2 Blade or sharply pointed

This section is aimed at creating a criminal offence for those who choose to carry particular bladed or sharply pointed instruments, which might not fall within the definition of 'offensive weapon', yet the possession of which might be expected to create risk of injury or risk of use to the detriment of public order. There is no *mens rea* required. If it falls within the definition and none of the defences applies, then the offence is made out. A Stanley knife would be caught. It is not a pocketknife but it is bladed. In the absence of one of the defences applying, it would be covered by the section, whether or not it was carried with offensive intent. A comb with a sharpened edge or a sharply pointed end would also be covered.

8.1.3 Public place

There is a definition section at s 7 but this is not an exclusive definition. There have been a number of cases describing whether places were or were not public. A staircase adjoining a block of flats is a public place if there is nothing preventing the public from using it (*Knox v Anderton* (1983)). A garden is not public merely because there is access to a house through it. The access is for a visitor rather than for the public at large. (*R v Edwards and Roberts* (1978)). A public house carpark with a 'patrons only' sign is not public (*Sandy v Martin* (1974)). Well after a shop has closed, its carpark will not be public (*Marsh v Arscott* (1982)). Whether a place is a public place is best demonstrated by the fact that the public do have access to it. It is a question of fact.

8.1.4 Has with him

This formula is not to be taken as meaning precisely the same as 'possession'. It has a connotation of more proximate connection than the word 'possession'. 'There must be a very close physical link and a degree of immediate control . . .' *per* Scarman LJ (*R v Kelt* (1977)). It is aimed at the person with such an article in a pocket or with him in a vehicle. Anything much beyond that in terms of proximity is unlikely to fall within the definition in practice.

8.1.5 Folding pocketknife

The folding pocketknife is given its own definition to prevent the absolute prohibition of carrying pocketknives. For a folding pocketknife to be caught by the Act it must have a 'cutting edge of its blade' which is more than three inches long. The cutting edge is that part of the blade which is sharpened. Only the sharpened edge should be measured and only that part of the sharpened edge which is actually sharpened to cut. That part of that edge towards the handle which has not been sharpened should not be included, as it is not the relevant part for the section.

Folding pocketknife does not include a lock knife. A lock knife is not readily and immediately foldable at all times. A lock knife needs the trigger mechanism to be used to close it. The length of a lock knife does not matter because it is not treated as a folding pocketknife (*Harris v DPP* (1993)).

8.1.6 Defence of good reason

The onus of proving the defence is on the defendant and the burden of proving it is on a balance of probabilities. The issue of reasonable excuse is one of fact and depends on the circumstances of the case. The defence has to be restricted for the section to operate and as a matter of public policy the courts will not easily be persuaded that the carrying of articles for self-defence in any context can be reasonable. A common defence in relation to folding pocketknives is that they are used for and needed for peeling fruit and similar non-hazardous practicalities. This cannot be a valid defence for either a pocket or a lock knife. In each case there is no necessity for the particular form of knife (either locking or bladed more than three inches) and therefore there is no good reason for having them. It is as easy to peel an apple with a two inch blade as it is with a three-inch one and a lock provides no assistance for such routine tasks in the absence of special and particular evidence.

Forgetting that an article is in his possession is not a defence of good reason (*DPP v Gregson* (1992)).

8.1.7 Defence of lawful authority

This defence seems only to apply to 'those people who from time to time carry an offensive weapon as a matter of duty—the soldier with his rifle and the police officer with his truncheon', *per* Lord Widgery CJ (*Bryan v Mott* (1976)). Thus, a soldier's bayonet would not be caught by the provision, but if he were carrying an article which was not authorised as part of his kit he would be caught.

8.1.8 Defence of use at work

This defence is designed to protect those who need to carry for their work, articles which would be caught by the Act. Thus a Stanley knife might well be a legitimate tool being carried by some workers, as might be any other sharp or bladed instrument such as saws, chisels, bradawls and the like. There is no general permission to carry them and a person who is carrying them other than en route to and from work should expect the additional burden of proving the need to carry them on occasions other than those journeys. Such proof is not impossible for people who might be on call, but ought not to be available for a person who has merely left such tools in a vehicle for convenience.

8.1.9 Defence of religious reasons

This is designed to protect religious groups such as Sikhs who, as part of their religion, are in certain circumstances required to carry a bladed article which might otherwise contravene the section. Each case must be looked at on its own merits to determine whether there is such a religious reason and whether that was in fact the actual reason of the person concerned.

8.1.10 Defence of national costume

Designed to protect those such as Scots who might have a bladed article in their sock as part of a national costume. Each case must be assessed on its own merits to determine whether the national costume requires the article and also whether the person was actually wearing it as national costume.

8.1.11 Defences generally

Each must be proved on a balance of probabilities. Once the elements of the offence are made out, then, in the absence of one of the statutory defences, the person is guilty (*Godwin v DPP* (1993)).

8.2 Offensive weapon

8.2.1 Checklist

- Offensive *per se* means designed to or adapted to injure people
- intent to injure required for items not offensive *per se*
- public place has a wide definition
- accused must know he has the article
- transferred burden of proof for reasonable excuse and lawful authority

Section 11 of the Prevention of Crime Act 1953, as amended, provides:

(1) Any person who without lawful authority or reasonable excuse, the proof whereof shall lie on him, has with him in any public place any offensive weapon shall be guilty of an offence, and shall be liable—
  (a) on summary conviction, to imprisonment for a term not exceeding [six months] or a fine not exceeding [the prescribed sum] or both;
  (b) on conviction on indictment, to imprisoment for a term not exceeding two years or a fine . . . or both.

(2) Where any person is convicted of an offence under subsection (1) of this section, the court may make an order for the forfeiture or disposal of any weapon in respect of which the offence was committed. . . .

(4) In this section 'public place' includes any highway and any other premises or place to which at the material time the public have or are permitted to have access, whether on payment or otherwise; and 'offensive weapon' means any article made or adapted for use for causing injury to the person, or intended by the person having it with him for such use by him or by some other person.

8.2.2 Offensive *per se*

The first category of offensive weapons involves those specifically designed or adapted to cause injury to the person. The question of whether an article is offensive *per se* is a question of fact but certain articles are automatically offensive *per se*. Flick knives are offensive *per se* and any of the articles set out in the schedule to s 141 of the CJA 1988 are offensive *per se*. This schedule sets out the articles which it is an offence to manufacture, sell or hire and includes such things as 'death stars', knuckledusters and swordsticks. These objects have no purpose but to injure and as such are offensive *per se*. Other articles which may have been privately adapted may be less clear cut. A stave with a nail through it might have been adapted for a reason other than to cause injury and it is for the tribunal of fact to determine from the evidence what the purpose of such manufacture or adaptation is. *R v Allamby* (1974) confirms that carrying such obvious items as flick knives demonstrates a conditional intention to use them and that that is sufficient for the section.

8.2.3 Not offensive *per se*

The second category of offensive weapon is that which requires that the person intends an article to be used by him or somebody else for causing injury to the person. Thus a non-offensive article becomes an offensive weapon if the person intends it to cause harm. The baseball bat in the car becomes an offensive weapon, not because it is capable of injuring a person, but because the person who has it intends to use it for that purpose. Many other articles have been deemed offensive weapons in particular contexts. Belts with studs (*McMahon v Dollard* (1965)), workmen's tools (*R v Dayle* (1974)) and kitchen knives (*R v Rapier* (1980)) have all been found to be offensive weapons.

Public policy requires the courts to be unwilling to permit the public at large to arm themselves for their own protection. That is the job of the police. Thus carrying objects with a provisional intention of using them, ie if someone attacks, will generally be deemed sufficient to make an object an offensive weapon.

The problem in court is that if the article is not offensive *per se*, and the person is sufficiently astute to deny carrying it for reasons of self-protection, then there is little basis for finding the necessary intent in the absence of other telling circumstantial evidence going to intention. Historically many such cases are proved because in interview the person denies an offensive intent but admits a defensive intent which provides the conditional intention to use which is sufficient to convict.

8.2.4 Injury to the person

In most cases the fact that an object is to cause injury will be evident from the evidence. Injury means physical injury caused by the object itself. The only difficulty in this context relates to the person who has with him an offensive weapon to frighten or intimidate and not to cause injury. Apart from the fact that tribunals of fact would generally find it difficult to accept that the object was for intimidation and not to injure it would also be difficult not to keep in mind the notion of conditional intention, ie if you carry it you have it in mind that you will use it if required. For public policy reasons, the courts have been slow to develop the distinction between intimidation and injury (see *Woodward v Koessler* (1958) and *R v Edmonds* (1963)).

8.2.5 Has with him in a public place

For this definition, see 8.1.3 for places defined as not being public and 8.1.4 for the definition of 'has with him'. The section incorporates the expression 'at the material time'. It follows that a place may be public at one time and not at another. The issue is whether the public have free or paying access at the material time.

8.2.6 Intent

There is no offence unless the defendant had the offensive weapon knowingly (*R v Cugggelere* (1961)). Where more than one person has a weapon or weapons, it is necessary to show that each person knew of weapons which the other had and that they had common purpose (*R v Edmonds* (1963)). Intent will either be shown by conduct which may be irrefutable, or words. Now that the law relating to interviews and giving evidence has been modified (CJPOA, ss 34, 35 and 36), it may be that offensive weapon cases might be more easily proved if persons in possession of particular articles answer questions either in interview or in court in an effort to avoid adverse inferences being drawn.

8.2.7 Defences of lawful authority and reasonable excuse

See 8.1.6, 8.1.7 and 8.1.11. The defences do not arise until after the prosecution have demonstrated the elements of the offence (*R v Petrie* (1961)) and forgetting that an article is with him will not afford a defence of reasonable excuse (*R v McCalla* (1988)).

8.2.8 Mode of trial

There is no reference to offensive weapons in either the *National Mode of Trial Guidelines* provided by the Lord Chief Justice, or the Magistrates' Association's sentencing guidelines. This may be a simple oversight, but in relation to mode of trial decisions the general rule is that 'except where otherwise stated, either way offences should be tried summarily'. It is hard to reconcile this view with the gravity of carrying such articles as flick knives and purpose-designed coshes which ought, subject to the particular circumstances of a case, to create the risk of an immediate and significant custodial sentence.

8.2.9 Sale of offensive weapons

Section 141 of the CJA 1988 makes it an offence for 'any person to manufacture, sell or hire or offer for sale or hire, or expose or have in his possession for the purpose of sale or hire, or to lend or give to any other person, a weapon to which this section applies'. The penalty is imprisonment up to six months or a fine to level 5 and the Secretary of State may direct the section to apply to any weapon except crossbows and weapons subject to the Firearms Act 1968. The list is set out in the schedule to the Act and contains such items as knuckledusters, swordsticks and telescopic truncheons.

8.3 Explosives

8.3.1 Explosives and public order

Offences contrary to the Explosive Substances Act 1883 may not be instituted without the consent of the Attorney-General (s 7). The proceedings are instituted when the person goes to court to answer a charge (*R v Elliot* (1984)). (See also the cases of *R v Bates* (1911) and *R v Cain and Schollick* (1975) on the question of consent which may be given in general terms, but if it is missing it invalidates the proceedings.) Historically possession of explosives has been regarded as related to public order law. These are serious offences and those who commit them in the context of public disorder place themselves at risk of immediate long-term prison sentences, whatever their motives.

8.3.2 Offences

Section 2 makes it an offence if any person:

> unlawfully and maliciously causes by any explosive substance an explosion of a nature likely to endanger life or to cause serious injury to property.

Section 3 makes it an offence if a person:

> (a) does any act with intent to cause, or conspires to cause, by an explosive substance an explosion of a nature likely to endanger life, or cause serious injury to property whether in the United Kingdom or the Republic of Ireland, or makes or has in his possession or under his control an explosive substance with intent by means thereof to endanger life, or cause serious injury to property, whether in the United Kingdom or the Republic of Ireland or to enable any other person so to do.

Section 4 states:

> Any person who makes or knowingly has in his possession or under his control any explosive substance, under such circumstances as to give rise to a reasonable suspicion that he is not making it or does not have it in his possession or under his control for a lawful object, shall, unless he can show that he made it or had it in his possession or under his control for a lawful object be guilty of a felony . . .

Sections 2 and 3 carry life imprisonment and s 4 carries up to 14 years' imprisonment.

8.3.3 Explosive substance

This is a very wide definition including any substance used in the making of any explosive substance (Explosive Substances Act 1883). It is expressed widely and includes the substances, the equipment for manufacture and, by way of an example, petrol bombs (*R v Elliot* (1984)).

8.3.4 Lawful object

Lawful object in s 4 might protect HM forces in certain contexts. In relation to the ordinary citizen, it has been reviewed in relation to self-defence where a person has made petrol bombs for self-protection following riots. So long as he can demonstrate on a balance or probabilities that his object was protection of self, family or property from imminent attack, by means which he believed were no more than reasonably needed to meet the particular type of attack, then he demonstrates a lawful object (*A–G Reference No 2 of 1983*).

The burden of proof transfers to the defendant to demonstrate lawful object and to that extent the provision differs from the rest of the provisions of the Explosive Substances Act.

Because ss 2 and 3 are extended to include acts committed outside the UK which would be offences in the UK, lawful object is not limited to a purpose taking place in the UK (*R v Berry* (1984)).

8.3.5 Knowledge (s 4)

It must be proved that the accused knew he had the substance and that he knew that the substance was a defined explosive substance under s 9. It must also be proved that the possession was in circumstances which gave rise to the required suspicion. His knowledge may be inferred from the circumstances (*R v Hallam* (1957)).

8.3.6 Unlawfully and maliciously (ss 2 and 3)

Legitimate demolition using explosives is not the target of these provisions nor is the use of explosives by HM forces in appropriate circumstances. Their use is not unlawful. The necessity for the word 'maliciously' is less clear in that it incorporates into the sections a level of intent requiring proof. The implication is that there is a category of cxplosion which is unlawful but not malicious which would not warrant the penalty range of these sections.

8.4 Fireworks and football

Section 2A of the POA 1986 provides among other things:

> A person who without lawful authority possesses a designated article in or whilst trying to enter a designated ground or in any area of a ground from which the event may be directly viewed commits an offence.

Section 2A(3) prohibits:

> any article or substance whose main purpose is the emission of a flare for purposes of illuminating or signalling (as opposed to lighting or heating) or the emission of smoke or a visible gas; and in particular applies to distress flares, fog signals, and pellets and capsules intended to be used as fumigators or for testing pipes, but not to matches, cigarette lighters or heaters.

There is power to enter grounds to search designated vehicles and people and to arrest on reasonable grounds for believing an offence is being or has been committed. The focus of these provisions is to reduce fire risk. Unfortunately there has been at least one case where such items, fired recklessly, have caused death.

8.5 Possession of, carrying or trespassing with a firearm

8.5.1 Firearms Act 1968, ss 16–20

Section 16 provides:

> It is an offence for a person to have in his possession any firearm or ammunition with intent by means thereof to endanger life . . . or to enable another person by means thereof to endanger life . . . whether any injury . . . has been caused or not.

Section 16A provides:

> It is an offence for a person to have in his possession any firearm or imitation firearm with intent—
> (a) by means thereof to cause, or
> (b) to enable another person by means thereof to cause, any person to believe that unlawful violence will be used against him or another person.

Section 19 provides:

> A person commits an offence if, without lawful authority or reasonable excuse (the proof whereof lies on him) he has with him in a public place a loaded shot gun or loaded air weapon, or any other firearm (whether loaded or not) together with ammunition suitable for use in that firearm.

Section 20 provides:

> (1) A person commits an offence if, while he has a firearm (or imitation firearm) with him, he enters or is in any building or part of a building as a trespasser and without reasonable excuse (the proof whereof lies on him).
> (2) A person commits an offence if, while he has a firearm (or imitation firearm) with him, he enters or is on any land as a trespasser and without reasonable excuse (the proof whereof lies on him).

8.5.2 With him, lawful authority, reasonable excuse

To prove that a person has a firearm with him is demonstrated by a close physical connection, not necessarily that he actually carried it. It might be in a holdall at his feet or in some equally proximate place. (*R v Kelt* (1977), *R v Pawlicki* and *R v Swindell* (1992)). 'Lawful authority' and 'reasonable excuse' are defined at 8.2.7.

8.5.3 Proof lies on him

This burden of proof on the defendant is on a balance of probabilities (*R v Carr Bryant* (1943)). Thus if he could persuade a court that he was, for example, a member of the forces acting in the course of his duties (lawful authority) or that he had found the item and was on his way to surrender it to the police (reasonable excuse), then he would have satisfied the burden of proof and be entitled to an acquittal.

8.5.4 Penalties

The penalties are as follows:

- section 16: life imprisonment or a fine or both (indictable only);
- section 16A: ten years or a fine or both (indictable only);
- section 19: *Summary* six months or a fine or both; *On indictment* seven years or a fine or both;
- section 20(1): *Summary* six months or a fine or both; *On indictment* seven years or a fine or both;
- section 20(2): *Summary* six months or a fine up to level 4 or both.

8.5.5 Mode of trial and firearms

The subject of firearms is a substantial one with increasing relevance during a time when firearms are more widely available. Most of the law relating to firearms is not sufficiently connected with the law relating to public disorder to justify detailed analysis. The provisions set out here deal with those parts of the law most directly connected with the protection of public order. All firearms offences are treated seriously and do not appear in the *National Mode of Trial Guidelines*. This is no doubt because of the presumption that either way cases involving firearms will be dealt with in the Crown Court except in the most exceptional of cases. These offences do not feature in the Magistrates' Association sentencing guidelines.

Chapter 9

Other Public Order Offences

9.1 Offences in connection with football matches: introduction

In recent years the law relating to sports grounds in general and football matches in particular has undergone radical change. Such changes have not only been necessitated by tragic events at Ibrox, Hillsborough, Bradford and abroad, but have also reflected the concern over safety and public order. The police have also developed strategies and tactics which have operated in parallel with the statutory changes and which have ensured that there has been a decrease in the level of offences at football grounds. The importance of the licensing provisions in assisting in the control or prevention of disorder cannot be underestimated. The unauthorised selling of tickets for football matches is now an arrestable offence under s 24(2)(h) of the Police and Criminal Evidence Act 1984 (see the CJPOA, s 166).

9.1.1 Sporting Events (Control of Alcohol etc) Act 1985

The 1985 Act, as amended, makes extensive provision for specific offences in connection with the possession of alcohol at football matches or on journeys to football matches. There are also other offences in connection with the possession of other items at football matches.

Relevant football matches or grounds are designated by order by the Secretary of State (see currently SI 1985 No 1151 as amended by SI 1987 No 1520 and SI 1992 No 1554). Essentially, the relevant grounds are the home grounds of association football clubs which are members of the Football Association in England or Wales, Wembley Stadium and any other ground used for international football matches, and the relevant matches are those which involve a team which is a member of the Football League or the FA Premier Division, and includes international games and games within the European Cup Winners Cup, UEFA Cup or the European Champions Cup. Designation also extends to football matches involving English and Welsh clubs abroad.

9.1.2 Alcohol in vehicles

The offences in ss 1 and 1A of the Sporting Events (Control of Alcohol etc) Act 1985 concern alcohol on coaches, trains and certain other vehicles. Section 1 applies to public service vehicles or railway passenger vehicles being used for the principal purpose of carrying passengers for the whole or part of a journey to or from a designated sporting event. Section 1A applies to any motor vehicle which is not a public service vehicle but which is adapted to carry more than eight passengers and is being so used to carry two or more passengers on a journey to or from a designated sporting event.

It is an offence knowingly to cause or permit intoxicating liquor to be carried in such vehicles. The offence may be committed by the operator of a public service vehicle (or his servant or agent) (s 1(2)(a)(b)) or, where the vehicle falls within s 1A, by the driver or keeper (or his servant or agent) or any other person to whom the vehicle is made available (or his agent or servant) (s 1A(2)(a)(b)). It is also an offence to be in possession of intoxicating liquor when in such a vehicle (ss 1(3) and 1A(3)), or to be drunk in such a vehicle (ss 1(4) and 1A(4)).

Section 7(3) of that Act contains the power for a constable to stop and search a vehicle which falls within the Act on reasonable suspicion that an offence is being or has been committed in respect of that vehicle.

9.1.3 Possession of alcohol at sports grounds

It is an offence for a person to be in possession of intoxicating liquor or a relevant article at any time during the relevant period of a designated sporting event when he is in any area of a designated ground from which the event may be directly viewed (s 2(1)(a)). The relevant period commences two hours prior to the event and ends one hour after the event (s 9(4)); there are additional provisions in respect of postponed or cancelled matches (s 9(4)(a)(b)). The offence in s 2(1)(a) is subject to s 5A(1) which prescribes a different period in respect of private boxes at sports grounds.

It is also an offence for a person to be in possession of alcohol or a relevant article while entering or trying to enter a designated sports ground during the relevant period. Relevant article is any article which is capable of causing injury to a person struck by it and which is a bottle, can, portable container used to hold drink and which is usually discarded, returned to or left to be recovered by the supplier (s 2(3)).

It is an offence for a person to be drunk in a designated sports ground at any time during the relevant period or to be drunk while entering or trying to enter a designated sports ground during the relevant period (s 2(2)).

Section 2A of the 1985 Act was inserted by the 1986 Public Order Act and makes it an offence to possess in the appropriate circumstances certain other articles whose main purpose is the emission of a flare or smoke or visible gas or which is a firework, see s 2A(1)–(4) and 8.4.

9.1.4 Additional police powers

A constable has power to enter any part of a designated sports ground at any time during the relevant period of a designated sporting event for the purpose of enforcing the provisions of the Sporting Events (Control of Alcohol etc) Act 1985, s 7(1). A constable also has power to search a person he reasonably suspects is committing or has committed an offence under s 7(2) of the Act. A constable may, when acting in support of the relevant football club, carry out a search with consent of the person searched where such a search is a condition of entry. A constable has power to arrest a person he reasonably suspects is committing or has committed an offence under the Act, s 7(2).

There is no specific provision to use force in connection with s 7, nor will s 117 of the Police and Criminal Evidence Act 1984 apply (which authorises the use of reasonable force in connection with powers in the 1984 Act), although s 3 of the Criminal Law Act 1967 may justify the use of force in appropriate circumstances.

9.1.5 Offences under the Football Offences Act 1991

There are three offences created under the 1991 Act and which may be committed only in relation to designated football matches, ie an association football match designated or of a description designated by order of the Secretary of State (s 1(1)). Essentially, these are the same as for the Sporting Events (Control of Alcohol etc) Act 1985 (see SI 1991 No 1565, as amended by SI 1992 No 1554).

The 'relevant period' for the application of the offences to such matters is the period beginning two hours before the start of the match or (if earlier) two hours before the time at which it is advertised to start, and ending one hour after the end of it (s 1(2)).

The three offences are:

(a) the throwing of missiles without lawful authority or excuse at or towards either (i) the playing area or any area adjacent to the playing area to which spectators are not generally admitted or (ii) any area in which spectators or other persons may be present (s 2);

(b) taking part in chanting of an indecent or racialist nature (s 3). 'Chanting' is the repeated uttering of any words or sounds in concert with one or others. A person who acts alone will commit offences contrary to ss 4, 4A or 5 of the Public Order Act 1986 but it is unlikely that s 17 of that Act would fall to be established in respect of a person acting alone in these circumstances. 'Racialist nature' means consisting of or including matter which is threatening, abusive or insulting to a person by reason of his colour, race, nationality (including citizenship) or ethnic or national origins (s 3(2)(b)). 'Threatening', 'abusive' or 'insulting' have already been considered at 4.2.4;

(c) without lawful authority or excuse going on to the playing area or on to any area adjacent to the playing area to which spectators are not generally admitted (s 4).

The burden of proving lawful authority or excuse in respect of ss 2 or 4 is placed by the Act upon the defendant.

The offences are arrestable offences within s 24 of the Police and Criminal Evidence Act, which brings into play the extensive arrest provisions of that Act (s 5(1)). They are triable summarily only and are subject to a fine not exceeding level 3 on the standard scale (s 5(2)).

9.1.6 Exclusion orders

Under ss 30–37 of the Public Order Act 1986, magistrates and Crown Courts have power to make exclusion orders and, in conjunction with such an order, a further order that a convicted person should be photographed by the police. Procedures under this power are similar to the procedures under the Licensed Premises (Exclusion of Certain Persons) Act 1980. In respect of matches abroad the terms of restriction orders made under the Football Spectators Act 1989 are relevant (see 9.1.12).

Exclusion orders may only be imposed following conviction for offences defined by reference to the circumstances in which they were committed. An exclusion order prohibits the person subject to it from entering premises for the purposes of attending a football match prescribed within s 30. There is an offence of failing to comply with such an order. Under s 37, ss 30–36 may be modified to apply to other sporting events.

Although exclusion orders are commonly made against spectators, there is no reason why such an order should not be made against others such as players, coaches or managers, provided of course that the overriding criterion in 9.1.7 is satisfied.

9.1.7 Criteria for making an exclusion order

The overriding criterion for imposing an exclusion order is that the court must be satisfied that making the order would help prevent violence or disorder at or in connection with prescribed football matches (s 30(2)). Further, the defendant must have been convicted of an offence which fulfils one or more of the following three conditions (s 30(1)), and the order must be in addition to a sentence imposed for such an offence or a probation order or an absolute or conditional discharge (s 30(3)):

(1) An offence committed during a period relevant to a prescribed football match (see s 31(6)(7)(8) for the meaning of relevant period) while the defendant was at, entering or leaving, or attempting to enter or leave a ground. Any offence will be sufficient, eg criminal damage, assault. Offences of dishonesty are apparently included.

(2) An offence which either:

   (a) involves the use or threat of violence by the defendant towards another person while either of them was on a journey to or from an association football match, eg where there is an 'ambush' of visiting fans (s 31(3)(a)). Note that any association football match will suffice for this section; it need not be a prescribed football match. Association football match is not defined. Section 31(5) extends the meaning of journey to include breaks, even overnight breaks. Violence is not defined for the purposes of this part of the Act but there is no reason why it should receive a different interpretation from that given in s 8 of the 1986 Act (see 3.2). An assault would suffice, as might criminal damage caused by bricks hurled at coaches. An offence under s 4 will usually fall within this category provided that the victim was put in fear of violence being inflicted by the defendant himself. Where the offence involves the provocation of violence, other than by threatening conduct, then the category may not be satisfied; *or*

   (b) involves the use or threat of violence towards property and was committed by a defendant who was on a journey to or from an association football match (s 31(3)(b)); *or*

   (c) was committed under s 5 or ss 18–23 of the Public Order Act 1986 while the defendant was on a journey to or from an association football match (s 31(3)(c)).

(3) Thirdly, an offence committed under ss 1(3)(4) or 1A(3)(4) of the Sporting Events (Control of Alcohol etc) Act 1985 (s 31(4)).

Factual difficulties as to the meaning of journey may well be common.

For example, a group of youths may agree to meet at a shopping centre or public house during the morning preceding a match. At what stage can it be said that the journey of each commences? Will it be at the moment each leaves his house, intending to go to the rendez-vous, or will it be when as a group they leave the shopping centre or public house and begin to make their way to the ground?

As far as racialist chanting is concerned, chanting by people in or trying to enter a ground will fall within the first condition; racially abusive gestures or behaviour outside a ground will fall within the second condition.

Where the facts have not been canvassed or are otherwise not accepted by the defendant, eg after a guilty plea, it may be necessary to hear evidence on important issues, eg the extent of the journey.

The requirement in s 30(2) is the overriding criterion and is not a requirement for the matter to be proved on any basis other than the court asking itself 'are we satisfied?'

When an order has been made, the clerk or appropriate officer in the Crown Court should (a) give a copy to the defendant; (b) send a copy to the chief officer of police; and (c) send a copy to any person prescribed by the Secretary of State (s 34(1)), eg the general secretary of the Football Association. Although the Act is silent upon the matter, the order will be effective from its pronouncement in court and not from the time of service on the defendant, if later. Thus, the operation of the order will be unaffected by non-delivery. Compare the reasoning of the court in *Walsh v Barlow* (1985) in deciding that community service orders were operative even though they had not been served.

9.1.8 Effect of the order and arrest (ss 30 and 32)

The order prohibits the defendant from entering any premises for the purposes of attending any prescribed football match (s 30(1)). The order may be made for a period of at least three months (or for three months plus the unexpired period of any other order still extant). It is common practice to issue a general order excluding a person from entering any premises for the purpose of attending an association football match, or to define the premises as the grounds of any club which is a member of or is affiliated to the football league. A person who enters premises in breach of the order commits an offence (s 32(3)). A constable, in uniform or not, may arrest without warrant any person he reasonably suspects has entered premises in breach of the order. He has no power to arrest someone he reasonably suspects is about to commit an offence although entry could be denied by the club or by the constable if he anticipates a breach of the peace.

9.1.9 Photographs

The court which makes an exclusion order may, on the application of the prosecutor, make an order requiring a constable to take a photograph of the defendant or to cause it to be taken, and requiring the person to whom it relates to attend a police station within seven days to have his photograph taken (s 35(1)).

A constable may arrest without warrant any person who fails to comply with the order so that his photograph may be taken (s 35(4)). Arrest is for no other purpose and failure to comply with the order is not an offence under the Act, although it may be wilful obstruction of a constable in the execution of his duty. The constable is not protected if he arrests when in fact the defendant has complied with the order, even if the constable has acted on reasonable suspicion.

Arrest under s 35 is not an arrest for an offence and a person arrested under s 35 is not in police detention for the purposes of the 1984 Act (see s 118 of the 1984 Act). Arrest under s 35 is akin to the power in the 1984 Act to arrest for breach of a requirement to attend a police station in order to be finger-printed. Section 28 (information to be given on arrest) and s 32(1)(2)(a) (search upon arrest) of the 1984 Act apply to arrest under s 35. The detention provisions of the 1984 Act (ss 34, 37–46) do not apply and neither does s 30 (duty to take to a police station) because there has not been an arrest for an offence. However, the common law will apply and the arrested person should be dealt with reasonably by taking him to a police station without delay for the photograph to be taken. Section 54 (duty of custody officer to record details of possessions), ss 56 and 58 (right to have someone informed of arrest and access to legal advice) and the Code of Practice on Detention apply to arrest under s 35.

One area of doubt is the use of force to conduct the photographic session; there is no express provision for the use of force. Merely photographing a person is not a trespass, but restraining him or compelling him to remain to have a photograph taken would amount to a trespass and would take the officers concerned beyond the execution of their duty in the absence of a power to use force. The better view is that the use of reasonable force will be implied since to do otherwise would render the section defective.

The Act refers to 'a photograph' and 'his photograph', it does not say 'to be photographed'. Strictly construed, this may mean that only one photograph may be taken without the consent of the individual. In common parlance, however, the phrase may mean no more than 'be photographed'. 'A photograph' may mean a photograph which is not blurred or otherwise defective. Deliberately making it more difficult to take a photograph will amount to an offence contrary to s 51(3) of the Police Act 1964.

9.1.10 Termination of exclusion order (s 33)

If the order was made by a magistrates' court, any magistrates' court in the same petty sessional division as the court which made the order may terminate the order. In the case of an order made by the Crown Court, the same Crown Court must terminate the order. An order may only be terminated if at least one year has elapsed since the making of the order (s 33(1)). Regard must be had to the applicant's character, his conduct, the offence and other circumstances (s 33(2)). Costs may be ordered to be paid by the applicant irrespective of the success or failure of the application. If the application is refused, then no further application may be entertained within the next six months (s 33(3)). The order to terminate the exclusion order must specify the date from which the exclusion order will cease to have effect. Section 34(2) prescribes the information which must be given upon termination and to whom it must be given.

9.1.11 The future

The Football Spectators Act 1989 provides that at a date to be appointed the Public Order Act, ss 30–37 will be repealed. The complex regulatory scheme envisaged by the 1989 Act centres on a national membership authority which would administer and enforce the membership scheme under which access to football grounds would be regulated. The 1989 Act was passed prior to the Hillsborough disaster and the report of Taylor LJ. In the light of the report, it is thought unlikely that the provisions in ss 2–7 of the 1989 Act will be implemented in their existing form, if at all. Accordingly no further description of the scheme is thought to be necessary at this stage. The provisions of the 1989 Act relating to licences to admit spectators have been brought into force (ss 8–14), as have the provisions below relating to restriction orders.

9.1.12 Restriction orders under the Football Spectators Act 1989, Part II

A restriction order is an order requiring the defendant to report to a specified police station on the occasion of designated football matches outside England and Wales (see SI 1990 No 732 as amended by SI 1992 No 1554). There is a specific enforcing authority (the Football Spectators

Restriction Orders Authority) which has particular functions in connection with restriction orders.

The power to make a restriction order is in addition to sentence or to the making of a probation order upon conviction of a defendant for offences within Sched 1 of the Act, which are broadly similar to the offences in respect of which exclusion orders may be made. The overriding criterion corresponds with that for the making of exclusion orders (s 15(2)).

In addition, s 22 allows a magistrates' court to make restriction orders in respect of offences committed in other countries which have been identified by Order in Council as corresponding to the offences in Sched 1. The proceedings are commenced upon information and either the issuing of a summons or warrant of arrest. There are similar provisions as in the 1986 Act as to the distribution by the court of relevant information (s 18) and termination of the order (s 17).

9.2 Intimidation under the Trade Union and Labour Relations (Consolidation) Act 1992, s 241

Section 241 of the Trade Union and Labour Relations (Consolidation) Act 1992 states that:

> (1) A person commits an offence who, with a view to compelling another person to abstain from doing or to do any act which that person has a legal right to do or abstain from doing, wrongfully and without legal authority—
>   (a) uses violence to or intimidates that person or his wife or children, or injures his property,
>   (b) persistently follows that person about from place to place,
>   (c) hides any tools, clothes or other property owned or used by that person, or deprives him of or hinders him in the use thereof,
>   (d) watches or besets the house or other place where that person resides, works carries on business or happens to be, or the approach to any such house or place,
>   (e) follows that person with two or more other persons in a disorderly manner in or through any street or road.
>
> (2) A person guilty of an offence under this section is liable on summary conviction to imprisonment for a term not exceeding six months or a fine not exceeding level 5 on the standard scale, or both.
>
> (3) A constable may arrest without warrant anyone he reasonably suspects is committing an offence under this section.

Prior to consolidation, this offence was to be found in s 7 of the Conspiracy and Protection of Property Act 1875. It has to be read together with s 220 of the Trade Union and Labour Relations (Consolidation) Act 1992 which now governs the legality of picketing at or near premises where pickets are employed. Section 220 does not provide an immunity from either criminal or civil law save in a very narrow scope of legalising peaceful picketing at such sites. The scope of s 241 extends beyond the context of industrial disputes (see *DPP v Fidler and Moran* (1992)).

9.2.1 Common features

The common features of the offences contrary to s 7 are that they should be done 'with a view to compel any other person to abstain from doing or to do any act which that person has a legal right to do or abstain from doing' and should have been done 'wrongfully and without legal authority'.

The phrase 'with a view to compel' has now been considered in *DPP v Fidler*. What matters is the purpose behind the activity rather than the motive. Where the purpose behind a watching and besetting contrary to s 7(4) is to embarrass and shock and shame, then this amounts to a purpose to dissuade rather than compel (*DPP v Fidler*, approving *R v Bonsall* (1985)). Compulsion and not mere persuasion is the necessary ingredient of the offence. Successful compulsion is not required since what matters is the intention of the defendant. The means employed by the defendant will assist the court in establishing the purpose; thus in *DPP v Fidler* the means adopted to confront women attending an abortion clinic were confined to verbal abuse and reproach and shocking reminders of the physical consequences of abortion. The police were in control of the situation and there was no attempt to use or threaten physical force. As to other charges in the context of abortion protests, see 4.4.4.

The phrase 'such other person' has been rather confusingly held to refer to any other person such as an employer or colleague or supplier, ie even if not the immediate subject of the offending behaviour (see *J Lyons & Sons v Wilkins* (1899)). This curious reading widens the scope of the offence.

There remains some confusion over the expression 'wrongfully and without legal authority'. It is probably now the case that it must be shown that the activity is unlawful outside the statute, eg as a tortious obstruction or nuisance. See *Thomas v NUM* (1986) and *Ward, Lock & Co v Operative Printers' Assistants' Society* (1906); *J Lyons & Sons v Wilkins* (1899) tended to the opposite view.

9.2.2 Offensive behaviour

Much of the behaviour within s 7 has received little judicial attention and the issues are principally issues of fact, eg as to whether or not following can be said to be persistent (*Smith v Thomasson* (1890)). Watching and besetting will receive their normal meaning. Using violence or injuring property need no further analysis, and other offences will be involved in such behaviour.

Intimidation in the context of s 7 has been judicially explained. In *Connor v Kent* (1891) Lord Coleridge CJ said:

> Intimidate is not, as has often been said, a term of art—it is a word of common speech and everyday use; and it must receive, therefore, a reasonable and sensible interpretation according to the circumstances of the cases as they arise from time to time.

Violence or threats of violence to the person fall within the meaning of intimidation and, despite initial doubts, so will threats or violence towards property. In *R v Jones* (1974) it was said:

> 'intimidate' in this section includes putting persons in fear by the exhibition of force or violence or the threat of force or violence; and there is no limitation restricting the meaning to cases of violence or threats of violence to the person.

A picket in the form of a mass demonstration is likely to intimidate others and to fall within s 7, especially in the light of the observations of Scott J in *Thomas v NUM*:

> . . . counsel for the . . . defendants submitted that mass picketing (by which I understand to be meant picketing so as by sheer weight of numbers to block the entrance to premises or to prevent the entry thereto of vehicles or people) was not *per se* tortious or criminal. In my judgement, mass picketing is clearly both common law nuisance and an offence under s 7 of the 1875 Act . . .

Even where the activity falls short of the picketing described above, picketing may still be intimidatory if accompanied by sufficiently serious threats or violence.

The mischief aimed at in s 7 is of people being deterred from going to work by threats of violence. In non-industrial cases the threats may be less obvious and more likely to be economic in nature. As such they will often not fall within the meaning of intimidate. For example, a picket of a company to persuade it not to invest in a particular country or not to experiment on animals might be backed up by threats of disinvestment or a campaign against the purchase or supply of that company's goods. Such action would not be intimidation. But as to whether the activity would fall within 'watching and besetting' see *DPP v Fidler*, and also *Hubbard v Pitt* (1976), a civil case involving picketing of an estate agent's premises. The limited immunity granted by s 220 of the 1992 Act, and its predecessors, does not extend to consumer picketing, although Lord

Denning in the Court of Appeal in *Hubbard v Pitt* attempted to assimilate the immunity into the common law of private nuisance.

The information should identify the acts which it was intended the relevant person should abstain from doing or be compelled to do (*R v Mckenzie* (1892), and *Ex p Wilkins* (1895)). For the purposes of s 7(1)(a), the information should specify whether it is alleged that there was intimidation (*R v Edmondes* (1895)). This would indicate that the section creates several offences, although there are authorities which suggest that the section creates only one offence capable of being committed in a variety of ways.

9.3 Disorderly behaviour in relation to meetings

As well as the offences dealt with in Chapter 4 and the preventive powers at common law dealt with in Chapter 2, there is a range of legislation which makes provision for offences at public meetings. These additional provisions seem rarely to be invoked, and the common law power to control those threatening to break or actually breaking the peace allows ample scope to police officers and stewards.

9.3.1 Public Meeting Act 1908, s 1

Section 1(1) of the Public Meeting Act 1908 makes it an offence to act or incite others to act in a disorderly manner for the purpose of preventing the transaction of business of a lawful public meeting. This offence is triable summarily only and punishable up to six months' imprisonment or a fine on level 5 of the standard scale.

Where a constable reasonably suspects a person of committing an offence under s 1(1), he may if requested to do so by the chairman of the meeting require that person to declare his name and address. Failure to do so or declaring a false name and address will be an offence (s 1(3)). This offence is triable summarily only and punishable by a fine on level 1 of the standard scale only.

The meeting must be shown to be lawful, and for these purposes a meeting on the highway is not necessarily unlawful unless some other factor is present, eg obstruction (*Burden v Rigler* (1911)). Section 1 does not apply to election meetings to which s 97 of the Representation of the People Act 1983 applies (s 1(4)). Putting questions to a speaker, shouting 'hear, hear' or simple disapproval are insufficient to merit action under the Acts (see *Wooding v Oxley* (1839). There must be conduct which seeks to prevent the transaction of the business.

The provisions as to arrest for failure to give name and address to a police officer acting on behalf of the chairman were repealed by s 7 of the Police and Criminal Evidence Act 1984, s 25 of which now contains the effective power of arrest in these situations and for the offences under s 1(1) and (2).

9.3.2 Local authority meetings

In so far as meetings of local authorities are concerned, reference may also be made to the Public Bodies (Admissions to Meetings) Act 1960 (see now also Local Government Access to Information Act 1985, s 1 which creates s 100A of the Local Government Act 1972). Generally the public are allowed access to meetings of local authorities, but for the preservation of order there is a saving in respect of powers to suppress or prevent disorderly conduct or other misbehaviour at a meeting. This preserves the common law power to expel or exclude from a meeting those who are causing or threatening disruptive behaviour. It is also possible to exercise the power in advance of the meeting provided that the discretion to do so is exercised properly (see *R v Brent Health Authority ex p Francis* (1985)).

9.3.3 Illegal election practices

Section 97(1) of the Representation of the People Act 1983 makes it an illegal election practice to act or incite another to act in a disorderly manner with the purpose of preventing the transaction of business at certain election meetings specified in s 97(2). A person guilty of an illegal election practice is liable to a fine on level 5 of the standard scale (Representation of the People Act, s 169).

Where a constable reasonably suspects a person of committing an offence under s 97(1), he may if requested to do so by the chairman of the meeting require that person to declare his name and address. Failure to do so or declaring a false name and address will be an offence (s 97(3)). This offence is triable summarily only and punishable by a fine on level 1 of the standard scale only. The arrest provisions, which were similar to those in the Public Meeting Act 1908, have been repealed by Sched 7 to the Police and Criminal Evidence Act 1984, and s 25 of that Act represents the effective arrest power for offences contrary to s 97.

9.4 Protection of worship

There remain extant a range of provisions which concern themselves with protecting worship from interference. These were reviewed by the Law

Commission in their report on *Offences against Public Worship* (No 145) which favoured retention of some and repeal of others. There are also powers at common law or under statute vested in church wardens to maintain order and decency in the church, including powers to expel those who create a disturbance.

Section 2 of the Ecclesiastical Courts Jurisdiction Act 1860 was reviewed by the Law Commission which favoured its retention. The Act penalises behaviour of two sorts. The first offence concerns 'riotous, violent or indecent behaviour' at any time in churchyards, burial grounds, churches, chapels and any other certified place of religious worship, whether during divine service or at other times.

Indecent is given a wide meaning which includes, but extends beyond, sexual connotations, and beyond that which tends to deprave or corrupt, although the offence is often charged in respect of activities of a sexual nature committed in churchyards (see the facts of *Blake v DPP* (1993)). Indecent will extend to anything which creates a disturbance in a sacred place (*Abrahams v Cavey* (1967)). The nature of the place is the context in which the behaviour falls to be construed rather than whether the behaviour would be condemned were it to have occurred elsewhere (*Worth v Terrington* (1845)).

In *Girt v Fillingham* (1890) a clergyman was properly convicted when he went with a crowd to a church and cried out during prayers, 'Idolatry! Protestants leave this House of Baal':

> It was pointed out that on the authority of Sir John Nichol in *Palmer v Roffey* (1824) 2 Add 141 that the sacredness of the place was the object of the protecting law, and that controversial matters could not bc dcalt with in church without a violation of the statute.

It might be otherwise where the words are spoken as an aside and not in a loud voice (see *Jones v Catterall* (1902)). See also *R v Farrant* (1973) (using magic incantations at night in a churchyard); *Abrahams v Cavey* (1968) (interrupting a Methodist service to protest about the Vietnam War was indecent behaviour). Interrupting a church service to complain about the church's views on Sunday trading was held to fall within the Act and merit a £30 fine (see *The Times* (1986) 22 May).

The second sort of behaviour penalised by s 2 of the 1860 Act concerns behaviour which obstructs a clergyman or preacher. The Act makes it an offence to 'molest, let, disturb, vex or trouble, or by any other unlawful means disquiet or misuse' any preacher or clergyman celebrating any sacrament or rite, etc in a church or burial ground. Offenders are liable on summary conviction to punishment by fine on level 1 or two months' imprisonment without fine. Other minor Acts relating to disturbances in cemeteries and burial grounds were recommended for repeal by the Law Commission but remain extant.

Section 36 of the Offences against the Person Act 1861 makes it an offence to obstruct by threats or force a clergyman or other minister from celebrating divine service. This is triable either way under the Magistrates' Courts Act 1980 and is punishable by up to two months' imprisonment.

9.5 Byelaws and miscellaneous legislation

Byelaws will often be applicable to the conduct of processions and assemblies or otherwise affect protest, demonstrations or more general matters relating to public order in public places. The licensing powers of local authorities in relation to activities on or near the highway, and associated offences, are also relevant in this context.

Typically byelaws will make provision relating to a wide range of activity including the display of posters, the use of particular language, the use of loud-hailers, the distribution of handbills, the collection of money, the use of musical instruments. Byelaws commonly restrict the holding of meetings in certain places or require consent to meetings and assemblies. Byelaws often make it an offence to use riotous, violent, disorderly, indecent or offensive behaviour, or conduct which causes annoyance. The use of indecent, offensive or obscene words may also be an offence. There are wide variations in the formulae employed in such instances, and there are extensive decisions upon specific formulae. The meaning attributed to some of the words employed has tended to be specialised in the context of byelaws; for example the meaning of 'indecent' does not necessarily bear the meaning attributed to it elsewhere in the law, and 'riotous' will not be synonymous with riot for the purposes of the Public Order Act 1986.

The principles of judicial review apply to challenges to the validity of byelaws, whether directly by way of application for judicial review or indirectly by way of defence to a criminal charge under the byelaws (*R v Crown Court at Reading ex p Hutchinson* (1988) and *Bugg v DPP* (1993), where the effectiveness of challenge to the validity of byelaws was emphatically demonstrated). In the case of byelaws the principles of unreasonableness have been applied with particular care to avoid undue interference with locally made decisions (see *Kruse v Johnson* (1898)). Challenge based on procedural irregularity not obvious from the face of the byelaws will apparently not be permitted as a defence to a criminal charge but must be pursued by way of application for judicial review, presumably concurrently with an adjournment of the criminal charge (*Bugg v DPP*).

Although punishment for breaches of byelaws will be by fine not exceeding level 2 on the standard scale, there is also the possibility of a binding over order. In extreme cases, a local authority will be able to obtain an injunction to prohibit persistent breaches of byelaws and in order to stop repetition (see *London City Corporation v Bovis Construction Ltd* (1992) and *Runnymede Borough Council v Ball* (1986)).

9.6 Town Police Clauses Act 1847, s 28

The offences contained within Town Police Clauses Act 1847, s 28 are legion and concern activities which obstruct, annoy or place in danger residents of a street or passengers in the street (which must be indicated: *Cotterill v Lampriere* (1890)). The offences range from those concerning housekeeping (beating or shaking a carpet) to childrens' games (flying a kite), from immorality (indecent exposure) to public safety (leaving a cellar unprotected). Section 28 also prohibits wilful obstruction of the highway.

The Vagrancy Act 1824, s 4 penalises a wide range of conduct including indecent exposure, which is also an offence at common law.

9.7 Prohibition on uniforms and quasi-military organisations

Of paramount importance at the time of the passage of the 1936 Public Order Act, the provisions of the 1936 Act relating to uniforms worn in connection with political objectives, and quasi-military organisations, have since had only sporadic application, although as a deterrent they remain important.

9.7.1 Public Order Act 1936, s 1

Section 1 of the Public Order Act 1936 states:

> 1(1) Subject as hereinafter provided, any person who in any public place, or at any public meeting wears uniform signifying his association with any political organisation or with the promotion of any political object shall be guilty of an offence:
>
> Provided that, if the chief officer of police is satisfied that the wearing of any such uniform as aforesaid on any ceremonial, anniversary, or other special occasion will not be likely to involve risk of public disorder, permit the wearing of such uniform on that occasion either absolutely or subject to such conditions as may be specified in the order.

The offence is triable summarily only and is subject to a maximum penalty of three months' imprisonment or a fine not exceeding level 4 on the standard scale or both (s 7(2)). A constable may arrest without warrant any person reasonably suspected by him to be committing an offence contrary to s 1 (s 7(3)). Although a person may be charged with an offence contrary to s 1 without the consent of the Attorney-General, such consent is required before further steps in proceedings may be taken (s 1(2)).

9.7.2 Definitions

'Meeting', 'public meeting' and 'public place' are defined by s 9(1) of the 1936 Act as amended by s 33 of the Criminal Justice Act 1972. Section 9 was unaffected by the 1986 Public Order Act:

> 'Meeting' means a meeting held for the purpose of the discussion of matters of public interest or for the purpose of the expression of views on such matters;
>
> 'Public meeting' includes any meeting in a public place and any meeting which the public or any section thereof are permitted to attend, whether on payment or otherwise.
>
> 'Public place' includes any highway and any other premises or place to which at the material time the public have or are permitted to have access, whether on payment or otherwise.

The meaning of public place was considered in a number of cases under s 5 of the Public Order Act 1936 to which reference may be made. Among those cases, see *Marsh v Arscott* (1982) (carpark attached to shop not a public place at 11.30 pm), *R v Edwards and Roberts* (1978) (the front garden or driveway of a house was not a public place since entry was under licence), *Cawley v Frost* (1976) (football ground is capable of being a public place even though there are places within to which the public do not have access, the premises should be considered in their entirety). Reference may also be made to cases on the meaning of public place for the purpose of other legislation (see cases noted at 8.1.3) but it should be noted that the definitions may vary from Act to Act, and that the context of each statute will affect the meaning to be ascribed.

9.7.3 Uniform

Early cases on the Act are *R v Wood* (1937) and *R v Charnley* (1937). Uniform is undefined in the Act, but it has been analysed in *O'Moran v DPP* (1975) where it was said that the use of the word 'wear' implies one or more items of wearing apparel such as beret, dark glasses, pullover, trousers, jacket. Whether one item alone will be sufficient will be a question of fact but there is no reason to doubt that it may be.

Whether or not the wearing apparel can be described as uniform will be decided without necessarily requiring proof that the apparel has been worn as such in the past; it is to be judged by reference to the adoption of the items to indicate that a group of men or women are together or in association. The deliberate adoption of identical apparel showing association will be sufficient to show that the apparel is uniform.

9.7.4 Association with a political organisation or object

It must be proved that the wearing of the uniform shows the wearer's association with a political organisation or object. Uniform worn in a range of contexts would clearly fall outside the scope of the Act, eg in a charity parade or a play. 'Association with' tends to suggest a willingness to adhere to the tenets of the organisation, even if falling short of membership. In any event 'association with' is an ordinary phrase and ought to receive no special construction (*Brutus v Cozens* (1973)).

The meaning of 'political' has not been reviewed in this context but it would seem to be capable of a very broad meaning. Whether a body could properly be said to be a 'political' organisation would be answered by reference to its central tenets and aims and objectives. In the context of the law relating to extradition, 'political' has been extensively examined and the meaning there may be adopted. A review of the meaning of 'political' in the context of the law relating to charities, extradition and the Broadcasting Act 1990, s 92(2)(a) was undertaken in *R v Radio Authority ex p Amnesty International* (1995). Since it is an ordinary word of the English language it ought to receive its ordinary meaning (see *Brutus v Cozens*).

A body which could not be said to be a political organisation may on occasion involve itself in trying to achieve a political object, and the wearing of uniform in that context might be an offence. Whether the wearing of a uniform on the occasion of a demonstration to press for a change in the law would fall foul of the Act is unclear, eg a protest march by uniformed firemen calling for a change in the law. And there is a serious issue whether clothing of a highly specialised sort, could be said to be uniform, eg the garb of a priest might be described as uniform and the wearing of it in connection with a protest outside an embassy as association with a political object. No doubt the prosecutorial discretion of the Crown Prosecution Service ensures that there will be no inappropriate use of the Act.

9.7.5 Other items

Where what is alleged to be worn is not wearing apparel but an object such as a badge, tie or arm band, then s 1 of the 1936 Act may not apply. In such an instance, consideration may be given to whether or not the article is likely to occasion a breach of the peace (see *Humphries v Connor*, 2.9.5) in the context in which it is worn, or whether it may amount to a visible representation within the meaning in ss 4, 4A, or 5 of the Public Order Act 1986.

The Prevention of Terrorism (Temporary Provisions) Act 1989, s 3 makes it an offence for a person to wear any item of dress or carry, wear, or display any article, in such a way or in such circumstances as to arouse reasonable apprehension that he is a member or supporter of a proscribed organisation. Proscription is dealt with in s 1 and Sched 1 of the 1989 Act, and currently applies to the IRA and the Irish National Liberation Army (INLA). There are similar provisions in the Northern Ireland (Emergency Provisions) Act 1991, s 29 in relation to organisations proscribed under s 28 of that Act.

9.7.6 Quasi-military organisations

Section 2 of the 1936 Public Order Act states:

> (1) If the members or adherents of any association of persons, whether incorporated or not, are
> (a) organised or trained or equipped for the purpose of enabling them to be employed in usurping the functions of the police or of the armed forces of the Crown; or
> (b) organised and trained or organised and equipped either for the purpose of enabling them to be employed for the use or display of physical force in promoting any political object, or in such manner as to arouse reasonable apprehension that they are organised and either trained or equipped for that purpose;
>
> then any person who takes part in the control or management of the association or in so organising or training as aforesaid any members or adherents thereof, shall be guilty of an offence under this section.
>
> Provided that in any proceedings against a person charged with the offence of taking part in the control or management of such an association as aforesaid it shall be a defence to that charge to prove that he neither consented to nor connived at the organisation, training, or equipment of members or adherents of the association in contravention of the provisions of this section.

As the preamble to the 1936 Act remarks, the gist of the offences is concerned with the development of private armies to usurp the functions of the state. Hence, the growth of private security firms patrolling housing estates would not fall within the scope of s 2(1)(a) or (b).

The overt use of 'political object' in s 2(1)(b) can be contrasted with the different emphasis in s 2(1)(a) where that phrase is absent. There is also a difference between being 'organised and trained' and being 'organised and equipped' (see *R v Jordan and Tyndall* (1963)). There are two limbs to s 2(1)(b). The first is, in essence, being involved in the management of an organisation whose members are organised etc for use or display to attain a political object. The second is being involved in the management of an organisation whose members are organised etc in such a manner as to arouse reasonable apprehension in the mind of a sensible man aware of all the facts that they are organised etc for such a purpose (see *R v Jordan and Tyndall*).

There is a specific saving in respect of the provision and proper identification of stewards at public meetings on private premises (s 2(6)).

The consent of the Attorney-General is required for the institution of proceedings (s 2(2)). A search warrant may be granted by a judge of the High Court to enter and search premises and anyone found on them; there is also a power of seizure (s 2(5)).

The offence is triable either way and is subject on summary conviction to a maximum of six months' imprisonment or fine not exceeding the statutory maximum, or both, and on conviction on indictment to a maximum of two years' imprisonment or to a fine, or both (s 7(1)).

9.7.7 Uniforms: other statutory provisions

There are various offences connected with the wearing of uniforms, including bringing contempt on a uniform (see the Uniforms Act 1894, ss 2 and 3; British Mercantile Marine Uniform Act 1919, s 1; Official Secrets Act 1920, s 1; Police Act 1964, s 52; British Transport Commission Act 1962, s 43).

There are also offences under the Unlawful Drilling Act 1819 which relate to being concerned in the training or drilling in the use of arms or military exercises (punishable by up to seven years' imprisonment), or attending a meeting where such training or drilling occurs for the purpose of being trained or drilled (punishable by up to two years' imprisonment). Meetings for such purposes are prohibited 'as dangerous to the peace and security of his Majesty's liege subjects and of his government'. Justices of the peace and constables have the power to disperse such unlawful meetings and to arrest and detain any person present (s 2).

9.8 Bomb hoaxes

Although there were offences which might have been committed by false claims as to the presence of a bomb, or similar device (eg Criminal

Damage Act 1971, s 2(1), Post Office Act 1969, s 78) and the common law offence of public nuisance (*R v Madden* (1975), *R v Norbury* (1978)), these offences were seen as defective and not appropriate to the mischief. Accordingly specific legislation aimed at the problem was enacted. Section 51 of the Criminal Law Act 1977 states:

> (1) A person who—
> (a) places any article in any place whatever; or
> (b) dispatches any article by post, rail, or any other means whatever,
> with the intention (in either case) of inducing in some other person a belief that it is likely to explode or ignite and thereby cause personal injury or damage to property is guilty of an offence.
> In this subsection 'article' includes substance.
> (2) A person who communicates any information which he knows or believes to be false to another person with the intention of inducing in him or any other person a false belief that a bomb or other thing liable to explode or ignite is present in any place or location whatever is guilty of an offence.
> (3) For a person to be guilty of an offence under subsection (1) or (2) above it is not necessary for him to have any particular person in mind as the person in whom he intends to induce the belief mentioned in that sub-section.
> (4) A person guilty of an offence under this section shall be liable—
> (a) on summary conviction, to imprisonment for a term not exceeding six months or to a fine not exceeding the statutory maximum, or both;
> (b) on conviction on indictment, to imprisonment for a term not exceeding seven years.

Penalties imposed tend to be high, bearing in mind the impact such hoaxes have both on the general public and the emergency services, and the need for deterrence.

9.9 Tampering with goods: Public Order Act 1986, s 38

At a very late stage in the passage of the Public Order Act 1986, the government introduced a late amendment, which subsequently became s 38, to reflect its concern with the apparent growth in the tampering with products carried out either with a view to extorting money from manufacturers or with a view to publicising a cause. Both before and after the 1986 Act, offences contrary to any of the following Acts may have been committed by those who tamper with goods: blackmail contrary to the Theft Act 1968, s 21; administering a noxious substance contrary to the Offences Against the Person Act 1861, ss 23 and 24; Criminal Damage Act 1971, s 1(1) and (2). Where death or serious injury occurs, then other offences may be appropriate.

All these offences present difficulties, eg as to *mens rea*. In criminal damage, for instance, it will frequently be the case that the property damaged is that of the defendant and there may be difficulty in establishing the necessary *mens rea*. In any event the offences are not principally designed to combat the mischief against which the Act is designed to operate, ie the creation of apprehension among consumers or the general public by actual or claimed tampering.

Section 38 creates offences to deal specifically with those who seek to promote a cause or objective by tampering with products supplied to the public or by claiming to have done so. Such tampering or claim must be accompanied by one of the intentions specified in s 38(1). Section 38 of the 1986 Act contains provisions which might sit more happily in other legislation, rather than a Public Order Act, although the government view at the time was that the offence, relying as it does in one respect on public alarm or anxiety, was appropriate to a Public Order Act.

There have been several examples of campaigns against particular manufacturers or stores within this country, but extreme examples of this sort of offence may be drawn from America and Japan where deaths or serious injury have occurred. The problem in the UK is apparently on the increase and each police force has arrangements to co-ordinate measures in the event of occurrences of this nature. The nature of the crime has led to the growth of insurance and the development of tamper-proof or tamper-resistant packaging. No doubt one of the problems inherent in dealing with this offence is the risk that publicising investigations by the police or affected companies may well lead to the very real risk of deterring the public from purchasing particular products, and thereby either achieving the very aim of some perpetrators or causing considerable damage to companies.

9.9.1 Provisions of s 38

Section 38 of the Act states:

> (1) It is an offence for a person, with the intention—
> (a) of causing public alarm or anxiety, or
> (b) of causing injury to members of the public consuming or using the goods, or
> (c) of causing economic loss to any person by reason of the goods being shunned by members of the public, or
> (d) of causing economic loss to any person by reason of steps taken to avoid any such alarm or anxiety, injury or loss,
>
> to contaminate or interfere with goods, or make it appear that goods have been contaminated or interfered with, or to place goods which have been contaminated or interfered with, or which appear to have been contaminated

or interfered with, in a place where goods of that description are consumed, used, sold or otherwise supplied.

(2) It is also an offence for a person, with any such intention as is mentioned in paragraph (a), (c) or (d) of subsection (1), to threaten that he or another will do, or to claim that he or another has done, any of the acts mentioned in that subsection.

(3) It is an offence for a person to be in possession of any of the following articles with a view to the commission of an offence under subsection (1)—

(a) materials to be used for contaminating or interfering with goods or making it appear that goods have been contaminated or interfered with, or

(b) goods which have been contaminated or interfered with or which appear to have been contaminated or interfered with.

(4) A person guilty of an offence under this section is liable—

(a) on conviction on indictment to imprisonment for a term not exceeding 10 years or a fine or both, or

(b) on summary conviction to imprisonment for a term not exceeding six months or a fine not exceeding the statutory maximum or both.

(5) In this section 'goods' includes substances whether natural or manufactured and whether or not incorporated in or mixed with other goods.

(6) The reference in subsection (2) to a person claiming that certain acts have been committed does not include a person who in good faith reports or warns that such acts have been, or appear to have been, committed.

9.9.2 'Contaminate' and 'interfere'

These expressions are left undefined and ought to receive a common sense and broad interpretation. They are wider than damage and will cover instances ranging from (a) the addition of a harmless but discolouring substance; (b) the addition of an adhesive label to a package or item indicating that it may have been tampered with; (c) the injection of a harmful substance into food; (d) the removal or damage of part of a product so as to create a danger, eg in an electrical item.

9.9.3 'Goods'

This is partially explained in s 38(5); that definition has been used in previous legislation (see the Consumer Safety Act 1978) and is wide enough to encompass ingredients or parts for incorporation into another product. Goods during all stages of the manufacturing, processing, cleaning, production, storage, and sale stages are within the scope of s 38.

The term 'goods' may be interpreted to include part of a building; thus, a claim that a lift has been interfered with may fall within the terms of the offence. A claim that a circus big top has been damaged or that apparatus in a fair has been interfered with seem to fall within the mischief of causing public anxiety and economic loss. Whether such instances fall within the meaning of goods is unclear, but in any event there remain other offences relevant to such conduct.

9.9.4 Relevant places

The phrase 'place goods . . . where goods . . . are . . . otherwise supplied' relates to the 'placing offence' and seems to create a genus of places where goods are supplied. The supply need not be to the general public or to members of the public, but the necessary *mens rea* must be demonstrated. Where a person places contaminated goods on a production line, eg on a conveyor belt leading to a packing system, he should be charged under the contamination or possession arm of the offence since the place will not be one to where goods are 'consumed, used, sold or otherwise supplied'. The placing type of offence seems to be aimed at the substitution of goods on supermarket shelves, in cafés, in warehouses, etc.

As the employment of the terms 'the public' and 'members of the public' indicate, the mischief at which the Act is aimed appears to be the creation of public alarm or anxiety, injury to members of the public or economic loss suffered in the avoidance of these matters. Where there is a campaign aimed at a company and where the intention is to cause alarm, anxiety or injury to that company's employees, then it may be difficult to hold that these are in fact 'the public' or 'members of the public' for this purpose, although a relevant consideration might be the size of the workforce.

9.9.5 Good faith defence (s 38(6))

Where a newspaper or TV or radio company reports an acknowledged claim of interference or contamination, it is hard to envisage a prosecution, but the good faith defence will apply. The good faith defence may, however, be more likely to be appropriate where a newspaper or TV or radio company runs a campaign to report alleged occurrences concerning a company who might well deny the suggestions. Even in the unlikely event that the relevant intention could be established, it might still be possible to demonstrate good faith, eg the editor's belief in the public interest in knowing about the alleged events.

9.9.6 Sentence

In *R v Smith* (1994) a defendant, without desire for financial gain, informed a journalist that goods in a warehouse serving a well-known chain of high street chemists had been contaminated. The story was untrue and had been simply a ruse to cause inconvenience to the company in question. The sentence of three years' imprisonment was reduced to 18 months in the light of the absence of publicity and interference with trade. In *Witchelo* (1992), a case of blackmail contrary to s 21(1) of the Theft Act 1968, a term of 13 years' imprisonment was reduced to eight years in the case of a defendant who had threatened food producers that he would contaminate products.

Index

(All references are to page numbers)

In the 1960s Sir Ranulph Fiennes was removed from the SAS Regiment for misuse of explosives but, joining the army of the Sultan of Oman, he received that country's Bravery Medal on active service in 1971.

He is the only person yet to have been awarded two clasps at the Polar Medal for both Antarctic and the Arctic regions. Fiennes has led over thirty expeditions, including the first polar circumnavigation of the earth, and in 2003 he ran seven marathons in seven days on seven continents in aid of the British Heart Foundation. In May 2009, Fiennes became the oldest Briton ever to reach the summit of Everest.

In 1993 Her Majesty the Queen awarded Fiennes the Order of the British Empire (OBE) because, on the way to breaking records, he has raised over £10 million for charity. He was named Best Sportsman in the 2007 Great Britons Awards.

Also by Ranulph Fiennes

A Talent for Trouble
Ice Fall in Norway
The Headless Valley
Where Soldiers Fear to Tread
Hell on Ice
To the Ends of the Earth
Bothie the Polar Dog (with Virginia Fiennes)
Living Dangerously
The Feathermen
Atlantis of the Sands
Mind Over Matter
The Sett
Fit for Life
Beyond the Limits
The Secret Hunters
Captain Scott: The Biography
Mad, Bad and Dangerous to Know: The Autobiography

RANULPH FIENNES

Mad Dogs and Englishmen

AN EXPEDITION ROUND MY FAMILY

HODDER

First published in Great Britain in 2009 by
Hodder & Stoughton
An Hachette UK company

First published in paperback in 2010

1

A CIP catalogue record for this title is available
from the British Library.

ISBN 978 0 340 92504 1

Hod ... ible
and r ... rests.
Th ... to

For my Lollick, with love

Contents

The Romans first with Julius Caesar came,
Including all the nations of that name
Gauls, Greeks, and Lombards, and, by computation,
Auxiliaries or slaves of every nation.
With Hengist, Saxons; Danes with Sueno came,
In search of plunder, not in search of fame.
Scots, Picts, and Irish from the Hibernian shore,
And conquering William brought the Normans o'er.
All these their barbarous offspring left behind,
The dregs of armies, they of all mankind;
Blended with Britons, who before were here,
Of whom the Welsh ha' blessed the character.
From this amphibious ill-born mob began
That vain ill-natured thing, an Englishman.

From 'The True-Born Englishman' by Daniel Defoe

⚭ – indicates marriage

⋆1070 – indicates date of birth

†1015 – indicates date of death

Charles Martel – indicates direct line

Charles Martel
715 – 741

Pepin, King of the Franks
752 – 784

Charles (Charlemagne)
768 – 814

Ludwig (Louis I) 'The Pious'
814 – 840

Charles II, Emperor, 'Charles The Bald'
†875

Judith
Count Baldwin II of Flanders
879 – 918
Adelof, 1st Count of Boulogne
918 – 933

Louis II, King of Neustria
877 – 879

Charles (Simplex)
893 – 929

Louis IV (d'Outremer)
936 – 954

Bonna d' Ardennes ⚭ **Charles, Duke of Lorraine**
953 – 994

Lambert, Count of Louvain, 'The Bearded' †1015 ⚭ **Gerberga of Lorraine**
975 – 1015

Eustace de Fiennes ⋆1070 ⚭ Adele de Furnes et de Selvesse, Dame of Ardres
Lambert II, Count of Louvain
Matilda †1049 ⚭ Eustace I, Count of Boulogne 1000 – 1049
Landrade of Louvain

Alice de Bournonville ⚭ Conon de Fiennes 1080 – 1127

St Ida de Bouillon ⚭ **Eustace II 'Aux Grenons' de Boulogne** 1014 – 1093 ⚭ Princess Goda

Beatrice de Mandeville ⚭ **Geoffrey de Boulogne de Tingry**
Baldwin 1058 – 1115
Godfrey Bouillon 1062 – 1100

Margaret de Guisms ⚭
Anne de Dreux ⚭
Françoise de Miraument ⚭
Eustace 'Le Vieux' Fiennes II

William de Boulogne
1080 – 1130

Mary ⚭ Eustace de Boulogne III

Picot de Saye

Agnes de Grentmesnil ⚭ William de Saye

Hawise de Clare ⚭ Geoffrey de Saye

William de Saye II †1144 ⚭ Beatrice Talbot de Mandeville

Matilda ⚭ **Faramus de Boulogne de Tingry**
1105 – 1183

Matilda de Boulogne ⚭ Stephen, King of England 1135 – 1154

Ingelram Enguerand Fiennes 1134 – 1189 ⚭ **Sibyl de Tingry**

Constance de France ⚭ Eustace de Boulogne

Mathew, Count of Flanders ⚭ Mary, Countess of Boulogne

Agnes de Danmartin ⚭ **William Fiennes I**
1160 – 1243

Thomas Fiennes

Isabelle de Warrennes ⚭ William de Boulogne

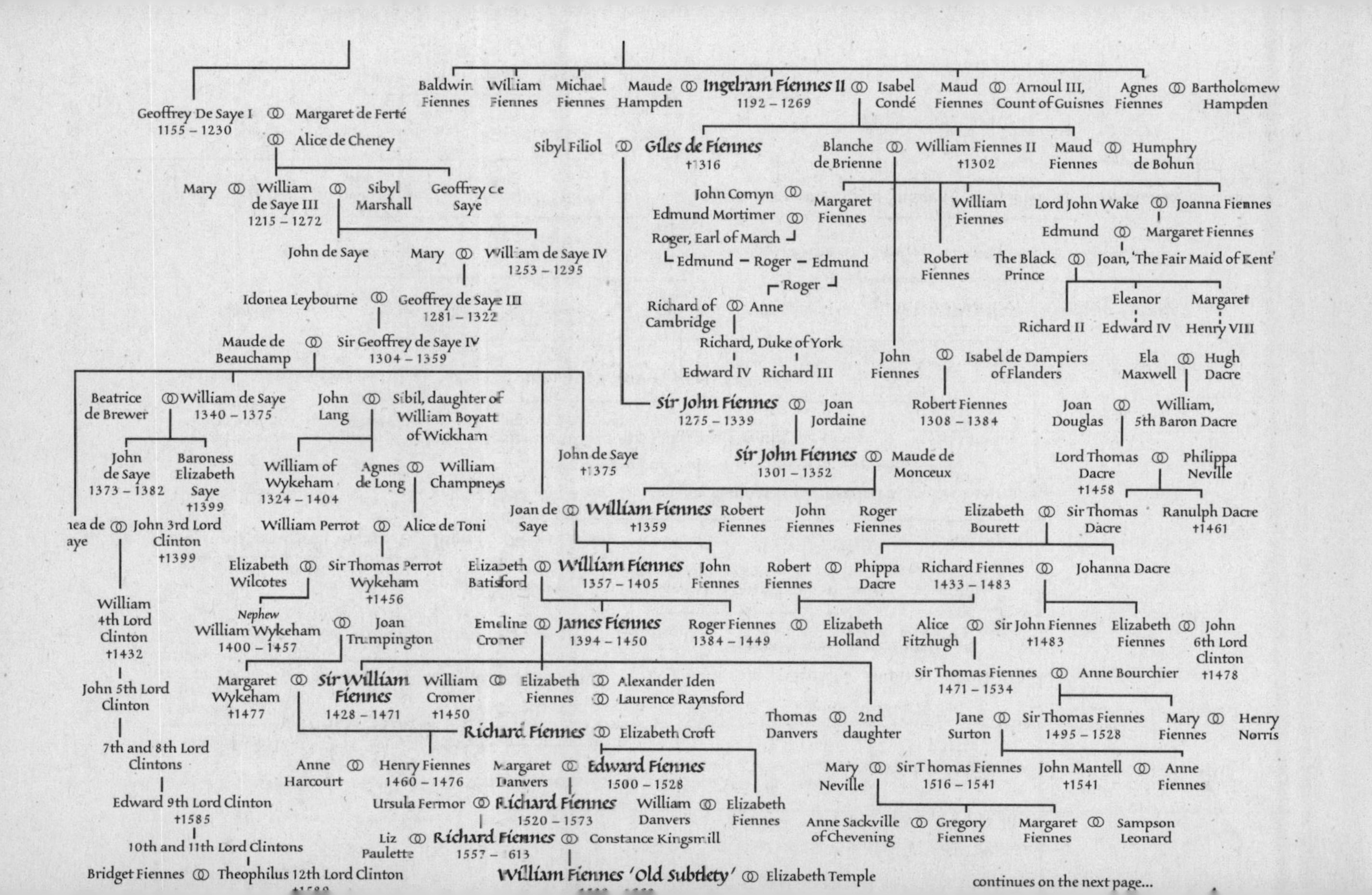

continues on the next page...

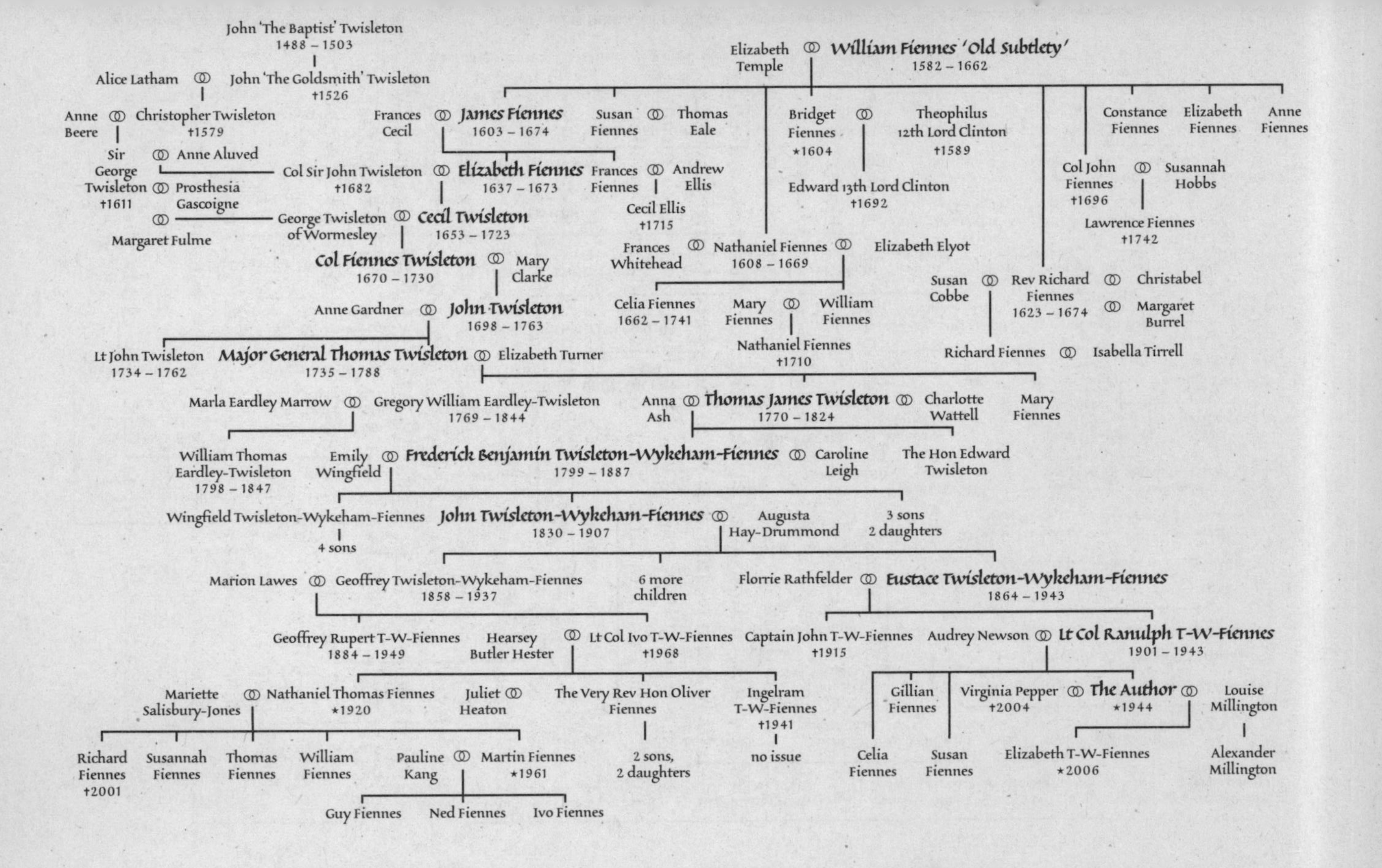
John 'The Baptist' Twisleton
1488 – 1503
Alice Latham ⚭ John 'The Goldsmith' Twisleton
†1526
Anne Beere ⚭ Christopher Twisleton
†1579
Sir George Twisleton
†1611
⚭ Anne Aluved
⚭ Prosthesia Gascoigne
⚭ Margaret Fulme
Col Sir John Twisleton
†1682
George Twisleton of Wormesley
Elizabeth Temple ⚭ William Fiennes 'Old Subtlety'
1582 – 1662
Frances Cecil ⚭ James Fiennes
1603 – 1674
Susan Fiennes ⚭ Thomas Eale
Bridget Fiennes
*1604
⚭ Theophilus 12th Lord Clinton
†1589
Constance Fiennes
Elizabeth Fiennes
Anne Fiennes
Elizabeth Fiennes
1637 – 1673
Frances Fiennes ⚭ Andrew Ellis
Cecil Ellis
†1715
Edward 13th Lord Clinton
†1692
Col John Fiennes
†1696
⚭ Susannah Hobbs
Lawrence Fiennes
†1742
Cecil Twisleton
1653 – 1723
Frances Whitehead ⚭ Nathaniel Fiennes
1608 – 1669
⚭ Elizabeth Elyot
Col Fiennes Twisleton
1670 – 1730
⚭ Mary Clarke
Susan Cobbe ⚭ Rev Richard Fiennes
1623 – 1674
⚭ Christabel
⚭ Margaret Burrel
Anne Gardner ⚭ John Twisleton
1698 – 1763
Celia Fiennes
1662 – 1741
Mary Fiennes ⚭ William Fiennes
Nathaniel Fiennes
†1710
Lt John Twisleton
1734 – 1762
Major General Thomas Twisleton
1735 – 1788
⚭ Elizabeth Turner
Richard Fiennes ⚭ Isabella Tirrell
Marla Eardley Marrow ⚭ Gregory William Eardley-Twisleton
1769 – 1844
Anna Ash ⚭ Thomas James Twisleton
1770 – 1824
⚭ Charlotte Wattell
Mary Fiennes
William Thomas Eardley-Twisleton
1798 – 1847
Emily Wingfield ⚭ Frederick Benjamin Twisleton-Wykeham-Fiennes
1799 – 1887
⚭ Caroline Leigh
The Hon Edward Twisleton
Wingfield Twisleton-Wykeham-Fiennes
4 sons
John Twisleton-Wykeham-Fiennes
1830 – 1907
⚭ Augusta Hay-Drummond
3 sons
2 daughters
Marion Lawes ⚭ Geoffrey Twisleton-Wykeham-Fiennes
1858 – 1937
6 more children
Florrie Rathfelder ⚭ Eustace Twisleton-Wykeham-Fiennes
1864 – 1943
Geoffrey Rupert T-W-Fiennes
1884 – 1949
Hearsey Butler Hester ⚭ Lt Col Ivo T-W-Fiennes
†1968
Captain John T-W-Fiennes
†1915
Audrey Newson ⚭ Lt Col Ranulph T-W-Fiennes
1901 – 1943
Mariette Salisbury-Jones ⚭ Nathaniel Thomas Fiennes
*1920
Juliet Heaton ⚭
The Very Rev Hon Oliver Fiennes
Ingelram T-W-Fiennes
†1941
Gillian Fiennes
Virginia Pepper
†2004
⚭ The Author
*1944
⚭ Louise Millington
Richard Fiennes
†2001
Susannah Fiennes
Thomas Fiennes
William Fiennes
Pauline Kang ⚭ Martin Fiennes
*1961
2 sons,
2 daughters
no issue
Celia Fiennes
Susan Fiennes
Elizabeth T-W-Fiennes
*2006
Alexander Millington
Guy Fiennes
Ned Fiennes
Ivo Fiennes

Foreword

My grandfather was born the second son of a family that has lived for six hundred years and twenty-one unbroken generations in the same house, Broughton Castle in Oxfordshire. This book is the record of my family and, through them, a simplified squint at the history of my country, England, warts and all, from its beginnings until 1944 when I was born. Churchill wrote: 'There is a forgotten, nay almost forbidden word which means more to me than any other. That word is England.' I go along with that.

I have spent fifty years of my life returning to England from abroad, and every now and again visiting the family at Broughton, as my father did before me. I always knew that just under the roof there was a secret tower room, 'a small room with no ears' they called it, where the leaders of the opposition to Charles I, including John Hampden and John Pym, had plotted against the king with the powerful 8th Lord Saye and Sele and I knew that the 1st Lord Saye and Sele had been beheaded by Jack Cade, the leader of the Peasants' Revolt. But beyond that, I had no knowledge of family history.

That all changed last year when I started to sift through often conflicting historical opinions alongside the voluminous family documents lent me by my cousin Nat, the 21st Lord Saye and Sele. I then became aware that one or two of my ancestors had played roles that almost certainly changed the course of English history.

On past expeditions and this year on Everest I have often conjured up the image of my father, my grandfather and long lines of Fienneses watching my flagging efforts and I pressed on because I didn't want to let them down. I never knew my father, much less the forty earlier generations, but since writing this book those vague shadows down the ages have for me become living people.

Ranulph Twisleton-Wykeham-Fiennes
written from Base Camp, Everest, May 2009

1

The Conquest that Nearly Wasn't

Many English people today point to Norman ancestry and boast, 'My lot came here in 1066.' Quite why that should be a point of pride rather than of shame, when one considers how those same ancestors behaved, is questionable and, as I shall reveal, the Fienneses are as guilty as anyone. Geoffrey Twisleton-Wykeham-Fiennes, Lord Saye and Sele (yes, that's just one man) writing in his book, *Hearsay*, in 1830 offers us a corrective viewpoint however.

> 'Your family history goes back a long way,' remarked a casual acquaintance to me.
>
> 'Yes,' I replied, my bosom heaving with pride, 'we came over with the Conqueror.'
>
> 'Ah!' he said. 'We were waiting for him.'

The 'English' who were sharpening their weaponry in anticipation were still a mongrel mix, a genetic goulash of a dozen racial origins who had arrived from what we now call Germany and the Low Countries of Belgium and Holland and the English language derives from these illiterate and pagan tribes, the Jutes from Jutland, plus the West Saxons (Wessex), the East Saxons (Essex) and the South Saxons (Sussex) from Old Saxony. The name England derives from the land of the Angles, a Germanic people from Angeln, now southern Denmark. Over the fifth, sixth and seventh centuries regional groupings of settlers fought each other for land and established their own kingdoms of East Anglia, Essex, Mercia (in the midlands), Sussex and Wessex.

By the eighth century a pecking order had emerged. Offa of Mercia (757–96) became direct ruler of all but the Wessex and Northumbrian provinces and was on 'My dearest brother' terms when addressing the most powerful man in Europe, his trading partner, the Frankish Emperor Charlemagne. And this is the point where I can introduce my family for the first time, as Charlemagne was my direct ancestor going back thirty-nine generations. In fact we have been traced back two generations more through his father Pepin the Short to Charles Martel, Charlemagne's grandfather and my great-to-the-power-of-forty-one grandfather. But it was to be a couple more centuries before we set foot on English soil and in that time Offa and his descendants had to cope with a brand new threat, the Vikings.

The English hero who stemmed the Viking invasions was Alfred the Great who penned the Danes into the so-called Danelaw along the eastern seaboard of England. Alfred was lauded as 'Engele hirde, Engele dirling' – shepherd and darling of England. It was his grandson, Edgar, who divided England into counties whose boundaries remained in place until 1974. He also started the tradition at coronation rituals of the great cry of fealty 'Long live the king, may the king live forever' which we still use in the twenty-first century.

The Danes made nuisances of themselves in Europe as well, laying siege to Paris and settling in the rich Frankish region which became known as Normandy, the land of the Norsemen. One of their villages was Fiennes, but more of that later.

No sooner had Alfred's successors thought the Viking problem had been settled than fresh waves of invasion panicked Edgar's son Ethelred the Unready into ordering all Danish men in England to be killed. A great many were massacred but the new Danish forces soon ousted and exiled the witless Ethelred whose unfortunate career I would not have mentioned had he not been a relation by marriage. His daughter Goda married my great-to-the-power-of-thirty grandfather, Eustace II of Boulogne.

The man who stepped into the power vacuum, King Canute, was luckily for us an anglophile and a sadly misunderstood one in popular mythology. When he let the waves on a beach near Chichester wash over his royal feet he was in fact demonstrating to his foolish courtiers the limit of human and kingly powers, not attempting to rule the tides. He did rule both England and Denmark pretty successfully from 1016 until his death in 1035.

His two sons, one of whom was an alcoholic, died a few years later, at which point the Wessex dynasty was restored to the English throne in the person of the late King Ethelred's son, Edward the Confessor, whose sister Goda, you will recall, was married to my cousin Eustace of Boulogne. I'm calling him my cousin Eustace because I am going to get sick of referring to various ancestors as ancestor this and ancestor that through the rest of this book. 'Cousin' is a much more user-friendly and less pompous general term.

During the reign of Canute and sons, Ethelred's immediate family had been in exile at the Norman court for twenty-five years, so when young Edward the Confessor found himself back in England as reigning monarch, he brought with him a goodly number of Norman friends, many of whom he appointed to senior positions of power, much to the annoyance of various influential English and Danish nobles, especially Lord Godwin, Earl of Wessex, the most influential noble in England.

An unhealthy power struggle now developed between the party of Edward, supported by the Dukes of Normandy, on the one hand, and Godwin of Wessex, the eminence grise behind the English throne – the man who would be king and was raising troops against Edward. It was this situation which sowed the seeds for the Norman invasion of Britain. Godwin bullied Edward into marrying his daughter, Edith. Edward, king in name only, had always loathed Godwin for having his teenage brother murdered, and he made sure that Edith remained childless by packing her off to a nunnery and taking a vow of celibacy himself.

At this point Edward's brother-in-law, my cousin Eustace, came, albeit unwittingly, to the king's assistance. Eustace had been having an eventful time in France rebelliously fighting against the forces of his overlord, the Emperor and, as if that were not enough grief, finding himself being excommunicated by the Pope for remarrying to too close a relation. Chastened, he begged forgiveness of the Emperor and prudently retreated for a spell to the friendly court of his English former brother-in-law. The two men were united in their hatred of Godwin and when Godwin's men killed twenty of Eustace's men in an affray at Dover, it was the last straw and the king had a perfect excuse to exile Godwin and his sons for not seeing the culprits were brought to justice.

But only a year after the Dover brawl the Godwins were back with a large Flemish army lent them by the Count of Flanders. Earl Godwin and sons once again became the power in the land and King Edward a mere puppet king who was anyway by then getting old and interested only in his pet royal architectural project of building Westminster Abbey.

No written evidence remains but during Godwin's brief exile, King Edward is said to have invited his friend, Duke William of Normandy, to his court, where he promised to make him heir to the throne of England. Nevertheless, on his deathbed only a year later Edward recommended to his council of nobles that Godwin's eldest son, Harold, should be his successor.

Another incident, of which there is also no written evidence, occurred during the year before Edward's death. Harold Godwinson, shipwrecked off Normandy or – less likely – sent there as an emissary to confirm Edward's promise of the succession to William, found himself in William's hands where he was forced over the bones of a saint to swear allegiance to the Duke of Normandy. The pictorial version of Harold's Oath is to be viewed on the Bayeux Tapestry which depicts Harold's ship sailing to France, his capture there by William's men, his joining William to fight the Duke of Brittany and, significantly, a friendly scene where Harold is thanked for his help prior to his making his oath of allegiance to William.

Edward died in 1066, the last of twenty-five kings of the Wessex dynasty, all of whom had lived in England. Harold Godwinson, an Anglo-Saxon-Scandinavian with no blood claim to the throne, but the mightiest earl in the land, was immediately proclaimed King of England.

Storm clouds gathered at once to the north and the south of the realm. King Harald Hardrada of Norway, a six foot four professional fighter of great military experience and with a clear claim to the throne of England due to his descent from King Canute, mustered his forces on the Norse island of Orkney. Duke William of Normandy worked feverishly on the Norman coast to prepare a fleet of over four hundred ships with which to attack from the south.

A good number of these vessels, according to historians, are likely to have been on loan from my cousin, Eustace of Boulogne, who was to ride beside Duke William in the heat of battle and carry his standard. Another strand of our family tree comes into the picture at Hastings. This was a Norman neighbour of Eustace's called William de Saye (from the village of Saye, near Argentan), who is described in all our medieval documents as 'companion of the Conqueror'.

Harold collected his 3,000 strong force of axe-men, or house-carls, and some 12,000 part-time soldiers (who owed the king forty days a year of armed service) and manned the beaches of the south coast. But bad weather delayed the Normans' attack and Harold's men began to wander off to tend their late summer harvests.

At this point came news that the Norwegian army, augmented by the forces of Tostig, the disaffected exiled brother of Harold, had landed north of York. Deciding that this northern threat was the more serious, Harold force-marched his men, recruiting more en route, for 190 miles in less than five days. At the ensuing Battle of Stamford Bridge, Harold's Anglo-Danish forces thoroughly defeated the Norwegians on 25 September. Victory celebrations must have been short-lived because William's army landed at Pevensey only three days later. So Harold turned back south, his force depleted and exhausted, to meet the well prepared Norman army a few miles north of Hastings. Here he gathered his men along the crest of a hill and formed a wall of shields.

Duke William initially divided his force into three groups, with Bretons on the left, his own Norman contingent in the centre and, on the key right flank, the main force of knights and mercenaries under my cousin Eustace. Harold's army was initially successful in holding off the first Norman attacks, but then a great many of his men broke ranks to pursue the Normans back down the hill. This was a costly mistake. The best known historian's description of the great battle, the last time England was ever successfully invaded, was by William of Poitiers, chaplain to Duke William. He describes the aftermath of the error by Harold's men.

> The Normans then surrounded several thousands of their pursuers and rapidly cut them down so that not one escaped. Heartened by this success, they then furiously carried their attack on to the main body of the English host, which even after their losses scarcely seemed diminished in number. The English fought confidently with all their strength . . . so closely massed together that even the dead had not space in which to fall . . . There were present in this battle: Eustace, count of Boulogne; William, count of Evreux; Geoffrey, count of Mortagnet . . . Haimo of Thouars; Rodulf of Tosny . . .
>
> But some of those who retreated took courage to renew the struggle on more favourable ground . . . These people, descended from the ancient Saxons (the fiercest of men) are always by

nature eager for battle, and they could only be brought down by the greatest valour. Had they not recently defeated with ease the King of Norway at the head of a fine army?

The duke . . . did not turn from his course when he saw these enemy troops rallying . . . Armed only with a broken lance he was more formidable than others who brandished long javelins. With a harsh voice he called to Eustace of Boulogne, who with fifty knights was turning in flight, and was about to give the signal for retreat. This man came up to the duke and said in his ear that he ought to retire since he would court death if he went forward.

If William had listened to Eustace's assessment of the situation the whole outcome of the Norman invasion might have been different. Duke William's historian continues.

But at the very moment when he uttered the words Eustace was struck between the shoulders with such force that blood gushed out from his mouth and nose, and half dead he only made his escape with the aid of his followers . . . In this dangerous phase of the battle many Norman nobles were killed . . .

The bloodstained battle-ground was covered with the flower of the youth and nobility of England. The two brothers of the king were found near him, and Harold himself stripped of all badges of honour could not be identified by his face, but only by certain marks on his body.

The Battle of Hastings and the events leading up to it are beautifully depicted on the Bayeux Tapestry, which is some two feet high by 230 feet long and is believed to have been commissioned either by William the Conqueror's wife or by his half-brother, Bishop Odo of Bayeux, or by his army chief, my cousin Eustace of Boulogne. Whoever inspired it, the tapestry disappeared for 500 years, turned up in Bayeux, was almost used as a cover for an ammunition wagon during the Civil War, and was removed to Paris by the Nazis. It is now back in its museum in Bayeux and cousin Eustace is depicted on it proffering his unheeded advice.

The Normans had arrived in style. They would make the Saxon English suffer for many a long year. As far as the family is concerned, it is at this point that we started to spend our time in England from our Boulogne base just over the Channel. The words of Daniel Defoe, in his 1703 poem 'The True-Born Englishman', are appropriate:

> And here begins our ancient pedigree,
> That so exalts our poor nobility:
> 'Tis that from some French trooper they derive,
> Who with the Norman bastard did arrive . . .

2

Stolen from the Saxons

Today, 934 years after the battle of Hastings, people still believe that the French conquered England on that fateful day in 1066. But, as we have seen, the two countries' leaders were as un-French and un-English as most of their soldiers. Duke William, whose nickname back home was the Bastard, was the great-great-grandson of Viking raider, Hrolf, whilst King Harold Godwinson's grandfather, Wulfnoth, had once destroyed most of the Saxons' royal navy. It was a case of one group of Viking vandal descendants clashing with another, something which both groups' ancestors had been doing all over Europe and back in their own Scandinavian homelands for centuries.

However, the genuine Wessex Saxons in Harold's army had been in England long enough to claim to be English, and their royal family had eventually, with interruptions, achieved a unique English way of living under Edward the Confessor and his dynastic predecessors. This fledgling nation was to be ruthlessly disrupted by the Normans, and it would take some 350 years before their DNA, their customs and their language eventually emerged with those of the Romano-British, the Anglo-Saxons and the Anglo-Vikings to form an island people quite distinct from their contemporaries in France, Germany or Scandinavia. They had by then earned a name of their own, the English.

I picture liquid grey cement, representing the pre-Romano-

Britons, revolving slowly in a mixer, and a pigment of imperial Roman purple being added to the mix. Then a blood-red dye to represent the Saxons and Vikings. And finally blue for the Normans. Eventually the cement attains its own distinct hue, unlike any other, and none of the separate additives are now recognisable in the hardened cement. At that point we have, for the first time, the English.

Daniel Defoe summarised this cement-mix result in 'The True-Born Englishman':

> But grant the best, how came the change to pass,
> A true-born Englishman of Norman race?
> A Turkish horse can show more history,
> To prove his well-descended family.
> Conquest, as by the moderns it is expressed,
> May give a title to the lands possessed:
> But that the longest sword should be so civil
> To make a Frenchman English, that's the devil.
> These are the heroes that despise the Dutch,
> And rail at new-come foreigners so much,
> Forgetting that themselves are all derived
> From the most scoundrel race that ever lived;
> A horrid crowd of rambling thieves and drones,
> Who ransacked kingdoms and dispeopled towns,
> The Pict and painted Briton, treacherous Scot,
> By hunger, theft, and rapine hither brought;
> Norwegian pirates, buccaneering Danes,
> Whose red-haired offspring everywhere remains,
> Who, joined with Norman-French, compound the breed
> From whence your true-born Englishmen proceed.

The post-Hastings Bastard, now King of England and Duke of Normandy, was well aware that he could never enjoy a peaceful holiday, since his subjects on either side of the Channel were both troublesome by nature and constantly threatened by their neighbours. He would have to travel back and forth to assert his presence as much in Rouen and Boulogne as in London and York. The key to keeping the lid on such a situation was to have eyes, ears and loyal allies everywhere.

Loyalty, William knew well, was a fickle beast at a time when neighbour fought neighbour and built castles for fear of predatory brothers or even sons. In Normandy he had spent his adult life at war with ever shifting alliances in and around his duchy and often against his official liege lord, the King of France. So he had developed a pyramid system of vassals, of barons, knights and serfs, which he quickly (he did everything quickly) replicated with brutal efficiency in England.

England's Roman, Saxon and Viking invaders had let the local leaders retain a good deal of their land and local authority, providing they paid tax to their new landlords and behaved themselves. The Norman invaders, however, intended to remove every last vestige of self-esteem and power from the natives of England. William marched his army from Hastings to London and had himself crowned King of England on Christmas Day 1066 in Westminster Abbey, even as his men burnt down Saxon homes in the vicinity.

The Norman army that remained in England the year after Hastings was made up of less than 8,000 men, but by the end of the twenty-one years of William's rule, some 5 per cent of the two million people in England were Gallic immigrants approved of or appointed by William to rule the natives with a rod of iron and by way of a rigid caste or feudal system. Many English Saxons escaped Norman oppression by emigrating, some to Nova Anglia, New England, an area which was later known as the Crimea on the Black Sea coast, and thousands responded to a recruiting drive to join the Varangian Guard of the Eastern Emperor in Constantinople.

Just as the Senate of Rome logged the name and status of each and every citizen in town, so William instituted his own census of Saxon England, the Domesday Book. His tax assessors recorded the wealth of every hamlet (some 13,000 settlements) down to the last goat and a measured tally of every productive acre, so that an unavoidable tax burden could be levied. One observer wrote at the time: 'So very narrowly did the King have his new land investigated by his inquisitors that there was no single hide nor acre of land, nor indeed . . . one ox or one cow or one pig which were left out and not recorded; and all these records were brought to him afterwards.'

Norman barons controlled the Welsh Marches, but the more inaccessible reaches of western Wales remained the land of the native British. The Scots succumbed from time to time to the Normans, but never for long, and even in southern England there were occasional revolts. One of these was spearheaded by my feisty ancestor, Count Eustace of Boulogne, who clearly felt badly treated by William, and his grievances were well known. So when the men of Kent decided to revolt while the king was abroad, they invited Eustace over with a force of Boulogners. (They knew him well due to his original fracas with Godwin thugs in Dover in 1051, which had caused Harold Godwin's temporary exile.) This was an extremely rash move, and it misfired at the outset because, although Eustace's men successfully occupied Dover town, they failed to overcome the garrison of Dover Castle. Eustace then sensibly retired back to Boulogne with his tail between his legs and, unsurprisingly, had various of his English lands forfeited by an apoplectic King William. Given to him by a grateful post-Hastings Conqueror and known as the Honour of Boulogne, they constituted a huge chunk of English land. After his failed invasion of Kent, Eustace made no further attempts to seize any part of England from King William. Some years later, and no doubt to ensure his loyalty, William gave him back most of his confiscated properties, including a huge collection of estates and manors that were part of the Honour of Boulogne.

For Anglo-Saxons all over England life under the Normans grew ever more miserable. If the serfs had always had a hard life, they were now hammered into the soil. To meet the Norman levies meant toil without respite. The best land was taken from its Saxon owners and given to Normans, whether they wished to live there permanently or, like my ancestors, the Fiennes, the Sayes and the Counts of Boulogne, to be absentee landlords. Domesday reveals that half the value of all England was in the hands of a mere two hundred men, including cousin Eustace. So much rental did this earn that Eustace introduced a standard of his own into England for weighing the moneys due to him. Some statistics from the Domesday Book reveal the truly ruthless nature of William's acquisition policies. He stole 5,000 estates from their Saxon owners and gave them to his barons. By 1087 when he died, only two out of the 190 big estate owners in England were Saxons. Only a hundred out of 1,400 medium-size estates were still Saxon owned. Many small holdings were confiscated and then leased back to their owners for rental. And of the sixteen bishops in all England, fifteen were Normans.

In exchange for their huge new Saxon estates and the acquired titles that went with them, the Norman barons had to remain utterly loyal to William and provide him with a set number of armed knights whenever he needed to raise an instant army. If they failed to come up with the goods, their land was confiscated.

In 1069 the citizens of York welcomed a Danish army as liberators from the Norman tyranny, so William rushed north to crush the rebels. His reputation alone must have impressed the Danes, for they fled before he arrived. The chronicles told of the vengeance exacted by the king: 'It was horrible to behold human corpses decaying in their houses, the streets and on the roads, swarming with worms whilst they were consumed by corruption with an abominable stench . . . There was no village inhabited between York and Durham; they became lurking places for wild beasts and robbers and were a great dread to travellers.'

The Normans in England during William's reign did not mingle or intermarry, spoke only French, tore down Saxon churches and imposed sky-high taxes. Saxons were now second-class citizens who were shunned socially by their Norman overlords. My Norman ancestors were clearly members of a nasty and arrogant bunch, and I feel, when I read about their behaviour, rather like Germans of my generation must feel about their Nazi forebears. All families have cupboard skeletons, and we had our fair share, alongside our saints and heroes.

The Twisleton and the Wykeham family branches stayed away from the Fienneses for quite a while, so I will concentrate at this point on Fiennes, Saye and Boulogne. The Counts of Boulogne took their name from their city, and the villages of Fiennes and Saye also became family names.

Normandy was divided into counties which waged constant war between themselves. These included Guisnes county, within which the town of Guisnes fought against the town of Ardres. Both had a castle and an army and both had supplies of rich young heiresses of great interest to the nearby village of Fiennes. Especially to the senior family there, who had taken on the village name as their surname, a fashionable thing to do. This family had become one of the twelve top baronies of Guisnes county, and their alpha male was, at the time of King William's death, Seigneur Eustace de Fiennes. There were a lot of Eustaces about at the time, which confuses things, but this one did well on the First Crusade and, as a local hero on his return, had no difficulty gaining the very profitable hand in marriage of Dame Adele of Ardres. Their son, Conon de Fiennes (1099–1127), failed to find a wealthy bride, but his eldest son, yet another Eustace but with the nickname of 'Le Vieux', the Old, focused on Guisnes and came up with a five-star lady named Margaret, who gave birth to one of our top heiress-grabbers, Ingelram Fiennes (1134–89), who married the sole heiress of the Counts of Boulogne.

Ingelram's father, Eustace Le Vieux, squandered some of the family fortune by terminally drilling an opponent at a local jousting tournament, which was not the done thing and the equivalent today of killing a man in a boxing match. As a penance

Eustace founded the magnificent, but expensive, Abbey of Beaulieu, not far from the village of Fiennes. In the year 2001 there were 821 people living in Fiennes, which is about halfway down the main road from Calais to Boulogne. Turn left at the Fiennes signpost and you will enter the region once covered by the Forest of Fiennes and overlooked by Mount Fiennes, from which, on a clear day, you can see the coastline of England.

To keep up with Guisnes and Ardres the Fiennes family built our own modest castle in the forest in 1049. It was burnt down in 1320 but rebuilt. Then in 1543 Henry VIII of England razed it to the ground, since when our only castles have been in England.

The very first Fiennes who, according to the family, went to England and settled there was John, who fought so well at Hastings that the Bastard honoured him with the accolade of Constable of Dover Castle and Warden of the Cinque Ports. This was a hereditary title, so the next three generations of John's family proudly retained it. Sadly, a close inspection of medieval records reveals no trace of any of these four Fienneses, and the 21st Lord Saye and Sele, my cousin Nathaniel Fiennes, believes that they probably never existed but were the complex invention of one James Fiennes (the 1st Lord Saye and Sele) in the 1440s, who was, for unconnected reasons, hanged, drawn and quartered. This James was an avid social climber and by suggesting that four of his forebears were Wardens of the Cinque Ports he would have gained much prestige. If he did indeed mastermind such a fraud, it clearly worked well for him, since he eventually became Lord High Treasurer of England before his gory demise.

Going back to ancestors who definitely did exist, you will remember cousin Eustace of Boulogne who tried to persuade the Bastard to retreat during the battle of Hastings and the following year conducted his own failed invasion of England. Eustace's eldest son, Geoffrey, more than made amends for his father's bad judgment by marrying the daughter of Geoffrey de Mandeville, a close companion and trusted adviser of King William who was given vast English estates stolen from the Saxons. Not only did Geoffrey win back the remainder of the lands his father had forfeited by his invasion stunt, but he further inherited, according to the Domesday records in 1086, major estates in eleven different counties. He styled himself Baron of Tingray and Lord of Clapham.

Meanwhile, his fellow barons resident in England were hard at work building formidable castles throughout the land from which they could dominate the locals. The most impressive of these was the Tower of London, built mostly of white stone from Caen in Normandy. From such centres, French culture was slowly but surely to become the culture of England and the way by which the new master race would eradicate the ways of the old Anglo-Saxon elite. Normandy and England were both now ruled by an aristocracy of Anglo-Normans, who moved between their estates in both countries, taxing and exploiting both sets of serfs. They were the new governing class of England, and, in the words of the contemporary historian Orderic Vitalis, 'The native inhabitants were crushed, imprisoned, disinherited, banished and scattered beyond the limits of their own country.'

The English language remained the tongue of the suppressed masses, but a well-educated Anglo-Norman who settled in England and stayed all his life there would be trilingual. His French would be fluent, he would know church Latin and he could understand English. The fact that, 350 years later, English had become the tongue of English royalty was purely because the vast majority of the island's inhabitants spoke it and their Norman overlords made no effort to penalise those who did. Nowadays the French, threatened by 'franglais', doubtless consider this to have been an extremely bad error and missed opportunity.

Half a dozen years after Hastings, William began to spend more and more time back in Normandy fighting various of his neighbours, including the King of France and, intermittently, his own rebellious elder son, Robert. On one of these campaigns, in 1087, William died of wounds, having appointed his second son, William, King of England.

Norman records of William's deathbed words include the confession: 'I persecuted the native inhabitants of England beyond all reason. Whether nobles or commons, I cruelly oppressed them; many I unjustly disinherited; innumerable multitudes, especially in the county of York, perished through me by famine and sword . . . I am stained with the rivers of blood that I have shed.'

The Bastard was buried in Caen, so corpulent that when the attendant bishops tried to force his body into the royal sarcophagus, his entrails burst forth and the resulting pestilent stench caused panic amongst the mourners, many of whom fled the ceremony.

3

Riding to Jerusalem

Despite the treasonable behaviour of his eldest son, Robert, King William left him the Duchy of Normandy. His second son, William, was speedily crowned King of England, and the third son, later to become Henry I, received 'innumerable treasures'. This turned out to be a recipe for fraternal strife and, quite possibly, murder.

The coronation of William II went ahead without immediate complaints from any meaningful party, but a powerful grouping of Anglo-Norman barons broke into open revolt in 1088. A firm reaction by King William won the day, but the unrest continued to simmer and major trouble was on the verge of exploding into civil war in 1095.

The main aim of the barons was straightforward. They wanted their king, whether Robert, William or even Henry, to be monarch of both England and Normandy. Since Robert, the eldest son, was clearly dissatisfied with his father's deathbed decision to give him the duchy not the kingdom, the barons reckoned he would cause endless trouble (and war taxes for them to stump up) until such time as he could win the crown.

Their rationale made sense. The historian Vitalis quoted the most powerful of the rebel magnates, the late king's half-brother, Odo of Bayeux, as saying, 'How can we yield good service to two distant and mutually hostile lords? If we serve

Duke Robert well, we will offend his brother, William, who will confiscate our land in England. On the other hand, if we obey King William, Duke Robert will do likewise with our Norman properties.'

There would doubtless have been civil war between the two brothers sooner or later, but for Robert's personal and heroic desire to be a crusader hero. To raise a meaningful army of his own with which to carry out this ambition, he would need a great deal of money, and his surprise method of raising the funds was to sell Normandy to brother William in 1095, the year of the First Crusade.

By the time he disappeared in a cloud of dust towards the Holy Land, Robert had already lost chunks of the Bastard's hard-won French territory to the King of France. Once William II took over the duchy, he waged war on France until he had restored all his father's French territories to their former frontiers and England and Normandy were once again a single sea-split land. Known as Rufus, due to his red hair, William II ruled his dominions with the same dedicated cruelty as had his father, the Bastard. He was not religious, and treated the church with contempt as a bottomless source of taxes. Even his barons received short shrift, for he preferred to give royal favours to the captains of his mercenary armies. He never married and his court was said to squirm with 'fornicators and sodomites'. He died, most conveniently, in the year 1100, which averted the long-postponed but imminent civil war with brother Robert, who was by then on the long journey back from his highly successful crusade.

Rufus died on a New Forest stag hunt, killed by a stray arrow. These things can happen in field sports even today. But murder conspiracy tales were soon rampant, with the chief suspect being William's younger brother Henry, who happened to be hunting in the same woods on the same day. Whether implicated in the king's death or not, Henry, knowing that brother Robert was heading home from Palestine, rode post-haste to Winchester to seize the Royal Treasury and thence to Westminster Abbey, where he had himself crowned Henry I of England, on the principle that possession is nine-tenths of the law.

William II's corpse did not explode, as had his father's, but the clergy refused to bury it in royal Winchester due to the bloody and sacrilegious nature of his thirteen-year rule.

The key factor that saved England from civil war between brothers Robert and Henry was and remained the First Crusade, and my family was into crusading in a major way. The response to Pope Urban II's call to arms was not only far greater than he had expected, it also proved uncontrollable, for he had loosed a vicious genie which stirred the worst leanings of the Franks, the latent bloodlust of their Viking forebears, and their subsequent actions were to horrify the Pope. Styling themselves pilgrims, they sewed crosses on their cloaks and marched away for hundreds of miles to lands and sights beyond their wildest dreams. They came from all levels of society: monarchs, bishops, knights, peasants and clerks. Their aim was indeed to fight the forces of evil, but they were themselves a devilish brew. The advance waves of some 60,000 fighting men, many with their families in tow, set out for the East in the spring of 1096 and, that autumn, another 100,000 in five armies followed their trail. Among their leaders were the charismatic preacher Peter the Hermit and the robber baron Count Emich from Germany, notorious for his cruelty, in charge of 20,000 men.

Peter the Hermit's message to aspiring crusaders was as anti-Semitic as anti-Muslim and posed the point that to march thousands of miles to kill the Antichrist in Jerusalem made no sense if you spared the killers of Christ, the Jews, back home. So the likes of Count Emich's army conducted widespread purges in Germany before their crusading marches began. Jews whose families had lived peacefully in their European homes for centuries were offered a choice of baptism or death. Most chose the latter and were burnt to cinders. Many family members killed each other to prevent any abandonment of the faith. All over Europe, wherever a crusading army gathered together, its first act was to kill any Jews within reach.

The first army to leave France in the summer of 1096 was led by two members of the family of my ancestors, Godfrey de Bouillon and his brother Baldwin de Boulogne. Their parents were Eustace de Boulogne (of Hastings and Dover fame) and his wife Ida of Bouillon. Being direct descendants of Charlemagne helped Godfrey and Baldwin as leaders of often fractious armies of proud Franks. Cousin Godfrey's background was military with a good deal of campaigning against the Pope during a papal war with the Bouillon region, a complex affair which even involved Godfrey fighting battles in Italy.

However, when the Pope proclaimed the crusade, Godfrey signed up and mortgaged much of his property to pay for the 40,000 knights and foot soldiers he would command. Many were armed mercenary bands of Germans, Walloons and Flemings. His army moved with speed and efficiency. In Hungary, like many other crusader leaders, he had trouble preventing his men from pillaging from the locals, their fellow Christians. But he still arrived at Constantinople in the vanguard and was the first crusader general to take an oath to the Byzantine Emperor who ruled there. Other lesser leaders heading for the Holy Land that summer included Eustace Fiennes, the husband of Dame Adele of Ardres, and Seigneur of the Fiennes Castle. Eustace was twenty-six years old.

For two years the crusaders fought the Muslim occupants of the Holy Land, many of whom were Fatimids from Egypt. Godfrey and Baldwin were at the forefront of the fighting, alongside Count Raymond of Toulouse, another Frank. In 1098 they successfully laid siege to Edessa, where Baldwin of Boulogne remained as commandant. Later in the year they took the major city of Antioch, where Godfrey fell out with some of the other leaders. He remained there whilst most of the army moved on south down the Mediterranean coast. For a while the local Sunni Arabs offered no resistance, for they feared the Fatimids, who were Shias, more than they feared the Christians.

Godfrey joined his army to that of William II's brother, Duke

Robert. Together they reached Tripoli in early May, then on to Beirut, Jaffa and Bethlehem. On 6 June they came at last to Jerusalem and learnt that the Fatimid commandant had poisoned nearby springs, burnt crops and expelled all Christians from the city. The gathered crusaders had struggled in all weathers from towns as far away as York or Hamburg, but they were still a long way from victory as they gazed at the high walls of the Holy City, the final goal of their long march. They had yet to cleanse Jerusalem of the Devil.

It is a sad reflection on human nature that Muslims, Christians and Jews, despite sharing the origins of their religions as People of the Book, have spent so much energy over so many centuries trying to eliminate each other, and are still at it today.

The crusaders, led by men of varying degrees of religious fervour or none, clearly believed that the only good Muslims were dead ones. The siege wore on through the hot month of June. Ladder-scaling attacks failed as boiling oil, rocks and flaming arrows rained down from the Fatimids along the battlements. The Egyptians' rigorous scorched-earth policy carried out over a wide area outside the city walls proved effective, and the crusaders' food supplies dwindled so that speedy success became critical. They convened a council and decided to build mobile siege towers. There was no available wood as the Fatimids had taken care to burn all nearby forests, but the timbers of two Genoese ships that had recently brought the crusaders some supplies were torn apart and three attack-towers were fashioned, which proved crucial in finally breaking the siege on 15 July 1099.

The Franks, with cousin Godfrey and his knights leading the way, swarmed through the city, hacking the inhabitants to death. Nobody but the garrison commander and his personal escort was spared. Blood, according to one participant, the chronicler Fulk, sloshed ankle-high around the corpse heaps in the stone alleys of the city. Fulk wrote:

> At the noon hour with trumpets sounding and with great commotion, the frenzied Franks broke into the city, and the pagans, demoralized, began to flee. Some Saracens, Arabs and Ethiopians fled to the tower of David, others to the temple of Solomon, where a great battle followed. They could not escape our gladiators. Those who fled to the roof were shot by arrows. Some ten thousand were killed in this temple alone. We spared the life of none of them, neither woman nor child.

During this massacre, cousin Godfrey stripped off his armour and walked unarmed and barefoot through the carnage to pray in the Church of the Holy Sepulchre.

After the last inhabitant lay dead or herded into groups ideal for slavery, the crusaders plundered the empty houses. Fulk wrote:

> They took whatever they found. Thus many poor men became rich. Our footmen discovered the Saracens had swallowed gold coins. So they burnt great heaps of bodies so that the stomachs and intestines of the dead released the precious metal into the human ashes. Afterwards the clergy went chanting to the Lord's glorious temple. It was the eleven hundredth year of our Lord when the people of Gaul, the Franks in their might, took the city, 285 years after the death of Charlemagne and twelve years from the death of William I of England.

The crusaders counted over 40,000 Muslim corpses after the massacre. They herded all the Jewish survivors together into one of the synagogues and burnt every last one to death. Then they all gathered in the Church of the Holy Sepulchre to give thanks.

Of their various army leaders, the crusaders selected cousin Godfrey to be Jerusalem's new ruler. He nominated the city as capital of the whole country, and was installed as the first 'Christian King of the crusader Kingdom of Jerusalem'. Over the next year he forced the Saracen strongholds of Ascalon, Arsuf and Caesarea into submission and rebuilt the city of Jaffa as a port of arrival for crusader reinforcements. In 1100 he died, struck by an arrow according to Arab legend, but more likely by one of the many exotic diseases rife at the time.

By the end of the twelfth century cousin Godfrey was a legend among crusader descendants all over Europe. Tasso made Godfrey the hero of his epic poem *Gerusalemme Liberata*. In his *Divine Comedy*, Dante sees the spirit of Godfrey in the Heaven of Mars with other 'warriors of the faith'. Godfrey is depicted in Handel's opera *Rinaldo* as Goffredo. In 1848 a statue of him was erected in the Royal Square in central Brussels, as Godfrey was born on the Belgium side of the French border and in 2005 he was voted seventeenth in the Greatest Belgian contest, a public vote of national heroes in French-speaking Belgium.

When he died, his title of King of Jerusalem passed to his warrior brother, Baldwin of Boulogne, which kept the Holy City in the family for a while longer.

4

A King's Ransom

When King William II died in the New Forest, his brother Robert became the rightful heir to the throne of England. But Robert was in the wrong place at the wrong time, being on his way back home from the capture of Jerusalem, which gave younger brother Henry his chance to leap in. Henry I, nicknamed Henry Beauclerc because of his learned ways, was the first King of England to speak English fluently.

Just a few weeks after Henry's coronation, Robert arrived back in Normandy, flushed with his crusading successes. Most of England's Anglo-Norman barons supported his claim to the throne, but a powerful minority, as well as the leaders of the church, preferred Henry. Civil war was only averted by the cunning politics of Henry. Robert would keep Normandy and be paid the huge annual sum of £2,000 by the king.

Fearing that, despite this agreement, brother Robert would sooner or later gather forces and funds sufficient to invade England, Henry set about enfeebling those barons known to support Robert, such as the powerful Marcher lords, the Mortimer family who straddled the Welsh border. He then began to woo the loyalty of many of the magnates (who William Rufus had alienated) by increasing their lands or handing out titles and other favours. He married Matilda, the daughter of a Scottish noble with no Norman blood, who bore him a son and a daughter. He later became infamous for extra-marital activities, resulting in over twenty illegitimate children, including a number of daughters who were to prove extremely useful when Henry needed to neutralise potential rivals. At least seven of Henry's bastard daughters were married off to likely threats, such as the King of Scotland and various French regional dukes. The historian, William of Malmesbury, summed up this royal tactic as sex 'for politics not pleasure'. One hopes Matilda found this an acceptable practice.

By 1106 Henry was ready to deal with brother Robert, so he invaded Normandy and, at the Battle of Tinchebray, captured him and took over the duchy. England and Normandy once again shared the same ruler, and Henry ensured that Robert would never again be a threat by locking him up in Cardiff Castle, where he learnt Welsh from his jailer and died twenty-eight years later. Some say he was murdered.

One of Henry's contemporaries wrote of him: 'God endowed him with three gifts, wisdom, victory and riches, but these were offset by three vices, avarice, cruelty and lust.' An example of his cruelty was when, at the tender age of twenty-one, he took a rebellious citizen of Rouen up a castle tower and threw him out of the window to his death on the cobbles far below.

After taking Normandy from Robert, Henry spent less and less time in England, which was possible thanks to the efficient and sophisticated system of government he left there, especially the apparatus for gathering the taxes he needed for his wars with Normandy's ever-aggressive neighbours. These included the King of France and the Counts of both Anjou and Flanders.

Keen that his only legitimate son, William, should be his heir, he had him groomed and educated to that end. In 1120 the king, his heir and many senior barons sailed back to England after a campaign. Young William sailed on the speedy 'White Ship' and handed out generous supplies of wine to the crew. Racing to catch up with the king's vessel, the 'White Ship's skipper hit a rock in the dark and only one passenger survived to describe the death of Henry's heir.

Henry's final years were heavily involved with his attempts to secure the succession of his dynasty for his surviving, legitimate child, his daughter the Empress Matilda. On her husband the Emperor's death and under threat from powerful forces in Flanders, he secured a new marriage deal for her with the Count of Anjou's heir, Geoffrey Plantagenet. The marriage went ahead, but without the approval of many of the Anglo-Norman barons, so when, in 1135, Henry suddenly died of food poisoning in Normandy, my ancestors in Boulogne were able to stir up big trouble. Let me explain.

Henry had a favourite nephew to whom he had given land and great wealth, Count Stephen of Blois, Matilda's first cousin, who clearly planned to grab nice uncle Henry's throne as soon as he died. The fact that Henry was not all that far from Boulogne when he died of food poisoning, and so news of his demise reached Stephen quickly, and that Queen-to-be Matilda was away with her husband Geoffrey in distant Anjou, all added up to a wonderfully coincidental opportunity for Stephen to hop on a speedy ship from Boulogne to London, where he knew he had the key support of the magnates. This worked well and Stephen, the grandson of William the Conqueror but nonetheless a clear usurper of the crown which Henry I had appointed for his daughter Matilda, was duly crowned King of England. He claimed that Henry had actually changed his mind on his deathbed and named him, Stephen, as heir. Very cheeky.

Where my relations enter the story is through the Counts of Boulogne. Cousin Eustace had three sons. We have met the two who went crusading but not his eldest son, Eustace III, who married Princess Mary of Scotland (the daughter of King Malcolm III) and produced a daughter confusingly also called Matilda, who in 1125 married Count Stephen of Blois, who ten years later usurped the English crown.

This not only makes Eustace's daughter the Queen of England, but it also complicates any précis of the next few years of English history by giving both the chief contenders for the crown the same name. To get round this confusing issue, I will follow the historians in calling my ancestor King Stephen's wife and loyal supporter, Queen Matilda, whilst Henry I's daughter and legitimate heir to his throne, is the Empress Matilda. At the time of Stephen's seizure of the crown, our Matilda was heavily pregnant with yet another Eustace of Boulogne. A few months later she joined Stephen in London and was crowned his queen.

Stephen set about the difficult job of placating his many and various enemies in England and France, doing everything he could to avoid open warfare. He allowed powerful barons to get away with murder and, even worse, to steal lands considered to be under royal ownership. To keep his rival and cousin, Empress Matilda, quiet, he accepted highly unfavourable terms in a treaty with her husband, Geoffrey Plantagenet of Anjou. In England he weakly gave way to all those with local pretensions to power. Anarchy ruled throughout the land, well portrayed in the Anglo-Saxon Chronicle.

> When the traitors perceived that he was a mild man, and a soft, and a good, and that he did not enforce justice, they did all wonder. They had done homage to him, and sworn oaths, but they no faith kept; all became forsworn, and broke their allegiance, for every rich man built his castles, and defended them against him, and they filled the land full of castles. They greatly oppressed the wretched people by making them work at these castles, and when the castles were finished they filled them with devils and evil men . . . never was there more misery, and never acted heathens worse than these. At length they spared neither church nor churchyard, but they took all that was valuable therein, and then burned the church and all together. Neither did they spare the lands of bishops, nor of abbats, nor of priests; but they robbed the monks and the clergy, and every man plundered his neighbour as much as he could. If two or three men came riding to a town, all the township fled before them, and thought that they were robbers. The bishops and clergy were

ever cursing them, but this to them was nothing, for they were all accursed and forsworn, and reprobate. The earth bare no corn, you might as well have tilled the sea, for the land was all ruined by such deeds, and it was said openly that Christ and his saints slept. These things, and more than we can say, did we suffer during nineteen years because of our sins.

This horrific state of affairs had already begun when Empress Matilda arrived in England to claim her throne in 1139. At the time of her arrival, Stephen was in a good position to seize and imprison her, but instead of confronting her feeble force with his army, he merely had her escorted to the south-west to Bristol, the seat of her brother, Robert of Gloucester. From then on there were, to all intents, two rival royal courts in England. Matilda and her brother began at once to ferment rebellion wherever they could. Civil war would ravage the land for the next nine years.

Empress Matilda's forces soon held sway in most of the west country, and in 1141 at the battle of Lincoln her forces captured King Stephen, imprisoning him in Bristol, her headquarters. Stephen's fickle brother, Henry of Blois, the papal legate, went over to Empress Matilda's side and helped her gain the key support of London – just. A few weeks later Stephen was deposed and the empress entered London in triumph.

Cousin Matilda of Boulogne, aka the queen, surrounded herself in this time of trouble with her close family, including cousin Faramus of Boulogne, putting him in charge of the royal family affairs as Comptroller of the Household, whilst Stephen languished in jail. She then rallied as great a force of loyalists as she could in the short time that remained before the date when the empress, then styled by a clerical council as 'the Lady of the English', was to be officially crowned in Westminster Abbey.

Fortunately for Stephen and Queen Matilda, the empress was hoist by her own rapacious petard. In no time at all, and ignoring the peace conditions laid down by the papal legate to woo the Londoners, she squandered their support so that when Queen

Matilda's force arrived and marched towards the city, the Londoners took up arms and forced the empress out. She was soon captured, but escaped by riding away from her captors at full speed, sitting astride like a man.

Stalemate ensued until, later that year, Robert of Gloucester, chief ally and brother to the empress, was captured by loyalists. She had no choice but to agree to a prisoner swap. The king for her brother. In double quick time the deposed Stephen was re-crowned at Canterbury Cathedral and the civil war flickered on in a see-saw fashion. The empress, as brave as she was proud, became quite a legend when she escaped Stephen's men on two further occasions: once from Devizes dressed up as a dead body, and then in 1142 from Oxford Castle 'gliding over the snows in a pure white gown'.

The trouble with civil wars is you find you have family on both sides. Two of my relatives, William de Saye and his brother-in-law Geoffrey de Mandeville, the Earl of Essex, were loyal soldiers of the empress, but both were killed in 1141 when attacking King Stephen's fortress at Burwell, near Cambridge. William's son Geoffrey de Saye may have been a chip off the old block when described as, '*vir in armis strenuus sed in mundanis rebus minus sapiens et incircumspectus*', meaning 'strong as a fighter but thick and rash in worldly matters'.

Stephen was grateful to those of his wife's relations who had remained loyal during his time in prison, and cousin Faramus, made Constable of Dover Castle and Warden of the Cinque Ports, was given lands in England which later ended up with his Fiennes descendants. Our family still owns a watercolour dated 1837, before Dover Castle was extensively rebuilt, showing the Fiennes Tower.

Over in Jerusalem meanwhile, a half century had passed since the victorious First Crusade. Cousins Godfrey and Baldwin de Boulogne, successive rulers of the city, were long gone, and Saracen raiders were overrunning crusader lands. When in 1144 the Pope called for a new crusade, Stephen wisely stayed out of it, but some 50,000 French and German crusaders, at vast cost to their nations' coffers, finally reached Damascus in 1147. Meeting a superior Muslim force before they could even begin their conquest plans, they were forced into an ignominious retreat.

This failed crusade did have an indirect effect on English history because, by sod's law, both the beautiful French Queen Eleanor of Aquitaine and her husband's uncle were on the crusade and had an affair, which naturally upset the King of France, who divorced his wife. Eleanor, clearly not a woman to waste time, married again eight weeks after the divorce, the then main rival of King Stephen of England, Henry, the son of Empress Matilda.

Henry had control of both Anjou and Normandy and now, by marrying Eleanor, also Aquitaine. Encouraged and financed by the feisty Eleanor, Henry took his army to England in 1152. There he found an ongoing situation of stalemate between pro- and anti-Stephen barons, which seemed insoluble until, in 1153, Stephen's eldest son and heir, Eustace of Boulogne, died suddenly.

The long drawn out civil war and resultant anarchy which had so ravaged England for nearly two decades had made most of the barons on both sides keen for peace, and a treaty was signed between the two contenders for the throne: one the grandson of Henry I, the other his nephew. It was agreed that Stephen, by then a sick and weary man, would keep the crown until he died and that Henry would be his heir. Stephen died of a heart attack a year later and Henry II took the throne. His father's family name of Plantagenet now became that of the English monarchy, a dynasty that would rule through fourteen kings over three hundred years.

From a family point of view, the close relationship of Faramus with King Stephen, through his wife Matilda, had for the first time given us a solid base and extensive lands in England to add to those in Boulogne. But a likely problem, common to all times of leadership change, was that the new King Henry would wield a new broom to sweep out the favourites of his predecessor and give their lands to his own cronies. Faramus ran that risk.

Henry II was the most powerful monarch in all Europe, with territory stretching between the borders of Scotland and Spain. Indeed, he ruled far more of France itself than did its nominal king. He established reforms of government and is still regarded by many historians as the founder of English common law. Henry II fathered eight children with his beautiful wife Eleanor, who had been accused by her previous husband, the King of France, of being barren. But his four sons were truly a Devil's brood, as nasty as their father was clearly likeable.

Richard, the eldest, later called Richard Lionheart, was happy only when at war. The fourth and last son, John, was born when his mother was forty-five, by which time Henry had already willed all his vast territories to his three elder sons. He nicknamed him John Lackland, which must have seriously irked the lad. In 1185 he was promised Ireland – a poisoned chalice if ever there was one. All four sons caused Henry trouble throughout his highly successful thirty-four year reign. On occasions Richard fought alongside his father against his brothers. The middle two died in 1183 and 1186 which cleared the ground, but not enough for Richard who correctly feared the king preferred his younger brother John and might will him the throne. In 1189 he allied himself with the French king and defeated Henry's army at the Battle of Ballans, forcing his father to name him officially as heir apparent.

A twist in the tail of this whole sorry family saga was when, not long after Ballans, as a sick Henry lay dying at his castle in nearby Chinon, he learnt that son John, his favourite, had secretly allied himself with his enemies. Despite his highly successful reign, both in military and in governmental terms, he died an unhappy man. Even his wife Eleanor betrayed him and plotted with their sons against him. He had her imprisoned and thereafter, according to well documented legends, kept his mistress, Rosamund Clifford, hidden within a forested labyrinth at Woodstock in Oxfordshire where Queen Eleanor's agents eventually tracked her down and had her poisoned.

Henry never cleansed his court nor the baronage of the favourites of his predecessor and longtime rival, the late King Stephen. So cousin Faramus lost none of the privileges gained through Stephen's patronage. Indeed, he remained a favourite of King Henry, who granted his daughter, Sibyl of Boulogne, many rich estates in England, including those of Ash, Martock and Widdicombe in Somerset. Faramus also retained lordship of Clapham and Carshalton in Surrey. Faramus, like other Anglo-Normans, still spent a good deal of time in France, where he was a close friend and adviser of Stephen's surviving son, William of Boulogne.

Since Sibyl was the only surviving child of Faramus, she inherited much land in England and France, which all passed on her marriage to her husband, Ingelram de Fiennes, the son of Eustace le Vieux, who founded Beaulieu Abbey in penance for killing a jousting opponent. Thanks to Ingelram, the Boulogne inheritance was now subsumed into the Fiennes family. It would require a few more decades for us to take over the Sayes.

The year before Henry died, the Holy Roman Emperor led the Third Crusade to the Holy Land to rescue Jerusalem from Saladin. The siege of the coastal port of Acre early in 1189 became one of the longest sieges in history and killed at least three of my ancestors. Over the next three years of siege and counter-siege and squabbles among the crusader leaders the situation in the Holy Land was at stalemate. The tide finally changed in favour of the crusaders when, in the summer of 1191, fresh armies arrived, including a hundred ships and 8,000 men, led by the English King Richard I who, three years earlier, had succeeded his father, Henry. Richard's entire adult life had involved fighting, very often against his father and brothers as well as the King of France, and the crusaders could have found no better military leader to pit against the wily Saladin.

Richard's crusader knights included Sir Ingelram Fiennes, his cousin Tougebrand Fiennes, and John Fiennes. All were killed during the crusade and John's family gave the land in England where they buried his heart to the citizens of London; a place now known as Finsbury Square.

Richard sent envoys to Saladin once he was sure the 5,000-strong Acre garrison was on its last legs following a major battle on 11 July. Saladin agreed to surrender the city on various conditions, and Richard's victorious armies entered the gates. At this point an apparently minor squabble occurred when Richard noticed the flag of Leopold, Duke of Austria flying over the city. He had it torn down, since he believed the Austrians had done little to help during the siege. Leopold's revenge was later to affect English history.

Saladin agreed to swap 1,600 Christian prisoners for 2,700 of the captured garrison but, when the return of some of the Christian leaders was delayed, Richard massacred over 2,000 prisoners, including many women and children, the story of which act of cruelty was told and retold by Muslims down the centuries.

Acre became the new capital of the crusaders in the Holy Land, and Richard went on to other major victories against Saladin's forces. Jerusalem, however, remained in Muslim hands. Acre would remain a Christian redoubt for one hundred years until 1291 when a force of Egyptian troops attacked and massacred the garrison. A few months later the last of the Crusaders was driven from the Holy Land.

During his ten-year reign, King Richard I of England, who spoke only French, spent just six months in England. Yet for his derring-do he has become, like King Arthur and Robin Hood, a romantic and essentially English hero. Does he deserve such reverence? His reign began with the sorry death of his father Henry II, an extremely good king, to whom he had behaved with determined disloyalty for many years.

Richard was crowned in Westminster Abbey, and the ceremony sparked a London mob to attack the local Jews. They knew the new king was off to save Jerusalem and, like crusade-enthusiasts all over Europe, they confused Muslims with Jews; all Christ-killers from their warped viewpoint. Richard's reaction was revealing. He had the London Jew-killers executed and allowed one Jew, who had survived by submission to conversion, to return to his own religion. This and his consistent treatment of both Jews and Muslims throughout his reign showed that he was neither anti-Semitic nor anti-Islam. The Jews were simply better than other Europeans at lending money, and the Muslims were merely another military enemy like, often enough, the French.

After Richard's successful siege of Saladin's forces at Acre, his army headed towards the main target of Jerusalem, harassed all the way by the Saracens, by thirst, disease, great heat, snakes, spiders and scorpions. Over the next year his men advanced twice to within sight of the Holy City but retreated on both occasions as they were too weak to take it.

It was time for Richard to cut his losses, particularly as back home his former partner in arms, the wily King Philip of France, was in cahoots with Richard's treacherous younger brother John. Philip wanted to expel the English from Normandy. John wanted the English throne. So Richard negotiated the Treaty of Jaffa with Saladin in 1192 which allowed Christian pilgrims safe entry to the Holy City in future. This was not exactly a triumph but it was better than nothing and the king set off to sort out home affairs.

Forced by a storm to land near Venice, he decided to travel overland via Austria to avoid hostile French territory. All went well until the royal party were recognised not far from Vienna and word of their presence reached Leopold, Duke of Austria. His men captured and imprisoned Richard, demanding a fortune in ransom money for his release. The politics of Europe were complex, and the Emperor of Germany soon paid up a large sum in order to gain a much larger one from the next bidder. Richard then languished in a German castle for some eighteen months, during which time John tried hard to ferment rebellion in

England, whilst Philip successfully took over big chunks of Richard's French empire.

The German emperor set the ransom at the equivalent of three tons of silver, or the total of three years of England's entire tax yields. Luckily for Richard, this was an amount that Philip and John, who would have loved to have transferred Richard into a French prison for life, could not sensibly afford. Somehow Richard's agents in England raised enough tax to pay the ransom and Richard agreed to an oath of alliance with his emperor captor. Once the money was handed over, Richard would be released.

A trusted group of barons under Chancellor William Longchamp, the bishop Richard had left in charge of his government in England, travelled to Germany in February 1194 with the ransom chests. My ancestor William de Saye II, his son Geoffrey and his father-in-law Geoffrey de Mandeville escorted the ransom out and the king back.

After a tumultuous English welcome, a re-crowning ceremony, a day's hunting in Sherwood Forest where, myth has it, he greeted Robin Hood, and a remarkably generous pardon of his treacherous brother John, Richard was off to Normandy to sort out his nemesis, King Philip of France. Both Geoffreys went too and stayed with him for his next four years of warfare, diplomacy, bribery and force of personality, by the end of which he had regained from the French king almost all the territory he had lost during his eighteen months in prison.

In the spring of 1199, during a minor siege operation, Richard was hit by a crossbow bolt and died of gangrene poisoning. He left his empire to his brother John, who had fought beside him over the past four years, together with three-quarters of his fortune. The rest he willed to loyal members of his retinue and to the needy. Although he spent a mere six months of his ten-year reign in England, he had selected a group of mostly brilliant ministers to govern in his absence. Despite the heavy taxation imposed to fund his crusading and Normandy campaigns, and despite the best efforts of John to cause trouble, the majority of the barons remained loyal to their absent king, and a highly efficient system of central government developed that was the envy of Europe.

5

'Across the reeds at Runnymede'

King John is portrayed by many teachers of English history as the worst of our kings by far – lecherous, treacherous, ugly and cruel. He had his men locate the money hoards of Jews by extracting their teeth, one by one, until they came clean and coughed up. On his accession he had only one obvious family rival, his twelve-year-old nephew Arthur, whose support lay with the barons of the Anjou region. At first Philip of France was friendly and the two kings signed a treaty of no interference the one with the other. But neither man trusted the other, and in 1202 the French armies poured into Normandy and Philip declared that the rest of John's lands in France were henceforward the property of Arthur.

John, with an army of mercenaries, managed to defeat and imprison his nephew in a tactical campaign worthy of his brother Richard, and gained some territory at the same time. But not for long. Philip's pressure was constant, and John resorted to murder, for he could see no chance of peace whilst Arthur still lived. History does not record quite how young Arthur died, but monastic chronicles relate that John ordered the baron in charge of the prison to blind and castrate the child and when this order was ignored, John himself, after a drunken dinner, murdered his nephew and dragged his body, lashed to a rock, into the Seine, where it was later found and recognised by a fisherman.

Philip gnawed away at the rest of John's Norman lands until, by the end of 1208, all Normandy was French, save for the Channel Islands. John, based back in England, reacted by confiscating the English lands of those who had accepted Philip as their king, an act which turned many of them from ambivalence towards him to outright hostility.

More to the point, he fell foul of the Pope, not the first English King to do so and by no means the last. John's choice for the prime job of Archbishop of Canterbury clashed with the Pope's nominee and, when John refused to accept the latter, the Pope excommunicated John and thus the English church for the next five years. This meant no official weddings, funerals or baptisms in churches, but nobody seemed to mind much.

Philip's invasion plans, now blessed by Rome, grew sufficiently ominous to alarm John into submitting to the Pope and even, in 1215, taking an oath to lead a papally-blessed crusade. This adroit move made England a bad place to invade if you feared, as the French did, papal wrath. Free from excommunication, John took his mercenaries back to France, where he did well for a while, but then suffered a catastrophic loss to Philip's forces at the battle of Bouvines. With very little land left outside England, John had no choice but to agree to a five-year truce with Philip and, back home, to concentrate on the threat of a major rebellion by hostile barons. There were several reasons for their unease, especially after John's major defeat in France.

Since the Norman Conquest, Anglo-Norman barons, including my Fiennes, Boulogne and Saye ancestors, had happily owned lands in and received annual income from various parts of England, whilst mostly basing themselves in Normandy. Now that their ancestral homes on the continent were owned by the French king, they had to make up their minds. Some stayed in France and lost their English properties, whilst others became solely English and wound up their affairs in Normandy.

Many officials who had enjoyed positions of power in Norman castles now headed for England and found a job shortage, which was exacerbated by John's habit of preferring jobs for his boys, meaning the officers of his many mercenary groups from various parts of France. To these foreigners he gave key castles, shires and other rich pickings.

The severance with Normandy also caused many barons to refuse to supply John with soldiers to fight outside England. This included involvement in the Fourth Crusade, which John had avoided and which had a poor attendance by the English. My ancestor Ingelram Fiennes I, the son of Eustace le Vieux, did join a Flemish contingent under Philip of Flanders and took his son, Thomas Fiennes, with him. This was a sad waste of Fiennes blood on a worse than pointless cause.

This Fourth Crusade was a shameful business. It was not even fought to kill Muslims or to recapture Jerusalem. The crusaders didn't get that far. Instead they set about destroying their fellow Christians, the Greek orthodox church in Constantinople. Ingelram disappeared during the crusade, and I imagine Thomas did too, since no record was ever traced of what exactly happened to either of them.

On the more positive side of military matters, John is often credited (as are three or four other kings) with having founded the English navy. Knowing that Philip was preparing a fleet to invade England, John had his own custom-built ships made in various ports and, in 1213, destroyed a major part of all Philip's navy with a surprise attack on the harbour of Damme, near modern-day Bruges. He seized three hundred French ships, a goodly haul for no loss of life.

John also built up an alliance with those French and Flemish coastal fiefs that had proved friendly to previous English kings. The most important of them was clearly Boulogne, the land of my ancestors. William Fiennes, grandson of Sibyl of Boulogne, had recently married Agnes de Danmartin, the sister of Count Renaud of Boulogne, and the count was a key ally of the English who, a year before the attack on Damme, came to London and paid homage to King John.

Philip was aware that the Counts of Boulogne were traditional anglophiles and, therefore, a weak French link and thought to put this right by marrying into the family. Arrangements were at one point made for his marriage to Maud of Boulogne, but the Boulogne marriage never came to fruition and, since the province was key to his plans for the invasion of England, Philip invited Count Renaud of Boulogne to a meeting at Vernon to woo him as an ally. This failed to work, for Renaud and his neighbour, the Count of Flanders, both visited King John in Lambeth in 1212 and again in 1214 and pledged themselves to a coalition with him. Philip's army attacked the Count of Flanders, but thanks to cousin Renaud's firm alliance with John, Philip never gained the best harbours for an invasion of England.

Early that year, John began to find out exactly which of the English-based barons he could count on. William Fiennes, Baron of Martock in Somerset, was a loyal supporter but John nonetheless reserved the power to take any Fiennes properties away at any time. William had been granted Martock in the first place as a favour from William of Boulogne, the son of King Stephen. But William, like many other barons, although a natural loyalist, was unhappy about the way he was so heavily taxed. So he wavered.

His cousin and friend, the hugely wealthy Geoffrey de Mandeville, Earl of Essex, was, however, virulently anti-John and, along with the Bishop of Hereford, sparked off a civil war by marching on the royalist castle at Northampton on 2 May 1215.

John, with his professional mercenary army, could have crushed the rebels at that point, and the Northampton garrison held out with ease. But John had no wish to provoke trouble, so he offered the rebels the chance of arbitration via a court with four of their men and four of his, plus a papal deputy to chair the event. He further promised to arrest none of them nor confiscate their land. He then offered the two leaders, de Mandeville and the Bishop of Hereford, personal olive branches, by promising to withdraw the huge fines he had recently imposed on them. Both men turned down the king's offer, for they and their rebel colleagues had the bit between their teeth and were spoiling for a fight. Two days later John ordered their estates to be seized, and the civil war began.

The general conception of many people today is that King John and his immediate cronies, with mercenary support, faced the massed aristocracy of England, but this is not the reality. At the time only forty barons and their vassals supported the rebels, and they came from different, often dispersed counties. Fathers, sons and brothers were in many cases split for or against the rebels. Even William Marshall, England's most respected warrior and statesman, loyal at all times to his monarch, had a son amongst the rebels.

The king's support came largely from the south-west and the midlands, but the most influential group were neutralists who, through the Archbishop of Canterbury, hoped to avoid war through discussion. Things may well have been different if John had had some dynastic rival hovering in the wings, but his own two sons were mere children, and no other figurehead existed for the rebels to promote. So they championed a new focus for their uprising; a people's charter, to right the wrongs to which they had been subjected by John, by Richard and by Henry II, mainly through unbearably heavy taxation for the endless Plantagenet wars.

John's patience grew thin, and he called up more mercenaries, this time from Wales, but after the rebels had occupied London William Marshall and the Archbishop of Canterbury rode back and forth between king and rebels to effect a meeting and a truce. This eventually worked in the form of an agreed safe passage for all concerned to a wide Thames-side meadow called Runnymede.

The meeting began on a glorious June day, and some say a thousand people attended. The twenty-five barons' or signatories' self-appointed task was to gain the king's agreement, seal and subsequent adherence to their charter of rights. Peace, it was hoped by the neutralists, would be the result. John hoped merely to gain time by affixing his seal and then ignoring it. The barons, believing he would either refuse to sign or sign and then renege, were ready for battle to follow.

The charter, possibly the work of the archbishop himself and his legal advisers, formed a legal and constitutional document which bound the king and all his successors to fully respect the liberties of his subjects, as stated in the charter's sixty-three clauses. These included forty-nine specific grievances. Once the full text had been prepared in the Royal Chancery and sealed with the Royal Seal, copies of this Magna Carta were sent out all over the land.

Four of the originals survive to this day, two in the British Library, one in Salisbury, and the other in Lincoln Cathedral. In 1987, the two hundredth anniversary of the American constitution, the Dean of Lincoln, my cousin Oliver Fiennes, younger brother of Lord Saye and Sele and descendant of the signatory Baron Saye, arranged to exhibit his cathedral's eight hundred-year-old copy of the charter all over the United States, where (since it forms the basis of the American Bill of Rights) it received great acclaim and interest. Cousin Oliver raised funds for Lincoln Cathedral on the side by selling tea imported by the very firm whose tea had been thrown into Boston Harbour back in 1773.

Cynics like to point out that the barons were actually only wanting an agreement to preserve their own baronial rights and to hell with the serfs. This is, of course, true, and the three members of my family who were signatories at Runnymede would surely agree and see nothing wrong with that. They were the rebel leader, Geoffrey de Mandeville, Henri de Bohun of Hereford and Baron Geoffrey de Saye (who had helped ransom King Richard from the Germans eleven years earlier).

The cynics notwithstanding, the Magna Carta, as the charter came to be called, is recognised worldwide as being the most significant and earliest influence on the historical process which led to the rule of constitutional law today. Government must be responsible to the governed. It also famously proclaimed: 'We will sell to no man, we will not deny or defer to any man either justice or right.'

It is still referred to in the twenty-first century as the bedrock of various legal arguments. In the year 2003, in the international court case of the Chagos islanders, compulsorily removed from their islands by Britain to facilitate the US military base on Diego Garcia, the islanders' counsel used the argument of 'unlawful exile', which he claimed was 'based on rights derived from Magna Carta'.

On leaving Runnymede the cunning John sent messages to the Pope complaining about the barons' infringement of his rights as the Pope's man in England, and in due course received exactly the papal reply he had hoped for which completely annulled the charter, 'this shameful and demeaning agreement, forced upon the King by violence and fear', and threatened anyone who might impede King John's papally-approved royal powers.

John had clearly signed and sealed Magna Carta under duress, and English custom as well as the law recognised that oaths taken in such a manner were meaningless. The majority of the barons in the country were not at Runnymede and would have been shocked, if they had been, by the revolutionary nature of the conditions forced on their king by the charter. There was also a large section of the aristocracy with personal and dynastic interests which dictated their loyalty to the monarch and to his young son and heir.

The man with a weak but existing link to the throne, who the rebels now chose to support, was King Philip of France's son Prince Louis, who built up a fleet across the Channel. John also sent for more mercenary troops from the continent to strengthen his army. By September 1215, awaiting his new troops at Dover, John listed the barons he believed to be on his side, including Baron William Fiennes. William had, however, decided to join the standard of Prince Louis, so John had him blacklisted as 'being with the King's enemies' and confiscated his properties in Somerset. William's cousin, and arch-enemy of John, Geoffrey de Mandeville, was killed at that time in a jousting match.

Since his new navy had been so successful at Damme, John decided to cross the Channel and bottle up Louis with his fleet in Calais. But a storm ruined his plan and, in May 1216, Louis landed unopposed and laid siege to John's headquarters in Winchester. William Fiennes, soon after joining Louis's army, decided for reasons unknown but, judging by other accounts of the time, due to the great arrogance of the French prince, to switch back to supporting King John. As a result, in September John gave him back his Somerset possessions.

By then the two armies were circling each other like snarling cats, neither with a clear advantage. In October 1216, crossing a swollen tidal river by the Wash, John's wagons containing the royal treasure and crown jewels were snatched away by the current. That night John went down with a severe attack of dysentery and soon died.

Had he lived and defeated the rebels, John would certainly have rendered Magna Carta a toothless and soon to be forgotten event. But his successors were to reissue the charter, slightly modified but legally binding. Within fifty years of John's death the first real English Parliament was to emerge.

John's loss of Normandy led to his title being altered from that shared with his Norman predecessors of 'King of the Anglo-Normans' to 'King of England'. English Normans were now simply English, even though their switch from use of the French tongue would take a touch longer. Normandy was now just another French province and England an isolated kingdom with no meaningful empire. However, in the year 2009, over two million British people own French properties, and, in the Channel Islands, the Queen of England still has the title of Duke of Normandy. After the loss of Normandy, some Fienneses and some Sayes saw themselves as solely French, whilst others became truly English citizens, and I will now, with one or two exceptions, focus on the English branch.

6

Marriages of Convenience

The rebel barons of England failed to capitalise on the death of King John because his nine-year-old son Henry III was crowned with alacrity by the royalist clique with solid support from two main areas of England, the south-west and the midlands.

The chief authorities in the land, Hubert de Burgh and William the Marshal, were sound strategists, knew their barons and saw that the young prince was a feeble-minded child who would be putty in the hands of his enemies if given sole charge of the country. With this in mind, de Burgh and the Marshal ensured that Prince Henry remained under close tuition (their shorthand for supervision) until he was in his mid-twenties. They also re-issued the Magna Carta soon after Henry's accession, despite the fact that it had been annulled by the Pope, which adroit move pulled the carpet from beneath the feet of those barons with rebellious inclinations.

One of the young Henry's most faithful supporters was my great to the power of twenty-four grandfather, Ingelram Fiennes II. In King John's reign he had held the top post of Constable of Dover Castle, and on Henry's accession he was made a Knight of the Bath and became the highest paid official in the royal household. Ingelram's second son Giles married Sibyl, the beautiful eleven-year-old daughter of the Filiol family who owned the manor of Old Court in Wartling, near Pevensey. On the night of 30 August 1223, seven years into Henry's reign, Sibyl was kidnapped by thugs and for three years was taken from one hiding place to another by a suitor named Richard Pageham, who had, so he said, been previously promised her hand in marriage by her parents. In the subsequent court case Pageham defended his actions by claiming that Sibyl's parents had given him 'the marriage, guardianship and nourishment' of Sibyl, after her father's death, for the sum of two hundred marks, of which he had already paid six marks. Perhaps Pageham was robbed of his rightful nuptials by my ancestor, Giles, her parents deciding he was a better bet for their daughter's future.

The case dragged on for years and is the first detailed record I can find of a personal event in the life of one of my early ancestors' families. Whatever its outcome, elder brother William was to become a favourite, like his father Ingelram, of King Henry III, who appointed him to oversee the education of his heir, the young Prince Edward.

Since most of the Anglo-Norman barons had spent much of their time (and now all of their time) in England for the past two hundred years, they not only felt English rather than French, but they were no longer much interested in the goings-on over the Channel. They became inward-looking and scarcely minded when Prince Louis, on becoming King Louis VIII of France, captured the remaining English possessions of Poitou and La Rochelle. Now only Gascony remained as 'English' land in France.

Henry would, in due course, try to defend Gascony, but back in 1225 he and his advisers were focused entirely on home affairs, in particular their attempts to avoid rebellion by the troublesome barons. To this end they proclaimed, with much song and dance and 'by the king's own spontaneous good will', a new and generous version of Magna Carta, and this 1225 charter was officially lodged in the statutes of the realm.

Henry III's heir, Prince Edward, was born in Westminster and named after the king's favourite saint, the last of the Anglo-Saxon kings, Edward the Confessor. Giles Fiennes, son of Ingelram, was brought up and educated alongside the young prince. In 1254, aged only fifteen, Prince Edward was sent to Spain to marry the nine-year-old Eleanor of Castile, and shortly before this arranged marriage King Henry gave him Gascony, the last remaining English province in France, along with parts of Wales and Ireland. Edward spent 1255 in Gascony and, when he left, Henry put his chancellor, Michael Fiennes, in charge there with his brother, Baldwin Fiennes, and a small army.

To keep Louis of France from predatory moves in the direction of Gascony, Henry agreed the Treaty of Paris with the French king and was, as a result, able to concentrate on the long festering trouble with the barons which by 1259 was about to burst into a new civil war. A sworn confederation of the most influential barons in England was mobilising its local armies against the government, and their main grievance, which had simmered and flared for nigh on a quarter of a century, was Henry's choice of advisers from a family circle, most of whom were recently arrived from the continent. It was the familiar old grudge against immigrants taking native jobs. Of course, the vast majority of these 'foreigners' were in reality Normans or Anglo-Normans switching their permanent domicile from France to England. But Prince Edward's young wife, Eleanor of Castile, naturally brought with her to her strange new country as many of her own friends and relatives as possible, the majority of whom were found positions of influence and wealth.

Ingelram Fiennes (whose mother was Eleanor's great aunt) would also count as a foreigner as far as the barons were concerned, and he rubbed a good deal of salt into their wound by marrying his son and heir, William Fiennes, to Blanche, the first cousin and personal friend of Prince Edward's wife Eleanor. Once settled into the ways of the English court, Eleanor generously and actively arranged top-class marriages for her Fiennes kin. This she continued to do for the rest of Henry's rule and well into her husband's.

Although the barons' anger was largely fanned by Henry's nepotism, it was a specific scheme, encouraged by the Pope, to make his second son Edmund into the King of Sicily that finally caused the barons to take the government out of Henry's hands. Henry's folly was to tell the Pope that he would finance the conquest of Sicily. A crippling tax burden on the barons would be the only way he could go ahead with such a plan, and this was the final straw.

Civil war did not break out at that point, which was a miracle partly due to Henry's non-aggressive, some say weak, character. An elected body, the Council of Twenty-four under the moderate guidance of the baronial leader Simon de Montfort, took all governmental decisions out of reach of the king, which can clearly be described as a revolutionary process. It was known as the Provisions of Oxford, and arranged for all Henry's Sicilian-linked debts to be met by the English taxpayer in exchange for a raft of reforms. For five years de Montfort and his barons fought the royalist clique by parliamentary means, but the king's intransigence eventually led to open civil war.

One of de Montfort's main supporters and planners was his son Henry, who, on a cross-Channel mission for his father, was arrested by William de Saye III, the Constable of Rochester Castle, and shut up in a Boulogne jail. Political pressure by the barons soon freed this young de Montfort, who returned to England in time to join his father's victorious army at the Battle of Lewes in 1264, where he fought against his neighbour, Sir Giles Fiennes.

Fighting valiantly by the side of Prince Edward was William de Saye, Lord of Sele (a village in Kent), who was famous for having captured six knights single-handed at the Battle of Saintes. At Lewes his fighting prowess was clearly not enough to prevent de Montfort's men winning the day and imprisoning Prince Edward as a hostage to guarantee the king's future subservience to the dictates of Parliament.

For the next sixteen months de Montfort assured himself a

place in English history by inventing and establishing the first elected and regional parliamentary democracy, while he himself remained content with the role of merely guiding the government, and with the modest title of Steward of England. Nonetheless many barons soon began to feel that he was swinging too far to the left (in today's parlance) and feared that they had unleashed a popular force that might quickly threaten their own positions of power. So, when Prince Edward escaped and raised a royalist army, de Montfort's baronial force was severely depleted. The two armies met at Evesham, where it was noted that cousin Ingelram Fiennes 'distinguished himself by his valour'. Prince Edward's much larger force annihilated the parliamentarians, and when the royalists located de Montfort's body among the heaped corpses of his men, a thunderstorm raged whilst they cut off his head, his limbs and his testicles as trophies to award to the main royalist generals.

De Montfort's head was displayed on London Bridge until it rotted, but his legacy to the English people lasted down the centuries, for it provided the first glimmerings of true democracy without the trauma of a bloody revolution. There would be another ten Plantagenet kings but, in terms of their post-1264 autocratic power, they would be as impaired as the genitalia-reduced de Montfort.

For the last seven years of his reign King Henry lapsed slowly into senility, and England was ruled by Prince Edward or, in his absence, his well-chosen ministers. He focused on reconciling the king and the barons, relieving the populace most affected by the years of bad harvest and famine and adopting most of de Montfort's social reform programmes.

Once Prince Edward was confident that even the most troublesome barons were quiescent and the populace reasonably content with their government, he decided to indulge in his long-cherished wish to join a crusade to the Holy Land. He took 1,000 soldiers, including 150 selected trusted knights, and appointed his most loyal supporters to responsible positions in government during his absence. These included, as his chancellor, Michael Fiennes, the brother of King Henry's senior official, Ingelram Fiennes.

Prince Edward and Eleanor set off on crusade in August 1270 with the intention of joining up with the crusading army of the French King Louis IX, St Louis, in the Holy Land. Louis and his impressive French army landed in Tunis and did well against their Muslim opponents until, stricken by a virulent plague, they ran out of steam and, when Louis himself succumbed to the plague, his entire army surrendered. One French general described the onset of this plague: 'The skin became covered with black and earth-coloured spots, just like an old boot . . . the flesh on our gums began to rot away.' One of St Louis' close companions on this disastrous eighth and last crusade was William Fiennes, who is shown in the crusade records as having 'nine knights' and as having 'dined in the King's lodging'.

When Prince Edward's tiny contingent of knights arrived in Acre, there was no longer a French force to join. Nonetheless he stayed in the Holy Land for over a year, making minor raids, supported by the Fiennes brothers William and Giles after Louis's death. Much of the crusade would have involved heat, disease and boredom, but excitements did occur, including a near-successful attempt on Prince Edward's life by an assassin, an agent of a secret order of Shiite Muslims. Eleanor is said to have sucked the poison from her husband's stab wounds and saved his life.

Back in England, after a reign of fifty-six years, King Henry III died, his last few years spent focused entirely on the rebuilding of Westminster Abbey as a memorial to its original founder, his hero Edward the Confessor.

Ingelram Fiennes, and his brothers Baldwin and Chancellor Michael, had all served Henry with loyalty and distinction throughout his struggles with the barons and his various campaigns in Gascony. The highs and the lows of what being in the constant service of a medieval monarch might involve can be seen from the family records of another kinsman, William de Saye III. He distinguished himself on expeditions in France, he witnessed charters and agreements, parcels of his lands were confiscated one minute and restored the next, he was allowed weekly markets and annual fairs, he was granted the right to hunt the wolf, hare, fox, cat and otter in certain of the king's forests 'if he take none of the king's deer', he was ordered to join the king's army at Shrewsbury, summoned to Windsor, to Westminster, to Oxford with horses and arms, he fought in the Battle of Lewes. He died in 1272, the same year as the king he had served so well for over forty years, and his heir was his son, William de Saye IV.

7

Dangerous Liaisons

Prince Edward was heading slowly home from his crusade when news reached him of his father's death. He took this in a very relaxed way and did not rush back home, as might have been expected. He had, after all, been proclaimed king in his absence, the barons had sworn allegiance to him, there was no rival claimant to his throne, and he was enjoying himself with his beloved Eleanor in interesting places. Everywhere he went he was acclaimed as a great crusader and 'the best lance in the world'.

He lingered in Italy, Sicily, southern France and Paris, and finally arrived in London to be crowned two years after his father's death. A good many kings, before and after him, would have sped home apprehensive of being usurped, but Edward I's position was unusually secure for a medieval monarch. He was an energetic leader with charisma and a violent temper. Capable of cruelty, arrogance and intolerance, he was also a faithful husband and, above all, a good, successful king. England was ruled in his initial absence by his nominees, and he had chosen well for they acted as his loyal regents and Edward I returned in 1274 to a peaceful realm.

Even before his crusading prowess, Edward had gained a reputation as a brave and skilled martial arts fighter. Tournaments were then, as football matches are today, highly popular spectacles, but jousting was dangerous even for the great and the bold. Henry II of France, for example, died when the splinter from a shattered lance pierced his eye. And the Earl of Salisbury killed his own son in a 'friendly' joust.

The Fiennes family, though not yet entwined with the Sayes, were doing well in their adopted land of England. Giles Fiennes, who had for so long enjoyed his enviable position in King Henry's household, benefited further through the marriage of his son, sister and daughters to various wealthy personages. Son John married the daughter of the Head Forester of Windsor Forest, and thereby gained an estate in Berkshire and two in Oxfordshire. Sister Maud married Humphrey de Bohun, Earl of Hereford and Essex and Constable of England. Maud Fiennes is referred to in the royal records as 'the noble damsel Maud, cousin of Queen Eleanor', and Eleanor, who appears to have personally arranged the match, agreed to pay Humphrey de Bohun £3,000 in instalments for which Maud's brother, William Fiennes, was to reimburse her. The fruits of Maud's marriage to this noble earl included two sons, who between them were to be largely responsible for a major defeat of the English army. But more of that later.

Giles's elder daughter, Margaret Fiennes, married Edmund Mortimer, and their eldest son Roger would later murder King Edward II. Their daughter would marry the Black Prince. Giles's second daughter, Joanna Fiennes, married Lord John Wake, Earl of Kent, and their daughter Margaret would later marry Edmund, Edward I's younger brother.

King Edward spent a great deal of time riding around his kingdom with Queen Eleanor in the baggage train. Despite this state of almost continuous travel, she bore him thirteen children, of whom four were sons. Three of these died young, and the youngest (Edward II to be) was born in Wales during one of his father's ongoing Welsh campaigns. He was known as Prince Edward of Caernarfon and grew up to be a foppish wimp. One of his guardians was Giles Fiennes' son, John, who the prince described in a letter in 1305 as '*consanguineus et alumnus meus*' – 'my cousin and teacher'.

King Edward's first priority was to mould the disparate parts of his kingdom into a single country under the rule of the crown, starting with Wales, whose leader, Prince Llewelyn I, was killed by Edward's men in 1282. The reason no previous English army had finally crushed the Welsh was mainly due to the mountainous terrain in the north, but Edward did not let this deter him. His navy blockaded the North Wales coast and his army was as big or bigger than any previously assembled in Britain by a king; over 15,000 men including 9,000 from South Wales.

Llewelyn's main supporter, Rhys Vychan, quickly surrendered to Humphrey de Bohun, Maud Fiennes' husband, who passed him on to the Tower of London for safekeeping.

In the king's army during the Welsh campaigns were two more of my kin. Giles Fiennes (whose swans were all stolen from his Wartling manor while he was away) and William Saye's younger brother, John.

Llewelyn's brother, Dafydd, carried on fighting, but was caught the next year and executed. The chronicles described his death, the first British political prisoner to be hanged, drawn and quartered.

> David was first drawn as a traitor, then hanged as a thief. Thirdly he was disembowelled alive and his entrails burnt as an incendiary and a homicide. Fourthly his limbs were cut into four parts as the penalty of a rebel. His right arm was sent to York, the left arm to Bristol, the right leg with hip to Northampton and the left leg to Hereford. The villain's head was bound with iron bands lest it should fall to pieces from putrefaction. This head was stuck upon a long spear for the mockery of London.

With both rebel leaders dead, Edward ensured that the status of Wales as an independent principality came to an end, and its land, like all England's, was divided up into shires ruled by English law. To ensure against further trouble, Edward built eight great castles along the Welsh border.

In 1286 he turned his attention to his lands in Gascony in the far south of France. He spent the next three years living there and avoided war with his arch-enemy Philip IV, the King of France, until in 1294 the latter brazenly attacked Gascony and forced Edward into a series of skirmishes which reclaimed only a part of the province for England, and an uneasy peace ensued. Edward's army in Gascony was led by his brother Edmund (married to Joanna Fiennes), whose close adviser, one of his officers, was William Saye.

Although Edward is remembered today as the Hammer of the Scots, he never actually managed to subdue them, as he so successfully had the Welsh. The royal house of Scotland had intermarried with my ancestors when Eustace III of Boulogne had wed a daughter of King Malcolm III of Scotland. (Their daughter Matilda had then married King Stephen of England.) Malcolm III's descendant, Malcolm IV, had a great great granddaughter who, King Edward I hoped, would marry his own son, Prince Edward, and thereby secure a family pact between the two countries.

When this plan failed to materialise, various Norman-Scottish barons who controlled lowland Scotland disputed which of them should inherit the throne of Scotland; the Bruce clan being the chief claimants. When their current king, Alexander of Scotland, died, the claimant barons called on King Edward I to arbitrate as to which dynasty should take over the Scottish monarchy. Edward duly nominated John Balliol as being the closest relative to royalty, and he was crowned. One of Edward's unnecessarily arrogant terms imposed on Balliol was that he should make no legal decision of any import without his, Edward's, advice. This naturally offended the proud Scottish barons who soon felt that Balliol should rebel against Edward. They therefore tried to put Robert Bruce (grandfather of King Robert the Bruce) on the throne whilst Edward was busy in Gascony in 1296.

Balliol decided to invoke the French on to his side against Edward; the Auld Alliance. With this in place, he felt strong enough to face Edward, so he renounced all previous agreements that he had made with the English. A furious Edward I, back from Gascony, caught up with Balliol's supporters in their stronghold, the border town of Berwick-upon-Tweed. When Balliol refused to parley, Edward stormed the town and, in the accepted practice of the time, spent three days killing over 7,000 of the inhabitants. Giles Fiennes was there, and I sincerely hope that he took no part in the killings. It was Britain's worst ever massacre, and Edward only called off his killers on watching a defenceless woman being hacked to death.

Balliol himself, a weak and vacillatory man, left Scotland and, after a brief sojourn in the Tower of London, retired for good to France. At this stage, instead of placing one of the other Norman-Scottish claimants on the vacant throne, Edward stupidly appointed three English bureaucrats as regents. He then left them to it.

A year later an outlaw knight, William Wallace (who has today, thanks to Mel Gibson's *Braveheart* film, greatly boosted the popularity of the Scottish National Party), raised the Scottish standard and reconquered the entire country, bar one or two border towns, within a year.

A few months later Edward was back with an army of 25,000 soldiers and defeated the Scots at the battle of Falkirk. Wallace escaped but was captured eight years later and executed in London. He became a Scottish martyr and has never been overshadowed by his successor, the next Scottish 'rebel' Robert the Bruce, himself a descendant of Norman invaders, who after a long and arduous campaign would finally defeat the English. But not until after the death of Scotland's nemesis, King Edward I, the Hammer of the Scots.

Lord John Wake, the eldest son of Joanna Fiennes, who, like Giles Fiennes, had been present at the massacre of Berwick, was a captain under the Bishop of Durham during the battle of Falkirk where he was killed. Joanna's sister, Margaret Fiennes, chose unfortunate husbands, the first being John Comyn of Badenoch, the Red Comyn, nephew of the exiled Balliol and possible claimant to the Scottish throne, who was murdered in a church by Robert the Bruce shortly before the latter was crowned King of Scotland. Margaret Fiennes' next husband was the youngest son of King Edward I, Edmund, who was beheaded in the reign of Edward III. Margaret's daughter Joan married Edward, Prince of Wales who died in 1376 and by whom she was mother to King Richard II who was executed at Pontefract Castle.

Despite all the husbandly deaths, Margaret Fiennes still managed to spawn the kings who led both the House of York and the House of Lancaster.

When Robert the Bruce defied Edward in 1306 the English king was sixty-eight years old and sick. But he raised another army and headed north yet again. He made it as far as Carlisle, where he died. Prince Edward of Caernarfon, his only son, was quickly crowned, but he was far too feeble a character to continue the Scottish campaign.

With Edward I and, some years previously, his wife Eleanor both dead and buried, the close relationship between the royal family and the Fiennes family wavered for a while but, unfortunately for the new king, Edward II, did not entirely vanish.

In England Edward I is still remembered as a great king. He maintained both the spirit of Magna Carta and many of the additional canons introduced by his old and vanquished enemy, Simon de Montfort, which expanded the number of people summoned to the parleys or Parliaments that Edward held twice a year. The motive behind many of Edward I's laws and his setting up of ever larger assemblies was the need to collect huge sums of money for his Welsh, French and Scottish campaigns. This worked well to begin with, but by the latter part of his reign, failed miserably to the point where, in chronic debt, he was refused help by the clergy, the Archbishop of Canterbury threatened him with excommunication, and the barons, some of whom refused to fight for him, began to mutter mutiny. Nonetheless he introduced many good new laws and promoted both the uniform administration of justice and the exposure of abuse by officials.

In terms of foreign conquests, always of importance to the reputations of medieval kings, Edward I held Wales, but not Scotland, and lost very little land in France, which was not difficult since, after his father Henry's reign, there was very little left to lose. In 1303 he successfully arranged a treaty with the French whereby the previously confiscated parts of Gascony were all restored to English rule, but his various attempts to spin a web of alliances to balance the power of France were generally ill-conceived or unlucky, and one, with the traditional allies of England, Boulogne and Flanders, ended with his earning the sobriquet '*perfidus anglorum rex*', the perfidious King of England, when he did a political about-turn, leaving both provinces at the mercy of the French.

Boulogne was soon to become an integral part of France, but the Flemings revolted in 1302 and, at the Battle of Courtrai, the 'Battle of the Golden Spurs', they astounded everyone by defeating a French army that included 2,000 mounted knights, the flower of the French cavalry, with a ragbag of Flemish foot soldiers armed with long spears. Helped by marshy ground, the Flemings not only withstood the French attack, but routed their fabled knights. They took no prisoners, and some contemporary accounts put the overall casualties at 10,000 dead, which included about 40 per cent of the aristocracy of France. One Fiennes who died that day on the French side was that William, son of Ingelram, who all those years before had accompanied Prince Edward and Queen Eleanor on their first crusade to the Holy Land. Flanders never became a part of France, and the date of the Battle of Courtrai is still celebrated in modern-day Belgium as a national holiday.

Edward II began his reign aged twenty-three, popular enough with his people but hampered by the legacy his father had left him, which consisted of huge debts, a war with Scotland which looked unwinnable and, worst of all, great expectations that he would be as powerful a character as his father.

He started badly by promoting the son of a Gascon noble named Piers Gaveston to ever more exalted positions of power and wealth in England. Rumour was rife that Edward was not only gay but, worse still for a king, on the receiving, passive end of a loving relationship with Gaveston. The more outrageous the favours, especially the Earldom of Cornwall, that Edward bestowed on this 'foreigner', as the Barons scathingly termed him, the more unpopular both men became.

A suitable marriage seemed to the king's dwindling band of loyal supporters to be the best way of ousting Gaveston and, at the same time with luck, cementing a sound relationship with some powerful royal family. When Edward II was still a young prince, his father had betrothed him to Philippa, a daughter of the Count of Flanders, and, when she had died young, to her beautiful sister Isabella.

At this point we need to take a closer look at John Fiennes, the son of William who was killed at the battle of Courtrai, for John was to become the lover of Isabella. His father William, who had gone to the crusades first with Saint Louis and then with Edward I, had taken the French side when trouble with the French reignited, and Edward had confiscated his land. A little later peace broke out and William was given back his land. After his death at Courtrai, there were disputes as to whether his son and heir, John, should inherit his English lands because, the records state, he was born 'beyond the seas' and had spent much time in France. All we know of son John (who did get his father's lands at some point) was that as a young man he was unruly when visiting his properties in the English west country. There exists a record of King Edward I writing to the Bishop of Exeter asking him to be gracious to John when John comes to ask for a pardon for 'breaking up the Bishop's property'. A further record, a few years later, accuses John with a gang of others of breaking John de Foscle's dyke at Asherugge in Wiltshire and felling his trees.

Both John and his brother Robert were involved in the post-Courtrai period, fighting for the French against frequent border raids by the ebullient Flemings. On one occasion French troops under John's command cornered and destroyed a large group of raiders. Following negotiations to end the fighting, John, acting for the French, became very friendly with the Count of Flanders, the father of Isabella, then betrothed (in lieu of her dead sister Philippa) to Edward II. John, therefore, saw quite a lot of Isabella.

At the same time, the King of France was using John as a royal commissioner to negotiate with King Edward about various disputes. At Broughton Castle, the Fiennes home for the past six hundred years, there is a record of a letter, in French, from John to the King of England on behalf of Philip of France.

At some point John Fiennes fell in love with Isabella of Flanders, the story of which may well have shocked both French and Flemings and is well described by the chronicle of Brother Mineur of Ghent. Luckily for John, his affair and subsequent marriage worried neither Philip nor Edward because, in a separate treaty, they betrothed each other's children to one another, Isabella of France to Prince Edward of England. From then on John became a favourite of King Philip, and when Edward II wished to do business with the Count of Flanders, he treated John as the count's equal.

In 1308, a year after Edward II became king, he went to France to marry Isabella and made the serious mistake of appointing Piers Gaveston as regent in his absence. This naturally infuriated the barons and was not improved by the arrogant behaviour of Gaveston. Soon afterwards and not far short of open rebellion, the barons enforced Gaveston's exile.

Edward somehow wheedled the return of Gaveston in 1309 to be his main man in Ireland, where he did surprisingly well subduing minor insurrections. But back in England he was as arrogant as ever, and this time the full hatred of the barons was directed by the most powerful magnate in the land, the Earl of

Lancaster, who determined to control the king and to preserve baronial powers. In 1311 he and his councillors drew up a series of ordinances to achieve his aims. The king spent the rest of his life trying to circumvent or ride roughshod over such curbs on his powers.

In 1312 one of Lancaster's cronies murdered Gaveston. He was mourned only by the king. In the words of a chronicler: 'Anon he had home his love Piers of Gaveston and did him great reverence and worshipped and made him great and rich. Of this doing fell villainy to the lover, evil speech and backbiting to the love, slander to the people, harm and damage to the realm.'

Gaveston's murder saved the land from almost certain civil war. Edward must have, briefly at least, climbed into bed with Isabella long enough to conceive a son and heir – or maybe John Fiennes did it for him. In any event, another little Prince Edward was born to the joy of the nation. Meanwhile, trouble a plenty was brewing north of the border, and Edward was lucky that the ever opportunistic Philip of France was focused on home matters at the time, busy annihilating the Knights Templar.

Whilst that was going on in France, Edward finally gathered an army to crush Robert the Bruce, who, ever since his murder of Margaret Fiennes' first husband, John Comyn, had gradually reduced virtually all the English strongholds north of the border, save for a few great castles. His initially small band of followers might be described as forerunners of the SAS, for they disdained sieges, preferring silent night raids with ladders, which proved highly successful, and his popularity helped swell his forces into a real army.

The most important stronghold that did not succumb to the Bruce's ladder-by-night methods was Stirling Castle, which the Scots therefore had to besiege in the traditional cumbersome manner. Edward's aim was to crush the Scottish army and to relieve Stirling Castle, and he set out northwards with confidence. Disaster ensued. The two armies met in a wood two miles from the castle and on a part of the Forth plain dissected by marshy streams. A place called Bannockburn. Not good for heavy cavalry, but a big plus for the Scottish army.

The Scots fielded a mere third the strength of Edward's force, but by clever tactics, a forest of sharp stakes held by foot soldiers, and especially by using the local geography in the same way as the Flemish had against the superior French force at Courtrai, they won the day with a massive victory, well followed up by efficiently killing off the vanquished English as they retreated through enemy country.

Edward II himself is surprisingly reported to have 'fought like a lion'. Parted from his shield-bearer, he lost his horse only to grab another and head anew for the heart of the fray. But once defeat was obvious, he and a small group managed to retreat to the still English-held redoubt of Dunbar, and thence by ferry to the border at Berwick.

Maud Fiennes, as you may recall, had married Humphrey de Bohun, Earl of Hereford during Edward I's reign. They had two sons, the elder of whom, another Humphrey, commanded the English army at Bannockburn and was captured by the Scots. His younger brother Henry was also partly responsible for the outcome of the battle by having himself sparked off an ill-timed and disastrous cavalry charge which turned possible success into a massacre of English knights.

Whether or not this can be said to have altered Anglo-Scottish history, who can say? But Robert the Bruce managed to ransom Humphrey for £200,000, a vast sum, plus the return from England of his own queen, his sister and his daughter. Once Robert the Bruce was crowned, the Scots would remain firmly independent for three hundred years until King James VI of Scotland became James I of England, at which point both nations were ruled from London by Scotsmen (just like nowadays).

Edward's tiny force arrived back in London where the king's main opponent, the Earl of Lancaster, bound Edward to adhere minutely to the ordinances that he and his cronies had previously installed in Parliament but which the king had, prior to the disaster of Bannockburn, largely ignored. Lancaster was not interested in the good of the country at large so much as the retention, and indeed the increase, of his personal powers. But he was a skilled PR man and for a while he was backed by the barons, the church and the people. He appointed himself as King's Councillor, checking every move the king made. Monarchical power was then at a very low ebb.

In October 1321 an event occurred which sparked off Edward's escape from the puppet string controls of Lancaster. Queen Isabella, on a personal pilgrimage to Canterbury, desired to spend a night at Leeds Castle in Kent. To her understandable anger, the governor of the castle, Lord Badelsmere (or rather his wife, since he was away at the time) refused her entry to the castle due to fear of Lancaster's reaction. He might, she presumably thought, assume that the Badelsmeres were in secret cahoots with royalty and sack her husband from his job.

A furious Isabella told her escort to storm the castle. They were unsuccessful and six were killed. Isabella complained to Edward who sent the ever-faithful Geoffrey de Saye to arrest and try all those responsible for the Isabella incident. One way or another the king found himself unexpectedly the popular man of the moment with many normally neutral barons right behind him due to this apparently minor event of discourtesy against the monarch. His force laid siege to Leeds Castle which surrendered in a week. Badelsmere and sixty-three of his garrison were hanged.

Minor clashes followed shortly between King Edward's group and the mixed forces of Lancaster, the Mortimers of the Marches, and others of the king's enemies. In May 1322 both armies had swollen and met up at Boroughbridge, north of York. The result gave Edward his first meaningful victory over his key opponents. He had Lancaster executed, along with his chief associates and all those previously implicated in the murder of Piers Gaveston. Others, including Roger Mortimer, captured just prior to Boroughbridge, were imprisoned in the Tower. Mortimer was the son of Margaret Fiennes, and Edward would have done well to have executed him while he had the chance. Another bitter enemy of the king was Lord Thomas Wake, the son of Joanna Fiennes, Margaret's sister, but he also escaped arrest.

Edward generously rewarded those few individuals who had remained constantly loyal through the dark Lancaster years, including Geoffrey de Saye, who had been at Edward's side since he was a prince in his teens and fought for him both against the Scots and against Lancaster. In 1318 Geoffrey had briefly been jailed 'for consorting with the outlaw Robert Coleman', but Edward soon had him released and fully returned to royal favour.

Also loyal to Edward, and to his father before him, with a few exceptions over the years, was Giles Fiennes who had arrived in England as a young, penniless cousin of Queen Eleanor, bride of Edward I, and had been appointed to her household. By the time of his death, just prior to Boroughbridge, his descendants were well established with at least six large estates in England. He was the first Fiennes to establish himself as an English, rather than an Anglo-Norman, resident. After him there were English Fienneses and French ones. You had to make your mind up quickly or it was made up for you. The records note: 'Moreover, John Fiennes had the living of the manor of Wendover but, being afterwards attainted for adhering to the French, he lost all.'

Edward used his post-Boroughbridge success and his recovery of power to repeal those of Lancaster's ordinances that had rendered him virtually impotent, but not those that favoured the populace in general. Unfortunately, Edward adhered to the rule that leopards never change their spots. He developed an unnaturally close friendship with an adviser, Hugh Despenser and his son (Hugh Junior) in much the same manner as he had with Gaveston. The Despensers were given wealth and power. A chronicler of that time, one Lanercost, observed that the young Despenser became 'the apple of the king's eye'.

A group of barons forced the Despensers into exile, as they had Gaveston. And, as before, Edward managed subsequently to retrieve and reinstate both men, gaining many powerful enemies thereby. The most venomous of these was Edward's own wife, Isabella, known to all as the 'she-wolf of France'. She plotted, with great diplomacy and secrecy, the downfall of the Despensers, even writing to the Pope to have them excommunicated, but that didn't work.

Her next ploy was to release from the Tower the man with whom at some point she had fallen in love, Roger Mortimer, the son of Margaret Fiennes. Isabella's co-conspirator, Bishop Orleton of Hereford, hired two Londoners who smuggled liquor and a rope to Mortimer's prison. After ensuring his guards were drunk, Mortimer abseiled the outer wall of the Tower and fled to his uncles, John and Robert Fiennes, in France, both of whom at that time had their English lands confiscated by Edward for 'adhering to the French'.

Edward II wrote letters to each of the Fiennes brothers, addressing them as 'my kinsman' but using strong language to persuade them to give Mortimer up. The king knew both brothers well, and in 1309 he had paid Robert five years' rental in advance for the use of his estate at Wendover. The records show no response from Robert, whose 'warhorse was confiscated'.

Back in England, Queen Isabella, who clearly hated her husband Edward as much as she did his right-hand man Despenser, carried out stage two of her plot. Edward obviously had no idea of what she had in mind, for he sent her as his ambassadress to parley with her brother, King Philip of France. He even, very stupidly, allowed her to take their son Edward, the heir to his throne, with her. Once there she persuaded Philip to restore Gascony and Ponthieu to the English. Whilst the details of this treaty carried on over the next year, she remained in France making love to Margaret Fiennes' son, Mortimer, and plotting with him and with his uncles, the Fiennes brothers, the overthrow of her husband and the crowning of her son.

John and Robert agreed to raise a force to help her and Mortimer invade England, whilst they raised their main army in

Holland. In 1326 their invasion force landed in Suffolk and, with a rapidly growing army, marched on London where they occupied the Tower once Edward II, and the hated Despensers had fled to the west country. Despenser aides unfortunate enough to stay in London were killed. The head of one was sliced off with a butcher's knife and sent to Isabella, who thanked the donor with a dignified speech of gratitude. She then promoted the two locals who had helped Mortimer escape the Tower, one becoming Mayor and the other Constable of the Tower.

Edward's party sought sanctuary in Bristol, which surrendered to Isabella, so they fled by ship bound for the Despensers' island of Lundy. But the wind blew them back to Wales, where they were soon captured. The Despensers were executed, the younger being hanged, drawn and quartered with an added twist. The Froissart chronicle reported: 'His member and testicles were first cut off because he was a heretic and a sodomite even if, it was said, with the King.'

Edward was imprisoned initially in Kenilworth Castle, and in 1327 was forced to sign his own abdication in favour of his son, the thirteen-year-old Prince Edward, who was very much under the control of his mother and her lover Mortimer and clearly unaware that their next move was secretly to murder his father. Edward was moved from Kenilworth, where his captors were friendly, to Berkeley Castle where they were not. His new custodians had both been captured at Boroughbridge and owed their release from prison to Isabella.

Edward's last months at Berkeley were for a long time kept secret from the public, but it was clear to Isabella that he must die. Soon after she and Mortimer gained power as regents for her son Edward III, the country and a growing number of barons realised that the new outfit was just as bad as the Despensers had been. A growing move in sympathy for the imprisoned Edward II gathered strength, so the latter's speedy death became vital to Isabella.

In September 1327 Edward's death from illness was announced, and his body was given to an official group of Bristol worthies to check that he had not been murdered. The truth came out slowly. Geoffrey le Baker's Chronicle reported:

> His wife Isabella was angered that his life which had become most hateful to her should be so prolonged. She asked advice of the Bishop of Hereford, pretending that she had had a dreadful dream . . . that her husband would at some time be restored to his former dignity and would condemn her, as a traitress, to be burned or to perpetual slavery. The bishop of Hereford was feared . . . And so letters were written to Edward's keepers. [These men] believed that the favour of Isabella and the bishop made them secure [and they] took control of the castle . . .

Then began the most extreme part of Edward's persecution . . .

> He was shut up in a secure chamber, where he was for many days and almost suffocated by the stench of corpses buried in a cellar hollowed out beneath him. Carpenters who worked beneath the window of his chamber heard his laments. When his warders perceived that the stench alone was not sufficient to kill him, they seized him on the night of 22 September . . . and held him down. They thrust a plumber's soldering iron, heated and red hot, guided by a tube inserted into his bowels and thus they burnt his innards and his vital organs . . . He shouted aloud so that many heard his cry both within and without the castle and knew it for the cry of a man who suffered violent death. Many in both the town and the castle of Berkeley were moved to pity for him.

There were rumours that Roger Mortimer was himself among the murderers, but there was no proof. I prefer to believe that he had no involvement in the cruel details of Edward's demise. Isabella, in widow's weeds, attended the lavish funeral of her late husband, and ruled the land with Mortimer, the son of Margaret Fiennes.

Under Edward II the people were far better off than under his father, with less taxation, far less conscription and no foreign service. In short, Edward II did not deserve his horrible death.

8

Fiennes on Both Sides

Prince Edward, son of the late King Edward II, grew up in the constant company of his adulterous mother and her murderous lover. Yet he was to flower into a great king, Edward III, who ruled for fifty years almost without civil strife. His secret was largely to recognise the monarchical limitations laid down by successive Parliaments over the past century and, above all, to keep the barons on his side. A seemingly simple recipe, but in fact one requiring endless tact, cunning and diplomacy. And bags of self-confidence, which Edward possessed from birth. He was well educated by tutors, especially by Richard of Bury (whom he later promoted to Bishop of Durham) who clearly honoured study:

> The value of books cannot be expressed . . . Yet a lazy youth will lounge over his book and, in mid-winter, when his nose is oozing mucus, he does not think of wiping it, but allows it to drop on the page before him. If only he had a cobbler's apron in front of him, instead of a book! His nails are black with dirt, with which he marks any passage that strikes him. He sticks in straws to remind him of the bits he had to learn by heart, so that the book becomes so stuffed it tears away from its binding. He eats fruit and cheese over it, and drinks wine, all of which leave their traces; and, always chattering, he waters the page with his spittle.

Edward, luckily and unlike his late father, was keen on and excelled at the martial arts. He would need above all to be a great military leader. The contemporary Chronicles of Froissart summed up the ideal English monarch:

> The English will never love and honour their king unless he be victorious and a lover of arms and war against their neighbours and especially against such as are greater and richer than themselves. Their land is fuller of riches and of goods when they are at war than in peacetime. They take delight and solace in battles and slaughter; they covet and envy other men's wealth beyond measure.

Only a year after his coronation in 1327, the teenage King Edward III was forced to sign a treaty with King Robert the Bruce, giving him full sovereignty and Scotland full independence. He said at the time that he found this deeply humiliating. In 1330 Roger Mortimer, son of Margaret Fiennes, made it obvious that he would stop at nothing short of the crown, when he successfully conspired to have Edward's uncle, the Duke of Kent, a potential future royal claimant but a harmless popular character, executed on a trumped-up charge of treason.

Young though he was, Edward III was no fool and he made the first move with a night raid on Nottingham Castle when his mother and Mortimer were over-nighting there. He killed their two room guards and personally arrested Mortimer in his bedroom, and in front of Queen Isabella denounced him for murder and other crimes. Mortimer was sent to the Tower and Isabella into comfortable, but carefully observed, retirement in Norfolk.

Mortimer was hanged, drawn and quartered in front of a huge crowd of enthusiastic voyeurs at a specially erected gibbet at Tyburn, which, from that day, became London's favourite and official place of execution.

Edward was too shrewd to kill off Mortimer's allies, or even those who were known to have been involved in murdering Edward II. These were men, or friends of men, whom the king would have to work with and fight beside. He wanted as few enemies as possible. In this he did remarkably well, having over the next forty years virtually no disagreements with great barons.

The Fiennes and Saye fortunes were definitely in the ascendant in Edward III's reign, during which they intermarried to become a powerful family entity. Geoffrey de Saye, son of the Geoffrey who was always loyal to Edward II, had two daughters, one of whom, Idonea, married John, Lord Clinton, who was one of Edward III's greatest warriors. And Geoffrey himself became Edward's Admiral of the Fleet, as well as a great land general at such battles as Crécy. His daughter, Joan, became the sole heiress of the Saye fortunes, and she married William Fiennes. During Edward III's reign the Fiennes family absorbed the name and fortunes of the Sayes through the marriage of Joan and William. The Wykehams would come next.

One family problem was caused in 1337 when Edward declared war on France and laid claim to the French throne. The last links whereby Fiennes members could happily feel both Norman and English were irrevocably split, at which point Ingelram's son Giles elected to be English, whilst his brother William's family became wholly French.

Ingelram's daughter Maud had married Humphrey de Bohun, the Constable of England, and their daughter Mary married King Henry IV. Mary's sister Eleanor (also granddaughter of Ingelram Fiennes) married Thomas of Woodstock, the youngest son of Edward III.

Not long after Ingelram's two sons went their separate ways, and during Edward's reign, one descendant, Geoffrey de Saye, was Admiral of the English fleet and the other, Constable Robert Fiennes, commanded the French army. On 5 March 1327 John Fiennes having 'declared for the French', Edward III promptly removed his estates at Martock and elsewhere and his manors were 'granted to other more faithful subjects of the house of Plantagenet.'

In 1338 the French King Philip VI was preparing to invade England. Naval raids took place at Portsmouth, Southampton, Dover and even up the Thames, and as a result deep stakes were placed along the riverbed against future attacks by the London route. Early in the summer of 1340 spies reported to Edward that a great armada of French, Spanish and Genoese ships were massing in the Channel port of Sluys, prior to invasion. The first big military move of the so-called One Hundred Years War had begun, and Edward ordered his Admiral, Geoffrey de Saye, grandfather of William Fiennes (my great to the power of twenty grandfather) to prepare the southern fleet for war. Edward and most of his court, including his queen, sailed with the fleet.

Against the advice of his spies, Edward ordered the fleet to attack without delay. The French ships, joined to one another by rope walkways, never left the Sluys channel into which the English sailed. Most of Edward's ships, square-rigged and oar-steered, were known as cogs. They had small crews of five and carried up to thirty soldiers. The chronicle of Geoffrey le Baker describes the battle.

> The whole fleet gave a terrible shout, and a shower of arrows out of long wooden bows so poured down on the Frenchmen that thousands were slain . . . At length they closed and came to hand blows with pikés, poleaxes, and swords, and some threw stones from the tops of ships, wherewith many were brained . . . many of the Frenchmen abandoned their ships and leapt overboard . . . during the night thirty ships . . . fled away . . . The fight continued all night, and in the morning, the Normans being overcome and taken, there were found in the ships four hundred men slain . . . . The number of ships of war that were taken was about 230 barges; the number of enemies that were slain and drowned was about 20,000, and of Englishmen about 4,000 . . .

No member of the French king's court dared give him the news from Sluys. Finally the king's jester was ordered to tell him, which he did by saying, 'Our knights are much braver than the English.' 'How so?' asked Philip. 'Because,' replied the jester, 'the English do not dare to jump into the sea in full armour.' In fact, many of those French soldiers who managed to swim to the shore were then killed by the hostile Flemings. The victory at Sluys gave Edward control of the Channel throughout his reign and enabled his forces to attack along the French coast as and when he wished.

His army was based on that of his grandfather, Edward I, who, for the first time, had paid his men wages to ensure that they turned up when needed, trained and equipped, and they did not disappear whenever some distant female or harvest needed attention. Edward III honed this professional system. Under him all ranks received daily wages. Thus his kingly ally, Edward Balliol, King of Scots, had fifty shillings per day, his eldest son, the Black Prince, got twenty shillings, down to an archer at six pence daily and ordinary foot soldiers at two. The majority of his unprofessional troops were from Wales and Cheshire and most were either archers or men-at-arms who wore intricate armed suits made up of more than two dozen separate items. Carrying a sword and a dagger, they were highly effective so long as they remained upright, but, once fallen, they usually needed help to stand up. Falling in bogs or shallow water, they would often drown.

The secret of much of Edward's military success lay in the six foot long wooden bow fashioned of oak or yew or maple, which could fire four hundred yards with relative accuracy, but only in the hands of an archer who had developed his skill over many years. To this end, English and Welsh villagers were encouraged to practise archery from an early age. Other nations, including the Scots, never indulged in this remarkable skill that built up the great, but lopsided, often body-deforming, muscle, needed to exert the necessary hundred-pound 'tug' on the bowstring. The government passed many laws forbidding such village sports as football and cockfighting, expressly because they distracted people from archery practice.

Because the French authorities forbade French peasants to carry any weapons of war, they never developed a force who could use longbows. The practical range of the crossbow, far easier to use with accuracy, was a mere hundred yards, and the act of reloading it was far slower. An experienced longbow archer could loose off an arrow every five seconds, which was six times quicker than a crossbow. To protect them from cavalry charges, they also carried long pointed stakes. Siege guns and simple cannons were just emerging but were of no import during Edward III's reign, other than for scaring all horses within earshot.

Nine years after the original declaration of war, in 1346, Edward launched his first major attack on northern France, with the idea of luring the French army into direct confrontation there, which would draw them away from the English lands in the south. One of his three chief advisers was the Earl of Warwick, whose son-in-law was Admiral Geoffrey Saye of Sluys fame, and one of his best army commanders-to-be, although only sixteen at the time, was his eldest son, Edward the Black Prince, whose great great grandfather was William Fiennes. Their forces laid waste to the countryside and plundered churches, anything to provoke a response.

When the French king finally did get his act together, he was quickly successful in raising a huge force of 80,000, including Genoese specialist crossbowmen, the cream of the French cavalry, together with forces from Bohemia, Germany, Savoye and Luxembourg.

Edward's army consisted of 4,000 knights and men-at-arms, 7,000 Welsh and English archers, and 5,000 Welsh and Irish spearmen. Additionally, there was a tiny contingent of cannoneers who lugged five cannons with them and a supply of stone cannon balls, the predecessors of today's Royal Artillery. Realising that direct confrontation with such a numerically superior force was a bad idea, Edward decided to retreat towards the coast. The

Seine got in the way, for its bridges were either destroyed or heavily defended. Not far from Paris one bridge was repaired and crossed, but the river Somme then caused a similar problem. Edward followed its course north to the sea and crossed the river mouth at low tide, just evading the French who advanced along the far bank.

Edward's army halted on a ridgeline between two villages, one named Crécy. He commanded from the hilltop. My relations were well represented that day. The Black Prince commanded the division of archers in the front line, assisted in command by the Earl of Warwick, and Geoffrey Saye fought alongside the king.

On the French side, Robert Fiennes was a senior captain who would soon rise to command the entire French army. Robert was the son of the John Fiennes who had incurred the displeasure of Edward II and, having had his English estates confiscated, had settled in the old Fiennes territory of Fiennes and Guisnes. When Edward III had laid siege to the key city of Amiens, Robert was the senior French army captain who forced the English to yield, not only at Amiens, but soon thereafter at Rheims, Tonnerre, Auxerre and Regennes. He met most of the costs of these campaigns himself, went bankrupt and, by the time of Crécy in 1346, appealed to the French king, who appointed him Constable or commander-in-chief of the French army, a job with a salary.

First to attack at Crécy were the massed ranks of the Genoese crossbowmen whose weapons fired iron bolts, stones or lead bullets with a flat trajectory that could pierce armour. The British longbowmen used high trajectory metre-long arrows which descended on their targets at an angle in showers. Horses were easy targets. At Crécy the average rate of fire was thirty seconds between each crossbow shot. The 15,000 Genoese crossbowmen were tired after their long march and before they advanced there was heavy rain with thunder and a terrible eclipse of the sun. Froissart tells us a great flight of noisy crows hovered over the battalions. Then the sun came out and shone into the eyes of the French. The Genoese advanced with great shouting but the

English, quietly, rose up, stepped forward and let their arrows fly, 'so thick it seemed as snow.'

Froissart also explains that the rain had the instant effect of making the archers unhitch their bowstrings (a three-second job) to keep them dry inside their hats, but the unwieldy crossbow strings could not be so easily kept dry, became loose and lost effectiveness.

The Genoese, with serious losses, sensibly retreated, but the heavy cavalry had begun a mighty uphill charge and rode down a great many of the Genoese, contemptuous at their cowardice. Horses stumbled in deep bloody mud, knights in heavy armour floundered among dying Genoese, and the heaps of bodies grew higher as successive flights of metal-tipped arrows found new targets.

Nonetheless, at one point King Edward received a breathless messenger from his sixteen-year-old son clad in black armour and thenceforth called the Black Prince. He and my kinsman Warwick needed support. The king surveyed the battle scene below and asked if his son was wounded. No, he was told, and so he replied to the messenger, 'I am sure he will repel the enemy without my help. Let the boy win his spurs.'

The battle continued far into the night, but at midnight King Philip VI of France abandoned the carnage, and his surviving knights and men-at-arms went with him. The English army stayed on their ridgeline until, cautiously at dawn, they could be sure the French had truly gone. I call the two armies French and English, as did the chronicles, but in truth they were clearly European and British.

Once Edward was certain that the French had not rallied, his men swarmed over the battleground. Those knights too wounded or crushed beneath dead horses were unable to be carried off for ransom, and the vast majority of the wounded not worthy of ransom were murdered where they lay by men with long daggers. These were inserted either through visor slits into the eyeball and brain, or through the armpit into the heart.

With an eye to ensuring maximum ransom revenue and good public relations back home, Edward arranged a meticulous tally of the dead by two nominated lords with three heraldic experts and their secretaries. The result of their grand post-mortem was a report that eighty battle standards, eleven princes, three archbishops, 1,200 noble knights and 30,000 common soldiers had been identified. When the English moved away towards Calais, their target, they flew the eighty French standards which caused ignorant onlookers to believe that their own king's forces had won at Crécy.

The battle enhanced King Edward's warrior reputation and that of his young son. The Black Prince was titled Prince of Wales and Duke of Cornwall, but he spent most of his life fighting in France, and French was his first language. At Crécy he chose for his battle standard the family crest of the dead King of Bohemia who had fought well, despite being totally blind, lashed to his horse and to those of two 'guide-dog' knights on either flank. The Bohemia crest of three white feathers is still that of today's Prince of Wales, as well as the Welsh Rugby Football Union. The Black Prince made sure that, on their return to South Wales, his brave Welsh bowmen were each given an acre of land, made freemen and exempted grazing tax for their cattle.

But first Edward's victorious army had to begin their siege of the fortified deep-water port of Calais, a convenient day's sail from Dover and a key position from both a military and commercial viewpoint. Calais was defended with a tidally-fed double ditch and high double walls, well built and strongly garrisoned. Edward surrounded and blockaded Calais for eleven months until, all supplies gone and the citizens starving, they desperately needed their king to relieve them. But Philip's memories of Crécy kept him firmly in Paris, and eventually the Calais garrison commander faced the hard fact that if he didn't surrender, the inmates would die slowly of hunger. On the other hand, surrender, according to the rules of war of the period, entailed the massacre of all citizens if their town or fortress had held out for any length of time.

Froissart's Chronicle tells the famous story of the garrison commander pleading for clemency for Calais, of the toing and froing of fruitless emissaries, and eventually Edward's deciding that if six leading burghers brought him the keys of the city and the garrison, 'I will do with those six as I please, but the rest I will spare.'

The chronicler continues:

> Finally the town's wealthiest citizen, Master Eustace de Saint Pierre came forward saying, 'It would be a terrible thing indeed to allow so many to die when there appears a means to avoid such misfortune. An act of such merit would surely find favour in Our Saviour's eyes. Let me be delivered into the King of England's hands.' Other greatly respected citizens volunteered to accompany Saint Pierre, including Jean d'Aire, brothers Jacques and Pierre de Wissant, Andrieu d'Andres, and [the youngest of them] Jean Fiennes.

When the six heroic burghers of Calais knelt before the king bare-headed, barefoot and with halters around their necks, they so impressed everyone present by their bravery that all begged the king to show them mercy. But he was adamant they should die in recompense for grievous English losses over the course of the siege.

> At this point, the Queen of England, Philippa, who was present during these events, was moved to intercede. Though she was pregnant at the time, she fell to her knees before the king and weeping said, 'My lord, since I crossed the sea to join you, at great danger to myself, I have never asked of you a single favour, but now I ask you in all humility, in the name of the Son of the Blessed Mary and by the love you have for me, to have mercy on these six men.'

> The king remained silent for a time and finally spoke saying, 'My lady, I might wish you were anywhere but here. Nevertheless I cannot refuse your request, though it be against my will. These men are yours to do with what you like.' And with that the queen thanked her husband the king and had the halters taken from the necks of the prisoners. They were presented new clothes and fed an ample dinner. Whereupon they were given safe passage through the English army and released to freedom.

In 1888 the famous French sculptor Auguste Rodin completed a life-size bronze grouping of the Burghers of Calais, the original of which still stands in the centre of Calais, but copies can be admired in London in the gardens below the Houses of Parliament, and also in Paris, New York, Washington, Jerusalem, Tokyo, Canberra and Copenhagen. In the year 2000 I went to look at one of Rodin's representations of my distant French kinsman, who was in his day as famous as his contemporary cousin, Constable Robert Fiennes. He helped to save King Edward from ordering a major massacre.

Calais remained a key English possession until 1558, but the war elsewhere in France continued, and this benefited those of my ancestors with military careers on both sides. Especially Captain Robert Fiennes who, the week after the Battle of Crécy, was sent by King Philip to defend the nearby key town of St Omer. When an English-allied force from the Flemish army came his way, Robert ambushed them, killing seven hundred. Fiennes together with the Governor of St Omer made continued raids on the English lines of communication. One night, not long after Calais was taken by the English, the two men plotted to attack the town by a sudden night raid. Unfortunately they were betrayed, and according to Froissart:

> The King of England was informed of the conspiracy and came into Calais with three hundred men-at-arms and six hundred archers. The English knew that a large detachment of French

remained at the bridge at Nieulay under the command of Robert Fiennes. The King put to flight or killed the crossbowmen of St Omer. He then came to the bridge believing he would seize it with ease. But Fiennes and his small troop fought through the night. Later, when his enemies increased, Fiennes sounded the retreat and returned to St Omer. This attempt against Calais failed but gave Fiennes, the future Constable, the occasion to show his valour.

Froissart uses the term Constable of France for the commander-in-chief of the French army. The position was vacant for a while after the battle of Calais, where Constable Raoul Eu was captured and taken to England for ransom. Whilst there, in loose captivity, he took an enthusiastic part in many court activities, especially the jousting. Word got back to King Philip and when the Constable did return to Paris, he was tried for treason and beheaded. Nonetheless Constable of France was the summit of ambition for a French soldier, and my French cousin Robert Fiennes was helped to achieve the honour by Raoul Eu's execution.

Edward III's personal popularity in England, just prior to his Crécy campaign and the subsequent success at Calais, had been waning due to his government's methods of raising money. There was also hostility to the expansion of compulsory military service. Victory at Crécy and Calais, however, renewed his popularity and put the brakes on growing parliamentary opposition, at least for as long as his French campaigns continued to succeed. Sadly a new threat was soon to cut short the national mood of post-Crécy jubilation.

The Black Death ravaged England in three separate pandemics during Edward III's reign. The bacteria-carrying flea was hosted by rodents, especially by the large black rat, and the symptoms included swollen glands which oozed pus and blood in the armpits, neck and groin, followed by heavy bleeding under the skin. Hence the 'black' appearance of victims. Accompanying tumours or 'buboes' could grow to the size of apples overnight.

Excruciating pains and vomiting of blood, which drove people mad, preceded death within a week. A mutated sister bacillus was hosted by human fleas causing additional septicaemia, and this would kill in less than two days. A third variety went for the lungs and was spread by the breath of the victim. The speed of the plague's onset, the terrible pain and the grotesque appearance of the victims all made it especially terrifying.

The disease was first spotted in central Asia in 1338, whence it spread inexorably through China and India. In 1346, the year of Crécy, a Mongol army besieging a Crimean port used the old tactic of catapulting decomposing bodies over city walls to infect the inhabitants. From the Crimea the plague spread within a year through all of Italy and soon reached Paris. In 1348 a French sailor arrived in Melcombe, near Weymouth, and brought the plague to England. It thrived in the warm summer weather and the pneumonic variety flourished in winter with much sneezing. By early 1349 Edward was forced to cease his military activities altogether, and even had to close Parliament, since it was unsafe to go to London like most towns, a centre of infection.

The Archbishop of Canterbury was an early victim. The aristocracy death rate was relatively low due to their more spacious houses shared with fewer rats. Nonetheless, 27 per cent of the English nobility and 40 per cent of the clergy were to die over the next three years, as did half the population of Britain; as many as two million people. In winter the plague dropped away, since fleas rest up in the cold, but in spring they were hopping about again from ratty host to human. Throughout Europe one third of the population died over four years; some twenty-five million people. The plague killed like no other illness. Boccaccio wrote of what he saw: 'Victims often ate lunch with their friends and dinner with their ancestors in paradise.'

Rural records tell of 5,000 sheep dying of starvation on a single estate where all the farmhands and the owner had died. Animal corpses littered the land. Cattle ran wild over untended crops. Nobody blamed the rats, they looked for culprits in society at large. Preacher Thomas Brinton wrote: 'We are not constant in faith . . . for that reason there exists in England . . . so cruel a pestilence, so much injustice, so many illegitimate children – for on every side there is so much lechery and adultery that few men are contented with their wives but each man lusts after the wife of his neighbour or keeps a stinking concubine.'

England recovered very slowly from the plague, partly because other epidemics followed in the ensuing years, but with fewer workers to till the land, the common people demanded and got higher wages, despite the barons. In France this same wages issue caused peasant rebellions and large areas of France became ungovernable. The man charged with dealing with this problem there was Robert Fiennes, in the years before he was made Constable.

The old French King Philip VI, died in 1350, and his successor, King John II, renewed hostilities against English territory in southern France. By 1355 the Black Prince was again at war in Gascony and the Mediterranean provinces, ravaging the land and gaining rich plunder and a Europe-wide reputation as a great warrior. In 1356 he decided to emulate his father's strategy of a decade earlier; that of causing so much damage that the French would confront him in a major battle which he, the Black Prince, was confident of winning. He left Bordeaux with an army of 10,000 soldiers, only three hundred of whom were mounted, soon to be pursued by the French king with 50,000 men. They met at the village of Poitiers with the Black Prince's men positioned on high ground approachable only up a single hedge-bound lane.

What followed was in many ways a carbon copy of the Battle of Crécy some nine years before. Once again the retreat of the first French attack clashed with the advance of the next. Once again the longbow arrow proved superior to all other missiles and, as before, French casualties were enormous, and the jewel in the crown of the entire battle for the Black Prince was the capture of John, King of France, who was taken to England and only released after a treaty was signed at Calais by both kings, a huge ransom was paid and the English gained full sovereignty over all their current possessions in France. In return, Edward renounced his claim on the French throne. The various talks and transactions that sealed this deal in the late 1350s were conducted, on behalf of the French king and his dauphin, largely by Constable Robert Fiennes, who travelled back and forth between his Guisnes headquarters and London.

In 1360 Edward III gave Robert Fiennes leave to travel all over the English possessions in France as a troubleshooter to negotiate problems and flare-ups. But when the estates of Fiennes and Guisnes were included in areas given to the English by King John of France, Robert refused to pay homage to the English and was briefly imprisoned in England before becoming Governor of Languedoc and retiring.

In the decade after Poitiers, King John died and his successor, Charles V, soon broke the treaty, and the war rumbled on. King Edward was growing old and less energetic but the Black Prince was as active as ever, although successes came less easily and less often. Nonetheless the long years of victory in France had given the English great self-confidence. The fighters who won the victories were men of every class, from humble village archers to lance-bearing nobles. A chronicle of 1373 stated: 'the English are so filled with their own greatness and have won so many big victories that they have come to believe they cannot lose. In battle, they are the most confident nation in the world.'

That may well have been true at the time, but the situation reversed over the next five years. Queen Philippa, loved by her nation and, above all, by her husband, died and Edward was never his energetic, decisive self again. He relapsed slowly into senility, and the Black Prince, a sick man for many years, died in 1376, a year before his father. It is easy with hindsight to focus on the bad times of any monarch, especially one who survived as long as Edward. His dotage saw the French regain nearly all the territory he had won for England in his glory years, but his capture of Calais was a longstanding and precious prize. Under Edward, trade prospered and increased, the language of English flowered, as did a great sense of nationhood, despite the horrors of the Black Death. He had also bucked the Plantagenet curse of civil war, thanks to his pragmatic and sensitive policies. His successor, the son of the Black Prince and great grandson of Joanna Fiennes, was crowned Richard II at the tender age of ten.

9

Founder's Kin

Richard II's rule was to be bedevilled at different times by his uncles, since they and their children would always have an eye on the throne. To have been royal with no uncles must have been wonderful in medieval times. Richard's grandfather, Edward III, was to blame for a great deal of strife by siring twelve children, seven of whom were male and likely, if they reached adulthood at the time of the Black Death, to be itching to get their claws on the crown. It was one of Richard's four uncles, John of Gaunt, Earl of Lancaster, who acted as his regent until he was twenty-four.

Somehow through a natural propensity for peace which clearly did not come from his father, the Black Prince, Richard managed to avoid civil war for all but the last few days of his reign. But following his twenty-two-year reign, the bloody War of the Roses, fought between the dynasties of two of his uncles (both directly descended from the Fiennes sisters Margaret and Joanna), would rage for over eighty years.

The Fiennes family members most involved with King Richard were the inmates of Herstmonceux Castle; an expensive place to run. To glimpse the finances of the estate of Herstmonceux (which looks pretty much in the twenty-first century as it did then, a unique red-brick crenellated manor, now called a castle), I am including text from a local record of the mid-1350s. The

Fiennes inmates at the time were William, whose father had inherited Herstmonceux from his heiress wife, Maud Monceux, and Joan Saye, an heiress of the Saye fortunes. William and Joan lived well and he served King Richard loyally as a rural bureaucrat. His jobs included serving on the Sussex commission for ditches and dykes, being Sheriff of Sussex and Surrey and, for many years, Constable of Pevensey Castle until, in 1399, the French invaded Pevensey and he surrendered it. His brother Robert had the hazardous job of Collector of Taxes for Sussex.

William died in 1361 and an 'inquisition' held after his death found that at Herstmonceux:

> there are 350 acres of arable land lying in the marsh, of which two parts can be sowed yearly, and that an acre is worth 9d a year, beyond the reprises, producing altogether £13 2s 6d; there are 199 acres of arable land, two-thirds of which can be sowed every year, of which each acre is worth 4d when sown, when not sown 3d, as pasturage for beasts; the other third is worth 2d an acre as pasture; there are 10 acres of meadow, worth 10s a year, the value of an acre is 12d and no more, because it is often flooded, and cannot be mown except in a dry season; 20 acres of bush, worth 3s 4d a year, for pasturage of sheep and other beasts; 8 acres of bush called Bemsell [a small farm in the northwest part of the parish of Watling is still known by the name of Bemsells]. Another farm not very far distant bears the name of Prinkle [one of the jurors on the inquisition held on the death of John de Fiennes, in 1251, being Alan Prinkle] worth nothing because they are copse, and were cut down before William's death; 80 acres of arable called Lewstrode, worth 20s a year; the price of a acre is 3d for pasture, because it cannot be sown and 'is overgrown with heath'. And they say that the rents from the free tenants and 'nativi' there amount to £17 16s 4d, and the labour of the bondsmen is worth 58s.

While William and Joan Fiennes lived out their rural existence in Sussex, Joan's sister, Idonea Saye, had married a career soldier who spent his life fighting for the Black Prince in Scotland and France and, to a lesser extent, for King Richard in the same countries. This was John, the 3rd Lord Clinton, whose family adopted the Saye title for several generations. Lord John was a senior commander in the English army at the time when the Constable of the French army was Robert Fiennes. As far as I can trace, there is no record of the two meeting up at the same battle. Both of them would have spoken French as their first language. But in England English was gaining ground slowly.

In 1330 a Chester Monk named Ranulf Higden wrote a history book in which he comments:

> [The] corruption of the mother-tongue is because of two things. One is because children in school, contrary to the usage and customs of all other nations, are compelled to abandon their own language and to construe their lessons and their tasks in French, and have since the Normans came to England. Moreover, gentlemen's children are taught to speak French from the time they are rocked in their cradle . . . and rustic men want to make themselves like gentlemen, and strive with great industry to speak French, in order to be more highly thought of.

John of Trevisa, another Chester monk who taught French and translated much of Higden's writing into English, wrote that French was 'much in use before the first plague [the Black Death] and since has somewhat changed . . . in the ninth year of Richard II, in all the grammar schools of England children are abandoning French, are construing and learning in English.' Under the cultured King Richard, such poets as Chaucer were encouraged and patronised. More practically, Richard's Statute of Pleading decreed: 'The king hath ordained that all pleas in the courts of the realm shall be pleaded, defended, debated and judged in the English tongue.'

As early as John's reign when Normandy was lost, the barons who committed themselves and their families to England, began also to adopt the English language and by 1400, the year Richard II was murdered, England's new king, Henry IV, would be a native English speaker for the first time.

Despite his ongoing efforts for peace Richard continued to have trouble in France and Scotland where victories of the calibre of his father and grandfather were a thing of the past. But he was an arrogant man and, like his great grandfather, Edward II (but without the homosexual factor), he favoured certain nobles above all others and caused enemies by promoting them unreasonably.

Then there was the uncle problem. Richard had only to look over his shoulder to spot one or another lurking in predatory mode. There was John of Gaunt, of the House of Lancaster, the Duke of Gloucester (who he eventually had executed), and the Duke of York, largely harmless but not to be trusted when it mattered most. There were many reasons for the unrest Richard faced, but few were of his own making. The feudal system was declining. Vassals enjoyed protection from their barons in return for their work and, if needed, their military service. But by Richard's day, compulsory enlistment had rendered much of this system obsolete.

The immediate cause of the uprisings, now known as the Peasants' Revolt, was the unprecedented level of taxation. The 1380 poll tax was three times higher than that of the previous year and, for the first time, taxed both rich and poor at the same rate. This was both unfair and extortionate, especially when viewed in conjunction with the Statute of Labourers which pegged wages to pre-Black Death levels. The peasant could not win, so he naturally revolted. Manors were attacked, officials beaten up or murdered. In Cambridge university archives were burnt, Norwich Castle was taken over, mobs of several thousands marched on London, mainly from Essex and Kent, and for several days mayhem ensued. Key buildings were ransacked and burnt, officials and foreigners were beheaded, prisoners were released from jails, and legal documents destroyed.

The chief leaders of the mob were a Lollard preacher, John Ball, and a Maidstone ex-soldier, Wat Tyler. As many as 60,000 rioters were involved, and one group gained entry to the Tower of London where they seized the chancellor, the Archbishop of Canterbury and the treasurer. All three were beheaded and their heads joined others displayed on Tower Bridge.

The king, only fourteen years old at the time, was not considered by the mob to be behind their troubles. He was, they felt, being duped by the regent, John of Gaunt, and his government. Gaunt was away in Scotland, so the young King Richard agreed to meet the rioters at Smithfield. A 20,000 strong armed crowd gathered to meet the king who, with sixty retainers, bravely rode towards them. Wat Tyler's ensuing insolence towards Richard infuriated the Mayor of London, who stabbed and killed him on the spot. Not, you would think, a wise action in the circumstances. King Richard somehow stilled the fury of the armed mob with promises that all their demands would be met as soon as possible. Ten days later with his army around him, Richard felt safe enough to revoke all his promises and execute those rebels who were traceable. He had proved, even at fourteen, that he was no pushover. The poll tax was reintroduced at a more realistic level, so in one way the peasants achieved their objective.

John of Gaunt returned from Scotland, once the English mobs were safely out of the way, and continued his reign. Four years later he involved English soldiers in protecting Portugal from a Spanish invasion, and cemented an Anglo-Portuguese alliance with a Treaty of Friendship which has endured for six hundred years and was last invoked in 1982 during the Falklands War. Gaunt's daughter married the Portuguese king, and their son, Henry the Navigator, became a famous sponsor of the nautical exploration which paved the way for the Portuguese empire.

One of the commanders of the English force who fought the Spanish for Portugal was Gaunt's highly capable general, Lord John Clinton, husband of Idonea Saye, who died on campaign at the end of Richard II's reign. His grandson would later hand over the title of Lord Saye to the Fiennes family.

Although, in Richard II's reign, our family's main home was Herstmonceux in Sussex, the manor in Oxfordshire where the family lives today was first purchased in 1377 by Richard II's chancellor, whose name was William of Wykeham. This house, Broughton Castle near Banbury, was to be inherited by Wykeham's nephew's great granddaughter, Margaret, who became Margaret Fiennes.

William was born into a farmer's family in the village of Wykeham in Hampshire and became a clerk in Winchester, graduating to be a clerk of the works for royal properties. At some point he oversaw building work at Windsor Castle and impressed Edward III, who liked and promoted him to Bishop of Winchester and eventually to chancellor of England. When Edward grew senile and his brother John of Gaunt became regent, William resigned after various disagreements with Gaunt. He had many ups and downs during the period of political turbulence between King Richard's troublesome uncles, successive Parliaments and loyal king's men, but when Richard eventually emerged from beneath the wing of Gaunt, William again became chancellor. He was clearly lucky not to be in that position during the Peasants' Revolt, or he would have lost his head and my family would never have inherited Broughton Castle.

William's main drive, especially after he resigned the chancellorship for a second time, was the furtherance of clergy education. Once he became one of the richest men in the kingdom, he founded Winchester College and New College, Oxford, to consolidate a firm link between public schools and universities. He made both places of learning available through scholarships granted to the 'poor and indigent'. He established the academic layout of large quadrangles surrounded by arched cloisters and, more than anyone else, he promoted the perpendicular style of architecture, strengthening the culmination of the gothic style. Although he hoped that his new schools would produce generations of learned and competent clerics, able to act independently of influential and often corrupt barons, William did not neglect the education of his own heirs.

To this end, he invented *Consanguineus Fundatoris* (Founder's Kin), a process by which his heirs into perpetuity could gain favourable rates for education at Winchester and New College. Sadly this excellent system ended in 1868 after only five hundred years, so I just missed out (by eighty-eight years) and had to go to Eton instead. During the centuries between the entry to Winchester College of the first Fiennes in 1465 until the Founder's Kin arrangement ceased, a total of fourteen Fienneses or Twisletons entered the college. Of those fourteen, one died in school and another was drowned during a holiday. Since then, when Fienneses had to pay up like anyone else, fifteen of them have been educated there, one of whom was head boy. Nathaniel Fiennes, Lord Saye and Sele, the current owner of Broughton Castle and William's heir, used to be a member of the College's governing body.

As for William of Wykeham, he was well out of it when he resigned the chancellorship for the last time, as things went from bad to worse between the king and his wicked uncles. In 1397 Richard's position was sufficiently secure for him to arrest the Dukes of Warwick and Arundel and exile his uncle, the Duke of Gloucester, to Calais where he was mysteriously murdered. With his main rivals now gone and his regal powers restored, he made friends with Uncle John of Gaunt again and appointed him his chief adviser. All went well until, in February 1399, Gaunt died and his son, Henry Bolingbroke (named after the village where he was born), claimed the vast Lancastrian wealth and estates which King Richard badly wanted for himself. Both men plotted in secret, but for a while were openly cordial to one another.

The king, making the first move, managed to have Bolingbroke permanently exiled to France, and, feeling at last completely safe at home, led an army to Ireland to deal with ongoing troubles there. This was definitely a mistake. Over in Paris Henry Bolingbroke made his move. He was, after all, the grandson of Edward III, as was Richard II, but he clearly shared more of that powerful king's aggressive genes than did Richard. Together with a substantial French army, Bolingbroke landed his fleet in Yorkshire, where the Percy dynasty of Northumberland rallied their considerable forces to his cause. They were then joined by various Lancastrian forces, and by the time King Richard heard the bad news and embarked from Ireland in July, Bolingbroke had time to muster further support in the south and west of England.

Richard's army had to stay and maintain the status quo in Ireland, so he had hoped to raise new forces in his traditional recruiting ground of Cheshire and North Wales. But the astute Bolingbroke knew this and reached Chester first. Richard then found himself, with only a small band of loyal supporters, stranded in North Wales. Surrounded by the forces of Bolingbroke, he could only surrender, and was taken to London where Bolingbroke and a quickly assembled Parliament accused the king of having broken his coronation oath and ruled for his own pleasure and not by the laws of England. He was forced to abdicate and the vacant throne passed to Henry Bolingbroke as King Henry IV of England.

Richard was imprisoned in Yorkshire and he died there in February 1400 aged thirty-three. Some say that, heartbroken, he starved himself to death, but the more likely explanation is that he was starved or suffocated to death on the new king's orders. His body was brought to London and buried without ceremony. Richard's death at the hands of his cousin created the seeds of the dynastic instability which would, in due course, explode into the Wars of the Roses.

Henry Bolingbroke of the House of Lancaster, murderer and usurper of his cousin Richard and now King Henry IV, hurried to make it appear to the nation that his four sons had been involved in the coup, lest they later turn against him and take a 'holier than thou' line to depose him. He obviously feared that usurping, like abusing, might run in families. The Fiennes connection to

King Henry IV was through his wife, Mary de Bohun, whose grandmother was Maud Fiennes, the sister of the William Fiennes killed at the Battle of Courtrai.

Henry IV was residually less Norman than his predecessors, in that he was the first English king since the Conquest to have been born on English soil to an English father and an English mother. Further, on the day of his coronation he made his induction speech, the first post-Conquest monarch to do so, in English, not French. The long-lasting habit of most aristocratic and bureaucratic conversations being in French was at last fading away, slowly but surely. One reason was the sense of English patriotism engendered by the many wars against the French and their identification as the number one enemy. The other reason had to do with the Lollards, the religious sect who had first appeared in Richard II's reign with their anti-papal, keep-religion-simple message and the Wycliff translation of the Bible into English which helped standardise midlands English as a dialect more and more people began to accept. The great writer of this new midlands English was Geoffrey Chaucer whose patronage by Richard II was one thing continued by Henry IV who doubled Chaucer's salary as court poet on the day of his coronation.

As things turned out for Henry the threats to his throne came not from his four sons but from Scotland, Wales and the north of England who sometimes even managed to liaise with each other, though not very efficiently. The Percys of Northumberland who had helped Henry achieve the throne grew resentful and over-ambitious. Their great champion, Harry Hotspur, was eventually put down by Henry's even more famous son and heir, Prince Hal of Shakespearean history fame, at the Battle of Shrewsbury. Although only sixteen at the time, the prince led the king's forces in an uphill attack on Hotspur's men, while they concentrated on mounting charges at King Henry's royal standard, knowing that to kill or capture the king would win the day. But the cunning Henry had dressed several of his own knights in royal surcoats to confuse the issue, which clearly worked well. In the thick of battle Hotspur was killed and the Percy rebellion crushed.

Prince Hal also led campaigns against Owain Glyndŵr (Shakespeare's Glendower) who at one point had managed the improbable feat of uniting the whole of Wales under his leadership. From Glyndŵr Prince Hal learnt about guerrilla tactics, as year after year the English army tramped aimlessly through endless rain and fog in search of an enemy that would only skirmish, then fade away.

Many of Henry IV's best army leaders during his Welsh campaigns were the sons of King Richard's top army men, who clearly saw no problem working for the great usurper. One of these was William Clinton who, with no legal basis, called himself Lord Saye, which had been the title of his mother, Idonea Saye, and which should have gone to the Fiennes family who had previously inherited the Saye fortunes. At the time, William Fiennes lived peacefully at Herstmonceux Castle, where he remained a loyal subject of Henry IV, the Sheriff of Sussex and Surrey and busy with 'several royal commissions to view the banks, seacoasts and marshes of Pevensey, Hailsham, Hoo and adjacent parishes in order to draw up the ordinances for Pevensey Marsh'.

Henry's policies towards the French were very different from the appeasement strategy of Richard II. Henry was convinced that, as King of England, he had taken over the Plantagenet claim to the throne of France. Once his home-grown troubles were quelled therefore, he turned his attention to gaining territory and glory in France. He was not bothered by the twenty-eight-year truce that Richard had engineered, since the French had already ignored it when, a few years back, they sent an army to help Owain Glyndŵr.

France, Henry knew, was engaged in three or four regional civil wars, the two main rivals in which were the Burgundians and the Armagnacs. King Charles VI was a mere figurehead who, medically insane, was incapable of sorting out the murderous strife between those of his various relatives who led the two warring dynasties. The great province of Brittany was also split between two rival groupings, so England was in a wonderful position to create alliances which would tip the balance of power in favour of one or other faction in return for land which Henry thought of as being his by traditional rights.

There was a period in the middle of his reign when two separate groups formed a council to decide such things as the best policy to follow in France. One group consisted of the king and his key advisers, and the other slightly bigger cabal was led by Prince Hal and his young colleagues. The older group favoured the Armagnacs and Prince Hal preferred the Burgundians. In 1410 the king believed that he and his advisers could do without Prince Hal's help, so he disbanded the council and thereafter decided French policy by himself.

Prince Hal became famous for his enjoyment of London's dens of iniquity and of wine, women and song. After all his teenage years spent marching through rain-sodden Wales, he deserved to sow his oats, but the king disapproved. The prince was ever-popular and there were, after 1410 when Henry fell ill, rumours of disloyalty. Twice there were open rows between father and son. But when an undiagnosed illness finally killed the king in 1413, Prince Hal was still as loyal and obedient a son as any monarch could wish for. French chronicles relate the dying Henry saying to the Prince:

> 'How shall you have any right to this Crown when, as you know, I never have?'
>
> 'My Lord,' Prince Hal replied, 'as you have kept and guarded it by the sword, so do I intend to guard it all my life.'

Prince Hal, the grandson of Maud Fiennes, was crowned, in the midst of a snowstorm, as King Henry V.

10

Once More Unto the Breach

Things were pretty good for most people in England at the time Prince Hal was crowned. The barons were peaceful, the rash of plagues had all but gone away, harvests were mostly good, and the government had reduced taxes to a reasonable level. Because of the plagues, there were fewer workers and the government was no longer trying to keep wage levels down to force peasants to remain as feudal serfs. Forced to pay more, it now suited many landowners to rent out land to peasants, who were, therefore, able to grow prosperous and better fed. Henry V was a lucky king to walk into such a placid scenario.

There was just one small blot on the landscape. The Lollards were increasing in number and spreading their heresy to all classes. Like his father before him, Henry believed in burning all Lollards who would not recant at the stake. A story told often about Henry and the Lollards involved a clothworker who was being burned in the royal presence. As the flames licked up the man's legs, he screamed for mercy. Henry ordered the fire to be put out and waited for the man to escape his fate by recanting. But, when he didn't, Henry had the fire relit and watched him burn to death.

Otherwise, England was at peace with itself for once, which enabled Henry to plan that which medieval English kings were seemingly designed for: to wage war on France. In Henry's case he had learnt to fight as a prince in many a long campaign in Wales, and an arrow scar down one side of his face was a reminder of his great victory at Shrewsbury. War would mean the chance to reclaim those continental parts of his rightful inheritance that his French cousin Charles VI, mad as he was, held tantalisingly across the Channel. He knew that both church and Parliament would support him and that circumstances were just right, due to the ongoing French civil war.

The barons, he knew, would salivate at the thought of a French war. They had been denied such fun throughout the reign of the pacifist King Richard, yet war was what they were trained and yearned for. It meant adventure, romance, glory and plunder. Especially in France.

And not only the barons looked forward to war. There were in England a great many outlaws on the run for whom military service was the only way they might redeem themselves in the eyes of the law. In some of the English armies of the fifteenth century, up to 5 per cent of the soldiers were murderers officially seeking a pardon. There was none of the ancient problem such as King Harold's army faced in the days of the Conquest, when men deserted in droves at the season of harvesting crops, because Henry's fighters were for the most part the landed classes and their servants, not field labourers. Three-quarters of all Henry's army were his archers, most of whom were professionals a great deal of their time. Then there were the cannon fodder troops from Ireland who, often enough, fought barefoot with great ferocity using daggers as their only weapons. As for the fully armoured men-at-arms (mostly dismounted in battle in Henry's day due to the ever-increasing vulnerability of horses to modern weaponry), their equipment was hugely elaborate and costly. From his all-enclosing helmet and visor to his steel-encased feet, a man-at-arms was completely sheathed in overlapping sections of plate armour. His eye slit was minimal, and only his arms and legs could move, puppet-like but sufficiently to wield his sword and his dagger. If he fell over, it would take two men to stand him up again, and if he fell into a puddle, he was likely to drown.

Henry planned his invasion of France down to the last detail. A huge amount of back-up equipment was involved, and to get it all across the Channel with the army meant a great many boats. These he simply requisitioned from every port in England. His eventual invasion fleet consisted of 1,500 vessels, including Dutch, Venetian and Genoese mercenary ships, a fleet twelve times the size of the Spanish Armada. Henry's entire army numbered at the outset some 10,000 men, or one per cent of the population.

Three Fiennes relations fought for Henry V at Agincourt: the same self-styled Lord Saye who had fought for Henry's father in Wales, and two Fiennes brothers from Sussex, the sons of William of Herstmonceux. The elder son, Roger, Sheriff of Sussex at the time, was given £1,086 to pay for himself and a company of eight men-at-arms and twenty-four archers to present themselves to the fleet at Southampton. This Roger was to spend a great deal of time serving Henry in France over the next ten years.

His younger brother, James, led a 'lance', or small section of infantry in the division headed up by the king's brother, Humphrey, Duke of Gloucester, and James outshone his brother to the extent that Henry later awarded him the lordship of Court-le Courte, the governorship of Arques and captain-generalship of various key towns along the River Seine. He was later to build the beautiful manor of Knole in Kent with the spoils of Agincourt and its aftermath.

The army landed unopposed on the north bank of the Seine and close by the walled city of Honfleur, which Henry considered as the key to Normandy. He sent his favourite brother, the Duke of Clarence, to block the far side of Honfleur and positioned his siege guns to batter its great walls from the north. Sapper groups began to tunnel under the walls with explosives, but the French dug counter-tunnels and fierce underground fights ensued where the skills of English archers were redundant. The city moat, wide as a lake, made ramming tactics unfeasible.

Pontoon-mounted scaling ladder attacks were met by showers of burning sulphur and lime or scalding streams of hot oil from the battlement guards above.

In the English siege camps along the salt marshes of the Seine estuary, dysentery struck, and hundreds died of the bloody flux. Fortunately for Henry, the town ran short of supplies, one of the key towers was taken, no relief army turned up and, five weeks after the siege began, the garrison surrendered.

Henry now had his foothold in Normandy, but his army, ravaged by sickness, was too weak to march on Paris. So he decided to march east to his only other secure base, the port of Calais some 160 miles away. His 6,000-strong force managed seventeen miles a day, baggage trains and all, and did well until they reached the Somme, when they found every bridge destroyed and every ford heavily defended. Food began to run out and the rain poured down, as it would five centuries later. The miles went wearily by as the weakened men toiled along the south bank of the river, searching upstream for a crossing point, but always losing ground to their goal of the coast and Calais. Soon a French force as big as theirs appeared on the far riverbank and shadowed their progress inland.

Wet, cold, sick and hungry, the English marched on, their prospects dire. It looked as though Henry had made a horrible tactical error. Hundreds of men had crutch-rot, a condition from which I have suffered for hundreds of miles man-hauling in the polar regions. This can result from walking when there are no washing facilities and one is suffering from diarrhoea. Henry's soldiers cut the backs out of their breeches to stop the bloody flux rotting the leather.

On this long and fearful march, James Fiennes was with the king's brother, the Duke of Gloucester, as was the king himself and various royal favourites, including William Wykeham, the heir of ex-chancellor William of Wykeham. William was only seventeen at the time, but his uncle Thomas had died at the siege of Honfleur, so he took command of the family standard and led his archers on towards Calais. One outcome of James Fiennes of

Sussex and young Wykeham from Hampshire sharing such memorable circumstances may well have been the subsequent marriage, twenty years later, of James's son to William's daughter and heiress, resulting in the Fienneses inheriting Broughton Castle.

As the long hellish march continued and bridge after bridge bristled with French troops, making, one imagines, gallic gestures, Henry may have regretted his decision to head for Calais. But what other option did he have after the long and disease-stricken Honfleur siege? He could hardly have taken his army straight back to an expectant England. His prestige would have sunk below zero with sullen soldiers, angry barons and an uppity Parliament, truly a potential rebellion scenario. On top of which, any future invasion of France would be well nigh impossible to finance. So the march to Calais, however disastrous its outcome, might yet be preferable to having gained Honfleur and then fleeing home.

At some point Henry received local information which led him to cut away from the river where it performed a great loop, thereby gaining ground on the French on the other bank. Then, when the English reached the river again at the end of its loop, they found and crossed two bridges that were intact. This involved feverish work destroying local wooden houses to provide solid approaches to the bridges, for the French had broken up the previous causeways. One can imagine Henry's apprehension as this work went on since, at any minute, the French army might arrive on the far bank before the English could cross. But their luck stayed good, they crossed and must have slept greatly relieved on the northern bank. That night, although they could not know it, the two armies camped only seven miles apart. Henry gave his exhausted men a rest day and sent out scouts to search for the French. Calais, he knew, was still a full eight days' march away.

The two armies then marched along on parallel roads but in the same direction until, converging near the village of Agincourt and from high ground, the English gained their first view of the enemy. They were shocked and dispirited by the sheer size of the French host of some 27,000 soldiers. The French continued northwards until, just ahead of the English, they deployed right across the approach roads to Calais and just outside Agincourt. The English camped a mile short of the enemy lines on the eve of the Feast of St Crispin. They were truly exhausted. Their mood must have been sombre as they camped, having seen the size of the army blocking their escape route. They were outnumbered more than four to one. Henry ordered silence in his camp. Then he moved around the groups of wet, hungry men with words of exhortation. Shakespeare's later version of his speech on the eve of battle was to make Henry famous down the centuries.

The rain poured down all night, but ceased at dawn when Henry rode down his lines. For four hours the armies faced each other 1,000 yards apart in a wide, muddy field with a slight dip between them and woods to either flank of the English. Six thousand men, mostly archers, against 25,000 men mostly men-at-arms with 1,200 cavalry behind them.

Henry made the first move, for his men were cold, wet and hungry. He gave the order 'Banners advance', his men cheered, drums beat and pipes played. Leaning with the weight against their bows, his archers loosed their first arrows to goad the French cavalry into a charge. Once the charge began, the archers planted sharpened stakes ahead of them and continued to shoot as the cavalry lumbered towards them through deep mud. Unable to pass the stakes, the cavalry wheeled about, but their subsequent rally blocked the oncoming waves of men-at-arms, struggling through the mud to reach the English. So the French living piled up on the French dead and when the English archers ran out of arrows they set about the French with axes and swords taken from the corpses, then sorted the living from the dead to keep the live for ransom.

One problem that the French men-at-arms clearly had at Agincourt was that their pages were left behind, leaving nobody to help them up when they tripped or overbalanced. If two men fell onto a third, the man beneath was likely to die, such was the weight of the plate armour. During the battle, the Duke of York, fighting in the front line, was pushed over and others fell on top of him. When the battle ended and his body was found, he was uninjured, but was dead from suffocation. He was the last of Edward III's grandsons.

As the English took their prisoners, a sudden new danger arose. French cavalry had successfully raided Henry's baggage train and carried off his crown, whilst others had rallied in a force still bigger than the entire English army and were spotted gathering for a new attack. Henry, realising that thousands of French men-at-arms, fallen but uninjured, could yet pose a big threat in any new battle, gave the immediate order that no Frenchman was to be left alive. Wholesale throat-cutting and eyeballing ensued, much to the displeasure of Henry's troops who lost fortunes in potential ransom fees. But they went ahead with the mass killings, saving only the likes of the Dukes of Orleans and Bourbon and other royal personages.

For reasons unknown, the new cavalry attack never materialised and the battle was over. That night the English set off for the safety of Calais where, after two weeks of rest and care of their wounded, they set sail for England.

Less than 1,000 Englishmen were killed at Agincourt, but 10,000 Frenchmen died in the battle, including three dukes, ninety lords and 1,560 knights – over half the nobility of France. This was surely England's greatest hour of triumph in the Hundred Years War. Back in England, King Henry and his men could do no wrong. Eighty years after Agincourt, an Italian visitor was recorded as saying: 'the English are great lovers of themselves . . . They think there are no other men than themselves, and no other world but England. And when they see a handsome foreigner they say that "he looks like an Englishman."'

In the year 2008 a group of French academics met in Agincourt on St Crispin's Day for a conference to mark the 593rd anniversary of the battle. They ridiculed the idea that it was a heroic English victory against overwhelming odds, saying the size of the French army had been grossly exaggerated and that the English had behaved 'like war criminals', setting fire to prisoners and killing French noblemen who had surrendered. In fact, Agincourt was, as Henry himself was quick to realise, just a small, if successful, beginning to his quest to become King of France. At a cost of a quarter of his army lost, mostly to sickness, he had merely captured one town and won a single battle.

Over the two years following Agincourt, Henry prepared for his second invasion by diplomacy, using as his main lever the ongoing civil war between the Burgundians in the north and east and the Armagnacs or House of Valois, in the south and west. Both sides vied for the favour of the mad French king and whichever of his sons was his dauphin at the time (they died off one by one). Henry eventually chose the Burgundians for an alliance, and only planned his next move secure in the knowledge of Burgundian aid, or at least their non-interference with his planned annexation of Normandy. His enemy would be narrowed down to the armies of the Armagnacs, and the dauphinists.

The Count of Armagnac was now also Constable of the French army, the position previously held by Robert Fiennes, and he attempted to forestall Henry's invasion by retaking Honfleur, having blockaded the mouth of the Seine. In August 1416 one of Henry's brothers, the Duke of Bedford, with a large English fleet, won the Battle of the Seine and lifted the siege. Henry then took Caen, after which other lesser towns yielded like falling dominoes, so that, by November 1416, he controlled all of Lower Normandy and could move on to the challenge of Rouen.

The garrison at Rouen knew the English were coming and burnt all the churches, abbeys, manors, castles, villages, harvests and barns, until a blackened wilderness surrounded the city for miles around. All families who could not prove they could provide for themselves for at least ten months were exiled. Several thousand died of starvation as a result.

One of Henry's fears had come to pass, for Paris had fallen to his former ally the Duke of Burgundy, who now felt powerful enough to ignore his truce with England and send troops to help hold Rouen. The city lies on the east bank of the Seine and its walls were five miles long. Henry never succeeded in a direct assault, but after six months the garrison were starving, holding out only because they believed the Duke of Burgundy would soon arrive with his main army to relieve them. But he never did, and inside the city the cost of a cat was ten times that of a mouse, whilst shoes made of leather were boiled and chewed. Finally, in January 1418 the garrison surrendered and Henry's men entered in triumph. Normandy could now be said to be the property of the English king 'Henry the Conqueror', 352 years after William the Conqueror and the Battle of Hastings.

Henry's two successful invasions gained Normandy, but he had yet to achieve his ultimate aim of gaining the crown of France. A third invasion would be needed and, before that, a great deal more diplomacy, particularly when he learnt the Burgundians and Armagnacs were about to bury their differences in an anti-English alliance. A grand meeting was fixed between Burgundy and Armagnac to agree terms. The Duke of Burgundy duly arrived at the rendezvous, in the centre of a bridge over the river Yonne, expecting to meet the dauphin. Instead the dauphin's Armagnac soldiers hacked off half of the duke's head with an axe.

Nothing could have helped Henry more, throwing as it did the Burgundians straight into his arms. A further outcome of the duke's murder was that the French Queen Isabella, the Burgundian figurehead, betrothed her daughter Catherine to Henry. She loved her daughter but detested her son, the dauphin, leader of the Armagnacs. In May 1420 Henry married Catherine of France and co-signed with her mother, the queen, the Treaty of Troyes which made him the next King of France as soon as mad King Charles VI died. Until then he would act as regent. The only drawback to the treaty was the promise Henry had to make to continue war against the southern territories still held by the dauphin. But, so what? Henry was King of France and England, and his new wife was young, beautiful and quickly bore him a son.

Henry and the new Duke of Burgundy were highly successful in their ongoing joint campaigns, but Henry's brother, the Duke of Clarence, was operating with a small force near Baugé in Maine when a dauphinist Scottish-French army of 5,000 blocked his way near Tours. Clarence rashly attacked when his archers under Lord Salisbury were still hours away, and was massacred. Clarence was Henry's favourite brother and trusty comrade-in-arms and, although the battle was in itself minor and led by the Scots, its effect on the morale of the dauphinists was great, for it was the first time in the Hundred Years War that the English had suffered a straightforward defeat in open battle.

The dauphin promoted the Scottish victor of the Battle of Baugé, the Duke of Buchan, to be the Constable of his army: a unique honour for a foreigner. At one point, due to the tiny force left to Lord Salisbury with which to defend Normandy, the dauphin may well have been able to retake much of the province. But he never pressed his attack, and Salisbury held out until he was reinforced.

In the spring of 1421 Henry set out from England for his third and last campaign. This was not, technically, an invasion force, since he was after all regent of France. He landed at Calais with 4,000 men, his aim being to defeat a powerful dauphinist counter-offensive and to subdue a minor regional rebellion. The successes that followed were as brilliant as ever, with no open battles but several hard sieges of diehard garrisons, such as Maux. But his main aim, to lure the dauphin into a major battle, never worked, and in 1422 he became too ill to ride a horse. By August that year he was confined to bed, probably with severe dysentery, at the Castle of Vincennes, where he spent his last three weeks putting his dominions in order and securing the inheritance of the baby son, his heir, whom he had never seen. His funeral cortege moved slowly and in great style through Normandy. The Normans would long remember the passing of King Henry the Conqueror.

II

Murdered by a Mob

Henry VI was born in July, only six months before his father, Henry V of England, and mad King Charles of France both died, leaving their thrones to him. He became the only monarch ever to be crowned king of both countries. However, King Charles's exiled and dispossessed son, the dauphin, was shortly to proclaim himself the rightful King of France and to dedicate his reign not just to getting Henry out of the way but to ridding France of the English once and for all.

English successes in France to date had been largely due to brilliant commanders but, more so, to clever manipulation by the English of the ongoing civil war between two royal dynasties, the Burgundians and the House of Armagnac (Valois), both having reasonable claims to the French throne. However, the rumblings of civil war in England between two similarly royal-contending dynasties, the Houses of Lancaster and of York, both claiming the right to the throne of England, allowed the French to slowly turn the tables and to rid France of the English. The seeds of this civil war were sewn largely by the unfortunate Henry VI, not through aggression on his part but through his very weakness and ineptitude, for he was as feeble a character as his father, Henry V of Agincourt, had been ultra-efficient and powerful.

During Henry V's final three weeks on his deathbed in France, he had made meticulous plans for his succession. He specified that his brother, the Duke of Bedford, was to be young Henry VI's regent in France and Normandy, that his brother, the Duke of Gloucester, was to be regent in England, and that his uncles, the Duke of Exeter and Bishop Beaufort, would be Henry VI's tutors.

This initially worked well, and in France, despite the loss of the ever-victorious Henry V, things carried on normally, even though there was a serious lack of troops to man the garrisons of the many hundreds of castles and fortified towns held by the English. Bedford and Talbot were the two great English generals of the time and, in the wings, the Earls of Salisbury and Warwick.

One great battle of the period was fought at Cravant in Normandy between a fairly small English/Burgundian allied force under Salisbury against a mixed Scottish/Armagnac army. Some 4,000 Scots were killed and 2,000 Frenchmen. By the mid 1420s a constant stream of Scottish reinforcements were joining the Armagnacs to fight the English, and in April 1424 the Earl of Douglas led an army of 6,500 Scotsmen against an English force. The dauphin later gave the earl the title of Duke of Touraine. At the subsequent Battle of Verneuil, Bedford and Salisbury defeated a Franco-Scottish force twice the strength of their own army and annihilated the Scottish contingent of 6,000. French writers of the time described the battle as another Agincourt.

All went well under the young Henry VI's regents, or at least it did so for the first five of years of his reign. And for the Fiennes clan of the period, things were also looking up. Two successive William Fienneses had lived at Herstmonceux Castle and both had been Sheriffs of Sussex and Surrey. The younger William had surrendered Pevensey Castle to French raiders some twenty years before the start of Henry VI's reign, but that had not affected his high standing in royal eyes. He had two sons, Roger and James, and passed all his lands to Roger, the elder son, who joined the royal household, took over as Sheriff of Sussex, was knighted, and spent many years as the influential Treasurer to Henry VI's household.

He and his younger brother James had both done well at Agincourt for Henry V and on subsequent campaigns, but James, who set out in life with no land, was extremely ambitious. He is my great to the power of eighteen grandfather, and I have to admit that both written history and William Shakespeare make him sound the sort of man who would and did do anything in the pursuit of power. He attended the young King Henry VI at his coronation in Paris, and was made Commissioner of the Peace for Kent, a lifelong appointment. At the time he began to cultivate and promote friends and relations into a veritable Kent mafia that would eventually affect English history.

The wealth James Fiennes made from his French campaigning helped him purchase two great estates in the south-east that are open to the public today: Knole, near Sevenoaks, and Hever at Penshurst. But the more James had, the more he wanted. Whenever he could he used his big brother Roger's influence, and that was considerable, especially after he had organised the marriage of the young Henry VI to a niece of the King of France, Margaret of Anjou. Before long both Fiennes brothers were Members of Parliament, representing Kent and Sussex.

Whilst these two Fiennes stars were in the ascendant, the English situation in France was deteriorating fast. The rot set in when a teenage peasant girl from eastern France, Joan of Arc, became the talisman of the dauphin's army with her 'divine voices'. Agincourt became merely a nightmare of the past for the French. The English were no longer invincible. This ensured that it would only be a matter of time before the Burgundian/English alliance collapsed, as the Duke of Burgundy always sought the stronger side. However, the alliance was still in place when, after a string of minor victories, Joan of Arc was captured by the Burgundians, sold to the English for 16,000 francs, condemned as a heretic by the French church and burnt at the stake. Joan's main beneficiary was, of course, the dauphin who, despite several reversals due to brilliant generalship by the likes of Lord Talbot, spent the next quarter century driving the English out of every corner of France, save for the port of Calais. In this he was greatly helped by one Jean Bureau, an expert designer of artillery who changed the face of siege warfare and, at length, rendered obsolete the previous advantages of the English longbow.

When the French captured the key town of Pontoise, they slaughtered five hundred English soldiers in the garrison and ransomed their commander, John Fiennes, the 6th Lord Clinton, who had married Elizabeth Fiennes, the granddaughter of that Roger Fiennes who was treasurer of the royal household. Like his father before him, this Clinton styled himself as Lord Saye. But the exorbitant ransom that John Clinton had to pay to escape the French clutches (twice, because he was later recaptured!) crippled his finances and, to retrieve his fortunes, he sold the title of Lord Saye to the Fiennes family, where it had rightly belonged since one of the William Fienneses of Herstmonceux had married Joan de Saye almost a century before.

The senior Fiennes who should have taken over the Lord Saye title from the Clintons was Roger, the royal treasurer, since he was the elder brother. But the ever ambitious James was, by the time of Pontoise, a close favourite and adviser of Henry VI, who agreed that he, James, should become Lord Saye. James added the name of his estate village, Sele, to his title, and so was officially thereafter Sir James Fiennes, the 1st Lord (or Baron) Saye and Sele.

In 1440, the new Lord Saye and Sele, James Fiennes, began a meteoric rise to the dangerous heights of political power in England. His methods may be described as occasionally dubious. He and his elder brother Roger were members of the inner circle surrounding the king, led by the Earl of Suffolk. James spent a great deal of time working with the king on two of the latter's more praiseworthy projects: the foundation of Eton College and King's College, Cambridge. In 1444 James became chamberlain to the queen, Margaret of Anjou, who was, much of the time, a powerful influence on the king. James received many other offices, wardships, estates and annuities to add to his growing wealth and influence. He was appointed Constable of both Pevensey and Rochester Castles. The same year the Archbishop of Canterbury gave him various church lands by the king's order, and recorded these appointments as 'havyng consyderacion how the seid James stondyng aboute the Kyng as he dooth, may dayly proufyte our church and us'.

The tangled plotting of different advisers to King Henry VI was further complicated in the mid-1440s when the king began to experience periods of madness. The Earl of Suffolk's influence vied with that of the regent, the Earl of Gloucester, and when the latter's star waned, Suffolk went in for the kill, successfully persuading Parliament to arrest and imprison Gloucester for his failed policies in France. James Fiennes was Suffolk's main crony and, when Gloucester died mysteriously in prison, he was accused of his murder. But nothing was proved and James, who had served alongside Gloucester at Agincourt, profited hugely from his death, since the day after its occurrence he petitioned successfully for various offices held by the duke.

His royal wages were greatly increased and he became chamberlain of the royal household, which gave him control over access to the king and membership of the Continual Council. For a period he became Constable of the Tower of London, whilst all the while adding to his web of influential friends in Kent, a regional mafia involved in heavy extortion of taxes and dubious land-grabbing tactics.

Many historians later accused Roger Fiennes of extortions in Kent alongside his brother, but his actions suggest that he had no sympathy with James's greedy and aggressive behaviour. There is no evidence of his ever lining his own pockets, nor did he have himself ennobled. Indeed, Roger resigned from his influential position at court at the exact time when James and the Duke of Suffolk reached the peak of their power on the back of policies which Roger clearly detested.

On the wider political front, Suffolk and James tried to buy peace with France through mediation and by marrying King

Henry VI to a French royal. They pushed a plan to surrender Anjou and Maine, providing they could keep Calais, Gascony and Normandy. Such appeasement was loathed by supporters of the possibly murdered Duke of Gloucester, including Roger Fiennes who had risked his life over the years to retain such French territories.

When the Suffolk policies collapsed in ruins and the French grabbed back everywhere but Calais, the vengeance of Parliament was immediate. The king tried to save Suffolk from execution by banishing him, but he was intercepted by a mob of Kentish sailors during his cross-Channel escape and was clubbed to death. To be fair to Suffolk and James Fiennes, their peace policy, with hindsight, looks to have been the most sensible option. If the English had retained Calais, Normandy and Gascony, they would have kept control of the Channel and the wool and wine trades. The alternative course was war, which may have looked good at the time but was an expensive no-win solution. As it was, the peace policy appeared to have allowed France to throw out the English, and James, with Lord Suffolk dead, must have known his days were numbered. But he did not go without a struggle.

The king appointed James lord high treasurer, to which the Commons responded by moving to have him arrested, and his fate was sealed by his past shady dealings in Kent. But the men of Kent were not the only folk in England with grudges to bear. In a world already ravaged by the Black Death, there followed outbreaks of plague, disastrous famines, wet summers, cattle and sheep epidemics and a slump in wool prices. Private armies of disbanded soldiers, most but not all owned by local barons, roamed, bullied and wrecked many local economies. King Henry VI, insane and weak, appeared to do nothing to alleviate the misery of his people.

In June 1450 a great crowd from all over Kent county met together on the road to London. Their aim was to punish those in government who caused their tribulations and, in their own words, to free the good king from the trickeries of these false ministers. The ringleader of the march on London was one Jack Cade whom history records as having been a part of the household of close Fiennes relations in Kent, but was often described as a mere peasant. Mere peasant he could not have been, bearing in mind the efforts made after his death to declare officially that 'his blood was corrupt'. Two years after his death, the king ordered that his goods should be forfeited, including his lands, rents and possessions. Had he been low-born, no such act of attainder would have been made. He himself claimed to be called John Mortimer, the family name of the Duke of York.

In July 1450 Cade's mob came to London, and the king, 'dredying the malice of the peple', committed James Fiennes to the Tower as a sop to the rebels who in a 'dyrge made by the comons of Kent in the tyme of their rysynge' wrote:

> 'So pore a kyng was never seene
> Nor richere lordes alle bydene;
> The communes may no more.
> The lorde Say biddeth hold hem downe,
> That worthy dastarde of renowne,
> He techithe a fals loore.'

James is berated in better prose and verse when he features in Shakespeare's *King Henry VI, Part 2*, where in true Elizabethan royalist style he is afforded the dignity of afflicted nobility whereas Cade is merely comic relief:

> Thou hast most traitorously corrupted the youth of the realm in erecting a grammar school: and whereas, before, our forefathers had no other books but the score and the tally, thou has caused printing to be used; and, contrary to the king, his crown and dignity, thou hast built a paper-mill. It will be proved to thy face that thou hast men about thee that usually talk of a noun and a verb, and such abominable words as no

> Christian ear can endure to hear. Thou hast appointed justices of peace, to call poor men before them about matters they were not able to answer. Moreover, thou hast put them in prison; and because they could not read, thou hast hanged them; when, indeed, only for that cause they have been most worthy to live.

Shakespeare replies for James Fiennes with the words:

> I sold not Maine, I lost not Normandy;
> Yet, to recover them, would lose my life.
> Justice with favour have I always done;
> Prayers and tears have moved me, gifts could never.
> When have I aught exacted at your hands,
> But to maintain the king, the realm, and you? . . .
> Have I affected wealth or honour?
> Are my chests fill'd up with extorted gold?
> Is my apparel sumptuous to behold?
> Whom have I injured, that ye seek my death?
> These hands are free from guiltless blood-shedding,
> This breast from harbouring foul deceitful thoughts.
> O, let me live!

At the Guildhall mock-trial James was accused of many things, including murder. The record states that he 'knowlachyd of the dethe of that notabylle and famos prynce the Duke of Glouceter'. The Bury Parliament 'was maad [set up] only for to sle the noble duke of Gloucestre, whoz deth the fals duke of Suffolk . . . and ser Jamez Fynez lord Say . . . hadde longe tyme conspired and ymagyned.'

He requested a proper trial, but the mob, enraged and beyond the control of anyone or anything but their immediate bloodlust, dragged James on foot to Cheapside, where they hacked off his head halfway through his confession and before 'the priest could shrive him'. His head was then impaled on a long spear and paraded ahead of Cade 'as he rode, like a lordly captain, thro' every street.'

At Mile End, James's son-in-law, William Cromer, the much hated Sheriff of Kent, was also decapitated, his head mounted on another spear and the mob then 'made both hedes kisse to gider'. James's body was stripped, tied to a horse's tail and dragged naked, 'so that the flesh clave to the stones all the way from Chepe to Southwark'. At London Bridge the two heads were rammed on to spikes and the bodies hanged and quartered.

Documents that Nat and Mariette Fiennes lent me from Broughton indicate a sub-plot behind the Cade killing of James Fiennes. For anyone interested in conspiracy theories this one rates a great deal more likely than most of those suggested for the deaths of Kennedy, Princess Diana or Michael Jackson. If you can't abide a touch of 560-year-old forensic dabbling, then simply skip the next page or so. The facts and deductions are as follows:

FACT Sussex records state: 'Cade drew with him a great company of tall [important] personages and vagrant persons from Kent, Sussex and Surrey . . . These musters were levied by the Constables . . . We have by name four hundred Sussex men . . . Lord Saye [James Fiennes] was unfavourably known here as having acquired his title by grant from his kinsman John Clinton of Sussex and it will be seen that the neighbours of Clinton and the men living closest to Fiennes's eldest brother Sir Roger and to Thomas Dacre, in whose service Cade had been, were the strongest in the list of Cade's Sussex men.'

DEDUCTION James's Sussex relations did not approve of him. His unpopular reputation and his closeness to the hated Suffolk were perhaps reflecting on them and they wanted him sacked but not killed.

FACT Of the Kent rebels with Cade only one was a knight, John Cheney, who was at the forefront of the rebellion. He shared a common Saye ancestry with James and his great grandmother was James's grandmother.

DEDUCTION Cheney was in league with the above Sussex Fiennes plotters and for the same reason.

FACT The above Fiennes plotters would also have received an unpopular backlash from the fact that the hated James and Suffolk clique was closely associated with yet another relation of theirs, Sir John Saye, the only man to be Speaker of the House of Commons in both a Lancastrian and a Yorkist Parliament, 'related to James Fiennes, Lord Saye and Sele, in whose company he is often recorded . . . brother to William Saye, Dean of St Paul's. Close associate to the Earl of Suffolk.' This Sir John was a favourite of both Henry VI and Edward IV, but in 1450 was 'attacked by the Cade rebels and in 1451 the Commons demanded his banishment from Court'.

FACT In addition to targeting James and his cousin John Saye, Cade's other main target was, as we have seen, William Cromer, Sheriff of Kent, who was married to James's daughter.

DEDUCTION A powerful group of the Fiennes/Saye/Dacre clan in Sussex and Kent were fed up with three family members who, as extortioners and cronies of Suffolk, were getting them a very bad name. So their plot was as follows.

They were influential enough to have friends in court and learnt of the king's plan to help Suffolk escape by sea. So they paid men to bludgeon Suffolk to death during his secretive flight. These same men were later listed as Cade followers.

Next the plotters instructed Cade (who had once worked for Thomas Dacre) to extract James from his refuge in the Tower and then to select Robert Danvers, the Recorder of London, as the man to judge James.

They selected Danvers because he was part of their plot, being brother-in-law to James's daughter Jane. Danvers would ensure that James, John Saye and Cromer were removed from their high-profile jobs but not actually killed.

All went well with the plan until Cade lost control of his mob. John Saye was indeed sacked but both James and Cromer were murdered. The plotters, fearing discovery, decided to have Cade silenced so, when Cromer's widow married the new Sheriff of Kent he was tasked to find and kill Cade, which he speedily did.

Many historians proffer the theory that Cade aka Mortimer was put up to the rebellion against King Henry's ruling clique in order to make way for a rival group under Richard Duke of York, whose family name was Mortimer. But the Fiennes versus Fiennes plot that I offer here is based on no less circumstantial evidence.

THE FIENNES VERSUS FIENNES PLOT

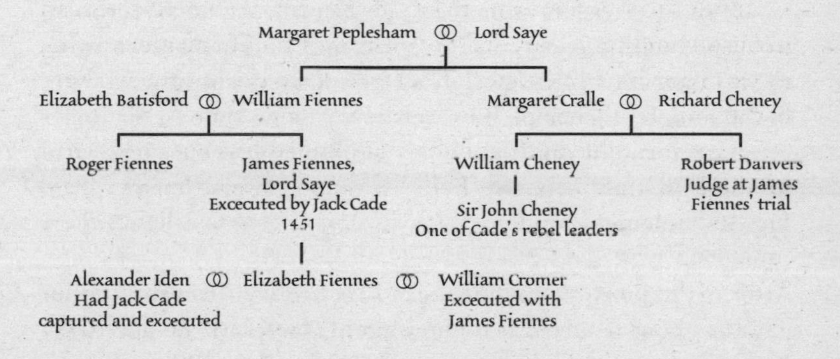

After the Cade revolt, English reverses continued apace in France, and soon after the final English bastions of Rouen and Castillon were lost, Roger Fiennes, ten years of whose life had been spent fighting for Henry V, died at his moated home, Herstmonceux Castle, which he had rebuilt and crenellated at a total cost of £3,800. At the time this was considered to be the greatest brick building in England since Roman times. Unaltered, in the twentieth century it would become the Royal Observatory in lieu of Greenwich when the London lights became too bright in the night sky for observation of the stars. When Herstmonceux also became too bright at night, the Observatory moved to the Canary Islands, and Herstmonceux became a Canadian-funded international study centre.

I believe that Roger was always as strait-laced as James was wily. Both brothers were for a long period full-time courtiers of Henry VI and both received many royal gifts as a result. One record of the Treasury from the 1440s records. 'An ouche [brooch] garnished with a baleys and a saphyr and six perles yeven by us to Sir James Fenys on New Yere's Day and an ouche of gold with, in the middle, a fleur de lys yeven at the same time to Sir Roger Fenys, tresorier of our household.' Both men had sons who were to shine in their separate fields with no adverse effects from James's lamentable end.

After 1453 Henry VI and his successors had little to worry about in France, but troubles at home soon made up for the next sixty years of peace with the French. The Wars of the Roses did not begin with a bang, nor were the warring parties divided along clean lines, although they clearly fought to place a Lancastrian or a Yorkist on the throne of England. Henry VI, the Lancastrian was directly descended in an unbroken male line from Edward III's third son. The claimant who was to take Henry's throne from him was Richard, Duke of York, who was descended from Edward III's second son, but through two women. In the male only line, he was also descended from Edward's fifth son.

BOTH THE HOUSES OF YORK AND LANCASTER WERE AT SOME POINT MOTHERED BY FIENNES DNA

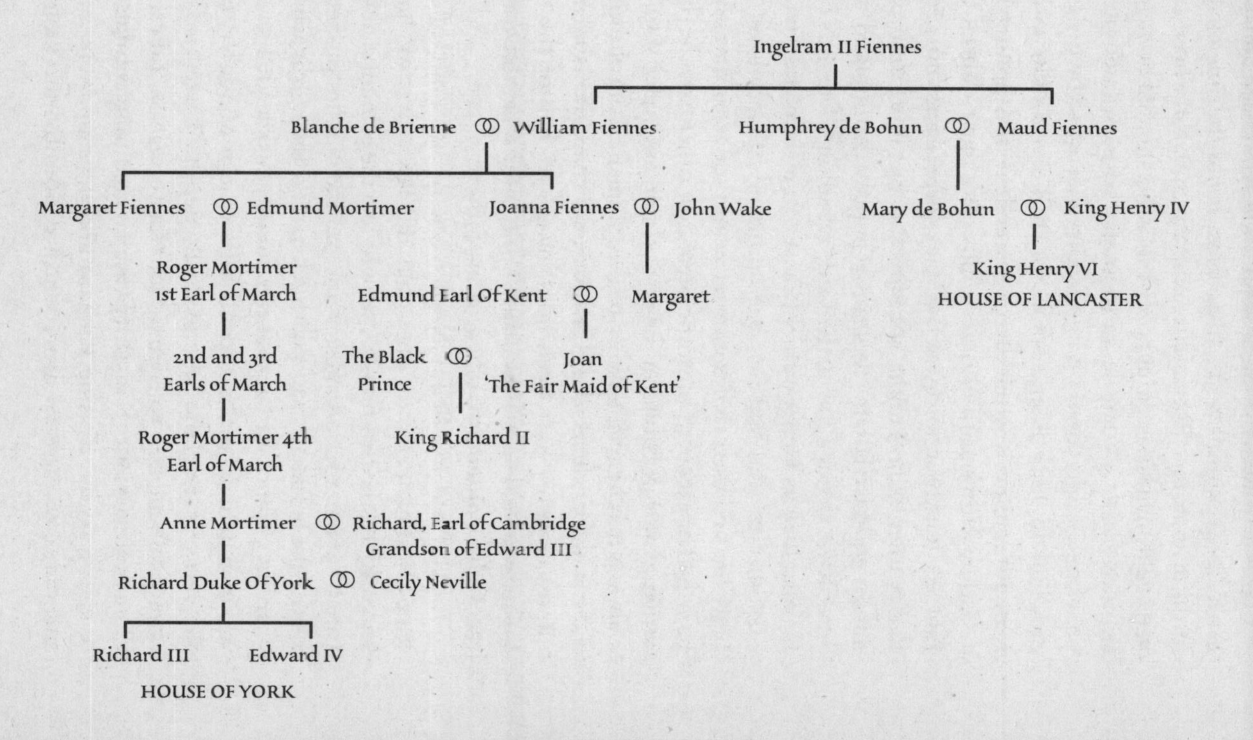

Quite who was the more legitimate contender and why is a matter long fought over by historians, but at the time of the Wars of the Roses both sides were certain that their king was the rightful heir. Both dynasties originated from the same family and both dynasties were at some point mothered by Fiennes DNA. On the Lancastrian side, Henry VI's grandmother was Mary, the granddaughter of Joan Fiennes. On the Yorkist side the soon to be King Edward IV was the direct descendent of Margaret Fiennes.

Although the Lancastrians could trace their descent back to Edward III, they were clearly already usurpers since their Henry IV had murdered the Yorkist ancestor Richard II. Richard of York's advantage was that he was more popular in England than the weak King Henry. One of the Cade rebellion's demands had been his installing as Henry's chief adviser, in place of Edmund, Duke of Somerset, who had just been promoted chancellor.

Richard realised that Somerset would sooner or later have him banished or executed on some pretext or other. So he struck first, arriving outside London with a small force and loudly proclaiming that he wished only to oust Somerset, not the king. This did not work, and Richard, who then disbanded his men, would almost certainly have been done away with but for the fact that his ten-year-old son, Edward of York, with a sizeable force from the Welsh borders, marched to his father's rescue.

Richard had married a Neville, one of two powerful families from Northumberland. They and the Percy dynasty hated one another, and the two families were to fuel the coming civil war. The Percys supported the Lancastrians and the Nevilles pushed for the rise of the House of York, with Richard as their great white hope.

In 1453 Henry VI became temporarily insane, due to madness in his maternal family, and his wife Queen Margaret took over the reins of England alongside Somerset. These two became implacable enemies to Richard and his young son, Edward. Early in 1455 King Henry's insanity disappeared long enough for him to regain power, causing Richard and his supporters, in fear of their lives, to raise an army which confronted the king's forces at St Albans, the first battle of the Wars of the Roses. This was in reality a one-hour skirmish, but the Duke of Somerset was killed and the king was captured.

Once again Richard was in charge and his main men, Salisbury and Warwick, got the top jobs. King Henry, weak and verging on new bouts of insanity, would surely have accepted the situation, but not his feisty Queen Margaret who plotted constantly to ensure that when her mad husband died, her young son Edward, and not the hated Richard of York, would take over.

The two armies clashed again at Northampton in 1460, and in no time the Lancastrian army dissolved, King Henry was once again in Richard's hands and, for a while, things seemed little changed. The mad Lancastrian King Henry was on the throne with a Yorkist government ruling the land in his name. But then Richard's personal ambitions to usurp and rule without awaiting Henry's demise grew too strong. He found soon enough that the country was not quite ready to remove its rightful king, but Parliament did sign an agreement that, on Henry's death, Richard's dynasty, not Henry's, would succeed.

This was too much for Queen Margaret. Her husband might be mad and accept whatever humiliation Richard threw at him, but she would somehow ensure that her son remained heir, as was his birthright. She raised support in Scotland and in the Lancastrian northlands, so Richard went north to deal with her. Overconfident and somewhere near Wakefield, he found himself with few troops and surrounded by a large Lancastrian force. He was killed, along with the Earl of Salisbury and others. Their heads were paraded on poles and then planted on the battlements of York.

A few days later Richard's son and heir, Edward of York, heard the news. His father, brother, uncle and cousin were all dead. He himself defeated a force of largely Welsh Lancastrian supporters near Hereford before heading for London. Meanwhile, the queen's large army of northerners behaved like Viking raiders as they also advanced on London over a wide front, looting, raping and causing devastation wherever they went. Known or suspected Yorkists were tortured and killed. The queen could not control her army, so, on reaching London, she camped on the outskirts. This allowed Edward of York, and his cousin and main supporter the Earl of Warwick, to outflank the queen's wild horde and secure the capital, the centre of power.

This time there was no beating around the royal bush. A speedily convened council agreed that Edward of York, who was neither mad nor in charge of an army of rapists, should be king in place of the mad King Henry and his haughty wife. So King Edward IV, only twenty years old, became the first Yorkist king. But there were now two reigning monarchs, a situation that would need speedy resolution.

Edward and Warwick sped north a week after the coronation to deal once and for all with Queen Margaret, her son and their army. The two armies, each numbering over 40,000, met at Towton in Yorkshire on 29 March 1461 in a blinding snowstorm. This was to be the bloodiest battle, since Roman times, ever fought on British soil, and the dead were counted at almost 30,000. Roger Fiennes of Herstmonceux's only son, Richard and his wife and Johanna's uncle Ranulph of Dacre were commanders of a large Lancastrian army at Towton. In the filthy weather, the Lancastrians manned the high ground so that the Yorkists had to climb to get at them. There were crude firearms around, but the main groups of fighters on both sides were still archers and dismounted men-at-arms.

A strong cold wind appears to have been the deciding factor of the day, blowing from behind the Yorkists as they toiled uphill. Their wind-blown arrows went that little bit farther and killed Lancastrians whose arrows, fired into the wind, fell short of their Yorkist targets. Present day archaeologists claim to have found the very first battlefield bullet, and have worked out that a total of over a million arrows were loosed in the first few hours of the battle. Rather than risk slow attrition, the Lancastrians advanced downhill and soon lost their uphill advantage. Close-quarter fighting was intense. Bodies had to be moved simply to get at the enemy as the hours of slaughter continued. Eventually Yorkist reserves arrived and outflanked the Lancastrians, who began to flee.

No quarter was given, no prisoners were taken and thousands of Lancastrians were slaughtered as they tried to escape. Yorkist horsemen rode them down for many miles through the night and the following day. My kinsman and namesake, Ranulph of Dacre, died at some point in the battle. At rivers with broken bridges hundreds of bodies piled up in the frozen water. Somehow King Henry, Queen Margaret and the Duke of Somerset survived and fled to Scotland. But their army was no more.

Edward IV and the man whose support had proved crucial, Warwick the Kingmaker, were soon back in London and feeling secure. For a while there was peace. King Edward must have had a sense of humour, for he appointed as Commissioner to 'look into the extortions in Kent' by the late beheaded James Fiennes and his crony, Cromer, the sheriff, none other than James's only son William Fiennes, 2nd Baron Saye and Sele. William must have done well, as he soon became vice-admiral and senior adviser to Warwick the Kingmaker.

12

Winter of our Discontent

The immediate aftermath of the bloody Battle of Towton saw Yorkist King Edward IV, direct descendant of Margaret Fiennes, fairly secure on the English throne, backed by his cousin and main adviser, Warwick the Kingmaker, a slimy character, who was the father-in-law of Geoffrey de Saye and grandfather of William Fiennes, my great to the power of twenty grandfather. In 1465 mad King Henry was captured in the north and locked up in the Tower of London. Although his queen and young son were still at large, an imprisoned mad king was better than a loose one, so Edward felt a good deal more secure. He gave the most powerful three positions in England to three men whom he trusted. Two of them were to let him down badly, Warwick the Kingmaker and his youngest brother, the slippery Duke of Clarence. The third, who remained loyal, was the eldest of his brothers, Richard, Duke of Gloucester.

Edward gratefully rewarded all those who had led his forces at the key Battle of Towton, including William Fiennes whom he knighted and made a Privy Councillor. Aged twenty-four, he had taken his beheaded father's title and so was the 2nd Lord Saye and Sele. He had also taken over various appointments his late father had held, including Constable of Dover Castle and Warden of the Cinque Ports, Sheriff of Kent and Sussex, and was owner of many estates in both counties.

However, William was as pro-Yorkist as his father and uncle Roger had been Lancastrian. He did a number of things which seemed to indicate that he was ashamed of the way his father had behaved. He sold his hereditary title of Constable of Dover Castle to the Duke of Buckingham and the superb manor and estate of Knole to the Archbishop of Canterbury. He sold the manor of Sele, and even Hever Castle (which his father had bought from Sir John Fastolf, Shakespeare's Falstaff) to Sir Geoffrey Boleyn, whose lovely granddaughter Anne would later be discovered at Hever and fatally courted by Henry VIII before giving birth to Queen Elizabeth I and losing her head. Many documents by various historians state that William sold his estates because he was twice held captive and ransomed whilst fighting in France for the king. But this is clearly a case of mistaken identity, since his cousin, Lord John Fiennes Clinton, *was* captured twice by the French, did become poor through paying ransom and did sell off the title of Lord Saye to William's father as a result.

Another reason for selling off estates in Sussex and Kent may well have been his acquisition of Broughton Castle through his marriage to Margaret Wykeham. The Wykehams were ardent Lancastrians, but nonetheless seemed to approve of young William. Our family has since that time lived in Broughton Castle for twenty-one unbroken generations and, from time to time, included the name of Wykeham as part of our surname. Broughton Castle came to public attention in 1999 when the film *Shakespeare In Love*, recipient of thirteen Oscar nominations, was filmed there with the titular role being played by my cousin, Joseph Fiennes. The castle was chosen for the film because it provided exactly the right period setting, complete with crenellated gatehouse overlooking the moat. Little is known of its early history save that in the Domesday Book it was owned by the Saxon thane, Turgot, and was later given by William the Conqueror to a Norman knight, Berenger de Todenai. He sold it to a family called de Broughton, who sold it to William of Wykeham, who sold it, over six hundred years ago, to us.

With Edward firmly on the throne, the country became relatively peaceful. History has portrayed England at the time of the Wars of the Roses as a land laid waste by civil strife and widespread carnage, but the reality was very different. There were battles, and I list them below, but their effect on the general population was minimal. There were exceptions, such as the last march of Queen Margaret's northern troops towards London, which ravaged the land over a wide front, but usually battles were short and affected few folk beyond the battlefield.

According to Shakespeare, the Wars of the Roses (white for York and red for Lancaster) got its name one morning when Richard of York met King Henry's men, the Duke of Suffolk and the Earl of Somerset, whilst they were walking round a rose garden in the Inns of Court. They argued. Richard said, 'From off this brier pluck a white rose with me.' And Somerset responded, 'Let him that is no coward nor But dare maintain the party of the truth, Pluck a red rose from off this thorn with me.'

THE WARS OF THE ROSES
Major Battles

King Henry VI's Reign

1455	St Albans	won by Yorkists
1459	Blore Heath	won by Yorkists
1459	Ludford Bridge	won by Lancastrians
1460	Northampton	won by Yorkists
1460	Wakefield	won by Lancastrians
1461	Mortimer's Cross	won by Yorkists
1461	Second St Albans	won by Lancastrians
1461	Ferrybridge	won by Yorkists
1461	Towton	won by Yorkists

King Edward IV's Reign

1464	Hedgeley Moor	won by Yorkists
1464	Hexham	won by Yorkists

1464	Edgecote Moor	won by Lancastrians
1469	Losecote Field	won by Yorkists
1471	Barnet	won by Yorkists
1471	Tewkesbury	won by Yorkists

King Richard III's Reign

1485	Bosworth	won by Lancastrians (Tudors)

King Henry VII's Reign

1487	Stoke	won by Lancastrians (Tudors)

The reasons that the Wars of the Roses involved few folk other than the direct protagonists were many and various. Most of the fighting was done by the noble families and their retainers. There was no conscription-raised army at the time, other than the soldiers of Calais. There were no long sieges involving troops, sometimes for many months, living off pillage and looting for miles around the city under siege. Great massacres of troops, other than at Towton, did not automatically follow a victory, since fleeing troops were not usually hunted down and the victors were often content to lop off only the heads of the opposing leaders. The overall death toll of executed aristocrats during the Wars of the Roses totalled nine dukes, a marquess, twenty-four barons, twelve earls, a prince and a king. Another factor which was important to both sides was to avoid upsetting the population for fear of losing their backing, and this was very easy to do, so both armies tended to behave well rather than alienate the locals.

In England in the fifteenth century the Wars of the Roses usually involved small armies, 5,000 men at most per side, and confrontation on some unpopulated moor or open fields. So many of the major historic buildings of the era, such as Roger Fiennes' Herstmonceux or William Fiennes' successors' Broughton, had thin walls, large windows and minor crenellations, since no foreign invasions were feared, nor sieges from neighbouring barons.

The main chronicler of the period, Philippe de Commynes,

Councillor to the King of France, wrote that, 'Of all the countries which I have known, England is that wherein public affairs are best conducted and managed with least destruction to the people.'

After the anarchy of mad King Henry VI's rule, the baronial mayhem, lack of police force and very little law, Edward IV took care to tour the country from end to end and to sit on the bench himself at assizes. He left what fighting had to be done in the lands of Lancastrian sympathisers, mainly the north and Welsh borders, to his trusted generals like Warwick. He made a successful truce with Scotland and considered alliances either with France or with their great enemy, Burgundy.

Warwick advised the king to marry the sister of the French queen, and thereby become allied to France against Burgundy. To the horror of Warwick and his supporters, the king in 1464 admitted in public that he could not marry Warwick's target bride, or anyone else for that matter, since he had already secretly married the beautiful daughter of an English duchess. This girl, Elizabeth Woodville, was descended from the French Dukes of St Pol, but was of no value at all in terms of a political marriage.

Robert Fiennes who, as the commander of the French army, had fought the English at the Battle of Poitiers, had died childless, so his inheritance as the senior French Fiennes had passed to his niece, Jeanne, and thence to the Dukes of St Pol and to Richard Woodville, the father of King Edward's surprise bride, Elizabeth, who, whether the Earl of Warwick liked it or not, was already the Queen of England.

Warwick took this very badly. He had loudly and in public proclaimed his initiative in arranging with the French king for Edward's French marriage. Now Edward's secret marriage made him look a fool, and his full support of Edward veered through 180 degrees to hatred. The members of Queen Elizabeth's family, the Woodvilles, were numerous and ambitious, and Edward helped many of them to positions of influence and power that upset Warwick still further, for he began to sense his uniquely powerful status was on the wane. King Edward's views on England's best foreign policy, especially with France, were also diametrically opposed to those of his chief foreign adviser, Warwick. The two men may have been cousins, but they were increasingly at odds.

Quietly, the worried Warwick the Kingmaker made his plans. If he could make one king, he could make two, and maybe he could even end up king himself. Secretly he approached the king's youngest brother, the Duke of Clarence, a sly serpent of a man who was deeply envious of his big brother Edward. Warwick was also aware that Edward's honeymoon period with his people was over, signs of Lancastrian conspiracies were abroad again, and both Warwick and Clarence were sufficiently two-faced to switch overnight from their previously ardent Yorkist loyalties to wooing their old enemies.

In June 1469 Warwick, Clarence and a mix of Lancastrian rebels marched on London, defeated a royal force at Northampton and locked King Edward up in Warwick Castle. This was a difficult time for many ardent Yorkists, including cousins William Fiennes of Broughton and Richard Fiennes of Herstmonceux, both of whom had fought for King Edward and for the Kingmaker. William Fiennes had fought for the king in England and France and been appointed Lord High Admiral of the Fleet for the major invasion of France that never happened. At home his perks included Commissioner for Sewage in Sussex.

William's cousin, Richard, being Lord of Herstmonceux in that south-east heartland of rural whingers (which produced both Wat Tyler and Jack Cade), was a valuable noble to be kept happy by any sensible London-based monarch. So he was elevated to the royal inner circle as Chamberlain to Edward's wife, Queen Elizabeth, made a member of the Privy Council, Sheriff of Surrey and Sussex, and Constable of the Tower of London.

Before he died, Richard's father, Roger, had rebuilt Herstmonceux as the very first redbrick castle in England, widened the moat and carved above the gateway the three lions rampant of Fiennes supported by wolfhounds. Unlike cousin William's Broughton Castle, which sported crenellated battlements but was soon to be proved useless as a defensive bastion, Herstmonceux was built to withstand aggression and guard the approaches to London from the coastline of the Pevensey Marshes.

The Lord Dacres of Fiennes lineage now owned a huge swathe of the Herstmonceux region, with many manors and villages. To name but a few, these included Arthington, Dacre, Risk-Oswald, Blackhall, Farlam, Branhanwarp, Lasingby, Brampton, Burgh-upon-the-Sands, Ayheton, Roucliss, and Glassenby, and 300 acres of land with 200 acres of pasture, 40 acres of wood and 50 shillings in rent in Newbigging, Mesdale and Starhull; also Castell-Harriot in Cumberland, Barton and Holf in Westmorland, Holbeche in Lincoln, plus Halton Fishwick, Relette and Eccleston in Lancashire.

There was one problem, however. The Dacre heiress, Richard's wife Joan, had even greater estates in the north, but disputes about these arose with one of her uncles called Humphrey who contested the inheritance so hotly that King Edward eventually, with the wisdom of Solomon, split the barony in two, so that Richard Fiennes ended up as the 1st Lord Dacre of the South, and Humphrey Dacre's dynasty became the Dacres of the North.

The northern Dacres had emerged from the mists of Cumberland where they were a rough bunch known as the Devil's Dozen for their exploits at avenging Scottish raiders and were ranked with the Nevilles and Percys as great defenders of the borderlands. Ranulpho de Dacre and his grandfather were both Sheriffs of Cumberland and Yorkshire and Governors of Carlisle.

Ranulpho had three sons, William who fought at Neville's Cross and was Sheriff of Dumfries, next was Ranulph II who was Warden of the West Marches but was murdered in bed, and lastly his little brother Hugh who was locked up in the Tower of London for murdering his brother. For some reason Hugh was released and became 4th Baron Dacre. His son William, the 5th

Eustace de Boulogne, my great grandfather times thirty, depicted second from left in the Bayeux Tapestry, led part of the Conqueror's army at Hastings in 1066. During the battle he advised the Norman leader to retreat.

Godfrey de Bouillon, the 1st King of Jerusalem and leader of the First Crusade, has become the greatest legendary figure of the Crusades. He was the son of Eustace de Boulogne and Ida de Bouillon, both direct descendants of Charlemagne. In 2005 he was voted 17th in 'The Greatest Belgian' contest.

Edward I and Queen Eleanor of Castile. William Fiennes (who was Edward's childhood guardian) and his younger brother Giles Fiennes, joined them and the French King Louis IX on the Crusade of 1270.

Queen Isabella, wife of Edward II, arrives at Hereford with her troops and her lover Roger Mortimer, the son of Margaret Fiennes. John and Robert Fiennes, uncles of Mortimer, had agreed to raise a force to help Isabella invade England in 1326.

Battle of Sluys, 1340. The first big military move of the Hundred Years War. Admiral Geoffrey Saye, grandfather of William Fiennes, prepared the Southern Fleet for war. Twenty thousand French and 4,000 English died.

The Black Prince was ready to massacre every citizen when he won the siege of Calais in 1347. But five brave city burghers, the youngest of whom was Jean Fiennes, volunteered as martyrs if the prince would spare the citizens. Urged by his queen, the prince finally killed no one.

Battle of Poitiers, 1356. My French forebear, Robert Fiennes, was made Commander (or Constable) of the French army, and led many defeats of the British.

Bishop William of Wykeham, a farmer's son, became Chancellor of England. In 1377 he bought Broughton Castle which was inherited by his great nephew's granddaughter, Margaret Wykeham-Fiennes.

James Fiennes (left), that 'bastard of renown', became Lord High Treasurer of England and was blamed for corruption, bankruptcy and military humiliation. During The Peasants' Revolt Fiennes' head was hacked off and rammed on a Tower Bridge spike.

Henry VI captured by Richard, Earl of Warwick, after the battle of Northampton, 1460, during the Wars of the Roses. Both dynasties were, at some point, mothered by Fiennes DNA. On the Lancastrian side, Henry VI's grandmother was Mary, the granddaughter of Joan Fiennes. On the Yorkist side, Edward IV was Margaret Fiennes' great grandson times four.

King Edward IV and Elizabeth Woodville, both direct descendants of Margaret Fiennes.

Henry VIII arriving at the Field of the Cloth of Gold, 1520.
The meeting was held in the heart of Fiennes country, in France,
where Henry's men burnt down Castle Fiennes.

Thomas Fiennes, Lord Dacre, was hanged at Tyburn for poaching his neighbour's deer and killing a game-keeper. Prior to this fatal indiscretion he had sat on the jury at Anne Boleyn's trial, and was a pall-bearer at Jane Seymour's funeral.

Herstmonceux Castle, East Sussex. The greatest red brick castle in Britain in the mid sixteenth century. Thomas's family lost this castle because of his bad behaviour but Elizabeth I gave it back to his descendants.

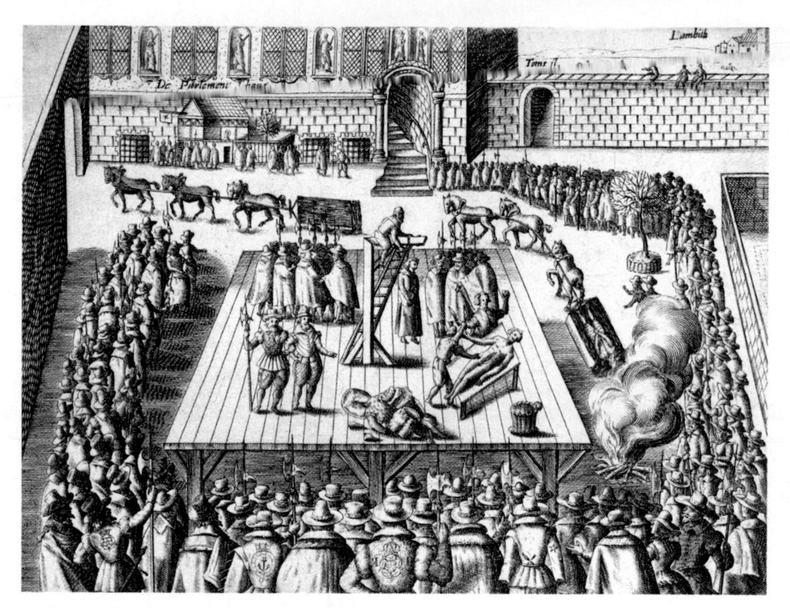

The Gunpowder Plot conspirators' execution, 1605. Similar fates befell Roger Mortimer – hanged, drawn and quartered; James Fiennes – head displayed on a spike on London Bridge, his body drawn and quartered; and Thomas Fiennes – hanged at Tyburn.

Broughton Castle, Oxfordshire, has been in the continuous ownership of the Fiennes family since 1377.

William Fiennes, 'Old Subtlety', 8th Lord and 1st Viscount Saye and Sele. His long life was a highly successful balancing act between king and Parliament. If any single individual controlled the destiny of Great Britain during the key years before, during and after Cromwell's reign, it was William.

The devil presides over Oliver Cromwell, 'B', and his cabinet in a Royalist print. William Fiennes is shown as 'K', with his back to us (left).

Nathaniel Fiennes, William's second son, at the time of the Civil War. He was almost hanged by Cromwell for losing Bristol too easily to the Royalists, and was later Speaker of Cromwell's 'Other House'.

baron, married the daughter of the Earl of Douglas, a family who had led Scottish armies against the English in France, and the 6th baron married a Neville whose sons all died, leaving the Dacre estates to Joan, who passed the southern lands by marriage to Richard Fiennes of Herstmonceux.

Joan's uncle, Ranulph, was killed at Towton. He, like his niece's husband and rival claimant to the Dacre wealth, Richard Fiennes, was a Lancastrian, but when his claim to the title was ready, Edward the Yorkist was on the throne, and poor Ranulph's claim failed dismally. Seven years later when his younger brother, Humphrey, renewed the claim, Edward had grown mellow, so Humphrey was pardoned with the words, 'The seid Humphrey is as repentaunt and sorrowful as eny creature may be of all which the seid Ranulph or he have doon or comitted.'

Edward still had the problem of two lords with the same title sitting in the Lords glaring at one another, so the records quote the king's judgement as: 'Richard Fenys shall be reputed, held, named and called Lord Dacre . . . Humphrey Dacre shall be reputed, held, named and called Lord Dacre of Gilsland and have, use and keep the place in parliaments next adjoining beneath the said place that the said Richard Fenys . . . now hath and occupieth.'

The Fiennes Dacres thus gained the superior spot in the lordship stakes, which must have made Roger and Joan a touch less miserable at losing all the northern Dacre estates to Uncle Humphrey. To summarise the status of the two cousins: William Fiennes, who was my great to the power of seventeen grandfather, did well under Edward IV and sat in the Lords as the 2nd Lord Saye and Sele of Broughton, while Richard Fiennes prospered equally as the 1st Lord Dacre of Herstmonceux.

King Edward IV himself, however, was by 1469 in bad trouble. The Kingmaker, having locked him up in Warwick Castle, proceeded to wreak vengeance on everyone he considered his enemy, including Edward's wife's father and brother. Heads were lopped off left, right and centre. The Kingmaker was clever enough to know that the English masses were definitely not ready for him to usurp their rightful monarch, so he kept Edward cooped up and had him sign the many edicts that he, Warwick, issued for Parliament to pass.

Edward, for his part, bided his time. He knew that the Lancastrians would jump at this major split at the Yorkist helm. When they did, up north, Warwick found that, without the king's presence, he simply could not raise a strong enough force to fight the Lancastrians. So he let Edward out of prison and the two cousins made a show of togetherness. Warwick, with the king's approval, went north and smashed the rebels. Edward grabbed his chance, gathered all his own supporters around him and returned to Westminster and to full regal power. His attitude to the traitors Warwick and his own brother Clarence was, surprisingly (and foolishly) forgiving. This merely resulted in their taking advantage of his clemency to raise another army of rebellion, this time in Lincolnshire, cunningly hiding their treachery from Edward until the very last minute. The king's army, equipped now with powerful artillery, defeated these new rebel forces at Huntingdon in March 1470. Warwick's hopes of ousting the king for whom he himself had fought since youth, and had put on the throne ten years before, had come to nought.

But he did not give up. With the slippery Clarence in tow, he proceeded to reverse all his past loyalties and turned to his previous enemies to aid his next step. He announced to England's current arch-enemy, the King of France, that he was prepared to work for the restoration of the mad King Henry, who was still languishing in the Tower of London where Warwick had imprisoned him ten years before. A more odious example of two-faced treachery would be difficult to devise, even in a work of fiction. The French king, Louis XI, welcomed the Kingmaker's offer to put back on the English throne the mad King Henry, whose wife, Queen Margaret, was French. Queen Margaret had spent decades loathing Warwick, but buried her hatred for this chance of revenge on Edward IV and the possibility of her seventeen-year-old son (another Edward) becoming king. Warwick's French-aided army landed near Plymouth and soon cobbled together a force of some 30,000 from Wales and various English counties. Edward IV, weary from fighting Lancastrian rebels in the north, found himself heavily outnumbered in Doncaster, and was forced to flee with a small band of supporters, including his faithful brother, Richard of Gloucester, and his ever-loyal supporter, William Fiennes, Lord Saye and Sele. They made it, just, to the relative safety of Burgundy, whilst Warwick was, once again, in charge back in London.

The Lancastrians who had helped him did not trust Warwick an inch. But nor did the Yorkists. So his new government included a mixture of both groups, and he removed poor mad Henry from the Tower to reinstall him as king (the only monarch in English history to be recycled in this manner).

The tit-for-tat fight between Yorkist King Edward IV and the Lancastrian-cum-Yorkist Kingmaker continued as soon as Edward mustered some thirty-six ships and 2,000 men with which he landed at Ravenspur on the Humber with William Fiennes, as ever, at his side. Gradually Edward's force grew to some 6,000 men, and at Coventry he was joined by his ever-treacherous brother Clarence with a further 4,000 men from the west country. This Clarence army was actually on its way to join Warwick in order to fight Edward, but Clarence changed his mind at the last moment.

The brothers embraced, apparently forgetting their past enmity, and so arm-in-arm, as it were, with brothers Gloucester and Clarence, Edward entered London in triumph where, the mind boggles, he met up with the 'other king', mad Henry, who shook hands with him and is quoted as having said, 'My cousin of York, you are very welcome.' To avoid King Henry falling into the hands of others, Edward kept him at his side when his army of 10,000 confronted the Kingmaker's force of 15,000 at Barnet on the Great North Road. At dawn and in thick mist, Edward's men attacked, and in less than four hours routed the Lancastrians. John Warkworth, the official chronicler of this key Battle of Barnet, wrote: 'and of King Edward's party was slain the Lord Cromwell, heir to the Earl of Essex, Lord Berners, Lord Say and divers other to the number of 4,000 men.' And so cousin William, Lord Saye, was killed in the heat of the battle, as was Warwick the Kingmaker, with whom he had once fought side by side against the French.

Edward had no time to mourn lost friends nor to savour his victory, for another Lancastrian army under Henry VI's wife Margaret and young son Edward had landed from France and was en route to meet up with Welsh reinforcements. Edward once again exhorted his weary men and met the queen's forces at Tewkesbury. Richard of Gloucester, Edward's loyal brother, saved Edward from certain defeat at one point, and their artillery did much deadly work. The Lancastrians fled, but many were caught and put to the sword. Queen Margaret was locked in the Tower, her son lay dead at Tewkesbury, as did her greatest general, Earl Somerset.

Back in his long-time prison in the Tower, poor mad Henry VI was soon reported to have died of melancholy. But when his bones were exhumed in 1910, forensic evidence concurred with the theory of most fifteenth-century chronicles, that the old king's dented skull and hair remnants were matted with blood, evidence of a violent death. Only King Edward would have had the motive and the right of access to carry out Henry's murder, but there was never proof that he did so. Either way, the main Lancastrian royal line was now extinct. The civil war seemed over and England settled down to a strife-free existence for the next twelve years.

13

The Sun of York

In the fifteenth century it was still common for people to die early. William and Margaret Fiennes of Broughton lost their first son, Richard, while he was still being schooled at Winchester. Their second son, Henry, died at twenty-three, leaving only their youngest son, Richard, who inherited their estates as the 4th Lord Saye and Sele at the age of five. King Edward IV, you will remember, had two younger brothers: the Duke of Clarence who was as slimy as a greased snake, and Richard, Duke of Gloucester, who was everything anyone could wish for in a brother. This Richard was utterly loyal to King Edward throughout the latter's life, and young Richard Fiennes was lucky enough to have him as his guardian and custodian. England's history was soon to be steered by Richard of Gloucester, a man who, thanks to Shakespeare turning him into a murdering hunchback, is still thought of as the ultimate villain. This, in my opinion, is grossly unfair.

After their twin victories at Barnet and Tewkesbury, Edward and Richard ruled supreme, the one as king, the other as Constable and Admiral of England. Richard Fiennes' father, William, would almost certainly have been his Vice-Admiral had he not been killed at Barnet. Edward was amazingly merciful to his defeated Lancastrian foes, those who had survived the war, fining them heavily rather than chopping their heads off.

The most troublesome areas of England were traditionally Kent and the north, so Edward placed his most trusted and capable men in both places. The Fiennes Dacres of the South retained the offices of Sheriff in Sussex, Surrey and Kent, and the Dacres of the North the governorship of Carlisle. Above him, as supreme Commander of the North, Richard of Gloucester dealt successfully with King James III of Scotland's intermittent raids. A marriage fixed between James's and Edward's children also helped.

After a few years Richard had tamed the north and decided to marry his childhood sweetheart, Anne, a daughter of the dead traitor, Warwick the Kingmaker, and extremely wealthy by inheritance. Richard's brother Clarence was at the time determined to grab the Warwick riches for himself and complained to his elder brother, King Edward. The latter, keen to avoid strife between his younger brothers, allowed Richard to marry Anne, but gave many of Richard's best estates and influential titles to Clarence as a heavyweight sweetener.

But, as a chronicler of the day put it: 'Clarence was born with a sour taste in his mouth and no amount of goods or honours could sweeten it.' True to his reputation for treachery, Clarence proceeded to conspire with King Louis XI of France and various Lancastrian magnates in exile to remove Edward from the throne. Both Edward and Richard, ever ready to forgive their brother Clarence for his intermittent acts of treason, did so again, but decided to make war on France anyway, starting by wooing the two provinces currently at odds with the French king: Brittany and Burgundy. In 1472 Edward sent a small army to help the Duke of Brittany, but it returned when the duke's nerve went and he sued for peace with King Louis.

In 1475 Edward signed a treaty with the Duke of Burgundy that they would attack France in tandem. So Edward raised an army of 11,000 men, landed at Calais and awaited the army of Burgundy. They camped for a couple of nights on the Agincourt battlefield, but things did not go to plan. A Fiennes descendant, the Count of St Pol, who had agreed to help Edward, changed his mind and fired artillery at the English instead. The armies of

Brittany and Burgundy never materialised, so Edward made peace with Louis XI and withdrew his great army without involvement in a single battle or siege. Not very glorious but politically sound; since King Louis agreed in return to pay Edward a huge annual pension, to marry his heir to Edward's daughter and to act with England in trade and in war.

With a rare trouble-free vista at home, up north and in France, Edward IV now enjoyed himself to the full. He grew fat through gross addiction to good food and wine and he ravished pretty much anything female that came his way, married or single, for he was a great charmer, handsome in an increasingly pudgy sort of way, and notably oversexed. Despite all this, he was a dedicated and effective monarch. He built many great palaces, libraries and chapels, some rated now as the very best examples of the English Gothic style. He started the first Royal Library and patronised William Caxton.

Sound financial management and solvency were hallmarks of Edward's reign, and his interest in the finances of the realm extended to encouraging extensive wool exports. This would form the basis of the Fiennes family business and that of their Northampton neighbours, the Spencers of Althorp, for generations to come. Edward's business acumen resulted in him becoming the first king for a very long time who did not have to beg cash from Parliament. As a result he never summoned one for six years, preferring a centralised monarchical government.

There was the odd hiccup in this unnatural medieval calm, as when the French urged their Auld Alliance partners the Scots into some border raids, quickly put a stop to by Richard. Then Clarence overstepped the mark yet again. This time the King had had enough. Clarence was arrested and placed in the Tower, the death sentence was pronounced and Clarence, according to tradition, was found drowned in a barrel of Malmsey wine.

Richard of Gloucester, according to the chronicles, was 'overcome with grief for his brother and thenceforward came very rarely to Court'. He preferred to stay up north where, for twelve years, he ruled the roost on behalf of the king. Edward IV was definitely set for a long, fine rule when his physical over-indulgence did him in and, without much warning, he fell gravely ill in the spring of 1483. His son, Edward, was but twelve at the time the king took to his deathbed, 'neither worn out by age [he was forty-four] nor yet seized with any known kind of malady'. He was compos mentis enough to appoint his beloved brother, Richard of Gloucester, as Protector of the Realm to be regent of all England until young Edward V was old enough to take over.

King Edward's sudden death put the fear of God into many Woodville relatives of his widow, Queen Elizabeth, who had been placed in positions of influence as royal favourites. The queen attempted to persuade the ruling council to pass a resolution that Richard of Gloucester should head, but not dominate, a body to be known as the Regency Council. A situation quickly arose where, with the late King Edward freshly buried, Richard of Gloucester headed towards London with a band of supporters, and the young Prince Edward, with his Woodville uncle Lord Rivers did likewise.

These two groups met up en route and agreed to arrive in London together as joint guardians of the prince. But the Duke of Buckingham, a peer whose treacherous potential was rivalled only by that of the late Clarence, somehow managed to persuade Richard that if he arrived in London with Rivers, he would be arrested once the Woodville clique had the prince under their wing. Persuaded to strike first, Richard arrested Rivers, then took the prince under his own protection. He and Buckingham, supported by the people of London, ousted the queen and the Woodville faction. They promised the people that they would soon have young Edward crowned.

The queen's supporters and the late Edward's key advisers, under the leadership of Lord Hastings, were deemed by Richard to be conspiring against him. He had Hastings executed and then sent both his nephews, the young prince and his brother, into that part of the Tower of London which, at the time, served as a royal residence. He then spread word that his late brother, King Edward, whose loyal servant he had been down the long years, had already been contracted to marry another woman when he married Queen Elizabeth. Were this true, the two princes in the Tower would be bastards and their uncle Richard would have the greater claim to the throne.

With help from the cunning machinations of the Duke of Buckingham, himself third in line for the throne, Richard engineered the switch from mere protector or regent to being crowned King Richard III and successor to the brother he had served so long and so loyally. No proof has ever been produced, but there is little doubt in the minds of most historians that Richard ordered the secretive murder of his two nephews in the Tower at some point soon after his coronation. In 1674 workmen demolished a staircase in the Tower of London and found a chest with the skeletons of two children aged ten and twelve. Forensic evidence does not point the finger of guilt at Richard of Gloucester, nor at any other specific character, but he and Buckingham are the most likely suspects.

It is easy to shake one's head in disbelief at how easily kings could be usurped and loyalties switched throughout medieval times and irrespective of so-called Lancastrian or Yorkist attachments. Family loyalty often took a poor second place to self-preferment. Uncles, brothers and cousins often enough fought and killed one another. Sudden treacherous turnabouts of whole armies were common. For Richard to switch from ultra-loyal subject to murderer and usurper more or less overnight does however seem out of character, but may well have happened because of the influence of the snake-tongued Duke of Buckingham. Whether or not this was the case, as soon as Richard III was King of England he appointed the duke as Constable and Great Chamberlain.

The new king set out at once on a royal tour of the south. Having been the de facto and popular ruler in the north for over a decade, he felt no need to make his presence felt in those parts. But he did choose York for the investiture of his own dynasty, his son (another Edward), as the Prince of Wales.

Very quickly, whilst Richard's royal tour trundled on, a rolling conspiracy gathered force down south. Where else, but in Kent! Part Lancastrian aficionados, part Edward IV's old friends and long-time advisers, part Woodville clan survivors, part ever-discontented Kentish men. All these elements came together and were stirred into outrage by the ever-growing rumour that King Richard had murdered the princes.

In order to stand any chance of removing the usurper Richard from the throne, the conspirators needed a suitable royal claimant of their own, and such a man they found in the twenty-seven-year-old Henry Tudor, the sole surviving heir to the claims of the House of Lancaster. Henry Tudor's grandfather, Owen, was a Welsh squire with no royal blood, but his grandmother had been Queen Catherine of England, widow of Henry V. Although the daughter of mad King Charles VI, she had not returned to France when Henry V died, but had retired to Wales as wife of Owen Tudor. Her grandson Henry was pretty much forgotten until, after the Lancastrian defeat at Tewkesbury back in 1471, he became the Lancastrians' last real royal claimant and so was taken to Brittany for safety.

The key link between the anti-Richard plotters in England and Henry Tudor over in Brittany was the ultimate traitor himself, the Duke of Buckingham. The duke, as Constable of England and Richard's right-hand man, was playing a long game. He considered his own royal claim more legitimate than that of King Richard or of Henry Tudor, but he needed to pretend loyalty to both. First he got rid of the Princes in the Tower through his influence over Richard of Gloucester. Next he was to oust Richard by backing Henry Tudor. For sheer effrontery and KGB-like covert plotting it would take some beating. But the best laid plans fall foul of spies, and King Richard's intelligence network soon knew of Buckingham's involvement with the Henry Tudor plot.

The various conspiring groups on both sides of the Channel agreed upon a simultaneous uprising to take place in October 1485, but swift moves by Richard cornered Buckingham, who was betrayed by his own servants and executed in September. Henry Tudor, who had set sail from Brittany with fifteen ships and 5,000 men, survived a major storm but found none of the support he expected, so he turned about and went back to his Breton refuge. The Buckingham revolt was over without a shot being fired.

Shakespeare goes well over the top in his caricature of Richard as Crookback Dick, the evil murdering hunchback, devoid of any redeeming feature. Others even accuse Richard of previously murdering Henry VI, but offer no evidence. I have read a great deal about Richard and come to the conclusion that he was a touch strait-laced, capable of a modicum of what we now call cruelty, as seen from an age where the death penalty is frowned on, and no great long-term strategist. But on the plus side, we have a great deal to thank him for. In the two years of his reign and with a group of able advisers, he concentrated on improvements to government with constructive, far-reaching results. He was a just man, as can be seen from the judicial records of the three northern counties that he ruled so successfully for over a decade. He introduced a good many new laws, including that juries must be kept free from intimidation, that individuals arrested merely on suspicion of a crime must be allowed bail, and that property buyers must be protected from malpractices such as gazumping. These laws, aimed often at corrupt and unjust nobles, showed that Richard had no compunction about upsetting the powerful en route to improving social justice. His loyalty to his brother the king helped keep the peace for a long period of prosperity, and for the most part his financial prudence helped alleviate the tax burden on the masses. Even his behaviour towards his unbelievably duplicitous brother Clarence shows him in a good light. Despite Clarence's repetitive treachery and his attempts to block

Richard's marriage to his beloved Anne, Richard tried his damnedest to stop Clarence's execution for treason.

The close group of skilled men who Richard chose to help him govern wisely were described in one famous and irreverent rhyme of the day: 'The Cat, the Rat and Lovell our Dog rule all England under the Hog.' The Hog was clearly the king, since the boar was his emblem, Lovell and Dick Ratcliffe were old friends from Richard's time in the north, and William Catesby was his closest confidant. None were big landowners, but Catesby's father, buried at Broughton, was married to Philippa Wykeham, whose sister was married to Broughton Castle's then owner. Catesby Junior was soon to be beheaded.

If luck had been with him, Richard III might well have ruled long and wisely, but in the spring of 1484 he was aware that the Scots were again spoiling for trouble in the borderlands, French fleets were raiding his vital export traders, and Henry Tudor was again raising an army of invasion. But far worse than these blots on his horizon was the sudden death of his own son and heir, the Prince of Wales, who died still a child and, since his wife Anne had been barren for a decade, Richard was faced with the supreme irony of being a childless usurper. Such a status would, he knew, encourage far greater support throughout the realm for the obvious alternative, Henry Tudor. Henry Tudor's own advisers were planning the betrothal of Lancastrian Henry to Edward IV's daughter Elizabeth of York, thus binding the two warring factions forever and ending the Wars of the Roses. Such a marriage would be intensely popular in war-weary England.

In order to avoid the Hastings fate of Harold Godwinson at the hands of the Conqueror, King Richard pressed the Scots hard by land and sea until a safe treaty and a three-year truce was forced on them. He could then concentrate on the southern threat from Henry Tudor, and a coastal watch was organised, including relays of fire beacons on high ground. Richard dealt harshly with spies, including one William Colyngbourne, a former servant of his mother who was caught sending information to Henry Tudor. He was also the rhymester responsible for the Cat-and-Rat doggerel. Colyngbourne was 'drawn unto Tower Hill and there full cruelly put to death, at first hanged (partially), then straight cut down and ripped and his bowels cast into a fire. The which torment was so speedily done that when the butcher pulled out his heart he spake and said, "Jesus, Jesus."'

Bad luck continued to strike Richard, for in March 1485 Queen Anne, his wife and friend since childhood, died, and gossipmongers accused the grief-stricken king of murdering her because he wanted to remarry someone who could give him an heir. The someone in question was his own niece, the late King Edward's daughter Elizabeth, who Henry Tudor was also keen to marry. Richard denied such rumours and concentrated on strengthening all defences against invasion.

In fine weather Henry Tudor's fleet set sail for Wales on 24 July 1485. Henry had spent half his life in exile, his first invasion had failed, and this time his entire army consisted of 2,000 French mercenaries. He relied on discontent in England and Wales to swell his ranks. His banner was the red dragon of the old Welsh princes from whom he claimed descent. The two armies met at Bosworth Field, a touch west of Leicester, Richard with 7,000 men and Henry with some 6,000. The king's army occupied the high ground of a single grassy hill, and both sides anxiously awaited the decision of two nearby armies, largely from Wales and Shropshire, under the Stanley brothers. Until the very last minute they appeared indecisive as to which side they would ally themselves. The only loyalties felt by these powerful magnates (and by a great many others on the battlefield that day) were to themselves.

The Lancastrian army attacked uphill under the veteran Lord Oxford. Henry, inexperienced at war, stayed behind at the foot of the hill guarded by a troop of horse. Archers on both sides loosed arrow storms and a division of the royal army rushed downhill into close combat between men-at-arms, who could only tell who their enemy were by nearby battle standards or clothing crests.

The king's leader of the Yorkists, the Duke of Norfolk, was killed and his men retreated back uphill. Richard ordered his rear division under the Duke of Northumberland to attack, but the duke, a known waverer, refused to budge for he had noticed that down on the plain at least one of the Stanley armies was static, awaiting the main outcome. Northumberland politely told the king he felt it prudent to stay on high ground until the Stanley army decided who to attack.

Ever a man of instant action, King Richard decided that, rather than await the moves of Stanley and other hedge-sitters, that he would take the bold, but risky, move of nipping down a flank of the hill with a cavalry charge straight at the weakly guarded Henry Tudor, easily identifiable by his battle standard. If he could kill Henry, the battle would be won whatever the Stanleys did. With only ninety mounted men beside him, King Richard charged down and around the battle front and straight at Henry's body-guards. The king fought hard, but his tiny force was surrounded and he himself was cut down before he could reach Henry Tudor. It was a close call and could well have worked.

The battle was quickly over as news spread of Richard's death. He was the last King of England to die in battle and the last of the long line of Plantagenets. He lost to a rival claimant with a numerically inferior army because of several factors. Enthusiasm for the war was at a low ebb, with many nobles ready to opt merely for the winning side of the day. Few folk cared whether Richard, the childless usurper, or Henry Tudor, the little known Welshman, held the throne. Peace was craved, not further dynastic conflict, so when all was said and done at Bosworth Field, the military skills of the Duke of Oxford for Henry's side versus those of the king's Duke of Norfolk were the factor that turned the day and King Richard's rash charge decided the outcome.

King Richard's body, stripped and flung over a packhorse, was taken to nearby Leicester, where it was exhibited as proof that the House of York was no more. The Wars of the Roses were over and Henry Tudor was crowned King of England.

From a family point of view, it is sad that Richard III, the descendant of sister Margaret and Joanna Fiennes, died childless, but his Welsh successor soon ensured that our DNA was reintroduced into the royal line (to keep them 'on the straight and narrow', as my mother used to say) by marrying another Fiennes descendant, Elizabeth of York, whose ancestor was that William Fiennes killed at the Battle of Courtrai.

14

Twisletons and Tudors

Henry Tudor, now Henry VII, relied on his heritage for Welsh support. He encouraged Cambro-British propaganda that he was the man long prophesied to return the Welsh to the throne of Britain. His legal claim to be a monarch of dynastic descent was tortuous, being through the illegitimate line of Edward III's fourth son, John of Gaunt. He was clearly a usurper, but then so was Richard, his childless predecessor, so, between the two of them, what mattered most was the outcome of the Battle of Bosworth, since possession is nine-tenths of the law and he who laughs last laughs longest.

Bosworth also killed off a great many key Yorkist supporters not already dead from previous battles, and on a more upbeat note, there was something very attractive to the whole country about a Lancastrian and Yorkist marriage to end all wars. Especially since Elizabeth of York quickly gave Henry seven children, including an heir in 1486 who he named, with an eye to Celtic nostalgia, Prince Arthur, and in 1491 she bore the future King Henry VIII. Both princes shared York and Lancaster blood and Henry seemed doubly secure on his throne.

However, just as all seemed most rosy, storm clouds crept over the horizon in the shape of a pretender claiming to be the legitimate king, being the elder of the princes in the Tower who had managed to escape. The real identity of this pretender was one

Lambert Simnel, the son of an Oxford organ-maker who had been selected by William Seymour, an eccentric priest who had dreamed that he was the tutor of the prince. To make his dream come true, Seymour taught Simnel to impersonate the prince; not difficult since virtually nobody had ever met the poor lad.

In startlingly quick time, great numbers of citizens rallied to the cause of this pretender. Died-in-the-wool Yorkists, such as the Earl of Lincoln, stirred support in Burgundy from the queen there who was Richard III's sister, hated Henry and raised a mercenary army. Sailing to Ireland, where they crowned Simnel as King Edward VI, he then landed on the Lancashire coast with a much larger army than that which Henry Tudor had wielded at Bosworth.

Luckily for Henry, few Englishmen, even in Yorkshire, had rallied to this pretender's cause by the time his army met the king's at Stoke-on-Trent. Henry lost 2,000 men but won the day, killed Lincoln and captured Simnel. Henry clearly had a great sense of humour, for instead of beheading Simnel, he had the young man put to work as a servant in the royal kitchens, from where he was later promoted to royal falconer, and he died peacefully long afterwards.

The next pretender, Perkin Warbeck, was an even less likely specimen, since he spoke not a word of English and, the son of a Flemish boatman, arrived in Cork with a load of fine silks. His only claim to possible fame was that the mayor and good citizens of Cork were impressed by his 'royal bearing'. But that was enough. He was taught to speak English (no doubt with a Cork brogue) and how to comport himself like the prince he had become. This time the pretender's patrons decided he should be the younger prince from the Tower and, as with Simnel five years before, support came in from parties interested in causing Henry trouble, including naturally the Scots and the French. No major battle was needed to deter Warbeck's intermittent 'invasions', for he was never well supported. Nonetheless, when King James IV of Scotland hosted Warbeck, married his cousin to him and addressed him as Prince Richard of England, Henry decided to raise money for a Scottish campaign.

For some reason this new tax went down especially badly in Cornwall. A lawyer from Bodmin, ironically the son of the local tax commissioner, noised abroad that honest Cornish folk were being taxed into the ground for a fight at the far end of the land that had 'nowt to do with them at all'. Fifteen thousand Cornish men armed with bows, arrows and pitchforks marched peacefully on London, where Henry's troops killed 2,000 of them, beheaded their leaders and heavily fined the rest.

Henry, soon after the Cornish tax revolt, sent his army north to relieve the garrison of Norham Castle, under siege by James IV's Scots. Lord Thomas Fiennes of Dacre excelled himself at Norham, as he had when defending London during the Cornish troubles. Henry obviously felt that he was reliable, for he made him Constable of Calais, England's only remaining property in France, and awarded him the Order of the Bath. James IV soon caved in and signed a seven-year truce with Henry who, for the rest of his twenty-four-year reign, suffered no further threat from any direction. Warbeck lasted a lot longer than Simnel, six years to be precise, before Henry had him imprisoned and eventually, since he proved to be a compulsive escapist, executed.

Henry married his son and heir, Prince Arthur, to Catherine of Aragon, a diplomatic marriage with the newly powerful royal house of Spain but, within a few months of the wedding, Arthur died, aged fifteen, to be followed very soon after by his mother the queen. Henry, who doted on them both, never recovered from his grief and became a morose semi-recluse.

His second son, Henry, now his heir, had been kept on a very tight rein and was never the apple of his parents' eyes, as Arthur had been. He was never instructed in the arts of government, never allowed to attend councils, nor witness court attendances of foreign ambassadors. Historians usually deduce from this that Henry Tudor feared the future, sickness and death, and jealously guarded all ruling activities for himself while he still could. By the time he was fifty he was visibly careworn and withdrawn. He died of no recorded sickness aged fifty-two and on his deathbed made his son Henry promise that he would marry Arthur's widow, Catherine of Aragon.

Compared with his predecessors, Henry Tudor had things pretty easy combat-wise. Apart from the two pretenders, the Cornish marchers and border strife with the Scots, all was peaceful. Remembering the carnage of Bosworth, which he had observed close-up, he must surely have thanked the Lord hugely, devout and spiritual man that he was. So instead of evaluating his prowess at war, it seems a good time to take a quick look at an England unusually at peace at home and abroad. Henry's rule began as the Middle Ages faded away: the age of the printing press, the discovery of India and America, the Renaissance and a time when many men no longer believed that the Pope was divine, nor the church supreme.

Life expectancy was still poor, whichever class you belonged to and no matter how great your wealth. The most famous teacher-preacher of the day, John Colet, Dean of St Paul's was the only child to survive out of the twenty-two born to his mother. Few marriages lasted more than fifteen years, since by then one of the couple was likely to be dead. There were very few divorces, but people often married twice or three times. England was not especially backward in medicine or any other science, and in 1499 the famous Dutch scholar Erasmus wrote of Henry's England: 'I have met with so much learning here; not hackneyed and trivial but deep, accurate, ancient Latin and Greek. It is marvellous how general and abundant is the harvest of general learning in this country.'

So far I have accounted for the parts of the family name that cover the Fiennes and the Wykehams, but this is the point where the Twisletons make their entrance. The name is Saxon and means a settlement on a river bend. The family heraldic symbol is three moles, or in Old English, moldiwarps. Our ancestral Twisleton came from Darrington, near Pontefract in Yorkshire, and in all the records is nicknamed John the Baptist Twisleton. He was a farmer who, in his will, left his cow to John Twisleton of Bolton and his windmill at Wentbridge to his wife. He died in 1503, but one of his sons was named John, and in his will he named a John Twisleton as his trustee.

I cannot tell which of these two later Johns was the father of John the Goldsmith Twisleton who, three years after Henry Tudor killed off Richard III, headed south like Dick Whittington to make his fortune in London. There are fifteen generations of Twisleton in between me and the Goldsmith. Apprenticed to Robert Johnson, Goldsmiths of London, he had by 1498 become a Freeman of the Company of Goldsmiths, and four years later entered that Livery. In 1508 he was the Renter Warden. In 1515 he had twelve apprentices under tutelage, and by 1523 he was in the exalted position of 2nd Warden of the Livery.

He never made it to Prime Warden due no doubt to his curmudgeonly nature. He once accused some fellow goldsmiths of using slanderous words about him in ale houses and other places, and this despite all the years he had spent in the Company. He laid down his Company hood and announced that he would never again wear it. Told to take it up, he refused. The order was repeated or he was to sit down and shut up. He then said that he might as well take it for he had paid for it. All this is on record. Nonetheless he ended up making and repairing plate for the Royal Court, grew wealthy and bought a manor back in Yorkshire at Barlow, where a derelict part of his hall still stood in the 1980s.

The Goldsmith's son, Christopher Twisleton, married Anne Bere, a Kentish heiress, and he moved down to Dartford. Such upward mobility happened all over England increasingly during Henry Tudor's reign, for by his own appointments of top ministers due to their talents not their rank or class, he showed that he believed that ability, good service and loyalty, irrespective of social origins and background, should be the yardstick for promotion, favours and rewards.

*

Both Edward IV and, for his short two-year reign, Richard III had brimmed with financial and administrative acumen, which made life a lot easier for Henry Tudor when he took over. His own handling of the nation's finances were extremely efficient, for he was a natural and dedicated accountant who derived great pleasure from devious new methods of squeezing blood from stones. His was the time of the saying, 'The sparing were to be pressed for money because they saved, and the lavish because they spent.' His attitude on taxation, according to one of his ministers, was, 'Heads I win, tails you lose.'

Europe was seething with aggressive leaders, and Henry needed all his natural Welsh cunning to maintain English influence and involvement without actually committing expensive armies to one side or the other. France was focused on invading Italy, and so spent less time than was traditional in plotting with the Scots against England. Henry was not expected, as were most of his predecessors, to wage war on France and to extend English territory there, because the public had become accustomed to Calais being the last bastion of the English empire abroad.

Henry began the slow process of curbing the private armies of the barons, whilst not banning them altogether, since they were the only source of a national army if and when it should be needed. In Kent and Sussex, where troubles for past regimes had often originated, Henry did forbid the hiring of armed retainers, and no man below the rank of baron could raise an army.

Today's green agenda was in Henry's day mirrored by chronicled warnings of shrinking woodlands. So more coal and fewer logs were being burnt. London's air, as a result, was beginning to thicken and maybe, even then, an embryonic ozone layer hole was forming. England was exporting coal, wool and textiles, and becoming unusually wealthy, which prompted the English to focus more on the world beyond little Europe. But so did other Europeans, especially the Hispanics. Italians had powered the Renaissance, rediscovered Greek philosophy, freshly interpreted the New

Testament, and encouraged humanism rather than narrow doctrinal religious obedience. All this led to new threats to the church and to bold voyages, sponsored by kings, to see what lay beyond the horizon.

The Portuguese led the way by rounding Cape Horn not long before Columbus crossed the Atlantic, found the West Indies and colonised Central America. De Gama reached India, and English fishermen, sailing ever further north with Cabot's guidance, discovered Newfoundland. From centuries of war within the kingdom and against the French, little England had begun to stir. Henry did not openly challenge the self-given rights of the Spanish and Portuguese (which the Pope described as 'God-given') to all 'the New World', but he did quietly encourage John Cabot, the Bristol seaman and others in their northerly search for a new route to the rich lands of Asia. Cabot disappeared on a voyage with five ships, one supplied by Henry, but his son Sebastian Cabot discovered Hudson's Bay before Henry died, the first of many British nudges at the great ice barrier that blocked the North-West Passage. Henry's reign saw the Spanish and Portuguese as the big winners of the new urge to colonise, along with vast wealth from the east. England, with its prowess in northern waters, ended up only with unlimited supplies of cod.

The Fiennes' local expansionism, fairly steady since Hastings, had stabilised in England with the Fiennes Dacres at Herstmonceux and the Wykeham Fiennes clan at Broughton. The wealth and the lands of the Counts of Boulogne and of the Sayes had been swallowed through marriage and inheritance, but the original Fiennes family remained 'over there' (near Boulogne), as they do today. Many of my expedition friends still call me Froggy, harping back to my ancestor at Hastings, but by the dawn of the sixteenth century all the Fienneses 'over here' were as English as roast beef.

Henry died in 1509, a sick, tired and stressed king who had fought no wars, kept a tight rein on the barons and on the nation's solvency. He should definitely go down in history as a good, successful monarch. His young heir, crowned King Henry VIII, took over a throne unchallenged from any direction, despite the fact that his father, a little known Welshman, had sprung from nowhere. Henry VIII was soundly imbued with Fiennes DNA through his mother, Elizabeth of York, the direct descendant of Margaret Fiennes.

15

Death of a Deer Hunter

Henry VIII, the most famous of English kings, was the great grandson of a Welsh tradesman once wanted for murder, whose son married the French widow of Henry V. His hereditary claims on the throne were negligible but, once on it, the strength of his character and the fear that he commanded in all around him kept would-be rival claimants from making an appearance. With Henry VIII you kept your head well below the parapet at all times, or you risked losing it.

Born handsome, intelligent, physically strong and full of the joys of life, Henry remains famous (or infamous) for his serial matrimony, his dissolution of the monasteries and his schism with Rome. What linked all this was his casual brutality to all who crossed him, whether closest family or oldest friends. In rereading English history, before writing this book, with no inbuilt bias for or against any particular monarch, I have come away with an active dislike for only one of them – Henry VIII. He was in every way a right evil bastard, as we used to say in the army, and with no redeeming features. Some historians have tried to whitewash this monster but without success.

Most of my kinsmen who had the misfortune to get close to Henry soon regretted it. One who didn't was the previously mentioned John the Goldsmith Twisleton, who caught the eye of the purchasers of the fine plate Henry was wont to dole out as new year gifts. Through his goldsmith's skills, John rose to the appointment of repairing the silver of the royal household and became wealthy. Seven times he applied to become an alderman of the City, and on the eighth was accepted for the Queenhythe ward. As well as the manor of Barlow back in his native Yorkshire, he bought three more manors in Nottinghamshire, four in Lincolnshire, plus property in London. One of his two sons was John Twisleton, the vicar of Windlesham church in Surrey where I was christened 390 years later. The other son, Christopher, prospered greatly, became Comptroller of Hull, bought large tracts of land in Yorkshire and married a Kent heiress.

Within three generations my ancestral Twisletons had elevated themselves from the lowest echelons of trade to the manorial class complete with their own heraldry. This was not an unusual shift at the close of the Middle Ages, especially for the great merchant tradesmen of London. The Hoares of Hoare's Bank began their rise soon after our Twisletons took off, and other goldsmiths, the Dunscombes, became the richest commoners in England and bought the Duke of Buckingham's prime estate in Helmesley.

But apart from this clutch of lucky Twisletons, the family, especially the Fienneses of Dacre at Herstmonceux, ended up in very deep water under Henry-the-butcher.

In his late teens Henry was, by all records, extremely handsome, spoke four languages, excelled at sports from tennis to jousting, was highly literate, a tenor of rare ability and an accomplished player of various instruments. He adored the hunt and was a skilled archer. He enjoyed elaborate masked balls, tournaments and royal ceremonies. He craved recognition on the wide European stage, especially if he could achieve it through battle, like Henry V.

He remained married to his first wife, Catherine of Aragon, daughter of King Ferdinand of Spain, for twenty years, and for the first ten appeared to be truly fond of her. In 1511 she gave birth to a son, and Henry was over the moon. But the child died two months later and Henry was desolated. His desire for a son was to rule much of his life, but fame as a warrior was surely a close second on his wish list, and for many years he dabbled in diplomatic conspiracies either with Ferdinand of Spain or Francis of France to fix a firm enough alliance to ensure a great military victory – anywhere, but above all, of course, in France.

Time and again over the next thirty years treaties were made by and between the three potentates and occasionally other parties, but treachery and double-dealing by one or all of them always interfered with Henry's ambitions. Nonetheless he built up England's navy from five to fifty ships with the latest artillery, and he has even been called the father of the Royal Navy, as have at least five other kings before him. In 1513 Henry's first invasion of France, after years of talk, successfully managed to besiege two well-defended towns and to defeat a lost group of French knights at the so-called Battle of the Spurs. The Emperor Maximilian's tiny force which had fought under Henry's command went home delighted, as did Henry. This was his first military command and also his last, although some of his army commanders did very well without him from time to time.

He learnt on his return home that King James IV of Scotland, to whom he had previously married his sister, had, with French connivance, led 15,000 Scots over the border and clashed with a smaller English army near Berwick. This battle, at Flodden Bridge, lasted only three hours but ended with 10,000 dead Scotsmen, including King James and many nobles. Henry's sister Margaret now ruled Scotland on behalf of her seventeen-month-old son, James V of Scotland, Henry's nephew.

One man who shared Henry's philosophy of the end justifying the means, no matter how cruel and ruthless they might be, was Thomas Wolsey, son of a butcher and servant of another. Due to Henry's innate dislike of the mundane side of government, Wolsey was given a loose rein to rule England in all but name for fifteen years. He was very much a self-made churchman, like many of Henry's top executives, and he remained in the number one spot, a lethal position with Henry VIII anywhere near, by simply doing exactly what Henry wanted at all times.

Ferdinand of Spain had proved a treacherous ally during the French campaign, and his daughter, Henry's wife Catherine, suffered a distinct lessening of kingly affections as a result. As the years went by and she failed to produce a male heir, Henry's philandering increased and he began to realise that he must look elsewhere to obtain the required son. With no royal heir to marry off to a powerful ruler's daughter, England was in a no-win position on the diplomatic chessboard of Europe.

In 1518 Wolsey used the mutual hostility of France and Spain to convene the so-called Treaty of London, which in turn led to an agreed peace meeting between England and France to be held in the halfway house of the district of Calais, the only English possession left in France. The exact venue for this meeting was halfway between Guisnes and Ardres in the very heart of Fiennes country, and came to be known as the Field of the Cloth of Gold. Henry's court and anybody who was anybody, or thought they were, had crossed the Channel to be seen at this event and all wore clothes of rich satin and velvet under cloaks of gold. Six thousand workmen put up costly tents and prepared the food brought over, much of it from England, including 2,000 sheep on the hoof. Wine flowed freely and with trumpets blaring, the mounted hosts approached each other from either side of the field, much as they had for hundreds of years with intent to kill. But this time they put aside the long years of mistrust and fear and, dismounting, joined together in a huge love-in of feasting, dancing, music, jousting and laughing. Wonders never cease. John Fiennes, Lord Dacre, who enjoyed the fun must have felt at home, for he had been the Constable of Calais twenty-seven years before. Yet within two years of all the many oaths of eternal friendship sworn at this Field of the Cloth of Gold, the two sides were again officially at war.

After fifteen long years of relying on his chancellor Cardinal Wolsey to sort out Europe, or at least France, by his much vaunted diplomatic cunning, Henry no longer valued him and that, as Wolsey knew, was a distinctly dangerous sign. Especially as his tax collection methods back home were causing great discontent verging, in Kent of course, on armed rebellion. Wolsey's additional failure, and the one that sealed his fate, was his inability to obtain a papal annulment of Henry's marriage to Catherine of Aragon and a blessing on Henry's desired replacement wife, Anne Boleyn, who he had met at Hever Castle, which Roger Fiennes had sold to Anne's father. Anne's elder sister had for a while been Henry's mistress, but Anne kept the king panting with desire, allowing no hanky-panky without a promise of marriage.

By 1529 Wolsey's star had fallen from on high, and he was stripped of office, wealth and privilege. He died a year later on his way to the Tower and certain execution. His place was partially taken by a lowly don named Thomas Cranmer who Henry promoted to Archbishop of Canterbury, but he never gained the supreme power that Henry had once allowed Wolsey, for the king had himself grown more involved with government and especially with the church, the body that was so frustrating his remarriage plans.

With Cranmer's help, Henry identified a groundbreaking new way around his problems, while the cunning vixen Anne Boleyn unearthed a treatise penned by the reformer William Tyndale which suggested to Henry that the monarch of England could be leader of both church and state; in short, his own Pope with his own divorcing powers. Cranmer proceeded to issue dozens of proclamations which ended England's ancient allegiance to Rome, installed Henry as Supreme Head of the Church of England and saw him married to Anne Boleyn (already pregnant) in no time at all.

A longstanding friendship between Anne's family at Hever Castle and the Fienneses of Herstmonceux was to be cemented by Henry's subsequent dealings with both families. Thomas Fiennes, the 2nd Lord Dacre, had served Henry VII well and had often done diplomatic duty for Henry VIII. But in 1525 Henry's judiciaries shut him up in Fleet prison and the court record states: 'The Lord Dacre confesste the bearinge of Theuves, and his negligence in ponyshement of them, and also his famylyer and conversaunte beinge with them, knowinge them to have com'ytted felonye and dyvers other his mysdoings.'

This Dacre's seventeen-year-old grandson Thomas and his sister Mary were called to Henry's court where Mary married courtier Henry Norris, a good friend of Anne Boleyn.

As soon as Anne's first child turned out to be a daughter (the future Queen Elizabeth I), Henry's infatuation with her began to fade. He was also no longer the handsome lover of yore, having suffered from smallpox, malaria, several jousting accidents and, as a result of the latter, a pus-producing leg ulcer that, together with migraines, gave him a good deal of pain. He was vain and jealous, so Anne was courting big trouble when she openly flirted with the likes of the fashionable sonneteer Sir Thomas Wyatt, and several others. Her reputation as a flirt was well-known, and one recorded epithet given her by the public was 'the goggle-eyed whore'.

At the May Day celebrations in 1536 Anne dropped her handkerchief as a token of admiration for a jouster. Henry Norris, Mary Fiennes's husband, witnessed this and, either because he was himself infatuated with Anne or merely to curry royal favour, he snitched on her. He probably knew that Henry's first minister, Thomas Cromwell of Putney, who had previously been Wolsey's chief executive and attorney, was in the process of collecting evidence of Anne's infidelity for the king.

In addition to Henry's ailments, he had by 1536 grown so obese (over twenty stone or, in modern EU parlance, about 130 kilos) that he needed a servant-borne litter, a shire horse, or, to go upstairs, systems of ropes and pulleys. The imagination boggles at the bedtime duties of Henry's wives, most of whom were petite. Small wonder that the flirtatious Anne failed to err on the side of caution.

Mary Fiennes' husband made a fatal miscalculation when he told

Cromwell about Anne's handkerchief, because the latter had, at a secret tribunal, decided to arrest Anne on charges of treason, adultery and incest with her own brother (patently untrue) and with half a dozen others including, ironically, Henry Norris himself. Anne was speedily put on trial in front of a jury of twenty-six peers under the chairmanship of her own uncle, the Duke of Norfolk. One of the peers, the brother-in-law and good friend of Henry Norris and his son, was the seventeen-year-old Thomas Fiennes of Herstmonceux who had to vote for the execution of Norris, the other equally falsely-charged adulterers and Anne herself. She was executed a few days later after spending a thousand days as Queen of England. Two queens down and four to go.

Not long before Anne's execution, ex-Queen Catherine had died a lonely death, exiled to an East Anglian priory, and, only a month after killing off Anne, Henry married one of her ladies-in-waiting, a quiet girl named Jane Seymour who, in 1537, gave Henry what he had wanted for so long, a healthy son who was named Edward. The birth was difficult, so Jane's surgeon cut her stomach wide open to ensure Edward's live exit, and this killed Jane. The king, utterly callous at the deaths of Catherine and Anne, showed genuine and long-lasting grief at Jane's death.

Thomas Fiennes of Herstmonceux was again called up from Sussex to act as pall-bearer at Jane's funeral.

Now that he had an heir, the king could more patiently look upon future marriages with a view to cementing advantageous diplomatic alliances. He and Chancellor Cromwell contemplated various matches with a number of European princesses, eventually settling on Anne of Cleves, a duchy in the Lower Rhinelands. Henry was never content with Cromwell's suggestions on political grounds alone. His bride-to-be must also look good, and to that end he always sent out the portrait painter Holbein to capture each potential bride's likeness for him to inspect. Holbein's picture of Anne of Cleves was clearly to his liking, but following their betrothal, he was in for a shock.

Anne arrived in England early in 1540 and was met by Thomas Fiennes of Herstmonceux and the Duke of Norfolk heading a cavalcade of knights 'all in coates of velvet with chaynes of gold'. They brought her to the king, who took one look, swore at Holbein and Cromwell for having deceived him, and described Anne as a Flanders mare whose ugliness 'struck him to the heart'. Without consummating the marriage, Henry divorced her six months later. Divorce was now no problem at all, since in that respect Henry was his own Pope. The faithful Thomas Cromwell, who had done so well for Henry and for so long, was executed in 1540, largely for the crime of having advised Henry to marry Anne and for having praised her beauty.

Henry lived his life to the end as a devout Catholic. He did not approve of the German Protestant Martin Luther, and was proud of his title, Defender of the Faith, awarded him by the Pope for writing a treatise against Luther. But the Church's wealth was quite another matter and he realised, with the earlier prompting of Cromwell, the great scope for enriching his Treasury at the expense of the hugely wealthy clerical establishment. The church, except in the north, was extremely unpopular with the population. A large percentage of the clergy led idle lives, never gave to the poor, kept mistresses in their benefices, sat on great hordes of wealth and levied heavy church taxes on their parishioners, including big fees to bury anyone in holy ground. The king used the anti-clerical mood to instigate and execute the dissolution of the monasteries. The church's wealth was now the king's. He would use it for his own ambitions, especially for any future wars against the French or Scots.

Removing England from under the power and influence of Rome had been no more unpopular than would, today, be withdrawal from the European Union. There were, of course, individuals who refused to sign declarations of loyalty to the king as head of the church. These included the famous philosopher and, briefly, Henry's chancellor, Sir Thomas More, and his friend

Bishop Fisher of Rochester. Henry naturally beheaded them both, alongside a trio of dissenting Carthusian monks who were lashed to hurdles, dragged to Tyburn, hanged, cut down alive, disembowelled, mutilated and cut into quarters.

Henry wanted Catholicism without the Pope. He did not want heresy, but he lived at a time when Protestantism was on the move all over Europe. William Tyndale was no Lutheran, but his driving passion was to translate the Bible into English and make Bibles available to all. Henry had anti-heretic spies at home and abroad, and Tyndale was eventually hunted down in Antwerp and executed.

Cromwell's purge on the church went ahead with ever increasing vandalism. Eight hundred major churches and abbeys were forced to close by 1540, and 9,000 monks and other inmates were turned out into the cold. Ancient tombs of the Anglo-Saxon kings were destroyed, as were priceless collections of books and manuscripts. Whole buildings were pulled down, while metalwork and jewellery were melted with the same determined but thoughtless vandalism as was later to be practised by the Chinese in Tibet and the Taliban in Afghanistan.

Not everyone kowtowed weakly to Henry's new laws. Various small uprisings occurred, mostly in the north, the biggest being the Pilgrimage of Grace which was led by Robert Aske and orchestrated by Thomas Fiennes' Dacre cousin, Lord Thomas Dacre of the North, in collusion with the Darcy and Hussey clans, all loyal Roman Catholics. They demanded that all powers seized by the state from the church should be returned. Together with a Lincolnshire-based rebellion, those involved were more than Henry's small available armies could hope to cope with, and Henry was lucky indeed that the main rebel leaders did not resort to armed conflict. Once they dispersed, following his vague promises to look at their grievances, his men exacted revenge with widespread hanging and burning of ringleaders.

The Catholics abroad were also incensed at Henry's shrugging off of Rome and of his treatment of the monasteries. A holy war, bringing France and Spain together, seemed imminent and so threatening to the English in 1539 that a major building of coastal defences was begun, and the navy was placed on alert.

At the same time, Henry's long-time paranoia about rival claimants to the throne resurfaced. Since his father, the Welsh usurper, had such a feeble royal lineage, there were several families whose claim was at least as strong, such as the Nevilles, the Staffords and the Poles. Henry had been plucking them off one by one over the years as the opportunity arose. Back in 1513 he had a Pole beheaded, and in 1521, on a feeble excuse, Edward Stafford, Duke of Buckingham, was executed. Henry now learnt that for the Franco-Spanish holy war on England, the Pope had selected as their figurehead Englishman another Pole family member, Reginald, once a great favourite of Henry's but a staunch Roman Catholic. Henry, with typical ruthlessness, forced Reginald's brother to save his own skin by 'confessing' to the involvement of the rest of his family. His eldest brother Henry was beheaded, as were their cousin the Marquess of Exeter, a close Neville friend, his own mother, Margaret Pole, and his little nephew, brother Henry's son. Other Poles were locked up in the Tower. Henry sent spies armed with poisoned daggers, the forerunners of KGB umbrellas, to search Europe for Reginald himself.

When Henry's defences were fully ready, his navy patrolled the Channel on alert under three main admirals, one of whom was Edward Fiennes Clinton, the Earl of Lincoln who eventually made it to Lord High Admiral a few years after Henry's death. The pride of the navy was the *Great Harry*, a monster with banks of heavy cannon set all along her waists and designed without the fatal flaws which caused the sinking in 1545 of Henry's equally ambitious *Mary Rose*. The *Great Harry* and the rest of the navy were not, in fact, needed because the Franco-Spanish invasion never materialised, since the two countries' leaders mistrusted each other.

This was as well, for by 1540 Henry was a great rotting hulk of a man who suffered more or less constant pain from his ever-pustulating leg ulcers. His irrational rages grew more frequent and he thrived, Stalin-like, on causing all those around him, especially his nearest and dearest, to live in constant fear of death.

His old warrior friends, the Dukes of Norfolk and Suffolk, seemed for many years to live charmed lives as year after year they arrested all Henry's top men one by one. But when Henry parted amicably from Anne of Cleves, without consummation of their six-month marriage, the Duke of Norfolk saw a chance to consolidate his royal links. He introduced his sexy, nineteen-year-old niece, Catherine Howard, to Henry, who fell hook, line, and sinker for her blatant charms. She was very soon his fifth queen but, having enjoyed sex with a number of men prior to meeting Henry, she foolishly saw no reason at all why she should not continue to entertain secret lovers now that she was queen.

Henry soon learned of the antics going on in the queen's bedchamber. One lover, her music teacher Mannox, confessed that he 'had commonly used to feel the secrets and other parts of the Queen's body', her handsome cousin Francis Dereham that he had 'known her carnally many times'. Catherine confessed that Dereham had often 'lain with me, sometimes in his doublet and his hose but I mean naked when his hose were put down.' Two of her lovers' heads soon adorned London Bridge, and she was executed sixteen months after becoming queen.

Looking at the records, it is painfully obvious that many of the treason trials were utter farces. The peers who sat in judgment parroted 'Off with his/her head' in order to keep theirs. Cromwell and the king maintained control through terror.

One who knew how easily people of his rank and standing could lose their heads was Thomas Fiennes, husband of Mary Neville, granddaughter of that Duke of Buckingham who was judicially murdered by Henry VIII because of the possible threat his Plantagenet lineage posed to the throne. Thomas himself had sat on the jury at the trial of Anne Boleyn and her brother, Lord Rochford, with whom she was accused of committing incest. Thomas had also been one of the jurors who tried and found guilty the rebellious northern lords, one of whom was his own cousin, the other Lord Dacre. As well as being a pall bearer at the funeral of Jane Seymour, he had been chosen to 'bear the spice plates' at the christening of Prince Edward.

Thomas Fiennes was clearly a young man in favour at court, but also one with an unfortunate addiction. Hunting the numerous deer in his own extensive parks was not as exciting a challenge as planning night raids on his neighbours'. But deer poaching was a capital offence, and unfortunately Thomas was caught at it, more than once.

I found a creepy little note the nineteen-year-old Thomas Fiennes wrote to Thomas Cromwell after one episode:

> I have received your lordship's letters wherein I perceive your benevolence towards the frailness of my youth in considering that I was rather led by instigation of my accusers than of my mere mind to those unlawful acts, which I have long detested in secret. I perceive your lordship is desirous to have knowledge of all riotous hunters, and shall exert myself to do you service therein.

Young Thomas was volunteering to be a grass. This did not, however, stop him having another go himself in 1541. According to court records, Thomas and thirteen cronies, mostly local tearaways, met up at Herstmonceux Castle to plot a two-pronged raid on the neighbouring park of one of England's most influential nobles, Nicholas Pelham. There had been territorial wrangles between the Pelhams and the Fienneses going back to the previous century when Sir John Pelham was allowed to enclose a road which led through the middle of Herstmonceux park and Roger Fiennes enclosed Herstmonceux and enlarged its park by 600 acres of Pelham land. All this no doubt still rankled down the generations.

I can't help having some kindred feeling for Thomas and his exploits, as in my own youth I was brought before the Assizes for night offences in Sussex, viz raiding a girls' school with smoke bombs and, on another occasion, for blowing up civilian property at Castle Combe with army property, Her Majesty's explosives. Like Thomas, I was addicted to wild behaviour at night. It must be something in the Sussex night air. Like him, I had been led astray by my colleagues. My fate was to be thrown out of the SAS. Thomas, however, was to fare far worse.

In the dark, one group of the Herstmonceux poaching party came upon three Pelham gamekeepers, which was not part of the script, and in the ensuing fracas one of the gamekeepers, John Busbrig, 'received such hurt that he died thereof'.

Everyone involved was arraigned for murder even though Thomas was not himself with the group that killed Busbrig. The lords who sat to judge him included many of his neighbours who had been co-jurors with him on previous trials. But the outcome of this trial showed him no mercy. The king himself ruled that Thomas and his three main ringleaders must die on commoners' gibbets. The London Chronicle records: 'The 29th day of June, Saynt Peturs day was my lorde Dakars of the Southe led . . . from the Tower to Tyburn and there he was hanggid . . . for robbre of ye Kingges deer and murther of ye Kepars.'

It was the talk of diplomatic circles. I found a letter from the French ambassador in London to the King of France dated 30 June, which said there was judgment on a young lord called Dacre of the South 'who, for assembling armed men with the intention of seeking a park keeper whom they wished to slay . . . was condemned to be hanged, and yesterday was executed at the common gibbet of London, called Tyburn.'

Another to the Queen of Hungary from the Emperor's ambassador ran: 'Lord Dacres . . . a cousin of this Queen, 23 yeares old and possessing a property . . . was hung from the most ignominious gibbet, and for the greater shame dragged through the streets to the place of execution, to the great pity of many people, and even of his very judges, who wept when they sentenced him, and in a body asked his pardon of the King.'

Of Thomas's friends, three were hanged at Saint Thomas

Wateringe, the official place of hanging for Sussex criminals. They included John Mantel, the husband of Thomas's sister Anne, who was Controller of Customs and a member of the select group of fifty courtiers known as the King's Pensioners. Herstmonceux and its estates were confiscated by Henry from the Fiennes family so, for a while, only the Oxfordshire branch at Broughton Castle, the Lords Saye and Sele, kept the Fiennes flag aloft.

The Fiennes Clinton branch, once claiming the Lord Saye title, had now dropped the Fiennes part of their surname. Edward, the 9th Lord Clinton, backed all the right horses under King Henry. He sat on the board that decided the dissolution of the monasteries and cultivated a close friendship with John Dudley, the Lord High Admiral. Together they led a fleet to attack Scotland in 1544 and, on landing, their army stormed Edinburgh. Later Henry sent them to France, where they successfully laid siege to Boulogne. Ravaging the surrounding countryside, they razed many castles to the ground, including our family castle in the village of Fiennes.

A decade later, a local duke reconstructed the castle less than a mile away, a tower of which stands today. Local road names still reflect both castles: the *Rue de Chateau* and the *Rue de Vieux Chateau*.

King Henry meanwhile decided to have another go at war with France and their Scottish allies. The latter under Henry's nephew, now King James V of Scotland, pre-empted the planned English invasion by their own southerly attack. The armies met at Solway Moss, the Scots were defeated and King James died soon after the battle. His week-old daughter was crowned Mary Queen of Scots, and Henry quickly arranged for his heir, Edward, to marry her once she was of age. Henry then focused on France, leaving an army in Edinburgh to ensure good behaviour. After the siege of Boulogne, the English army's planned advance on Paris petered out, along with their supplies, near mutiny of the troops ensued and Henry had to make do with a vague peace treaty.

To conduct even these minor military meanderings cost Henry an arm and a leg and destroyed the financial independence of the crown which his father had won through his policies of peace. The resultant tax gathering did nothing to enhance Henry in the eyes of the populace. Nor did his ongoing reign of terror endear him to his nobles. Even his old friend and loyal general, the Duke of Norfolk, forgiven over the years for tempting the king into marrying two adulterous Norfolk nieces, was finally tabbed for execution, largely due to his son's tactless arrogance.

But the night before Norfolk's head was due to roll, Henry VIII died in his pain-wracked bed in the presence of his loyal adviser, Thomas Cranmer. Before he died, Henry made clear his wishes for the future of England. His heirs, in order, must be Edward, his son by Jane Seymour, then his elder daughter Mary by Catherine of Aragon, and, after her, Elizabeth, the daughter of Anne Boleyn. His sixth wife, Catherine Parr, became queen in 1543, gave him no children, but served as a good companion for Henry's last few crotchety, inward-looking years.

Henry ruled for thirty-eight years. He started out in a blaze of popular glory as bluff King Hal. He died a wounded bull who killed many of those with whom he worked or bedded, a callous megalomaniac with a fifty-four-inch waist, weighing over twenty stone and crippled by festering ulcers. The most famous King of England he may always remain, but also, in my opinion, speaking on behalf of Thomas Fiennes, Lord Dacre, by far the nastiest.

16

Stately Homes of England

Prince Edward, son of Jane Seymour, was a sickly child, and his six-year reign as King Edward VI was punctuated by ever-worsening illness until his death from tuberculosis in 1553. His uncle, Edward Seymour, who had been appointed by the late king to act as a member of a Council of Regency during Edward's minority, seized power, became sole regent and promoted himself to the dukedom of Somerset, with the title of Protector Somerset. He could see that Edward was likely to die long before he came of age and that if, as the late King Henry had wished, Edward's elder sister Catholic Mary then took over, there would be big trouble in an England which, under the guidance of the protector with young Edward's fervent approval, had become ardently Protestant.

Anne Boleyn's daughter, Elizabeth, was brought up as a Protestant, but not fanatically so. She lived with her stepmother, Henry's sixth wife, Catherine Parr, who was good to her until a troublesome third party entered their household in the shape of Thomas Seymour, the brother of Protector Somerset, who first married Catherine Parr, and then began to flirt with the fourteen-year-old Princess Elizabeth. When Catherine found out what was going on, poor Elizabeth was sent packing, and when Somerset lost patience, his brother ended in the Tower.

Protector Somerset had bigger troubles than his philandering brother, for his rule was under threat at home and abroad. The French sent an army to Scotland, where the child Mary Stuart was queen. They took her 'to safety' in France and betrothed her to the dauphin. Various plans by the protector to avoid just such a Franco-Scottish alliance had come to nought, and embryonic Protestant England was threatened by hostile Catholic coalitions from all sides.

The protector's chief rival for power was John Dudley, who was the close friend of both Edward Fiennes Clinton and Richard Fiennes, Lord Saye and Sele of Broughton Castle. Richard was attendant to the Privy Chamber of young Edward VI. To what extent he and Fiennes Clinton were involved in John Dudley's plots to seize power from the protector is not clear, but they were certainly close colleagues, and John Dudley's faction was successful, deposing Somerset in 1549.

John Dudley, promoted to the dukedom of Northumberland, ruled in much the same manner as had Somerset, but with more efficiency and enough new regional controls to prevent the spreading anarchy. He sued for peace with the French and Scots and worked closely with the highly intelligent and precocious teenage king. From an early age, and backed to the hilt by Thomas Cranmer, still the Archbishop of Canterbury, Edward VI worked to make the Anglican church created by his father (Catholic in every sense but adherence to Rome) into a genuinely Protestant body of worship. He was described by a famous Protestant writer of the day, John Foxe, as a 'godly imp'. He loved listening to sermons by Cranmer and was proud to read at least twelve chapters of scripture daily. He reinvigorated his father's robbery of church property, and issued the first English language Book of Common Prayer, which with various revisions is still in use today. Church services were made more simple, Mass became Holy Communion and was conducted in English, altars were turned into tables, stained glass windows, icons and holy pictures were removed, and priests' robes toned down. Priests could also marry, if they wished.

*

This period of dynastic uncertainty and religious zeal was curiously also a time of great architectural expansion as the Fienneses, the Dudleys and the Seymours vied to employ the services of the top English architect, Sir William Sharington, and his brilliant mason, John Chapman. The superb quality of his workmanship at each castle, all of which are now open to the public, is as impressive today as it was back then, though Sharington turned out to be a rogue who was executed for fraud whilst Master of the Bristol Mint. My cousin Nathaniel Fiennes, the 21st Lord Saye and Sele, has lived at Broughton for much of his life and he sees the modifications made to the castle by Richard Fiennes during the reigns of Edward VI and Mary as being the most important in the entire six hundred years that our family has lived there. Richard's son, another Richard, spent most of his short life completing the works, and much of the fortune that it cost derived from the wool of the Broughton sheep.

Many of the new rooms and the ninety-foot long gallery of Richard's time were designed, not for family life, but to receive royalty. New windows were installed, along with flamboyant plasterwork ceilings and extensive oak panelling. On one chimney the date identifying the completion of the exterior building work is inscribed as 1554. The style of the work relates uniquely to the short-lived style of King Edward VI's court. Today the comparisons can be made by visiting the castles or manors of Longleat (the Thynnes), Sudeley (the Seymours), Dudley (the Dudleys) or Sharington's own Lacock Abbey. The other main patron of the style was Protector Somerset himself, and the old Somerset House, now owned by the nation, is another example which is worth viewing.

Quite how Richard Fiennes, a mere lord in the company of the king and his top dukes, came to occupy such dizzy heights was through his father's close friendship and family ties with the Norris family. Henry Norris, executed on the trumped up charge of adultery with Anne Boleyn, had been guardian of Richard Fiennes back in the 1530s, at which time he married Richard's cousin, Mary Fiennes of Herstmonceux. Mary had a son, Henry Norris II who, as a child, spent much time playing with his young cousin, Richard, his father's ward. When this Henry joined the court in the Privy Chamber of Edward VI, he introduced his long-time friend Richard Fiennes to the boy king.

Edward, who became seriously ill, named his fifteen-year-old cousin, Lady Jane Grey, an ardent Protestant and John Dudley's daughter-in-law, as his heir, specifically excluding his two sisters, Mary because of her Catholic tendencies and Elizabeth so he could be seen to apply the same rule to her as to Mary. Among the last recorded words of the dying Edward was the plea, 'Oh, Lord God, defend this realm from Papistry.' Richard Fiennes was one of the signatories of Dudley's 'Device for the Succession' to nominate Lady Jane Grey as Edward's heir. So on Edward VI's death, Dudley needed to speedily ensure that Lady Jane Grey was crowned before Henry VIII's elder daughter, Mary Tudor, could, as feared, try for the throne.

Unfortunately for Dudley and for Lady Jane, Mary, the daughter of Catherine of Aragon, was a canny lady who had hidden her hardcore Catholic leanings from the general public, whose long-time expectation was that she would become their queen. So they refused to acknowledge Lady Jane, and only nine days after Northumberland's council had her crowned, Mary, with a large force of supporters, marched on London, and Jane was betrayed by every one of her supporters, even Cranmer. Mary was crowned, to the (temporary) joy of the people, and later that year the sixteen-year-old Lady Jane was executed, as were her father, her husband and the Duke of Northumberland.

The most famous 'heads' man, King Henry VIII, had gone, but folk who hovered too close to the throne of England were still living in a fairly risky environment. Mary Tudor's honeymoon period as queen did not last long, for no sooner was she on the throne than she revealed the fanatical nature of her Catholicism and her determination to return England to Rome, reversing everything her father and brother had done to reform the church. Worst of all, she announced her firm wish to marry Philip, the heir to the throne of Catholic Spain, who would swallow England in one gulp once he became King of Spain, which was at the time the richest, largest and most powerful empire in the world. The marriage went ahead.

At twenty-seven Philip was already a widower of nine years. His future as King of Spain was to be a rule of forty-two years and, thirty-four years later, he would send the Armada to attack England. Mary, at thirty-eight, was eleven years older than Philip, highly neurotic and lacking in teeth. Philip wanted England, but not her queen's body. Mary wanted his support to help her re-Catholicise England, and she desperately wanted a good Catholic son and heir. Whether or not Philip ever consummated the marriage is not known, but Mary did suffer a number of phantom pregnancies. She was to die childless, and Philip, engaged in enlarging his empire, seldom visited her or, indeed, England.

Mary became instantly unpopular on her marriage to Philip and then a figure of hatred when she started burning Protestants at the stake, 274 of them according to the records of John Foxe's *Book of Martyrs*. Sixty of the fried victims were women and several were Lollards who would probably have come up for burning sooner or later even if Edward VI had stayed around longer. Mary Tudor grew to be detested by her people, and the epithet Bloody Mary is still current today. It is also a rather evil-looking drink.

The most famous of her victims were the priests Ridley, Latimer and Archbishop Cranmer, but the *Book of Martyrs* tells the detailed sufferings of each and every known martyr. The story of the immolation John Hooper, the Bishop of Worcester and Gloucester tells of the executioner's inability to get a good fire going that would have shamed a Boy Scout. The faggots were green and the first two attempts went out.

> After the second fire was spent, he wiped both his eyes with his hands, and beholding the people, he said ... 'For God's love,

> good people, let me have more fire!' and all this while his nether parts did burn; but the fagots were so few that the flame only singed his upper parts.
>
> The third fire was kindled within a while after, which was more extreme than the other two. In this fire he prayed with a loud voice, 'Lord Jesus, have mercy upon me! Lord Jesus receive my spirit!' And these were the last words he was heard to utter. But when he was black in the mouth, and his tongue so swollen that he could not speak, yet his lips went until they were shrunk to the gums: and he knocked his breast with his hands until one of his arms fell off, and then knocked still with the other, while the fat, water, and blood dropped out of his fingers' ends, until by renewing the fire, his strength was gone, and his hand clave fast in knocking to the iron upon his breast. Then immediately bowing forwards, he yielded up his spirit.
>
> Thus was he three quarters of an hour or more in the fire.

The *Book of Martyrs* remains controversial among historians in terms of its accuracy, but the background of Mary's reign of terror is indisputable and was masterminded as chief inquisitor by the notorious Roman Catholic Bishop of London, Edmund Bonner. Foxe emphasises throughout his book that the stand of brave individuals, like John Hooper was all about freedom. Freedom of religious choice and the ability of individuals in England to read the Bible in their own language.

Quite apart from her notoriety as the scourge of Protestants, Mary was deeply despised as being responsible for the loss of Calais, England's last possession in France. Her marriage to Philip of Spain naturally involved her agreeing to help his ongoing fight with the French, and this led to the loss of Calais, despite the valiant efforts of Edward Fiennes Clinton and his garrison to withstand a determined French siege with no hope of relief. Mary came to recognise the morale-boosting effect which Calais had for so long given to Englishmen but only after she had lost it. She is reported to have said on her deathbed,

'When I die, you will find the words Philip and Calais written on my heart.' That assumes that she had a heart. Certainly she had no conscience about the torture she had loosed on so many of her citizens. She once said that a good bout of burnings enhanced her appetite for dinner. The loss of a French town may have disturbed her on her deathbed, but not the blood she had spilled.

Although she burnt up many leading Protestants, many also escaped through exile or through hiding with friends whilst promulgating subversive religious propaganda, in the manner of *samizdat* pamphlets in the darkest days of the Soviet Union.

Religious mania aside, and she was certainly not the only religious maniac around at the time, Mary was relatively successful in some ways. She reorganised and redesigned the financial system with intelligence, played cleverly with recoinage and customs taxation, and completed the more sensible financial reforms of the beheaded Duke of Northumberland.

That Queen Mary's soul was not entirely black is evident in that she failed to have her little sister Elizabeth poisoned, beheaded, smothered or anally skewered with a red hot poker. The temptation, though, must have been great, for Elizabeth was used by a number of anti-Mary conspirators as the most obvious and highly popular successor to the throne. Elizabeth was a born survivor. She knew from late childhood as heads rolled all about her, favourite uncles disappeared and the smoke from pyres of human flesh wafted over London, that she must tread with care and avoid too open a commitment to one side or another, for life at the top was a game of roulette.

In 1555 Queen Mary sickened, probably with ovarian cancer which, through the resultant bloated stomach tumour, made her think she was suffering yet another phantom pregnancy. She feared death in childbirth, and she knew her only feasible successor, due to her failure to produce her own heir, must be her sister Elizabeth, and during the last year of her life the half-sisters grew closer.

In November 1558 the Spanish ambassador, representing Philip who was as usual 'abroad on business', called together the ruling council and gave Philip's approval for Elizabeth to succeed Mary. Mary, near death, at last gave her own assent, with the pitiful request that Elizabeth maintain the Catholic religion. A week later she died, and the great Elizabethan age began.

The mad dogs of England, puppies as yet, heard the bells chime out all over their land and stirred in their kennels. Elizabeth had witnessed the loss of Calais and the last English 'empire', but she was destined to sow the seeds of the greatest empire the world had ever known. She gave the English – for they were not yet British – a sense of national pride. Here, for the first time, was a monarch who preached no overt form of religion and stood for no Red or White Rose. She preached only the glory of England.

17

Begging for a Barony

King Alfred has been remembered for his burnt cakes, Canute for sitting on a sandy beach with the sea lapping his feet, and King Harold for the arrow in his eye. Queen Elizabeth I spawned many a myth, including the cloak that Walter Raleigh was said to have thrown over a puddle to keep her dainty feet dry. She is said to have owned two thousand magnificent dresses, to have been fluent in Greek, Latin, Spanish and French by the age of twelve and, later in life, to have plugged her cheeks daily with cotton buds to disguise her lack of teeth, made rotten by chewing sugar cane. Her face, they say, was layered with lead paint in her middle age to make her look younger and hide smallpox ravage. Yet she held the adoration of the English for forty-five difficult years and is still revered today as a highly successful monarch.

She was celebrated as Gloriana, Deborah, Virginia, Diana, Cynthia, Astrea and Belphoebe. Hers was the so-called Golden Age of England. Only moderately religious and described by the reformer John Knox as 'neither a good protestant nor yet a resolute papist', she always steered England towards the middle ground and ended with a bland form of Protestantism very similar to that of today's Anglican church. She achieved the return of the Book of Common Prayer from Latin to English, but not in time for her own coronation which had to use the traditional

Latin format. The crowds outside Westminster Abbey for that service, like Beatles fans or Berlin Wall souvenir hunters, tore off strips of the carpet she had trodden to enter the Abbey.

A great many nobles, scared stiff of the late Mary Tudor, homed in on Elizabeth and her council for the righting of long held grievances. The Fienneses led the charge: the Fiennes Dacres from Herstmonceux, and the Saye and Seles from Broughton. The first Fiennes appeal reached the queen in early January 1559, and this begged that Gregory Fiennes, the son of the poacher-lord Thomas, hanged by Henry VIII, be given back all that which had been confiscated by the crown. Gregory's wife Anne was at the time the queen's lady of honour which may have helped his claim. The queen and her senior adviser, William Cecil (whose great granddaughter would marry a Fiennes), were keen to gain the support of as many of the nobles as they easily could by the simple expedient of bestowing favours. So to Gregory the queen said yes or, to be precise, '*Soit fait comme il est desiré*'. Gregory and Anne remained in Elizabeth's close court and were given a 'convenience house' in Westminster. Later they bought the Chelsea home of Sir Thomas More from the Bishop of Winchester, who had taken it over when Sir Thomas was executed by Henry VIII.

At the same time that Gregory had his appeal agreed, Richard Fiennes of Broughton (applying to have the dormant title of Baron Saye and Sele reinvigorated, in case of a nominal lapse) was turned down. Not taking no for an answer, he kept on pestering the queen and Cecil for decades. Although Richard was, like Gregory, an intimate of the royal court, the queen had, before her coronation, long observed how the nobles of England were often, if not always, the greatest of all pains in the neck to their current monarch. So, once she was in firm control, she did all that she could to cut down their number and created new ones only when she had no alternative.

Her religious policies were naturally less simplistic, especially since they were directly entangled with most threats to her very existence from a number of Roman Catholics, the most obvious being her second cousin Mary Stuart, Queen of Scots. Her most likely enemies were English Catholics, the Pope, the French and the Spanish, or a Catholic alliance of them all with the aim of planting Mary Stuart on her throne. England had for a long while counted on enmity between France and Spain to keep both countries occupied, but in 1562 a bloody civil war broke out in France, enabling Spain at the height of her power to focus on Elizabeth's heretical new-look England.

The ministers that Elizabeth selected to advise her included a great many experienced councillors of the three previous monarchs, even some of Mary's. However, the man who, along with William Cecil, would be the greatest companion of all to the queen for the next thirty years was Robert Dudley, whose father and brother, the latter married to Lady Jane Grey, had been executed by Mary. Dudley's aunt married Sir Thomas Fiennes and this connection remained of value to the Fienneses throughout the reign of Elizabeth, at least until Dudley's death.

Dudley was the queen's age and, although already married at seventeen, had begun to flirt with Elizabeth even before her coronation. Although they are thought never to have made love together, they had numerous tiffs over the years, and Dudley served the queen loyally as a close adviser, admirer, and sometimes successful army commander. The queen gave him the title of Earl of Leicester, but often spoke of him as 'My dear Rob'. There was a period after his wife died in suspicious circumstances when marriage to the queen was an option, but Elizabeth declined, as she would a dozen or more ardent suitors well into her fifties.

Elizabeth's sexuality has long been a subject of debate by historians and psychiatrists, but none deny that she adored male admirers and maintained a constant flow of them at her court, delighting to play one off against the other. By far the most enduring was Robert Dudley, but if ever he acted above himself, she kept him in his place, at one time shouting, 'if you think you rule here, I will take a course to see you forthcoming. I will have here but one mistress and no master.'

The queen's other main man was her first minister, William Cecil, who she promoted to Lord Burghley. He had served in the governments of her three predecessors and was a pragmatist, survivor and, apart from one or two exceptions over forty years, totally obedient to Elizabeth. He and Dudley often sparred and held opposing opinions, but both died in their queen's service.

William Cecil's great granddaughter, Frances, was to marry James Fiennes, my great to the power of eleven grandfather. She was a woman of scandalous behaviour who had an adulterous affair with James Fiennes' steward at Broughton Castle. Still, Queen Elizabeth's William Cecil can hardly take the blame for that, and he did a truly wonderful job for his queen and for England, unsurpassed by any prime minister past or since.

In 1562 Elizabeth caught smallpox and nearly died. This caused near panic among ministers and, like worms at dawn, a clutch of claimants surfaced. Elizabeth merely instructed her anxious councillors to appoint Robert Dudley as regent, and named no successor of her choice. There was method in her apparent madness, for she had seen, when a girl, how a named successor can instantly become a rival queen bee and disrupt the hive.

One of the claimants, Henry Darnley, was the son of Henry VIII's niece. He married Mary Stuart Queen of Scots, and their son would one day become King James VI of Scotland. Darnley was an arrogant drunkard who was murdered, some say on the orders of his wife. The Protestant Lords of the Covenant forced Mary Stuart to abdicate and to appoint her Protestant step-brother, the Earl of Murray, as regent. Mary fled to England, requesting her cousin Elizabeth's support to regain her throne. This was, of course, a major conundrum for Elizabeth, since Mary was her main Catholic rival for the throne of England, or could become so at the turn of a coin. The French and Spanish certainly rated Mary as their best chance of re-Catholicising England. Elizabeth decided not to send Mary back to Scotland, nor yet to let her loose in England. Instead she placed her under house arrest in a northern castle policed by a loyal Protestant commandant.

Two of my relations now figured as major players on the queen's chessboard, for the chief villain in her biggest English rebellion was Leonard, Lord Dacre of the North while the 9th Lord Clinton was Elizabeth's chief of staff. When Leonard Dacre and other northern Catholic lords, including, of course, the Percys and the Nevilles, ignited what became known as the Rising in the North of 1569, John Fiennes Clinton was sent north to deal with it. The danger to Elizabeth was very real. She possessed no standing army, so she shut herself up in Windsor Castle and had Queen Mary (who the northern lords aimed to crown Catholic Queen of England) imprisoned well south of the rebel forces. Luckily for Protestant England, a harsh winter thinned out the northern forces, the rising was defeated, and the Dacre lands were confiscated, as were most of the Percy and Neville estates, to be given to loyal courtiers. Over seven hundred rebels were executed, hundreds of Catholic clergy were deprived of their livings, and the previously moderate queen pronounced a repressive set of laws against all Catholics which would last into the nineteenth century.

After his defeat, cousin Leonard fled to Scotland, but his younger brother managed, fifteen years later, to retrieve some of the Cumberland estates which he believed were his. In the courts he carried on a family land feud until 1591 when, feeling his family would never receive justice under Elizabeth, he joined the Spanish army in the forlorn hope of helping to throw her out.

The next plot to overthrow Elizabeth, and many subsequent conspiracies, were foiled by England's first spymaster, Sir Francis Walsingham, previously the English ambassador in France. William Cecil spotted his counter-espionage talents which, in cunning, deception and inventive forms of torture, were at least on a level with the Inquisition. One of the queen's cousins, the Catholic Duke of Norfolk, plotted with the Spanish to put Mary on the throne. But Norfolk and his co-plotters were careless in using the sixteenth century equivalents of their own mobile phones. Walsingham discovered hidden letters, broke ciphers and then put suspects on the rack, and Norfolk was sent back to the Tower, where he had already spent nine months for a part in the Northern Rising.

Elizabeth knew now that she was beset by hidden dangers, papal poisoners and treacherous courtiers. If Norfolk, her cousin and senior peer, was mired in intrigue, who could she trust? Even Dudley had briefly involved himself with a previous plot, but had then sworn devotion and been forgiven. William Cecil and other ministers forced the queen to agree reluctantly to Norfolk's execution three full years after his intrigues were first revealed. Cecil advised Elizabeth to put a stop to the ongoing papist plots by agreeing to have her cousin Queen Mary executed, but for nineteen long years, remembering, no doubt, her own teenage imprisonment at the mercy of Bloody Mary, she stayed her hand. So the plots against her continued. Jesuit priests, the chief arbiters of the Inquisition, were sent to England under cover, but Walsingham's agents were everywhere and Tyburn awaited his annual catch.

All monarchs and presidents risk madmen with pistols, and Elizabeth had her fair share. John Somerville of Warwick was caught in the act, as was Francis Throckmorton of the so-called Babington Plot. Walsingham's agents shadowed would-be assassin Throckmorton for six months, intercepted his mail, cracked his ciphers, eavesdropped, and finally placed him on their most successful rack. Somehow he survived his first full session, but spat out everything he knew on the second, including the identity of all his colleagues. Walsingham then used a double agent to entrap the imprisoned Mary Queen of Scots into accepting the Babington Plot, and she wrote to its French sponsors stating that she would prefer Elizabeth's assassination to precede her own rescue from captivity.

Walsingham now had his trump card which, despite Elizabeth wriggling every which way to avoid such an outcome, ended with cousin Mary's Catholic head, minus its orange wig, rolling off the block. A little terrier was then found to be lurking among the petticoats of the headless body. Elizabeth, when she heard of the execution, was furious and blamed her councillors, especially William Cecil, for acting without her go-ahead, despite the fact that she had signed her cousin's death warrant a week earlier.

The year of the Babington plot saw Europe's other Protestant monarch, Prince William of Orange, assassinated by papist agents, so Elizabeth, once she recovered from her initial fury, must have recognised the good sense of her cousin's execution.

Elizabeth Throckmorton, the daughter of the conspirator's uncle, married Sir Walter Raleigh and, after his death, carried his embalmed head about with her in a bag. This must have been upsetting for her next husband, Richard Fiennes, the 7th Lord Dacre of the South.

Through much of the 1570s the queen steered England along a path of peace, relying on internal troubles in France, Scotland, Spain and Holland to keep them occupied elsewhere. Nevertheless, Elizabeth sent a batch of top courtiers, including Gregory Fiennes of Herstmonceux, over to France to agree the Treaty of Blois between herself and the French regent, Catherine de Medici (an unusually merciless ruler, even for those inhuman times). This Gregory Fiennes, the son of the poacher, was sent on various political missions by Elizabeth, but historian William Camden describes him as 'a little crack-brained' and dominated by both his mother and his wife Anne, whose inherited fortunes had helped restore the depleted-due-to-poaching fortunes of the Dacres.

Elizabeth numbered two other Fienneses amongst her tightly controlled household retinue of top ladies. One was Lady Fiennes Clinton, whose husband Edward, the Lord High Admiral, she promoted to Earl of Lincoln. Another was a French girl, Françoise Fiennes, a younger daughter of Eustache, the head of the French clan and the brother of Guislain Fiennes, Viscount de Fruges. This Guislain Fiennes was a naval officer and top-level diplomat who fought all his life against Spanish tyranny. In 1572 he commanded the Protestant fleet against the Spanish and was William of Orange's personal envoy to negotiate with the Emperor Charles IX. The King of France also engaged him to negotiate with Charles IX on the delicate matter of France ruling the lower Catholic Netherlands. Fiennes proved himself '*de beaucoup de zèle et d'habilité*', in other words, an industrious and foxy negotiator. As a reward, he was buried with great honour in Paris in the Cathedral of Notre Dame.

The English Fienneses and Twisletons, as far as I can trace, were generally inclined to Puritanism at Broughton, wishy-washy Protestantism at Herstmonceux and, up north with the Yorkshire Dacres, Catholicism. In all cases they were better off being English, since Elizabeth's religious dealings were infinitely milder than those of her contemporary rulers on the continent. Her main punishment of well-heeled determined Catholics was to make them recusants, confiscate their properties and 'imprison' them in the castles or manors of loyal Protestant nobles, forbidding the latter to fraternise with their 'prisoners'.

Like most appointed hosts, Richard Fiennes at Broughton found the recusants' unwelcome presence an extreme imposition and, since the government paid nothing towards their keep, a considerable expense. Since Broughton, despite all the new wings Richard and his father had added, was not as vast as most top noble manors, he was forced to send his wife and children to the nearby rectory to avoid accusations of fraternisation. Many of the sixteen recusants, 'men of quallitie and calling', dumped on Broughton brought their own families and servants too, so the poor Fienneses were greatly put out for at least eight years from 1589. Richard was still on good terms with his old friend William Cecil, the boss of the recusancy system, and wrote him many pleading letters, one of which states that he would gladly send ten horses for the queen's military service, rather than the five he was due to send, and even do military service himself if only he could be freed of the recusants.

Cecil's answer was to point out that Richard could charge his recusants for bed and board at a higher rate than they would have to pay the government if they were in Fleet Prison.

At no time over Elizabeth's remaining years at the helm did Richard stop pestering Cecil to officially reinstate him as Baron Saye and Sele, which title his immediate forebears had allowed to lapse into dormancy, but Elizabeth steadfastly refused. Richard sold off his remaining manors in Hampshire and Somerset to help fund his ongoing building work at Broughton. There were extensive attics where the servants who ran the household slept with their own strict *Upstairs Downstairs* hierarchy. Other manors at the time were also allotting attics or basements for their servants and, as at Broughton, creating or appointing other rooms as drawing rooms or long galleries hung with portraits and manned by pedestal-mounted ancestral men-at-arms in full gear staring through their visor slits at their children's children. Log fires crackled from another popular new feature – brick chimney fireplaces ornamented with armorial bearings. Cooks were experimenting with new ingredients, including potatoes, and daring nobles were puffing at pipes stuffed with a weed called tobacco, both goodies which Sir Walter Raleigh brought back from his expeditions beyond the horizon and his daring, highly successful raids on Spanish treasure galleons.

By 1587 Elizabeth had spent a great deal of money and effort helping the Dutch against the Spanish, while both Francis Drake and Walter Raleigh had raided Spanish ports with her blessing and financial support. She had also executed Catholic Queen Mary of Scots. So King Philip II of Spain decided to undertake a holy crusade against England and to occupy the throne, this time by invasion not by marriage. He felt sure that the estimated 25,000 English Catholics would welcome his invading army under the Duke of Parma launched from Spanish-held Flanders, whilst his much-vaunted Armada ruled the Channel.

A system of high beacons was erected and tested along the cliffs of the south coast, local Dad's Armies were formed, and Drake was sent on a pre-emptive strike against Cadiz. Elizabeth had long been in the habit of nominating her oldest friend Robert Dudley, the Earl of Leicester, as commander of her military missions, and now she placed him in charge of the defence of the realm because, sixty years old and a spinster, she cared more for loyalty than military brilliance. Nor did England possess much of an army beyond the amateur volunteers who had long served in the Netherlands in support of Dutch Protestants fighting their Spanish overlords.

As it turned out, the English didn't need an army, for the navy that set out to meet the Armada in July 1588 was well led by the powerful personality of Lord Howard of Effingham, keeping under iron discipline a pack of brilliant naval commanders, including Drake, Hawkins and Frobisher. The two navies eventually met off the Isles of Scilly. The great Armada of 130 ships with 8,000 sailors and 19,000 soldiers appeared to Lord Howard to be unbeatable 'with lofty towers like castles' stationed across the entire southern horizon 'like a crescent moon'. For five days both fleets fired long-distance broadsides at one another, doing little damage and running out of ammunition. A council of war of the English admirals decided to send fireships amongst the Spaniards when they anchored off Calais. Drake offered to fire his own ship, and other commanders followed suit. Tar, gunpowder and other inflammables were duly lit or fused and drifted with a suitable wind into the Spanish lines. Chaos ensued, Howard's men excelled in close-quarter fighting, and the Spanish only avoided immediate disaster due to a sudden storm.

To escape, the Spaniards sailed right around the perilous seas off northern Scotland and Ireland, and only eighty-six of their 130-strong original fleet made it back to Spain. Nine thousand Spaniards died en route. The English navy never chased the Spaniards, due to their own lack of gunpowder, rations and water. Some sailors were, by the time they made port, already drinking their own urine. Not one English ship was sunk by the enemy, and their subsequent victory medals boasted the legend: 'God breathed and they were scattered.'

Nobody told the queen of the victory, so she and Robert Dudley spent anxious days with their army at Tilbury. She rode about, part Boadicea and part Joan of Arc, in a shiny suit of armour making sturdy speeches. Dudley shared in the victory celebrations when news of the Armada's defeat eventually reached London. But he died the following week causing great grief to the queen, a sadness which in the course of time was mended by the new love of her life, Dudley's young stepson, the Earl of Essex.

Essex had been a close attendant of the queen since a teenager, and he was a keen soldier with handsome looks and great charm, spoilt only by his arrogance. Unlike Dudley, whose long-term loyalty and love of the queen had been genuine, Essex flattered her for his own ends. However, he was addicted to the glory of soldiering and would periodically grow bored with the honey platitudes of court life beside the old queen and, disobeying her direct orders, would sail over to the Netherlands for a quick punch-up with the Spaniards.

He upset the queen when, without telling her, he married the daughter of her old spymaster, Walsingham. She forgave him, however, and in 1596 sent him with Lord Howard of Armada fame on a second attack against the Spanish fleet in Cadiz. Henry Fiennes Dacre, the grandson of Thomas Fiennes the Poacher, went too, but I have no record of his part in the raid except that he came back alive and was knighted by Essex. By then Drake and Hawkins were both dead, but Howard's fleet nonetheless surprised Cadiz, destroyed the Spanish fleet there and captured the town. The popularity of the handsome young Essex blossomed overnight back home and remained so high that his natural arrogance overtook his meagre supplies of common sense.

On a new voyage to the Azores, he argued violently with his admiral, Walter Raleigh, and back home, encouraged perhaps by the queen's ongoing forgiveness of his ever-greater public effrontery toward senior ministers and even herself, Essex soared, Icarus-like, too close to the sun. When, at his request, Elizabeth put him in charge of an army in 1599 to subdue Irish rebels being helped by the Spanish, he not only made a mess of the mission and disregarded all her specific instructions, but, on being summoned back to England, arrived in a towering rage and entered her bedchamber unannounced, to find her wig-less and unmade-up. Anyone else would have lost their head, or certainly their freedom, but the queen merely imprisoned him briefly, removed his state titles and kept him from court.

This was too much for vain Essex who conspired in 1601 to overthrow her. He was undeniably popular, but not sufficiently so to unseat the queen. Arrested and tried for treason, he was quickly executed in a manner to which his family must have become almost accustomed. His grandfather had been executed for his support of Lady Jane Grey, and *his* father had also lost his head for treason; a triple whammy.

Only five years after the Armada the greatest of queens died of old age without naming her successor, other than by her answer to her councillors' urgent queries, 'Who but our cousin of Scotland.' By then there was no question in anyone's mind but that the cousin she referred to was James, the Protestant son of Mary Queen of Scots and of her husband of brief duration, Henry Darnley. James was already King of Scotland and a direct descendant of Henry VIII.

Elizabeth's chief minister of four decades, William Cecil, had been succeeded by his equally talented second son, Robert Cecil, who had long been in secret communication with King James VI so that a speedy and painless takeover would follow the queen's death. Robert Cecil, who was to become as vital a minister to James as his father had been to Elizabeth, was neither as religious nor as moral as the older man. He was out for himself, open to quiet corruption and enjoyed power, not just for itself but as a route to ever greater wealth. If anything blemishes the queen's record, it is the increase of bureaucratic corruption which flourished in her last few years.

On the plus side, her diplomacy allowed for a prolonged peace in England in which great artists could thrive, and she refused to allow the ever-growing menace of Puritanism to stifle the performing arts. Her brave new world of the arts was symbolised by Shakespeare's own Globe Theatre on London's South Bank. Elizabeth patronised Shakespeare, Ben Jonson and Christopher Marlowe and a drama company called Queen Elizabeth's Men was formed in her name. In the 1980s I sat on a committee founded by the actor Sam Wanamaker to rebuild the Globe, burnt down in 1613, on its original site.

Under Elizabeth the English also began to widen their horizons. They realised the riches of the world could be theirs. We had been local, mostly inshore, sailors for centuries, but after the Armada we found our destiny on the great seas in which, wrote Shakespeare, our realm was set like a precious stone. Drake, Raleigh, Hawkins and Howard of Effingham showed the way to make their country rich as well as great. All the English thenceforward needed was to maintain the most powerful navy in the world.

18

A Failed Poisoning

Though knighted by the queen, and a good friend of William Cecil, Richard Fiennes of Broughton never managed during Elizabeth's reign to regain the barony of Saye and Sele for which he had so frequently petitioned. But fresh from Scotland, James I of England needed all the friends he could make down south, and he readily granted his courtier Richard Fiennes the 'favour' he and his wife so fervently requested. So in 1603 we were back in the barony business, thanks to the persistence of Richard, 7th Lord Saye. He and his wife Anne had done incredibly well to keep up with the Inigo Joneses at court and still find time to manage the estate and finish the building work at Broughton. By 1597 he had been able to write to the elder Cecil saying, 'I have the estate in such order that I can free it from debt nor lose a foot of land.'

Richard Fiennes survived five straight years of poor harvests due to successful selective sheep breeding, timely consolidation of his various estates into a single Broughton-centred block, and by judicious land enclosure. Enclosure for cattle and sheep grazing purposes often involved depopulating an entire area which was naturally highly unpopular. Somehow Richard managed his enclosures without depopulation and without local resistance. He switched most of his tenants from copyhold to leasehold, thereby avoiding the countrywide reaction to enclosures which included the murder of certain landlords in Oxfordshire, not all that far from Broughton. To Robert Cecil he could eventually boast, 'Never did any tenant find himself grieved, their living being much better and now estated.'

Once Richard had the barony officially back in his hands, he quickly switched his focus to ways of increasing his income by various, usually ludicrous, schemes. He urged Cecil to have Winchester College, founded by his ancestor William of Wykeham, send him the college annual revenues worth £7,000, which were, he claimed, 'lineally descended to me as heir to the Founder's sole sister and heiress'. He offered to lead an army 'under my Royal master, to recover those lands in France which to my noble ancestor were given'. Cecil would know very well that such French lands had plenty of French Fienneses in them and that they had not been the property of any English Fienneses for at least two hundred years. So he fobbed Richard off by sending him, in an ambassadorial role, to the Archduke of Austria.

On King James's arrival in London, he had already ruled Scotland for twenty-nine hectic years, spoke with a strong Scottish accent and was in many ways the antithesis of his cousin, the late Queen Elizabeth I. She had adored and encouraged ceremony and the adulation of the common people. James shunned both and put up with them only as an unfortunate necessity. He loved to hunt and to read. His youth in Scotland had, like that of many Scottish kings, been plagued by the plots, rivalries and religious differences of clan nobles. But above all else, he believed that all kings had a Divine Right to rule and to make laws, a belief which had gone down like a lead balloon in rebellious Scotland and would fare little better in his new expanded kingdom of what he described as 'Great Britain'.

James came south with the full approval of the English people. After all, he was no usurper, and he *was* a sane male leader, adult, experienced and Protestant. What more could anyone want? He also had five children, including two sons. His rumoured homosexual tendencies did not at first worry anyone and, since he needed to make friends in his new realm, he sensibly handed out knighthoods like confetti; over two hundred of them.

The Fiennes clan did well out of this largesse. We have seen how Richard Fiennes, Lord Saye and Sele, had his barony restored, and it was on the basis that it could be inherited by 'heirs general', since the lawyers were under the impression that the original 1447 barony (of the Jack Cade'd James Fiennes) could pass through both sexes. Another relative, one of the Clinton family still using the surname Fiennes Clinton when it suited them (and about to marry back into the family), was the 11th Lord, Thomas, who was given the barony of Clinton and Saye in 1610 and who helped James greatly in his ongoing attempts to formalise the official Union of Scotland and England.

Most of today's Fienneses are adamant that this bunch of Fiennes Clintons should not have used our name and were no longer relatives, but the records of the Star Chamber during James's reign detail the trial of 'Sir Henry Fiennes, a gentleman of the King's Privy Chamber and a younger son of the Earl of Lincoln'. This identifies him as a younger brother of Thomas, the 11th Lord. The Star Chamber's jury on 19 February 1622 found Sir Henry guilty of attempting to murder his wife, Lady Fiennes, by poison, robbery and other grave charges. He was fined £2,000 and imprisoned, but was let off lightly through the intervention of King James. There is a detailed description of the trial in *The Genealogists Magazine* of March 1942 from which I have taken the gist of events.

Grace Somerville, daughter of Sir William, a Warwickshire knight, who by tradition was a friend of Shakespeare, went, when her father died, to live with her aunt, Lady Gresley, a woman of bad character, and there she met Sir Henry Fiennes, who did everything in his power to seduce her, telling her that his wife was ill and might die any day. They agreed on marriage as soon as Lady Fiennes died, and Sir Henry, who owned houses in Westminster, had two rooms furnished for Grace. He would visit her there regularly, having made a secret way from his mansion in

Cannon Row, through his garden and stables, and into a shoemaker's house, where he made a special door and stairs to reach a garret with a trapdoor down to Grace's rooms. There is a letter today in the British Library written by one of Grace's uncles, Sir George Gresley, who grew suspicious and forbade Grace further entry to his own house.

After two years Grace grew discontented. Sir Henry had given her a false report of his wealth. He was, in fact, hated by his own father, Henry, 2nd Earl of Lincoln, who refused to make adequate provision for him, and he was driven to such straits that Grace had to come to *his* assistance. Her shameful life distressed her mother and her friends and, what's more, caused her to let slip many good chances of marriage. As for Lady Fiennes, she lived on and proved no more likely to die than did Grace.

Sir Henry decided to force the issue and procured from an apothecary two little gallipots full of a poisoned confection which he gave to Lady Fiennes, telling her they were special cordials against the pains of wind and stone. In June 1620 she did become very ill, and Grace began to invite her friends to her wedding, which was to be in the Tower of London. But Lady Fiennes recovered. After four years of dashed promises, Grace began to hate Sir Henry. And Lady Fiennes, long fed up with her husband's infidelity, decided to send a petition to King James by way of her first cousin, Sir Henry Montague, who was the Lord Treasurer of England. Whether her petition ever reached His Majesty is not known, but Grace went off with an ex-Cambridge student named Harrison to the Isle of Wight, where they were married.

Sir Henry, furious, followed them there with two retainers and confronted the couple at a Yarmouth Inn, wearing 'swords, daggers, stilettos, pistols, petronels and guns'. Grace and Harrison somehow remained married, and Sir Henry, blinded by his anger and jealousy, filed proceedings against Harrison in the Star Chamber in the name of the Attorney-General. One of the witnesses that Harrison called against Sir Henry was one of the latter's own retainers called Armitage, and to keep this man quiet, Sir Henry had him murdered by contracted ruffians just before the trial.

Ironically, Lady Fiennes died a few months after the trial and Sir Henry's incarceration in the Fleet prison. Harrison, still married to Grace, was sent to the Fleet as a debtor. When Sir Henry was set free, he remarried, and his descendants fill a great deal of space today in *Burke's Peerage* in the pedigree of the Dukes of Newcastle.

In 1605, only two years after James's rule began in England, plotters of both ultra-Protestant and Catholic persuasions began to surface. The Protestants approved of the king's great work, the beautifully phrased Authorized Version (now called the King James Version) of the Bible, but otherwise they disliked his adherence to the middle episcopalian way, not far enough distanced, in their opinion, from Catholicism. The Catholics, for their part, despised him for retaining the penal laws against them and enforced limitations on their form of worship.

The so-called Gunpowder Plot of 1605 involved half a dozen Catholics, led by one Robert Catesby, who planned, as every schoolboy knows, to blow up the House of Lords during the State Opening of Parliament on 5 November, when the Lords, the Commons and the king would all be there. Somebody betrayed them in the nick of time, and Guy 'Guido' Fawkes, who was caught red-handed amongst the barrels of explosive, was tortured on the rack to get him to confess and name his colleagues, all of whom were subsequently executed, with the brutal sentence of disembowelment whilst yet alive and after semi-suffocation on gibbets.

That such acts of brutality should still be acceptable in the seventeenth century may seem surprising, but England's penal system was slowly becoming less harsh. This was definitely not a universal trend and, in 1616, the Japanese dictator or *shogun* united his country by subjugating the last independent province, Osaka, and beheading every single soldier who had defended it against him, lining the long road from Kyoto all the way to Fushimi with tens of thousands of severed heads.

The cruel deaths of Guy Fawkes and his fellow plotters certainly put a stop to all further meaningful Catholic plots, but King James faced a far more serious threat to his powers from an ever more rumbustious Parliament which would in thirty-seven years' time lead England into civil war. The House of Commons, especially its Puritan-inclined members led by three or four men including William Fiennes, Lord Saye, was showing ominous signs of opposition to royal authority, especially in the matter of granting tax moneys to the king.

By no means profligate in the playboy sense, James nonetheless ran up big debts by way of the many favours he handed out to his favourites, quite a few of whom had accompanied him from Scotland and were sneered at by English aristocrats. James's wife, Queen Anne, enjoyed the good life and specialised in elaborate masked balls, while James openly favoured the Scottish courtier Robert Carr, to whom he gave the Earldom of Somerset and whose lips he openly kissed, to the disgust (or jealousy) of many of his nobles. Somerset was later murdered, and the king's next favourite, and probably lover, was one George Villiers who James knighted and then made Duke of Buckingham. The king once wrote to him, 'Sweet child and wife; I naturally so love your person and adore all your other parts, which are more than ever one man had.'

Buckingham achieved very considerable influence throughout the last decade of James's life, a fact which greatly favoured William Fiennes, Lord Saye, whose sister Elizabeth married Buckingham's brother.

The most sensible minister, who had sufficient influence with James to curb his high-flown ideas of the Divine Right of Kings, was Robert Cecil, but he died in 1612. Soon afterwards the House of Commons and the king fell out in a big way. James believed in his prerogative, and the Commons, did not. So the king dissolved the 1613 Parliament in a high dudgeon. The previous year his eldest son Henry, of whom he was extremely proud and who was popular with the people, died, leaving James in a state of mourning and gloom for many months, while James's remaining male heir, Prince Charles Stuart, eleven years old at the time, became the focus of the nation's curiosity. For a long while James planned to marry young Charles off to the Spanish Infanta to complement his existing treaty with that powerful nation.

In 1614 he called another Parliament to raise much needed funds, but the members of this congress were so good at bitching about every wish of the king and made such hate-filled comments about his cabal of courtiers, advisers and ministers 'imported' from Scotland, that James, exasperated, dissolved this Parliament as he had the last, but without obtaining his badly needed funds. One tax that he did refine was his Tobacco Tax, whereby all Virginian tobacco, no matter what its eventual destination, must pass through English ports and be taxed there. This was levied with great zeal, despite his personal aversion to smoking. He once pronounced: 'Smoking pollutes men's inward parts . . . with an unctuous and oily kind of soote, as hath been found in some great tobacco takers who, after their deaths, were opened up.' He added for good measure that smoking was: 'a custom loathsome to the eye, hateful to the nose, harmful to the brain and dangerous to the lungs.'

King James twice took his queen to stay in the newly decorated Broughton Castle, with the newly decorated (or, to be more accurate, redecorated) Baron Saye and Sele, and there he would have met the strong-willed young William Fiennes, only heir to the barony and recently out of New College, Oxford at the conclusion of his Founder's Kin free education.

William Fiennes, my great to the power of twelve grandfather, was to become in the next reign the number one pain in the royal backside. Known to king and Cromwell alike as Saye, it was not for nothing he acquired the popular nickname of 'Old Subtlety', as his life became one long and highly successful balancing act between the Royalist and Parliamentary forces. William Fiennes took over the barony in 1613 and was soon to be one of the half dozen individuals who would help mould the destiny of Great Britain during the key years leading up to Oliver Cromwell's Protectorate.

To begin with, his friendly relationship with his sister's brother-in-law, the king's favourite, George Villiers, Duke of Buckingham, had proved of great value, but as he, Saye, felt increasingly at odds with most of the king's policies, Buckingham slowly became an enemy. The contemporary historian Lord Clarendon detested William Fiennes as the man behind all the king's worst troubles.

> The Lord Saye, a man of mean and narrow fortune and of the highest ambition had for many years been the oracle of those who were called Puritans in the worst sense and had steered all their counsels. He was a notorious enemy to the Church and to most of the eminent Churchmen . . . He was in the truth the pilot that steered all those vessels which were freighted with sedition to destroy the government.

Clarendon's ongoing diatribe against Saye underlines the fact that he appeared to be a self-interested hypocrite.

> a man who had the deepest hand in the original contrivance of all the calamities which befell this unhappy Kingdom, though he had not the least thought of dissolving the monarchy and even less of levelling the ranks and distinctions of men, for no man valued himself more . . . His parts were not quick but so much above his own rank that he had always great credit and authority in Parliament; the more so for taking all opportunities to oppose the Court. He had with his milk sucked in an implacable malice against the government of the Church.

This refers to William's Puritanical leanings, and the problem with James I, as far as he was concerned, involved the king's desire for tolerance in his new Great Britain for all forms of religion, including Catholicism. William loathed Catholics and therefore fought every move by James for an alliance with Spain. James had married his daughter Elizabeth to the main German Protestant leader, Frederick, the Elector Palatine. Spain had later caused Frederick to be deposed, and thereafter James had to tread a diplomatic tightrope trying to become friendly enough with Spain to have them reinstate Frederick.

At home James and his ruthless Archbishop Laud of Canterbury reacted strongly against fundamentalist Puritans who, tied to the dour ethics of the Old Testament, insisted that they, like the Jews before them, were God's chosen people and should observe every last biblical ruling, such as strict observance of the Sabbath. The most troublesome Puritans like William, Lord Saye, were imprisoned, and many fled to ultra-Protestant Amsterdam to start a community there. In 1620 another group set sail from Plymouth in the *Mayflower* to form a Puritan settlement in America.

In Ireland James pursued what he called a 'plantation policy', which dispossessed hundreds of native Irish Catholic families whom he replaced with thousands of Londoners (mostly in the region of Londonderry) and with even more settlers from lowland Scotland. By 1641, 100,000 English, Welsh and Scots settlers had arrived in Ireland, and, in Cromwell's time, another 100,000 followed them. Over 150,000 Scots settled in Ulster. Despite this ethnic flooding of the area, the majority of the population were still Catholic Irish, but whereas they made up 98 per cent of the population in 1600, the Stuart 'plantations' reduced them to 75 per cent and stored up big troubles for the future. So James, the Scotsman, was the godfather of the first British colonists. At the beginning of his reign there were no British colonies, but by his death, in both Ireland and America, they were thriving. This is the point at which, to be accurate, I will often need to switch from using the term English to British, especially when describing our activities abroad.

In addition to the Pilgrim Fathers' voyage, new settlements soon sprang up in Newfoundland, Virginia, Massachusetts, Bermuda, India and the East Indies. Scotsmen were at the forefront of many of these adventures. Trade began to flourish, which was just as well as, in the second half of James's reign, Britain suffered a sudden dire rise in the cost of living and a severe depression.

As with many leaders who strain to follow policies of pragmatism and peace, James often came to grief by upsetting extremists. This was especially true of his balancing act with Spain, for his colonial missions naturally clashed with Spain's foreign policy. He let Sir Walter Raleigh out of prison (where he had languished since Elizabeth I put him there) in order to have him search for gold up the Orinoco. Raleigh, against royal orders, clashed with various Spaniards, and on his return, at Spanish insistence, James had him beheaded. This infuriated the likes of Saye, who increasingly saw the king as a mere Catholic lackey.

When Robert Cecil had died back in 1612 and James needed a new first minister, he had chosen a friend and neighbour of Saye, Sir Walter Cope, a valuable choice for Saye's ongoing influence. The man who had thought he should get the top job, Sir Francis Bacon, was thereafter hostile to those who had helped Cope get his job. That included Lord Saye. In 1621 James needed to placate a Parliament he had called yet again to raise cash and he used the sacking and imprisonment of Francis Bacon, demanded in the Lords by Saye, as a bargaining chip. Saye had clearly become a major influence even then; a sign of what was to come.

Saye's next rebellion was over James's plan to marry off his heir, Charles, to the Spanish Infanta at some suitable future date, but only if such a union became sensible. Unfortunately for James, as he grew older and more plagued by introspective gloom and crippling arthritis, his son Charles, arrogant and self-willed, formed an alliance with the king's old favourite, the Duke of Buckingham, and the two men frequently, when requested to fulfil a mission for the king, simply waved two fingers at the old man and followed their own, usually foolish, designs. They both liked the idea of Charles's marriage to the Infanta, but without the baggage of key diplomatic conditions that James specified. They badgered the king until he allowed them to go to Madrid where they were kept waiting for many months and failed to gain any reasonable diplomatic agreement to go with the proposed royal marriage. Eventually, in disgust, they returned to England, now wanting an immediate war with Spain, which was precisely what Saye and the other Puritan lords had long been advocating.

The king wanted peace and his son wanted war. Buckingham, knowing that Saye, by 1624, was the most influential figure in the Lords, promoted him to viscount, which meant that William now had two concurrent titles, as 8th Lord Saye and 1st Viscount Saye.

Why was Saye so hostile to Catholicism and to Spain? Since he wrote a good deal which survives today but never dwelt on his feelings towards the Spanish, I can only wonder if he was deeply affected by the fear that rippled through England in the year of the great Armada threat when, aged only eight, he would have watched from Broughton the rehearsals of the beacon fire-keepers on nearby Crouch Hill and the training of the local Home Guard in readiness for the expected invasion.

A British force was, in due course, sent off to help rescue the Protestant Elector Palatine. The result was both dismal and expensive. Nobody was happy and, only months after accepting his viscountcy, Saye was openly hostile to the Buckingham faction once again. Saye began at that time to hold clandestine meetings of leading Puritan lords and others in an upper tower room at Broughton, well away from the ears of spying servants. As Clarendon's history recounts: 'Saye gave them instructions how to behave themselves with caution and to do their business with most security.'

He was not known as Old Subtlety for nothing.

19

The Small Room with No Ears

Old, sick and arthritic, James I of England died in late March 1625, having warned his heir, Charles, to call as few Parliaments as possible, for they were increasingly big trouble. He gave the same advice to his old favourite Buckingham, Charles's chief crony. Buckingham was assassinated three years later and, after a brief honeymoon period, Charles alienated a great many people by his lack of subtlety, his apparent arrogance and even his unimpressive personal appearance. Most historians paint successive monarchs as part good, part bad, like every other human, but the only redeeming features any of them allow Charles I are his lifelong chaste behaviour, patronage of the arts and the dignity of his final tragic days. Otherwise the adjectives applied to him make sorry reading: prudish, cold, shifty, runt-like, autocratic, offensive, indecisive and a stutterer with a thick Scottish accent. His better known abuses of power include arbitrary arrests, a lifelong desire to rule without reference to Parliament, insensitive and harsh taxation systems, and use of Catholic troops to enforce his will on his Protestant subjects.

For the first five years of his reign, Britain warred with the Spanish in order to regain Protestant territories which the Spaniards had taken from Charles's brother-in-law, the Elector Palatine. Charles also warred with France to make them honour a marriage treaty which had been designed to keep the two countries friendly. He married the French king's sister, Henrietta Maria, which must have been quite a sacrifice for him, judging by a contemporary account from a bitchy Bohemian royal lady following a visit to Britain. 'Van Dyck's portraits had so accustomed me to thinking that all English women are beautiful that I was amazed to find a small creature with skinny arms and teeth like defence works sticking out of her mouth.' The US state of Maryland is named after her.

Charles, like his predecessors, had to raise funds for the fighting by calling Parliament, who would, he hoped, then raise the necessary taxes. Simple but effective when it worked, but with Charles, even when Parliament approved of a particular foreign campaign, they often still refused to raise the relevant taxes unless Charles agreed to extend their powers, to the direct detriment and dilution of his own royal prerogative. This was simple blackmail and, as Charles was stubborn, the result was usually stalemate. Charles refused to hand over meaningful powers, and Parliament gave him minimal funds. As a result, a mercenary army sent to help the Protestants in Germany was a total failure, as were various naval attacks on French and Spanish coastal strongholds. Francis Drake and Elizabeth I no doubt squirmed in their respective graves.

In 1630 a number of Puritan nobles got together to launch a grand design. Those who had since the *Mayflower* landings established a tentative foothold in cold and rocky New England had done so to escape persecution from the regime of the Stuarts, which they wrongly believed to be steering the nation back to Catholicism. Lord Saye and his Puritan friends, including John Pym, Lord Brooke and the notorious semi-pirate the Earl of Warwick, all hostile to King Charles and his Spanish appeasement policy, decided to increase the colonisation process in a big way and with a long-term grand design. The chief planner was Saye who in 1630 formed the Providence Island Company to colonise the island of New Providence, 130 miles off the Mosquito Coast of Nicaragua. He and Lord Brooke also bought from the Earl of Warwick a large tract of land on the Connecticut river. They appointed John Winthrop, a close friend and neighbour of Saye, to be governor of a fort at the mouth of the river, called the new colony Sayebrook (nowadays Old Sayebrook) and sent off shiploads of hopeful colonists, including many friends, neighbours and acquaintances from the Banbury region. Then in 1633 Saye and Brooke invested in a large plantation at Cocheco, in what is now New Hampshire. Saye, Brooke and the buccaneer Warwick were among Britain's most active early imperialists and entrepreneurs for colonisation.

My godfather, Lawrence Fiennes, who first told me about Lord Saye, used to refer to this ancestor as Bill Fiennes, in an irreverent but nonetheless admiring sort of way. To me 'Bill' epitomises the sort of entrepreneur who has very big ideas and loves to plot them with a group of close friends and in the face of lots of opposition. His group included many with whom he was to engineer the launching of the Civil War in Britain.

By the mid-1630s Saye grew discouraged by the setbacks of the North American settlements and by the attitude of their local governors to his suggested system of choosing future leaders. They should, he and Brooke demanded, select governors from 'gentlemen of approved sincerity and worth'. When the governors of what is today Massachusetts flatly refused, Saye turned his back on them and focused his attentions on the Caribbean and his Providence Island colony.

Since Providence was at the epicentre of the Spanish trade routes, it was bound to be attacked, so Saye had to work extremely hard to attract settlers. The name Providence was calculated to act as a lure in the same way that medieval Danes hoped the name Greenland would entice settlers to that icy and barren island. In his zeal to attract greater numbers of settlers, Saye appealed to the experienced but often disgruntled colonists already in New England under John Winthrop. The 'Colonist Captain' Saye sent to Providence was another old friend, the ex-Mayor of Banbury, fifty-four-year-old Henry Halhed, a staunch Puritan who had imbibed from Saye many of the lessons learnt from Winthrop's experience. These included the tendencies of largely middle-class families, arriving in harsh and alien environments, to clash with one another and to need very firm leadership to avoid anarchy.

Knowing this did not stop Halhed, who spent the next eight years on Providence with his wife and young family, from experiencing constant trouble with his co-islanders. The Spanish attacked twice but were repelled, the English buccaneers who were based on Providence upset the more Puritan settlers with their ribald ways, and the successive governors, mostly ex-navy types, quarrelled with the clergy and neighbours. The last of the governors, rightly accused by Halhed of dereliction of duty during a Spanish attack, countered by putting Halhed in irons and sending him back in disgrace to England: Saye immediately released and praised Halhed and sacked the governor. Very soon thereafter a massive Spanish fleet attacked and took over Providence in order to stop further depredations on their treasure ships by the island's buccaneers.

At the time Saye's Providence dream came to this abrupt end in 1641, there were over 25,000 British immigrants settled along North America's east coast, and Governor John Winthrop agreed that 'some men should be appointed to frame a body of law, in resemblance to Magna Carta which . . . should be received for fundamental laws'. Such Magna Carta-based liberties appear today in the founding charters of Maryland, Maine, Connecticut, Rhode Island, Georgia, and other states.

Sadly, the nation failed to take advantage of Saye's colonising vision but his enterprise did lead to certain other islands being settled and developed into the British sugar islands, which formed the foundation of a great commercial empire. As for Providence Island, now part of the South American state of Colombia, my cousin David Fiennes went there in 1977 and found that the inhabitants, including many descendants of English pirates, spoke not Spanish but their own version of English, and sported surnames like Huffington, Hawkins and Henry.

The eleven years of the Providence Island Company's Caribbean survival coincided with the eleven years of King Charles's personal rule, and when the island fell to the Spanish, the board meetings of Saye and his shareholders ceased. No longer able to create their new world across the Atlantic, they switched their full attention to building a new world at home and became the leaders of the Puritan Parliaments of the 1640s. They met in secret in each other's houses, mostly in John Pym's lodgings in Gray's Inn Road and William Fiennes, Lord Saye's Broughton Castle's 'small room with no ears', which today is known as the Council Chamber. Apart from Saye and Pym, the plotters included John Hampden, the Earl of Warwick, Lord Brooke, and Benjamin Rudyard.

For five years, Charles I ruled alongside three noisy and hostile Parliaments, but by 1629 he had had enough and decided he would rule, for as long as he could raise his own taxes, without a Parliament of any sort. The tax which had sparked off the Saye group's anger, was known as Ship Money. Its purpose was to fund the defence of the nation. Since the state of the navy was abysmal, most Englishmen were for a few years willing to pay to have the Channel cleared of Dutch privateers and of pirates from as far away as Algeria and Turkey, who were turning trade with Europe, and coastal fishing, into risky activities. But then, when the tax was extended far inland and reached Banbury, Lord Saye, his tenants and his sympathisers in North Oxfordshire all refused to pay up.

Warwick advised the king against the tax and, when this failed, Lord Saye personally sued the government. Cleverly enough the latter responded by counter-accusing Saye of enclosure and depopulation of one of his estates in Gloucestershire and summoned him to trial in the Star Chamber. The inference was that the trial would not take place if Saye dropped his Ship Money case. Saye was famous for his anti-enclosure stance and he had, years before, become a celebrity through physically tearing down hedges put up by his neighbour, a senior judge, and winning major victories for anti-enclosure laws in the Banbury area. So the accusation that he had enclosed in his own demesne was calculated to cause him maximum embarrassment.

Only one other senior peer joined Saye in suing the government, and that was Theophilus Fiennes Clinton, the 2nd Earl of Lincoln, who was married to Bridget Fiennes, Saye's daughter. He also became the only peer that year to be imprisoned in the Tower for tax refusal. His son, Thomas, was called to Parliament in 1610, and at that time he combined his title of Lord Clinton with that of Lord Saye. Despite this, he, his family and the real Lord Saye, William Fiennes, seemed to be good friends.

Here is a statement of the position from the Bulletin of the Institute of Historical Research which gives Saye his proper due:

> Ship Money will forever be associated with John Hampden and his challenge to its legality. Popular history has glowingly described the courageous Hampden refusing to pay a mere 20 shillings for the sake of the liberties of all Englishmen and being dragged to trial. Closer examination reveals a much more complex picture for, surprisingly, Hampden appears to have played a passive role whereas . . . the genesis of the challenge to the King's policy came from William Fiennes, Viscount Saye and Sele, and by implication the other directors of the Providence Island Company, one of whom was Hampden. There can be little doubt that Saye, through his tenacity and through the effective manipulation of his connections, outmanoeuvred the government and finally forced a legal confrontation that Charles could neither control nor afford.

Saye was not imprisoned, but he and his heir, James Fiennes, were sacked as North Oxfordshire Justices of the Peace. Banbury was the foremost town in Britain for tax refusal, and one of its most avid mutineers was Thomas Halhed, the son of Henry Halhed of Providence Island. Nevertheless, Charles won in the end, for 90 per cent of the tax was eventually collected, if a lot more slowly than planned.

*

By 1637 the king was at the height of his power with a balanced budget and a secure throne. His main troubles were caused by the unbending ways of William Laud, Archbishop of Canterbury, whose goal was to harness everyone in Britain to the 1559 Prayer Book. This upset pretty much every shade of Puritan in the land, whilst many of the church practices of Laud and his colleagues smacked of Roman Catholic ritual. This made Puritans apprehensive that he and the king, who supported Laud's every edict, were planning to re-establish popery and rule by bishops.

The Saye group loathed Laud and, although not keen on Scotsmen per se because Charles was, in their eyes, a Scot, they were sympathetic to their co-religionists, the Scottish Covenanters. So when in 1639 Charles, falling back on an almost obsolete prerogative, summoned his peers to York to join his army to squash the Covenanters, Saye and his friend, Lord Brooke, obeyed only with great reluctance. Once there, Charles demanded that they take a military oath committing them to the struggle. Both men refused. When his turn came, Saye 'kneeled downe and told His Majesty that he would take the Oath of Allegeance to adventur his lyfe for the defence of this Kingdome of England against any that should invade it. But to goe and kill a man in Scotland he was not satisfyed of the lawfullness thereof.' Saye went to prison for four days for this refusal.

The king's plans to invade Scotland fizzled out through poor organisation, so he abandoned the idea, which allowed the Scots to attack southwards and to occupy Newcastle late in 1640, refusing to head back home until they obtained a favourable treaty from the king.

One of Saye's four very capable sons, Nathaniel Fiennes, had gone to Geneva, where he was immersed in the Calvinist doctrine before returning home via Scotland, where he established links with the Scottish opposition which later helped his father. Saye helped Nathaniel's election as MP for Banbury so, when Charles was forced to call Parliament for funds in 1640, it was Nathaniel in the Commons who called a motion to block any taxes they raised being used against 'our Scottish brethren'. When the king found this Parliament altogether too stroppy to warrant its existence, he dissolved it and it became known historically as the Short Parliament. Saye later claimed that its dissolution was above all a strategy to block the success of his son's pro-Scottish motion.

Charles had tried to prevent Saye even participating in Parliament by not recalling him (and Brooke) to the Lords at all. This ploy failed, Saye turned up and, true to form, was the only peer who spoke out directly against an attempt by the king to distance the Lords from the Commons. This royal move was caused by Charles's worry that, whereas the Commons had long proved troublesome, only recently had there been an ominous alteration of temper in the Lords, and this he attributed to Saye, Brooke and their clique.

The king ruled largely through Lord Strafford and Archbishop Laud, and all three were keen on the re-establishment of powerful bishops throughout the land. On one occasion in the Lords various bishops had not turned up and Laud moved that 'this House adjourn because the Bishops are not present'. Saye objected, 'that the presence of the Bishops is not necessary to give legality to the proceedings. They have such absolute dependency upon the King that they sit not here as free men.' Saye then made a long speech to push a bill to restrain bishops from meddling in secular affairs.

Lord Strafford and Laud had had a bellyful of Saye at this point, so they imprisoned him in the Tower, alongside Pym, Hampden and Brooke. Men were then sent to Broughton Castle and to Saye's London house to search for evidence of treasonable collaboration with the Scots. None, of course, was found. The plotters were released due to lack of evidence against them and immediately went back to their schedule of secret meetings at Broughton. Fiennes family records simply state: 'Between the dissolution of the Short Parliament and the meeting of the Long one, there met in this room at different times Mr Pym, Mr Hampden, St John, Vane, Brooke, Bedford, Warwick, Nathaniel

Fiennes and Lord Saye to take steps to oppose the arbitrary measures of the King. From this room they would pass on to the leads [the castle roof] in discussion.'

Lord Strafford continued to advise Charles to arrest Saye when, for various reasons, Strafford was himself arrested and Saye escaped to become eminent in the subsequent Long Parliament of 1641, which impeached both Strafford and Laud, gained several powers over the king and voted Saye to be Privy Councillor, Master of the Court of Wards and Commissioner for the Treasury.

Saye heavily criticised the rigidity of the Church of England and its Book of Common Prayer and denounced Laud's attempts to impose 'certaine prayers and formes of divine service . . . upon all persons in all times to be used and none other . . . as if, because some men have need to use crutches, all men should bee prohibited the use of legges and injoyned to take up such crutches as have been prepared for those who have no legges.'

During that August of the Long Parliament, the king went north to Scotland and, in his absence, Lord Saye was appointed one of a select group of regents. By the time the Long Parliament came to a close, apart from removing the king's chief bully boys, they had also abolished the juryless royal courts which Charles had used to imprison MPs he disliked, and had secured a Bill preventing kings from dissolving Parliaments without their own consent. Saye had a leading role in all these 'triumphs of the people'.

Charles, who had called the Parliament only because he had no other way of raising the money he urgently needed, but ended up without, had to resort to desperate means. In 1641 his wife Henrietta Maria even went as far as pawning the crown jewels to raise money for the king's army.

Over in Ireland, meanwhile, the Catholics of Ulster, fearful of the huge influx of Scottish and English Protestants the Stuarts had 'planted' there and thinking that the English were about to introduce new repressive Protestant legislation, decided to attack the Protestant settlers by way of pre-emptive action. They slaughtered over 3,000 men, women and children, the direct cause of Cromwell's subsequent retribution a decade later. Fatally for the king, the Irish Catholic killers in Ulster claimed to have acted on his authority and produced a forged document to prove it. This served to convince wavering Parliamentarians that Charles really was plotting with Irish Catholics, with the Pope, and probably with Catholic Spain to get money to invade Scotland.

This was followed by Nathaniel Fiennes' discovery that Charles was planning to dissolve the Long Parliament by force, and by the unprecedented arrival at a Parliamentary session of the king himself, with armed troops at his back, demanding the arrest of five Parliamentarians, including Pym and Hampden. No arrests were made as the five wanted men slipped away, but the next day, when news of the king's attack on Parliament was noised about, mobs roamed London in fury and Charles fled the city.

Since the king had resorted to armed threats against his own Parliament, Parliament set about raising its own troops. To this day no sovereign has ever again been allowed into the House of Commons. John Pym led a motion that Charles was unfit to reign, and over the next eighteen months a majority of the Commons and a minority of the Lords came round to Pym's viewpoint. On 22 August 1642 the king raised his standard at Nottingham, declaring war, from a Puritan's point of view, on his own country.

The bulk of the Royal or Cavalier army came from the Catholic north and the west, including Wales, with a strong contingent of Irish troops and foreign mercenaries, whilst the Roundheads, so-called due to the shaved heads of the London apprentices who supported Parliament, came mostly from the more prosperous south and east, and from the Scottish Presbyterians. This was a general rule to which there were a great many confusing exceptions. Close kin often ended up on different sides, and the Fienneses were not immune to such splits.

William Fiennes, Lord Saye, had the close support of his three younger sons, all of whom became Roundhead generals, but his eldest son and heir, James, was a shy, gentle type who would nowadays be described as apolitical or agnostic, in terms of his commitment to either side during the Civil War. If anything, his proclivities appear to have been on the Royalist side. One of his sisters, Saye's younger daughter, married into a Royalist family, but the rest of the eight-strong brood were definitely anti-Royalist.

Most people throughout Britain (for Scotland and Ireland experienced as much or more bitter internal strife) only wanted peace, but they were sucked inexorably into the conflict and followed the line of least resistance. Some areas were let off lightly, having no key defensive installations on either side. Others were constantly fought over, and life there was hell on earth for the local people. At the height of the conflict in 1643 there were some 150,000 fighting men in England, a total which dropped by the late 1640s to 25,000.

At the outbreak of war Saye was made Lord Lieutenant of Oxfordshire with the power to call out and command the militia. He lost no time and the Oxfordshire Regiment was soon 1,200 strong and his own Saye and Sele Bluecoats vied for efficiency with the troops of his friends, including Hampden's Greencoats and Brooke's Purple. Saye additionally raised four troops of cavalry, three commanded by himself, and his sons, John and Nathaniel, while a fourth was led by a Captain Francis Fiennes and his ensign, Cornet Henry Fiennes. The family today are uncertain who exactly these two rogue Fienneses, presumably brothers, were, but think they were Fiennes-Clinton cousins.

Another Roundhead colonel, and one who achieved local fame by turning up with his regiment late for the battle of Worcester, was one of the Yorkshire Twisletons who had moved south and lived in Kent where he became a Puritan militia officer. He married four times and was the third husband of Elizabeth Fiennes, the granddaughter of Old Subtlety by his heir James, and my great to the power of ten grandmother. Her father was of Royalist inclination, despite being heir to Broughton, at the very time his father was plotting the downfall of the monarchy in the upstairs room.

Poor James must have kept his politics very much to himself, for not only were his father and three brothers active leaders of the Roundhead army, but his daughter's Twisleton husband was a Roundhead colonel knighted by Cromwell, whose elder brother, Colonel Philip Twisleton, was also Cromwell-knighted and whose younger Roundhead brother, George Twisleton, was the army colonel who settled North Wales for Parliament. He later married there and his memorial is still to be seen in the church of Clynnog, near Caernarfon.

The first real battle of the Civil War took place at Edgehill, only five miles up the road from Broughton, and was well attended by at least six Fiennes relatives, all leading Parliamentary forces.

20

Old Subtlety

The king's cavalry at the Battle of Edgehill was led by his nephew, Prince Rupert, and the Roundheads' army by the Earl of Essex, the son of the longtime favourite of Elizabeth I. His title was Parliamentary General, and Saye disliked him, but Saye's fourth son, Richard, was at Edgehill one of Essex's personal bodyguard, 'one hundred men of rank and fortune'. Colonel John Twisleton also belonged to it from time to time.

I have been to the site of the battle and could see how well chosen was the start point of the Royalist army. The king himself stayed on the high ridgeline out of harm's way, whilst the prince's ill-trained cavalry swept down on the Roundhead left flank, capturing their cannon and chasing them way back. But Saye's sons in the Roundhead centre did well and forced their opponents to retreat. The Broughton Horse with Essex's bodyguard cut down Wilmot's Royalists and killed many of the gunners of the king's artillery. They then fought a pitched battle with the royal foot guards, which they won shortly before dusk.

Back at Broughton, Saye's wife Elizabeth listened to the thunder of the cannon and must have kept her fingers crossed, for three of her beloved sons were there. The sixty-year-old Saye was himself in London addressing Parliament. The reports Elizabeth heard and diarised included one that her son, Colonel John, had been seen running away from the battle. This turned out to be false, since he was merely joining the fighting late, having collected much-needed stores and ammunition.

Rupert's initial charge would have won the day, despite the Roundhead presence of over 14,000 men, but he failed to regroup to protect the royal infantry. Nonetheless, the king's men felt that they had won and the road to London, their overall goal, was at least for a while free of Roundheads. The king then directed Rupert, his cavalry and artillery to attack Saye's two castles in the immediate vicinity, Banbury and Broughton. The Royal infantry under the Earl of Northampton laid immediate siege to Banbury.

In London Saye received a message from his son Nathaniel that the Earl of Essex had withdrawn to Warwick, leaving the road to London open for the king's army. Saye reacted with a Churchillian speech to a demoralised Parliament:

> My Lords and Gentlemen, that little I have to say shall not be to emphasize your approaching danger but rather to apply myself to stir up your spirits, to encourage you . . . This is now not a time for men to think with themselves that they will be in their shops to get a little money . . . In common dangers let every man take his weapons in his hand, let him offer himself willingly to serve his God . . . Let every man therefore shut up his shop, let him take his musket, let him offer himself readily and willingly, let him not think with himself who shall pay me, but rather think this, I'll come forth to save the Kingdom, to serve my God, to maintain his true religion, to save the parliament, to save this noble city . . . Let every man arm himself and arm his apprentices, and come forth with boldness and with courage and with cheerfulness, and doubt not but God will assist you . . . Be not daunted, let not malignant parties that go up and down and would go about to inform you that there are these fears and these dangers, let them not make you be wanting to yourselves; fear them not at all. I shall conclude with this, that that good King said, up and be doing and the Lord will be with you.

A revealing point of this text is that Saye was not anti-king *per se*. As with different forms of worship, where he saw no particular sect as omnipotent, he viewed no particular form of government as singled out by divine commendation. Mixed monarchy seemed to him to be the best system for the Britain of that time. There must, he believed, be a king or queen, but one who ruled *with*, not against, the wishes of the people's Parliament. The aim of Saye's Civil War, as plotted with Pym, Hampden and his other friends at Broughton, was to control, not to evict, the king.

Four days after Edgehill, the combined troops of Colonels Nathaniel and John Fiennes attacked the siege force of Royalists around Banbury Castle, especially keen to save Lord Brooke's artillery from falling into enemy hands. They failed. The Saye and Seles had for many years owned Banbury Castle and been MPs for Banbury. (I am today the 3rd Baronet of Banbury, my grandfather having chosen the town where he had long been the Liberal MP when he was made a baronet.) But that castle was extremely well built to withstand the strongest of sieges. The fact that it fell in only four days to Prince Rupert's troops and the metal cannon balls of a single small gun was entirely due to a large part of the garrison being disaffected and, after the siege, going over to the Royalists. Banbury Castle spent the rest of the war as a Royalist stronghold. Once Banbury Castle was in Prince Rupert's hands, the king ordered him the very next day to 'attack and plunder Broughton Castle'.

Personal animosity against Saye explains why the king, with a major war on his hands, should send his senior cavalry general to attack what amounted to a mere country house, for although crenellated with a moat and drawbridge, Broughton was never built with serious defensive features in mind. A Banbury complaint record states:

> When our Mayor showed Prince Rupert the King's hand and royal seal that the towne should not be plundered, Prince Rupert threw it away and said, 'My uncle little knows what belongs to the wars.' And so he commanded his men to plunder which they did to a purpose. But that which touched us most is a warrant under His Majesty's hand for the plundering of Lord Saye and Sele his house, demolishing of it and invites the people to do it with a grant to them of all the material therein.

Broughton was held only by a single troop of horse whose billets were the extensive attics, still known to the family as 'the barracks', which is where cousins Nat and Mariette, the present Lord and Lady Saye and Sele, took me to locate many of the documents quoted in this book. The castle is also overlooked from rising ground nearby, ideal for cannon fire. The defenders had lashed large bales of wool along the battlements, but this proved a useless gesture and the garrison sensibly surrendered after twenty-four hours. Prince Rupert's diary for Friday, 28 October 1642 simply states, '28. My Lord Saye's howse was taken.' Cannon balls dredged up from the Broughton moat are on display to the public today, along with a coat owned by Cromwell, which is displayed in the Great Hall. Like Banbury, Broughton remained in Royalist hands for the rest of the war.

Soon afterwards, General Essex, the Roundhead army commander, ordered the Fiennes cavalry to push forward ahead of the army towards Worcester. In charge of this reconnaissance force were Nathaniel and John Fiennes with Colonel Sandys. Unfortunately, the Royalist cavalry under Prince Rupert attacked them in strength at Powyck Bridge. The Fiennes force was heavily defeated, Sandys was killed and the brothers were among the last survivors to leave the battle, Nathaniel killing a Cavalier officer with his sword. A Royalist victory song results from the Battle of Powyck Bridge:

Thither came Fiennes with arms complete
The town to take and Biron defeat
Provision was made but he stayed not to eat
Which nobody can deny'o
Which nobody can deny.

For as soon as he heard our great guns play
With a flea in his ear he ran quite away
Like the lawful begotten son of Lord Say,
Which nobody can deny'o
Which nobody can deny.

After this setback, the Fiennes brothers with the remnants of their force were sent by Essex to other campaigns. John was commissioned as colonel of a cavalry regiment, later involved in many actions in the Oxford area. He commanded the siege of his home town of Banbury from August to October 1644, when he finally succeeded. He was singled out by Oliver Cromwell in a commendation the following year: 'His diligence was great and this I must testify that I find no man more ready to all services than himself . . . I find him a gentleman of that fidelity to you and so conscientious that he would all his troop were as religious and civil as any and makes it a great part of his care to get them so.'

When a temporary treaty was mooted in Oxford in November 1642, the king gave his grant-of-safe-conduct to all the Peace Commissioners put forward by Parliament, with the sole exception of Lord Saye. The latter gradually grew in influence and reputation in the Lords, as did his sons, Nathaniel and John in the Commons. Saye's position was one of hostility to both religious extremes, the Presbyterians and the episcopalians. He took a middle, relatively tolerant line and became the leader of the Independents, or middle party.

His greatest friend and ally, Lord Brooke, was killed at the siege of Lichfield. Sir Walter Scott celebrates him in verse: 'fanatic

Brooke, the fair cathedral stormed and took.' In fact, Brooke was merely inspecting entrenchments there when he was shot through the eye. 'That very eye,' crowed his enemies, 'with which he had said he hoped to see the destruction of all the cathedrals in England.'

Saye's main allies, fellow Independents, after 1644 were the Earl of Northumberland and Lord Wharton in the Lords and, in the Commons, his son Nathaniel and Oliver Cromwell. Cromwell was slowly ascending the army ranks and agreed with Saye that the current overall commander, the Earl of Essex, was getting too powerful and too autocratic; just like his father who Elizabeth I had eventually beheaded. Saye led the plot to deal with Essex, and when the Earl started to receive Royalist peace proposals in person rather than as head of Parliament, Saye pounced. He put forward a proposal for a joint Anglo-Scottish governing body called the Committee of Both Kingdoms. This radical new bill was engineered through Parliament by Saye's powerful cliques in both houses. The Scots acquiesced, for Essex had arrogantly claimed jurisdiction over their army, too. The Scottish Minister, Robert Baillie, wrote: 'The proposal was gotten through the House of Lords with little difficultie, where most was expected, my Lord Say being somewhat of the General.' The proposal established an alliance between the Parliamentarians and the Scots. That is, of course, those Scots who were not for the king.

At this time Saye also proposed a bill known as the Self-Denying Ordinance, an attempt to depoliticise the army, and began the move to form an efficient 'New Model' Parliamentarian Army with Sir Thomas Fairfax as its commander-in-chief. Saye was everywhere at once and always one jump ahead of his many adversaries. To some extent the parliamentary system and its two houses made this easy for him because the politics of the English revolution were dominated by members of the House of Lords. Being at the tip of the pyramid of English society, individual lords used their power and prestige to control the government. Powerful non-peers in the Commons, such as Nathaniel Fiennes, John Pym and Oliver Cromwell, were briefed by their patrons in the Lords; secretly briefed since the Commons was proud of its independence. Hence the ongoing cabals at Broughton Castle and, later on, in Saye's London rooms. As they stood to address the Commons, King Pym, King Cromwell and King Fiennes never owned up to their co-movers in the senior house.

In February 1643 Nathaniel was sent as a troubleshooter to keep Bristol from the Royalists. The current governor's loyalty was under suspicion, the garrison had been dangerously denuded by the army of the west, and the city aldermen were openly sympathetic to the king. Nathaniel Fiennes was clearly the man for such a job. His first move once there was to execute two men caught plotting to open the city gates to Prince Rupert. Then he pestered Fairfax for more men and supplies but, only five months after his arrival, Prince Rupert's 25,000-strong army attacked on all fronts, including from the sea, for the ships in Bristol harbour declared for the king. With the citizens hostile, supplies running low and the city walls breached in several places, Nathaniel had no option but to surrender after a week of desperate resistance. His 3,000 troops were allowed to leave under 'partial arms'.

Various MPs, shocked by the collapse of such a key city in the west, accused Nathaniel of treason and cowardice. A trial before a Council of War found him guilty of improper surrender, and he was sentenced to death despite fierce support from his brother, Colonel John Fiennes, who had shared the Bristol defence with him. The prosecution made use of one Dorothy Hazzard, the Baptist leader who had established Bristol's first dissenting church three years before and who, with two hundred other women, had held the city's Frome Gate against Prince Rupert's men. Nathaniel received a last minute pardon, doubtless due to the influence of his father and other friends in high places, but his own considerable influence waned until, two years later, Prince Rupert was forced out of Bristol by a Roundhead siege, and it then became clear that the city was indefensible without huge commitment and expense. Nathaniel, fully vindicated, regained his powerful position as an Independent leader in the Commons. He is remembered in the records of Winchester, which city his men once took from the Royalists, with great gratitude for the firm hand he took with Roundhead troops found desecrating and smashing memorials, including the tomb of the city father, William of Wykeham, Nathaniel's ancestor.

After the Bristol debacle, Nathaniel's brother John returned to Oxfordshire and, in April 1644, laid siege to Banbury Castle. Letters which he sent from his siege tent to his parents in London were intercepted, as was incoming mail, by Royalist spies, and published in the public *Court Journal*, presumably by way of ridicule. One from Lord Saye said: 'Jack, I fear you must get into the Castle by a golden bridge. Try if you can get a fit instrument. Spare not cost. No matter for the clamour of bribery. £500 given were well bestowed and would soon be gotten up again.'

Another letter from Colonel John's mother runs: 'Sonne John, Whatever you want, send earnestly for it before you want it or else you will go without it when you most need it. I pray you, do not engage yourself more than in keeping them in and in keeping others from them.' That sounds like a typical worried mum, hoping her son will keep safe by taking minimal risks.

The Royalists had also managed to get hold of an executive order sent by John to the Constable of Roxton, presumably prior to a planned attack on Banbury Castle.

> These are to charge and command you that upon sight hereof you gather together all the ladders in your town with a load of hay bound hard together with thumb ropes, and one load of good brush faggots and bring the said things into the churchyard in Banbury by one of the clock this day week at the furthest;

hereof fail not upon pain of death and forfeiting your whole estate.

Given under my hand the 20th April 1644

John Fiennes

Colonel

The largest battle of the war, a Roundhead victory, took place a few weeks later at Marston Moor involving 45,000 soldiers, but most Civil War engagements were mere skirmishes or sieges. At Marston Moor Prince Rupert, in admiration, called Cromwell Ironside, and thereafter his personal cavalry were known as Ironsides. 'Cromwell's troops moved to victory,' wrote historian Lord Macaulay, 'with the precision of machines and the fanaticism of Crusaders. From the time it was remodelled to its disbandment it never found an enemy who could stand its onset whether in Britain or abroad. These Puritan warriors, even contending against threefold odds never failed to conquer, to destroy and break in pieces whatever force was opposed to them.'

The New Model Army gradually took shape as Saye's Self-Denying Ordinance removed the old commanders, leaving Fairfax and Cromwell in charge. Their chief recruitment areas were in and around London. At the beckoning finger of Cromwell, like Kitchener's subsequent 'Your country needs you', thousands of Londoners would be rapidly deployed to augment the standing army.

Cromwell wrote a condolence letter to his brother-in-law just after the Battle of Marston Moor:

> The Left Wing which I commanded, being our own horse saving a few Scots in our rear, beat all the Prince's horse. God made them as stubble to our swords. We charged their regiments of foot and routed them . . . Sir, God hath taken away your eldest son by a cannon shot. It brake his leg. We were necessitated to have it cut off, whereof he died. There is your precious child full of glory, never to know sin or sorrow any more.

After the battle Cromwell was promoted to commander of all the Model Army's cavalry units. A succession of chess-like moves by both sides, various sieges, siege reliefs and skirmishes eventually led to a major confrontation near Naseby, where Colonel John Twisleton's men fought by chance alongside those of Colonel John Fiennes, both on the right wing and directly under Cromwell's command. Their forces were critical to the final outcome of the three-hour battle in which over 5,000 Royalists were killed. Fairfax's men pursued and slaughtered many fleeing Royalists and, unusual for Puritan troops, raped and mutilated dozens of Rupert's female camp followers. Those responsible later said that they did this because the women spoke Irish. In fact, they were Welsh.

After Naseby the Roundheads were all-conquering. Chester, Leicester, Taunton and other major bastions fell to Parliament. The king managed to last out until the fall of Oxford in 1646, but after Naseby he never really stood a chance.

Amongst the royal baggage coaches captured at Naseby were compromising copies of letters written by Charles seeking support from Catholic Europe. The Roundheads published these with much righteous indignation and gained popular support to carry on fighting to the finish. But there were increasing signs of anger in many regions that the war was ruining people's lives and achieving nothing. Groups of neutralists or 'clubmen' throughout the west country tried to drive both warring sides out of their area and demanded an end to the war by negotiation. In Dorset there was even an armed clubmen uprising that Cromwell had to quash.

Eleven months after Naseby the king's troops had withered away, disillusioned by constant defeat, and, unlike the Roundheads, unpaid. So Charles surrendered to the Scottish in the hope that he could enlist their support by promising to establish Presbyterianism as the official form of worship throughout Britain. But the Scots did not trust him, and anyway hoped to achieve their religious aims through Parliament. So they handed the king over to the Roundheads for £400,000. 'Cheap at the price,' was

Charles's recorded comment. So he still had a sense of humour. (The £400,000 was also to pay the Scottish army to go back home.) The first Civil War was over.

Parliament put the king under comfortable house arrest at Hampton Court Palace and began a series of internal squabbles between various factions. One small act by Lord Saye at that time revealed that, although an outwardly cold individual, he was kind at heart, for he was the only peer who paid for the royal children to be well looked after whilst their father was 'away' and before Parliament voted the money for their care.

To win the war, Parliament had imposed tax on two key commodities: beer and salt. People needed salt to preserve food, and they drank beer as today we drink tea and coffee. So to tax such items was a sure way of losing support. Bad weather, in fact the worst harvests for a century, led to exorbitant food prices and economic recession. The poor became desperate. Large numbers of redundant soldiers found no work and Parliament enraged the army, early in 1647, by trying to disband most of the soldiery without pay.

Parliament, by that summer, was far more unpopular throughout the land than the king had ever been and, unable to see an alternative, a majority in both houses felt that the only way forward was to restore the king to his former position with the best terms they could squeeze from him. But such a course was anathema to the many whose loved ones had died to change the system. To admit that the whole hellish struggle had been fruitless and futile by bringing back the king to his former powers would be a betrayal to God and to the dead.

The dominant faction in Parliament's Committee of the Two Kingdoms was the Scottish-orientated Presbyterian grouping who had, in order to win the war, promised their Scottish allies that they would dismantle the Elizabethan Church of England and refashion it in the Presbyterian model. This they had done with edicts throughout the land banishing the Prayer Book, the episcopacy, cathedrals, and all festivals like Easter and Christmas.

Nobody was exempt from the authority of this new national church and nobody could receive Holy Communion without the approval of their minister and a Certificate of Worthiness.

The reaction of the populace to all this was to hate the source of it all: Parliament and the Puritans. Congregations everywhere chucked out ministers who tried to impose the new rules. There were riots in London. The Independents, led by Lord Saye in the Lords and, in the Commons, by Colonel Nathaniel Fiennes (his reputation fully restored since his near-hanging after his surrender of Bristol), pursued a path that led between the various radical factions. A letter sent to the king at that time by his adviser, Lewis Dye, stated: 'Cromwell and his Cabinett which are the Lord Say, St John and Vayne-the-younger, now steer the affaires of the whole Kingdome.' Only five days after the London riots, Sir John Maynard wrote to the court, 'On my knowledge the greatest enemies the King had be my Lord Say, St John, old and young Vane and Evelyn.' The Royalist publication *Mercurius* summed Saye up: 'He is as smooth as a butterbox. Oh! how the Presbyterians sneare in their sleeves to see with what dexterity this spider weaves his nets to catch the silly flies of the Army.'

The views of the Fiennes faction, which at that stage included Oliver Cromwell and the other army generals, were reflected in a document drawn up by Saye known as the Heads of the Proposals. In this they told the king that they believed that nobody in Britain should be treated as a heretic, except aggressive papists or way-out Low Churchers, and that no one should be prosecuted for failing to attend parish services 'if he could show a reasonable Cause for his absence'. Saye believed that 'beyond ensuring order and punishing blasphemy, the State had no brief to police men's thoughts and that congregations were free to choose their ministers and forms of worship or use the Book of Common Prayer. But the old episcopal order should be abolished.'

On the monarchy, Saye's bill proposal stated that the king's executive powers were to be strictly limited. 'He himself,' Saye wrote, 'hath brought this necessity upon us; not to trust him with that power whereby he may do us and himself hurt but with so much alone as shall be sufficient to inable him to do us good.' Restoration of the king, Saye stated, was to follow immediately upon his agreement to the concessions demanded in Saye's proposals.

In such a complex and contrary environment as Parliament in 1647, Saye's proposals could only be implemented by cunning and influence. Only Saye had the necessary web of contacts and allies in the Lords, the army and the Commons.

'Colonels Nathaniel and John Fiennes,' Sir William Waller claimed, 'acted as tame draftsmen for the Lords who gathered at Saye's house'; and another contemporary observed that: 'it made little difference which of Saye's parliamentary siblings was involved [with an appointment to control the Exchequer] since, no matter which of them it is, both may do well enough with their Father's Money Baggs.' Political prisoner in the Tower, John Lilburne, wrote in a letter: 'Cromwell is now closely glued in interest and councelle to the Lords Say and Wharton.'

In October 1647 the king's men responded that royal assent would be given to Saye's proposals as passed by the Lords, but not with the amendments applied by the Commons. The king, however, still believed that he could win the day without making any concession to anybody. He eluded his guards at Hampton Court and fled, to Carrisbrooke Castle on the Isle of Wight. Saye went to see him there, in defiance of Parliament, but negotiations came to an abrupt halt when Civil War broke out again as the army faced a Royalist invasion from Scotland and a series of regional uprisings. Charles had promised the Scots he would Presbyterianise the whole of Britain in return for their support.

This second phase of the Civil War, as bloody as the first, ended at the Battle of Prestonpans, where the Scots were crushed by the New Model Army and the king was again imprisoned. Back to square one, and Saye, Nathaniel and John Fiennes again pressed in both houses for settlement with the king. Thomas Coke wrote of Saye:

> Of all the parlement commissioners, the most inward man with the King, he undertooke most on his behalfe with his interest in the Houses. The Duke of Richmond and hee were very intimate and by him the Lord Saye conveyed his intelligences still to the King. He was so confident of the successe of the treatie that he had bespoke of himselfe to be Lord Treasurer. He did all that he could to work upon the King to yield to what was proposed to him. And, afterwards, to persuade the Parliament to be content with what his majesty had yielded.

Likewise, in the Commons Nathaniel Fiennes strongly supported the king's response to the Saye proposals and, on 1 December, made a powerful speech urging that the king had 'done enough' to safeguard religion and the constitution and that therefore they should negotiate and settle with him.

The majority of the Commons clearly agreed with Fiennes, but a large section of army men, disgusted by the king's secret alliance with the Scots, pre-empted any further discussions with him by Parliament by simply raiding the Commons. Colonel Thomas Pride arrested over half the members and forcibly prevented them taking their seats. Two-thirds of the remainder, appalled, boycotted their violated house.

In the revolutionary months that followed, less than one in six of all MPs returned to the house, and many of those that did wished only to moderate proceedings. The decision to put King Charles on trial was approved by less than one in ten of those who had made war on him five years before. Nathaniel Fiennes was amongst those arrested by Pride's men who proclaimed 'a Republic' and, when released, he, like his father and brother, took no part in it. The House of Lords, meanwhile, was abolished to be later replaced by Cromwell's 'Other House'.

Saye wrote gloomily: 'Had the King only passed those Four Bills [his proposals], a Peace had been settled, safe and just to the subjects, as Honourable to himself, and all troubles and confusions ended. When they will now end, the Lord only knoweth.'

Unforgiving of the recaptured king's treasonable dealings with the Scots, Cromwell pressed for the trial of the 'tyrant, traitor and murderer, Charles Stuart'. On 2 January 1649 a bill was brought before the remnants of the Commons, known as the Rump Parliament, ordaining that 'a high court of justice for the trial of the King be erected'. All the peers were ordered to attend and, from my point of view, an interesting note was the reaction of a hitherto timid, non-participatory Fiennes relative. Lord Francis Dacre normally kept well clear of trouble, and therefore of attendance at the Lords. I have a copy of a letter he wrote from Herstmonceux some five years earlier addressed to the Deputy Speaker.

> On Wednesday night last I received your lordship's of the ninth of this month, and would have most gladly obeyed the commands of the House of Peers, by coming . . . to wait on the affairs of the kingdom on the 22nd, had not the ways ever since been so extremely clogged by a very deep snow, that men pass not without much difficulty and danger: I beseech your lordship to add to this reason the weakness of my own health, not being able to endure the rigour of the journeying on horseback in such exceeding cold weather, as now it is; and to represent this to their lordships' favourable constructions; not that I intend to make long use of any way to excuse myself from that duty, which I shall ever owe to the commonwealth, but very shortly shall give my attendance on their lordships with all willingness and readiness. And so I rest
>
> Your lordship's
>
> Most humble servant,
>
> Francis Dacre

However, so strong were his feelings about the impending trial that on a cold January day he not only made it to the Lords, but was one of only twelve peers who had the courage to speak out in defence of their sovereign, an act of loyalty which so upset

Cromwell's men that they suggested that the twelve lords should be impeached 'as favourers of the grand delinquent of England and enemies to public justice and the liberty of the people'. Good Marxist stuff.

Later that month the trial went ahead and the king was tried for his life. He was found guilty of treason and sentenced to death. The court decided that the king 'be put to death by the severing of his head from his body'. On a wintry morning outside Whitehall, Charles was beheaded in public which, in time, turned out to be a great propaganda mistake by his enemies. The crowd, watched over by the army, were stunned and sympathetic to their king.

Charles wore several layers of underclothes on his way to the block, for it was cold and he did not wish the public to see him shiver and mistake this for fear. One record of the event is a letter home from an Oxford student in Whitehall by chance. 'I stood amongst the crowd where the scaffold was erected. The Blow I saw given, at the instant whereof there was such a Grone by the Thousands then present as I never heard before and desire I may never hear again.' The crowd were allowed to rush forward and dip their handkerchiefs in his blood. It was the Puritan poet Andrew Marvell who wrote:

> He nothing common did, or mean
> Upon that memorable scene
> But with his keener eye
> The axe's edge did try . . .
> And bowed his comely head
> Down, as on a bed.

Four months later England became a Republic, with Oliver Cromwell the chairman of the Council of State.

21

Adultery at the Castle

A popular image of Oliver Cromwell, the man who killed the king and then usurped the throne, is of an angry, prudish commoner who, like Idi Amin, quickly climbed the ranks and ruled as a tyrant. But Cromwell's grandfather was a wealthy landowner who regularly entertained King James I and his court on his estates. Cromwell's father, a younger son, inherited a lesser part of the family wealth, and young Oliver, after studying at Cambridge University, farmed his land and looked after his seven unmarried sisters.

He was thirty-nine years old and suffering from depression (for which he consulted doctors) when he underwent, like St Paul on the road to Damascus, a religious conversion which was to propel him from middle-aged obscurity into national power and a fame which has remained so durable that at the millennium he was voted one of Britain's Top Ten Men in History.

Through his wife, whose family had extensive estates in Essex, he met the Earl of Warwick and through him Lord Saye, both vociferous members of the Independent party of liberal Puritans, at that time the group whose aims most tallied with Cromwell's. As MP for Cambridge by 1640, Cromwell first became known for his frequent fiery speeches in the Commons, which mirrored those of the Saye group in the Lords. He remained friends with Saye through the Civil War, and in 1647 tried to push Saye's Heads of the Proposals through Parliament. But, when the king proved recalcitrant and escaped from house arrest, Cromwell's anti-Royalist side hardened and, unlike Saye, he no longer saw a way forward that included King Charles as monarch. After Pride's Purge cleansed Parliament of MPs wishing to continue negotiations with Charles, Cromwell was one of the main architects of the king's subsequent trial and execution which so disgusted Lord Saye.

The Rump Parliament was set up after the Purge to run the new Republic. Cromwell, very powerful by now, tried at first to bring together Saye's group of Independents and to work with them, but only one participated in the Rump. The rest were too alienated by the regicide and, like Saye, left Parliament. The Fiennes family was not at this stage politically split, and 1649 saw both Nathaniel and John unsympathetic to the Rump. Neither brother had anything to do with the Republic, nor did they approve when Cromwell abolished the House of Lords, leaving nobody but the blinkered and intolerant Rump to run the Republic.

Although Broughton was by then out of Royalist hands and back with the Fienneses, the seventy-year-old Lord Saye, probably because his beloved wife Elizabeth had died at Broughton the previous year, did not go back there, but spent the next three years in self-imposed exile on the Isle of Lundy, a pirates' haven for centuries in the Bristol Channel halfway between Wales and North Devon. I boated to Lundy in 2003 and noted the puffins nesting along the high cliffs, the seals in the Atlantic surf below and the total lack of trees or permanent inhabitants. I failed to find the ruins of the 'castle' where my great to the power of twelve grandfather had spent those three Cromwellian years. Yet in his day, and certainly in the first half of his century, the place was a hive of piratical activity and not the sort of place I would have chosen to bunker down in an anti-Cromwellian huff. Lundy was one of the very last Royalist strongholds in England to surrender to Parliament, the governor eventually handing the island over to Colonel Richard Fiennes, representing General Fairfax.

Richard lived there for a while, then when his father Lord Saye arrived, fed up with Cromwell and with the Lords abolished, Richard moved with his family to Broughton, where he settled, although his elder non-military brother James was heir to the castle and, while Saye stayed away on Lundy, its proprietor. The two brothers clearly enjoyed each other's company, and James was otherwise alone as his wife had left the castle due to what seems to me to have been a bad case of in-house adultery. Not exactly *Upstairs, Downstairs* so much as Upstairs and along the Corridor to the Chief Steward of the Household's suite.

At that time many great houses with estates were run by stewards, who were often younger sons of nobles with good university qualifications. Lord Saye at first took on Thomas Dudley, a scion of the famous Elizabethan favourite, but then Saye did a favour to his son-in-law, Theophilus Fiennes-Clinton, 4th Earl of Lincoln, by lending him Dudley, who did such a good job for the earl that he never returned to Broughton. He was replaced by one William Sprigge of Banbury, an excellent steward who went on to become the steward of New College, Oxford, but was the father of a prudish Puritan, Joshua Sprigge, who, behind James Fiennes' back, seduced his wife in his own castle.

The adulterous Frances Fiennes, Lady Saye and Sele, was herself an extreme Puritan of the sort who could do no wrong and made a study of hypocrisy. Lady Frances Cecil (her maiden name) was the great granddaughter of Queen Elizabeth's great statesman, Lord Burghley, and with James Fiennes she had produced six little Fienneses, including three sons. Two died as infants and the eldest, after a Winchester education that did not include swimming, went to Paris aged nineteen, where he drowned in the Seine. In his rooms in Paris he had a miniature painting of his father which the owners kept when he died. Over two hundred years later a French family returned this miniature to Broughton. Two of his sisters survived to carry on the Fiennes inheritance.

Fiennes relations, the Verney family, are famous for having kept family letters down the centuries, and one of them in 1648 mentions: 'Your cousin James Fiennes and his wife are parted. They say the reason is they cannot agree in disputes of conscience and that she does not think him holy enough, but in my opinion there is very little conscience in parting from husbands.' Contemporary gossip-mongers described Joshua Sprigge as the 'Gallant of Lady Saye', and when James died, they married.

Quite when the adulterous goings-on at Broughton became general knowledge it is difficult to say, but James was married to Frances for at least sixteen years before she went off to live with the slimy Joshua. The scandal would have been all the greater due to the extreme Puritan prudery that they both preached. Indeed, to confuse things, Sprigge had a post as chaplain in Fairfax's army and wrote a popular account of various battles, called *Anglia Rediviva*, but he was a monarchist nonetheless and wrote a forceful argument against the king's execution as part of Saye's effort to stop the regicide.

So James, no doubt smarting in public as a known cuckold, lived at Broughton with his two surviving daughters and the family of his brother, the retired Colonel Richard Fiennes. How long their father would have stayed away on Lundy is difficult to deduce. It is said that he wrote a romantic novel there or, together with his other son Nathaniel, a famous Parliamentary tract called *Vinducii*. Either way, one of his supply ships from the mainland was in 1651 captured and a ransom was demanded, which must have turned him off Lundy.

Royalist vessels based in France routinely harassed parliamentary ships, and one Captain Will Hinton who hijacked Saye's boat sent him a ransom note on behalf of his exiled master, Charles II to be, which read:

> My Lord,
>
> Not far from that pretty island whereof your Lordship is petty prince, it was my fortune last evening to fetch up a small vessel laden with provisions of your garrison. I could wish it have been

> of some considerable value . . . so famous is your Lordship for your activity against your Liege Lord, the King's Majesty of ever beloved memory. Yet, as little as it was, it did me good to seize upon it by virtue of my commission from his Majesty that now is, were it but to keep it in your Lordship's memory that there still is a King.

The letter went on to threaten Saye that future supply ships to Lundy would also be liable to seizure. So Saye returned to live out his old age at Broughton and keep a jaundiced eye on his number one enemy, once his good friend, Oliver Cromwell.

The Royalists had, following the regicide, regrouped in Ireland after signing a treaty with the Irish Catholics, and Cromwell was chosen by the Rump Parliament to lead a Roundhead army to deal with this Irish threat. First on his list of targets was Drogheda. Cromwell's first attack on well defended Drogheda was repulsed, which annoyed him, but after the defenders began to waver, all hell was let loose. By his own estimate he put some 2,000 to the sword. 'In the Round Tower they refused to yield to mercy whereupon I ordered the fire. One of them was heard to say in the midst of the flames, "God damn me, God confound me: I burn. I burn."'

Cromwell starved out some sixty defenders of another tower, and when they at length gave up, he had their officers clubbed to death, every tenth soldier shot after the Roman fashion of decimation, and shipped the rest to the Barbados. Cromwell's report added: 'I am persuaded that this is a righteous judgement of God upon these barbarous wretches who have imbrued their hands in so much innocent blood.' The final toll of the massacre included 2,700 Royalist soldiers, many of whom were actually English, anyone with arms, many civilians, Roman Catholic priests, and even prisoners. Wexford was in the process of surrendering when Cromwell's men broke into the town in his absence, killed 2,000 Irish troops, murdered 1,500 civilians, and set fire to the town.

In the conquered areas, Cromwell's officers confiscated the land of 'all rebels', as a result of which nearly 40 per cent of all Ireland was redistributed from Catholics born in Ireland to Protestants born in Britain. The public practice of Catholicism was banned, Catholic priests were killed when caught and somewhere between 12,000 and 50,000 Irish folk were sold into slavery. Cromwell is still a figure of hatred in Ireland, his name being associated with massacre, religious persecution and mass dispossession of Catholics.

Parliament then sent Cromwell's army to Scotland, where Charles I's son had been proclaimed Charles II by the Scottish Presbyterians. Cromwell was far less harsh with the Scots, many of whom had been his allies in the Civil War. At the Battle of Dunbar the Roundheads smashed the main Scots army, killing 4,000 and taking 10,000 prisoners before capturing Edinburgh. Despite this, Charles II with a small army of Scots invaded England, hoping to gather support en route to capture London. But Roundhead armies closed on Charles near Worcester in September 1651 and surrounded his 15,000 men with twice that number. Charles had made a crucial error in assuming that traditional Royalist supporters in Lancashire and the Welsh border area would rush to his standard, but Parliament had done a successful PR job convincing the populace that this was a Scottish Presbyterian invasion first and foremost, never mind the king.

The river Severn figured strongly in Royalist Worcester's defences, but Cromwell's men built pontoon bridges which circumvented the king's defensive plan. Charles II fought with brain and bravery, but the battle was eventually lost. There were very few Parliamentary dead, but 3,000 Royalists were killed, over 10,000 captured, English prisoners were conscripted into the Parliamentary army still in Ireland, whilst 8,000 Scots prisoners were sent to labour in New England and the West Indies.

Prior to the battle, King Charles II had contracted the Worcester clothiers to outfit his army with uniforms, but the £453 bill was never paid. In June 2008 Charles, Prince of Wales, paid off the debt. Charles II managed, just, to escape, via an oak tree hide and many other adventures, to exile in France.

Three Fienneses were involved in the Battle of Worcester: the three elder sons of John Twisleton, all of whom were colonels in the New Model Army. The eldest one, Colonel John Twisleton, had two years previously married Elizabeth, the eldest daughter and co-heiress of James Fiennes, whose inheritance would include Broughton Castle. He was Colonel of the Kent Militia and had been summoned to help surround Charles II at Worcester. For some unrecorded reason he was very nearly late for this, the last battle of the Civil War. A stern order was sent to him (27 August 1651): 'Council of State to Col. John Twisleton: We are sorry that, in a time when there is such a necessity for forces, there should arise such difficulties to get out your regiment and we desire you to march forthwith with it to Lt Gen Fleetwood with all expedition to Banbury or to such place as he shall direct, and use all diligence as your regiment is so far behind.' Twisleton and his men did just make it and helped Fleetwood secure the key south bank of the river Teme, south of Worcester. Cromwell even knighted him.

The battle was Cromwell's last and his victory over the Scots contributed to his ever-growing eminence in the early 1650s. Over in Broughton, 'Old Subtlety' Saye must have thought all his life's work had been to no avail, but he was to live long enough to have the last laugh.

Whilst Cromwell was in Ireland and Scotland, the Rump Parliament, with no king as a common enemy, squabbled amongst themselves and failed to convince Cromwell, when he returned to active politics, that they could effectively achieve his goals to set election dates, to unite the three kingdoms under a single government and to put in place a single tolerant, national church. In April 1653 Cromwell and other army commanders decided that the Rump was a waste of time, so they used gentle force to 'help' the Rumpers out of their Commons seats, in the shape of a squad of forty musketeers under the command of Major General Charles Wolseley (who was married to Lord Saye's daughter, Anne Fiennes). Cromwell took away the mace, symbol of parliamentary authority, and gave it into Wolseley's safe keeping.

The Rump was replaced by a group of 140 men considered by Cromwell and his army colleagues to be the 'most godly men in England'. This 'holy parliament' was nicknamed the Barebones Parliament, after one of its members, Praise God Barbon, and was tasked by Cromwell to agree upon and implement a permanent constitutional and religious settlement. After five months of useless deliberation, they gave up and voted that Cromwell take over the reins of government. At this stage the army leaders asked Cromwell to accept the crown and to rule as king, but he refused, even though he approved of monarchy in principle. He was even, at the time of Charles I's execution, discussing with colleagues the case for restoring one of his sons to the throne.

However, Cromwell did agree to become Lord Protector of the three kingdoms, a title which brought with it most of the trappings of royalty without the embarrassment of becoming king and being known as the usurper. For the next five years until his death, he ruled through a Council of State with a sitting Parliament, but to all intents and purposes his Britain was a benevolent military dictatorship, in order to avoid being an anarchy or a monarchy. People started to address him as 'Your Highness', and he did not object. He signed his name regally as 'Oliver P', standing for 'Oliver Protector'. He was paid £100,000 per annum and would clearly remain undisputed boss of the realm so long as he stayed popular with the army.

The new constitution which he initially tried out was based on the Heads of the Proposals which Lord Saye, Pym and he himself had put together years before. When it failed to work, he tried a number of other forms of government, and none were revolutionary. He was perfectly happy to keep the country's class structure the way it was. He approved of a wide measure of religious liberty. His state church did not require folk to attend it, and all citizens (except Catholics) were allowed to follow their own conscience as to how they chose to worship. He was, like old Lord Saye at Broughton, violently anti-Quaker, but his Protectorate was, looking back, a remarkable period of religious freedom in Britain.

He even encouraged Jews to come back to Britain. Edward I had sent them all packing, but Cromwell's welcome back invitation was well-timed, since only five years before the Ukrainians had massacred 100,000 Jews and deported the rest. Cromwell saw Holland as Britain's main trade rival, and Amsterdam was full of Jews. He felt that, if tempted to Britain, they could lead an economic revival to help the country recover after the Civil War. He gave them full freedom of religion. Many soon arrived from Holland, Spain and Portugal, bringing invaluable information to assist the British trading empire in the Atlantic which Cromwell envisaged. Seventeenth-century British emigration across the Atlantic reached its peak during Cromwell's rule, many going for a better life, others for religious reasons, like the Catholic emigrants to Maryland and Puritans to New England. Thousands were also deported, often for minor crimes such as vagrancy.

Despite his policy of overall religious tolerance, Cromwell, like some fundamentalist Ayatollas of today, cracked down on what he regarded as frivolous pleasures which offended his work ethic. Many sports were selectively banned and theatres were closed. Women were not allowed brightly coloured dresses nor cosmetics, and Puritan soldiers would patrol the streets and rub the make-up off offenders' faces. Festivities at Easter and Christmas were abolished, and patrols would confiscate holly decorations and, by following their noses, roast goose and plum puddings would also be requisitioned.

In 1657 a major split occurred for the first time between Lord Saye and his two actively Puritan sons, Colonels Nathaniel and John. They had both left Parliament by the time the Rump was formed but, unlike Saye, both had made friends again with Cromwell and, when he became Lord Protector, both joined his Council of State. When they were invited to join Cromwell's Other House, a replacement for the Lords, both Fienneses agreed and became active members. Nathaniel rose to be the Speaker of the House, Keeper of the Privy Seal, and officially known as Lord

Fiennes. He was one of the main movers in 1657 who attempted to convince Cromwell to take the crown because, as Protector, he officially possessed unlimited powers whereas, as king, he would be subject to legally limited authority.

In 1658 Nathaniel, as Speaker of the Commons, opened the new Parliament's first sitting with a rousing speech to both houses in which he described Cromwell as 'His Highness' and urged an ongoing war against the evil empire of Spain. Nathaniel's brother John did not shine in any way, and one Republican pamphleteer describes him as 'such a one who they call a sectary, but no great stickler and partly under the influence of his brother'.

Their father, although well into his seventies, was also summoned to the Other House by writ, but he refused and objected strongly to his two sons acquiescing with the king-killer. He also despised his son-in-law, Major General Charles Wolseley, who had become Cromwell's chief adviser and army supporter. No doubt to Saye's satisfaction, Cromwell sickened suddenly from septicaemia, some say malaria, and died in September 1658 with Nathaniel Fiennes at his deathbed strongly supporting his proposal that Cromwell's son, Richard, take over as Lord Protector.

Oliver Cromwell was buried with royal pomp in Westminster Abbey but, three years later when the monarchy was restored, his body was dug up, beheaded (on the same date that Charles I was executed), his body was hanged in chains from a Tyburn gibbet, then thrown into a pit. His severed head was displayed on a pole outside Westminster Hall for the next twenty-five years. Afterwards his head was auctioned several times, most recently in 1814, and was finally buried near the chapel of his alma mater, Sydney Sussex College, Cambridge in 1960.

His son and successor, lacking both his character and, crucially, top army support, was widely known as Tumbledown Dick. He ruled for only eighteen months of relative chaos. Army commanders with widely differing ideas of what should be done fell out with one another until the most powerful grouping under General Monck decided that there was only one answer, and that was to call back from exile the son of Charles I. Free elections were called and the man who had hidden in an oak tree after defeat at Worcester nine years before was recalled from France to be King Charles II of Britain.

As his ship brought him over from France, another vessel transferred the exiled Richard Cromwell to Paris, where he tactfully remained for twenty years before returning under an assumed name to live quietly in England until he died in 1712. His father had left Charles II a legacy of unusual religious tolerance but, after an eleven-year Republic during which he had experimented with many ways of changing the government system, nothing very much had actually happened since the killing of Charles I.

Scotland and most of Ireland were now fully integrated with the rest of Britain (under a continued dynasty of Scottish kings!) and, abroad, Cromwell's foreign policy had accelerated the road to empire. His invincible armies allied with the French to defeat the Spanish in 1658, but his grand 'Western Design' to defeat the Spanish in South America was a dismal failure. He did, however, capture Jamaica.

His 1651 Parliament passed the Navigation Act as a direct challenge to Dutch shipping. This provoked a brief naval war with the Dutch which Cromwell's powerful navy under General Monck had won by 1653. The Navigation Act confirmed Britain as an aggressively outward-looking nation, soon to become a commercial world power with an extensive merchant marine and a big-gun navy to protect it.

Cromwell was an undeniably successful ruler at home and abroad and, although originally a minor sheep farmer, he has today more roads named after him in England than anyone else but Queen Victoria.

But it is arguable that without his original friendship and political affinity with William Fiennes, Lord Saye, he would never have made it to be head of state.

22

A Restoration and Elopement

My great uncle, Geoffrey Twisleton-Wykeham-Fiennes, the 19th Lord Saye and Sele, spent many years researching the history of his predecessors at Broughton, especially Old Subtlety, and observed: 'It was Saye's rare and strange fortune after being the mainspring of the Revolution to become also the mainspring of the Restoration.' Although Saye was nigh on eighty years old at the Restoration, the king acknowledged his key role (despite the fact that Saye had been among the first to plot and take up arms against his father) and made him Lord Chamberlain of the Household and a Privy Councillor. Other ardent Fiennes Cromwellian fighters were also forgiven, including Colonels Nathaniel and John Fiennes, Colonel John Twisleton and Theophilus Fiennes-Clinton, Earl of Lincoln, whose wife was Old Subtlety's daughter.

Saye, back in his old seat in the Lords, was appointed Councillor of the Colonies and chairman of the committee to settle the government of New England. The Puritans there were naturally apprehensive of their changing status under the new Royalist motherland. Saye did his utmost to use his unparalleled influence with army, Parliament and king to ensure that the colonies were treated well under the new management. Near the end of his life he wrote to John Winthrop, the Governor of Massachusetts: 'I was loth to omit writing because it may be my last, my glass being almost run out. I have not been wanting, both to the King and Council, to advance your interest; more I cannot do but earnestly pray the Lord to stand with you.'

Old Subtlety's glass did indeed run out in April 1662, a few weeks before his eightieth birthday, and he was buried at Broughton, to be succeeded by his eldest son James, the least Puritan of his brood. Old Subtlety was undeniably the chief architect of the Puritan movement to which the United States looks for its origins and to which England owes three centuries of constitutional government.

The recalled Charles II set sail from exile in Holland in May 1660. Naval Secretary Samuel Pepys was on board the good ship *Royal Prince* (a quick name switch from *Naseby*) sent by Monck to collect the thirty-year-old king-to-be. Also on board was Charles's younger brother, James, Duke of York. Pepys was ready to weep at Charles's stories of his escape from Worcester and charmed by the king and the Duke of York's willingness to eat ship's diet of pease, pork and boil beef. He got into a barge to disembark with, 'one of the king's footmen with a dog the King loved (which shit in the boat which made all laugh and me to think that a King and all that belong to him are just as others are).'

Charles had been asked back to rule by a people who had experienced twelve years of Republican, Puritan-type experiments at government without a monarch, and so much did they hate the experience that they reverted to square one and, with great relief, welcomed back the son of the man they had allowed to be executed. They asked Charles back, surprisingly without conditions. They knew his history well enough to respect him as a man and in all probability (although you never really knew with the Stuarts) as a Protestant likely to keep the hated Catholics at bay. So the Parliament that welcomed Charles back had no greater governmental powers than it had possessed under Queen Elizabeth and the early Stuarts.

Charles would always live in fear of another revolution and would never forget the trial and decapitation of his father, but that did not much shake his inner conviction that he should be an absolute ruler, not a parliamentary puppet. And he was shrewd enough to see that he could pretty much get away with murder, since England had witnessed life with no king. Oppression had got worse, not better. So Charles knew that he could push his Parliaments hard, and if they didn't like it, he could keep dissolving them. By the time he died twenty-five years later, he had become an expert at the king versus Parliament game.

Charles built up his regime on a broad base with power-sharing at every governmental level. Old enemies and all religions (except way-out non-conformists and, of course, Catholics), as well as Cromwellians and Royalists alike, were all to be involved in handling the future of Britain. Charles devised an act to prevent religious intolerance, but Parliament blocked it and, because he desperately needed funds (the dilemma of all English and British monarchs in the days they had to fund their own wars), he gave in to the Clarendon Code which was a good deal less tolerant to both extreme Puritans and Catholics than the king had wanted.

The first war Charles became involved in was the Second Anglo-Dutch War. The First Dutch War, back in Cromwell's time, had been caused by English interference with Dutch trade. The second was fought for similar reasons and started well for the English, who captured New Amsterdam from the Dutch and renamed it New York in honour of the Lord Admiral, Charles's younger brother, James, Duke of York.

The big problem that Charles was to face through much of his reign was his need to constantly confirm to his Parliament that he was doing nothing that might bring back Catholicism to Britain. This meant that he would have to favour the Dutch against the French and Spanish. Yet he was related by marriage to both sides, a conundrum for any ruler. Both the Dutch and the French needed British help over the years, and Charles, often

Brigadier of Cavalry Maximilian-François de Fiennes who over the next twenty years fought on opposite sides to Fiennes Twisleton at all the major battles and many of the great sieges, including Namur (above) in 1695.

Battle of Culloden, 1746. General Henry Hawley, Susan Fiennes' great grandson, was known as 'Hangman Hawley'. General James Wolfe said of him: 'the troops dread his severity, hate the man and hold his military knowledge in contempt'.

My ancestor Samson Gideon 'the great oracle and leader of Jonathan's Coffee House in Exchange Alley' hugely helped the nation through his financial wizardry.

Major General Thomas Twisleton, great grandfather times six of the author, saved the Bank of England from the mob, killed as few rioters as possible and averted national chaos. He later committed suicide with a razor and sword.

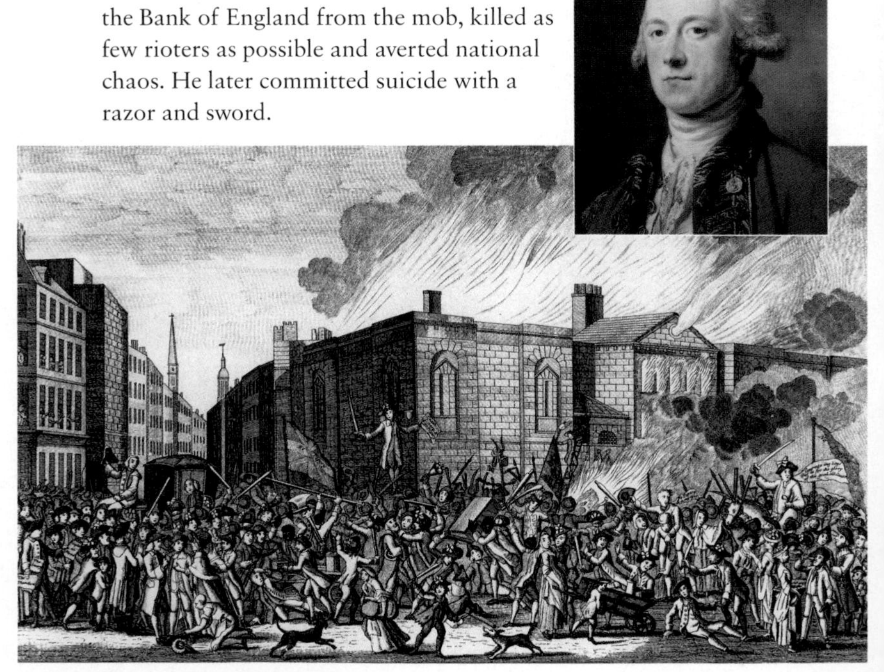

Gordon Riots, 1780, burning of Newgate Prison.

Elizabeth Fiennes, second cousin of Jane Austen, whose mother said of her; 'poor Lady Saye is to be sure rather tormenting though sometimes amusing and affords Jane many a good laugh. But she fatigues me sadly on the whole.'

A late nineteenth century illustration from *Sense and Sensibility*. The Twisletons not only afforded Jane Austen a good laugh, but also a good deal of material for her novels.

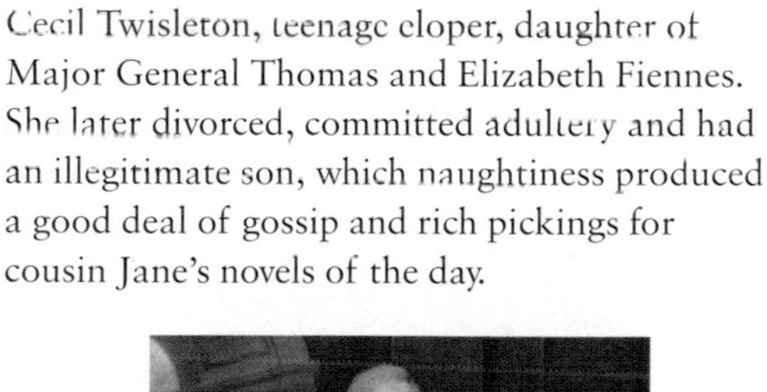

Cecil Twisleton, teenage eloper, daughter of Major General Thomas and Elizabeth Fiennes. She later divorced, committed adultery and had an illegitimate son, which naughtiness produced a good deal of gossip and rich pickings for cousin Jane's novels of the day.

Thomas James Twisleton, actor and eloper to Gretna Green aged 18, whilst still at school.

William Thomas Twisleton, a dandy and friend of the Prince Regent, Lord Byron and Beau Brummell, once said to a man-servant, 'Place two bottles of sherry by my bedside and call me the day after tomorrow'.

Life of a dandy. William's extravagance resulted in the abandonment of Broughton.

Frederick Benjamin Twisleton brought back the old family name of Twisleton-Wykeham-Fiennes by royal licence. His descendants include the author and the actors Ralph and Joseph Fiennes.

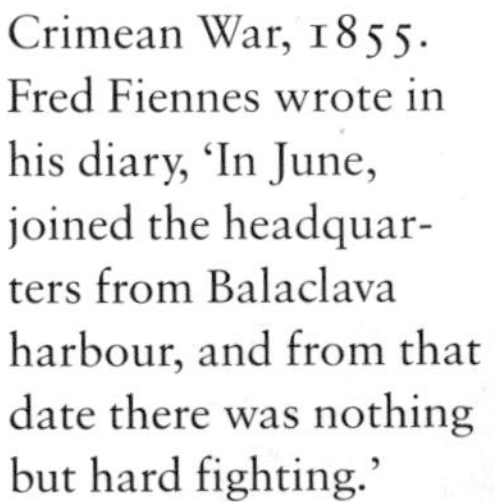

Crimean War, 1855. Fred Fiennes wrote in his diary, 'In June, joined the headquarters from Balaclava harbour, and from that date there was nothing but hard fighting.'

Eustace Fiennes (seated left) in the British South Africa Company's Police (1890-2), was just stopped by the British High Commission from chasing Portuguese troops to the sea.

Southern Command was extremely generous to Fiennes and Churchill. 'I recommend that these officers be excused this examination, Major Churchill has also to attend to official duties and Major Fiennes has a city business to look after. Both officers are natural leaders and thoroughly competent in every way.'

Captain John Fiennes, the author's uncle, was killed in 1917 aged twenty-one. He led a company of the 2nd battalion, the Gordon Highlanders, against German trenches at Arras. The carnage was unimaginable.

The author with the 2008 Master of Fiennes (the Institute) and Matron. Eustace Fiennes, Governor of the Leeward Islands 1921–9, built amenities for the sick and poor beyond his permitted budget. 'It is hoped,' noted the Colonial Office, 'that Sir Fiennes will pay more attention to Colonial Regulations.'

The author's father, Ranulph, leading 300 Royal Scots Greys, mounted, on exercise in the 1930s, prior to switching to tanks in Palestine in 1942.

THE "GREYS" AND THE DRAGON

Punch cartoon, 1937, 'in commemoration of the good news that this famous regiment has successfully defied mechanisation.' Nobody had seriously considered the sacrilege of 'mechanising' Scotland's Waterloo-famous and only cavalry regiment.

The author's father after Alamein, with Royal Scots Greys and crew. He was wounded on five separate occasions before dying of wounds in Italy in 1943.

Oliver Fiennes, Dean of Lincoln, with Ronald Reagan and Magna Carta at an exhibition in United States, in the 1980s.

Nathaniel Fiennes, 21st Lord Saye and Sele, his heir Martin, and eldest grandson Guy, with the author at Broughton Castle in 2009.

Meeting of the Fiennes clan at Broughton Castle at the Millennium, 2000. The author's mother (front row, third from left) was the oldest person there.

at odds with his Parliament, formed secret alliances and treaties with one or other, or even both at the same time.

Jokers in the pack were the Catholic Portuguese who wanted to be independent from both Spain and France and were happy when Charles, in 1662, married the Portuguese royal heiress, Catherine of Braganza. This brought Charles a considerable and desperately needed dowry, as well as control of Tangiers and Bombay, and a lovely, modest, loyal wife whom he loved all his life and who put up with his outrageous behaviour with dozens of mistresses, and a small army of illegitimate children. The English were initially highly suspicious of their new king taking a practising Catholic wife but her obvious harmlessness soon soothed their worries. However, Charles put up another black the same year by selling Dunkirk (which Cromwell's army had captured) back to his Catholic French cousin, Louis XIV for a hefty price.

Given a choice of aligning himself with his Catholic French relations or his Protestant Dutch ones, Charles chose France, primarily because they seemed to have an exhaustive exchequer, and in return for ongoing secret alliances Charles received vital funds which enabled him to yield over lesser issues to awkward, sometimes hostile, Parliaments. He could, in essence, survive without them so long as he kept cousin Louis happy (but did so always in secret).

One of Charles's biggest problems throughout his reign was that Queen Catherine never gave him a male heir, which meant that his younger brother, James, to whom he was always loyal, even under great provocation, was destined to become king on his death. Unfortunately, James was a not-so-secret practising Catholic who did not worship openly (which was against the Clarendon Code) but Parliament was highly suspicious of him throughout Charles's reign even when he made pregnant and married Anne Hyde, the daughter of Charles's Protestant Lord Chancellor, Clarendon.

Of the king's many loves, he acknowledged seven kept mistresses and, from them, fourteen children. He was good to them all, paid their upkeep and gave many of them titles. He became known as The Merry Monarch or Old Rowley, after a stallion known for producing many fine foals. The actress Nell Gwynne was the best known of the mistresses and most popular with the public, who nonetheless objected to paying taxes that were part spent on maintaining their ruler's many mistresses and illegitimate children. Of all the royal bastards, surprisingly enough, only one was to cause big trouble, mostly after Charles's death, and that was his first son James who he made the Duke of Monmouth and was from time to time a popular choice of some Parliamentarians as a better successor to the throne than Catholic James.

Rumours of ongoing debauchery at court did not help in 1665 when the war with Holland was going badly, and for the first time in many years an outbreak of the rat- and flea-borne bubonic plague scythed through the country. Despite being called the Great Plague at that time and ever since, it was in fact a pale image of earlier such pandemics. In London it began in early summer, and the king, court, mistresses and all fled to Salisbury, and Parliament to Oxford that July. Seven thousand people died in a single week, 75,000 in all and a fifth of the London population.

The law, unaltered since the plagues in Elizabeth's time, involved victims being sealed up in their homes along with all other current occupants, infected or not. Food and water, if they were lucky, would be put by the local watch-keepers into baskets which survivors lowered from upper windows. Doctors in fearful robes with masked beaks and waders were few and far between, as were priests to give last rites. The wealthy infected who could entice a doctor to attend them would invariably undergo vicious bloodletting, the infected blood being black, thick and vile-smelling, mixed with a green scum-like substance.

Not a good time for rumours of court debauchery, but the king and his brother received a timely boost to their waning popularity with the outbreak in 1666 of the Great Fire of London, which most people believed burnt so many rats, fleas, dirty hovels and putrid corpses that it stopped the plague, the last such bubonic outbreak to ravage England. In contrast to President Bush who received public odium for failing to react properly to the New Orleans flooding, King Charles and James, Duke of York were greatly applauded for their reaction to the great blaze which in four terrifying days of strong winds turned 14,000 houses, St Paul's Cathedral and eighty-seven churches into smouldering cinders. Working together with groups of volunteers and dangerously close to the inferno, the royal brothers joined the chain gangs of bucket-heaving firefighters for hours on end.

The public naturally blamed the Catholics for starting the fire and making 100,000 Londoners bereft. In the long term and entirely thanks to the influence and encouragement of the king, new London was rebuilt using the talents of Sir Christopher Wren.

Soon after the fire, the Second Dutch War came to a disgraceful end, from the British point of view. Following on from a series of naval defeats (including the drowning or burning to death of 6,000 British sailors at the Battle of Four Days), a masterful sally up the Medway by the Dutch navy, guided by two traitorous English pilots, put to the flames the pride of the anchored Royal Navy. Peace was made soon afterwards, but there were growing murmurs of dissent through the land, and the main target was, as ever, the unseen but ever present Catholic menace.

The king's scapegoat for the disgrace of the Dutch war was the Earl of Clarendon, who had been at the right hand of Charles for a quarter of a century. Politics are cruel. If Clarendon had stayed he would have been impeached and probably executed. As it was, he fled to France and power passed to the largely aristocratic grouping of Clifford, Arlington, Buckingham (Charles's childhood friend in exile), Ashley and Lauderdale. Their surnames spelled CABAL, and by that acronym they became known. Some of the Cabal favoured friendship with the Dutch and others with the French. The king ignored them in a polite and crafty manner, made a Treaty with Holland and, a year later in 1670, a similar Treaty with France. The second one, like several others, he naturally kept secret.

Despite the sometime failure of the Royal Navy, often under the capable command of James, Duke of York, Britain did well during Charles's reign in terms of increasing both colonies and trade. He granted the British East India Company the right to autonomous acquisition of territories, the right to form its own armies, build fortresses, make war and peace and, in their new lands, to be solely responsible for justice. In Canada he granted a royal charter to establish the largely Edinburgh-controlled Hudson's Bay Company, which is today the oldest corporation in Canada. Based on fur trading with the Indians, it ended up governing and colonising over three million square miles of North America. Not so successful was the Royal African Company which traded in slaves.

On the strictly domestic front arranged marriages were still the main way of ensuring that your family wealth and status increased, or were at least maintained. So elopements were anathema, and often blamed on the loose living example of the court. In 1670 an elopement seemed to spell disaster for the Broughton family.

After Old Subtlety's death, his son James became the 9th Lord Saye and Sele and 2nd Viscount Saye and Sele, and his eldest surviving daughter, Elizabeth, married Colonel John Twisleton who inherited Broughton. She was the only descendant from Old Subtlety's eight children to provide an heir for the barony. So the importance of who John and Elizabeth's only child, a daughter called Cecil, should marry could not be underestimated. After much consideration, John decided that the ideal match for their precious daughter would be her first cousin, another John Twisleton, who was three years older than she was. This John's father, Philip, was John Senior's younger brother, but first cousin marriages were common at the time. With Cecil marrying young John, all the Twisleton estates would be reunited in the family name.

John Senior was wont at the time to ask cousin John Junior

to many merry weekend parties, and another cousin (of a poor Twisleton branch) called George Twisleton was also invited, since both he and John Junior were of a similar age and both were training at Gray's Inn to be lawyers. John Senior had lost his Cromwellian-awarded baronetcy at the Restoration, but had since been made Sheriff of Kent, where most of his estates then were. My opinion of him is of a gloomy, but kindly, status-proud man. His wife, Elizabeth Fiennes, seems to have had many of the prudish traits of her mother, the scandalous yet ultra-Puritan wife of James, Lord Saye, who had gone off with the equally prudish Joshua Sprigge. So neither of Cecil's parents were likely to have been good company for their only daughter. She may well have pined for some excitement. This may explain why sexual attraction to her poor, but exciting, cousin George far outweighed her feelings of duty to her parents to marry her rich, but boring, cousin John Junior.

The 'wicked' George waited until three days after Cecil's fifteenth birthday before pouncing. He and a group of wild friends carried Cecil away on horseback at night, and the two young cousins married before her furious parents could prevent them. Today, in America, their marriage would have been illegal, for they shared the same Twisleton grandparents. But modern medical belief claims that genetic deformities in the children of first cousins are only 2 per cent higher than those of unrelated couples. The twenty-two-year-old George and his new teenage bride proceeded to live it up in London, and Cecil's father the furious Colonel John retaliated by leaving his entire estate to his nephew, John Junior. His will read: 'Whereas I have but one child living who has been very disobedient, married without my consent and has then run into great debts above the sum of two thousand pounds, I have therefore bequeathed all estates to my nephew John Twisleton and his heirs. To my daughter and her husband George I bequeath the sum of one hundred pounds.'

Even this miserly sum had twenty-seven conditions attached to it. He also tried to make sure that even if his nephew had no children, the estates could never revert to George and Cecil's line. Fate, however, was to favour the teenage elopers in the course of time, for they bred a healthy son who survived and to whom they gave the Christian name of Fiennes. This young Fiennes Twisleton had an unfortunate childhood because, not only did he see little of his merrymaking parents but was brought up by trustees, none other than the prudish Joshua Sprigge and the runaway former Viscountess Saye and Sele, who was now merely the ultra-Puritan, elderly Mrs Sprigge. From such subdued beginnings Fiennes was to go on to great things after the reign of Charles II.

When he was only two years into his reign, Charles had raised enough funds to commence the Third Anglo-Dutch War jointly with the French, and with his brother James still as Admiral of the Fleet. The war went badly and, after four major sea battles lost to the Dutch, Charles made peace on reasonable terms to all parties, but to the disgust of Parliament who turned down another attempt by Charles at that time to enact a law favouring religious tolerance, and substituted for it a new act that made things even more difficult for Catholics. James, Duke of York's wife Anne Hyde died, leaving him with two daughters and the duke's next wife Mary of Modena was an ardently Catholic lady whose mother was the niece of the notorious Cardinal Mazarin. The English, horrified that the wife of their future king was so dangerously Catholic, dubbed her 'the daughter of the Pope'.

The ruling Cabal faltered in 1673 (Clifford being sacked as scapegoat for the failed Dutch War) and their power as a group was eclipsed by the rising star of the Earl of Danby. Two of the Cabal, Buckingham and Ashley (who had become Lord Shaftesbury), formed a new party consisting of all the disparate elements who were discontent with the government. This party was to become the Whigs.

In 1677 powerful French armies attacked Holland and provoked an outcry for the English to help their Dutch Protestant neighbours. The powerful Danby agreed with this course before

Charles II, bearing in mind his secret alliance with France, could procrastinate. Tiny Holland saved itself by flooding some of its sea walls and, advised by Danby, Charles made an important pro-Dutch manoeuvre by marrying his niece Mary, one of his brother James's daughters, to William of Orange.

At about this time Thomas, a Lord Dacre descended from that Thomas Fiennes Dacre hanged for poaching, and the son of one of only twelve peers who had dared to object to Charles I's trial, made a name for himself by marrying one of Charles II's illegitimate daughters. He was promised £20,000 as a dowry which was never paid, and made the Earl of Sussex. Nonetheless, in later life he was to find enough funds to improve the old Fiennes family castle of Herstmonceux. This Thomas was the last descendant of the ancient families of Herst, Fiennes and Monceux to run Herstmonceux.

In 1678 a believable weirdo named Titus Oates, who had been both an Anglican and a Jesuit in his past, gave warnings of a complex Popish plot to assassinate the king and put Catholic James on the throne. He implicated several innocent ministers, various Catholic peers and even the queen in his fantastical conspiracy. Such was the anti-Catholic hysteria of the day that Oates was widely believed. Judges and juries condemned the long list of accused plotters, all of them innocent, and many were executed. Lord Danby himself was impeached and saved from death only by the king dissolving Parliament. Danby's supposed sin was to have planned the king's secret alliance with France (which was eventually revealed to the public). The next Parliament refused to allow Danby's acquittal, and he was confined to the Tower for five years.

Parliament's next attack on Charles was known as the Exclusion Bill and was designed to legally prevent the, by then, openly Catholic James, Duke of York becoming James II on Charles II's death. The ex-Cabal member, Lord Shaftesbury, was the bill's main mover, so the Whig Party that he had formed became synonymous with the Exclusion Bill, whilst their political rivals, who came to be known as Tories, opposed the bill. Tories were named after dispossessed Catholic Irish bandits, and Whigs, or Whigamores, was a term for rebellious Scottish Presbyterians.

To avoid the passing of the Exclusion Bill, Charles dissolved Parliament four times in three years, and by 1681 popular sentiment turned against troublemaker Shaftesbury and his Exclusion-bent Whigs. The bottom line was the national fear that, if excluded from his rightful succession, James would start a new civil war, and that was just about the only thing that none of the rival factions wanted.

In the spring of 1681, Charles felt ready to make a master move because another secret alliance with Louis XIV had assured him that France would back him against Parliament, with force if need be. First Charles, by a royal prerogative never before used, summoned Parliament to meet in royalist Oxford away from the Whig crowds of London. And when they did, he surprised them all with another prerogative by turning up in full royal garb and declaring Parliament dissolved until further notice. For the rest of his reign he ruled without Parliament, supported by funds from France and the basic fact that his country was at peace and desperately anxious to avoid more civil strife. A trade boom helped, and a new plot to murder both the king and James and to re-establish a Cromwellian style government backfired and provoked sympathy for him. This led to the arrest of the alleged plotters, who included the old arch-enemy of the king, Lord Shaftesbury, and even Titus Oates.

By 1685, the year he died and the twenty-fifth year of his reign, Charles II had handed over much of the running of the kingdom to his brother James. He still signed the documents, but mainly he spent time with his many mistresses and children, with his beloved wife, and in his private science laboratory where he loved to experiment. Science had prospered greatly under Charles, the founder of the Royal Society. Anatomy, physiology and the discovery of blood circulation, along with much of Isaac Newton's work, had taken great strides. So too had chemistry, geology and the predictable movement of heavenly bodies. The country's agriculture and economy still depended on human and animal power, but the world of magic and spells had, by 1640, become outmoded and the cruel centuries of witch prosecution ended.

Charles died in his bed at Windsor Castle after a short illness and the diarist John Evelyn wrote of him, 'He was a prince of many virtues and many great imperfections, debonair, easy of access, not bloody or cruel.'

He left a nation governed by those who believed in the Divine Right of Kings, the divine right of the Church of England, and the divine right of local regions to run their own affairs. After all the traumas of the Exclusion Bill and so many hostile anti-Catholic Parliaments, Charles had the last laugh, for his brother was now secure in his succession from his Protestant rivals, the Duke of Monmouth and William of Orange.

When Charles II died and James II came to the throne, my great to the power of eight grandfather, Fiennes Twisleton, had been at Winchester College for two years but was still in the bottom form. Only four years later he would command the forces that favoured the middle way against absolutism from left or right.

23

Ride a Cock Horse

James Stuart, long-time Duke of York, long-time royal heir in waiting, came to the throne of Britain in 1685 as an acknowledged Catholic prepared to accept Protestant ways, and as such was just about acceptable, providing he did not rock the boat, because both his daughters were Protestant. This acceptance, grudging by many factions both religious and political, was hugely helped by all those who still remembered the bloodshed of the Civil War and the grey gloom of the Interregnum.

So when, with a reasonable amount of celebratory joy that his accession had at least been peaceful, his people welcomed his crowning, James expected to be succeeded by his Protestant daughter Mary and her Dutch Protestant husband, Prince William of Orange. He had been a loyal, if sometimes irritating, supporter of his brother Charles II throughout the twenty-five years of that reign and was already fifty-two when crowned. The basic difference between the two brothers was the degree of their attachment to and belief in the Catholic form of worship.

Once on the throne James forgave the Whig Exclusionists who had tried in vain to block his accession. He kept most existing ministers in their jobs and was granted by Parliament a very generous life income. It seemed, after a month or two, that all would go reasonably well between the new king and his Parliament, even though he clearly worked harder and paid more attention to the governance of the realm than had his brother. And he was less prepared to compromise when his ministers disagreed with his wishes.

Trouble, unfortunately, arrived only a few weeks after the coronation in the form of two co-ordinated Protestant rebellions, both of which were planned in Holland with the full knowledge of William of Orange. The Scottish rebellion was led by the powerful clan leader of the Campbells, the Duke of Argyll, who sailed from Holland and raised a meagre host of Highlanders, but was easily defeated and captured at Inchinnan. This was a mere eight weeks after James was made king, but the royal reaction was instant. Argyll's head was severed on the Edinburgh block.

The other more menacing part of the rebellion came from James's nephew, the illegitimate James, Duke of Monmouth, who had long been personally popular in England, especially in the south-west. So with eighty-two followers he landed at Lyme Regis and had already raised over 4,000 armed men when, at Sedgemoor, near Taunton, he was confronted by the Royalist army under John Churchill (later to be the famous general and Duke of Marlborough). The Royalists won the day and King James's revenge was ruthless. Sedgemoor was the last battle ever fought on English soil and is remembered to this day.

I live on Exmoor, near Taunton, and pass the Sedgemoor battlefield twice weekly on the M5. My late wife's ancestor was King James's 'Bloody' Judge Jeffreys, who hanged suspected Monmouth men for months after the battle and left their bodies swinging at crossroad gibbets until they rotted. Local families, whose ancestors were gibbeted, still had meaningful words with my wife in the 1980s.

Monmouth himself, clearly a spirited character and thirty-six years old at the time, was clapped in the Tower, whence he sent letters to his uncle pleading mercy. He received no reply, and nine days after the battle he faced the axe-man, Jack Ketch (notorious at the time for making a mess of various aristocratic lopping jobs), and said, 'Do not hack at me as you did my Lord Russell', whereupon he gave Ketch six guineas to ensure a good clean cut. History recalls that on the fourth blow Monmouth's head came clean away and 320 others of his fellow rebels were hanged, drawn and quartered for good measure.

The king was determined to ready himself for attacks from other quarters. Maybe he had his Protestant son-in-law, William of Orange, in mind. After all, he had been Lord High Admiral in two wars against him. So he began to recruit an enlarged standing army, something which was completely contrary to the English tradition of raising a national army only when needed (and thereby avoiding a huge drain on the exchequer). This act by the king rang alarm bells for many, even loyal, subjects: Charles II had not needed such an army, so why should James, unless he had some Popish plot up his sleeve? Worse still, many of the commanding officers of James's new regiments were practising Catholics. The previously supportive Parliament objected strongly to James's military behaviour, so he prorogued them never to meet again during his reign.

His religious activities were to trigger his downfall, and one year into his rule his true colours began to show. Previously, like Charles II before him, his attempts to help Catholics were always disguised as a search for overall religious tolerance because they were always bracketed with similar favours for Dissenters. But James was a pig-headed believer in the straightforward Divine Right of Kings. What he wanted, nobody should stop him from obtaining. Unlike Charles II, who ruled for twenty-five years through the art of compromise, pragmatism and procrastination, James was a bull let loose in a china shop. A few of his early faux pas, which alienated friend and foe alike, included allowing Roman Catholics into the highest of offices, inviting a papal nuncio to visit his court, the first such liaison since Bloody Mary's day, and replacing the holders of court offices with Catholic favourites. In 1687 he issued the Declaration of Indulgence, which negated the effects of the existing laws that punished Catholics and Dissenters. He then, in 1688, reissued the divisive Declaration and commanded that it be read out in every church in the land. The Archbishop of Canterbury and six bishops naturally objected to the king, who promptly arrested them all for seditious libel.

In a very short time the king's insensitive, indeed stupid, behaviour had lost him the support of great chunks of the populace who he could previously have counted upon as loyal. The final crunch came in June 1688 when his Catholic wife produced a male heir. Previously, people could put up with his reign in the knowledge that his successors were his Protestant daughters, Mary and Anne by his first marriage, but not with this new threat of a permanent Catholic dynasty.

James was blind to the dangerous pit he was busily digging for himself. He believed that if he insisted that his way was best, then aristocrats, gentry and Tories would go along with him through lack of an alternative. He was, of course, forgetting that his own Protestant daughter Mary was married to Prince William, the heroic defender on mainland Europe of all Protestant states against the powerful Catholic armies of the French.

By the summer of 1688 enough was enough, and Anglican leaders secretly invited James's daughter and son-in-law to help them remove their king. Plainly speaking, they were plotting to replace the Catholic Stuarts with Protestant Stuarts. From Prince William's point of view, this was a great chance to increase his anti-French power base whilst ensuring that Britain ceased being a potential French ally. The resulting agreement by Prince William and his English wife to 'invade' England and protect the English from their king's Catholic ambitions came to be called the Glorious Revolution: glorious partly because it came about through the unlikely agreement of anti-Catholic Whigs and previously Stuart-friendly Tories in a settlement designed to avoid bloodshed. Assuming its success, England would switch from a Catholic monarch to, not one but two Protestant rulers who would, if that's what they wanted, become Queen Mary II and King William III.

When, in September 1688, it became clear that William was

about to sail for England (after many rumours that had proved false), individuals had to show where their true sympathies lay. Only a minority were willing to join the invasion by taking up arms, but even fewer were willing to show any meaningful support for their king. James refused assistance from Louis XIV of France because he believed that he could deal with things himself and that he would only blot his copybook forever if he invited a French Catholic army to help subdue his own subjects.

Before James could even raise his battle standard, his hoped for adherents began to jump the sinking ship like so many rats. Importantly, John Churchill, his senior army leader, defected to join the prince's forces. The king, stricken by nosebleeds and behaving in a bizarre and erratic fashion, halted at Salisbury, and before the two armies could meet he fled back to London where he was netted by William's men. He escaped and, seeing the hopelessness of his situation, put to sea but, visiting a Kent port for vital ballast, was seized, placed under guard and presented with a summary of Prince William's proposals. This, which was probably his last chance of remaining at least a parliamentary puppet-king, he refused, and the prince, not wishing to have James made any sort of martyr, happily let him flee to France.

John Evelyn wrote: '18th: I saw the King take barge at Gravesend at twelve o'clock – a sad sight! The Prince comes to St James's and fills Whitehall with Dutch guards . . . All the world go to see the Prince at St James's, where there is a great Court. He is very stately, serious and reserved. The English soldiers sent out of town to disband them; not well pleased.'

On arrival in France James was given a palace and a pension by his cousin and ally Louis XIV, whilst back home his daughter and son-in-law set up their Protestant shop by convening a Convention Parliament. Instant deposition was not on the cards, but since James had effectively abdicated the throne, the resulting vacancy was therefore declared filled by his daughter. She was crowned Queen Mary II and her husband King William III. A Bill of Rights was quickly passed which declared James to have forfeited his crown and which stipulated that no Catholic would ever again be permitted to ascend to the English throne or be married to an English monarch. William and Mary agreed to everything put forward by the Convention, which was made up entirely of the propertied classes, and so was in no circumstances a social revolution like the one in France would be.

Nonetheless, the Declaration of Rights agreed between the new dual monarchs and Parliament in 1689 did curtail the previous royal prerogative and established a parliamentary monarchy which, with absolutist monarchs prevalent through most of the world at the time, was a huge step forward towards the ideal of genuine democracy. From then on no monarch in Britain could rule without the majority support of Parliament.

Mary had married William in 1677 when she was fifteen and he twenty-seven. She had lived in Holland for eleven formative years and learnt to treat it as her home. She and William had, after a slow start, fallen in love with one another, and when in 1688 they became King and Queen of England, they were patently homesick for Holland. Mary had to stick it out, but William escaped whenever he could to command his Dutch forces in their ongoing fight against the French and to train a fledgling British army from mostly raw recruits into, eventually, the most effective army in Europe some twenty years later.

William, already the most determined of France's enemies, now became their formidable foe, not only because he had stopped any likelihood of England joining forces with Stuart-supporting France, but whatever English forces he could now muster would definitely be used *against* the French. The direct result of the Glorious Revolution was therefore to involve Britain in major European warfare. Firstly, the Nine Years War from 1688 to 1697 and, in Queen Anne's reign, the War of Spanish Succession from 1702 to 1713, England's first continental warfare since the days of the Elizabethan struggle with Spain.

In 1689 William and Mary were forced into war with France as a matter of survival, for there was a very real danger that

Louis XIV would try to restore James II to the throne. As it was, in March that year, with a powerful force of 6,000 French troops, James did land in Ireland where the Irish Parliament declared that he was still their king. In the two years prior to William's arrival in England, Irish Catholics had retained their ascendancy over Protestants, and many of the latter had begun to sell up and sail for England. By the time James arrived in Ireland with his French or 'Jacobite' army, Catholics controlled everywhere except Londonderry and Enniskillen in the far north. James ordered these towns to surrender, but neither would, so his army laid siege to both.

The key to subsequent Protestant survival in Ireland depended entirely on whether or not these two vital strongpoints could hold out long enough to provide the secure landing points for the army that William was desperately putting together in England. William decided to send a naval force to relieve the 30,000 starving and disease-ridden citizens of Londonderry and the man chosen to lead the tiny relief force was none other than young Fiennes Twisleton, sole heir of the teenage elopers, first cousins George and Cecil Twisleton. I must explain the background to his arrival at the Londonderry siege as I left him as a young lad in penury and cut out of his grandparents' will.

His CV can be found on a plain stone slab in the church at Broughton Castle, the home he loved and where he died after fighting for Britain for many years in many lands. Aged twelve, he went to live with the ultra-Puritan trustees appointed by his grandfather. Somebody must have realised that, despite the disgraceful behaviour of his parents, Fiennes could benefit from a free Wykehamist education. So he was sent to Winchester aged twelve, and was there aged thirteen and a half when both his Sprigge trustees died and he presumably returned to his gadabout parents. School records show that, of the five years he was at the college, he spent three of them in the bottom form, so he naturally chose the army for a career.

Many years later I took my Common Entrance exam for

Winchester, hoping to get some advantage in the 1950s from the long-ago family connection. But my results were so low that they would not accept me, and I had to go to Eton where, after five years, I failed to pass the A-Levels necessary for Sandhurst. The British army had obviously become a lot fussier in between Fiennes Twisleton's day and mine.

Fresh from college, Fiennes joined the Oliver Nicholas Regiment of Foot as an ensign on 25 November 1685. He rose through the commissioned ranks rapidly and, as a captain, was sent by ship to relieve Londonderry in command of a small force who ran the gauntlet of Jacobite patrols up Lough Foyle, cut the siege-force boom that blocked the river and managed, after much excitement, to deliver two ships laden with vital provisions to save the starving garrison. The Londonderry success fired up the only other Protestant garrison in Enniskillen, who broke out and beat up their besiegers. These two successes gave William a firm base in Ulster from which to start reconquering Ireland. Records show that Fiennes Twisleton married an Irish girl, one Mary Clarke, at Dublin Castle in 1692.

When William replaced the last Stuart king of England, there was surprisingly little resulting trouble from the Scots. In the Highlands the Viscount Dundee did rally the clans, who clashed successfully with William's men at the Pass of Killiecrankie. Two thousand Highlanders with claymores charged a thicket of musket-firing troops and cut off the heads of all those who could not reload quickly enough. Sadly for the clans, Dundee was killed and his men went back to their farms, where they were ruthlessly murdered by William's patrols. There would be no further trouble with the Jacobites in Scotland until the time of the Hanoverians.

William's army, once fully established in Ireland, numbered some 30,000 and was a far more complex mix than merely a Protestant force arrived to save Irish Protestants from their Catholic oppressors. That was, of course, William's immediate aim, but the wider context was pan-European and crossed religious boundaries. The Pope had become just as worried as William by the huge territorial gains of the all-powerful King Louis XIV, the long-time friend of the Stuarts and instigator of James II's invasion of Ireland. So, weird bedfellows indeed, the components of William's army included Dutch Catholics, French Huguenots, English and Scottish Presbyterians, Italians, Poles, Danes, Germans, Norwegians and Protestant Irish.

James's force, lined up against the above mongrel horde, was mainly made up of Irish Catholics and some 6,000 French regulars with a few English and Scots Jacobites thrown in. The ensuing battle was fought around the river Boyne, and although over 50,000 soldiers were involved, a mere 2,500 were killed, mainly because when James's army retreated, William's did not follow them up, due to the difficult terrain. In purely Irish terms, the battle was the saving of the Irish Protestants. From a British point of view, the Jacobite threat – the return of the Stuarts – was from then on a lost cause. And, in a European context, the Boyne was the first victory of a multinational force of combined Catholic and Protestant groups come together to block further French control of Europe.

King James II fled back to France immediately after the battle, where he was to die a distant Jacobite menace, eleven years later. Ironically, one of the titles, bestowed on him by the French King, was Duke of Normandy. After the Battle of the Boyne, William no longer had to worry overmuch about Ireland, Scotland, the Jacobites or, indeed, lingering Stuart supporters in England. So his focus returned to the main drive of his life: to stop the spread of the French empire over Europe, especially the Netherlands.

From 1691 to 1697 he therefore spent every campaigning season on the continent, for he knew, without conceit, that only he – a simple Calvinist who was perfectly happy with any and all other forms of worship including Catholicism but hostile to domination by any one power – could hold together the international alliance which had worked so well fighting together in Ireland. In these wars Fiennes Twisleton fought for William against the

French general, Maximilian-François de Fiennes, their ancestral connection going back to Henry III.

Although King William spent a great deal of his time fighting abroad (whilst Queen Mary proved a more than competent and much loved ruler of Britain in his absence) and although he kept a mistress throughout their marriage (Betty Villiers was originally one of Mary's ladies-in-waiting), William nonetheless loved his queen very much and they worked extremely well together as joint rulers. They had no surviving children and were always happy that they would be succeeded by Mary's younger sister, Anne Stuart who, married to Prince George of Denmark, also had no surviving children.

Mary's conscience was never at rest over her father's exile and the usurping of his throne by her husband, even though her motivation in going along with it in the first place had been her sincere Protestant beliefs. The public always loved her and she was revered as much as was Elizabeth I, although she was queen for only five and a half years and died aged thirty-two. Although no great beauty, several love ballads were printed during Mary's reign which featured illustrative woodcuts depicting the queen with exposed breasts. These sold in great numbers.

Her sister Anne was a shy girl who rarely responded to Mary's normal lively chatter but was for many years in platonic love with and in thrall to her childhood friend, Sarah Jennings. This Sarah later married the senior army commander, John Churchill, who had deserted James II in his hour of need. King William disliked Churchill as a turncoat, and in 1692 dismissed him from the army. When Anne continued to consort with the sacked Churchill's wife in public, Queen Mary was furious, and the two sisters never spoke again. This is the only record of 'unpleasant' behaviour by Mary. In 1694 Mary caught smallpox and took a week to die, during which a distraught William slept by her bedside and was inconsolable. When Mary died, William sacked his mistress Betty Villiers (a bit late in the day) and never married again.

William then ruled alone but was never popular. For no good

reason, other than the fact that he was foreign. The country prospered under his sensible rule, as is witnessed in a uniquely valuable description of the country during his reign by a lone horsewoman who wrote meticulous notes on all her travels through every county in England. The result is still available in most bookshops as *The Diaries of Celia Fiennes*. Historians of the late seventeenth and early eighteenth centuries quote heavily from her text.

Celia's grandfather was Old Subtlety and her father was his second son, the famous General Nathaniel Fiennes (almost hanged by Cromwell for losing Bristol to the Royalists). She often stayed at Broughton. Celia was born in 1662, the year of Old Subtlety's death, and little was known about her unique travels until her remarkable and extensive diary was first printed in an unedited version in 1887. Edited versions in 1947 and 1949 suffered from nasty post-war paper and printing, but attractively illustrated versions have been constantly reprinted since 1982.

Three of her four sisters died as babies, but the survivor married a merchant who traded with the Turks in London, and there Celia based herself after her mother died. In 1697 she decided that she would do what no other woman did at the time, never mind ones of her social class. She would travel and see the world outside London, or at least as much of England as possible, and make notes of all she saw. She set out on her first journey aged thirty-five and rode side-saddle. She put up with the most uncomfortable, dangerous conditions, being stared and hooted at in towns, sleeping and eating in filthy inns, facing up to highwaymen (who frequented wild areas like Hampstead Heath), fleeing from floods, falling into deep mud in which her horse floundered, and getting badly lost in remoter areas.

In the 1940s I was brought up by my mother to recite the nursery rhyme 'Ride a Cockhorse', and was assured that the words were based upon the travels of my ancestor, Celia. The line 'Ride a cockhorse to Banbury Cross to see a fine lady upon a white horse' I was told was a corruption of the original 'see a

Fiennes lady'. This seemed all the more likely to me due to the fact that I was born the 3rd Baronet of Banbury and one of my elder sisters was called Celia. Whether or not the Fiennes version of the rhyme is true, nobody has been able to confirm.

The first official signposts were erected in England in 1697, the very year Celia set out on her first journey accompanied by her manservant, William Butcher. 'At all cross wayes,' she noted, 'there are Posts and Hands pointing to each road with the names of the great towns that it leads to, which does make up for the length of the miles that strangers may not lose their road. 'Sadly, she later found many a crossroad further from London where signposts had either been removed by locals, rotated by highwaymen or simply never erected. She never explored Scotland or Wales in great depth, although arriving near Mount Snowdon, she was told that nobody knew what was 'up there' because 'there be dragons'. 'At Holywell,' she wrote, 'they speak Welsh, the inhabitants go barefoot and bare legged, a nasty sort of people.'

She also had a poor and ill-informed opinion of the Scots. 'Thence I went into Scotland . . . all here about which are called Borderers, seem to be very poor people which I impute to their sloth . . . two or three great wenches as tall and big as any women sat hovering between their bed and chimney corner all idle doing nothing, though it was nine of the clock when I came thither, having gone seven long miles that morning.'

Further south in a Durham 'chappell', she observed: 'here is the only place that they use these things in England (fine embroyder'd Coapes), and severall more Cerimonyes and Rites retained from the tymes of Popery; there are many papists in the town and popishly affected, and dayly encrease . . . I happen'd to get into a quiet good inn . . . two maiden sisters and brother kept it, at the Naggs Head.'

In Halifax her focus was on their unique system of dispensing justice, 'The town now being almost ruined . . . and the Engine that the town was famous for – to be head their criminalls at one stroake with a pully – this was destroyed since their Charter of Liberty was lost or taken from them because they most barbarously and rigourously acted even with an absolute power which they had of all the town; on these informations I resolved not to go to that ragged town.' The engine in question was used for the instant execution of cloth thieves in the local market. It was the model for the 'Scottish Maiden' which was later the inspiration of Dr Guillotine's finished article in Paris.

In Northwich Celia excitedly made a financial investment in the very first discovery of rock salt in England, 'It's not very large,' she noted of the town, 'it's full of Salt works, the brine pitts being all here and about and so they make all things convenient to follow the makeing the salt, so that the town is full of smoak from the salterns on all sides.' At Land's End she described tin and copper mining in great detail, and praised the Cornish for their cleanliness and their ales.

She loved the spas in Bath, but that of Harrogate, called 'The Sulphur' or 'Stincking Spaw', she described as 'not improperly termed for the Smell being so strong and offensive I would not force my horse near the Well.' In Bristol Celia describes an almshouse for better-off folk. 'The one side is for the women, the other for the men . . . and a middle room in common for washing and brewing . . . They have their coales and 3 shillings per weeke allowed to each to maintaine them; this is for decayed tradesmen and wives that have lived well.' Of the city itself she writes: 'The streets are narrow and sometimes darkish because the roomes on the upper storys are more jutting out, soe contracts the streete and the light . . . This town is a very great tradeing citty as most in England, and is esteemed the largest next London; the river Aven, that is flowed up by the sea into the Severn and soe up the Aven to the town, beares shipps and barges to the key.'

From the shore, Celia described the Eddystone Lighthouse. 'You can just discover a light house which is building on a meer rock in the middle of the sea. This is 7 leagues off. It will be of great advantage for the guide of the shipps.' Soon after Celia wrote this, in 1697, the resident Eddystone architect, Henry

Winstanley, was captured on the rock by the French, but Louis XIV agreed to liberate him as 'a benefactor to humanity'. However, he was drowned six years later when a huge wave struck the rock.

Celia also made polite comments on the structurally brilliant design of Mount Edgcumbe, 'a seate of Sir Richard Edgcomes'. This was the magnificent manor on the Cornish coast spotted by the Commander of the Spanish Armada, who told his officers that once they had command of all England, he would reserve it for his own possession.

Celia was always at her most enthusiastic when describing the various sights and scenes in the London area. The countryside between Westminster town and London itself, she noted, had just begun to be urbanised but you could still shoot woodcock in what is now Regent Street. There were nearly one million people in the whole of the newly expanded London, out of a total English population of nearly seven million. Celia wrote: 'there is alsoe one Nobleman's house . . . Parke House, which is a very curious building.' She later noted of this place, 'Arlington, now the Duke of Buckinghams, being newly built.' She was talking about Arlington House, which was pulled down a few months later, then became Buckingham House, and finally Buckingham Palace. Of London Bridge, Celia wrote: 'The Bridge . . . with 18 arches, most of them bigg enough to admit a large barge to pass it; it's so broade that two coaches drives abreast and there is on each side houses and shopps just like any large streete in the Citty.' The houses on the bridge had been rebuilt after the Great Fire of 1666, but were again burnt down in 1758 and never replaced.

Celia visited Parliament and observed: 'Westminster Hall has appartments, the one for the House of Lords and called the Upper House, where all the Lords which are not Papists and which are of age do sitt in their order on benches covered with scarlet cloth; the Bishops likewise sitt as peers of the realme and have voice in all causes but in bloud.' This meant that bishops could not be involved in sentencing which might lead to death or mutilation.

Celia observed further that these Lords 'which are peeres of the realme are born Councellors to the King and are looked on as such; it's true tho' at all tymes, they may and should give the King their advice, yet the King has power and do make choice of a Privy Councill.'

Moving on to the fashion centre of town, Hyde Park, Celia wrote: 'Hide-Park is for rideing on horseback but mostly for the coaches, there being a Ring railed in, round which a gravel way that would admitt of twelve if not more rowes of coaches, which the Gentry to see each other, comes and drives round and round; one rowe going contrary to each other affords a pleasing diversion. The rest of the Parke is green and full of deer; there are large ponds full of fish and fowle.'

All travellers made comparisons between London and Paris. Paris, the largest city in France, had 350,000 citizens, Rouen and Lyon a mere 90,000. London was bigger than the next fifty towns in England and had a near stranglehold on overseas trade, but most of the towns Celia visited offered her a wide choice of produce, including American tobacco, Yorkshire ironmongery, West Indian sugar, fancy metalwork from Sheffield, pottery from Stoke, and cloth goods from Leeds.

All this trade led to innovations in banking, which included the setting up of the Bank of England, which made big, much-needed loans to William's government in the 1690s. During William's wars these loans were vital to his ongoing success but, in the longer term, the development in London and Edinburgh of experiments in long-term credit enabled Britain to emerge from the wars more quickly than France, a country with a larger population and far greater resources. London soon overtook Amsterdam as the financial capital of Europe. For a while Isaac Newton was Master of the Mint, which reflected the fact that in both economics and scientific theory, the Britain of William and Mary led the way. The number of new patents for new British inventions also increased greatly at the time.

Despite all this, the British public never took to King William, nor did his Parliaments. He, in turn, hated them, complaining in public that 'the Commons use me like a dog'. William's military triumphs abroad were eclipsed by Commons xenophobia. They even disbanded most of the hugely efficient and experienced British army that he had fashioned. William rightly, but futilely, warned against further troubles. Parliament, he said, had done in a day to his army what Louis XIV had been unable to do in eight years. He even considered abdicating, furious at the ingratitude of the British.

After Mary's death, William, basically a kindly and polite man, reconciled his family with Princess Anne and her Danish princely husband. He gave her St James's Palace and even restored her favourites, the Marlborough family, to Royal favour. He had, after Mary's death, retired into the company of his mostly Dutch courtiers and, when he needed a society hostess, he would ask Anne to fill the role. In February 1702 William's horse tripped against a molehill whilst he was riding in Richmond Park. This led to his final illness, and vindictive Jacobites (the general term for pro-Stuart folk) were later prone to drink many a toast to 'The little gentleman in the velvet waistcoat.' William died a month later and was found to be wearing a lock of his beloved Mary's hair around his neck.

His death was not lamented in Britain, although by all he had done as king, it should have been. Daniel Defoe summed it up well. 'The dislike of the English people ate into William's very soul, tired it with serving an ungrateful nation and absolutely broke his heart.'

24

Fiennes vs. Fiennes

The childless Anne became Queen of England and Scotland in March 1702 in the knowledge that her Catholic half-brother, James III, considered himself the rightful heir. He lived in exile with his father James II, hovering like a vulture, or rather like some French-controlled hawk, just across the Channel. His supporters, the Jacobites, kept a low profile in England, but less so in Scotland and, over in France, proclaimed him loudly as the rightful English king.

The year before Anne's succession, Parliament had passed the Act of Settlement, which finalised the succession process that is still in force today. It overruled the hereditary rights of the House of Stuart (apart from Anne) and the legitimacy of fifty-seven potential Stuart Catholic claimants, and thereby gave priority to take over, as constitutional monarchs subservient to Parliament, a Hanoverian dynasty who were Anne's cousins, being the descendants of James I's daughter Elizabeth. They were middle-of-the-road Protestants with no real power base in Europe, being merely junior German princes. Parliament ignored the fact that none of them spoke a word of English, because they were the perfect answer to the succession should Anne remain childless.

Unfortunately, the Scots put their usual spanner into the works by passing their own bill in 1704 which emphasised their absolute right to choose their own ruler. The English hit back with a stick (to deport all Scots living in England) and a carrot in the shape of a huge financial settlement and an Act of Union which would unite both Parliaments. The Scots finally accepted this new joint state set-up, even though it specified, should Anne die childless, that their own independent monarchy going back to the ninth century would cease to exist. This new Anglo-Scottish state would be called the Kingdom of Great Britain, with a Union flag (designed by James I), a British government, and a British army to look after the ever-expanding British empire.

William of Orange had left Anne a legacy, in England at least, of a fairly liberal, if argumentative, political system in a reasonably free society which would become before long the wonder of eighteenth-century Europe. He had also developed the British army into a force of 60,000 men which formed the foundation of the efficient machine that John Churchill, Earl of Marlborough, would later use to conquer the mighty forces of Louis XIV.

So Anne's foreign policy was a simple continuation of William's. The Grand Alliance of Holland, Britain and the Emperor would continue to keep the greedy French in their place. In May 1702 Anne declared war on France in response to aggressive moves by Louis XIV. Her declaration of war was a fair one, but the war was to last for twelve long years and provide a main issue of contention between the grandees of the Whig and the Tory parties.

Anne firmly believed in the monarch's right to choose her own ministers, and amongst her chosen batch during her twelve-year reign was Lord Godolphin, whom she had known since childhood and who was neither Tory nor Whig, for he saw his task as managing government. As lord treasurer he sought support in Parliament from wherever he could muster it, Whig or Tory. He was a man of the centre, as was Anne's great general, the newly promoted Duke of Marlborough, who she made, to all intents, into her foreign secretary. Her third main man, Robert Harley, whom she described as dark, cunning, disagreeable and ambiguous, was selected due to his remarkable way with the

Commons, where his oratory and instinct could sway the most intractable opposition.

Ambitious men wanting to be ministers would often seek out the queen's long-time favourite, Sarah Churchill, Duchess of Marlborough (often cattily called 'Queen Sarah') as the best stepping stone to royal favour. The duke did not like Sarah's Whiggish views but, being as indulgent a husband as he was fierce a warrior, he refrained from tackling her politics. Theirs was a life-long love match and it was said that on return from campaigns he would 'pleasure her with his boots on'.

In 1702 the duke's armies did well in Flanders, with Fiennes Twisleton a senior commander with his foot soldiers, and Maximilian Fiennes a brigadier of cavalry in the French army. He was later promoted to marshal. 1704 was a good year for Marlborough and his armies, starting with the Battle of Blenheim which was long, complex and vicious. Marlborough, the victor, made his name that day. The myth of French invincibility on the European battlefield was destroyed, and a grateful nation, recalling the days of Henry V and Agincourt, hailed Marlborough as their hero. His reward was Blenheim Palace, named to rub salt into French wounds.

In 1704 the French did well in Spain and their Marshal of the Army, Maximilian Fiennes, commanded at the Siege of Gibralter. The Duke of Berwick joined him that November and the two cooperated to take the vital city of Carthagena, after which Fiennes was promoted to lieutenant general. It is confusing enough to accept that the English Duke of Berwick was a senior commander in the French army, but even more so when one remembers that he was also the nephew of the Duke of Marlborough.

In 1706 Marlborough struck back with a victory at Ramillies, during which affray a cannon ball flew between his legs and blew off his equerry's head. His army killed 15,000 Frenchmen to only 4,000 of their own dead and won back nearly all the Spanish Netherlands, gaining in a single day what all the years of William III's campaigning in the region had failed to achieve.

The next year, however, saw the Duke of Berwick and his colleague General Max Fiennes crushing the allies, including Colonel Fiennes Twisleton, at the Battle of Almanza. Cousin Max followed this up by a famous victory at Lerida. From a foreign affairs point of view, therefore, it was a bad year for Anne but, back home, her government finally concluded the Act of Union.

On 6 March 1707 parliamentary and royal assents were officially accorded to three items on the agenda of the day: to the Act to Try to Stop the Escape of Convicts; to the Act to Repair the Road between Hockliffe and Woodborne; and, almost incidentally, to the Act of Union with Scotland. In November that year the queen drove to open the very first Parliament of Great Britain which was to remain the greatest domestic achievement of her reign.

That arch-strategist, Louis XIV, did not take long to notice the considerable disquiet which the Act of Union was causing amongst Jacobites. So he energised the twenty-year-old Pretender, James Stuart, and provided him with troops and a fleet to help him on his way to rally all Jacobites and to claim his throne. In the event the whole invasion plan foundered with the French fleet off Scotland failing to co-ordinate with the Jacobites and being chased back to France by the British fleet. The scare, however, played into the hands of the Whigs, Anne's self-appointed loyalty party. They removed Anne's minister, Harley, and forced her to accept five peers she disliked. In the tussle over all this Anne received no support from those she most relied upon – Sarah, Duchess of Marlborough (now fifty and irritable in the extreme) and her husband, the duke, who simply went along with Sarah. Just before the duke left on his next European campaign, Anne wrote to him begging him to stop Sarah being so unreasonable, unfriendly and even hostile to her in public. The duke's response, unhelpfully, was that Sarah was being just as nasty to him. She has at present, he wrote, 'a resolution of living with that coldness and indifference for me which, if it continues, must make me the unhappiest man alive'. He went on to another great victory over the French at Oudenaarde, which paved the way for the allies to enter France and capture Lille, the strongest of all the French frontier fortresses. The following spring he fought the bloody Battle of Malplaquet, which he 'won' at a cost of 20,000 of his own troops to a mere 12,000 Frenchmen.

Max Fiennes, now working alongside the Duke of Orleans, took the key city of Tortona and received awards for his gallantry at the Battle of La Gudina. Thence he helped Berwick in the Piedmont and finally at the siege of Gerona. He was made head of that province and remained there until peace was agreed in 1713.

Despite his victories at Oudenaarde and Malplaquet, the Duke of Marlborough's star was on the wane back home, mostly through the ongoing rude behaviour of his wife Sarah to the long-suffering queen. In October 1708 Prince George died and Anne was heartbroken. She had nobody left who loved her, and Sarah, determined it seemed to break their friendship, continued to sour their relations, until in 1711 Anne finally snapped, dismissed Sarah from all her court positions and became more and more of a recluse.

Desire for peace with France led to the anti-war Tories taking over from the Whigs. Ministers came and went, the longest lasting being Lord Harley who Anne had grown to rely upon. Secret negotiations were continued with the French. Marlborough became less and less a key figure as these negotiations advanced, and in 1712 he was finally dismissed along with much of the expensive British army. The Treaty of Utrecht, when it was eventually signed by all parties in 1713, was preferential to Britain and resulted from the great diplomatic skills of Harley's Secretary of State, Henry St John, Viscount Bolingbroke. It gave Britain a monopoly of the Spanish-American slave trade, Gibraltar and Port Mahon as permanent bases in the Mediterranean, and Acadia and Newfoundland in North America, as well as the restoration of all Hudson Bay Company properties and forts in Canada. The French negotiator conceded, after the treaty was signed, that its terms gave to the British 'such considerable advantages as must absolutely ruin all commerce but their own'. By his diplomatic skills, St John had laid the basis for Britain's great era of trading and supremacy at sea for the next two centuries.

By the summer of 1713 the queen was too ill to attend the great celebrations of the signing of the Treaty of Utrecht. Her health continued to worsen with ever-present pain from gout, and it was clear to all that she would soon die childless. Who did she wish to succeed her? Her half-brother James, the Old Pretender, who had been in exile all his life but who was avowedly Catholic? Or the Hanoverian Protestants, as currently represented by her eighty-year-old cousin Sophia, a fairly distant descendant of James I? Anne refused to make up her mind. In Parliament she acknowledged the existing Act of Succession which officially nominated Sophia as the next queen.

The Old Pretender wrote to Anne from France to encourage her to vote for him. He reminded her that they shared the same father (James II) and asked her 'to prefer your own brother, the last male of our name, to the duchess of Hanover, the most remote relation that we have who will leave the government of our country to foreigners of another language'. A most appealing fraternal letter, but Anne did not send a reply. In June 1714 the duchess Sophia, thirty years older than Anne, collapsed and died suddenly in her garden, which handed the Hanoverian claim to her son, Prince George, who Anne had always disliked. Only two months after Sophia's death, two months of great pain for an increasingly sick Anne, she finally accepted that her own demise was imminent and announced that her choice was for the German prince, rather than her own Catholic half-brother. Her Privy Councillors immediately appointed a Board of Regency, who took rapid steps to safeguard the country against invasion by the Pretender. Coastal defences were made ready and troops placed on patrol.

In the event, the Jacobites everywhere stayed quiet when, on 1 August 1714, Queen Anne passed away, and such was the lack of panic that the new monarch, George I, took over a month before deigning to visit his new kingdom. He could speak hardly a word of English – just like William the Conqueror.

25

Bankers, Bubbles and Bonnie Prince Charlie

George I took his time, but then why should he rush? No Jacobite stirred, and, aged fifty-four, he had spent his whole life in the state of Hanover which he ruled as a benevolent despot with orderly subjects who showed him respect. He had been warned that such a commodity might well be in short supply with the British Parliament and their bickering Whig and Tory set-up. So he slowly put his Hanoverian affairs in order and leisurely sailed to his new kingdom a month after Anne's death, arriving at Greenwich in a thick pea-souper fog.

Things were at once awkward for him because not all his ministers spoke French and very few spoke German, whilst he spoke virtually no English. His own past behaviour did not recommend him to his new subjects as a pleasant character, for he had imprisoned his own teenage wife for two decades for unproven adultery and had for many years refused to speak to his own son. His family seemed to consist of his two ugly German mistresses with unpronounceable names, one of whom was grossly fat and the other as thin as a string bean. The British called them Elephant and Maypole.

As soon as George arrived in London, the Regents dissolved themselves and left the king to appoint his own ministers. This he did, choosing able men from both parties on the advice of those of his Hanoverian supporters who had been in England for some time. James, Earl Stanhope was a good choice as foreign secretary, and among his most able new men were two Norfolk lower echelon nobles who were brothers-in-law, Charles Townshend and Robert Walpole. In his first few months as king, George identified himself with the Whigs and made many high-level Tory enemies. He himself put people off by his cold, uncommunicative manner and by the pack of Hanoverian courtiers with weird names who surrounded him at all times.

Two top Tories went to France and encouraged the Old Pretender that the time was right to invade. In September 1715 the Earl of Mar raised the standard of rebellion at Braemar and marched on Perth which quickly succumbed. He sat there waiting for the expected arrival of the Pretender with French troops and when they failed to arrive, sent part of his 7,000 strong army south to join up with a force of Lowland Jacobites, to march into Lancashire, where they were confronted by a Hanoverian army. After a bitter battle at Preston, and another at Sheriffmuir near Stirling, there was stalemate, but Mar's Highlanders dispersed, as was their wont, when their leaders showed signs of getting them nowhere.

Five weeks later the Pretender himself finally made it to Scotland with 5,000 excellent troops and entered Perth where, like Mar before him, he dallied for five weeks until a powerful English force under the Duke of Argyl headed his way, whereupon he re-embarked for France, for the very good reason that the major army the French had promised him never turned up. His lack of success, whether his fault or not, was viewed as pathetic by many a Jacobite, and, his stay in France no longer being welcome, his exiled court moved to Italy.

The invasion attempt had proved that no violent anti-Hanoverian sentiment existed in England or Scotland, and this greatly strengthened the Whig/Hanoverian administration. But James was still alive, and knowing the Jacobite threat had not actually gone away but was merely latent was an ongoing incentive for the Hanoverians and their ministers to govern with moderation. Peace seemed the order of the day, both in England and in France. Marlborough and his wife Sarah retired to their glorious Blenheim Palace, whilst Maximilian Fiennes, the Marquis de Fiennes and Lieutenant General of the French army, retired to glory and awards in Paris where he died in 1716.

Colonel Fiennes Twisleton, meanwhile, had experienced many ups and downs since his famous relief of Londonderry. In 1710 he was promoted and sent as adjutant-general of the British expedition to Canada under Brigadier-General Sir John Hill, where, often in extreme weather and in arduous conditions, he fought many bitter engagements in the contest with the French for that country. Back home, Fiennes had a great stroke of luck with his Twisleton inheritance, which his grandfather had blocked from his teenage eloping mother Cecil and her descendants. By good fortune, the cousin who had inherited Broughton became a very good friend to Fiennes, and was, indeed, godfather to Fiennes' only son. This cousin, having no children of his own, had passed the inheritance back to Cecil and Fiennes, who therefore owned Broughton to which, after his extensive military career spanning two long wars, he looked forward to retiring.

Cecil had remarried some years before but when her second husband died, the sixty-year-old widow moved in with a surgeon, Will Burman, at his home in Holborn and left her entire inheritance to him. Fiennes was left not a penny, not an acre, and had to spend a good deal of money, trouble and time at the Courts to prove Cecil had no legal rights to disinherit him.

In 1718, finally living with his family in Broughton, the first Twisleton to do so, he was made assistant to the Banbury Borough Council and local magistrate under the charter of George I. What he did not do, which was years later to cause his grandson much trouble, was to reclaim his due right to the title (then in abeyance) of Baron Saye and Sele. Barony apart, Fiennes had the last laugh over his grandfather, whose measly will had, with obvious reluctance, stated that he was leaving 'an education allowance for

Cecil's only son, Fiennes Twisleton, secured on the rent of the Bull Inn at Dartford, so that he may be fitted either to be an apprentice to a merchant or other trade, or to study the law, phisick or any other learning.' One way or another, Fiennes, my great to the power of eight grandfather, did pretty well for himself and his descendants.

King George meanwhile made no attempt to hide his preference for Hanover over England. He escaped there whenever he could and, once the Jacobite 1715 scare was over, he took another trip 'home'. Parliament needed to appoint a regent, if only to sign the daily paperwork, and the Prince of Wales, George's heir, seemed the obvious candidate. But George had probably always disliked, and distrusted his son, and the last thing he wanted was to entrust him with Britain while he was over in Hanover. A compromise was reached which gave the Prince of Wales a nice sounding title, Guardian of the Realm, but minimal power. Both Georges were happy with this, but in 1717 a serious rift occurred between them due to a complex misunderstanding at the christening service of a newborn son of the Prince of Wales. This ended with a furious king banishing a furious prince and his sexy wife Caroline from the palace. The prince and Caroline set up a far more lively court at Leicester House, where one of the frequent attendants was the brilliant young minister, Robert Walpole. Walpole manoeuvred cleverly to close the rift between king and prince, eventually succeeding in 1720. They were never friends, but nor were they again outright enemies, and Robert Walpole was clearly responsible for this royal rapprochement. This coup leveraged him into the top all-Whig group of four ministers, along with his Norfolk colleague, Townshend, and the Lords Stanhope and Sunderland, all highly efficient and competitive men.

Quite how long these four star ministers would have survived working together without a major rift is anybody's guess, but the explosion that was to blow them apart occurred soon after the establishment of their power group, and it was known as the South Sea Bubble. In many ways it resembled a number of subsequent international, if not global, financial disasters, including that of 2008. Its history went back to 1694 when a group of City Whigs formed the Bank of England, which helped the Hanoverians to the throne since they promised Britain greater stability than did the Pretender. In 1711 the Tories, seeking a counterbalance of their own to the Whig Bank of England, agreed to the foundation of the South Sea Trading Company, which took on £9 million of the national debt in return for a monopoly of all trade to South America.

The directors of the trading company observed that a Scots banker, John Law, had in 1716 founded a bank in Paris that took on all the French national debt in return for a monopoly of all foreign trade. Law had then printed and circulated paper money so that from a deep economic depression, France had soared into wonderful (but inflationary) prosperity. By 1719 Law had founded his own trading company in which everyone bought shares which initially proved highly successful. The South Sea Trading Company in Britain followed suit, took on £30 million of the national debt and, with the deal approved by Parliament, saw its shares go sky-high, with nearly everyone in Britain and Hanover who had any money at all rushing to buy stock.

In a month or two a few wise men saw danger signals, and the so-called Bubble Act was passed to cool things down, but too late. Public confidence dropped overnight, share prices plummeted, and financial ruin was everywhere the result. The clever old Duchess of Marlborough had early on muttered, 'This project must burst in a little while and fall away to nothing,' and kept her money in the bank. But she was the exception to the rule.

Most of the king's ministers were deeply implicated in the Bubble, but Robert Walpole managed to avoid the appearance of involvement and cleverly used the disaster to overhaul his rivals and continue his rise to the top spot. Walpole was not himself a financial whizz-kid, but he knew someone who was, and in the immediate aftermath of the Bubble, this genius broker and investor saved Walpole in the same way that, years later, he would save Prime Ministers Pitt and Pelham. Samson Gideon, through a maternal link, was my great to the power of eight grandfather, and was also the first Jew to penetrate the peerage, an incredibly difficult task which he achieved through obtaining the favour of prime ministers and twice saving Britain's national debt. In the disastrous period of 1721 when the Bubble burst, Gideon was famous in the City for his lack of panic and for his positive investments. His services to Walpole in restoring the public credit gained great public admiration. From then on he and Walpole remained close and clever colleagues.

Walpole's success and the prosperity he brought to Britain naturally reflected on his king, but although the populace accepted George as a tolerable monarch, they never grew to love or venerate him. The writer John Jesse, in his *Memoirs of the Court of England*, wrote:

> It may be remarked . . . that, with the single exceptions of social pleasantry and constitutional good-humour, he seems to have been possessed of no redeeming quality which reflected dignity on him as a monarch, or rendered him amiable as a man. Profligate in his youth and libidinous in old age, he figures through life as a bad husband, a bad father, and, in as far as England is concerned, a bad king. He wanted even those graceful qualifications of the Stuarts, a love for polite literature and the fine arts; he possessed no taste for the one, and extended no patronage to the other. The only thing he seems to have had a regard for was his own ease; the only being he hated heartily was, probably, his own son. Many of these unamiable characteristics were unquestionably owing to his indifferent education; for, notwithstanding his wrong-headiness, he is said to have meant well.

In the summer of 1727 the king took one of his many trips back to Hanover and overnighting in Holland, gorged himself on ripe melons and soon afterwards, with severe indigestion, suffered an apoplectic fit and died. News of his death reached London by a speedy messenger who went straight to Walpole. He, in turn, rode forthwith to Richmond Palace, where the Prince of Wales was in bed. The story goes that, irritable and holding up his breeches with one hand, he received Walpole, who managed to lower his great bulk into the kneeling position and told the prince he was now the king. The confused king, according to Walpole, responded with the words, 'Dat is one big lie.'

Nonetheless, the crown changed hands smoothly and Walpole, who had for years taken trouble to cultivate the prince and, even more so, the Princess Caroline, soon became even more indispensable to George II than he had been to George I.

George II was a touch less alien to the British than his father had been, and at least he spoke English, albeit with a heavy German accent. He would be the last British monarch to be born abroad. He did very little ruling in terms of dictating politics, for he left that to his all-powerful prime minister, Robert Walpole. Nevertheless only two years into his rule, and despite the urgent requests of Walpole to desist, George was itching to declare war on Spain. Walpole worked on Queen Caroline who adored him, and she managed to persuade the bellicose king to go easy with the Spaniards, but Walpole was well aware that George continued to spoil for a fight and that peace hung by a thread.

As it was, the British army had shrunk quickly after the last war and many experienced veterans of battles all over the empire had hung up their boots. This included Fiennes Twisleton, whose only son John inherited Broughton on his father's death in 1730 and lived there until his own death thirty-three years later. In 1733 John put in a petition to claim the barony of Saye and Sele, which Colonel Fiennes Twisleton had not bothered about. The petition, initially unsuccessful, was deferred and John was subsequently discouraged from following it up by his cousin, Lawrence Fiennes, the 5th Viscount Saye and Sele.

Disappointed by his failed attempt to claim what, in his eyes, was rightfully his, John Twisleton proceeded to act strangely. For an unknown reason, perhaps to ensure that his progeny were all legitimate and in strong positions for future claims on the barony, he clandestinely married one Anne Gardner at the chapel of the Fleet prison, a place then notorious for granting unchecked, pre-dated marriage licenses for small fees. John did this on 30 December 1733, just inside the year of his baronial claim, which may or may not be pertinent.

Who exactly was Anne Gardner? Family tradition over the next two centuries maintained that she was a Broughton parlourmaid. Her apron remained until very recently hung on one of the castle walls by way of evidence of her station. More recent family research has upgraded her to housekeeper. Whatever the truth behind the conundrum, Anne and John remained a devoted couple living happily at Broughton until she died aged sixty-nine, having produced three gallant soldier sons.

Such domestic harmony was not mirrored at court. The king had an explosive confrontation with his heir, Frederick, Prince of Wales, who he threatened to banish to the colonies, and did banish from the palace. Then George's beloved wife Caroline died, which greatly reduced Walpole's influence over the king who, despite his prime minister's elegant advice, declared war on Spain.

This conflict was originally nicknamed the War of Jenkins' Ear, after a sea captain, Robert Jenkins, who claimed that his ear had been sawn off by the Spanish navy and, to prove it, waved the severed organ above his head in the House of Commons, sparking an outcry for vengeance. (The Spaniards had obviously made an error of judgment in allowing Robert to keep the ear.) The resulting Anglo-Spanish conflict soon melded with the Europe-wide War of the Austrian Succession, which was to last eight years and cause a heavy national debt. Walpole, the traditional peacemaker, was powerless as the Europeans squared up to one another, and in 1742 he retired. His place was taken by George's favourites, Lords Wilmington and Carteret, and then by Henry Pelham of Herstmonceux.

Britain found herself fighting the Spanish overseas and a powerful French coalition on the continent. George's prime aim, which naturally gained him no plus points in Britain, was to protect his beloved Hanover. But there were other reasons for fighting which definitely did enhance British interests, since it gave the British ever increasing opportunities to snatch more trade from Spanish South America, more bullion and more highly attractive tropical products.

At the same time, the growing importance of Britain's thirteen great colonies in North America was becoming obvious to both the French and the British. Demand for all sorts of merchandise was huge and British manufacturers were clamouring for export markets, not just for finished textiles, but for the newer, metal-based industries, everything for the household, tools, utensils, weapons and simple machines. In short, the made-in-Birmingham products destined in time to supply the world as made-in-China goods do today. One result of the 1740s conflict was, therefore, realisation that North Atlantic dominance would soon become the big issue between Europe's main naval powers.

On the European front George II personally led his troops into the major Battle of Dettingen in 1743 (the very last time a British monarch was to fulfil this function). The battle was fierce and bloodthirsty, and once again my ancestors turned out to fight on opposing sides. General Henry Hawley, the great great grandson of Old Subtlety, led successful cavalry charges as part of the army of Sir John Cope whilst, on the French side, General Charles-Maximilian Fiennes was made colonel of the army. When the battle was over George's men had won a significant victory, with under 3,000 casualties, compared to 8,000 French dead.

Such was Henry Hawley's personal popularity with both George and his army commander and favourite son, the Duke of Cumberland, that rumours abounded that Hawley was George's natural son. This did not stop his subsequently famous brigade-major, James Wolfe, from writing: 'The troops dread his severity, hate the man and hold his military knowledge in contempt.' The war in Europe continued for four more years, and Colonel Charles-Maximilian Fiennes fought at the sieges of Menin, Ypres, Furnes, Ath and Mons. He died in 1750, but his son, Christian-Maximilian, was later also a colonel of the army.

Shrewdly, in 1745 King Louis XV of France, knowing that the bulk of Britain's army of, by then, 62,000 men was fighting on the continent, stirred up the Old Pretender's son, Bonnie Prince Charlie, with the promise of 12,000 French troops if the prince could establish an army of Jacobite supporters in Scotland. This, it appeared, should not prove too difficult, especially in the Highlands, due to the extreme unpopularity there of the recent Enclosures Act imposed by George's government. Even in southern England this law had caused much hardship, for the poor could not afford the fences, ditches and hedges needed to demarcate their tiny land plots. One southern contemporary wrote: 'The poor in such parishes may say with truth, "Parliament may be tender of property; all I know is, I had one cow and an Act of Parliament has taken it from me."' And the effects in northern Scotland were infinitely worse.

Bonnie Prince Charlie landed in the Hebrides in July 1745, raised a Highland army of 2,500, took Edinburgh and nearly all Scotland, apart from the big, industrialised towns, defeated a British force at Prestonpans and marched south into England with 5,000 men. He took Manchester at the end of November without a shot fired. Many residents waved approving crosses of St Andrew at Charlie's men, but didn't stir a finger to help. Why should they? Times for most folk in prosperous towns were at least comfortable and secure under the Hanoverians. The prince moved on to Derby, but there was still no pro-Charles or anti-George reaction. So the prince went back north to await the promised French troops. The clock was ticking and George sent a force north under his son, the Duke of Cumberland, soon to be remembered in history as 'The Butcher'.

My kinsman, General Henry Hawley, had by then been

promoted first to Lieutenant General and then, in December 1745, to Commander-in-Chief in Scotland. A month after getting this top job, his army was defeated at Falkirk. Normally such a defeat would have warranted his immediate demotion, but such was his closeness to Cumberland that he retained his command and followed the prince north to Inverness, close to which, at the field of Culloden, the two armies faced off. The prince, at a desperate stage of the battle, charged his men uphill at Cumberland's centre. Yelling Highlanders were ripped by musket balls or impaled on bayonets. They died in their thousands, and when at last they turned and fled they were mercilessly hunted down by Hawley's cavalry. For weeks afterwards his dragoons continued the hunt to the north, sparing no suspects and earning the general the sobriquet Hangman Hawley in his mission to ethnically cleanse all rebel areas.

Culloden was the last battle ever fought on British soil. The French support for the prince never arrived and there were more Scotsmen fighting under Cumberland than under the Pretender. Young Charles did escape back to Europe, but the Jacobites never rose again and the Stuart cause withered away. Unlike the earlier lukewarm Stuart rebellion, which George I had treated with leniency, retribution this time was harsh in the extreme. The last of many resulting executions, that of the famous Highlander clan leader, Lord Lovat, took place at Tower Hill in April 1747, and that was to be the last official beheading in Britain.

As for Hawley, he went back to the war on the continent and led the allied cavalry at the Battle of Lauffeld. He retired to become Governor of Portsmouth and was buried in his home parish of Hartley Witney in Hampshire, one can only hope with a clear conscience.

The War of the Austrian Succession finally ended in 1748 with Maria Theresa's accession as Archduchess of Austria being accepted by all parties (although she soon dropped Britain from her list of key allies as being too liable to shift sides). With the end of the war and with no further threat to Hanover, King

George lost all interest in politics and in military matters. His son and heir, Frederick, whom he had disliked from an early age, died in 1751, so Frederick's son, George, became the new heir apparent.

A succession of French visitors to Britain at the time, including the highly critical and observant genius Voltaire, recorded their impressions of Britain compared to the rest of Europe as being far less class-bound. The social ladder, they noted, was, in Britain, there to be climbed by anyone with initiative. Aristocratic privileges were fewer in Britain than elsewhere, and they approved of peers being hanged in public for their crimes, just as commoners were. They also emphasised that, unlike on the continent, any person who cared to dress like a gent and had the money, could ape a higher rung of society and become a gent. The lower class could soon become the middle class if they were so minded in Britain but not in pedigree-conscious Hanover.

With George no longer bothered overmuch with the politics of the realm, and with Walpole no longer at the helm, there was in 1753 a vacuum and a need for a new effective supremo. Parliament was becoming a touch somnolent, especially in the House of Lords, and efforts were made in 1754 to sweep away the cobwebs. One of the officials of the Secretary to the Treasury, John Namier, drew up a list of a dozen peers who were, against the basic rules of the House, in receipt of financial assistance from the 'secret service budget'. Namier was at pains to point out that these payments were merely charitable and benevolent, and he titled them 'the aristocratic dole'.

One of Namier's Dozen, Richard Fiennes, the 6th Viscount Saye and Sele, explained to Prime Minister Newcastle that he could only afford to attend the House if he continued to receive his parliamentary handout of £600 per annum. Namier suggested that he and others in this situation would be unlikely to prove critical of government motions. One could see his point. Looking into Richard Fiennes' domestic situation, it is clear that whatever Namier's deliberations, Richard was still drawing his 'secret service benevolence' eighteen years later, despite, in 1753, having married a very rich widow, one Christobella, who had by then got through two previous and wealthy husbands.

She was descended from Sir Walter Raleigh, and married Richard when he was thirty-seven and she was fifty-eight. When he died, she was quoted as saying that she had married her first husband for love, the next one for money, and Richard for his title. When she eventually died in 1789, the *Gentlemen's Magazine* recorded: 'she tasted the good things of this world and enjoyed them long . . . she dressed, even at the close of her life, more like a girl of eighteen than a woman of ninety.' Quite how her husband, Richard Fiennes, got away with nineteen years of such a wealthy wife *and* £600 a year, due to being 'too poor to attend' the Lords, shows just how slack the Revenue had become at the time at checking MPs' expenses claims. A recurring theme.

However, the mid-1750s did see a considerable sharpening up of governmental and Commons efficiency with a fresh set of leaders and a new sense of urgency as another war loomed. William Pitt the Elder was the second son of a family who were often in debt, but he married the daughter of one of the great Whig families, the Temples, related by marriage to William 'Old Subtlety' Fiennes. Pitt made his name in Parliament as a fiery young orator who raged against the Hanoverians in general and George II's Hanover-protecting war antics in particular. By 1746 he was a minor minister, but 1754 saw the death of Lord Pelham, and the next prime minister was Pelham's brother, the Duke of Newcastle, then living at Herstmonceux. With the Seven Years War breaking out, the Newcastle administration started badly, missing a glaring opportunity to smash the French navy in the Atlantic and losing the key harbour of Minorca in the Mediterranean. Leadership brilliance was needed, and Pitt proved to be just the man to provide it. He was made Secretary of State but was effectively prime minister, and over the next few years, starting in 1757, became the most successful minister of war in British history.

Due largely to Pitt's brilliance, Britain won a whole series of engagements and switched the focus of the war to a global battle between the two great mercantile nations of the world – France and Britain. In North America France fought to establish a chain of influence from Quebec down to Louisiana which would cut off the east coast British colonies. In the West Indies they attacked the British 'sugar islands', and in India they made trouble for the East India Company. Somehow, against the most powerful army and navy of the day, Pitt's forces on land and sea decisively defeated the French throughout the Seven Years War.

The war was, of course, hugely expensive, and this was where my great to the power of eight maternal grandfather, Samson Gideon, saved the government by his financial wizardry. He had come a long way since boosting Walpole's post South Sea Bubble reputation in the 1720s. When Bonnie Prince Charlie invaded in 1745, panic ensued in the City with investors selling stock at any price, but Samson continued without a blip to buy good securities which doubled his huge fortune and helped calm public hysteria in the process. From 1742 onwards he was consulted by the government and loaned the nation vast sums. In 1750 he raised £1 million at 3 per cent at par, whilst at the beginning of the Seven Years War he paid a bounty from his estates to help army recruiting at a desperate time.

His main motive behind all this munificence was a peerage for his family, which for a Jew at the time would have been hitherto unobtainable. Nonetheless, in 1758 he pressed Newcastle, then prime minister, for a baronetcy, the first step up the ladder, but the PM could not oblige with such a blatant perk. As a compromise, and to keep the invaluable Samson on side, Gideon's son, then fourteen, was made a baronet in 1759 and sent to Eton. By 1754 Samson realised that however much he saved the British from financial chaos, his religion would always block his dreams of nobility. So he resigned his membership in the Sephardic congregation and raised his children in the Christian faith.

The two greatest triumphs of Pitt's colonising success were

undoubtedly those of Plassey in India in 1757 and Quebec in 1759. The origins of the Battle of Plassey go back to the establishment of the East India Company which, independent of England's close control, established autonomous areas of influence on the subcontinent. The Company, in the 1750s, was violently opposed by the Nawab of Bengal who overran the Company's Calcutta headquarters and crammed 146 officials and some of their womenfolk into a small, over-hot guardroom. One survivor, the senior British official there, wrote:

> We had been but a few minutes confined before everyone fell into a perspiration so profuse, you can form no idea of it. This brought on a raging thirst which increased . . . as the body was drained of its moisture.
>
> Various expedients were suggested to give more room and more air . . . I believe every man stripped (myself and three others excepted). Every hat was put in motion to produce a circulation of air . . . Almost a quarter after six in the morning, the poor remains of 146 souls . . . came out of the black hole alive.

There were said to be only twenty-three survivors.

One Robert Clive, the son of a Shropshire squire and a soldier of the Company was told to avenge the Black Hole, and with a force of 3,200 he confronted the Nawab's army of 50,000 soldiers, including French artillery, at Plassey. By a mixture of brilliant tactics and luck, Clive's meagre force defeated the Franco-Bengali host, and even pursued them for six miles. This was the turning point in the east which stopped French ambitions in India and established the British empire there.

Pitt turned his attention to North America, where the French had made a number of incursions into British held areas of Canada. In the summer of 1757 the famous French general Montcalm attacked Fort William Henry with a force of 8,000 French regulars, Canadian militia and their Indian allies. Their aim was to drive the British out of New York State. After six days the British surrendered, and during the ensuing retreat many, including children and women, were tomahawked or dragged off into the forest to become slaves. The story of the defeat was told by Fenimore Cooper in *The Last of the Mohicans*. The French went on to many further victories until, in 1759, the tide turned when the British attacked the main French stronghold of Quebec.

The British general in charge was the eccentric James Wolfe who, at Culloden fourteen years before, had described my relative, General 'Hangman' Hawley in such hostile terms. When George II was advised of Wolfe's eccentricity, he replied, 'Oh! he is mad, is he? Then I hope he will bite some other of my generals.'

The key to the attack on Quebec was Wolfe's unorthodox planning. The French defenders had discounted any likelihood that they could be attacked from the flank known as the Heights of Abraham, protected as it was by a river and high cliffs. The battle that followed was closely fought, bitter and bloody, but Wolfe's Commando-style approach had the great advantage of surprise. He himself was killed, but his victory at Quebec secured British control of Canada and eastern America.

Twelve months later George II died suddenly at the breakfast table, and his grandson succeeded to the throne as King George III. George II, like his father before him, died unloved by the British but, thanks mostly to William Pitt the Elder, his reign saw the emergence of Great Britain as the greatest empire-builder in the world.

26

Riot and Romance

George III is today remembered for being mad. The film of Alan Bennett's play *The Madness of King George* (shot partly at Broughton Castle) rammed this point home. But although his last nine years (1811–20) were indeed spent suffering from a cruel form of insanity, he was an active and often effective monarch for fifty-one years, during which Britain went from strength to strength, even if most of the credit for this can be put down to strong prime ministers and foreign secretaries, including the two Pitts.

The new king had one or two things going for him. He spoke good English and was married to a solid Protestant, Charlotte, a German princess of a minor state, who quickly gave him a son and heir, and as he grew older he chose very reasonable ministers when circumstances allowed. In 1770 King George selected as his prime minister Frederick, Lord North, the man who was to go down in history as having 'lost America'. British attempts to institute a revenue-raising Stamp Act had already caused the Americans to denounce King George's 'tyranny', and rioting ensued in many cities. British goods were boycotted, causing bankruptcies in Liverpool and Bristol, and the famous cry 'No taxation without representation' was raised across the thirteen colonies, leading by 1773 to the equally famous Boston Tea party when taxable tea arriving on three British ships was tossed into the Charles river. London ministers and commoners alike had failed to grasp the ability of a distant and independently-minded population of two and a half million colonials to obstruct any and all imperial edicts. The Stamp Act of 1765 led directly a decade later to the Declaration of Independence and war.

In 1778 Pitt the Elder, the last great figure from the reign of George II, had a stroke in Parliament and died. Lord North, after seven years in the hot seat, ached to retire but wanted to solve the American problem peacefully first. He offered the colonials any terms they wanted, short of actual independence, but by then they had the freedom bit between their teeth and would settle for nothing short of full severance from the mother country. The War of Independence (or what Americans call the Revolutionary War) started in Lexington in April 1775. At first the British did well, but then, with both the French and the Spanish offering the colonials their naval assistance with relish, things went from bad to worse.

Forty per cent of the immigrants, about 250,000 colonials, who settled in America in the Hanoverian century were from Ulster, and half as many again were from the Catholic south of Ireland. When the American statesman, Benjamin Franklin, for a long time very pro-British, realised that war was inevitable and travelled to Europe to raise support for his American brethren, it is hardly surprising that his first call was to Dublin in 1771. After all, nearly half of all his countrymen were of Irish stock.

On the other hand, in February 1776 an army of 1,000 kilted Highlanders with muskets and claymores, and to the sound of drums and bagpipes, attacked an American militia force at Moore's Creek, North Carolina. The Scottish were beaten and three-quarters were taken prisoner. These Highlanders were mostly recent immigrants who chose to fight as loyalists to the British crown rather than remain neutral or join their new country's forces. Many remembered the brutal aftermath of Culloden thirty years before, when most of their enemy had been from the Scottish Lowlands and Ulstermen Protestants. Many of them spoke only Gaelic and were still resolute in their hatred of these same Protestants who faced them at Moore's Creek.

Two of those imprisoned by the Americans after the battle were the husband and son of Flora Macdonald, who had led Bonnie Prince Charlie away from Culloden and his pursuers in a narrow escape to the Isle of Skye. For this deed she was later imprisoned and, when released, she and her family had eventually decided to emigrate to the New World.

In 1777 the British Army under General Burgoyne surrendered after the Battle of Saratoga and this changed the mood in Britain. War taxes were high and success was clearly evading George's generals. So Britain sought peace, especially when the French began to negotiate an alliance with Benjamin Franklin. The British quickly saw the very real threat of a French invasion whilst their navy was mostly far away supporting the troops in North America. The Channel was vulnerable in the extreme.

So on 30 November 1782 America received full official independence and a treaty was signed between France, Spain and Britain in January 1783 which, bearing in mind the circumstances of Britain being decidedly on the back foot, was lucky to lose George only Minorca and a few islands in the West Indies. The loss of the American colonies did not, in fact, harm Britain in any way, since the ex-colonials, friendlier now they were free, continued to trade as before with the Old Country, which in turn was now able to switch its full imperial focus to the East.

After a decade of fluctuating popularity, George III had, by the early 1780s, become as canny as many of his ministers. Trade was booming, confidence – at a low ebb during the defeats of the American War – quickly returned, agricultural yields were improved, largely thanks to encouragement by 'Farmer George', as the king was affably known, and to successful new methods of farming by innovative owners of great estates, like the Duke of Bedford and Lord Coke of Norfolk.

George's reign saw Edward Jenner's discovery of vaccination against smallpox. Dockyards turned out not only revolutionary steam-powered ships, but also sail system designs so sophisticated as to rival steam at sea. The new turnpike trusts funded major repairs to all roads, especially between manufacturing cities, so that, whereas in 1745 it took a fortnight to reach Edinburgh from London, in 1796 that journey was cut to two days. In the 1760s the Duke of Bridgewater's dead-water canals and lock-gate systems revolutionised river transport, linking major coal regions with manufacturing sites.

The burgeoning middle class underwrote new manufacturing companies and then spent a great deal of their money keeping up with the neighbours' acquisitions. 'The English,' according to Josiah Tucker, 'have better conveniences in their houses and affect to have more in quantity of clean neat furniture, and a great variety of such as carpets, screens, window curtains . . . polished brass locks, fenders, etc. – things hardly known abroad among persons of such rank – than are to be found in any other country in Europe, Holland excepted.' Quality was considered of great importance, and British goods soon obtained a global reputation for excellence and reliability. Eighty per cent of Josiah Wedgwood's pottery was sold for export.

And Britain also exported her inhabitants in great numbers throughout George's sixty years as king and as the empire grew and grew. By 1803 the great Mogul Emperor of India finally capitulated to the British army in India (most of whose soldiers were Indians) and Britain thereafter ruled over forty million Indians. Many Britons settled there, mostly as bureaucrats, but thousands succumbed to the heat and disease. More popular temperate parts of the empire included Canada, Australia and New Zealand. In the 1770s emigrants flocked to these vast areas of free land, and by far the most zealous were Scots-Irish, who outnumbered everyone else six to one. The phenomenally powerful fur trading giant of Canada, the Hudson Bay Company, employed 80 per cent of its new labour force from the Orkneys alone (and when I spent months on the rivers of the North West Territories and British Columbia in the 1970s, the HBC was still hiring many of its bureaucrats direct from Edinburgh).

Meanwhile, the number of immigrants into Britain was, apart from Europeans fleeing from persecution, such as Huguenots and French aristocrats, difficult to tally. Black immigrants were counted, however, and in 1770 there were 14,000, most of whom were the servants of West Indian planters who looked after their children sent back to British schools.

Generally, and against the backdrop of bloody revolution in France, the British working class, along with various middle-class intellectual troublemakers, stuck to the occasional low-grade riot, machine-smashing and, once or twice, stones were thrown or pistols fired at the monarch. But in June 1780 a rabid Protestant, Lord George Gordon, furious with recent concessions granted by Parliament to Catholics, roused a London mob to hysterical and homicidal violence against king and government. All too easily that month, a Paris-type revolution could have engulfed London. Magistrates seemed powerless to intervene and in the face of imminent catastrophe, one man Thomas Twisleton, held the line between revolutionary madness and democracy. As he was my great to the power of six grandfather, I need to take a short diversion from the Gordon Riots to explain his place in the family fortunes.

His father was John Twisleton, Lord Saye and Sele, who had clandestinely married the parlourmaid. Their sons, John and Thomas, joined the army, serving with the Coldstream Guards during the Seven Years War. During the Battle of Brüchemühle in 1762 the enemy cannonade was so violent and the British detachment, composed chiefly of the Foot Guards, suffered so severely that the soldiers piled up the dead bodies of their slain comrades and sheltered behind them as behind a parapet. Thomas Twisleton, at the height of the slaughter, reprimanded a sergeant whom he heard utter some exclamations of horror, and was answered by him, 'Oh, sir, you are now supporting yourself on the body of your own brother.' This sergeant had been a servant in the family.

So Thomas, the younger brother, ended up inheriting Broughton and had the foresight to marry Elizabeth the eldest daughter of the chairman of the East India Company, Sir Edward Turner, which allowed him to spend money on repairing the castle's neglected state. Elizabeth Turner turned out to be an excellent, house-proud Lady Saye and Sele. She was also highly extravagant and a determined party-giver, so Thomas sold off long-held Twisleton properties to fund her fun and her updating of the castle, whilst he continued to gain high promotion in the army, reaching the exalted rank of major general by the time of the Gordon Riots.

In terms of the property market, Thomas was lucky. His own father was not long dead but, prior to his demise, the last male heir of the other Twisleton line had also died, leaving Thomas property in Dartford, Kent, which had been in the family for a century.

Then in 1780, just before the Riots, Judith Twisleton, the last Twisleton heiress, died, leaving Thomas the large Yorkshire estates east of Selby which John Twisleton, the London goldsmith, had bought in 1519. Thomas and Elizabeth lovingly redecorated much of Broughton in the fashionable gothic style, with sash windows and Chinese hand-painted wallpaper in the Star Chamber hall, which is still there today.

By 1780 Thomas had enjoyed a long period of peacetime soldiering and was stationed in the London area. All army officers were well aware of the infectious dangers of the revolution just across the Channel. Many of the country labourers who had been attracted by the Industrial Revolution had, like Chinese peasants in the early twenty-first century, wandered into the big cities and had lost their old country ways, including traditional deference to the squires. The 1780 Riots served to demonstrate to the ruling class just how quickly life could become highly dangerous.

The London riot that summer was costly in lives and property. Big English cities were ripe for riot, and any access to looted supplies of gin was fatal. On 2 June 1780 the semi-deranged

George Gordon led a 50,000-strong howling mob to Westminster, from where they fanned out in a maelstrom of hatred and destruction, the result of long-simmering political discontent. They quickly destroyed the mansions of various senior ministers, including the Lords Rockingham, Devonshire, Mansfield and Savile. They violently assaulted both Houses of Parliament whilst in session. They attacked gentle folk who they caught riding in hackney carriages, including Lord Sandwich, breaking the windows, slashing his face and beating him up. He sent for a guard unit, mounted and on foot, but the mob dealt with these part-time constables in no time at all.

One witness, George Crabbe, later described what he saw:

> I met a resolute band of vile-looking fellows . . . armed with clubs. [I passed by to the Old Bailey] . . . The new prison was a very large, strong building, [as was the house of the keeper, Mr Akerman.] How he has escaped . . . I know not . . . they set fire to his house. [A mob of 500 passed by.] . . . They broke the prison gates with crows . . . They broke the roof, tore away the rafters [and let loose the prisoners] and they were conducted through the streets in their chains . . . You have no conception of the phrensy of the multitude.

Hundreds of Catholic homes were destroyed, and eventually, after three days of government paralysis, George III himself ordered the troops to go in, and a small force of three hundred under Major General Thomas Twisleton marched into the City thirty-six bullets having been doled out to each of his men.

Cousin Thomas was the chief liaison officer between the War Office and the action force he was himself commanding. The situation was lethally confused. He tried to appeal to the Common Council of London, the same legislative body who, urged on by the inveterate troublemaker, John Wilkes, had delayed appealing for troops for three full days of rioting simply because they hoped that a really good riot would bring down Lord North's government which they disliked. Fortunately, by the time Thomas confronted the councillors they had seen the fearful results of their irresponsible behaviour, and they agreed to give him a free hand. This being settled, Thomas sent off detachments to those key buildings not yet destroyed, including the headquarters of the South Sea Company, the Navy Office, and the Excise Office.

Thomas knew that the Fleet prison and the king's Bench had been burnt to the ground the previous night, and he now received a report of growing trouble in Holborn. A family company, Langdales, had built a huge distillery there and had very recently laid in enormous stocks to avoid an imminent new duty on gin. The mob, intent on murdering Langdale and his twelve children en route to liberating the gin, had set fire to all Langdale property, and in doing so had managed to start a huge alcohol-fuelled inferno. Rioters, blind drunk and on fire from head to foot, were staggering about the labyrinthine cellars. Looters were everywhere and Thomas despatched as many men as he could spare to that part of town. On the evening of 8 June, hearing that mobs were closing in on the most vital British institution of the time, the Bank of England, and that the guards there were insufficient, Thomas made best speed to Threadneedle Street, where he commanded the defence against two mass attacks by determined mobs, by all later accounts the key actions of the Gordon Riots.

Under Thomas's direct command, his meagre troops did their best to kill as few of the mob as was necessary to avoid being overwhelmed. This judicious restraint in all likelihood saved hundreds of lives. By the end of the riot only three hundred dead were counted. Although Thomas did not trust John Wilkes, he used him to help cool down the mobs until peace eventually came back to the smoking streets of London. Various neighbourhood groups subsequently offered, if armed, to act as voluntary patrol groups, but Thomas maintained that only the War Office had the right to re-establish public order. His cool behaviour in the most stressful circumstances did a great deal to assure a good outcome to a riot that could have grown into who can tell what national chaos. A few months later Thomas was busy fighting a very different sort of campaign.

Back in 1624 his ancestor, Old Subtlety, already Baron Saye and Sele, had been made the 1st Viscount Saye and Sele, a title that could traditionally pass through male heirs only, unlike the barony which in the Saye and Sele case could go through both male and female line. Soon afterwards a male shortage of Saye and Seles meant that the barony passed to a nephew, and the viscountcy ended up with the teenage eloper Cecil Twisleton's grandson trying to claim back the barony in 1734. He dropped his claim, probably for fear of offending Lawrence Fiennes, who was at the time the 5th (and penultimate) Viscount Saye and Sele and opposed the family barony being officially resurrected. He probably liked being the only Lord Saye and Sele in the House of Lords.

In 1781, with advice from his lawyer and probably with the encouragement of his wife, Thomas Twisleton decided to try to claim back the barony himself, despite his father's failure to do so. He needed, his lawyer advised, to put his claim in quickly because the current 6th Viscount Saye and Sele was about to die without male issue, so would not be likely to object to a resurrected barony but more important, Thomas would have to prove his own legitimacy since his father had previously been unable to present the appropriate documentation. Thomas's lawyer worked out that to find suitable witnesses who would agree to remembering Thomas's birth details, they would have to hurry, since, in his words, such witnesses were very aged and infirm. They must have found such survivors for they won their claim to the barony. Seven years later, Thomas began to suffer from a violent pain in his head due to a condition which his doctors declared was incurable. He committed suicide in his Harley Street rooms by cutting his throat with a razor and falling on his major-general's sword. He was buried that summer at Broughton.

Apart from the Gordon Riots, 1780 was quite a good year for King George. Admiral Rodney won a great victory against the

Spanish in the West Indies, went on to raise their siege of Gibraltar, already a key British port, and then, when the Dutch entered the war against Britain, Rodney trounced them, too. Ministers came and went. Then came again. The troublemaking hedonist, Charles James Fox, was up and down the popularity charts, except with George with whom he was on a permanent down, largely because he encouraged the Prince of Wales, whose loathing for his father was mutual, into dissolute ways with women, drink and obscene language.

George III was especially blessed by the arrival on the ministerial scene of William Pitt the Younger, if anything even more brilliant than his father had been. George made him chancellor of the exchequer at twenty-three years of age and, when North resigned and Rockingham died in 1784, Pitt became the youngest prime minister ever at twenty-four and the perfect political beast to work with George. For twenty-five years the king had fought hostile Parliaments, as had George I and II before him. Now at last, through guile and persistence, he had the man he wanted at the top of the tree.

For four years after his appointment of Pitt, George felt free enough to enjoy himself, although the binge drinking and general obnoxious behaviour of his two eldest sons did upset him. Then in 1788 the same strange symptoms, which had briefly attacked him twenty-three years before, recurred. His eyes turned yellow and his urine dark purple. He rambled constantly on disconnected themes, and his eyesight deteriorated. He believed, long before his doctors did, that he was going mad; a terrible prospect for anyone, let alone a king in the prime of his life. At times he could be violent. He smashed the Prince of Wales's head against a table. The queen believed he would murder her. Doctors put him in a straitjacket. If he objected to various agonising 'treatments' to which he was subjected, he was gagged.

Then, in spite of (rather than because of) brutal treatment by his medicos, George recovered fully about five months after his first fit, and he remained fully sane for the next twelve years. The

Prince of Wales and the Whigs, who had hovered hopefully in expectation of the king's death, retreated. Ironically the king's illness and subsequent recovery made him more popular and the Prince of Wales less so. By 1790, aged fifty, George had ruled pretty well for thirty years and outlived most of his earlier critics.

He was by nature an even-handed king. He hated mob violence as much as he avoided despotic government. Unfortunately, the bloody horror and absolutism of the French Revolution had, by 1792, so frightened him and a great many Englishmen, from ministers to country squires, that they became far less willing to grant any concession towards simple democracy for fear of it leading to a British version of the French anarchy. Some Whigs and most Tories, including an odd mixture of Edmund Burke and William Pitt, were, with George, amongst the alarmists, whilst Fox and Lord Gray welcomed the French Revolution and hoped it would help their quest for more liberty in Britain, not to cause a revolution but to prevent one.

For a while, whilst Austria and Prussia took up arms against Revolutionary France to crush the frightening incubus of the infant Republic, Britain hung back, for Pitt was a good peacetime leader. In 1790 the Revolution had still seemed relatively harmless to most British and many liberals thought the French were merely conducting a modest constitutional movement. Then came 1792, the year when the tumbril carts, with their abattoir-bound loads of condemned aristocrats, first rumbled their sad way towards the guillotines. George wept when he heard that King Louis XVI himself had lost his head to the 'blue blood blade'. But his grief was tempered by his recent anger at the way the French monarchy had given armed support to the American revolutionaries.

The European monarchies, far more vulnerable than sea-girt Britain, declared all out war on the French Revolution in 1792, and the French retaliated with their newly indoctrinated people's armies. In 1793, believing Britain was herself ripe for revolution, France declared war and began plans for an invasion. George's army of

45,000 men was unprepared, and less than a tenth of his navy was seaworthy. The new French armies were proving invincible against their continental opponents, and by 1797 only Britain still held out against them. The Royal Navy defeated the French at Ushant and prevented one of three major invasion attempts in as many years. In 1798 the French fleet again confronted them at the Battle of Aboukir Bay, near Alexandria, and this battle of the Nile gave Britain dominance in the Mediterranean. It also brought to the fore a new British hero – Admiral Horatio Nelson. Three attempts by the Revolutionary army were made to land in Britain, two via Ireland, where the French force spent two weeks before being chased away, and one at Fishguard in Wales, the last invasion of the British mainland, where on one occasion a French patrol mistook Welsh women in their black hats and red flannel for redcoats and beat a hasty retreat.

In Ireland, as the nineteenth century dawned, the Protestant ascendancy sought political union with the rest of Britain on the same terms as had the Scots in 1707. Irish MPs thereafter went to Westminster, and a new Union Jack was unfurled that included the Irish cross of St Patrick. This new sense of British togetherness was well timed because in February 1800 the glamorous thirty-one-year-old Corsican general, Napoleon Bonaparte, who had won glory for the Revolution in Italy and in Egypt, became Consul of all France. Whilst he consolidated his position, his forces and his territorial empire, Britain enjoyed a brief peace. The Revolutionary War was over but the Napoleonic Wars, which would last until 1815, were about to begin.

Britain had already spent the incredible sum of £1,500 million on the war, on the navy, on foreign subsidies and on creating a complex coastal defence including a ring of Martello towers, some of which still stand. Whilst the war went on, British trade continued to expand worldwide, and as the Royal Navy blockaded French ports, the midlands textile industry achieved such a global lead that British manufacturers were soon clothing the French army.

Although Trade Unions were treated like revolutionary societies and suppressed, as were all attempts to achieve a minimum wage, serious social consequences were avoided, largely by the traditional and relatively generous poor relief systems adopted by many rural and urban parishes after the 1790s.

Suddenly, during the 1801–3 spell of peace, King George again became sick, or temporarily 'mad', returning to normal after a short while. But the Prince of Wales, impatient as ever to rule, stirred up ministerial animosities. Pitt was out; then back in again, and in October 1803 Napoleon invaded Hanover and prepared again to invade Britain. At sixty-six and going blind, the king struggled on with Pitt, despite perennial quarrels.

1805 brought better news through the naval victories of the amazing Horatio Nelson. His famous advice to a newly reporting midshipman is recorded as: 'There are three things, young gentlemen, which you are constantly to bear in mind. First, you must always implicitly obey orders, without attempting to form any opinion of your own respecting their propriety. Secondly, you must consider every man your enemy who speaks ill of your king. And thirdly, you must hate a Frenchman as you do the devil.' During his formidable victory at Trafalgar over the combined French and Spanish fleets, the enemy lost twenty-two ships, the British not one. Nelson was killed, but Britain literally ruled the waves for the next hundred years and well beyond.

Sadly, in 1806, the greatest of all war ministers, Pitt the Younger, witnessing Napoleon's invincibility on land, died aged forty-six, to be followed as prime minister by a relatively minor man. His long-time opponent Fox, then foreign secretary, tried to make peace with France but found Napoleon far too shifty to deal with and he also died that year. George, for a blind man of sixty-eight, was doing quite well in between mad spells and the scandalous behaviour of his unpopular sons, two of whom were soon to become Kings of England. The king himself was by now a national treasure, like a favourite and much valued piece of fine furniture that you have grown up with. He was more popular than ever before, trade was booming, and so he could afford to relax. He loved to read novels or, when his eyesight worsened, to be read to.

His favourite novelist, Fanny Burney, was also the second keeper of the robes to the queen. Burney became a great gossip, but always restricted herself to praiseworthy comments when writing of the royal family. About others she could enjoy letting rip. Some years before his heroics at the Gordon Riots, she was asked to a party by Thomas Twisleton and his wife Elizabeth, Lady Saye and Sele, to celebrate the completion of their redecoration of Broughton. Of the forty-one-year-old Lady Elizabeth Burley she wrote with typical author's venom:

> I met Lady Saye and Sele who seems pretty near fifty – at least turned forty. Her head was full of feathers, flowers, jewels and gee-gaws, and as high as Lady Archer's. Her dress was trimmed with beads, silver, persian sashes and all sorts of fine fancies. Her face is thin and fiery, and her whole manner spoke 'a lady all alive'. She gushed and condescended to me, 'I think your novel is the most elegant I have ever read.' Her sister Cassandra was there, to whom she introduced me saying, 'She has a novel herself, so you are sister authoresses, a most elegant work it is, I assure you, almost as pretty as yours but not quite so eloquent.' The authoress then proceeded to quote to me from it as follows, 'If, when he made the declaration of his love, the sensibility that beamed in his eyes was felt in his heart, what pleasing sensations and soft alarms might not that tender avowel awaken!'

This younger sister, Cassandra, Lady Hawke, was clearly not to Fanny's liking either, for her letter continued in an equally catty vein: 'I took the first opportunity of Lady Hawke's casting down her eyes and reclining her delicate head to make away from this terrible set, but not before a square man, middle-aged and humdrum was introduced.' This last 'square' character turned out to be Thomas Twisleton, Lord Saye and Sele.

THE TWISLETONS AFFORDED JANE AUSTEN A GOOD DEAL OF MATERIAL FOR HER NOVELS

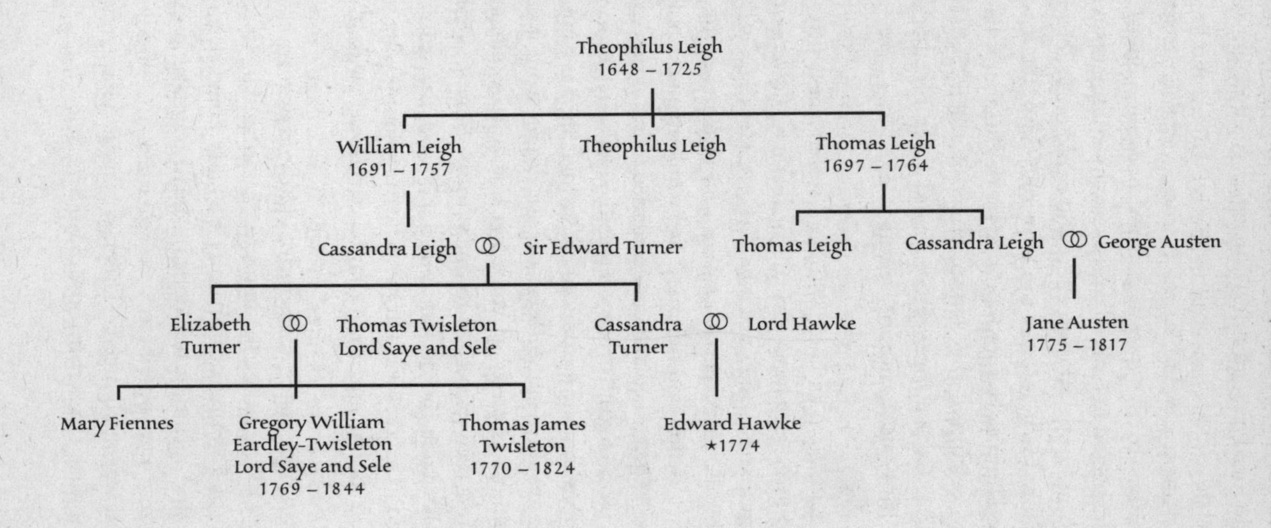

All my life I have admired two large oil paintings owned by my grandmother and passed to me on her death in the 1950s, which are portraits of Thomas and Elizabeth Fiennes, and I neither agree with Fanny Burney's description of them, nor with the following extract from a 1795 letter between two local neighbours: 'When you do me the favour to write next, do mention Lord Saye and Sele's family who live at Broughton Castle, near Banbury. I am anxious to know how they go on. I know the late good-humoured Weak Man and his romantic Wife.'

Thomas could never have been described as weak, active soldier as he always was, but Elizabeth loved life and, from her portrait, you can spot the twinkle in her eye. So romantic is perhaps an apt adjective for her. Her second cousin through the Leigh family was the novelist Jane Austen, who used various Twisleton scandals to flavour her novels. The Saye and Seles and the Austens would often visit one another. In 1806 Mrs Austen, Jane's mother, wrote a family letter at the time when Thomas was long dead and Elizabeth was sixty-four: 'Poor Lady Saye and Sele is to be sure rather tormenting, though sometimes amusing, and affords Jane many a good laugh. But she fatigues me sadly on the whole.'

The Twisletons not only afforded Jane Austen a good laugh, but also a good deal of material for her novels, including *Mansfield Park* and *Lady Susan*. Jane, who recognised a good scandal when she came across one, included them, hook, line and boudoir, when they came her way in her own family circle. The Twisletons were most obliging.

Thomas Twisleton's suicide was too serious a subject for Jane's pen, but eighteen years later, by which time Jane's novels were in full flow, her favourite sister Cassandra recalled: 'We offered Lady Saye and Sele some boiled chicken, to which she firmly replied, "No, I cannot. When my husband destroyed himself I ate nothing but boiled chicken for a fortnight in my chamber and haven't been able to touch it since."'

More in the Austen line was Thomas Twisleton's younger son, Thomas James, while still at school, eloping with an actress to

Gretna Green. This spawned much high society gossip and confirmed Jane Austen's opinion that theatricals, especially conducted in private manors (such as young Twisleton and his co-eloper had frequented), were a breeding ground for dalliance of an unhealthy manner. Shortly after this scandal Jane's own parents stopped their long and excellent tradition of producing plays in their rectory home. As for Eloper Thomas James, his actress wife later proceeded to commit adultery and to produce an illegitimate son, so he divorced her and became a priest. All very rich pickings for Miss Austen's novels.

If you thought the Twisletons had run out of copy for Jane Austen at that point, you would be sadly wrong, for the disgraced young Twisleton had two sisters, the elder of whom married one of Jane's cousins, and the younger, Mary Twisleton, conducted her own highly publicised adulterous affair and, at sixteen, eloped with and later married a Mr Ricketts at a society wedding in Marylebone. Seven years later Ricketts discovered incriminating letters between Mary and her lover, one Charles Taylor MP of Cavendish Square. Ricketts instigated divorce proceedings in the House of Lords and at the hearing, a popular event for the media, several witnesses swore they had seen Mary visit her lover's home by night, others mentioned her ruffled and unkempt state as she left his house, and her maid testified that Mary had often bragged in minute detail of Taylor's prowess as a lover, compared with Ricketts' performance as a husband.

Some years later Jane Austen went to a party in Bath, knowing that the fairly large family group there would include her adulteress cousin Mary, whom she had never met. She wrote to her sister Cassandra: 'By 9 o'clock [we] entered the rooms . . . and I am proud to say I have a very good eye at an Adultress, for tho' repeatedly assured that another in the same party was *She*, fixed upon the right one from the first! She was not so pretty as I had expected, her face has the same defect of baldness as her sister's, and her features not so handsome. She was highly rouged and looked rather quietly and contentedly silly.'

As a Twisleton myself, I met my future wife of thirty-six years when she was nine, and started to take her out, contrary to the forcefully expressed wishes of her father, when she was thirteen. We did not elope, but we did enjoy a good dinner in Gretna Green some years after marrying. The DNA elopement gene has obviously faded over the generations.

George III's family scandals were forgotten in 1810 when his many children put their differences behind them and turned up in strength at Windsor to the celebrations of his fiftieth year on the throne of Great Britain. But in January 1811, aged seventy-three and exhausted, he finally gave in to his rapidly declining health and yielded to the appointment of the Prince of Wales as regent of the realm. On 21 May that year, the old king made his very last public appearance, after which he was never seen again outside the walls of Windsor Castle, although he lived on, insane, for another nine years. In 1814 he was said to have had a brief interlude of clarity, when he was overjoyed to be told that various allied victories over Napoleon had included the recapture of Hanover. His life's work, and that of his great premier, William Pitt, had not, after all, been in vain. Whether or not in the following year George ever comprehended the crowning glory of the victory at Waterloo, history does not relate.

George's queen died in 1818, sadly estranged from her mad husband, who followed her to the grave in February 1820. He had brought his country safely through sixty years of great change and great danger. It is surely a travesty of fate that such a ruler should merely be remembered as 'mad King George'. Abroad, the gains of his reign had been immense. Britain's grip on India was tightened, Ceylon was conquered, Singapore and the material rich Dutch East Indies were dominated, South Africa was seized from the Dutch, and trading rights were secured with all the former Spanish colonies of Central and South America. The Prince of Wales, who for so long had waited impatiently in the wings, was now King George IV and, arguably, the most powerful man in the world.

27

A Dandy Road to Ruin

Just as there was a lot more to George III than his years of madness, so there were other achievements to George IV's reign beyond the dandy image of the Beau Brummell period, the works of Byron and the domes of Brighton Pavilion.

His Regency had taken him through stirring times, starting in 1811. This period saw Wellesley invade Spain and drive the French out of the Peninsula with some bloody sieges; it saw Napoleon and his Grand Army wasting their substance in Russia at the wrong time of the year for an invasion; it saw Napoleon's decline and exile to Elba, followed by his escape and the final showdown with Wellesley, now Duke of Wellington, at Waterloo.

My own regiment, the Royal Scots Greys, gained their cap badge of the Napoleonic Eagle, still worn today, at Waterloo by seizing the Imperial Eagle standard of the French 45th Regiment in the heat of the battle. The Greys had charged with Gordon Highlanders clinging to their stirrups, a novel combination attack. (In 1916 my uncle was killed leading a company of Gordon Highlanders and in 1943 my father was killed commanding the Scots Greys.) Eighteen years after my father was killed commanding the Greys, I commenced eight years serving the same regiment (in Centurion tanks, not on grey horses and ranged against Marxist, not Nazi or Imperial forces).

Here is an account of the fighting at Waterloo from a young

infantry officer, Ensign Wheatley, who was in the thick of that momentous fight:

> About 10 o'clock came the order to clean our muskets and fresh load them. Half an allowance of rum was then issued and we descended into the plain, and took our positions in solid Squares ... we were ordered to remain in our position but, if we liked, to lay down ... [Behind us I saw the cavalry and artillery] in excellent order as if by a magic wand. [Including all] the horse Guards ... A Ball whizzed in the air. Up we started simultaneously ... It was just 11 o'clock, Sunday ... In five minutes a stunning noise took place and shocking havoc commenced. One could almost feel the undulation of the air from the multitude of cannon shot. The first man who fell was five files on my left. With the utmost distortion of feature, he lay on his side and shrivelling up every muscle ... in acute agony, [he died] ...
>
> A black consolidated body was soon seen approaching and we distinguished ... the iron-cased cavalry of the enemy. Shouts of 'Stand firm!', 'Stand fast!' were heard from the little squares around and very quickly these gigantic fellows were upon us ... No words can convey the sensation we felt on seeing these heavily-armed bodies advanced at full gallop against us, flourishing their sabres ... the sun gleaming on the steel ... We dashed them back [with] sharp-toothed bayonets ... and we presented our bristly points ... like porcupines ... The horse Guards then came up and drove them back ... The French made repeated attacks ... for two long hours ... [Then] the warfare took a new turn. In order to destroy our squares, the enemy filled the air with shells, howitzers and bombs so that, every five minutes, the whole Battalion lay on its face, then sprang up again when the danger was over ... An ammunition cart blew up near us, smashing men and horses. I [was] shocked at the sight of broken armour, lifeless bodies, murdered horses, shattered wheels ... Here and there a frightened horse would rush across the plain trampling on the dying and the dead. Three or four poor wounded animals standing on three legs, the

other dangling before them. We killed several of these unfortunate beasts and it would have been [as well to do likewise to] the wriggling, feverish, mortally lacerated soldiers as they rolled on the ground.

About 4 o'clock the battle was renewed . . . We still stood in line. The carnage was frightful. The balls which missed us mowed down the Dutch behind us [or the] cavalry behind them. I saw a cannon ball take away a Colonel of the Nassau Regiment so cleanly that the horse never moved from under him . . . [I kept] the men firm in their ranks, closing up the vacuities as the balls swept off the men, inspecting the fallen to detect deception. A regiment of Cuirassiers came like a thunderbolt among us. At the instant, a squadron of horse Guards dashed up to our rescue. In the confusion of the moment I made for the Colours to defend them. And we succeeded with infinite difficulty in rallying the men again.

Ensign Wheatley was injured soon after this, and his colonel killed. Captain Kincaid of the Rifle Regiment describes the end of the battle:

Our Division [had numbered] 5,000 men but . . . had gradually dwindled down to a solitary line of skirmishers. The 27th were lying, literally dead, in square, a few yards behind us. My horse had received another shot through the leg and one . . . in his body, sending him a step beyond the pension list. The smoke still hung so thick about us that we could see nothing. I walked . . . to each flank . . . to get a glimpse of what was going on, but nothing met my eye except the mangled remains of men and horses. I had never yet heard of a battle in which everyone was killed, but this seemed likely to be the exception.

Presently, a cheer which we knew to be British commenced far to the right . . . It was Lord Wellington's long-wished-for orders to advance. It grew louder . . . We took it up by instinct, charged [downhill] and [our enemy flew before us.] Lord Wellington

> galloped up . . . and our men began to cheer him; but he called out, 'No cheering, my lads, but forward and complete our victory.'

Napoleon was imprisoned finally on the island of St Helena, the twenty-year war against expansionist Revolutionary France was won and the British empire continued to expand.

As for the Regent Prince George, he was still king-in-waiting, for his mad father was still alive. In 1817 his only child, a daughter called Charlotte, died along with her stillborn son. The nation had been following her pregnancy closely in the press and was now furious, blaming the doctor (who committed suicide) and even Prince George for not being at his daughter's side when she died. The tragedy changed the prince, who suffered a nervous breakdown. It also sparked off a worry about the royal succession as the prince had long been separated from his hated wife Caroline of Brunswick, so there was no other offspring. This accelerated the marriage intentions of George's younger brothers, three of whom quickly married German princesses.

In January 1820, George III finally died after a sixty-year reign, and George IV was crowned, although unpopular, obese and almost certainly addicted to the laudanum which staved off the agony of his gout.

Six months prior to George III's death, the Tory government was over-harsh with prevalent industrial unrest. In Manchester 50,000 people rallied in St Peter's Fields. The yeomanry were sent in by the local magistrates and, at the subsequent 'Peterloo Massacre', eleven of the crowd were killed and four hundred injured.

Only four weeks after George IV's succession a group of revolutionaries was seized, the Cato Street conspirators who planned to assassinate all the cabinet ministers. Five were quickly executed, but the general atmosphere was menacing and the new king stayed away from London with its threat of mob violence. Into this uncertain scene Queen Caroline trod centre stage. She and the king still loathed each other. Both had had numerous adulterous affairs, but she had remained mostly abroad. Nonetheless, she was still popular and George's refusal to recognise her as queen and allow her to attend his coronation did not go down well with the people. George tried to obtain an official divorce through a parliamentary bill and an enquiry into her past adulteries. Neither move succeeded but, by fate (some said by poison), Queen Caroline died and saved the king a good deal of trouble.

George IV's coronation turned out to be an unexpectedly popular event and very soon after the ceremony, George, aged fifty-nine, became the first monarch since Richard II to pay a state visit to Ireland. The visit went well and the king followed it up with a fifteen-day jaunt to Scotland, entirely organised and orchestrated by the novelist, Sir Walter Scott. The King wore full Highland apparel, including the Stuart tartan. In earlier, less obese years, he had been adept at Scottish reels and was a well known lover of the bagpipes.

After Scotland and Ireland, George visited his other kingdom, that of Hanover, but thereafter until the end of his reign he retired, forever plagued by gout, to the seclusion of Windsor Castle, from where he continued to interfere with politics. One of his brothers, the Duke of Kent, died seven months after the birth of his daughter, the future Queen Victoria, of whom Uncle George grew very fond. The issue that filled his last years was that of Catholic emancipation, which he and most Whigs were against. The Tory premier, George Canning, tried to push it through on the retirement of Lord Liverpool. When Canning died, and the Duke of Wellington eventually became prime minister in 1828, he persuaded the king, against his will, to finally sign the Catholic Relief Act, which certainly soothed the southern Irish for a while.

Wellington, the great general, did his best as prime minister, but leopards do not change their spots and, in office, he spent a good deal of time suppressing democratic reforms and generally favoured elitism over enfranchisement. This made him a prime target of the London mob, many of whom had once toasted his victories. He acquired his nickname of the Iron Duke from the metal shutters he subsequently fitted to protect the windows of his London House

– Number One, London. According to tradition, after his first cabinet meeting he remarked to an aide, 'It was an extraordinary affair. I gave them their orders and they wanted to stay and discuss them.'

Another minister of George's, very able but over-sensitive and, like Wellington, from Ireland, was Robert Castlereagh, briefly a superb foreign secretary who, overworked, had a nervous breakdown and slit his own throat with a penknife, provoking the following epitaph from Lord Byron who was less than a fan:

> Posterity will ne'er survey
> A nobler grave than this.
> Here lie the bones of Castlereagh:
> Stop, traveller, and piss.

The king, as his gout worsened, spent most of his last three years in bed. His waistline by then was fifty-eight inches and his weight in excess of 350 pounds. A massive stroke finally killed him, aged sixty-seven, in the summer of 1830. *The Times*, always critical of George since his very early days, commented: 'There never was an individual less regretted by his fellow creatures than this deceased King.'

As for Broughton, it did not fare well over this period, despite Maria Twisleton following the royal fashion of marrying an extremely wealthy Prussian count. Maria's mother, Maria Marow, was the daughter and heiress of Samson Eardley, the son of the famous Samson Gideon, who saved the nation by paying off the National Debt and converted to Christianity in order to establish an Irish peerage for his son. Through his friendships with Walpole, Pelham and Pitt he had a private act passed by Parliament which enabled him to buy the magnificent manor of Belvedere in Kent, which he stocked with great art, largely bought from Walpole. Unfortunately, for all this dynastic planning by Gideon, his son Samson died without male issue, and so his eldest daughter (Maria Marow), or rather her husband, Gregory Twisleton, Baron Saye and Sele, inherited Belvedere and other large chunks of Gideon's rich estates. Gregory, being the heir of the late Thomas Twisleton of Broughton, could have chosen to live at either place but, having selected Belvedere, he let Broughton become dilapidated and rented it out to a succession of careless tenants.

Gregory had a fetish about his surname and changed it more than once. Even before meeting and marrying Maria, which enabled him to take on her family name which was Eardley, he had already appended his own old ancestral name of Fiennes. Gregory ended up as Baron Eardley-Twisleton-Fiennes and sat in the House of Lords as a Whig peer, which was consistent with the Fiennes and Twisleton political tradition, with one Tory exception, since pre-Cromwell days. Gregory also supported the Reform Bill of 1832, was offered and declined an earldom (despite marrying his daughter off to a Prussian count), and was a founder member of the Reform Club, in the entry hall of which you can still see his portrait. He lived to be the oldest member of the Whig party in the House of Lords and was greatly favoured by both the Grey and Melbourne administrations. He was also a famous patron of the boxing ring, and is still mentioned in descriptions of the sport of that time.

Gregory died in London aged seventy-five, and was buried at Broughton which, in its uncared for state, he left to his only son, William Thomas, who was unmarried, a Liberal and the Provincial Grand Master of Freemasons of Kent. He was also, to use the term as politely as possible, a dandy after the image of Beau Brummell. He was close friends with three famous bon viveurs, the Prince Regent, Lord Byron and the Count d'Orsay. William needed constant financial support for his merry life from father Gregory, who usually obliged, if necessary selling off more of the Gideon lands in Kent or Lincolnshire.

William, like Gregory, let Broughton go to the dogs. He was, after all, a distinguished member of the prestigious Royal Thames Yacht Club and a leader of fashion, both in style of clothing and in the latest cuisine. Belvedere's magnificence was a great deal more in keeping with his image than the Puritans' old country rendezvous of Broughton Castle. A report in the 1820s on the state of Broughton mentioned that the coat of arms of the Fiennes family had, in a great gale, fallen from the front of the castle's walls and lay smashed below. The walls themselves were covered in a profusion of destructive, creeping ivy, the living rooms were 'daily dilapidating from misuses', and by 1837 William Eardley-Twisleton-Fiennes had sold off all the saleable contents, even the swans on the moat, to pay off debts. (Many of the portraits he sold were subsequently bought back by later Saye and Seles and can be seen today in the Long Gallery.) William survived his father Gregory by only three years, dying aged forty-eight and much loved by his many friends, including the well-known gossip Count Gronow, who wrote of him in his *Reminiscences and Recollections*:

> Twisleton Fiennes, the late Lord Saye and Sele, was a very eccentric man, and the greatest epicure of his day. His dinners were worthy of the days of Vitellius. Every country and every sea was searched and ransacked to find some new delicacy for our British Sybarite. I remember, at one of the breakfasts, an omelette being served which was composed entirely of golden pheasants' eggs! He had a very strong constitution and would drink absinthe and curaçao in quantities which were perfectly awful to behold. These stimulants produced no effect upon his brain, but his health gradually gave way under the excesses of all kinds in which he indulged. He was a kind, liberal and good-natured man, but a very odd fellow. I never shall forget the astonishment of a servant I had recommended to him. On entering his service, John made his appearance as Fiennes was going out to dinner, and asked his new master if he had any orders. He received the following answer. 'Place two bottles of sherry by my bedside and call me the day after tomorrow.'

The next king, William IV, sandwiched for seven brief years between his brother, the unlamented George IV, and his niece, the great Victoria, is rarely remembered and there is little to be said about him. He was, at sixty-four, the oldest person so far to become a British monarch. Being the third son of the long-lived George III, he never expected to be king. He was happy in the Royal Navy which he joined as a midshipman aged thirteen, and he was often known as the Sailor King. He saw very little action, although he was at the Battle of Cape St Vincent in 1780, and, when based in New York during the American War of Independence, George Washington agreed to a plan to kidnap him, since he would often walk around the city alone. British spies learnt of the plan and appointed a detachment of guards to watch over him. The problem of what to do with heirs to the throne in the British armed forces is still to be resolved.

In the Caribbean he became great friends with Horatio Nelson, who respected him for his naval proficiency. They often dined together and William gave away Nelson's bride at his wedding. William greatly improved the standard of naval gunnery and banished the cat-o'-nine-tails as a punishment, except for mutiny.

For most of George III's reign, William was overshadowed by his two fractious elder brothers, while living in semi-poverty with his actress mistress, Mrs Jordan, by whom he had ten illegitimate children. He was an affable old seadog, much given to loud obscenities and unregal behaviour. Eventually, sorely needing cash, he left Mrs Jordan and married Princess Adelaide of Saxe-Meiningen, with whom he was happy but had no children. He was as surprised as most people when his elder brothers produced no heirs and he inherited the throne.

William IV sacked all George IV's French and German chefs and artisans, gave most of George's art collection to the nation, and often walked about in town markets without his court in order to chat to anyone he met. He was for a year very popular, but then became mixed up with the Reform Bill to extend the suffrage by 50 per cent, which the Commons had passed but which the Lords blocked. Wellington resigned and Lord Grey, who took over, advised William to simply pack the Lords with new peers who would pass the bill. For various reasons William refused, so it looked to the public as if he was the chief bill wrecker. In 1832 the bill was passed anyway, and William soon regained his popularity. The bill refashioned the national electoral system and lost the Lords a good deal of credibility.

Most of William's ministers found him to be a sensible, hard worker. Wellington said that he could deal with more business in ten minutes with William than in ten days with the late George. A later premier, Lord Brougham, said William would always ask good questions when wanting advice, whereas George IV never did, for fear of revealing his ignorance, and George III had asked many questions but never listened to the answers.

On foreign affairs William, unlike his aggressive foreign secretary Lord Palmerston, was naturally non-interventionist, distrusted the French, and had a flair for flattering those foreigners he could see were important to Britain, including important visitors from the former colonial America.

He disagreed with Wilberforce about abolishing slavery, on the grounds that the slaves he had observed whilst in the Caribbean had a higher standard of living than many Highlanders. But, on other issues, he was clearly liberal, pushing for the removal of all penalties against religious Dissenters, for a bill to allow adulterers to remarry if they so wished, and child labour was drastically restricted during his reign.

Although, compared to his predecessors, he very rarely engaged in political fracas, he was the last monarch in Britain to appoint a prime minister of his own choice against the will of Parliament. He died of a heart attack aged seventy-one and the crown passed to his favourite niece, Victoria, the only child of the eldest of his younger brothers. No other subsequent monarch was related to William, but he had many illegitimate children.

In Oxfordshire the future of the barony of Saye and Sele, plus ownership of poor dilapidated Broughton, were once again up for grabs on the death without issue of the extravagant William Thomas, he of the golden pheasant egg omelettes. The heir should have been the issue of William Thomas's uncle Thomas James, T.J., as I shall call him to avoid confusion and because letters to his family were always signed 'T.J. Twisleton'. But there was a snag caused by his early behaviour.

T.J.'s passion was acting, which he indulged both at school and in the holidays, at private theatres like the one at Adelstrop House, the home of Jane Austen's family, the Leighs, who were, over the years, thrice married to the Twisletons. These plays were described in *The World* as 'Lady Saye and Sele's Theatricals'. She had her son T.J. sit for a large oil painting dressed for his part of Phaedra in *Eunuchus* by the Roman playwright Terence, and when the painting, today in the Long Gallery at Broughton, was cleaned some few years ago, the cleaner exposed handcuff chains on the young T.J.'s wrists. Nobody quite knows why these were there in the first place (or, indeed, why they were later painted over), since they were in no way applicable to that play.

In 1788, shortly after his father's death, T.J. eloped to Gretna Green, aged eighteen and still at school, with an amateur actress, Charlotte Anne Wattell, with whom, after marriage, he then had five sons and a daughter. Within ten years all of the sons had died. Soon after his elopement T.J., in deep disgrace with his family, had stopped acting and went to Oxford where he matriculated in Divinity and became a poor curate with his brood of children in deepest Northamptonshire. Charlotte hated the life; not what she had expected when marrying the second son of a baron with a castle. So she fled the nest for the excitement of the professional stage. She acted, according to still existing handbills, under the name of the Hon. Mrs Twisleton, first on the Dublin circuit and then in Edinburgh, where she committed adultery with a Mr John Stein and had a baby boy. This boy was either the illegitimate son of Stein, or he just could be T.J.'s own son and a later heir to the Saye and Sele barony.

T.J. divorced his errant wife, suffered further scandal in doing so, and married again, this time to the suitably and boringly devoted Anglo-Irish Miss Anna Ash, whose ex-Bengal army father was

Governor of Bath prison. In 1804 Anna and T.J., together with their first son Fred (Frederick Benjamin, my great great grandfather), went to Ceylon, where nine years earlier a British naval force had landed at Trincomalee and occupied Colombo. Quite why T.J. took up a job in such a place is not difficult to guess, because in England he was clearly an embarrassment to his lordly Whig brother, Baron Gregory Twisleton.

Gregory was a good friend and, at Broughton, a close neighbour to Lord North who, in 1802, was appointed the first Governor of Ceylon when the Treaty of Amiens with Napoleon attached the coastal zones of Ceylon to Britain. So pushed in all likelihood by his big brother, T.J., Anna and little Fred landed in Colombo, where T.J. became initially the minister of the British garrison church and then the first Archdeacon of Colombo. For twenty years he was priest, local JP and director of forty-seven new schools he helped set up, with a salary of £2,000 a year.

Apart from their own children, T.J. and Anna also looked after T.J.'s surviving daughter Julia from his marriage to Charlotte, the actress. Julia married an English Captain James Brown, but he was shot dead in a duel by another officer after a petty argument. T.J., as judge, had the sad job of putting the surviving duellist in jail for a week and burying his son-in-law. Julia and her fatherless son, Tom Brown, returned to England on the breadline where Tom went to Winchester College and New College Oxford (as Founder's Kin) and became a priest in Dorset.

T.J. and Anna's other children after Fred included Edward who married Ellen Dwight, the daughter of the Senator for the State of Massachusetts (part founded by Old Subtlety). Edward was commendably involved in one of the most productive areas of social progress towards the end of William IV's reign, the reform of the Poor Laws. Much of the research and hard work behind their subsequent success was down to him and he went on under Queen Victoria to become leader of the 1843 enquiry into the Scottish Poor Laws, and in the terrible years of famine and repression (1845–9) he was the Chief Commissioner of Poor Laws in Ireland. He served on more government-appointed commissions than anyone else in his time. The situation in Ireland, however, was so dreadful for the poor and so apparently intractable that Edward resigned his top post in despair. Edward and his American wife Ellen had no children, but his elder brother Fred was destined to be the saving grace of the Saye and Sele line and of Broughton. Aged six, he was sent back from Colombo to Britain to be educated. He travelled alone. (His younger sister, Anna, on a subsequent voyage was shipwrecked and drowned.) On that childhood voyage, Fred's passenger ship, with its great square sails, would have been part of an armed convoy, for fear of the Napoleonic navy, and en route from Ceylon would have called at Cape Town (as I did, aged two in 1946, and stayed there for ten years).

Back in England, Fred's Saye and Sele cousins and his aunt, having discussed what was best for young Fred, earmarked him for the church, like his father in Ceylon and, funds for him being short, they took advantage of the Founder's Kin free education available. At Winchester he became a notable scholar being brilliant at memorising Latin. He won the King's Silver Medal for English and later gained his Doctorate of Civil Law at New College. He was ordained in 1823 became rector of Adelstrop and Broadwell and joined the staff of Hereford Cathedral in 1825, just after his father, T.J.'s death from typhoid in Ceylon.

In 1827 William Eardley-Twisleton, lover of golden pheasant eggs and 16th Baron Saye and Sele, died a bachelor and, in normal circumstances, the barony would have passed directly and without question to his first cousin Fred who by then had married a daughter of Lord Powerscourt, who had given him five sons and two daughters. Fred had meanwhile advanced up the hierarchy of Hereford Cathedral, via treasurer to canon residentiary, and was forty-seven years old when William died. But because of the complication of his father, T.J.'s first wife having had an adulterous relationship and possibly an illegitimate son, he was forced by law to claim the barony at an official proceedings at the House of Lords.

This he did by hiring good barristers to locate first Mr John

Stein, late of Edinburgh, who had run off with T.J.'s first wife and, secondly, the lad Charles himself. Not an easy task, but Stein, well into his eighties by then, was duly located and confronted by Fred's barrister. It must have been quite an ordeal for the old man, but he was still clear-headed and he stated the facts as he remembered them. A boy had, indeed, been born to Stein and T.J.'s wife up in Edinburgh and they had looked after him until he was fourteen when, since Stein and Charlotte were then on the breadline, he had been sent to sea. Stein had met him only once since then and remembered that he was in common sailor's garb at the time. Mr Stein repeated all this under oath before the Committee of Privileges. The barristers' agents then located exact dates from the Advocates' Library in Edinburgh, where all playbills of the Theatre Royal had been preserved for a century. So they knew exactly when T.J.'s errant actress wife had been in that city.

To locate the lost sailor son involved searching the Register of Seamen kept at Custom House. The full family name was not, of course, found, but the adopted one supplied the clue and the sailor, whether Charles Stein or Charles Twisleton, was traced on to an outward-bound ship. He was then met on his next return to England and happily, in a guileless fashion, told the story of his youth and birth as he knew it. The case was submitted to the House of Lords by Fred's lawyer where, upon investigation of the dates involved, the Lords decided that the child was Stein's, not Twisleton's. Stein and his now proven-to-be-illegitimate son gave evidence, no doubt delighted to have been reunited. So Fred became the 17th baron Saye and Sele without the ever-lurking fear of some unknown claimant appearing one day out of the blue.

Fred did not simply forget sailor Charles Stein and his old father, whose honesty had been the key to the outcome of the case. In 1863 Stein's solicitor wrote to Fred:

> Many thanks for your cheque for £20 for the poor sailor. A short time since I thought the little annuity would have ceased. He had a very severe illness, with erysipelas, but the constitution of his

old father seems to have descended to him and he rallied and now walks here from the region of the Docks near Limehouse every Monday morning to receive the allowance and then walks back. He is of a peaceable contented disposition, gives no trouble, his wants being satisfied by the occasional gift of a second hand coat or pair of shoes, and a little meat at Christmas. I often think the history of his life would make good materials for a novel – he used to say of himself that his existence and identity was always a subject of doubt and perplexity to himself, and he never could understand who or what he was, or where he came from.

The very next year, having begun long overdue restoration work on Broughton, Fred and his family grew to love the place and to revere the generations of their ancestors who had lived and loved there. In honour of all the Twisletons, Wykehams and Fienneses whose blood ran through Fred's veins, as the Sore brook runs through Broughton's moat, he altered his surname to Twisleton-Wykeham-Fiennes, which all my ancestors since have happily born, as, until she marries, will my daughter Elizabeth. The same year Fred re-established the close relations the family had long held with Broughton's nearby town, when he was appointed High Steward of Banbury.

Following the death of his first wife, Elizabeth, Fred married again in 1857 the much younger Caroline Leigh of the Jane Austen family, into which previous Twisletons had also married. Since the Leighs were from Adelstrop and Fred had long been their rector, he had actually baptised Caroline when she was a baby. In 1863 he became Archdeacon of Hereford (where a stained glass window commemorates him to this day) and still found time to take his duties at the House of Lords very seriously.

When he was seventy-nine and on his way into the House of Lords to discuss the highly unpopular County Franchise Bill, a riotous mob gathered outside the House to hustle and jeer the lords as they entered. Fred might well have tried to avoid the unpleasant attention of the hecklers, but instead he shouted back, 'Here is one of the Lords you are hooting – aye, and one who has always been a friend of the people.' This, in tones so hearty and with a bearing so upright that the crowd made way and cheered as he passed into the courtyard.

Sometimes when checking how repairs were going at Broughton, Fred would go up the curved stone steps to the roof immediately outside the council chamber where Hampden and Pym had plotted with Old Subtlety, and stand by the parapet. His staff below would hear his stentorian tones, well practised in Hereford Cathedral, ring out with his favourite watchwords, 'Peace, Retrenchment and Reform!' and 'No Taxation without Representation!' But life is never perfect. A nightmare gradually unfolded for Fred in his well-earned old age.

When in 1847 Fred inherited Broughton, he and his second wife, Caroline, took on the challenge of restoring the castle to its former glory. The entire contents had been auctioned off in 1837 by Gregory, probably to pay off his dandy son William's debts, and he had then rented the castle out unfurnished. Fred and Caroline had to spend a great deal over many years in their labour of love, renewing beams, replacing baths and basins, opening blocked doorways, replacing rotten woodwork, and redecorating walls. They did not neglect Broughton's church, either. As the work went on, so the clouds of bankruptcy gathered. Huge imports of North American wheat had drastically cut the annual agricultural income from the Saye and Sele's farm estates, as was the case all over Britain at the time. Then to add to the ongoing costs of the restoration, there was the inexcusable behaviour of Fred's eldest son (he had four), John Twisleton-Wykeham-Fiennes, the heir to Broughton and my great grandfather. In the recent words of the 21st Lord Saye and Sele, 'John, I regret to record, was a *bad* man.'

As early as 1855, when John was only twenty-five, Fred had to bail him out of Oxford prison, whence he had been committed by a moneylender to whom he owed £3,300. He gambled heavily and Fred's lawyers were constantly having to pay off his debts. He borrowed large sums to buy racehorses under an assumed name, and was inordinately proud of his one real success. He owned one brood mare, his only stud, and by her he bred Placida who won the Oaks in 1877, which gained John £10,000 in stakes and, when he sold her, a further £2,000.

John hid much of his borrowing from his parents in expectation of his inheritance. Fred's three other sons were at least honest about their ongoing requests to their bankrupt father for funds he didn't have. One letter of 1886 from his fourth son, Wingfield, who was at the time the Rector of Milton Keynes and with five children, ran:

> My Dearest Father
> . . . The chief problem at the present time is how to live at all, and it is my opinion that if the country is misgoverned much longer by the Grand Old Goose, only bankers and brewers will survive the general wreck. Every day brings some fresh application for money, and as there is so little incoming I fear it will before long end in a grand smash so far as I am concerned – and yet we have not even a pony trap, and drink no wine or beer, and have hardly a rag to our backs except what is handed over to us as old clothes . . . it is the inevitable result of Gladstonism! My son Alberic is cramming . . . for the examination required for a clerkship in the Bank of England. I am told that, if he does well, he may be able to secure £500 a year when he is sixty years old!
> Your very affectionate son,
> W.T.F.

Things must have looked truly dire for poor Fred. Huge debts and no remaining funds. Every inch of land mortgaged to the hilt and beyond. But tradition and family loyalty from Fred's brothers and cousins eventually paid the debts and saved Broughton. When Fred died, John took over, but tenants remained in occupation of the castle throughout his lifetime. He deserved it.

Under Queen Victoria, Broughton must have hoped the family would do better.

28

Uncle Geoffrey in Zulu Land

When King William IV, the Sailor King, died in 1837, his little niece, aged eighteen and less than five feet tall, became queen of the greatest empire in the world. She looked very unimpressive and her nickname was Drinny. She had slept all her life in the bedroom of her mother, who was convinced that her wicked uncles, the previous Kings George IV and William IV, wished to kill her.

One of her later prime ministers, the Tory Benjamin Disraeli, wrote in 1847 in his novel *Sybil* that Victoria reigned over two nations, the Rich and the Poor; 'between whom there is no intercourse, and no sympathy; who are as ignorant of each other's habits, thoughts and feelings as if they were dwellers in different zones, or inhabitants of different planets; who are formed by a different breeding, are fed by a different food, are ordered by different manners, and are governed by the same laws.'

The basic problem was that Victoria coincided with a time of huge and ever-accelerating change, but she was saddled with a tried, tested but inflexible framework of governmental machinery. The political system, into which the young Victoria found herself slotted, had been designed over the centuries for the benefit of landowning aristocrats in a rurally based nation. It had not kept up with the recent and startling transformation of Britain into an urban industrial society. The ever expanding working class had few non-violent ways of expressing their frustrations legally available to them, and there was an increasingly uppity middle class with a great capacity for radicalism but still without the vote. The Reform Act of 1832 had only extended the franchise to certain categories of adult males, so a great many workers still felt voiceless and betrayed.

Parliament's frightened response to these people's increasing agitation was to clamp down on them. Six Dorset labourers were sentenced for transportation merely for trying to organise a trade union, but countrywide protests eventually secured their pardon. They were known as the Tolpuddle Martyrs. Old-fashioned Tories, like the Duke of Wellington, believed in holding a tough line on these 'troublemakers', but such rigid views were on the way out. The Whigs, soon to metamorphose gradually into Liberals, believed there were two main social classes – property owners and rabble – and that the former must stick together or be overrun by the latter.

A factor of change which did help the urban poor in very real terms was the Municipal Act that empowered urban councils to raise local taxes and spend the results as they felt best. This sparked many an ambitious and aggressive council in the 1840s and 1850s to greatly improve the lives of their tax-paying citizens. Cities such as Liverpool and Bradford spent millions of pounds on water and sewerage schemes. Glasgow's city fathers spent £1.5 million to stop cholera epidemics caused by the filthy waters of the Clyde. But the shiny new water closets of the middle-class streets often drained into the workers' water supplies.

1858 in London was known as the Year of the Great Stink when the Thames, according to Disraeli, became a 'stygian pool reeking with ineffable and intolerable horrors'. The foul stench pervaded the Commons and forced the Metropolitan Board to spend £4 million on the construction of an eighty-two-mile, multi-levelled sewer to take London's sewage to the sea.

In the latter half of Victoria's reign, great hospitals were built in many cities, and in forty years the supply of doctors increased from 14,000 to 23,000. Chloroform stopped surgery from being the terrible experience of earlier times, but faulty hygiene practices and overzealous use of forceps still meant that 10 per cent of pregnant women who entered maternity wards left them in coffins. The safest place for delivery was still at home.

Strangely enough, in the mid nineteenth century crime figures dropped, despite the industrial tensions and the rapid population growth in crowded cities. An explanation of this phenomenon may well have been the Education Boards, instituted by the Liberals, making it compulsory for schools to be set up wherever no church schools existed.

Such was life in Victoria's great new cities in the mid- to late nineteenth century where, despite a background of poverty, the Tory party under Disraeli and later Lord Salisbury did very well through the 1870s onwards. This started with Disraeli's realisation that political success was becoming as much a matter of presentation as of actual policy. The beginnings of what we now call spin.

Victoria's greatest and longest serving minister was the Liberal coalitionist, aggressively patriotic Lord Palmerston, who personified the arrogant self-confidence of his country, which he described, accurately enough, as the 'only world power'.

One of many examples of how British forces in the mid-nineteenth century reinforced this view was that of my first cousin Lord Nigel Napier's ancestor, General Sir Charles Napier and his 1843 successes in India. There is a bronze statue of him in Trafalgar Square.

When Hindu priests had a go at Napier for upholding the British law against their ancient *suttee* practice of burning widows alive on the funeral pyres of their husbands, he replied: 'You say it is your custom to burn widows. Very well. We also have a custom: when men burn a woman alive, we tie a rope around their necks and we hang them. Build your funeral pyre; beside it my carpenters will build a gallows. You may follow your custom. And then we will follow ours.' Later that year Napier led a force of four hundred British and 2,200 sepoys to decisively defeat 30,000 Baluchi soldiers at Miani, fighting hand-to-hand (and Napier was sixty at the time) before entering and gaining control of all Sind Province. His cable back to army headquarters simply read 'Peccavi', the Latin for 'I have sinned.' (The general was descended from the John Napier who invented Napierian Logarithms, still in use today.)

Back home, a stable Britain took in the French royal family fleeing the Parisian mob in 1848, and also two middle-class German revolutionaries, who had fled to London after involvement in a failed revolution back home, and in the calm of the British Museum produced a joint work entitled *The Communist Manifesto*. Karl Marx was twenty-nine and Friedrich Engels only nineteen, but their London scribblings were, over the next hundred years and more, to spawn the monstrous Marxist-Leninist nightmare that caused countless millions to die in misery, especially in Eastern Europe. I spent five years with a tank troop of the Royal Scots Greys, waiting for the Communist Warsaw Pact armies to pour over the East German border in the early 1960s. Now, thank the Lord, the *Manifesto* has proved a mere failed political experiment.

In London Marx despaired at the resistance of the working classes to the socialist ideas of middle-class intellectuals such as himself. In 1851, the Great Exhibition in the specially built Crystal Palace in Hyde Park, set up by aristocrats to celebrate the dominance of Britain's goods in the global marketplace, was visited by great numbers of honest proletarians who, far from voicing even the mildest revolutionary themes, beamed with monarchic chauvinism and revelled in the popular London ballad of the time, which ran: 'O, surely England's greatest wealth is an honest working man . . .' Over six million tickets were sold for the exhibition, and for many it was their first visit ever to London thanks to the special trains that brought in visitors from all over Britain. The profits were used to build the museums of South Kensington.

The next year over a million people lined the route of the Duke of Wellington's funeral procession from Horse Guards to St Paul's Cathedral. People remembered his great victories over 'Boney' of forty years before, his prickly ministries and, much later, his quaint behaviour, in his seventies, patrolling the London streets on horseback with cocked pistols on his belt as he searched for Spring-Heeled Jack, a serial killer who slashed his female victims with metal claws.

Victoria's Crimean War army of the 1850s could have done with a commander of Wellington's stature, but it seems to have suffered instead from a series of lordly buffoons, the most infamous of whom, Lords Raglan and Cardigan, sent Britain's finest cavalry into murderous cannon fire at Balaclava. The Crimean War had a complex background, but was mainly caused by Russian determination to take over the sprawling and weakening Ottoman empire of the Turks. France and Britain agreed to send armies by sea to prevent such Russian expansionism in the Crimea, and the result was extremely bloody, with the Russians doggedly holding on to a number of key coastal towns, such as Sevastopol. I have the 1850s diaries of Frederick Fiennes, 16th Lord Saye and Sele-to-be, which for 1855 simply states: 'Left Broughton and joined the depot of The 23rd [Royal Welsh Fusiliers] at Winchester . . . Left England for Malta in the *Great Tasmania* troopship . . . [joined the headquarters] in Balaclava harbour [on 16 June] and from that date there was nothing but hard fighting. Spent the Christmas in Camp before Sebastopol.'

A few months prior to Frederick's arrival, the famous cavalry charges took place. My own regiment of the 1960s, the Royal Scots Greys, together with the Enniskillens – three hundred men in all – charged uphill against a dense mass of Russian cavalry over 3,000 strong. This, the charge of the Heavy Brigade, has since been described by many war historians as the most desperate but successful cavalry versus cavalry charge in history. The tragic charge of the Light Brigade, which took place later the same day, was made famous by Tennyson with the words:

> Theirs not to reason why,
> Theirs but to do or die.
> Into the valley of death
> Rode the six hundred.

Six hundred and seventy-three of Britain's elite cavalry charged thirty Russian guns, which scythed them down as they kept coming along a mile of open ground. Survivors reached the guns, killed the crews and rode back. Only 198 lived to tell their tale. A French general who watched, said, 'It's magnificent but it's no way to fight a war.' George Orwell commented later: 'The most stirring battle-poem in English is about a brigade of cavalry which charged in the wrong direction.'

The Times pioneered a new method of telling folk back home immediately what was going on. This was the telegraph dispatch, and a new breed of war reporters were quick to expose how ill-equipped and poorly led were many of our troops. The scandal of the charge was soon overshadowed by the conditions in Crimean field hospitals, where more soldiers were dying from infections contracted in the wards than from their battlefield wounds.

Florence Nightingale, whom news reports immortalised as 'the lady with the lamp', vastly improved sanitation. Until her arrival, bedding was never washed, rats and fleas abounded and water sources were polluted. Nurses up till then were considered little better than prostitutes, and certainly never came from respectable families. Florence Nightingale, when officers obstructed her hospital reforms, simply contacted Queen Victoria direct, and Victoria always backed her requests and complaints. The queen visited the wounded and created the Victoria Cross to honour the brave. She personally knitted scarves for many an army veteran, gave nursing her full approval as a career for any caring female whatever her background, and helped Miss Nightingale establish nursing career structures at King's College and St Thomas's Hospitals.

For all the improvements in hospital care, it was typhoid from the cesspits of Windsor Castle that killed the queen's consort, Prince Albert, in 1861. Victoria wore only black for the rest of her long life and for years avoided public appearances to the point where she became very unpopular with her own subjects.

At the time of Prince Albert's death, the profligate owner of Broughton Castle, John Fiennes, the 17th Lord Saye and Sele, was renting out the castle and estate to pay for his horse racing addiction and gambling debts. He married the diminutive Lady Augusta Hay-Drummond, who gave him ten children, the second of whom was my grandfather, Eustace, born in 1864. Tradition dictated that Eustace, as second son, would end up as a priest, a soldier or an upholder of the empire in some faraway colonial outpost.

The year he was born, the papers were full of tales of the American Civil War, an affray Queen Victoria kept well clear of and indeed clear of all involvement with the ultra-sensitive ex-colonies, particularly after a recent diplomatic incident instigated by my grandfather's cousin, Sir John Fiennes Twisleton Crampton, minister plenipotentiary and envoy extraordinary to the United States. Lord Palmerston was in the process of instructing all his ambassadors to recruit foreign corps who would be paid by Britain to fight the Russians in the Crimea. These included German, Swiss and Italian legions, and Crampton recruited actively in the United States. President Franklin Pierce, in order to gain popularity and a fresh term of office, complained bitterly against such recruitment and demanded the immediate recall of Fiennes Crampton 'as prime mover in a scheme which he knew full well was contrary to the law of the United States and that he continued to recruit after it had been pronounced unlawful.' Despite Lord Palmerston's initially robust response to Pierce's posturing, he then relented and withdrew the offending diplomat.

Trade, Palmerston ruled, was master of all else and master of the empire.

London sometimes instituted small imperial beginnings, the thin end of new wedges, by way of chartered companies, trading bodies with governmentally guaranteed rights to trade and administer a given region. Rhodesia, East Africa and Nigeria all came under British rule in this insidious manner. Following the Indian Mutiny in 1857, the East India Company was wound up and all its vast territories became British-administered with, in 1876, the queen as official Empress of India.

Self-rule of colonies followed sooner or later (sometimes much later). Canada became a Dominion in 1867, and Australia a Commonwealth in 1900, but the latter half of the nineteenth century witnessed the annexation by Britain of vast new parts of the Pacific, East Africa and the Far East. World trade on the high seas was absolutely dominated by British shipping, and this carried over into the twentieth century, well after British dominance in trade goods had declined. Religious indoctrination by a thousand British missionaries, including David Livingstone, backed up trade activities, and by the 1880s a quarter of the entire world was coloured British pink on the map. In those days German tourists did not put their towels on British sunbeds.

Tory claims to be the only effective and dedicated empire party were severely dented by their handling of wars in Afghanistan where two expeditions were costly and catastrophic failures, and in South Africa where first Zulus, then Boers gave the great British army a very bloody nose. In 1879 some 5,000 British troops crossed into Zululand intent on forcing the Zulu king to accept the status of a British protectorate. Whilst the troops were camped at Isandlwana they were attacked by 10,000 Zulus with spears. The British fixed bayonets but were soon massacred. The Zulus swept on to the isolated garrison of Rorke's Drift, held by 120 mostly Welsh soldiers who somehow repulsed the attacking horde and earned eleven Victoria Crosses before breakfast, a greater number of medals for extreme gallantry than ever awarded for any other single engagement.

My great uncle Geoffrey, 18th Lord Saye and Sele, was part of Disraeli's response to the massacre, a second army of 23,000 men sent out to avenge the dead of Isandlwana. He was decorated for bravery in the fighting which captured the Zulu King Cetshwayo. On his return home he was appointed Comptroller of the Royal Household and High Steward of Oxford, and later wrote a family history called *Hearsay*.

Geoffrey, his younger brother, my grandfather Eustace, and their eight other brothers and sisters grew up spending their winters at Broughton and their summers in London. This was because family fortunes remained at a low ebb and dependent upon intermittent rental income. Broughton was rented out throughout the period from 1885 until 1912 to society figures like Lord and Lady Gordon Lennox who entertained the royal family there. Fienneses had long since learnt that they must go out individually and earn a living. They could no longer rely on the current head of the family inheriting or marrying oomph – oomph being the Fiennes slang for lots-of-money.

My grandfather Eustace decided to avoid the regular army and priesthood and to head instead for the other traditional second-son option of a colonial career. He had read of the romantic life to be found in northern Canada as a fur trapper, mining for gold on the side, and so in 1882, aged eighteen, he arrived in Alberta and tried his luck with pick, sieve and snares. He ran out of money long before finding even fool's gold and had to sign up with the North West Mounted Police as a trooper. After training and happily receiving his first salary, he picked up his first medal for his part in a campaign to quell the Plains Indians and métis of mixed race in the wilds of Saskatchewan. But there was little other excitement and he began to yearn for a more colourful existence somewhere where the pine forests or prairies did not stretch to the horizon, where summers did not mean clouds of mosquitoes and winters long months of white wilderness.

So he resigned in 1888 and hitched his way to Egypt with the job of news reporter for the *Morning Post*. There he joined the staff of General Kitchener, who was busy retaking Sudan after the rebellious Dervishes of the Mahdi had earlier killed General Gordon at Khartoum. Eustace fought with Kitchener's army at the Battle of Gemaizah but it would be ten years before the final defeat of the Mahdi's successor, the Khalifa, at Omdurman and the annexation of all Sudan by Britain. Eustace left Kitchener's forces in March 1890 and joined the British South Africa Company's police as a sub-lieutenant in Kimberley. This force had been formed by Cecil Rhodes the previous year to help protect pioneers travelling north into Mashonaland (now part of Zimbabwe). Eustace did well and was soon promoted to full lieutenant with his own police troop.

Just as the East India Company in India and the Hudson Bay Company in Canada preceded British territorial gains in those countries, so Cecil Rhodes' British South Africa Company expanded British territory in southern Africa. Hence Rhodesia. Eustace did his bit. The *History of the British South African Police* described Eustace (spelling his surname ffiennes) as: 'Not a regular soldier, he was the son of a lord and a member of the London Stock Exchange although he had served, by some unexplained circumstances, in the Canadian militia.'

Pennyfeather's Column of Pioneers to Southern Rhodesia, which began in late June 1890, made a confrontation with Portugal, Britain's oldest ally, inevitable because Portugal had laid claim to the whole area through which the Rhodes pioneers had to travel to reach Rhodesia, and many of his men, including Pennyfeather and, later, grandfather Eustace, were dead keen to grab territory for the motherland wherever they could. Shortly before Eustace joined the BSAP, an energetic Portuguese soldier, Major Paiva d'Andrada, formed a Rhodes-type commercial company and established a fortress at Massi Kessi, twenty miles from where Eustace's police were based at Umtali.

In November 1890, a small armed force under Eustace attacked three hundred Portuguese levies on the ridge above Massi Kessi. Andrada was captured and his fort seized. Andrada was sent back to Portugal where he caused a great stir against British aggression on Portuguese territory. Later, when four separate Portuguese forces arrived to retaliate, including a thousand volunteers with artillery, they found overland travel a harder foe than the British. It was easy to get lost in the dense tropical vegetation. Rations were meagre. Malaria and dysentery struck men daily. Horses died or contracted tsetse fly-induced sickness. Rivers had to be crossed, swollen and full of crocodiles. Tracks were deep in mud. The heat and humidity were exhausting.

In March 1891, according to the book *Men Who Made Rhodesia*, Eustace was stationed at Umtali when he received a messenger. Two of his men were down with fever at an outpost.

> Fiennes at once called for volunteers who were good swimmers, and selected [two. The three] set out on a 23 mile journey over slippery mountain paths at the height of the rainy season when all rivers were in flood. Rain had fallen incessantly for months, and 52 inches had been recorded for the season against a normal 30 inches. When they got to the Revue River they found it to be 'raging like a miniature sea, mountainous waves roaring like thunder'. In spite of this, Fiennes attempted the crossing alone; he was carried down the stream for half a mile and was once entangled in reeds. Nevertheless he managed to gain the far bank after half an hour in the water.

At the outpost he found that one man had been dead for a week and Glover, the other, was in a dreadful condition. He began to dig a grave with his own hands. Building a small raft, Fiennes and another man got Glover back over the crocodile river and, in a rough litter, over the mountains to their base. Glover lived until 1950. The account continued: 'Fiennes' part in the rescue was one of calculated courage of the highest order; the odds in favour of his crossing the Revue were very slender.'

On 11 May Eustace took part in the Battle of Chua Hill when a Portuguese attack was repulsed. Next day the Macequece Fort's garrison was found to have fled and Fiennes was sent forward with six mounted men along the paths towards Beira to follow up the enemy and keep going east to the sea. At Chimoio, 130 miles from Umtali, he located a manned Portuguese fort, observed it and decided to attack the next day. Whilst preparing the attack he was surprised by a white man whom he nearly shot for a Portuguese. But this was the British Bishop of Mashonaland who told him not to attack the Portuguese as the arrival of Major Sapte, the Military Secretary to the British High Commissioner, was imminent. This man duly arrived and ordered Eustace not to attack because peace had been made by the two governments the previous day.

According to the official *History of the British South Africa Police*: 'when Rhodes heard what had happened, and that the swashbuckling attempt to add Portuguese East Africa to his territories had again been abandoned, he said, "Why didn't Fiennes say Sapte was drunk and put him in irons?"' On 30 May Lord Salisbury and the Portuguese government finally signed an agreement, which has lasted until the present day. At the time, Queen Victoria was greatly relieved, being closely related to the Portuguese king. Eustace, unaware of the narrow scrape he had experienced in sparking off a potentially major international embarrassment, was sent back to Umtali.

That July, Rose Blennerhassett, in charge of a group of nursing sisters posted to the Umtali region, wrote in her book, *Adventures in Mashonaland*: 'Foremost amongst our friends was Lieutenant Eustace Fiennes whom we came to regard as a special providence. He saved us as far as possible from difficulties, was kind, courteous and helpful, to say nothing of being a very jolly young fellow and excellent company.' In December however, Eustace's health broke down and he resigned his commission.

His subsequent attempts to buy stakes in the Kimberley gold mines and to start a farm in Matabeleland quickly came to nothing. He was a bad businessman. He ran out of funds, as he had in Canada, and sought work in Cape Town. There, in 1894, he met and married my grandmother, a South African of Prussian descent, born Florence Agnes Rathfelder, whose first husband, a Scotsman named Arthur Fletcher, had been thrown from a horse and killed, leaving Granny Florrie fairly wealthy. My godfather, Lawrence Fiennes, told me with great mirth how well he remembered the breakfast when he and the rest of Eustace's large family at Broughton read aloud the telegram from Eustace in Cape Town, which simply proclaimed, 'AM MARRYING OOMPH. EUSTACE'. In 1895 Eustace and Florrie had their first son, my Uncle Johnnie, and they returned briefly to England until Eustace again became bored.

Two years later, Queen Victoria's Diamond Jubilee confirmed that, after sixty years on the throne, and despite abandoning her people during her long period of mourning, she was still highly popular. She wrote in her diary after the Jubilee celebrations: 'The crowds were quite indescribable, and their enthusiasm truly marvellous and deeply touching. The cheering was quite deafening, and every face seemed to be filled with real joy. I was much moved and gratified.'

In 1899 Eustace, back home with his little family, various medals and tales of derring-do, contested North Oxfordshire as the Liberal candidate. He was defeated by some 700 votes. That same year, in the nearby parish of Chipping Norton, the local vicar experimented with the medical properties of willow bark, and the aspirin was invented, still the most popular and useful drug in the world. Since his political aspirations had not initially worked out, Eustace kept his ears attuned to the South African scene. In October that year the Dutch, or Boer, leader in South Africa formally declared war on Britain unless British troops were withdrawn from the twin Boer republics of Transvaal and the Orange Free State. Since one of Britain's main geo-political goals was to bring both these gold-rich Boer provinces under direct British rule, war was exactly what Prime Minister Salisbury wanted, especially (PR-wise) if the Boers were seen to make the first aggressive move. Militarily Britain was confident of quickly defeating them. Eustace, along with many other Liberals, did not approve in principle of the idea of fighting the Boers to gain their gold. So he said so in public and was promptly labelled 'pro-Boer' by prominent Tories.

Originally the Cape, already settled by the Dutch, had been occupied by the British to safeguard the route to India. Various plans to incorporate the Boers into a federation were discussed and then, in 1877, imposed on them, but four years later the Boers had rebelled and their two states were given a loose independence. This had worked until both gold and diamonds were discovered on Boer land, and Cecil Rhodes goaded the Boers' leader, Paul Kruger, into his 1899 declaration of war.

Eustace, fresh from his electoral defeat as the great white hope of the North Oxfordshire Liberals, and despite his personal views on the Boers, discussed joining up for the Boer War with a friend, Winston Churchill, who had a similar background of fighting in various foreign wars, including the Sudan, and had also reported on them for the *Morning Post*.

Churchill's family, the Spencers, owned the Blenheim estate close to Broughton, had inter-married with the Fienneses years before and, although Winston was at this stage a Tory, before switching to Liberal and then back again, he thought along similar political lines to Eustace on most things. They would later work well together but, back in 1900, Eustace was attracted by Winston's war stories, not his politics. The previous year Winston had achieved brief fame through his own *Morning Post* reports by rescuing an armoured train from the Boers and then, after being captured, effecting a daring escape. So Eustace, like Winston, signed up with the local regiment, the Oxfordshire Imperial Yeomanry, said goodbye to Granny Florrie, Uncle Johnnie and all his brethren round the Broughton log fires, and shipped back to sunny South Africa to kill Boers instead of Portuguese.

Unfortunately, things did not go as planned for the British army. The superior mobility, field skills and firepower of the Boers led to many embarrassing British defeats and the siege of various garrisons, including Mafeking. Britain's enemies all over the world sniggered and gloated, though Eustace did well and was twice mentioned in dispatches, adding to his colourful collection of medals. Such had been the humiliating effect on the British public of the previous long history of defeats by the Boers that the May 1900 relief of Mafeking was greeted by nationwide rejoicing. The garrison commander, Colonel Robert Baden-Powell, who years later founded the Boy Scout and Girl Guide movements had saved many lives during the siege by boiling whole horse corpses in vats to provide 'the Colonel's Soup'.

At the close of 1900, Kitchener of Khartoum took over in the Cape with a Commonwealth army of half a million troops to clean up the remnants of a Boer army that never exceeded 50,000 soldiers. The latter resorted to the guerrilla tactics at which they were adept and to which the terrain was ideally suited. To retaliate, the British invented concentration camps and long lines of blockhouses, 8,000 of them, connected by tangled hedges of barbed wire. Boer farms were burnt and civilians shut up in the camps, where 25,000 died of disease. Finally, in May 1902 Kitchener signed a peace treaty with the Boers, whose two states became British colonies but with internal self-government.

Forty-two years later, when I arrived in Cape Town to spend my youth there, Brits and Boers lived happily together. But, in the words of historian Thomas Pakenham, the Boer War 'proved to be the longest (two and three- quarter years), the costliest (over £200 million), the bloodiest (at least 22,000 British, 25,000 Boer and 12,000 African lives) and the most humiliating war for the British between 1815 and 1914'.

Queen Victoria died before the war ended (in January 1901) aged eighty-one and after sixty-three years on the throne. Although the British empire peaked in every way during her reign, its economic decline also began in her time. By 1900, Britain's share of world manufacturing output had dropped from over 60 per cent fifty years before to 18 per cent, with America at 23 per cent and Germany rapidly catching up. Victoria's nine children's progeny included her two grandsons, George V of England and Kaiser Wilhelm II of Germany, whose nations were to fight each other at great cost in human lives and misery.

29

Eustace and Winston

Victoria's eldest son, Edward, like our own Charles, Prince of Wales today, had, since coming of age, waited over forty years in the shadow of his mother's rule. So he was well known to the nation and, aged sixty, unlikely to provide any nasty surprises when, on Victoria's death, he became King Edward VII. His Danish wife, Alexandra, was well loved, innocuous and seemingly inured to Edward's ongoing stream of scandals and mistresses, including Mrs Keppel and Lillie Langtry. Edward seldom interfered with home politics but was often useful to his ministers where foreign diplomacy was concerned, since most relevant heads of state were his first cousins; the most important and troublesome being his nephew, Kaiser William II of the ever more menacing Germany. Over the next nine years Edward used his charm and his cousinly links to encourage various treaties and alliances between Britain, Germany, Russia and France.

In the 1870–90 period, France had seemed, as ever, to be Britain's looming enemy and Germany Britain's ally, but that changed when in 1898 Germany's great naval construction programme and global ambitions preceded German encouragement of and backing for the Boers. Britain secured treaties or alliances with the Japanese in 1902, the French in 1904, and the Russians in 1907. Gradually, as German military power flexed its muscles on parade grounds, tensions mounted in Europe, and

Britain sided increasingly with the Franco-Russian alliance against Germany and Austria. In a series of incidents in the Balkans, Turkey and North Africa and, in its ongoing naval build-up, Germany grew ever more hostile to Britain.

Edward, a long-time fan of the exotic delights of Paris, became popular with the French people and is credited with beginning the process still known as the Entente Cordiale, a diplomatic agreement that put an end to a thousand years of intermittent warfare. It did not, of course, stop the two nations constantly sniping at each other because it is difficult to break an enjoyable habit. Two reasons for traditional Francophobia were suggested by the actor Robert Morley in 1974: 'The French are a logical people, which is one reason the English dislike them so intensely. The other is that they own France, a country which we have always judged to be much too good for them.' A worthy riposte about the English came from Jacques Chirac: 'You can't trust people who cook as badly as that. After Finland, it's the country with the worst food.'

When Victoria died, she drew her last breath in the loving arms of her grandson, the Kaiser, but Edward, though always polite, never liked his German nephew. He agreed with Admiral Fisher, in charge of the Royal Navy, that, 'Our only probable enemy is Germany. We must therefore keep a fleet twice as powerful concentrated within a few hours of Germany.' Not long before his own death in 1910, Edward noted: 'If the Kaiser goes on in that way [refusing a naval limitation agreement], a conflict between us and Germany is only a matter of time.'

Eustace returned from the Boer War with many medals. Of his nine brothers and sisters, he was definitely the most romantic. He stood for Parliament again in 1906 and this time won Banbury for the Liberals, a seat he held until 1918 through the period of his party's major social welfare reforms, including old age pensions, free school meals, sickness and unemployment benefits, national insurance, and many other rights that are now taken for granted.

His elder brother Geoffrey became a Liberal peer in 1908 on the death of their spendthrift father, John, my great grandfather, thanks to whose early debts Broughton was still, until 1912, rented out in summer to the Gordon-Lennox family. One visitor who was given the run of the castle by Lord Saye was the Baroness Orczy, whose most famous novel was *The Scarlet Pimpernel*. Keen to write about Broughton and its Parliamentarian experiences at the time of Old Subtlety and his sons, Orczy chose the Royalist-inclined eldest son and heir, James Fiennes, as her hero and called the book *The Honourable Jim*. Lord Saye disliked the resulting novel intensely, and told her so. He subsequently wrote about the Orczy visit to Broughton: 'The Baroness and her husband stayed here at my invitation to get, as she prettily put it, "the local colour". On the morrow she came down in a picturesque muslin frock and going into the garden, she sat on one of our newly painted seats and got "the local colour".' He was also very cynical about Tories in general, even when he liked them as individuals. He once wrote: 'I crossed the Channel with an intimate friend, a Tory peer, who remarked to me that, as a Liberal, I was sure to get some office quickly, for we had so few among us who could be trusted not to steal the spoons – a cheery specimen of Tory mentality.'

Brother Eustace was basically bored with life as a Liberal MP commuting between Banbury and Westminster, so he joined the local Territorials (the Oxfordshire Huzzars Imperial Yeomanry) along with his friend and fellow Liberal MP, Winston Churchill. Judging from correspondence that I have been sent by Churchill College, Cambridge, both men received 'special treatment' from relevant authorities. Here is a note from a senior officer in Southern Command dated January 1907:

> With reference to your letter asking for a report on the case of Major Winston Churchill MP and Major the Hon. Eustace Fiennes MP and their failure to present themselves for examination for Field Rank on promotion, I recommend that

these Officers be excused this examination for the following reasons . . .

Both officers have exceptionally long and meritorious experience on active service. Both officers are occupied with Parliamentary duties. Major Churchill has also to attend to official duties and Major Fiennes has a City business to look after. Both officers are natural leaders and thoroughly competent in every way.

Some sixty years later, with the British Army of the Rhine in Germany, I requested permission to miss my captain to major promotion exam, owing to special circumstances (an expedition to Africa). I was refused and subsequently failed the exam. It's all right for some.

The Fienneses and the Churchills of Oxfordshire, were traditional peers whose status came largely from the great estates they had inherited. However, during Edward VII's reign new peers in the Lords were no longer necessarily large landowners. Landed estates all over Britain were fragmenting and being sold off to previous tenants; a true sign of the times. In Edinburgh in 1900 half of Scotland was for sale in the hands of a single Edinburgh lawyer. By 1910 eighty of the hundred wealthiest families in Britain had made their fortunes from manufacturing and not, as had been the case at Broughton for centuries, from rental and wool.

Churchill, Lloyd George and their Liberals, the Fiennes clan included, were in the vanguard of a raft of proposed taxes, including a super tax on the incomes of the very rich, and various taxes on property. Forty years earlier, governments had treated Britain's poor as 'those vast, miserable, unmanageable masses of sunken people' and 'that enormous mass of paupers'. Only in Edward's reign did the Liberals believe that they could actually alter the status of the truly poor by clever handling of the economy. Poverty was neither inevitable nor a necessary result of capitalist societies. Edward's reign also saw the trades union movement double its membership to over four million, with the new Labour party gaining ground against both Tories and Liberals.

Edward VII was the first ruler to experience the full development of the national political parties and a franchise which included the greater part of the adult male population. He no longer held any royal veto on governmental legislation, could no longer sack ministers he disliked, nor alter the direction any Cabinet had decided to take on any matter at home or abroad. He once wrote to an adviser: 'The Cabinet is apparently so powerful a body that neither I nor the Prime Minister can gainsay them.' Edward died of a series of heart attacks in May 1910 and was much mourned, as was summed up in a note by one of the secretaries of state: 'The feeling of grief and personal loss throughout the country, indeed through Europe, is extraordinary. It is in a way deeper and keener than when Queen Victoria died – more personal. He had just the character that Englishmen, at any rate, thoroughly like and understand. He combined regal dignity with good nature and strict regard for form with entire absence of pomp.'

The Prince of Wales was crowned King George V and was to prove as popular over his twenty-five-year reign as his namesake, George IV, had been unpopular. As prince he had been sent by his father on a good many royal tours of the colonies and dominions. He was politically savvy but content to be a constitutional monarch, much as is Queen Elizabeth, his granddaughter, today.

Two years after George's accession, Geoffrey Fiennes, Lord Saye, finally moved his family back permanently into Broughton (after twenty-five years of on-off rental), but then the Great War broke out, so both Geoffrey and three of his sons joined up, as, once more, did Eustace. By then Eustace had spent two years (1912-14) in the crucial pre-war period as principal (parliamentary) private secretary to the First Lord of the Admiralty, his old friend, Winston Churchill. In the new world of the early twentieth century, Churchill's star had definitely begun to shine, though it was to suffer a good number of ups and downs. Never afraid of switching his stance (or even his party), Winston was a good friend of Eustace down the years. Both men were of the Victorian era, but the great personalities of those times were, by 1914, long dead: Gladstone, Salisbury and the old queen herself. Those years and their prevailing views were quickly eclipsed by the roar of the new century. Now there were telephones, electricity, typewriters, fast cars and good roads, wireless and aeroplanes. Even public cinemas. And everyone who did not have them, wanted them, or so it seemed. The biggest changes of all were to be the results of the catastrophe of the Kaiser's war.

The month before the war began, July 1914, was not exactly peaceful on the home front, either. Miners, railway and transport workers were threatening mass strike action, 200,000 men were under arms in Protestant Ulster and in the Catholic South, with civil war imminent. Nationalist groups were fermenting rebellion in Egypt and India, all of which demanded a strong, calm response from government and a reliable, sympathetic monarch as figurehead for a nation under threat. Lloyd George and King George V were to provide both.

Nobody in Britain wanted war. Of the various countries involved, she had less to gain from the fighting and less to fear from staying out of it. As the world's first industrial nation, Britain had evolved a liberal, capitalist, democratic system that needed both world peace and free trade to thrive. Its success on a global basis was thwarted by the Kaiser and his Prussians. The spark that kindled the Great War, as many a schoolchild has been taught, was the assassination in Sarajevo of an Austrian archduke. But the tensions which finally exploded in the summer of 1914 had accumulated over many years.

Herbert Asquith, the Liberal prime minister, voiced his thoughts on 1 August 1914, the day Germany declared war on Russia:

> I am quite clear in my mind as to what is right and wrong. 1. We have no obligation of any kind either to France or Russia to give them military or naval help. 2. The dispatch of the Expeditionary Force to help France at this moment is out of the question and would serve no object. 3. We must not forget the ties created by our long-standing and intimate friendship with France. 4. It is against British interests that France should be wiped out as a Great Power. 5. We cannot allow Germany to use the Channel as a hostile base. 6. We have obligations to Belgium to prevent it being utilized and absorbed by Germany.

All over Europe young men volunteered to fight the Germans. Britain had not fought a major war for over a century. Her few professional soldiers were less excited and their favourite song of the day was:

> Send out the Army and the Navy
> Send out the rank and file
> Send out the brave Territorials,
> They'll face the danger with a smile
> Send out the boys of the old brigade
> They will keep old England free
> Send out my mother, my sister and my brother,
> But for Gawd's Sake, don't send me

Eustace left Winston's department on the outbreak of war and went to fight with the Oxfordshire Yeomanry in the Flanders mud. His son, my uncle Johnnie, joined the Gordon Highlanders fighting nearby. Johnnie's younger brother, born in 1902, was my father Ranulph (named after our ancestor killed at Towton in 1461) but he was, of course, too young to sign up. He and Johnnie had spent happy times at Broughton, but were brought up at Studland Bay in Dorset. Their South African mother, my grandmother Florrie, was always the centre of a hive of activity and opened two convalescent homes for the war-wounded, one in

Dunkirk and one in her own Studland House. Her French hospital was shelled by the Germans, after which she had to close it down and escape. She was awarded a French medal and the OBE.

After being fortunate enough to survive Flanders, Eustace was sent as intelligence officer of the Royal Naval Division to help defend Antwerp for the Belgians. Eight thousand men of the division went with him, and Churchill arrived that October to assess the situation. His report to General Kitchener summed up the Belgian army as 'weary and disheartened and the ground so waterlogged, nobody can dig trenches'. With the division cooped up in the city, Eustace borrowed Churchill's driver (Lord Bellew) and headed south to meet informants. To his surprise, he found that the German chief, von Moltke, had decided to surround Antwerp and his divisions were already on the move. Eustace rushed back to alert his bosses, General Paris and the Belgian General de Brockville. Thanks entirely to his initiative and to his brave Belgian informers, most of the Royal Naval Division escaped the German trap two days before the city surrendered.

The original plan of the Kaiser, to finish his lightning war in only forty days, foundered due to unexpected Belgian resistance which slowed down the German advance, so that by the time they did reach France, the French army and British Expeditionary Force were there to meet them. And thereabouts they stayed for the next four years of murderous trench warfare.

In 1915 Churchill and Lloyd George, against the advice of Kitchener, Admiral Jackie Fisher and others, encouraged an alternative front to be opened up by the navy against Germany's Turkish allies in the Dardanelles. Eustace was heavily involved with Churchill in the planning and execution of the subsequent Gallipoli campaign. In the spring of 1915 Eustace wrote with an optimistic tone:

> My dear Winston
> Everyone is pleased with what you've done for the Division, not only getting it into this show but having supported us in every

way. Three ships are already here in Malta and others expected tomorrow. The men's health is excellent. All inoculated. Strenuous training and lectures on board. I will write and keep you updated. They talk a lot about the Canal here, but I think that is just a clever Turk move to detain a large force here. The division should do well.

Eustace

The whole Gallipoli idea was intended to circumvent the stalemate and huge loss of life on the Western Front but, due to gross mismanagement, the plan failed dismally and Churchill was sacked. The main problem with the Gallipoli plan was that, when Eustace and his naval force arrived there and the army contingent landed, they found themselves unable to break out of a narrow bridgehead on a rocky, sun-beaten, disease-ridden peninsula overlooked by enemy artillery. Naval bombardment did little to help. One Leonard Thompson, a farmhand from Suffolk, wrote about landing as an infantryman at Gallipoli:

The first thing we saw were big wrecked Turkish guns, the second a big marquee . . . [like at a] village fête . . . we all rushed to it, [but it was] laced up. We unlaced it . . . It was full of corpses. Dead Englishmen, lines of them with their eyes wide open . . . I'd never seen a dead man before and here I was looking at two or three hundred of them . . . I was very shocked [and] thought of Suffolk . . .

[One night] we had to move on to the third line of trenches . . . but, when we got to the communications trench, we found it so full of dead men we could hardly move. Their faces were quite black and you couldn't tell Turk from English. There was the most terrible stink, and for a while there was nothing but the living being sick on to the dead. I did sentry again that night . . . I knew the next sentry up quite well. I remembered him in Suffolk singing to his horses as he ploughed. Now he fell back with a great scream and a look of surprise – dead. It is quick anyway, I thought. On June 4th we went over the top . . . On June 6th my favourite officer was killed and no end of us butchered . . . Of the sixty men I had started out to war with, there were only three left.

We set to work to bury people. We pushed them into the sides of the trench but bits of them kept getting uncovered and sticking out, like people in a badly made bed. Hands were the worst; they would escape from the sand, pointing, begging – even waving. There was one which we all shook when we passed, saying, 'Good Morning', in a posh voice. Everybody did it. The bottom of the trench was springy like a mattress because of all the bodies underneath. At night, when the stench was worse, we tied [anti-gassing] crêpe round our mouths and noses . . . the flies entered the trenches by night and lined them completely with a density which was like moving cloth. We killed millions by slapping our spades along the trench walls but the next night it would be just as bad. We were all lousy and we couldn't stop shitting because we had caught dysentery. We wept, not because we were frightened but because we were so dirty.

When the survivors were evacuated along with their nightmares, they left 46,000 bodies behind. Eustace was on one of the last ships to depart back to the hell-hole of the Western Front, which the Gallipoli experience had been designed to circumvent.

For Eustace's many activities for the empire over several decades and for his dedicated years as a Liberal MP in Banbury (but presumably not for his part in the planning of the Gallipoli debacle), Eustace was made a baronet by the king. He chose to be Baronet of Banbury, the title I inherited at birth. Edward Heath put a stop to hereditary titles in the 1970s, so we baronets are a dying breed.

At fifty-two Eustace was a touch old for the front, so he accepted the job of quartermaster general of the Royal Naval Division in Plymouth. In August 1917 he wrote to Winston, complaining about the leader of their party. 'There are no two men I have fought harder for and stuck more faithfully to than Lloyd George and yourself, but the former has treated me very badly and I cannot make out why.' I have tried to unearth the facts of Lloyd George's dislike of Eustace, but without success. It is unlikely to have been due to Gallipoli since, like Churchill, he was fully in favour of that campaign.

In July 1916 the British army chief, grim Scotsman General Haig, commanded the great offensive of the Somme, which broke all manner of appalling casualty records by insanely attacking the strongest German defences, barbed wire, machine guns and massed artillery with 100,000 British and Commonwealth soldiers. By nightfall on the first day 20,000 British corpses festooned the wire and another 40,000 were injured or (the lucky ones) in German hands. For this ghastly toll, the greatest recorded one-day loss ever sustained by an army in history, two miles of pock-marked mud was the total gain. The entire four-month Somme offensive gained the British seven miles and cost them 420,000 casualties.

Germany's chief allies, the Turks, were eliminated by a clever campaign waged under General Allenby (with help from Colonel T. E. Lawrence 'of Arabia') and launched from Egypt through Palestine into Syria. But the Western Front continued to stagnate, and in May 1916, in order to counter the ongoing death toll, conscription was imposed. Each British attempt to crack the stalemate in the trenches ended in yet more carnage. Eventually huge financial, material and manpower support from the United States enabled the allies to overwhelm the Germans who, by the war's end, had committed eleven million men, of whom 1,774,000 were killed and four million wounded. British dead totalled 750,000, with 2,500,000 wounded, and many disabled for life. European, Commonwealth and American casualties were also huge. It is surprising, therefore, that in Britain at least, steady support for pursuit of the war lasted throughout the four years of the conflict.

In 1917 at the Battle of Arras, my only uncle, Captain John

Fiennes, led a company of the 2nd Battalion of the Gordon Highlanders against German trenches and was killed, aged twenty-one. Eustace and Florrie were devastated.

When Lloyd George formed a two-party coalition to conduct the war through an all-powerful war cabinet, a mighty state war-machine enervated the nation and brought about massive industrial and social change. Collectivist control and state power dominated, to the extent that Ramsay MacDonald, the first Labour prime minister, noted with irony that the war had achieved far more for social reform than had all the campaigns of the trades unions and of progressive do-gooders over the previous half century. Social welfare, housing policy, the status of women: all were affected, to the benefit of the poor. Coal mines, railways and the merchant navy were placed under state control. Edward VII's Liberal Britain was now an evolving corporate state. Marxism was not needed. A new Ministry of Health was set up to co-ordinate health and national insurance. Women, and they were numerically in the majority after the slaughter, were at last given the vote with universal suffrage for all men over twenty-one, but for women over thirty.

Abroad, the colonies, whose citizens had died in their thousands for the empire and the king, naturally flexed their muscles for greater independence from the mother country. But the empire did not shrink. In fact, due to the many secret treaties between the Allies during and after the war, Britain gained vast new territories in the Middle East, oil-rich Mesopotamia and the Persian Gulf. Meanwhile, thanks to the insatiable demand for wartime munitions workers and merchant seamen, there were well over 10,000 black citizens in Britain by the war's end.

Germany, and all things German, remained unpopular for a long while, and the king sensibly switched the title of the royal family from Saxe-Coburg to Windsor. At the same time, at Crufts dog show, German Shepherds were renamed Alsatians.

The coalition government of Welshman Lloyd George, the great wartime leader, triumphed in the first post-war election.

But soon after, he lost his reputation with Labour when he responded to mass unemployment rallies and strikes by using troops as strike-breakers. There were many minor strikes between 1919 and 1922. Then, after Baldwin's Conservatives' defeat of Lloyd George, a period of peace until, in 1925, Baldwin fell out with the miners and the Trades Union Congress (TUC). The General Strike followed, with the unions challenging the government with their full economic strength. This was billed as an all-out class war, but there was no violence either from or against the police or armed forces. Coppers and strikers played football together and the middle classes enjoyed the novel excitement of strike-breaking by driving buses and lorries. After nine days the TUC called off the strike, acknowledging the abject failure of its main aim (to achieve a subsidy for the miners), despite having brought Britain to a virtual standstill. Britain's class war had been a brief, but bloodless, event at a time when, throughout Europe, governments were being toppled, workers rebelling and fascists menacing. At the very time Lenin was the great hero of the people in Russia, King George V was all-popular in Britain.

Lenin died of a stroke in 1924, his corpse was reverently swathed in a red flag saved from the bloody Paris Commune of 1871 and his brain was removed for Soviet studies to identify the precise location of the cells responsible for his revolutionary genius. So died the man who replaced one form of Russian tyranny with another that would keep his (and many other) people oppressed for eighty long years. He once said: 'Liberty is precious – so precious that it must be rationed.'

The British National Debt, largely caused by the need to pay for wartime loans, soared by 1920 to £7,875 million. Irish troubles, renewed with vigour by the Fenians in the Easter Rising of 1916, led to vicious repression by the crown, but in 1920 Lloyd George granted the Republic of Ireland Home Rule, a concession eagerly noted by nationalists in India.

After the war Eustace joined the Colonial Office and was appointed Governor General of the Seychelles. He had hoped for

New Zealand because he felt he had got on well with the New Zealanders at the Dardanelles but he was told not to be over-ambitious when he not very tactfully applied for a transfer after only two months in the Caribbean. Settling down in the Seychelles, he was shocked at the lack of humane provision for the poor and the lepers and began to institute all sorts of social legislation to look after them, which included building a poor house which survived right up until 2006, and a hospital. While his good works put the Seychelles in the forefront of British colonies in their care for the destitute, the Colonial Office was to note that the major criticism of my grandfather's administration was his propensity to embark on projects without considering how they would be funded. His successor found he had been left with the bill for the imported building materials for the hospital.

In 1921 Churchill, recovering his Gallipoli-dented reputation, became colonial secretary and turned part of the remains of the defeated Turkish empire into Iraq. He promoted Eustace to Governor-General of the Leeward Islands. Granny Florrie, still mourning my uncle's death at Arras, had persuaded Eustace to ask my father Ranulph (then sixteen and at Eton) whether he would prefer to stay there or have a tutor and shark fish in the Caribbean. He chose the latter and was sad when the time came to head for home and Sandhurst, aged eighteen. Eustace and Florrie loved Antigua and the Antiguans. They stayed there far longer than most governors' families, from 1921 until 1929, and both worked to relieve the poor, the homeless, the sick, and those left bereft by the perennial hurricanes, with sleeves rolled up in the heat personally administering inoculations in little villages.

And Eustace continued to spend money without permission. Sir Samuel Wilson, Head of the Colonial Service, was quoted as saying: 'What can we do with Fiennes? He asks to spend thousands of pounds on village water services. We tell him to wait. He cables back, "Could not wait. Money spent. Villagers drinking water."' Once more his passion for improving the lot of the islanders took over, regardless of economics. As well as the water supply, he introduced electricity and a radio link with other islands, he built a jetty and encouraged tourism. Bakers had to have health certificates and the first city bus service was inaugurated – the first bus being named Florrie. There was also another home for the poor which was such a success that it was soon grossly overcrowded. An island historian records how Eustace and Florrie dealt with this:

> The Governor and Lady Fiennes, who were both keen dancers, arranged for a dance to be held there, during which those who were seen to be dancing in too sprightly a manner were later told to leave and find work. It was a method of weeding out the unworthy which annoyed no one, greatly appealed to the population at large, and only enhanced the Governor's reputation as a man of the people. His impact on ordinary black Antiguans was summed up by one of them, a man named Samuel Smith, whose colourful and often moving memoirs provide a unique record of estate life in the first half of the twentieth century: 'He [Fiennes] was a melle (well-informed) man. He love nega (black people's) business and he got to know what was happening in the island. I think he very well understood the feelings of the negas. He took pride in his work and he wanted that his term of office would mean something to the people. For me, he was entirely different to all the governors that reach the island before and I believe he will remain the best ever.'

Eustace retired, aged sixty-seven, and raised funds for the Hammersmith Hospital, of which he was the appeals chairman. He remained an ardent Liberal in an age of Labour and Tories. He was very proud of my father, Ranulph, who joined Scotland's only cavalry regiment, the Royal Scots Greys in India and was in 1929 appointed aide-de-camp to the Governor General of Canada. They spent many happy weekends, when my father was on leave, at Broughton. He used to swim round the moat for exercise. That was a time, the late twenties, when in southern England and the midlands there was growing contentment and prosperity. Suburban middle-class estates sprang up in mushroom clumps, subsidised by Neville Chamberlain and Stanley Baldwin. By 1930 there were over a million privately owned cars, wirelesses over which the BBC spread the news in prim voices, whilst bad memories of war and the General Strike grew dim. The danger of a Marxist revolution in Britain faded as Stalin and his gulags alerted would-be radicals against the perils of the left and, down in Munich, Hitler had only just begun to rant. Forty-three million folk lived in Britain, and many were simply content with the status quo. The empire was still, just, loyal to the king, and Kipling, still churning out his wonderful prose and verse, assured the nation that this was so.

In 1929 and the early thirties a worldwide downward spiral of trade and employment hit Britain hard, followed by despair in declining industries, hunger marches, and life on the dole. Nonetheless, the monarchy remained popular at all levels of society, and George V's annual pilgrimage to the Wembley Cup Final continued to be greeted with deafening applause and folk stood proud for the National Anthem. Meanwhile, 'over there', totalitarianism engulfed Germany, Italy and Austria, whilst France and Spain writhed painfully within their republics. Never mind the hell of Eastern Europe.

My father, back from Canada in 1931, met and married my mother, Audrey Newson, whose parents lived much of the time in Calcutta, for her father was Governor of the Imperial Bank of India. My parents had three daughters in the thirties and lived wherever the Royal Scots Greys needed my father. In 1934 he was posted to MI5 and did a stint of spying on Britain's French allies whilst attached to a French cavalry unit in the Pyrenees. His spying spree continued into 1936, and a later note in my mother's diary mentions a connected incident.

> Eustace had been entertaining Hitler's great friend, the Princess Hohenlohe. He [Eustace] was not one of the Anglo-German Fellowship but, like them, he believed the Nazis were a key obstacle to the Soviets. They were all later shocked when the two countries made a pact.
>
> Eustace asked Ranulph to invite the Princess and her colleague Hauptman Weiderman, Hitler's equerry, to the Aldershot Military Tattoo. They accepted with alacrity, clearly hoping to gain information on the latest military tactics and equipment. Weiderman even refused an invitation he had that evening for dinner with Neville Chamberlain, our Prime Minister.

As it turned out, the theme of the tattoo that year was the Cromwellian period, so the 'latest technology' on show was frock coats and muskets. Scotland Yard arrested the princess soon after and she was imprisoned in the USA. Despite all this, Eustace, in his eighties, developed a hatred of the Soviets and decided 'that German chappie Adolf is the best thing since sliced bread to halt the Commie advance'. A lot of people shared his view until too late. Even his old friend Churchill had, at the Treasury, been keen to encourage naval cuts and other savings from the War Office budget.

In 1936 George V died, his eldest son, the Duke of Windsor, briefly Edward VIII, soon abdicated in order to marry an American divorcee, and Edward's younger brother became King George VI, a nervous, shy man with a bad stutter, chronic gastric problems, knock knees and a lovely Scottish wife, later to become Queen Elizabeth the Queen Mother, who died, beloved by the nation, in 2002.

30

Colonel of the Greys

The utter horror of the Kaiser's War lived on in the nightmares, the burnt lungs and the limbless stumps of many millions, especially the Europeans, in whose midst that trouble had begun. Surely, a mere twenty years later, nobody would be stupid enough to risk causing a repeat performance? And yet Germany, one of the most civilised, culturally brilliant nations on earth, the home of Einstein and Beethoven, voted for Adolf Hitler and his Nazis to govern them.

In the year of King George VI's succession to the throne of Great Britain, on 18 July 1936 to be exact, Hitler found a wonderful way of testing tactics and military equipment for his coming Apocalypse – the Spanish Civil War. All those Spaniards who hated their country's republican status joined General Francisco Franco's side, including monarchists, Catholics, all branches of the army, the Fascist party, the landowning class and the bourgeoisie. Franco's opposition, who supported the Republic, included the unions, the Socialists, the Communists and the Anarchists. As in all civil wars, brother killed brother and the bitterness echoed down the generations. After three long years, Franco eventually triumphed and signed a five-year friendship treaty with Hitler. Five hundred thousand people had died, including 100,000 from disease or starvation and 100,000 by murder or execution.

For the Germans, the interlude provided excellent practice for the Second World War. Meekly the British and French failed to react (except for loud calls for military intervention by an isolated, unpopular, back-bencher in Britain called Churchill). For the rest, the way forward was appeasement and non-intervention at all costs. Chamberlain clearly favoured this craven policy, and Hitler certainly believed that Britain would stay out of any conflict he caused that did not involve its precious empire.

Eustace and Florrie joined my mother and three sisters in bidding my father goodbye as the Royal Scots Greys, complete with their five hundred grey horses, were sent out to Palestine in 1938. Nobody, even then, had seriously considered the sacrilege of 'mechanising' Scotland's Waterloo-famous and only cavalry regiment. So, while just about every other cavalry unit everywhere slaughtered their horses and taught professional horsemen the theory of cogs and pistons, the Scots Greys settled down in Rehovot, one of the oldest Jewish settlements in Palestine, helping the local police keep the peace between Arabs and Jews and search for known rebels and hidden arms caches. My father was the major in charge of 'B' Squadron (which I joined twenty-four years later), and my mother joined him in a 'very hot bungalow' for a while in between his patrols, cordons and searches.

Meanwhile Churchill's call to arms caused Chamberlain to begin rearmament in a rush and to commit Britain to defend Poland, should Hitler attack it. When he did so that September of 1939, Chamberlain declared war on Germany with the full support of all the British nations and dominions. As twenty years before, the British found unity at the last moment and plunged with full commitment into the fray.

For six months of Phoney War nothing happened, which allowed Britain feverishly to get its act together just in time. Then, in April 1940, Hitler took Norway and Denmark with his fearsome *blitzkrieg* or 'lightning war', followed four weeks later by equally crushing victories in the Low Countries and France. The Nazis seemed utterly invincible, as all-powerful as the Mogul hordes of Genghis Khan or Caesar's legions. Britain's entire army in Europe and the French military remnants were forced to retreat in confusion towards Dunkirk, and only just escaped thanks to a flotilla of naval and civilian craft which removed them from the snapping jaws of the Nazis at the very last minute.

With all mainland Europe under Hitler, co-Fascist Mussolini sensibly joined the war as his ally, which overnight made the Middle East a new theatre of war, since Italian forces in Libya and North East Africa posed an obvious threat to key Allied strategic features, including the Suez Canal. My father and his fellow Scots Greys eventually (in September 1940) received the long awaited news that they would not, after all, have to attack German panzers with a cavalry charge. A telegram from an ex-cavalry officer, the new prime minister, Winston Churchill, to the chief of staff stated: 'I am very pleased about the Cavalry in Palestine. It has been heartbreaking for me to watch these splendid units waste away for a whole year. The sooner they form . . . armoured units the better. These historic regular regiments have a right to play a man's part in the war.' As training major, my father had the job of removing the horses that his men loved, and most of which had names as well as mere army horse numbers. He also rented bicycles and had the Jocks learn basic tank tactics and troop formations, as per the relevant British army training manual.

After Dunkirk, Britain herself was Hitler's next target and Churchill was everybody's choice to stand up to Hitler, for he embodied the national sense of patriotic unity which none of his contemporaries could match. His famous oratory of June 1940 was an example of his ability to inspire:

> Even though large tracts of Europe and many old and famous States have fallen or may fall into the grip of the Gestapo and all the odious apparatus of Nazi rule, we shall not flag or fail. We shall go on to the end. We shall fight in France, we shall fight on the seas and oceans, we shall fight with growing confidence and growing strength in the air, we shall defend our island,

> whatever the cost may be. We shall fight on the beaches, we shall fight on the landing grounds, we shall fight in the fields and in the streets, we shall fight in the hills; we shall never surrender.

It's a familiar quotation but worth pondering still. And he continues:

> What General Weygand called the 'Battle of France' is over. I expect that the battle of Britain is about to begin. Upon this battle depends the survival of Christian civilisation. Upon it depends our own British life and the long continuity of our institutions and our Empire. The whole fury and might of the enemy must very soon be turned on us. Hitler knows that he will have to break us in this island or lose the war. If we can stand up to him all Europe may be free, and the life of the world may move forward into broad, sunlit uplands; but if we fail then the whole world, including the United States, and all that we have known and cared for, will sink into the abyss of a new dark age made more sinister, and perhaps more prolonged, by the lights of a perverted science. Let us therefore brace ourselves to our duty and so bear ourselves that if the British Commonwealth and Empire lasts for a thousand years men will still say, 'This was their finest hour.'

But the destruction of Hitler was a long way off in the summer of 1940. In June he took the Channel Islands and ordered Operation Sea Lion, the invasion of Britain. The Luftwaffe would first neutralise the RAF to ensure the safety of the invasion fleet, and Air Chief Goering, with over 3,000 aircraft only twenty-five minutes away from Britain's key airfields, was confident of success in the skies. On 15 September, seventy-five German fighters were shot down to a loss of thirty-four RAF planes. The Battle of Britain was under way; Spitfires and Hurricanes against Messerschmidts. Goering's prophecy that he would crush the RAF in four days proved hollow for, by late September, the air was still full of Spitfires, and Hitler, knowing when he was beaten, switched to a massive night blitz of London and other major cities to crush British morale.

In mid-September, the Luftwaffe lost sixty bombers on one London raid. The 2,500 pilots of Fighter Command had by then shot down 1,268 aircraft for the loss of 832. Hitler cancelled the invasion, having suffered his first defeat. Britain and her dominions stood alone against him until, eventually, the Soviet Union and then the USA joined in. The king and queen stayed at Buckingham Palace throughout the blitz, although the building was damaged during nine different raids. On one of many royal visits to the bombed areas of London, the queen remarked, 'I'm glad we've been bombed at the Palace. It makes me feel I can look the East End in the face.'

At Broughton, Lord and Lady Saye and Sele were in mourning from the spring of 1941 when their second son, Ingelram Fiennes, was killed in action aged nineteen, flying with the RAF Volunteer Reserves.

Rommel and his Afrika Korps grabbed Libya in 1941, while Greece and Cyprus were lost to Axis forces and a pro-German government took over Iraq. A detachment of the newly-armoured Scots Greys was immediately sent from Haifa to Baghdad to tie up with troops from India who landed at Basra. Between them they achieved the surrender of Baghdad before new Axis troops could reach that key city. This Scots Greys' success was rewarded by the delivery of their brand new 'General Stuart' light tanks to replace their grey horses. The Jocks, hardly a man of whom had not been a highly proficient horseman, soon became efficient as gunners, loaders, radio operators and drivers.

That December the Japanese attacked Pearl Harbor and, three days later, came across the two finest battleships of the Royal Navy leaving Singapore with no air cover. Dive bombers sank both ships and, two months later, Japanese armies reached Singapore where they forced the surrender of 80,000 British and empire troops. Churchill described the event as 'the worst capitulation in British history'. Malaya and Hong Kong also fell to the Japanese.

Two days after the fall of Singapore my father took command of the Scots Greys, by then consisting of two heavy squadrons of Grant tanks and a light squadron of Stuarts. They were part of the Eighth Army and confronted Rommel's Afrika Korps veterans, whose dreaded 88 mm anti-tank guns could pierce the armour of my father's tanks at ranges of 3,000 metres. My father wrote home, using careful phraseology to appease the censors: 'I am now taking care of the baby, and you know what trouble they can be when they are teething.' I wonder if he meant the men or the tanks.

Rommel's aim was to break through the British lines in order to seize Cairo and Suez. But thanks to superior strategy by General Montgomery, Rommel was halted in the region of Alam Halfa and largely cut off from his fuel supply lines. At the end of August Rommel attacked with cover from Stuka dive-bombers and using many of his Mark IV special tanks with their highly effective new 75 mm guns. A tank regiment of the London Yeomanry was soon wiped out by the Mark IVs, leaving a vulnerable gap in the British defence line. My father ordered the Scots Greys to 'charge' downhill to close the gap at the critical moment, and thus prevented further German progress. By nightfall twenty-six German tanks, 'bagged by the Jocks', burnt fiery red in the desert dusk, but at dawn Rommel attacked again. This time, still unable to break through, he gave up his attempt, and the Battle of Alam Halfa was won. The Scots Greys had done well in their first major fight with no horses.

Rommel's toll in the battle was 53 tanks, 700 motor vehicles, 70 anti-tank guns and 4,500 soldiers killed or wounded, against 1,600 casualties on the British side. The battle proved critical to the whole desert war, for it lost Rommel the last good chance he had of overall victory in Africa before Montgomery's build-up would make such an outcome impossible, even for Rommel.

In October the far better known, but actually less crucial, Battle of El Alamein again involved my father and the regiment in the key tank role against Rommel. My father, directing operations from his turretless Stuart tank, 'Astra', was slightly wounded in the neck and leg. With only slight exaggeration, Churchill later commented: 'Before El Alamein we never had a victory, after El Alamein we never had a defeat.' Various vicious tank battles then followed in quick succession as the Scots Greys caught up with detachments of Rommel's men. 'I had to move very fast to keep in front of the Colonel,' one Scots Grey officer wrote in his post-Alamein report. My father was known throughout his army days as 'Lugs' Fiennes, presumably on account of his slightly prominent ears. At the later Battle of Nofilia, as one squadron leader reported: 'The going was all soft sand. All the time I was getting stick from Lugs over the air for not coming on quicker . . . How Lugs ever managed to find his way round, up and down wadis, over about four miles of country, and arrive in the right place plumb on the flank of the enemy, I don't know. However, I am sure his quick decision and quick action won the day.'

My father wrote home to my mother:

> 19.7.42 When will this cursed war be over? When I see the things going on around me I can't help thinking that most of us must be mad. Why we ever allowed these filthy Germans to get up again after the last war, I can't think. I hope they give them hell for all the misery they've caused . . .
>
> 18.8.42 I've slept the last 2 months under the stars and on the ground, whether sandy, stony, hard or soft. No bother with those lilo things . . .
>
> 6.9.42 If the Russians can hold out a little longer, the winter will arrive and I very much doubt that the dirty Huns can last out another. Anyhow I doubt whether they will survive the 2nd Front which I daresay will start next spring.
>
> 29.10.42 I'm in a Casualty Station 12 miles back. I will go back up tomorrow. It is like having been peppered by a shot gun.

I have small wounds all the way up my thigh, right side and arm. We had no sleep for 3 nights. My knee swelled up. I was about to take a pot at an Eyetie outpost with the Browning when an explosive bullet hit its side and the bits got me. But it was fun seeing the Eyeties bolting from their holes like rabbits. I don't think many of them waited long enough to get killed.

23.12.42 I am in No. 9 General Hospital Heliopolis. I have a deep wound in the thigh on the inside; it missed the femoral artery although it laid it bare for 2 inches, *just* missed other vital parts and ruined my beautiful green cord trousers. It was caused by a bit of a shell which penetrated the tank. A second direct hit missed me but killed Mark Bodley's son, my operator, outright. I also have a gash in my forearm.

Against this we got 200 German prisoners, 6 anti-tank guns and 4 big German tanks. I'll be in bed, they say, for ten days. I've got a steel bit travelling round my neck. When it comes out, I'll keep it for the children . . .

My father was sent to America for two months whilst recovering from his wounds, in order to lecture to US troops about desert warfare, but he returned to the regiment in time to command it for the Eighth Army at Salerno, the toe of Italy and the key to attacking the soft underbelly of Europe.

As at Alam Halfa and El Alamein, the Scots Greys' role at Salerno proved critical to the outcome of the fierce battle for the beachhead. The regiment withstood German counter-attacks, fought hard and knocked out a great deal of German armour. At one point two Jocks, briefly captured by Germans, escaped to rejoin the regiment and reported that their interrogators, following their capture, had wanted to know the correct pronunciation of the names of each of the three colonels of the Greys: Twisleton, Wykeham and Fiennes.

One Greys' counter-attack forced a large enemy contingent to retreat, another killed two hundred enemy by night, and the Jock tank gunners generally outgunned their German counterparts at most close and long distance encounters. Although they did not know it at the time, this four-day battle just inland from the beaches had seen off a real pending crisis, for the Germans had succeeded in driving a wedge between the key British and American units and almost defeated the Fifth Army before the Eighth Army could cement their post-landing link-up.

My father now needed to find the regiment a safe route through the mountain pass overlooking the Bay of Naples, so he went with the brigade commander and his intelligence officer to check the road. A shell burst near them and all were hit by shrapnel. My father was, as before, not badly hurt, although by that time his body was host to a fair number of steel splinters. Two battalions of American infantry were put under his command for the next advance, but his tanks were unable to support them closely, due to rough lava beds spawned by Vesuvius, so the enemy was not dislodged. Eventually they made it to and through Naples city and were much kissed by Italian girls.

North and west of Naples, the country was hilly, wooded and dangerous for tanks. So my father reconnoitred every part of the route prior to letting any of his tanks advance. He found one bridge fully prepared for demolition and surprised three German sappers resting in a nearby cave. He had forgotten his revolver, but pointed his briar pipe at them and said, '*Hände Hoch*!' Their hands duly shot up and, taking them prisoner to his driver, he retrieved his gun and made them remove the bridge explosives.

Unfortunately, his habit of going out ahead ended on 11 November when he and one of his officers both trod on S-Type anti-personnel mines and were wounded. My father died of his wounds in Naples General Hospital twelve days later. He had briefly come home on leave four months earlier, and I was conceived then. So I never met my father; nor my grandfather Eustace, for he died earlier in 1943.

My father was awarded the Distinguished Service Order for his leadership at Salerno. The colonel who took over the Greys from him, wrote:

> Lieutenant-Colonel Sir Ranulph Fiennes will always be remembered by those who served under him as an outstanding leader and a vivid personality with a keen sense of humour . . . he had played a major part in the Regiment's conversion to armour . . . He nursed the Regiment successfully through its early battles and made it a confident and effective fighting instrument, with a high reputation both on and off the battlefield . . . A Royal Horse Artillery Commanding Officer . . . said that he had supported many armoured regiments, from the earliest days in the desert, but had never seen one fight like the Greys. To him [Lugs] more than to any other individual it was due that, when mechanisation came at last, the traditions of the cavalry trooper who fought under Marlborough, Wellington and Haig were carried over to the trooper of the armoured regiment, who was soon to fight again on the same well-worn battlefield of the Low Countries, confident that he belonged to a Regiment, which in its old role, but with new weapons, was still 'second to none'.

One of his lieutenants, Lord Althorp, the father of Princess Diana, told me years later that my father had been the best commanding officer any man could hope to serve under. I dearly wish I had met him. I grew up with only one ambition: to command the Royal Scots Greys, as he had.

A psychologist would probably say that my growing up without ever meeting my father or grandfather, nor having had brothers, uncles or any other male relatives, was bound to make me keen to trace my forebears. Whether or not that is so, I have no idea, but I do know that I have enjoyed every minute of rootling about with the history of my ancestors, of Broughton and of my country. You should give it a go, as you never know whose blood may run through your veins. It could be Genghis Khan, Florence Nightingale, or even Caligula.

Our national characteristics

Here are a couple of generalisations about England that would be accepted by almost all observers. One is that the English are not gifted artistically. They are not as musical as the Germans or Italians, painting and sculpture have never flourished in England as they have in France. Another is that, as Europeans go, the English are not intellectual. They have a horror of abstract thought, they feel no need for any philosophy or systematic 'world view'. Nor is this because they are 'practical', as they are so fond of claiming for themselves. One has only to look at their methods of town-planning and water-supply, their obstinate clinging to everything that is out-of-date and a nuisance, a spelling system that defies analysis and a system of weights and measures that is intelligible only to compilers of arithmetic books, to see how little they care about mere efficiency.

George Orwell, *England, Your England* (1941)

Acknowledgements

A very big thank you to everybody who made it possible for me to write this book, especially for the hospitality and patience of Nat and Mariette Fiennes (Lord and Lady Saye and Sele) who made available boxes full of documents, letters and old books from Broughton, many of which came from the attics where once the Parliamentary soldiers of Lord Saye's Bluecoats slept prior to the Royalist attack on the castle.

Also to Martin Fiennes, eldest son and heir to the Saye and Sele barony, for his kind agreement to check the details of the family history (but not the national history!), and to Martin's family for their time and patience. (Go and visit Broughton some time. It is near Banbury and open to the public, www.broughton-castle.com.)

To the Reverend Oliver Fiennes who gave me details of his tour of the USA with Magna Carta, and to my surviving sister Gillian who gave me details of our South African heritage. I am also grateful for useful input received from various members of the extended family. My wife Louise spent many months involved in travel, research and photography for the book, and I must also thank our family, Alexander (14) and Elizabeth (3) for their patience and for tuning down the background noise at home (drum beat stereo and screams respectively).

For producing the book, my thanks to Ed Victor, Maggie

Phillips, Rupert Lancaster, Maggie Body and Jonathan Boff and, above all, to Jill Firman.

For South African data and photos, my thanks to Ian Johnstone, Andrew Field, Fraser Edkins, Bob Manser, James 'Tackie' Bannerman, Tim Tanser, and other members of the History Society of Zimbabwe.

For Churchill data, my thanks to Lynsey Robertson (Churchill College Archives Centre), Colonel Tim May and Harry Staff and all of the Oxfordshire Yeomanry Trust and Hugh Babington Smith and Stanley Jenkins of Soldiers of Oxfordshire.

For Herstmonceux data, my thanks to Angela Minchin, Dr Scott McLean and Ann and Cheryl Friar. For Broughton and related Banbury data, to Jeremy Gibson of the Banbury Historical Society and editor of *Cake & Cockhorse*, and Brian Little. Also to Major Robin Maclean of the Royal Scots Dragoon Guards Museum. To Ralph Fiennes, William McAteer, Robert Stewart, the Archivist and members of the Derry City Council Heritage and Museum Service, and the archival staff from the Bristol Museum City Record Office.

Also, for making it possible to complete research work (between climbs from the Everest Base Camp in 2009), Henry Todd who had all the research books, maps, etc. yak-carried up from Lukla and fixed up a tent with heat and light. And to Mark Georgiou of BBC News, who patiently photographed 360 pages one by one, despite snow and wind, to send back to the UK just in time.

Plus big apologies to anybody else who helped but is not mentioned above.

RTWF

Picture Acknowledgements

Author's collection: 13 top and centre right, 14, 15 bottom, 16 top. © The Art Archive: 10 top and bottom. ©Bibliothèque Nationale Paris/photo Bridgeman Art Library: 3 bottom. © The British Library Board 2009. All rights reserved: 2 top left (Cott Nero D II f179v), 2 centre/photo Bridgeman Art Library, 2 bottom (Roy 14 E IV f276), 5 top (Harl 7353) 8 centre (G3538), 9 bottom/photo Bridgeman Art Library. © Chateâu de Versailles France/photo Bridgeman Art Library: 6 top. © Corbis: 1 bottom, 4 bottom. © Mary Evans Picture Library: 12 top right. © Mark Fiennes: 7 bottom. © Cheryl Friar: 6 bottom. © Getty Images: 13 bottom. © Kunsthistorisches Museum Vienna/Bridgeman Art Library: 9 top. © Lambeth Palace Library London/photo Bridgeman Art Library: 3 top, 7 top. © Lebrecht Music and Arts Photo Library/photo Alamy: 10 top right. © Musée de la Tapisserie de Bayeux/photo Bridgeman Art Library: 1 top. © National Army Museum London/photo Bridgeman Art Library: 12 bottom. Courtesy of The Warden and Scholars of New College Oxford/photo Bridgeman Art Library: 4 top. © Nigel Owen: 16 bottom. Private Collection/photo Bridgeman Art Library: 5 bottom left and right. © *Punch* Ltd: 15 top. © Graham Trott: 8 top and bottom, 10 centre right, 11 top left and bottom left and right, 12 top left and centre right, 16 centre.

Family trees © London Calligraphy Lettering.

Sources

The Life and Times of series (Weidenfeld & Nicolson/Book Club Associates): *Alfred the Great* by Douglas Woodruff, *William I* by Maurice Ashley *King John* by Maurice Ashley, *Richard I* by John Gillingham, *Edward I* by John Chancellor, *Edward II* by Caroline Bingham, *Edward III* by Paul Johnson, *Richard II*, by Michael Senior, *Edward IV* by Gila Falkus, *Henry V* by Peter Earle, *Richard III* by Anthony Cheetham, *Henry VII* by Neville Williams, *Henry VIII* by Robert Lacey, *Elizabeth I* by Neville Williams, *King James VI of Scotland & I of England* by Antonia Fraser, *Charles I* by D R Watson, *Charles II* by Antonia Fraser, *James II* by Peter Earle, *William & Mary* by John Miller, *Queen Anne* by Gila Curtis, *George I* by Joyce Marlow, *George III* by John Clarke, *George IV* by Alan Palmer, *Edward VII* by Keith Middlemas, *George V* by Denis Judd. *The Reign of King Henry VI* by Ralph A Griffiths (Sutton Publishing). *Queen Victoria, A Personal History* by Christopher Hibbert (HarperCollins). *England: The Autobiography* ed. John Lewis-Stempel (Penguin). *A Leap Year of Great Stories from History for Every Day of the Year* by W B Marsh & Bruce Carrick (Icon Books). *The Tribes of Britain* by David Miles (Phoenix). *England: 1000 Things You Need to Know* by Nicholas Hobbes (Atlantic Books). *A History of Antigua* by Brian Dyde (Macmillan). *To Be a Nation*, by William McAteer (Pristine Books). *A Brief History of Medieval*

Warfare by Peter Reid (Running Press). *Holy War* by Karen Armstrong (Macmillan). *The English* by Jeremy Paxman (Michael Joseph). *Churchill* by Roy Jenkins (Macmillan) *Peerage & Family History* by J Horace Round M A (Archibald Constable). *The Oxford Illustrated History of Britain* ed. Kenneth O Morgan (BCA). *Britons: Forging the Nation 1707–1837* by Linda Colley (Yale). *Hearsay* by Lord Saye and Sele (Nisbet & Co). *The Agincourt War* by Lt-Col Alfred H Burne (Wordsworth). *Second To None* by Lt-Col R M P Carver (McCorquodale & Co). *The Vikings* by Jonathan Clements (Muramasa Industries). *A Brief History of The Magna Carta* by Geoffrey Hindley (Running Press). *The Day of the Barbarians* by Alessandro Barbero (Walker). *The Journeys of Celia Fiennes* ed. Christopher Morris (The Cresset Press). *Jane Austen The Woman* by George Holbert Tucker & John McAleer (St Martin's Press). *Cake and Cockhorse* Banbury Historical Society Mags. *Foxe's Book of Martyres* by John Foxe. *The Men Who Made Rhodesia* by Col. A S Hickman (Memories of Rhodesia, Inc). *Studies in Peerage and Family History* by J Horace Round. *Oxford Dictionary of National Biography*. *Sussex Archaeological Collections relating to the History and Antiquities of the County* (The Sussex Archaeological Society). *The Battle Abbey Roll* by the Duchess of Cleveland (John Murray, London 1889). *Complete Peerage of England, Scotland, Ireland, Great Britain & the United Kingdom, Extant, Extinct or Dormant* ed. G E C (William Pollard & Co.). *Royal Descents and Pedigrees of Founders' Kin* by Sir Bernard Burke, LLD (Harrison, 1864). *Proceedings of the Massachusetts Historical Society 1873–75*. *The Genealogists' Magazine*, March 1942. *Topographer and Genealogist*, vol. 3, 1858. *Aristocratic Century: The Peerage of 18th Century England* by John Cannon (Cambridge University Press). *Settlements in the Americas* ed. Ralph Bennett (University of Delaware Press). *Dictionary of National Biography* ed. Leslie Stephen (Macmillan & Co., New York). *The Genealogist Magazine* ed. H W Forsyth Harwood (George Bell & Sons). *The Original Baronage of England*

1066–1885 by James E Doyle (Longmans, Green & Co. 1886). *Genealogie de la Maison de Fiennes* (Pere Anselme on the House of Fiennes). *The Peerage of England, Vol. VI* by Arthur Collins. *The History and Antiquisities of the County of Buckingham* by George Lipscomb (J & W Robins, 1847). *Bulletins of State Intelligence, etc. 1848* (F Watts). *Journal of San Diego History,* vol. 25, no. 1, 1979 (San Diego Historical Society). *The Principles of the Christian Religion Explained* by William, Archbishop of Canterbury (T Cadell, 1827). *The Historic Lands of England* by J Bernard Burke (E Churton). *Dictionnaire de Biographie Francaise* by Roman d'Amat (Librairie Letouzey et Ane). *The Baronage of England 1387–1676* by William Dugdale (Tho. Newcomb, 1676). *The Vindiciae Veritatis* by J S A Adamson. *Marshall's Genealogists' Guide. Histoire Genealogique et Chronologique de la Maison Royale de France. Medieval Kent Wills at Lambeth,* Book 26. *Patronage, Culture and Power: The Early Cecils* ed. Pauline Croft (Yale University Press). *The Commune of London* by J H Round (Archibald Constable & Co). *St James's Magazine and Heraldic and Historical Register, 1850. The House of Lords Cases on Appeals and Write of Error, Claims of Peerage, and Divorces 1847 and 1848* by Charles Clark & W Finnelly (Little Brown & Co. 1870). *The Antiquary,* vol. III (Frederick William Monk, 1873). *English Genealogy* by Anthony Richard Wagner (Oxford, Clarendon Press). *The New Century Cyclopedia of Names* by William D Halsey (Appleton-Century-Crofts, Inc). *Heraldry of the Royal Families of Europe* by Michael Maclagan (Clarkson N Potter, Inc). *A Genealogical and Heraldic Dictionary of the Peerage and Baronetage* by Sir Bernard Burke (Harrison & Sons). *The Herald and Genealogist* ed. John Gough Nichols (J G Nichols & R C Nichols, 1870). *Alumni Oronienses: The Members of the University of Oxford 1500–1714* by Joseph Foster (Parker and Co). *The New England Historical and Genealogical Register 1962* (N.E . Historic Genealogical Society). *Burke's Peerage & Baronetage. Dictionnaire de la Noblesse. The Pedigrees of the English Peers,* vol. II. *Bibliotheque de l'Ecole des*

Chartes, vol. III (J B Dumoulin). *The Great Governing Families of England* by John Langton Sanford & Meredith Townsend (William Blackwood & Sons). *The Publications of the Harleian Society. The English Nobility and the Projected Settlement of 1647* by J S A Adamson.

Index

Index

RANULPH FIENNES

MAD, BAD & Dangerous to Know

'Sir Ranulph has earned his place in the heroic roll call of Scott, Shackleton and the rest.' *Daily Mail*

The triumphs and the tragedies of a life lived at the limits of human endeavour are recounted with compelling honesty and passion by Sir Ranulph Fiennes in his bestselling autobiography.

'His book is not all about hairy-chested adventure: he also tells deeply movingly of his love for his first wife . . . His courage, determination, stamina – and madness – are truly awesome.' *Daily Express*

'Even readers with a broadly low tolerance for macho heroism will find themselves gripped . . . compelling.' *Time Out*

Available in Hodder paperback

www.hodder.co.uk

HELL AND HIGH WATER

Also by Sean Conway

Cycling the Earth

HELL AND HIGH WATER

My epic 900-mile swim from Land's End to John O'Groats

SEAN CONWAY

EBURY PRESS

1 3 5 7 9 10 8 6 4 2

Ebury Press, an imprint of Ebury Publishing,
20 Vauxhall Bridge Road,
London SW1V 2SA

Ebury Press is part of the Penguin Random House group of companies whose addresses can be found at global.penguinrandomhouse.com

First published by Ebury Press in 2015
This edition published in 2017

www.eburypublishing.co.uk

A CIP catalogue record for this book is available from the British Library

ISBN 9780091959753

Printed and bound in Great Britain by Clays Ltd, St Ives PLC

Penguin Random House is committed to a sustainable future for our business, our readers and our planet. This book is made from Forest Stewardship Council® certified paper.

CONTENTS

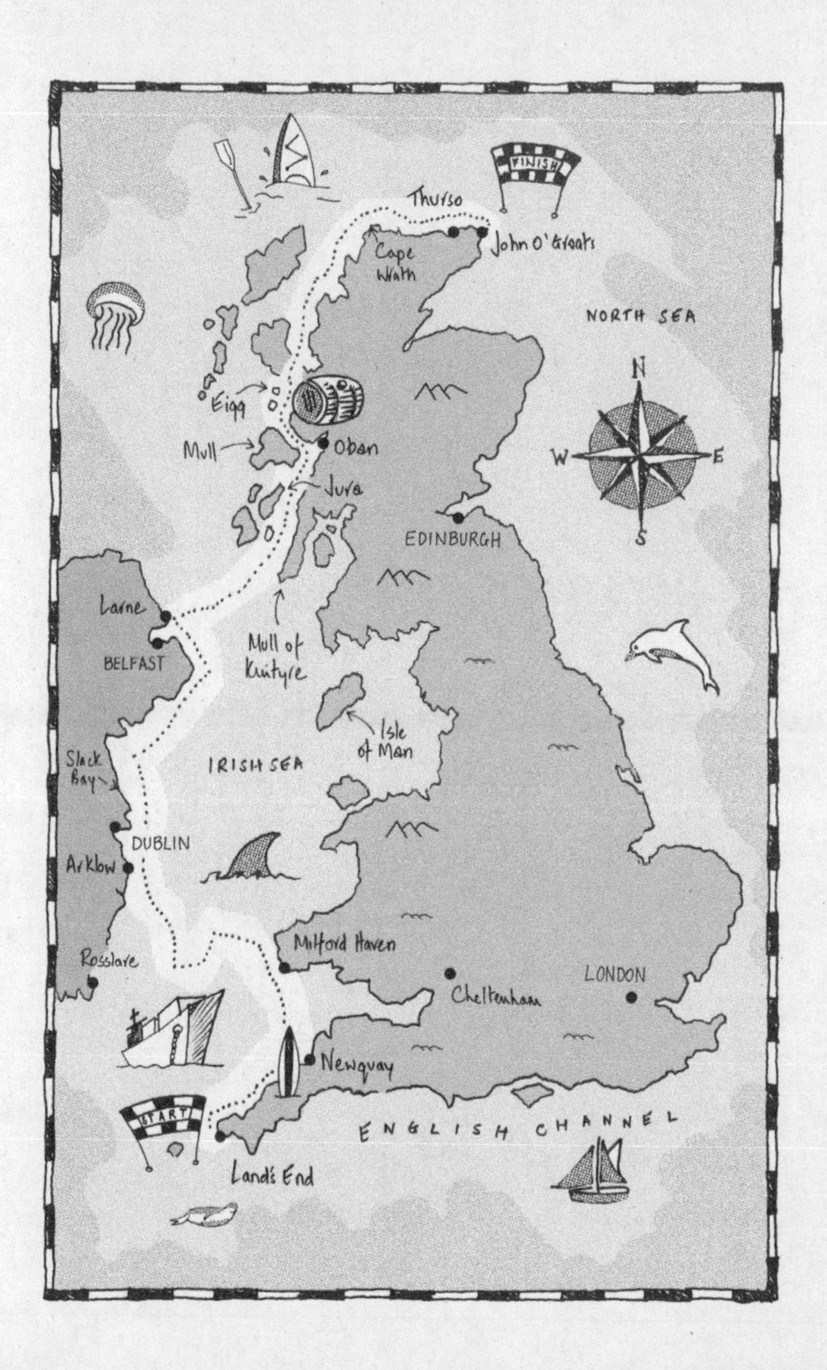
FINISH
Thurso
John O'Groats
Cape Wrath
NORTH SEA
N
W
E
S
Eigg
Mull
Oban
Jura
EDINBURGH
Larne
BELFAST
Mull of Kintyre
Isle of Man
Slack Bay
IRISH SEA
DUBLIN
Arklow
Rosslare
Milford Haven
Cheltenham
LONDON
Newquay
START
ENGLISH CHANNEL
Land's End

PROLOGUE

A mouthful of salt water rushed down my throat as I tried to breathe into a wave. I nearly vomited. Rain pelted down and ran into my mouth as I struggled for air. Off in the distance a horn started booming across the sea. I looked up to see where it was coming from. A lighthouse possibly? I wasn't sure. Was it a rescue siren for me? My heart started to race as I imagined being rescued on Day 2. That would be embarrassing. The horn carried on for a few minutes as a mist started to roll in, reducing my visibility to nearly nothing. Ah. A foghorn! I felt strangely relieved, but also nervous that perhaps I looked like I needed rescuing. No one in their right mind would swim in this cold, windy and foggy sea by choice.

I pushed on towards the headland where the foghorn was sounding and got caught up in a fast eddy. I pushed and pushed but no matter how hard I tried I wasn't moving. My tired arms, which had now been working for over five hours, just couldn't do it. Em, in the kayak next to me, had a look of despair.

'We're not moving!'

The tide was too strong at this time of day and I had nothing left in the tank. I tried for another 10 minutes but then had to make a decision. I told Em to go ahead to the beach and I looked for a way to get out of the water, as I started to float backwards. The rocks to my right were sharp and broken, and the waves rushed past them with daunting ferocity. I'd surely be knocked out if I got too close. The rise in water height was about one and a half metres. There was one ledge which was about the same height as the crest of each wave. If I timed it correctly, I could get beached on the top and avoid getting washed off. I waited and waited before the right wave lifted me right up to the jagged edge. I kicked hard and landed right on top of the ledge. I held on tight as the wave flowed away. I frantically tried to scramble up the rocks out of the reach of the water but nearly fell back into the sea again. I couldn't feel my feet at all. It was if they were completely separate from my body – numb bits of rubber at the end of my tired legs. Eventually I made it to the safety of the grass above and collapsed.

It was only Day 2 and I couldn't push through one eddy. I guess this was why so many people kept telling me this swim wasn't possible. I lay there for what seemed an eternity wondering if I had in fact completely misjudged the enormity of this challenge.

One thing was for sure, I'd never be able to take two months of this type of swimming.

1

GETTING TO THE START

Two months to go ...

'Sean, my boy. Would you like a cup of tea?'

I sat up and bumped my head on the ceiling. Damn it, I thought. I'm too bloody old to sleep on a bunk bed.

I climbed down the child sized ladder, my weight nearly toppling the bed over. I'd sleep on the bottom bunk but my entire life seemed to be piled on there. I'd moved back in with my mother almost a year ago. Partly because she has been ill, but mainly to save money for my swim. So, 32 years old and living at home, on a bunk bed. It was depressing to think about it but I really needed to save as much as possible.

I left my tiny room and headed a few metres down the hall to another tiny room at the back of the flat in which I'd constructed a sort of logistical headquarters. It had no windows and the landlord had forgotten to plaster the walls. The upside was I could draw and stick various things onto the wall knowing it would be covered over at some point. One of the first things I bought was a huge poster of the British Isles which I pinned right in front of me. I'd spend at least an hour staring blankly at it, wondering if it was possible to complete such a long sea swim. My heart rate always rose a little when looking at places like Cape Wrath. Yachts have come off second best there, how would a swimmer cope? So many questions to which I'd probably never get answers until I was underway. At this point everything was pure speculation.

Firstly, I had decided, I needed a support boat. I'd toyed with loads of ideas. Initially I was going to do it with just a few kayaks, but then realised we couldn't carry enough water and finding places to come ashore at the exact moment the tide changed would be impossible. The second idea was to get a motorboat, but I soon gave up on that idea when I realised the fuel bill would run into thousands of pounds. The best option was to get a yacht. I started by trawling through eBay. My budget was £4,000. Who was I kidding? I'd never find a 4-berth yacht that was ready to sail for £4,000. I had no other option though. I was planning on getting the money from credit cards, and I'd have to sell the yacht at the end to hopefully make some money back as long as I didn't trash it.

The second brainwave I had was to put a post on a yachting forum. Surely some kind-hearted gentleman who 'just didn't have the time to sail any more' would possibly lend me a yacht? It was a long shot but worth trying.

So the previous night I had posted the following:

In July 2013, I'm going to attempt to become the first person to swim the length of Britain. I'm swimming from iconic Land's End to John O'Groats up the west coast. It's going to be one of the hardest swims of all time and I am trying to raise money for War Child in Africa. I'll be swimming the equivalent of the Channel every day for two months as I battle the 1,000-mile coastal swim.

I am looking for anyone who has a 30-foot yacht that needs a bit of TLC. I'm proposing to get it cleaned up for you if you would be so kind as to lend it to me as a support boat. I'll need it from mid-June to the end of September.

Regards, Sean

There must be someone out there wanting his or her boat fixed for free?

The next morning I was delighted to see quite a few emails in my inbox. Brilliant. I excitedly opened the first one, which came only half an hour after I posted the topic. Keen, I thought. He must know someone.

It read:

'you need to do much more reserch and it will take more like 6 months'

No punctuation and bad spelling. He didn't even answer the question. Never mind. I moved on to the next email with slightly less positivity.

'Frankly I think this idea is totally daft. But you certainly didn't ask for my opinion, nor do you need anyone's permission to try.'

Well, that was helpful, I thought, but he was right on one thing. I didn't need his, or anyone's, permission. A stubborn anger started to build. Emails like that made me want to do it even more. I moved on to the next email.

'A project like this might be better supported with a RIB?'

A short answer and not exactly what I asked but at least we were getting somewhere. I moved on.

'I predict that you will have more problems trying to find a place to berth the yacht every night, 20 miles apart, than you will doing the swim. All-weather ports down the west coast are very few and far between. This will be repeated all the way down the Irish Sea and St George's Channel. A fast MOBO is the only possibility IMHO, a small yacht not an option.'

Logistical advice was great but not quite what I was asking. Also, what was a MOBO? Next.

'I don't want to be too pessimistic but Florence Chadwick who broke the England-France Channel record for both men and women after years of training, was not able to complete the Portpatrick–Donaghadee crossing: about 22 miles.'

What does that have to do with lending me a boat? Next.

> 'A lot of negative feedback here. If no one tries it we will never know whether it's achievable or not, best of luck with it and I will follow it with interest.'

Well someone at least feels sorry for me. Next.

There was no next. That was it. Not one person giving any useful advice. I turned my computer off and stared at the map of Britain. This swim was looking like a pipedream, but I was determined for it to become a reality. Nothing suggested it wasn't possible, but proving that the impossible is actually possible, before you even start, was proving to be near impossible. This is quite a common scenario with big adventures, I guess. If it seemed possible then it would probably have been attempted already and therefore not attract as much attention, which excites sponsors. It was a hard game to play because I needed to sound confident to potential sponsors that I'd be able to complete the swim without sounding too naïve about the task at hand. Sponsors can work out straight away if you have looked into everything or not.

Finding a company to sponsor the swim was turning out to be increasingly difficult. I always seemed to get into meetings but inevitably got the same answers: 'We love the idea but just don't think it's possible, so it's too big a risk for us. But if you want to use our kit we'd happily supply you with it.'

I didn't need kit. I needed money to pay for fuel for the support boat and food for the crew. I emailed 350 companies and most expressed no interest at all in becoming a title sponsor. A few said they'd think about it, but with less than two months to go it was looking unlikely. I never thought it would be this hard. All I was asking for was £10,000. Surely for these sorts of companies that's a small price to pay for the potential publicity? Some even said they didn't want to get involved in case I died. That's always a positive email to get.

While I struggled along to find a sponsor, I started to look for crew. I needed three crew members: someone to skipper the boat, someone to take care of press, PR, take photos, help with prepping meals and be a general deck-hand, and lastly someone to kayak next to me so that I didn't get lost. A kayak could also carry food and water so I could eat and hydrate while in the water.

I had no idea where to start so thought I'd write a blog and share it on Twitter and Facebook. I added questions like, 'Do you suffer from seasickness?' and 'Can you kayak?' Within a day I got an application from Em Bell. Em Bell? I recognised the name but didn't know why so I Googled her.

Ah, yes! She was part of the crew that supported my friend Dave Cornthwaite when he swam 1,000 miles down the Missouri River. She was 28 years old, had no commitments like a job or a husband and knew a thing or two about swimming-based adventures. On paper she sounded perfect. But I remembered that Dave had had quite a few problems with his crew so I decided to give him a quick call to see what he thought.

'Hello buddy. How's the swim prep?' Dave asked when he picked up the phone.

'Good. Just trying to find crew. Got any tips?'

Dave laughed.

'More to the point,' I said, 'Em Bell just applied. Is she any good?'

'Mate, she is incredible. Say yes to her NOW, before she finds something else to do. She was the best person in my crew and by far the hardest working person I have ever met. Honestly, you won't regret it!'

I emailed Em straight away to arrange a meeting. One crew member found, two more to go. Who knows how I was going to find a skipper. Most people who can sail a yacht probably own one and have better things to do, like run a successful business, than follow a swimmer going at two knots for two months.

Feeling a bit disheartened, I decided to do some work on the fundraising side of things to take my mind off logistics. I had chosen the charity War Child specifically to help children in the Central African Republic. Raising money for charity is an important motivator when taking on a challenge like this. I knew I would get a huge boost when people donate some money through the JustGiving page I had set up.

One month to go ...

I finally had my crew. Surprisingly, my Tweets and Facebook posts had resulted in more than 30 applications, which I'd narrowed down to five finalists. It was a hard decision as they all had pretty impressive CVs – two had even climbed Mount Everest. In the end the position of Head of Press and PR and general deck-hand went to Owain Wyn-Jones, a 35-year-old chap originally from Wales, now living in Shropshire. At first, he didn't seem the most adventurous of the applicants and even when I called him for the interview his reply was 'Really? I never expected a call from you', but he had a good eye for media, could take a great photo and said he loved fishing. My one concern was that he was married with a child but he convinced me that this wouldn't be an issue. His wife was the one who found the opportunity for him. I had a good gut feeling about Owain. This would be a big challenge for him and I knew he'd work hard at making the most of it.

I was really happy with having Em and Owain, but finding a skipper was still proving tricky. None of the blogs or forums I used came up with anything. Out of options, it was time to try my one and only lead, my good friend Jeremy. Jez was a teacher and had hinted that he'd like to come and find me during my swim for a few weeks during his holidays in August. Jez lives on a narrowboat in London and can sail, although he never formally trained. To get him for July too he'd have to get a lot of time off work right at the end of the school year. It was a long shot but I was desperate. I gave him a call.

'How's the boat?' I asked, knowing that he was busy installing a shower.

'It's coming along slowly. I've been showering at school for six months; a few more days won't kill me. How's the swim prep? Not long now, what's it, four weeks to go?'

'Just over four.' Saying it out loud gave me a slight panic attack. I had no skipper, no support boat, no kayak for Em, no RIB (Rigid Inflatable Boat), no sponsor and no food. How was I going to sort all that out in four weeks and still have time to train?

'You must be excited. Who's skippering it? Can I still come in August?' asked Jez excitedly.

'Well, that's why I am calling. I really can't find a skipper anywhere. Fancy being the skipper?'

There was a long pause.

'Interesting.'

I had no idea what he meant by that.

'When is it you start?'

'On 30 June.'

'Mmm. It's not a no, but I'd have to check with school. It could be fun!'

'Please, mate, I'll pay for you to do your VHF licence and a day skipper course if you want.'

'Well, legally I need the VHF licence and I don't need to do a day skipper course but it's always good to learn I guess. What boat have you got?'

'Yeah, um, I haven't got one yet. I was hoping a skipper might be able to help with that. I have no idea what I am doing.'

'Fair enough. Let me call you tomorrow.'

'Thank you. I am desperate.'

Jez hadn't said yes, but he hadn't said no either. I'd done my bit; it was up to him now.

*

I didn't hear from Jez for three days and I was close to giving up. Then my phone rang one morning when I was in the shower. I ran to my phone, dripping water all over the floor. It was Jez.

'Hello, mate,' I said, nervously, and slightly out of breath from my ten-metre dash from the bathroom. That was worrying, and probably reflected how little training I'd managed to fit in.

'Right, I've handed in my notice. My last day is Friday 28 June. I'm all yours from then.'

'Really? I thought you were going to ask for time off?'

'Yeah, but they said no and I didn't like the school anyway so it was a good excuse to leave.'

'Wow. This is awesome. Thank you so much. I owe you everything.'

I jumped around my bedroom, completely naked, doing a silent scream. I had a full crew now. I couldn't contain my excitement.

'I've also been thinking,' Jez continued in a calm, matter-of-fact way. 'I have a sea kayak too and I know a guy called Arthur who lives on a boat near me who has an old RIB with an outboard engine that is just sitting there. I'm sure if you service it for him he'd let you borrow it.'

'Really?!' My day was getting better. Not only had I got a skipper, who was a good mate of mine, I now had a kayak and a RIB with an engine.

'I can only ask him but he is really cool.'

'You are my hero. Thanks so much.'

'No worries at all. This is going to be fun. I'll send you

a list of things I need, like charts, etc. What do you want me to do?'

I gave Jez a long list of things he'd need to be in charge of, such as tides, route, navigation and safety, and most importantly, researching a support boat. My £4,000 budget, fuelled completely by a credit card I managed to squeeze out of Lloyds Bank, really wasn't bringing up anything suitable on eBay but I hoped Jez's knowledge might help.

I grew up in Zimbabwe, in Mana Pools National Park, where my dad was a conservation ranger. At my school swimming was compulsory and, even if you were spluttering around in the shallow end on the verge of drowning, our swim teacher, Mrs Morrison, would still shout at you to carry on. A few kids really weren't made for swimming, or wearing speedos to be fair. I wasn't a natural swimmer but I did at least learn the strokes. And I must have got reasonably good at it, as when I was 14 I took part in the Midmar Mile, a huge annual open water swimming event in South Africa.

But that was probably the last serious swimming I'd done. I was now 32 years old and apart from fetching the occasional Frisbee from the sea on Brighton beach, I hadn't actually swum for the sake of swimming for the last 14 years. So why on earth had I set myself such a huge swimming-based challenge?

Back in 2011 I was miserable and discontent, and very much just existing rather than living. I hated the life I had made for myself and was operating on autopilot. It was very much a case of, 'Get up! Do something you hate just so you can afford the flat you only sleep in and a car you need just to do the job you hate!' It was my own fault really. I'd arrived in London in 2002 with only £100 in my pocket. I did a few jobs just to get some cash, like cutting lettuces in a pre-packed salad factory in Cambridgeshire, and working six days a week developing other people's holiday photos at Snappy Snaps, before starting my own photography business. But instead of going out and chasing creative work that fuelled my imagination, I decided to chase the money and spent 99% of my time doing corporate portraits of bankers in the city, who, after the banking crisis of 2008, really didn't want to be photographed. When I wasn't photographing angry bankers it was crying babies for school portraits. Headshots in front of a white background. I was a glorified passport photographer photographing people who didn't actually want to be photographed. It was soul destroying, but it paid the bills.

I did this for almost ten years until, a few months before my thirtieth birthday, I'd had enough. I finally admitted I was miserable and walked into the office and asked my business partner, James, to buy my shares. He offered me £1. I agreed and, a month later, after helping him restructure operations so he could work on his own, I walked away. I knew what I needed now was to challenge myself to do something radically different.

Growing up on the banks of the Zambezi River meant there were some amazing opportunities to do adventurous stuff, and I have always loved getting outside. In my teens

I was really into canoeing, and competed in several river marathons including the Dusi Canoe Marathon, which takes place over three days on a 75-mile course in South Africa. I also once climbed Kilimanjaro dressed as a penguin for charity. I realised that this was the sort of stuff that made me happy.

I'd been reading a lot about round the world cyclists like Mark Beaumont, Vin Cox and Tommy Godwin. This was exactly the sort of adventure I wished I could have. Then I realised, why couldn't I do it? Honestly, I had two legs and could cycle. What was stopping me?

So that's how I came to join nine other cyclists all competing in the first ever World Cycle Race. It was the brainchild of round the world cyclist Vin Cox who, on returning home from his ride, realised his record could easily be beaten and invited people to attempt it. The idea that I might be able to break a world record was inspiring, and exactly what I needed. I worked incredibly hard training and getting ready for the challenge before setting off from Greenwich in February 2012. It was going to be one hell of a race.

A month into my ride I was way ahead of the world record, averaging 180 miles per day self-supported, when I was run over in America by a careless driver. This effectively ended my world record attempt. After a month off the bike recovering in America I carried on as I still wanted to raise money for my chosen charity, Solar Aid, but I was a lot slower and eventually limped back to London having cycled 16,000 miles in 116 days. In many ways it had still been the adventure of a lifetime, but there was one thing missing. I had failed in my attempt to break the world record for round the world cycling. I had worked so hard and really hoped to do something that no one else had.

This was the idea behind this swim. I was sure it was possible, but no one had done it. If I succeeded I would be the only one. I would really be pushing myself to my limits. Physically, as I would be battling the sea, but mentally too, as I would have to cope with being in the water for hours on end. I really wanted to make it happen to give myself the confidence back that I could do something physically and mentally on the 'extremely difficult' scale. Swimming 1,000 miles up the coast of Britain certainly ticked that box.

So, that's how it happened that ten months on from returning from my failed round the world cycle record attempt I was in the shallow end of my local pool, staring into the water. This was my first training session and I kept thinking to myself – I hope it's like riding a bicycle; you never forget.

As is turned out I had pretty much forgotten, and was so awful I had to get out after ten lengths because I felt dizzy and nauseous. I was rubbish. In between sorting out crew, logistics and finding a sponsor it was proving very difficult to fit in swim training. I was already resigned to the fact I'd have to do all my training in a pool and wouldn't be able to do any sea-training sessions; Mum lives in Cheltenham which is a good three-hour round trip from the nearest beach. It wasn't ideal, and far from the serious training sessions I did for my cycle, but I was just running out of time. I figured I would get fit along the route. If I didn't drown first.

I was told by various people who knew what they were talking about, which was almost anyone who has swum, ever, to get some coaching sessions. So, eventually, after not much progress in the pool, I decided to enlist the help of triathlon legend Mark Kleanthous who has completed more than 450 triathlons around the world. He had access to an 'endless' pool, which is a small pool that pushes a flow of water towards you. This allows you to swim in one spot while he films your technique. After my session, Mark sent me a long list of things I needed to change. He said my technique was pretty awful, but if I just changed a few little things I'd become more efficient in the water. I didn't need to be the fastest; after all, it wasn't a race. What was more important was strength – both mental and physical – as well as endurance. I would be tested to the limit and I really had no idea if I would be up to the task.

I did at least realise that getting enough fuel into my body every day would be really important, so I went to see Steve, the nutritionist I worked with before the round the world cycle. As ever, he was a fountain of useful information. He also helped me with a training program too. No one really had any idea how to eat enough calories for my body to deal with the cold water for so long, but Steve's 'eat EVERYTHING' concept seemed to be the best solution for now. There was no point in planning to eat certain food and then not being able to stomach them.

'If you can stomach it mate, then eat it,' he'd say. Seemed a good compromise for when conditions are against you.

Two weeks to go ...

I still didn't have a boat or a sponsor. I decided to go down to see Jez and meet Arthur, who was lending me his RIB and outboard.

Jez lives on a canal in east London and has one of the best local pubs I've ever been to. It's called the Anchor & Hope and sits right on the towpath. It's a proper East End pub that specialises in real ale. On weekdays, there's no food except for a few packets of crisps and nuts behind the bar. Jez has his own mug which they keep especially for him. It is one of those German-type mugs with the lid you open with your thumb. He even has a special order which they have ready for him even before he reaches the bar. It's half of one ale and half of another. Most afternoons you can buy eel and fish from a chap who walks through the pub with a tray. I decided that this would be a good place to catch up with Jez and look at a few yachts I had saved to the eBay app on my phone.

Every yacht we looked at either didn't have an engine, or was missing a sail, or had no navigation equipment – all of which can be expensive to sort out after you've bought the boat. Eventually we came across an old wooden 26-foot yacht built in 1961. It was a SCOD (South Coast One Design) and was currently at a bid of £3,500, which was just in budget, and had a few days to go on the auction. Jez read the description and he was surprised how good the condition was for the price. She had good sails, was sea-worthy already, had a separate toilet that wasn't between the two front bunks as with many smaller yachts, and had all the GPS navigation and depth sounders we needed. Her name was *Friday While*, and, although 52 years old and wooden, she looked like she had character. We decided to have another ale each and carry on searching.

Two more ales later and having seen nothing remotely as good, we had another look at *Friday While.* Twenty-six foot was a little on the small side, but she had a very large keel – five foot, six inches – which would make her more stable in bigger waves. I decided to Google SCODs. They had some great reviews: steady at sea, very well engineered and lovely to sail. The only thing people said they didn't like was that they were very slow. This could become an issue in trying to fight the tides and get us to safe anchorages, but to be honest, I didn't really have a better choice. Could this be the boat for Swimming Britain?

The auction had two more days to run, but I was leaving for Jersey to do some talks at schools to earn some money as I still had no sponsor. I had no way of going down to look at her before I left and the auction would end while I was on the ferry to Jersey. It was a case of bid now on the phone or miss out. I bought another pint while I mulled it over. Several ales later, after changing my mind constantly, I decided I didn't really have much choice. I hadn't seen anything like it at all for the price. I plucked up the (Dutch) courage and, with a small amount of difficulty, I took out my phone and put a maximum bid of £4,007.51. Nervously,

I pressed BID and waited. There was a slow internet connection and the spinning wheel symbol seemed to take forever. Eventually the screen flashed green and my heart jumped. It said, 'You are the highest bidder at £3,632.'

Jez and I looked at each other. He was smiling. I was smiling too but it was more of a nervous smile. Had I just bought a yacht on the eBay app? We had a few more ales to celebrate.

I woke up the next morning with a slight headache. Had I really bid on a yacht in Jez's local? I looked at my phone. I was still the highest bidder for *Friday While*. My heart raced. Last night was all a bit hazy but I remembered Jez saying it was worth it, and I trusted him. I now needed to pack for Jersey. I'd only know when I got there whether I had won the auction or not.

The ferry crossing to the Channel Islands felt impossibly long. I was meant to be working on my talks but couldn't keep my mind off the fact that at that very moment I may or may not be the owner of a yacht. A mile offshore I got phone reception but no 3G. Then a voicemail came through. It was Jez.

'Mate, we got it. We have a boat! Final bid was £3,890 which I think is a bargain. Well done, Mr Boat Owner! Anyway, let me know when you are back, it's down on the south coast. I need to start thinking about getting it to Penzance, which will take about six days.'

An overwhelming feeling smothered me and I started to hyperventilate a little. This was it. Owning a yacht was something I never in a million years thought I'd do, and buying one the way we did probably wasn't the best idea, but nevertheless, I now had a boat and a crew. Things were looking up.

Except that I still couldn't pay for the trip.

The truth was that Swimming Britain was still a fantasy. I was acting confident and telling everyone it was happening. I'd bought a yacht and convinced three people to give up their entire summer to live on it with me. But without financial help from sponsors there was no way on earth I could afford to feed a crew and pay all the costs. If I couldn't find a sponsor I'd most certainly have to delay the swim by an entire year, or more. Apart from everything else that I'd need to start all over again with, finding another crew would be the hardest – after all, who knows where Jez, Owain and Em might be in a year. That would be so disappointing. I was excited about our team.

I knew I was probably going to need more than the £10,000 in sponsorship I was asking for, but I didn't want to scare potential sponsors off with a higher figure.

On Tuesday morning, ten days before the start of my swim, I woke up and opened my laptop to see if I'd had any luck with emails to sponsors from the day before. It was always disappointing seeing an empty inbox but this time I noticed an email from a lady called Sally at Speedo. I'd had two meetings with Speedo, and although they said they were interested nothing had been confirmed. This was probably to say they didn't want to fund it, just like the other 350 companies I'd contacted. I hesitantly opened the email.

Hi Sean

We just wanted to let you know that we're in for the full £10,000. What you're doing is remarkable and it is exactly what we believe in – normal people using swimming to explore and get fit.

Attached is a contract. You should get the funds in ten days or so!

We're really excited to be part of this.

Chat soon.

Sal

I couldn't believe it. I screamed out loud and Mum came running into my room.

'I got it Mum, I got the money!'

'Well done! So proud of you!' She hugged me.

I could feel the tension running out of my shoulders. It had been a few hard weeks of getting nowhere with anyone. Having a brand like Speedo on board was perfect because I now had funds to feed the crew properly and also they had great ideas about sharing the adventure. I couldn't have asked for a more appropriate partnership.

As if my day couldn't get any better, I then received another email from a company called Stowaways who make high-end sailing food in a bag. They wanted to provide me with 500 meals for the swim. It was exactly what I needed: good quality packet food I could just heat up and that didn't need rehydrating. That was it – pretty much everything was in place! Swimming Britain could definitely go ahead! I was brimming with excitement and nerves.

One week to go ...

My plans were finally coming together. I had been working with Jez, Owain and Em on getting most of the logistics sorted. Jez had taken *Friday While* to Penzance with the help of an amazing skipper called Lou. She and her brother Jim run a sailing school called Nomad Sailing on the south coast, and had kindly offered to donate four days of their time to give Jez a refresher course in sailing and help him get the boat down towards Land's End. I tried to go out with them on the first day but got so seasick I decided not to do the rest of the journey. This was not a good sign. I hoped I wouldn't get seasick while swimming, although I'd heard that can happen.

The last week before the start was a hive of checking things, sorting last-minute kit and making sure the crew had everything they needed. The only slight hiccup was that Speedo hadn't received my signed contract and I only realised a few days before the start when the funds hadn't arrived. I had to send another one through, and that delay meant the money would only clear a few days after the start of the swim. Normally this would be fine but I literally had no money left at all. I had borrowed everything I could from friends and family, and maxed every credit card and all overdrafts possible. It was so bad that I didn't even have enough money to fill my car with diesel to get to Land's End.

My last resort was to go grovelling to my bank manager with the email from Speedo to ask for £250. It took an hour for Robert, the bank manager, to call various people at Lloyds head office, or wherever they make decisions, before they eventually decided to give me another £250 on a two-week extension to my current overdraft. At least I could pay to service Arthur's outboard, which I hadn't done yet, and fill my car so I could actually get to Land's End and the start line.

2
LAND'S END

'Hey mate, really sorry but I've missed my bus by two minutes.'

Jez hadn't got his bus from London to Penzance and therefore would not be here for the start of the swim, which was set for midday tomorrow.

'Shit. OK. When can you get here?' I asked, trying not to sound annoyed. He had quit his job for me after all. The reason I needed Jez there was because the only way to get to the tip of Land's End was to drive a mile up the coast to a place called Sennen Cove, which has a harbour and access to the sea. From there I was going to take the yacht to the tip of Land's End and jump in to start the swim.

'Tomorrow evening is when the next one comes in. Sorry,' he replied in an annoyingly calm voice. Why wasn't he stressed out? I would soon learn that Jez never gets stressed out about anything, which has its advantages.

'I guess there is nothing we can do. I'll try to find a fisherman or something.'

I put the phone down and put my head in my hands. Getting to the start line had been so difficult, but here we were. Everything was meant to be in place and I had hoped to have a relaxing evening, get some food and then an early night. I now needed to go and find a fisherman to help me, so I headed down to Sennen Cove for some advice. Em came along as I figured a girl might have more luck asking for things.

Em started working her magic straight away with a pretty convincing 'we're desperate' sob story. First stop was the café. They were incredibly friendly, and when Em told them what I was attempting they sent us to find a fisherman and also suggested that the RNLI might help.

So we asked the RNLI if they had a small dinghy that someone could take us in a mile up the coast and then drop me in the water.

'No, we can't do that!' the old lady replied as if it was absurd to ask. 'We take people out of dangerous situations and out of the water. We can't be seen to be putting people into the water and into dangerous situations!'

I was initially annoyed with their logic because I was going to swim no matter what and surely having them close to me was better than me going it alone but, after thinking about it, they did have a point. Imagine I did get into trouble and it was revealed that the RNLI had put me in that position. It would not look good for them. I guess I was just going to have to get used to the idea of this 'sorry we can't help in case you die' attitude for this swim.

The next stop was to ask a fisherman called Bob. Apparently he was still out fishing but was due back in about an hour, so Em and I sat on the beach and looked out to the sea. Although typically overcast, there weren't that many waves and conditions looked pretty good for swimming.

'I hope it's like this tomorrow,' Em said, looking a little worried. Em had actually never kayaked in the sea before; the only kayaking she had done was an hour on the Thames a few weeks before. (She had travelled down the Missouri by stand up paddle board as part of Dave Cornthwaite's crew.) It was a risky choice as we didn't know what the sea conditions would be like, but her swimming knowledge was well worth having and of all the people who had applied she was the most enthusiastic, and that counted for a lot.

'Me too. It's hard to imagine it all stormy and violent on days like today. Let's hope it stays like this,' I replied.

Off to our right was Sennen beach, which had a few kids building sandcastles and running around being mischievous. It was Saturday 29 June 2013, which meant the beach was probably at its busiest but, even so, it was still pretty quiet. Land's End is a very long way from anything really. So far away in fact that none of my friends had managed to visit. Just my mum and her friend Cathy had made it to see me off. I didn't really expect my mates to come all the way down, but it would have been nice.

My friends have become used to me doing big challenges after my round the world cycle, so they're not that surprised by anything I do now. It's fine because sometimes the planning of a big adventure like this can somehow turn into an all-encompassing monster that takes over your entire life. This can be a massive contradiction to the reasons you want to go off adventuring in the first place. You want to get away from the rat race, expand your mind, push yourself and not get caught up in the bullshit that modern living can throw at you. If you're not careful you can get just as caught up in the adventure bullshit, where your challenge starts to own you and all other parts of your life fall by the wayside. My friends keep me really grounded, and on occasions when I am telling someone at a party what I do, all my mates shamelessly just turn around and walk away yawning, as they've heard it a million times.

Mum, on the other hand, like all mums, loves everything I do and spent most of the preceding months telling everyone she met about the swim. Even people in the queue for an ATM, where engaging in conversation could be misinterpreted as an invasion of privacy, Mum doesn't care, she goes straight in with, 'My son is just about to swim the length of Britain.' No introduction or anything. Just bang, right for the jugular.

It was a shame Dad wasn't here but coming all the way from South Africa seemed a little over the top. He has always been bit more aware of the practicalities of what I do and worries a lot about my safety, especially after I got run over in America. It was a traumatic time for my family who could do nothing to help me from the other side of the world. But, although he was concerned, Dad was still supportive of the swim. I'd set him up with a Twitter account on his phone so he could keep up to date with my progress.

*

Bob eventually came ashore in his fishing boat. It was a lovely wooden open-top 15-foot boat, painted white with a blue rim. It was full of fishing boxes, various coloured nets and small plastic buoys. Bob was in his late fifties, wore typical fisherman dungarees and sported the most spectacular beard. I was envious.

'Hi Bob,' said Em, smiling from ear to ear.

'Hi there! You must be the swimmer. I've heard about you. Has anyone told you, you are mad?' He laughed.

'Mainly my mum!' I replied trying to keep the conversation light-hearted.

'Anyway, our skipper can't make the start for tomorrow,' continued Em, 'and we were wondering if there would be any chance we could hire your services for an hour to take us to the start? We need to leave at midday or thereabouts.'

'Midday? The tide would have just turned then. It won't be possible to swim.' He said with quite a worryingly stern look on his face, a stark contrast to his friendly smile earlier.

The way tides work in Britain is that for six hours you get the tide running north and then for another six hours the tide runs south. When it's running south, you can't swim northward as you'd just go backwards. This presented various logistical issues that we'd have to think about seriously because the tide affects where the boat can get to each night. Jez was in charge of all this but Jez wasn't here, so we were kind of in the dark.

The rest of the swim would be governed by tidal times that are related to High Water Dover. This is a sailing term which tells you when the tide is running in which direction, sort of like Greenwich Mean Time but for tides. High Water Dover is the benchmark for when the tide changes. The tide would turn at Land's End at High Water Dover +2. High water in Dover is at 10am. This means the tide at Land's End would turn at midday. My start time tomorrow, however, was determined by when the media could get here. I was set to start at midday and, although not ideal for the tides, I figured if I kept close enough to the shore I could avoid the big rush of tide that goes past Land's End. I had no research to back this idea up, more of a gut feeling really, as I was yet to do my first open-water sea swim. However, seeing as I was only going to swim one mile tomorrow and then carry on from Sennen on Monday, I wasn't too worried.

'I'm sorry. I wouldn't feel comfortable dropping you in the sea there. It's a nasty stretch of water and at full rush, not even my boat can cope against that tide,' said Bob while hauling large boxes of fish onto the sand.

Em tried everything and even explained it was all for charity, but nothing was going to make him budge. We asked if there was anyone else but he said we'd get the same answer from everyone.

Feeling a little terrified, we made our way back to the hotel at Land's End. Although I'd become quite used to people's default answer of 'no' or 'you can't do that' or 'it's not possible', I'd tended not to take them too seriously. This time was a bit different.

The sea can be a nasty place, and when it comes to nasty, Land's End is up there near the top of the list, apparently! Although I was hearing the local advice, I wasn't listening, or at least trying not to listen to it, and I was determined to display fake confidence, which was important for me and the crew. That this had never been attempted before meant there was always going to be a huge amount of guesswork involved, I just wished it wasn't on Day 1. A few days' easy swimming to get into the swing of things really would have been nice.

The hotel had kindly let us stay the night for free. If they hadn't I'd have probably had to spend the night in my car, as the last of £250 I had borrowed from the bank was gone. At least we had Stowaways to eat on the boat. All 500 meals were stuffed in the front of *Friday While*, or *Friday* as she was now known.

Once back at the hotel, Em, Owain and I tried a few more leads for getting a boat but no one was willing to help, so we sat down, ordered beers and decided what our options were. The first was to delay the start by a day, when Jez would be here. The problem was that we had arranged for the media to come on Sunday, and our friends and family who had come down for the weekend needed to get back to work on Monday. Too many people had made the effort – I couldn't let them down.

The second option, and the only really feasible one, was to swim from Sennen Cove to Land's End, turn around and then swim back. This meant that on one of the routes I'd be against the tide. We worked out that at midday I'd have tide heading away from Sennen Cove and then be fighting it on the way back. Any later than midday and the tide would be way too strong. In the grand scheme of things an extra mile didn't matter, but I liked the idea of waving at everyone on the cliffs from *Friday*, who was all kitted out in Swimming Britain stickers, having a big countdown and jumping in. Instead I was going to swim with Em in the kayak next to me. I then realised we didn't have the kayak. It was still on the yacht in Penzance, ten miles away. I'd have to go collect it in the morning.

I spotted *Friday* rafted four boats down in Penzance harbour. She seemed a lot smaller than I remembered. I hadn't seen her since I joined Jez and Lou taking her from Shoreham-by-Sea towards Land's End, but I was so seasick I had my eyes closed for half the time. She was now fully laden with everything we needed to survive for two months at sea.

Not really knowing what the etiquette was, I scrambled over other people's yachts and eventually stepped onto her. I was surprised at how much she heeled over to one side when I stood on her, but at 26 foot I guess that was to be expected. To put her size into perspective, most four-man Atlantic rowing boats, which are considered small and cramped, are just less than 30 foot. *Friday* really was tiny.

Her deck was made of wood and, although in fairly good condition, she had started to fade in patches where the sun had taken its toll over the last 52 years of her life. Her mast was made from one solid piece of wood and rose a good 30 foot or so into the sky. I looked up to the top of the mast and then felt a little seasick so looked back to the harbour wall to gather my balance. That didn't bode well considering the water was glass flat, as you'd expect in a marina.

At the stern was a wooden tiller arm for steering. This could be done while sitting on either side of the rear cockpit depending on which way she was listing. There was just enough room in the cockpit to sit four people but it would be a squeeze. Through the door and into the cabin was a really old paraffin stove on the port side and a chart table on the starboard side, each about half a square metre in size. Next along were two bunks just about long enough for Owain, who is 6 foot, 2 inches tall. It was so tight that the leg space went under the sink and the chart table on each side. Up against the wall was a fold-down table which we could use for meals and team bonding. The bunks were also the seats for the table.

The toilet (or 'heads') was on the starboard side and then a cupboard on the port side, which contained all my swimming kit, suncream, and carb/protein recovery nutrition powder.

Getting a yacht with a separate toilet was a bonus because most small yachts had the toilet under the V between the front two bunks. That would not have been ideal as there was no way I was going to let someone take a dump right where my head was going to be. I had also stuck a map of the UK on the toilet door and the plan was to mark off our progress each day. It looked dauntingly large so I opened the door to hide the map. I didn't need any more negative thoughts.

Moving to the front, there were two bunks angled together. Under the front part of the bunks were the

Stowaways meals and stuffed into the front (or 'forepeak' as Jez corrected me) were all our sails. Each of us had about one bin liner's worth of space under each of our bunks, and I did actually tell the crew to bring their kit in a bin liner as we didn't have enough space to store rucksacks and bags. So that was it, our little home for the next few months. 'Cosy' was a good way of putting it but 'claustrophobic' probably more apt. It would be a miracle if all four of us managed to survive on *Friday* without falling out at some point.

After some more faffing, I loaded the kayak onto the car and drove back to Land's End. It was 10am and I needed to get ready for a midday start.

Everything was laid out on the bed in the hotel room: wetsuit, goggles, thermal cap, outer cap, booties, fins, gloves and watch. This was the kit I was going to swim in. Next to that was some stuff I needed Em to take in the kayak. I had some bottles of water, some energy bars, some rope (you always need rope) and most importantly a SPOT tracker. The tracker would send a signal off every ten minutes showing my location on my website. This was primarily for my family to see where I was when I didn't have phone signal out at sea. There was also an SOS button that, if pressed, would alert the coastguard and send them our co-ordinates. Hopefully I'd never need to use it but it was good to know we had that as backup.

I hadn't had the time to feel nervous since arriving at Land's End due to all the admin I had to do, but walking out of the hotel in a wetsuit and onto the cliffs overlooking the Atlantic, knowing that I'd be out there for the next two months, suddenly made my stomach turn. Now it was real. I was also slightly embarrassed walking around in a wetsuit in front of so many onlookers. It was the first time I had tried on this wetsuit. Most people would have tested it out before but my local pool had a no-wetsuit policy, which meant I couldn't have done even if I wanted to.

It was pretty overcast again and the wind had picked up slightly. There were a few people around but generally Land's End was pretty empty. In fact, most of the people there were friends and family of Em and Owain, along with Ryan and Holly from Speedo, and the hotel staff who were keen to have a photo with me. There is a wall in the hotel with photos of various people who had made the length of Britain journey in interesting ways. Actually, there was already someone in a wetsuit but he was in a small pool on the back of a flatbed truck. I enquired as to what he did and was told he did laps of the pool as they drove from Land's End to John O'Groats. I liked that. Good old British sense of adventure and eccentricity. I also looked for a photo of my mate Dave, the one who swam the Missouri, from when he skateboarded the route but couldn't find it. I wondered if they would put a photo of me up there if I completed the swim.

There was a small queue for the official Land's End sign so I waited my turn. There were a few cyclists, some just starting and some finishing their adventures, both with equally big smiles on their faces. I cycled it in 2008 and know exactly how they were feeling. Back then it was by far the biggest thing I had ever done and I loved every moment of it.

Eventually it was my turn and I walked below the sign.

'What words would you like on the sign?' asked the lady in charge.

'I think let's go with SWIMMING BRITAIN and the date.'

'Are you swimming it?'

'That's the plan.'

She just smiled ever so slightly and kind of shook her head. I'm not sure what she meant by that but she didn't seem fazed at all and proceeded to get the relevant letters together in one hand. There was a slight buzz in the small crowd gathering as the letters went up. This was it. As soon as those letters spelt SWIMMING BRITAIN, it became official. There would be no turning back. The proof was there for everyone to see.

One man with his wife and kids shouted across to me.

'Mate, are you really swimming it? What? How? I don't understand?'

All of a sudden I noticed everyone looking at me and felt embarrassed.

'I'm getting in the water here and swimming up the west coast until I reach John O'Groats.'

'Shit! No way! Sorry, honey!' he apologised to his wife for swearing. 'That's amazing. How long will it take?'

'I hope two months but it all depends on the weather.'

'Fair play, mate. Good luck.'

'Cheers.'

At least he seemed impressed and didn't give me any 'you are going to die' vibes.

I stood under the sign for a while, having some photos taken by a press photographer. We had hoped the BBC or ITV might send a TV crew but in the end only one photographer turned up. Not even the local Cornish newspapers bothered. It wasn't that I wanted to be in the press for this, that's not the reason why I was doing the swim, but I had promised to raise £10,000 for War Child and getting publicity helps me spread the word. Maybe they thought it was a waste of their time as the risk of failure was quite high.

After the photographs, I went over to the edge of the cliff and looked out into the vast, empty Atlantic Ocean. It looked deceptively calm out there.

'Sean, come on, it's time to go,' said Em, taking control. That's exactly what I wanted from a crew captain. I wanted to be able to focus on the task at hand and let the crew make the decisions for me.

I walked away from the cliff and towards the car park, the sounds of the waves slowly disappearing into the distance. My stomach started turning on itself. I jumped in my car – which was a lot harder than expected wearing a wetsuit – and drove down to Sennen Cove.

I was a little behind schedule and it was 12.30pm by the time I got everything together and Em got in the kayak.

'You OK?' I asked, knowing this was Em's first time kayaking at sea.

'Yeah, totally fine.'

'Right, let's do this.'

I slowly walked into the water and was surprised at how cold it was. I turned around and waved at the few people who were there. I then sat in the water to put my fins on. Throughout the lead-up I had questioned whether I needed fins or not, and ideally would have liked to dispense with them as they put strain on your legs. However, after hearing that Martin Strel, the world's most accomplished open-water swimmer and the only person to have swum the Amazon River, used fins for his swims to fight currents, I figured I should at least try them out.

After faffing with the fins, I stood up again and looked out to sea. I was filled with apprehension and excitement at the same time. I turned back to the ten or so people on the shore. Everyone had huge smiles on their faces and a few were taking photos. In a weird way this made me feel quite pressured to succeed, as if those people were unconsciously saying, 'Sean I've come all this way to Land's End to see you off. You better bloody do it!' I knew that wasn't the case but I still didn't want to let them down.

I gave one last wave and dived in. Time stood still for those first few seconds as I was completely submerged before coming to the surface. This was it, I was now underway in the world's first ever length of Britain swim attempt. It was strange to think that for the next couple of months this would be my environment, my home, my life. Swim, eat, sleep, repeat. At two months long, it would be one of the longest swims in history, time-wise, and most certainly one of the longest sea-swims in history. I had no idea what lay ahead of me. What I did learn quickly, however, was that the sea was bloody cold. I hadn't thought to test the water temperature and although I knew it would probably be cold, I didn't think it would be that cold and immediately felt like an idiot.

Would there be animals? A few people online said I'd get eaten by killer whales. Turns out there are killer whales up in Scotland but luckily the figures were in my favour as no one has ever been killed by an orca in the wild. The few deaths that have occurred have been in captivity.

There was also the question of whirlpools, back-eddies, undercurrents and rip tides. These were some of the other reasons people told me this swim wasn't possible. I had convinced myself that they were incorrect and it couldn't be that bad, but the reality was I really had no idea.

Bursting through the surface to take my first breath of salty sea air, I felt a jet of cold water rush down the back of my wetsuit, which took my breath away. The water temperature was 13 degrees and it was a shock. The pool I trained in was around 20 degrees. I could feel the sting on my face and cheeks as I made my way out of the harbour, Em following close behind me.

I pushed on along the dramatic cliffs towering above me and headed towards the small island just off Land's End, which would be the official start point. I was about 100 metres offshore and seemed to be making good progress when I remembered I had the tide with me; I still had to turn around and fight it on the way back. On and on I swam, getting used to the new feeling of swimming in salt water and having to deal with, albeit small, waves for the first time. I reached the little island in about 40 minutes and was surprised how fast I zoomed past it. This tide was strong. I figured I'd swim another 50 metres past just to make sure I didn't miss anything. I'd hate to get back to Sennen and be told I wasn't quite at the End of Britain. I put my face down and suddenly something darted below me. My heart jumped. I looked up at Em and she had a look of fear on her face. Suddenly a fin popped out the water and went back again, and then another one. In a moment of panic I was certain they were sharks, but then realised they must be dolphins and I relaxed a bit. There were about ten of them that zoomed past me right as I was at the tip of Land's End. What an honour. It was as if they were coming to wish me luck. Then as fast as they appeared they disappeared again.

'How amazing was that?' I asked Em.

'Amazing!' replied Em, still looking concerned.

In the frenzy of dolphin activity, I had been swept quite far away from the island. It was definitely time to officially start my swim. I could see a crowd of people gathered at the top of the cliffs outside Land's End Hotel and waved at them. They all waved back. I turned around and started to swim back. I could feel the flood of water running over me. I felt like I was flying. It must have been the adrenalin from seeing the dolphins. I was still breathing to my left, which was away from the cliffs now. Stroke, stroke, breath. I did this for a good few minutes and then looked up expecting to be past the island again and heading back to Sennen. I was very surprised, then, and a little worried to see I was still 100 metres from the island.

'Em, can you come to my right?' I asked. 'Are we even moving?'

'Slowly, but we are moving.'

I carried on for another five minutes and didn't make much more than 20 metres progress. I looked up at Em again.

'Keep swimming. Every time you stop we drift back.'

I looked up at the cliff and could see some people coming down to the edge. It must look as if I was in trouble.

Again I pushed for another five minutes, but eventually Em shouted at me, 'Right, now we are not moving!'

She was also struggling to kayak against the tide.

My heart sank. This couldn't be happening. The tide was getting stronger and stronger, and the half hour delayed start might have meant I had missed my opportunity. What if I got swept way out to sea? There wasn't a beach for miles in the other direction to Sennen. I'd have to call a mayday, which involved pressing the SOS button on my tracker. This would alert the coastguard and probably the RNLI, and the old lady who laughed at us would get a message giving her our location. I could just imagine the look on her face. If there was ever a 'I told you so' moment, this was probably it.

I then remembered that I had planned to swim right along the edge of the cliffs. I was a good 100 metres offshore still, so decided to try swim towards the shore.

'Follow me Em. I'm going to swim to shore, maybe there is less tide there.'

'OK!' Em shouted back.

It took nearly ten minutes to swim the 100 metres to the shore but eventually, and utterly exhausted, I was just underneath the little island. The tide was kind of pushing past the island and flicking around, which meant I could rest in the water. There was no way of being able to fight the tide coming around the outside of the island. My only option was to try swim through the two-metre gap between the island and the mainland. It was hard to tell what it was like, how deep it was or whether I'd get smashed up against the rocks.

'Em, can you go have a look?'

'Are we going through there? It looks bad. Can't you go round?'

'Don't think so. It'll be fine! Please check it out.'

Em paddled off hesitantly towards the gap, which was being battered by a few waves. She went through and disappeared around the corner. I felt very exposed and alone. It felt like minutes but was most likely a few seconds before she came back through and waved to me to come. I put my head down and started towards the gap. The nearer I got the shallower it became. I was soon right between two rocks and the rise and fall of the water was about a metre. I looked down to see some very sharp rocks just below the surface. If I wasn't careful I could easily get washed onto one. I pushed hard with my head down and got another bucket load of freezing Atlantic water down the back of my wetsuit. My wetsuit was now full of water. Maybe I hadn't put it on properly?

Eventually, and completely out of breath, I pushed through the other side and into the open sea again. I was spent. It had been well over half an hour since I turned around to start the swim and I had done all of a few hundred metres.

'I need to rest, Em, and get the water out of my suit,' I called.

I went to a section of the cliff with a large flat rock and scrambled ashore, which wasn't easy wearing fins. It was a good thing I had fins though because there was no way anyone could swim against that tide without them. I stood there shivering, cold to the core, for a good ten minutes while Em circled around in the kayak. Em's boyfriend, Rob, who had been on the cliffs watching, appeared above us.

'You guys OK? That looked pretty sketchy.'

'Yeah, just a bit cold. I'll get back in in a bit. Tell everyone we're OK.'

I stood there for another five minutes and then decided to jump back in. It wasn't as cold this time and my theory of swimming along the shore worked. It took another hour to do that mile back to Sennen, and I arrived completely exhausted and collapsed on the beach.

'Well, that was a little harder than I thought,' I said to some onlookers, trying to keep it light-hearted, and so as to not stress out my mum who had an uncharacteristic look of worry on her face. Em got out the kayak and hugged Rob, who seemed relieved and also impressed that we survived and both made it back in one piece.

At least I had started and got all the chores out of the way. Tomorrow would be the real start to the adventure. We walked back up to the car and as I was getting in to head back to Penzance a chap came running up to me.

'Hi there. I'm Simon. I heard about your attempt. Amazing! I live in St Ives and do a lot of open-water swimming. Anyway, I see you're in a rush but here is my number. I'd love to come swim with you when you reach St Ives.'

'Sure thing. I hope to be there in a few days so keep a look out at my tracker online.'

'Will do.' With that he rushed off.

That afternoon Owain, Em and I said our goodbyes to friends and family, and headed to Penzance to sleep on the boat and wait for Jez. Although it was nice to have everyone around giving us support, it was hectic and I was looking forward to my first night on the boat.

Jez eventually arrived at 7pm and we had one beer each, which was all I could afford. The deal I made with the crew was that all expenses would be covered by me, and that would include a few beers and entertainment here and there. We all deserved a beer after today.

We retired to the boat for an early night. Jez and Owain took the two bunks in the main saloon, and Em and I had the shorter bunks up front. At least we'd have a calm sleep in the harbour. As I was getting into bed I noticed some pain on the inside of my left foot. I looked down to see a layer of skin, about one centimetre long, had rubbed off. I wasn't sure when it had happened but my feet had obviously been too cold to feel it. It wasn't bleeding or anything, so didn't think anything of it and fell fast asleep.

3

SEASICK AND SENNEN

It was good to have the whole team together finally and we were all keen to get going. We got up at 5am to make our way from Penzance to Sennen Cove. I had some porridge to fuel myself for the day, and then we left the harbour and started heading west with the RIB and the kayak dragging behind us on a long piece of rope.

'How long till we get there?' I asked Jez, as I started to get my wetsuit out of the cupboard.

'No rush, mate. Probably four or five hours,' replied Jez, while he loaded up the navigation app on his iPad.

'Really? How far away are we?'

'About 15 miles or so, but *Friday* can only go three or four knots, maybe five or six if we have a good wind, but we don't have a good wind.'

This was the first time I properly understood just how slow *Friday* was. The reviews I read weren't wrong.

It was great to be at sea finally and although overcast it was warm. It always takes a while to get a system together on expeditions. We were all still bumping into each other and falling over while we got used to the motion of the ocean, as they say, especially Owain, as he was the tallest by quite a bit. Within the first half hour he had hit his head on the roof in the main cabin about 20 times.

'Shit, bloody shit. Bloody roof! Argh!' he'd shout every time while rubbing his head, and we'd all burst out laughing. Our spirits were high and we were all thrilled to be underway.

'Right, first person to get seasick has to have two Jägerbombs,' I joked.

I was making light of it to the crew but the reality was that seasickness could in theory end my swim and I was quite nervous. I wasn't worried about Em and Owain as they both said they didn't get seasick on the questionnaire when applying to be part of the crew, and I knew Jez would be fine as he had already sailed *Friday* down to Penzance. But if I threw up too often I'd have no energy in my stomach to swim efficiently and keep warm, and therefore not be able to make the mileage I needed each day. Seasickness on a trip like this can completely ruin you. It is dehydrating, saps your energy and is one of the worst feelings in the world.

The next half an hour went by as we powered, slowly, through the averagely sized three-foot waves along the Cornish coast taking in the scenery. We were even joined by a pod of dolphins dancing in front of the boat like happy children. I wondered if they were the same ones from yesterday. I'd like to have thought they were coming back to make sure we were having a safe journey onwards. They gave me a strange sense of safety as they jumped in and out of the bow waves almost smiling at us. Then as soon as they came they were gone, back down into the depth of the sea, looking up at us. I liked the idea that the dolphins were making sure no other nasty animals were coming to bite me.

Another hour went by and I started to feel seasick, so went below and closed my eyes, which helped a bit.

'Please, don't get sick. Please don't get sick,' I kept saying to myself in a kind of anti-seasickness chant, hoping Neptune would hear me. Em too decided to have a nap, although she said it wasn't because of seasickness. I had my doubts though; yawning and sleepiness are often the first symptoms.

Seasickness is an imbalance of the inner ear that confuses your brain. I'm not sure why it makes you throw up or feel uncontrollably ill but that's just how our bodies cope with it. However, if you close your eyes you can't see that you are moving so your body doesn't get as confused.

I slept for another hour and rose again happy to be feeling a little better. Maybe I would be all right after all. I walked into the main cabin. Jez and Owain were in the rear cockpit and not talking much. Owain had his gaze fixed on the horizon.

'How you feeling, Owain?'

He just shook his head slightly.

'Seasick, mate?'

He nodded while keeping his eyes fixed on the horizon. Jez had given him the tiller arm to hold to give him something to do and take his mind off feeling nauseous. Then I saw Owain let the tiller go, do a kind of backward side bend over the edge and begin vomiting, while Jez tried to regain control of *Friday* as she veered off-course.

'We have a winner!' Jez shouted. 'Two Jägerbombs for Owain,' he laughed, now with *Friday* under control again.

Em came running through from her bunk.

'Owain, did you vom?' laughed Em. 'I feel a bit sick too,' she admitted.

'But you both said "no" to getting seasick on your questionnaire!' I exclaimed.

'Actually I said: Not that I know of!' she replied.

Owain still had his head overboard and clearly wasn't in the mood for any banter.

After a good five hours, we eventually reached Sennen Cove. Owain had retired to his bunk and Em was getting my swim kit ready. I had started to feel sick again and it was quiet on *Friday*. The waves were a lot bigger than they had been the day before and anchoring in the bay was pretty hairy. I went up on deck with Jez to help. *Friday* started to go side-on to the waves, throwing me left and right. I immediately felt really sick. I started to walk to the bow of the yacht and about halfway along, and without much warning, a torrent of the previous night's food mixed with this morning's oats came rushing up from the depths of my stomach. I leant over the side rails, while holding on to one of the shrouds to avoid ending up in the sea, as I turned the dark blue water into a murky white haze, vomit coming out of my nose. I hung over the edge for about a minute until there was nothing left in my stomach, my nose and throat burning. I was just dry heaving. I was frustrated because I hadn't lasted more than a few hours at sea and I had also just wasted some pretty important calories, which were now feeding the fish. I really didn't feel like eating so would have to have a liquid nutrition shake to fuel me instead. It wasn't ideal but I really needed to get calories in me.

Owain had thrown up once more too, and Em didn't look any better but was putting on a brave face. We just needed to get to land. We dropped anchor and Jez rowed the RIB to shore (I didn't have enough money to buy fuel for the engine yet) while Em kayaked alongside. I had all my swimming kit in a bag ready for the day's session but honestly didn't feel like swimming at all. Owain unfortunately had to stay on the yacht as it was too rough to leave it unattended at anchor. I knew the pain he was going through and I felt incredibly guilty. I knew if I were in his shoes, feeling like that, I'd have let the boat sink instead of stay on it. He looked helpless sitting in the back cockpit by himself as we rowed away from him, his head close to the edge of *Friday* in case he needed to throw up again. Eventually we got to shore and I collapsed on the sand, my world still swaying from side to side.

'You guys all right? Why did you row in?' asked a man standing halfway up the slipway.

'We haven't got any fuel for the RIB yet,' I replied.

'You're the swimmer, right? Hi. I'm Norman, nice to meet you. I'll tell you what, I'll go get you some if you want?' he said with a big smile on his face. He was from

Yorkshire. I didn't know what to say because I had no money to buy any fuel so just made an excuse.

'Thank you but I left my wallet on the boat. We'll get some in St Ives.'

'No, don't be silly. I'll donate it to you. Come, give me the tank. The wife and I will go now. It'll take us half an hour. Hope that's OK?'

'Wow, thank you so, so much. Very kind of you.' I said, as the sense of gratitude I felt unfortunately coincided with another sudden urge to vomit.

'Ah shit, Em, sorry! I forgot my energy shakes on the boat. Any chance you could kayak back and get them?'

In my haste to get off the boat I had left them in the cupboard. I really needed my shakes today as I was all out of nutrition in my stomach. As well as crew captain, Em's job was to get my nutrition and kit ready each day. She would basically be like my mum on the swim. I had some carb and protein powder, which Em would carry in the kayak.

Each shake was around 500kcal and that was a much-needed energy source between meals to keep me going. Em kayaked back to *Friday* and Jez faffed round with bits on the RIB, like attaching a small anchor to it and fixing a bigger rope used to drag it behind *Friday*. I slowly started to get dressed but started to feel sick again. I was still swaying from side to side. I hoped that getting back into the freezing water might snap me back to life.

Twenty minutes later Norman came back with our outboard tank filled. Jez could now motor back to *Friday* instead of having to row. I looked to see where Em was.

She wasn't on deck and the kayak was still rafted alongside *Friday.* Jez connected the fuel tank and decided to go and see what was happening. He zoomed out the harbour and into the now worryingly big waves. On one occasion he hit a wave so big I thought he might topple over backwards he went up so high.

When he arrived back on *Friday*, both Em and Owain weren't in a good state. Em was throwing up in a bucket and Owain was throwing up in the toilet. Em eventually managed to get up and back into the kayak, and paddled back to shore looking a little dishevelled.

'You all right?' I asked, not knowing what had happened.

'Yeah, fine, just been vomming, like, everywhere.'

'Really, can you kayak? Let me know if you can't.'

'No, I'm fine. Let's go Ginge,' joked Em, obviously trying to stay positive.

I was now in my wetsuit and ready to go. I jumped in and got the same shock from the cold water on my face as I had before.

This was it. This was my first proper day of swimming. I was a day behind because of Jez missing his bus and was hoping to get eight to ten miles up towards St Ives in the six-hour tide window before it swapped direction and I'd have to stop. The waves were coming at me from the left as I made my way towards *Friday*, bobbing from left to right in the bay. I tried bilateral breathing, where you breathe on every third stroke, which helps with your rhythm, but after drinking a few waves and nearly throwing up again whenever I breathed to the left, I settled with breathing only to my right on every stroke. This meant I was also looking at land, which gave me something to keep my mind busy.

I reached *Friday*, which was on my route north, and Jez was battling to get the anchor up with his hands because the waves kept knocking him off balance and he'd let it go. I later found out that he was even considering cutting the anchor because it was so hard to haul up.

The waves were starting to pick up as I carried on swimming towards the end of Sennen bay. Every now and then a jet of cold water rushed down inside my suit taking my breath away. I had tried to drink some of my energy shake but there wasn't nearly enough food in my stomach to help keep me warm. When your body is metabolising food and creating energy, it acts as a heater. When your heater runs out of fuel, you get cold very quickly. My heater had been out of fuel for hours. I was shivering with every stroke.

Em wasn't looking happy either, although managed to force a smile. I looked back to see Jez had finally hauled up the anchor and was coming towards us. Owain was nowhere to be seen and was apparently lying down with his eyes closed in his bunk. I waited for *Friday* to get alongside us.

'Mate, I'm freezing and everyone is feeling sick. Should we call it a day?' I asked Jez.

'Up to you, but it's another five hours to St Ives which is our only safe anchorage.'

I turned around and started to take a few more strokes. I really needed to get some miles in, and get away from bloody Sennen. It seemed cursed. I went another 50 metres and as I went to breathe, a wave engulfed my face and I swallowed what must have been a pint of seawater. I came up for air and nearly vomited again. I looked up at Jez running around the boat trying to sort out ropes, sails and steer all by himself because Owain was down below. Although *Friday* was a small boat that could be sailed single-handedly, if there was an emergency situation, having a second pair of hands was critical.

I had come up with a set of priorities for the swim and priority one was crew and boat safety. Nothing else mattered. If the crew or the boat was in danger everything stopped and we needed to make for cover. Second priority was for me to make progress. Me spending time in the water was more important than media, photos or exploring. Third priority was to document the adventure as much as possible, share the story and blog about it.

This was a time when there was a bit of a blurred line between priority one and two, but seeing as we were all feeling ill and probably not in any state to help Jez should we need to, I decided to abandon the day's session, get some proper food in me, take some seasick tablets and start again in the morning. I climbed back on the yacht feeling pretty disappointed with myself. I knew there would inevitably be problems to iron out in the beginning, but when the problem is not being able to do the main thing you're meant to be doing – i.e., swimming – then that makes it worse. I had wanted to start with a bang and get some good miles in. I knew if I swam like a fish on Red

Bull for the first few days everyone would start believing in me and the swim. I'd talked a big game in the lead-up, partly to try to convince people the 'impossible' is possible, and party because I listened to too many Muhammad Ali speeches on YouTube. I also put a lot of pressure on myself to do well at the start. Right now though I had swum two miles in two days and was very behind schedule. I could feel the naysayers' words in my ears. If I carried on like this it would take me just over two years to complete the swim.

I hoped tomorrow would be better. I had heard that you do eventually get your sea legs and prayed that we'd get them soon because there was no way we could carry on like this.

It was early evening by the time we reached St Ives and were all pretty desperate to get to land. We clambered into the RIB and motored to the harbour. Feeling our feet on solid soil was incredible. Even though we were still swaying from side to side after the long day at sea, especially Owain who had been in the yacht all day and still looked a little green. The one bit of good news was that my sponsorship money had cleared, which meant I could now get some proper food. First on the list was a nice big plate of lasagne from the closest restaurant to the harbour. It was the best lasagne I have ever eaten.

It was only halfway through the meal that I realised we had one big logistical problem to solve. How were we going to get the kayak to Sennen in the morning? Taking *Friday* all the way back wasn't an option and it was nearly a 20 mile drive. I then remembered Simon, who we'd met on the beach. He said he lived in St Ives and wanted to swim with me. I had his number so Owain decided to call him to ask if he could help us. It was a long shot but I wasn't sure we had any other options as hitch-hiking with a kayak would be near impossible.

'Morning. How you feeling? Owain tells me you were all seasick yesterday,' joked Simon, as he pulled up in his little silver Peugeot.

I'm glad he saw the funny side; although we tried to make light of it, it really hadn't been great for team morale. Simon and his wife Innes had really gone out of their way to help us. As they had lent out their van, which could have taken the kayak easily, to a friend, they had gone to the effort of finding some roof racks for their small car late last night. I was blown away by their kindness.

We spent half an hour trying to tie the kayak and paddle to the small roof rack before Em and I jumped into the back of the car and zoomed back to Sennen Cove. Simon and Innes chatted away, asking me questions and insisted we give him a call in the afternoon if we needed picking up from somewhere. It had started to rain slightly by the time we reached Sennen and unpacked our gear. We said our thank yous and decided to get a quick bacon and egg sandwich before my session. Just as I was finishing up and getting into my wetsuit, a large van with a satellite dish came into the car park. A lady jumped out holding a microphone.

'Are you Sean, the swimmer?' She asked with a big smile on her face.

'Yes, that's me.'

'Great. I'm from BBC Radio Cornwall and wanted to get a few quick words if that's OK.'

I told her all about what I was going to expect from the swim and also how we were all seasick, which is why I was a few days behind schedule already. She seemed to love that we were all seasick; I guess there was some sort of tragicomedy in the fact that everyone, on a sea-going adventure, couldn't actually handle the sea at all. I finished the interview and helped Em carry the kayak down to the beach. Sennen bloody Cove. We had been here for the best part of four days and I couldn't wait to get away from it. I knew that once we were round the corner from the bay I'd feel the journey was properly underway.

It was just Em and I today as Jez and Owain still had some boat admin to do in St Ives, and it would have taken too long to sail back to Sennen anyway. Both Em and I were really nervous as this part of the coast is lined with towering, jagged cliffs and the nearest beach is just over seven miles away, which meant there would be nowhere to get out if we got into trouble. If the tide changed before I reached the beach then I'd land up floating all the way back to Sennen again. So I had five hours (I was an hour behind schedule) to swim seven miles. To the average open-water swimmer that's a simple task, but I had no idea how I would cope and what my speed would be in the big Atlantic waves.

Em got in the kayak and I tried to push her into the sea but she just got caught in the mud. It took us three attempts before she was finally away. I had made it to the far side of Sennen beach the day before, so I ran around so that I didn't have to swim across the bay again. It also helped me warm up a little as the typical Cornish drizzle started to settle in.

Having a good night's sleep and a good meal certainly helped and I didn't feel nearly as cold as I had previously when I'd got in the water, and felt much better than yesterday. I swam through the breakers towards the end of the bay where I'd told Em to meet me, but when I got there I couldn't see her anywhere. The waves were just big enough that we both needed to be on the crest of a wave at exactly the same time to see each other. If either of us were in the trough we were hidden from each other's sight. After a good few minutes I eventually saw the end of a paddle above a wave. Em was kayaking away from me. I shouted and she turned around and we made our way towards each other.

'I thought you had started swimming without me,' she said.

'Yeah, can't believe how hard it was to see you in these waves. We need to come up with a system, like put your paddle straight up in the air if you can't see me,' I suggested.

Just then Em let out a huge gasp.

'What?' I asked nervously.

'I dunno, there is something big in the water over there and it wasn't a dolphin.' She looked worried.

My heart began to race. I looked all around and into the water below me.

'Look! There it is,' Em shouted.

I looked over to see a seal about 20 metres away, poking his head up and looking at us inquisitively.

'It's only a seal.' I said.

'Can they bite?' Asked Em nervously.

'I'm not sure. Come on. We need to go to make that beach.' I had never questioned if seals would bite someone but was almost certain they didn't. You never see pictures or graphics of angry seals, do you? They are always fluffy and cute. That was my logic anyway.

Within a few minutes I was finally around the corner from Sennen Cove and alone at sea. It was a strange feeling. There was no turning back now. I wasn't feeling confident at all in my ability to swim in big waves and knew these first few days would be a steep learning curve. I only wished that I was doing my first real session along a nice calm stretch of water with loads of beaches to get out and rest on should I need to. This was literally being thrown in at the deep end, the very deep and treacherous end at that.

That first mile seemed to take forever; I was trying to work out what to do with my arms as they kept getting pushed all over the place with every wave that came from my left. I hadn't quite achieved the muscle memory and had to concentrate really hard on every stroke in order to actually make progress. There were a few times when my hands and feet were doing the right things but I was in fact staying completely stationary.

On and on I swam, trying my best not to drink any salt water as I knew it would make me vomit. I stayed within

30 metres or so from the edge of the towering Cornish cliffs that rose from the crashing sea to a dramatically dark sky above. I didn't want to stop swimming as I knew my pace was slow, so just kept my head down. Stroke, stroke, breath. Stroke, stroke, breath.

It was coming up to the end of my five-hour tidal window and it had rained for most of the day. My body was starting to shut down. I could feel my pace dropping even further and I knew the tide was starting to turn against me. I still had no idea how far away the beach was. I knew it was just north of Pendeen Lighthouse but we hadn't seen a lighthouse all day. Would I make it? I was starting to get nervous that I wouldn't. I felt so very tired both physically and mentally, trying to remember what to do with each arm and then making that arm fight each battering wave.

'You all right Em?' I asked looking up at Em, who was soaked to the core. She looked freezing. I was at least keeping relatively warm due to being active.

'I'm OK, Ginge. Keep swimming.'

The waves were picking up and the tide was starting to push me backwards. I told Em to go ahead and it was then that I heard the foghorn, and thought it might be a rescue siren for me. I knew the bit at Land's End would be hard because I got my timing wrong but right here, right now, I should have been able to make some progress. I felt afraid for the first time, both for my safety and at the increasing reality that maybe I had bitten off more than I could chew.

'You go ahead Em. I'll stop here.'

'Are you sure?'

'Yeah, I'll be fine. I'll see you at the beach.'

Em paddled away from me and I eventually managed to clamber ashore and fell onto the grass, exhausted.

'You OK, mate?' a voice asked as I lay there with my eyes closed. A young guy had seen me struggling and came down the bank to see how I was. I barely heard him over the sound of the foghorn still blaring over the ocean.

'Yeah, just tired. Quite strong tides on that corner.'

We chatted for a bit and I got the impression he hadn't heard about my attempt so I decided to keep quiet. I wasn't in the mood for many questions. I just wanted to rest. After a bit more general chat about the weather and other irrelevant small talk I started to make my way round to the beach. I eventually reached it and found Em trying to empty the kayak, which was filled with a mixture of rainwater and seawater from waves that had crashed over her. She was wearing a spray deck – a waterproof covering for the kayak's cockpit that encircles you when you are sat in the kayak – but some water was still seeping in. Too much water and she'd eventually sink. It was unlikely, but she still really needed to tighten the straps on the spray deck.

'What a day, hey?' I said as I used up the last of my energy to help her empty the kayak.

'Well done. That bit on the rocks looked scary.'

I had made the seven miles stretch to the beach and that was enough for the day. There was no way I could attempt the next section now. I was just too tired.

Em and I needed to get back to St Ives, which was about 15 miles away on the roads but that would involve carrying the kayak about a mile up the steep cliff path. I had no energy left in my arms and it was far too heavy for Em to carry on her own.

'Should we call Simon? He said we should,' suggested Em.

'I feel bad. He's been so helpful already.'

'I know, but he did offer. I'll call him.'

There was no reception on the beach so Em headed back up the path to try and call Simon. I lay down on the beach and closed my eyes. I don't remember falling asleep but when I next opened my eyes, Em and a sweaty man carrying a huge tripod and broadcast camera were standing over me.

'Hi Sean, I'm Chris from BBC Points West. I followed the tracker and am here to do a piece on the swim. Hope that's OK?'

Chris was sweating profusely from having to carry all that kit about a mile from the car park. I felt sorry for him but he sure had dedication. I repeated most of the same things I had said in the morning's radio interview, including the bit about us all being seasick. This seemed to be the story everyone wanted to hear, and not the fact I was attempting the first ever length of Britain swim. I wasn't bothered though. The seasickness joke gave us all something to smile about and kept the mood light-hearted, instead of us getting overwhelmed and serious by the enormity of the swim and just how badly we were coping. I didn't want the swimming side of things to dominate. I wanted to have a coastal adventure that was using swimming as the means of transport. Much like you would on a cycle trip. The cycling gets you from A to B but the adventure is what you have in the middle.

I found it quite funny that no media bothered to come to Land's End to see me off but one mention that we were all seasick and they were all over us.

After the interview, Chris asked if I would just get back in the water and do a few lengths of the bay. It was the last thing I wanted to do as I had just started to dry out but I agreed nevertheless. I'm sure he got the shot in the first 30 seconds but I had to do about 300 metres up and down before he waved me in. Chris packed up and slowly walked back along the steep path carrying his heavy gear. His report would air on the news later that night.

'Simon is coming in an hour,' said Em, excited that we had a lift to St Ives.

'Awesome. Thanks for sorting that. I'm not carrying the kayak up there. I think we should leave it here. We can bury it by those rocks.' I pointed to a hidden part of the beach where no one would see it. It was unlikely that anyone would even come to this beach between now and tomorrow morning but it was Jez's pride and joy and I would feel happier if we hid it. So Em and I dragged the kayak up, hid it behind some rocks and then spent 20 minutes covering it in sand and seaweed.

We walked up to Pendeen Lighthouse and waited in the car park for Simon to arrive. He zoomed in, all smiles, in his little Peugeot.

'Good work, guys. I've been following your tracker all day. It's addictive seeing how far you go every ten minutes,' said Simon with great enthusiasm. 'I've spoken to Owain already, and Innes and I would like to have you round for dinner. She's making spag bol. Hope that's OK.'

Spaghetti bolognese is actually one of the best meals for recovery as it is high in fat, carbs and protein. I sure could do with a hearty meal.

Not only did we get an amazing meal and a few beers but we also had a shower. *Friday* had no running water, let alone hot water, so we knew having a shower would be a luxury to be taken at every opportunity possible. It was a nice ending to a pretty tough day and good to make new friends.

Unsurprisingly, I slept incredibly well. This was going to be the first day where I would swim on both north-going tides, one in the morning and one in the evening. The northerly tide would start running at High Water Dover +4. (The time of high water moves forward each day.) I needed to do ten miles to get to St Ives but had two tides to do it in. Jez had shown me one beach about halfway along that was inaccessible from land but we could get out of the water there and wait out the southerly tide. The only thing we didn't know for certain was if Google Earth had taken the photo at low or high water. If at low water then the beach might actually be covered at high water. The charts, however, showed some sort of sand, which gave us a little security. If that were to happen then we could always call Jez to come and collect us. High Water +4 meant I needed to start swimming at 7am.

Simon couldn't take us back to Pendeen because of work commitments, so the only way to get back to the beach was to take the 7.05am local bus from St Ives harbour, change somewhere along the route to another bus and then walk for 45 minutes. I'd then get in the water at around 8.30am, which was a little later than I wanted but at least meant I would have a faster tide to help me along. The middle three hours of every tide are the most important hours to be in the water as that's when I would make the biggest dent in my daily mileage goal.

So at 7.05am, already dressed in my wetsuit, Em, Owain and I caught the bus towards Pendeen. It was pretty surreal as the few people on the bus knew I was the swimmer and that we were all seasick. It seemed to be the running joke and certainly lifted our moods as we chugged along the Cornish country lanes laughing and joking with other passengers.

Just before getting in the water, I noticed the rubbing on my foot had turned to a small scab. I showed Em and asked her to look for something in the first aid kit. There was nothing but as it wasn't painful I put my booties on and jumped in. The sea was a lot calmer, which was a nice change. I also felt much warmer than I had the day before. I think it was a mixture of acclimatising and eating more food. The flatter water gave me the opportunity to work on my style somewhat. I tried various techniques to see what was best.

Eventually I settled on pretending to crawl along a ladder that was on the floor. Reach ahead, grab a rung, pull it towards me keeping my hand fairly close to my body and then push the rung below, then repeat that with the other hand. I wasn't sure if that was even correct, and was pretty certain my coach Mark would be pulling his hair out if he knew how bad it was, but it felt the best and with every stroke I was gaining confidence. It's amazing how a sunny day without waves can completely change your mental state. Yesterday, I had doubted whether the swim was possible, but today I felt good.

The only thing that was still a problem was the freezing cold jet of water that kept shooting into my wetsuit. That mixed with all my pee (you have no option but to urinate in your wetsuit when swimming for hours), which would gather around my torso area, meant that three hours of swimming made me not only look like the Michelin Man but also weigh me down a lot. I had been for a wetsuit fitting at Speedo and we had decided on a men's small wetsuit at the time because I was planning to put on some weight before the swim. Unfortunately I hadn't put on much weight at all and probably needed a men's extra small. This size was too big for me now and I was only going to get thinner. My starting weight was 67kg, which was far too light, but I've always battled to put on weight. This is normally a good thing but this time I could have done with a few extra pounds. My lack of body fat was definitely contributing to my inability to deal with cold conditions.

Settling into my ladder-crawl swimming technique for the day meant I could now begin to appreciate the incredible Cornish coastline. In the sunshine it wasn't nearly as dramatic as before, but the towering cliffs and jagged rocks were spectacular to swim along. I hadn't drunk nearly enough water the previous day so asked Em to make sure I had some every 20 minutes. Em too was getting more confident in the kayak and we managed to have some fun as we went along. The tide was due to turn around 1pm and we managed to get to our beach just in time. It wasn't the easiest of beach landings for Em due to the steepness of the rocks. It wasn't a beach at all really and had only become one due to what must have been a pretty big landslide once. I swam ashore and then Em did a run up to the rocks where I was ready to help pull her ashore. Even though the waves were no more than a foot high Em still managed to fall out the kayak.

'Noooo! I had just got dry.'

This tiny rocky beach would be our little home for the next five hours or so. The plan was to wait again for High Water +4 which was at around 6pm, but I figured I'd try swimming at relatively slack water, which would start at around 5pm. If the tide was too strong I'd just wait until I could make progress.

Both Em and I were pretty tired and it wasn't long before we had both found a little nook in the rocks and were fast asleep.

Crack!!! I heard some rocks smashing together a few feet from my head. I jumped up to see the remains of a cricket ball-sized rock split up into five or six different pieces and shoot off in all directions. I looked above me to see a few more pebbles rolling down the hill. A beach created by a landslide wasn't an ideal place to sleep but we had no option. I woke up Em and told her to find another large rock to hide behind in case more rocks came tumbling down. I found another spot behind another suitably large rock and soon passed out again. I was too tired to actually care. I just needed to sleep.

I got back in the water at 5pm and, although slightly against the end of the weakening southerly tide, I was still making progress so decided to get on with it. Having a nap certainly helped and along with hydrating every 20 minutes, I felt strong. It always takes a while to get into the flow of things and work out a system. It was incredibly reassuring to know that the struggles I had over the first few days were in fact teething problems and not challenge-ending problems. For the first time since I started I felt a smidgeon of hope that I could do this.

We reached St Ives at 8pm, and were too tired to do anything much other than eat a Stowaways dinner and go to sleep. The ten miles we'd managed was below the average I needed to do, but I knew this would be the case in the first week as I found my legs, and arms, so to speak.

4

CORNISH HOSPITALITY

Friday was rocking up and down more than usual when I went to bed but after finding a comfortable position I eventually fell asleep. I couldn't have been asleep more than an hour when all of a sudden the rocking changed from lengthways to sideways and I was flung right over and onto Em's bunk, pinning her against the side of the boat.

'So sorry! What happened there?' I apologised, while frantically trying to move back to my side of the bunk. I still didn't know Em well enough to know how she'd react to me invading her bunk.

'Don't worry, I can't sleep anyway,' she said.

I tried to get back into a comfortable position but the sideways rocking meant that with every wave I was still flung over towards Em's bunk. Unlike Jez and Owain's bunks, our front bunks didn't have sides preventing us from falling off in rough weather. Generally the wind and the waves come from the same direction, but sometimes in harbours the waves get flicked around the wall or headland and come in at a different angle to the wind. A yacht will always stay into the wind/tide so if the waves are coming from the side you will rock from side to side. It took a good few hours to work out the best position for my legs to create some sort of anchorage to avoid falling out of bed again. Eventually I fell asleep at around 3am.

Breakfast was dry oats and an energy shake which I was starting to dislike already. Normally I made the shakes with milk, but milk was at a premium on a boat with no fridge. So instead I had them with water which made them taste pretty disgusting. We all then went ashore to say goodbye to Simon who worked in the café along the edge of the bay. I decided to have a second breakfast from the café, which Simon said was on the house. What an amazing chap.

The section from here was a lot easier logistically. There was a town or beach every five miles, which meant I could get out and rest every few hours. Also, today I'd have *Friday* following me. The plan was to swim as far as I could and then anchor in St Agnes bay.

Em got ready in the kayak and instead of walking through the town, Jez decided to take me round in the RIB. We jumped in and fired her up. This was the first time I had been in the RIB properly and it was a good feeling bombing through the waves. We went round the corner of the bay heading west and then all of a sudden the engine died. Jez and I looked at each other as we came to an abrupt halt. Jez tried to start her again but she just spluttered. We were now drifting in the wrong direction and slightly out to sea. Jez tried a few more times and was getting tired so I decided to give it a go. Eventually after five attempts she fired up. Jez and I gave each other a ceremonial high five and carried on along the coast to yesterday's end point.

'Good luck, mate. We'll see you in a bit,' said Jez as I jumped in.

Jez followed me for the first few hundred metres until I was at the edge of the bay where Em was waiting in the kayak. He then waved us off and as he was zooming away I heard the engine die again. I looked up.

'Don't worry,' he shouted. 'I can row from here anyway. See you later.'

The tide was quite strong but I completed the four-mile crossing of St Ives Bay in just less than two hours. I looked back across the bay to see where Jez was but I could still see *Friday* anchored up near the harbour. Maybe they had gone for breakfast or Owain was arranging some media from shore. There was no real reason for them to be right by our sides all day, and as long as they met us at some point we'd be fine.

Our first beach was just east of St Ives Bay and as we came ashore the sun came out. The sand was white and the sea crystal clear. We could have been in the Caribbean if it wasn't for the freezing water. This was another beach that you could only access from the sea and at only 50 metres long we felt as if it was our own little paradise. I found a chair that had been washed up and sat down to rest and have an energy shake while the sun warmed up the rubber on my wetsuit. It suddenly dawned on me why wetsuits are black: to help absorb more heat, which certainly made a difference.

After about half an hour it was time to leave, so I got up and turned and got the fright of my life. There on the beach about 20 metres behind us was a guy in his late twenties sunbathing. He was completely naked with his blindingly white bum on full show. Em and I looked at each other. How did he get here and why was he naked?! There were 100 foot vertical cliffs all around the beach. He was just lying there reading a book and didn't even acknowledge us. It was all too strange so we just decided to get back in the water and keep going. We left the naked bum man and continued along the coast. The sun was out, the water was clear and there were no waves. The only thing still on our minds was that Jez hadn't passed us and we had no way of getting hold of him as we had no phone reception.

The next stop was Portreath, five miles away. I was making good progress and reached the beach by mid-afternoon. There were some slightly larger waves in the bay and Em took a pretty impressive tumble, which resulted in a Baywatch-style run in from a few of the ridiculously toned lifeguards on duty. I think Em capsized on purpose. They were exquisite examples of the human form as they ran in to help her drag her flooded kayak onto the shore. I too got dunked by a wave from behind as I walked into the beach but didn't even get a second glance.

At last, we had phone reception so Em called Jez. After a lot of chatting Em put the phone down with a concerned look on her face.

'He had engine failure.'

'On *Friday*?' I asked, worried.

'No, the RIB. He said he'd tell us later. They are about half an hour from us.'

Damn RIB engine. I had spent £220 getting it serviced and it still didn't work. That left us with the small problem of food. Em and I hadn't brought our wallets as we thought we'd have the boat with us, and I was all out of recovery shakes and really needed to eat something.

'I'll go beg for some food,' Em said confidently, as if that was a totally normal thing to do.

'Really, are you sure?' I've always hated asking people for things.

'Yeah, I'll find something.'

With that, Em wandered off and I lay down on the sand soaking up the warmth of the sun above and the hot sand below me. I could feel the tightness draining out of me.

Em came back about half an hour later with some soup, hot dogs and two flakes. Amazing! We gobbled it down with our hands while sitting on a pavement in a somewhat caveman style. We didn't care though, we were so hungry.

The next tide was only due to start running at around 7pm so we had a good few hours to kill before carrying on. I had done just over nine miles and wanted to at least get to Porthtowan by nightfall to bring my total up to 12 miles.

Half an hour later we saw *Friday* sail past, bobbing up and down in the waves. We called Jez again.

'Hey. How's it going?' I asked.

'Nightmare. Couldn't start the RIB and wind was stronger than I could row. I ended up drifting across St Ives Bay for two hours before embarrassingly giving up and calling the coastguard to drag me in. Damn Arthur's engine.'

'Shit. You all right?'

'Yeah, just very sore arms now,' joked Jez. It was good to see he still had a sense of humour.

'So where we anchoring tonight?' I asked.

'That's the other thing. Looking at the wind and the waves there might be nowhere to anchor except Newquay, which is six hours from here. We'll try in St Agnes but I think it will be too rough.'

If *Friday* went all the way to Newquay then I'd have no support boat for the next three days and Em and I would be stuck with the kayak each night, and have to hitch rides to and from Newquay, which would take forever. My heart sank. I hadn't thought these logistics through at all in preparation. There were just so many factors to take into consideration.

Jez continued, 'Owain and I need to go ahead to see if St Agnes is OK otherwise we'll have to push on to Newquay so we can't hang around. Sorry, but we gotta keep sailing.'

'OK, mate. Let us know.'

I now had a decision to make. Em and I had no clothes, no money and no food. If I did the next section to Porthtowan I'd get there at around 9pm. Jez would potentially be in St Agnes, which we could probably hitchhike to, but he could also very well be on his way to Newquay. We'd then be stranded at night at Porthtowan with nothing.

'What if we stop for the day? I'm sure we can find a place to crash here tonight. We still have time to do that,' Em suggested.

I hated the fact I was cutting another day short.

'I could then hitch to St Agnes, get our sleeping bags, clothes and wallets off Jez there before he needs to carry on, if he does.'

It did make sense. For the sake of losing three miles I guess it was the only option we had. I agreed and Em jumped into action. I called Jez to tell him to wait in St Agnes so we could get our stuff while Em went off to find somewhere to stay. About 10 minutes later Em came back.

'I found the most amazing lady. She is called Beth and she said we can stay in her house tonight. She's coming down for a surf in an hour so I said you'd be here. You'll like her.'

Em was buzzing with excitement. We now had a bed. All we needed was our spare clothes and money so Em decided to go and hitchhike to St Agnes.

With Em gone, I had some time alone to take things in. The last few weeks before the swim and these first few days in Cornwall had been so hectic that I hadn't had much time to absorb it all. The sun was still high in the sky, people were laughing and playing on the beach and I had swum here from Land's End. Although I had only swum 25 miles it still felt good to say that. My one concern was that I was still quite far behind schedule. I knew it would be slow to start but my competitive side was eating away at my fatigued mind because I wanted to do more miles. I was yet to hit double figures in one day and that annoyed me. In the lead-up I had planned to swim around 15 miles per day. That was worked out at a pace of 2–2.5mph for seven to eight hours a day in the water. Five hours in one tide and three hours in a second tide. My route was said to be 1,000 miles but I figured it might be a bit shorter if I cut across some of the big bays. A distance of 900 miles at 15 miles per day gives me 60 swimming days. I thought I'd have at least one rest day a week and a few bad weather days, bringing my expected swim time to be around two-and-a-half months, which meant finishing around the middle of September.

The waters stay warm until the end of September but the weather gets worse and worse the closer you get to October, so it's a case of make hay while the sun is shining. All these figures were good to write on paper but in reality it was complete guesswork. I really had no idea how the sea would treat us and how we'd cope mentally being cramped up in a small yacht for 75 days. Many expeditions in history have failed not because of the enormity of the task, but because of people's state of mind. With no one to ask for advice we knew there would be a lot of thumb sucking and supposition, especially in the first few weeks while we worked things out.

Jez had also said the first week would be hard from an anchoring point of view and that it would get easier. It was just difficult to think that way when there were so many things that weren't related to my swimming ability getting in my way. I lay down and closed my eyes for a while waiting for Beth.

'Sean? I'm Beth,' I heard a voice say and opened my eyes to see a lady standing over me. She had very short greying hair and was wearing a pretty well-used and characterful wetsuit. I felt very unadventurous in my shiny new suit that hadn't seen nearly as many stories as Beth's. I stood up immediately and then nearly fell over again because of a head rush. That was a sign I needed to eat and drink more.

'Listen, you're more than welcome to stay at mine but I'm just going for a surf for an hour if that's OK.'

'Of course. Thank you so much,' I said, still a bit dizzy as Beth went to get her board from the clubhouse and then disappeared into the waves. It had been a few hours since Em left and I had had a call from her to tell me she had got lost, been given a lift to someone's house, had a shower, some tea and cake, and was now on her way to meet Jez in St Agnes. She sounded like she had everything under control and gave me confidence in her ability to just get things done. Her bubbly personality mixed with her shameless ability to approach anyone and ask them for help was certainly going to be a good asset for the expedition.

Beth eventually came back from her surf and arranged with one of the lifeguards for me to leave the kayak in their clubhouse. She had cycled down to the beach from her cottage a mile up the road and instead of just giving me directions insisted on walking with me. I didn't have any shoes so was a bit slow over the pebbles but I was grateful to Beth for being so kind and patient.

I quickly noticed that Beth's bike had a Rohloff hub on it. Now, if you're into cycle-touring the Rohloff hub is the Rolls-Royce of gearing systems. You only buy one if you are going to be having some serious adventures. I have one on my touring bike and it's done over 16,000 miles and still hasn't missed a beat. It's amazing. Naturally I asked Beth what cycling she has done and she began listing off all the off-beat places she had cycled. Burma, Morocco, (back in the days when cycling in Morocco alone, as a woman, was pretty adventurous) and other far-flung places. Beth said she had been one of the first people to surf in Cornwall in the 1960s. When she started so few people surfed that she knew who owned every surfboard and who had owned them previously. This was before they even had built-in rip-cords and she told me how she experimented with doctor's tubes, the ones used on drips, which she would tie to her ankles. She had some wonderful stories. I was captivated by her adventurous life, which she seemed to still be living. Just then my phone rang. It was Em.

'Quickly, my phone is dying. Jez tried to anchor on St Agnes but too rough so has gone to Newquay. I'll hitch back. See you in a few hours. Gotta go. Bye!' With that she put the phone down.

I told Beth what had happened and she immediately said to tell Em we'd go and collect her. I was blown away. Cornish people are so very generous. I texted Em and she replied so I knew she had got the message.

Beth's house was at the end of a terrace, surrounded by all sorts of flowers and plants. I didn't want to get in Beth's car all smelly so quickly jumped in the shower. I had no clothes but borrowed a shirt and towel to go fetch Em. Yes, I was going commando. I'm not sure Beth was up to lending me her underwear just yet.

That evening we were treated to a delicious dinner, which included a salad made entirely with veg from Beth's garden. Em and I listened all night to her stories. She really was a remarkable woman. Considering we landed on Portreath beach with no food, clothing or money, we had done pretty well for ourselves. It was the best day of the swim so far.

The slight downer to the day was that we found a blog written by a guy at the café at Sennen Cove (not our friend Simon from St Ives café) who helped Em and I look for a skipper on Day 1 to get me to the tip of Land's End – completely mocking my swim attempt. What a back-stabbing idiot. Nice to my face but once back in the safety of his computer, he wrote:

> 'The poor boy is doomed. The tides around here may be bad but around Wales they are ten times worse and in some places downright dangerous. If he does complete his challenge he will certainly have every right to quote the cliché "they said it could not be done". From where I am standing just now they are saying it for a very good reason.'

The one other worry was the scab on my foot. It seemed to be getting bigger. I showed Em again.

'Ah, Stuart is back!' she said.

'Stuart?' I asked.

'Yeah, Stuart the Scab, that's his name now.' Em's light-hearted reaction made me feel a bit better.

'Damn Stuart. It seems to be getting worse, bigger and deeper.'

'We'll get some iodine or something at Newquay.'

I towel-dried Stuart, who was seeping a little, and fell asleep.

After we had big bowls of porridge for breakfast, Beth drove Em and me back to the beach for an early start. After missing three miles yesterday I was keen to get going. It was sunny again and fairly calm as I swam out of Portreath bay. A seal decided to come and say hi briefly, which was nice. I decided to try and push on to St Agnes for my first stop. It was seven miles away, which was the same distance that I had done on the first day out of Sennen that had nearly killed me. I felt a lot stronger and with a shorter day yesterday was confident I'd make it. We passed Porthtowan to our right and pushed on towards the far headland. That was my main marker for this session as I knew St Agnes was just round the corner.

My ladder-pulling technique seemed to be working and my pace was a steady 2mph. Em and I didn't talk much as I kept my head down, working on my style and breathing. My neck was starting to hurt and chafe on the right side from all the single-sided breathing. I figured I was turning my head too much so decided to try and roll my body more to breathe.

It took a while to master the technique but after a while I noticed I wasn't straining my neck as much and didn't chafe either. The only downside was that rolling my left shoulder in the water meant I kept swimming off to the left. I did that anyway because of an old injury I got while cheese-rolling in Gloucestershire a few years ago and this new technique was definitely making it worse.

My mother has lived about a mile from the bottom of Cooper's Hill, which is near the little village of Brockworth, for years. Every year on the late May bank holiday thousands of spectators gather to watch a few dozen people chase a large cheese down an incredibly steep hill. No one knows when exactly the tradition started or where it comes from, but in recent years it's become world famous. Probably because of the sheer eccentricity of this funny English event!

I'd kept promising to get involved, but when it came to it I would always wimp out (this hill is seriously high!). Then in 2009 I decided to tell my friends I was definitely doing it and that they should come and watch me. Then I'd be committed.

To get a place in one of the official races you have to get there early. The first race was at midday, but when I arrived at 9am it was already packed. I managed to make it into the second race and went to the top of the hill. My heart was thumping. I had just seen the first 15 people tumble down the hill and it looked way worse than the YouTube videos. According to the rules the cheese gets a one-second head start, and then the chasers are allowed to start running/falling down the hill. Being the honest guy I am, I followed the rules whereas most of the other guys went as soon as the cheese went!

I bolted down as fast as I could, lasting about three metres before everything became a blur: sky/grass/sky/grass ... I took a massive bump to the head when I collided with another tumbler. For a moment we were entangled together in one ball of craziness. Then I broke free and somehow landed up on my feet again, running, arms flailing in a double windmill fashion. I was heading down the steepest bit, which was just about to flatten out, and had managed to work my way into third place by now. However, as the flatter bottom of the hill neared, I realised I couldn't stop, and I was inevitably going to end up in a huge heap, face-planting the ground. Before I knew it I was face-first in the dirt, bounced twice and then skidded and rolled over the line where some hefty rugby players from the local team were waiting to stop us.

I had somehow managed to come a close second. I was a bit gutted as I would have won with a better start but at least I was uninjured... or so I thought. Once the adrenaline had worn off, I discovered I had actually dislocated my shoulder and torn muscles in my back.

It was one of the most exhilarating 23 seconds of my life, so I didn't mind the injuries too much. However, it did mean that my left shoulder was always a bit weaker than my right, so I had to pay attention to Em to make sure I didn't swim off in completely the wrong direction, which when tired, was happening in a worryingly short distance. If I didn't concentrate I was swimming at 90 degrees within 100 metres.

It took just under three hours to get to the far headland and I was ready for a break. On passing the headland we came across a huge patch of foam. It was about ten inches thick and covered an area the size of a football pitch. I didn't know what it was and whether I could swim through it. Em and I discussed it for a while but decided it was probably fine and going round it was going to take too long. The first few strokes were very strange because I couldn't breathe at my normal height otherwise I'd breathe in some foam. It also didn't smell too good. I therefore had to roll onto my back with each stroke just to breathe. Eventually I made it through and started to head inland for St Agnes. Going right into the bay was a good mile detour but there was no other choice. Just then I started to feel a rumble in my stomach. I hadn't been to the toilet in days, a number two that is. I think my body was still in shock from what I was putting it through. I looked up but couldn't see St Agnes at all. I was certain it was just around the headland. Em got out her phone and checked on Google Maps.

'It's a good mile and a half still.'

'Really? That's at least an hour, 50 minutes if I push it!'

'Why? What's the problem?'

'I might need the, er, actual toilet, if you know what I mean.' With that, I cramped up immediately, as if saying it out loud was my body finally giving up.

Em burst out laughing – she didn't seem to have an ounce of sympathy for my predicament.

'It's not funny, dude,' I said lightly, but was worried.

I pushed on for another 20 minutes as the pressure built up in my stomach. It was getting worse and worse, and still a mile from the beach I had to curl into a ball to try to stop a disaster. There was no way I was going to shit in my wetsuit. If it came to it I'd unzip it and then swim the last bit without a suit. It was just so cold though and I really didn't want to do that.

'Sean's going to shit himself. Sean's going to shit himself, la la la la laaaaa,' Em was singing away, happily.

'No! I won't. I can't!' I curled up in a ball, face-down in the water as if I had just done a splash bomb. If I wasn't careful I'd do a different kind of bomb pretty soon.

I carried on and eventually could see St Agnes bay. I scoured the beach for a place I could run and go to the loo but there were kids everywhere. I'd definitely get arrested for shitting on a beach near small children. There was no other option but to swim all the way into the beach and find a public toilet. Those last minutes were agonising as I swam through the breakers. Em's beach landings hadn't improved at all and she had another Baywatch lifeguard run in, but I didn't have time to help her and hobbled out the waves towards somewhere that might have a toilet, past a very smiley man with a dog who looked like he wanted to talk. Desperately, I rushed past him. There was a toilet in the car park, which I was directed to as I clinched my bum cheeks with so much force they started to hurt. Eventually I made it into the cubical and proceeded to make that cubical 'out of order' for the next, I'd say, year or so thereafter. I did, however, feel like a new man, when I came out.

I headed back to Em to find she was completely soaking wet from her little tumble. She really needed to work on her beach landings. She was chatting away to the friendly chap with the dog who I'd rudely ignored. I felt guilty and went over to say hi.

'You must be THE Sean?'

I laughed. I've never have anyone refer to me with an accentuated THE before my name.

'I'm Steve. I've been following you along the cliff top for the past hour. You've made good progress today. How's the seasickness?'

Steve knew everything about me, the crew and our journey so far, and informed me that his wife was a keen swimmer.

'Yeah, it's not bad. Good to make the beach though as I've needed the loo for the last hour.'

We all laughed. I was honoured to have someone actually go out their way to not only come and find me but also to follow me along the cliff tops. It was easy to forget that anyone was actually watching, let alone caring enough about my swim to come out and find me.

'So where are you staying tonight?' he asked.

'Our yacht is in Newquay, so probably swim to Perranporth and hitch a ride from there.'

'My wife and I would love to have you over for dinner, and if you wanted a shower and an actual bed, we've got the space.'

'Really? Thank you! We might take you up on that.'

We chatted for a bit longer before Steve left and Em and I went to find some lunch, and to wait out some of the southerly tide.

After a good break the plan was to swim round to Perranporth, have some more food as I needed to start eating more, and then try to do another three miles towards the north end of Perranporth beach. It was beautifully sunny and still fairly calm, but getting out of St Agnes bay seemed to take forever.

A few hours later we were starting our approach towards the beach at Perranporth when something felt wrong. We started to hear huge waves crashing. Em and I stopped. I climbed onto the back of the kayak to get a better view. Then we heard someone shout. There were a group of people on the cliffs above us shouting and signalling for us to get back and go further out to sea. Just then a huge roller came in from behind us. It wasn't breaking yet but it lifted us a good 10 feet in the air. From the top of the wave we could see why they had been shouting at us. Perranporth beach was experiencing some of the biggest swells it had seen all year. They were so big that not even the surfers were out.

'Shit, Em. I'm knackered. I'm not sure I can carry on.'

'Yeah, but they look huge. I can't do beach landings in one-foot waves. These would kill me.' Em said, looking scared.

I hadn't seen that look on her face before. I really needed some food and had run out of water too because

I'd drank it all thinking we'd stop. We looked back up at the cliffs where more people had gathered. They seemed to be pointing to the far end of Perranporth beach, which was a good three miles away.

'I might go in and just rest and get some food. Would you wait here?' I asked.

Em didn't reply but I knew she wasn't comfortable with that. Our only other option was to carry on swimming. The next beach, which was just round the corner from the far end of the long Perranporth beach, was four miles away. Doing this with no food and water would take me three hours. I just had no more energy and at times, even though I looked like I was swimming, I was just flapping around in the same spot.

I carried on swimming, getting lifted high into the air with every long roller that came through. I was questioning whether we could have made it to the beach and getting slightly annoyed with Em's inability to stay upright in waves, when I looked back to see the now even larger Atlantic waves crashing up against the cliffs. We had definitely made the right choice. Not even an experienced kayaker would have managed those waves. Knowing I had no other choice meant I just put my head down and forgot the 'but we might have made it if we tried' thoughts going through my mind. It was time to commit to the task at hand and get to the next beach.

By early evening I had made it round to Holywell Bay. I was exhausted. I couldn't move my arms any more and was starting to shiver. The problem was that we couldn't get into Holywell either because of the surf. No matter how I put it to Em she didn't want to do it. My heart sank. What were we going to do? Em looked terrified and I was so tired that treading water became so difficult that without the kayak to hold on too I feared I'd sink.

'We could call Jez,' Em suggested

Newquay was three miles away, which would take Jez at least an hour to get to us. Em and I would then have to just float at sea for an hour. The tide was turning, which meant even if my now-broken body wanted to I couldn't carry on swimming.

'Do we even have reception?' I asked.

Em took out my phone.

'One bar!'

We tried to call Jez but lost reception. It seemed to come and go but eventually Em got through. The conversation didn't last long before we were cut off again. I started to shiver uncontrollably as my core temperature dropped now that I wasn't swimming to keep me warm.

I tried to climb onto the back of the kayak and nearly tipped Em over as I fell off over the other side, like a lazy seal sliding into the water off an icy ledge.

On the fifth attempt, we managed to get through to Jez and tell him our situation. There was nothing we could do now except float aimlessly at sea until he arrived in *Friday*.

Eventually, after many tries, I found a way of getting onto the back of the kayak, and I lay there shivering and fatigued. I could feel my body burning away my muscle tissue in an effort to recover. This was the last thing I

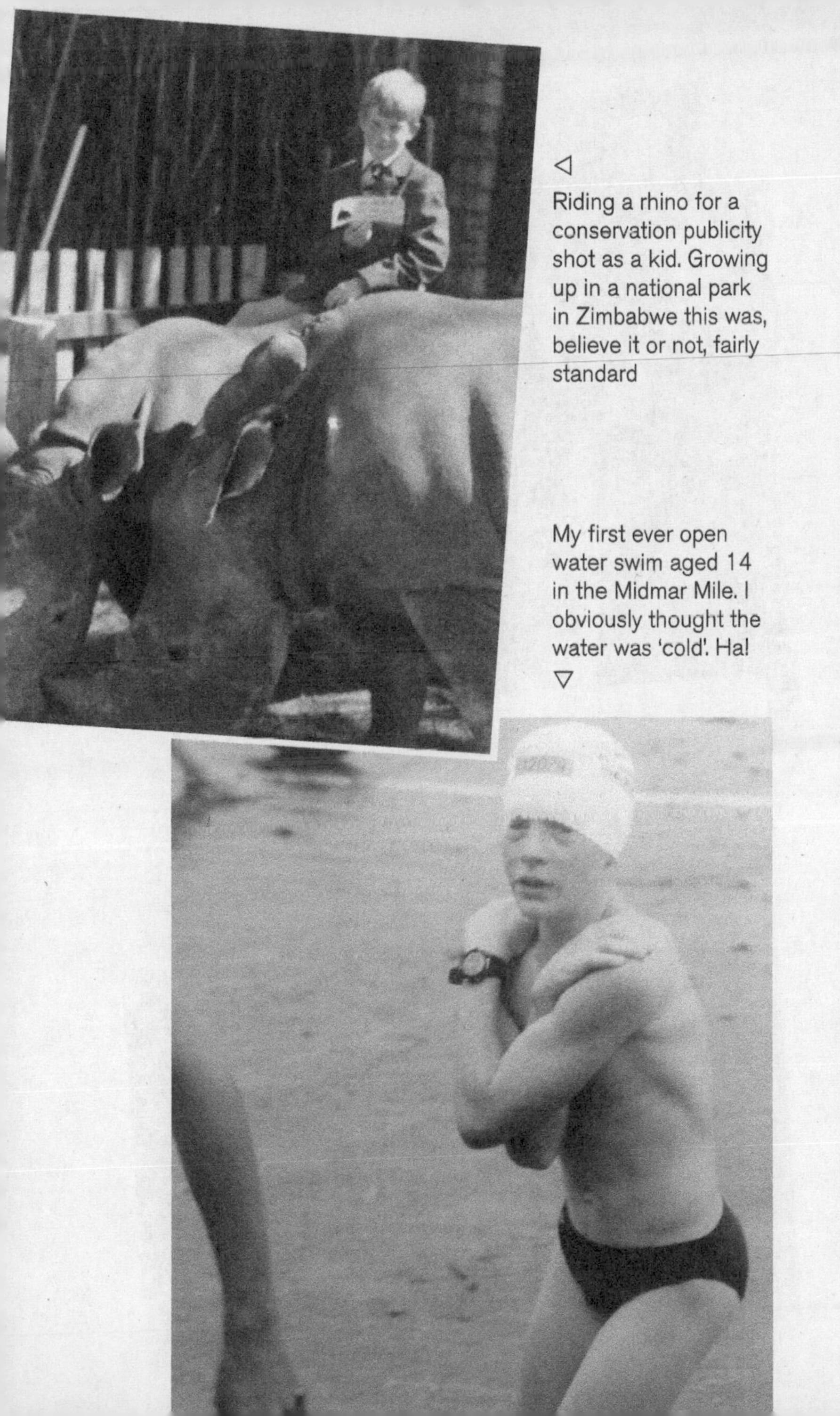

◁

Riding a rhino for a conservation publicity shot as a kid. Growing up in a national park in Zimbabwe this was, believe it or not, fairly standard

My first ever open water swim aged 14 in the Midmar Mile. I obviously thought the water was 'cold'. Ha!

▽

◁ Clean shaven at the start with my mum

Standing under the iconic Land's End sign looking seriously nervous ▽

Friday in all her glory. Jez is sailing, while Em's in the kayak and I'm swimming ahead

▷ *Friday*'s rather cramped and somewhat leaky interior. Four of us lived in here for over four months. I don't know how we didn't kill each other!

△

Coming back in the RIB from a trip to shore to get supplies. Judging by the look on Em's face she's forgotten something she wanted!

◁

Jez (otherwise known as 'The Hoarder') was always finding interesting ways of using flotsam and jetsam

△

Waiting out the southerly tide on a landslide in Cornwall. It wasn't the safest place to have a nap, admittedly...

Em, despite later admitting that she was actually terrified of water, was always smiling

Trying to prepare mentally for
another difficult session

△

Swimming with seals

▷

My arch enemy: the lion's mane jellyfish. I grew my own lion's mane to try to stop them stinging me in the face

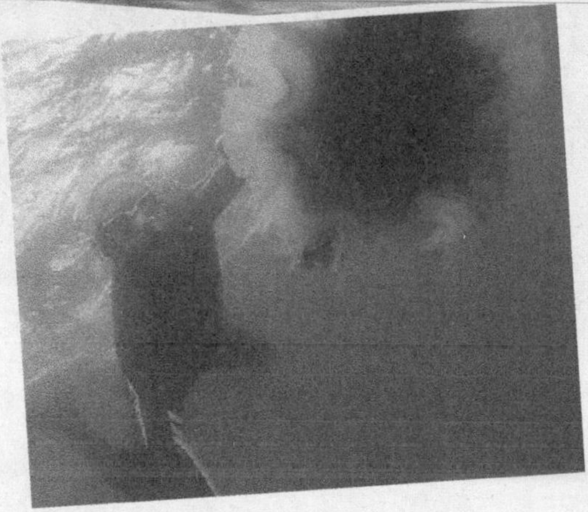

Enjoying a night ashore round the campfire cooking the fish Owain had caught that day. It was moments like this that really made the swim

▽

△

An ocean selfie with *Friday* in the background

◁

Trying to stay out of the way of the huge container ships around the Bristol Channel gave us a few hair-raising moments

needed. Less muscle means less power in the water. I was already below weight and couldn't afford to lose any more.

An hour later Jez arrived in *Friday*. To get out the water I had to wait for the RIB we were towing to come near me and grab one of the straps and haul myself into it. I then had to accomplish the even more acrobatic task of waiting for the back of *Friday*, which was moving up and down about a metre every second, to be at the right height before jumping on. This was hard normally, and after swimming for five hours, I wasn't sure how I was going to do it. Once on board I collapsed on my bunk and decided to nap on the way back to Newquay. I'd been asleep all of five minutes when I heard Jez shout.

'Sean! Can you help us?'

I got up slowly and walked into the cabin still half asleep.

'What's up?'

'The kayak has overturned, can you come help me?'

Friday was too small to bring the kayak on board so we were dragging it along with the RIB. A wave must have knocked it over and it was filling with water fast. Jez needed someone to help pull it onto the RIB and empty it.

Owain took the tiller arm and Jez did a very impressive Indiana Jones-style flying jump into the RIB, which was a good few metres behind *Friday*.

'Shit Jez, how'd you do that?' Em shouted.

There was no way I was going to manage that as I had started to stiffen up already from the swim.

It took Jez and me about ten minutes to try and bring the kayak onto the RIB, turn it upside down – which then just put the water in the RIB – before letting it go back into the sea.

Once back in Newquay we got our kit and prepared for a land evening. We had to row into the harbour again as Arthur's engine was still not working even though both Jez and Owain, who knew about outboards, had both had a look at it. It was a nice surprise to find out Owain knew a thing or two about mechanics. I hadn't actually asked this in the interview or the questionnaire, which I really should have, as I am sure I'd be needing his expertise at some point in the future.

We were lucky enough to stay with Steve and Kate that night. I spent the evening getting loads of advice from Kate, who was a seasoned open-water swimmer, while we all had a few beers, ate good food and had the hottest shower in the world. It was a great end to my longest day at sea. To top it off, when they found out we'd probably use Newquay as a base tomorrow they invited us back again for a barbecue. Cornwall seemed to be full of such kind, generous people. It was reassuring my faith in humanity.

I had finally done my first double-figure mileage day. Although completely shattered from doing the last few hours using muscle tissue as an energy source, I felt happy. Total distance swam: 12 miles.

I had the best night's sleep in a king-sized bed. It was nice not to have to try and hook my legs into anything, although a few times in the night I still felt I was rocking from side to side. Jez was the only one who didn't have a land-bed, as we now called them, because he said he didn't feel safe leaving *Friday* unattended on a mooring buoy outside Newquay harbour all night, so went back at around 11pm. His row back to *Friday* had all the ingredients for something bad to happen: dark, a few beers under the belt, a broken engine and some large Cornish waves, but thankfully he was safe.

I decided that I was only going to swim the four miles to Newquay the next day as I felt we could do with an afternoon off and a few beers to celebrate getting there; Newquay was the first major town on the map and something we had been looking at for days. Originally we were going to use *Friday* to get back to Holywell Bay where I ended my swim yesterday, but Steve and Kate insisted they take Em and me there with the kayak on their roof. After heading back to *Friday* to get my kit, Jez rowed me back to the harbour. Em kayaked and predictably fell out at the first sign of a wave, which was still hilarious. Her inability to kayak in any sort of wave was a skill in itself. Luckily she saw the funny side of it.

I absorbed as much open-water swimming advice as possible from Kate as we drove round to my swim start, especially on the diet side of things, which I had truly failed at. She said I should be eating every 45 minutes to avoid getting cold. Up till now, I was just drinking water every half an hour and eating every few hours. She also recommended I get a hooded thermal to fill out my chest space if my suit was too big. This seemed like a good idea and also helped with stopping cold water hitting my skin directly as it went down my neck. I figured if there was a place to get surf gear, Newquay would be it, and I'd sort it out in the afternoon.

It was a calm and sunny day, and knowing I only had four miles to swim meant there was time for some joking around on the beach before heading out. Em kayaked through the breakers, and didn't fall out, and I followed a few minutes later. I was just out of the other side of the breakers when I swam right into something hard, and sudden thoughts of swimming into a shark came rushing into my mind. I looked up and it was one of my water bottles that Em carried in the netting part of the kayak. I grabbed it and swam towards Em. She hadn't even noticed but had lost it in the breakers. We needed to come up with a better system for carrying water and food on the kayak. If I had been planning to swim further that day, not having water would have been disastrous.

I made it round to Newquay without much problem and then took the crew out for a few beers. It was nice to have the afternoon off and relax a bit.

Rest time not only allowed my muscles to recover but, essentially, allowed the crew to let their hair down. I knew all too well that following a swimmer doing 2mph was pretty boring and I wanted to show that I appreciated what they were doing for me. My way to do this was beer. It seemed to work. After a few hard days at sea, I could see the crew losing motivation. Three pints in the pub though and all of a sudden they were raring to go again. I have to admit the theory worked on me too. Added to that, beers are calories too. 200kcal a pint in fact.

We also stocked up on some supplies and fresh food, which included luxuries like toilet paper, red meat, pasta, potatoes, broccoli, cheese and milk. It was hard to keep food fresh and the only place we found that was remotely cool was under the floorboards in the bilge of the main cabin. The problem with this area was that it was always wet because poor little *Friday* leaked a lot, not to mention the fact there was excess diesel from many spillages over the years. I also managed to find a hooded thermal top without sleeves which would go under my suit. This would add more volume to my chest area thus avoiding the rush of water running down my back.

That evening Steve and Kate put on a barbecue the size of Russia for us, and we sat outside chatting and laughing. We were at the end of our first week and it was exactly what we needed. Just when we thought our friends couldn't get any more generous, on hearing about our problems with Arthur's engine, Steve offered to lend us his outboard, take ours to be fixed and then come find us in a few days to do the swap back. What a true gentleman.

I had another amazing night's sleep, which of course had nothing to do with the four beers I had the night before. Jez had again missed out on a land-bed and went back to *Friday* after even more beers than the previous night. He didn't answer his phone the first few times we tried to call him but happily it was because he was fast asleep and not washed up on a beach somewhere.

We said our goodbyes to Kate but knew we'd see Steve again in a few days with Arthur's engine. We did the swap over and motored back to the yacht. What a difference it made not having to row.

Today was going to be the first day where I'd be swimming with the yacht next to me. This meant I could eat a lot more, but more importantly it reduced the risk of me shitting myself as I could always get out if I needed to. It also meant that I could swim directly from headland to headland. Up till now I had been following the shoreline, even though there were so many cliffs I couldn't have gone ashore anyway. I still wasn't that comfortable at sea, and the idea of being a mile offshore with only Em was terrifying.

The going was steady and seeing *Friday* in action, zooming past as Jez sailed circles around me, was a joy to watch. She really was beautiful, despite her faults. Today's main challenge was to come up with a system of eating and drinking in the water. Kate's other recommendation was to drink warm liquids, which would keep my core temperature up. Owain was set the task of boiling the kettle and filling my flask with warm water, adding some juice and then working a way of getting the flask to me in the water and then me being able to get it back to him, bearing in mind once *Friday*'s sails were up it was hard to keep her in one place for long. He initially tried to throw the flask to me, which was attached to a piece of string, but inevitably Owain ran out of string as *Friday* slowly moved away from me in the wind, and he'd have to let his end go. There would then be 15 metres of cord in the water that we didn't want to get caught on *Friday*'s rudder or around the propeller, which still spins freely when the engine isn't running, so I'd have to frantically gather it in.

The next stage in the process was for me to try and launch the flask back at Owain. This felt like grenade-throwing practice as the only way I could throw it was with a straight arm and over my head, back at the boat. This obviously didn't work as I have never thrown a grenade before and I missed the boat by a mile.

Next, Em, who was trying to assist from the yacht today instead of the kayak, tried jumping into the RIB being dragged behind *Friday*. This made things a little easier but inevitably we had the same problems as from the yacht. After an hour, Em decided that it would actually be better if she kayaked next to me and did the food collecting. This was better not only for feeding but because my cheese-rolling shoulder meant I was swimming off to the left a lot more without her next to me. Every 100 metres I would hear everyone shouting, 'Swim straight!' and pointing to where I needed to go. It was almost impossible to get the direction right being so close to the surface of the water. Em said she was feeling seasick in *Friday* anyway, so all in all it made perfect sense.

It was great swimming with the whole team near me and it finally felt like the adventure I wanted it to be. Em was enjoying kayaking. Owain, being a keen photographer, was taking photos and videos, both of me swimming and some amazing landscapes for himself. Jez was happy sailing and playing with ropes, looking at charts and various other sailing-related things I didn't understand. Everyone was in high spirits.

We were in the switch-over tide period where all of the second tide was at night, so I had only had one session to swim in. By early evening I had swum a distance of 11 miles, all the way up to Polventon bay. This was just around from Booby's Bay, which, when reading the name on the map resulted in at least 15 minutes of predictable childishness between Owain and Em.

We managed to find a perfectly calm anchorage in a secluded bay near a lifeguard station and, while Em prepared our Stowaways dinner, Jez went for a swim and then a quick kayak to explore some of the coastline. It was a beautiful evening and we didn't want to waste it, so we went ashore and decided to make a beach fire and cook some marshmallows that Em's friend had given us. There wasn't much in the way of firewood so I went inland to see what I could find.

One hundred metres down the road I found a few chopped down trees that were lying in a pile of overgrown weeds and bramble. They were in a field but there was no gate so I went in. I untangled one branch, which was just big enough to have a fire to roast marshmallows and make a great end to our best day. Just then I heard a voice shout from one of houses on the other side of the road.

'Put it back!'

I turned around to see an old lady shouting from her fence, reading glasses on the end of her nose and kitchen towel over her shoulder. I dropped the branch and went over to her.

'Put it back. You didn't ask for permission.'

'I'm so sorry. Is this your field?'

'No, but you didn't ask.'

I was confused. It wasn't her field. Why did she care? Also it was a rotting tree in a pile of weeds, hardly a stack of prime wood.

'I'm so sorry. Who owns the field? I'll go and ask them.'

'No it's too late, you should have asked first.'

She then shrugged and turned away from me and gave one more flying comment, 'Now go away!' while flicking her hands at me. What a grumpy old lady. If I had scaled a fence to take an organised pile of wood then yes, but surely this was just foraging? I decided it wasn't worth the conflict and sulked all the way back to the beach empty-handed. Our marshmallows would have to wait for another night.

It was strange sleeping back on *Friday* and I struggled to get a good night's sleep. She was just rocking way too much. I had, however, managed to work out a way of locking my legs into the corners, which, although not comfortable, meant I wouldn't land up on Em's bunk in the night.

We had another day where I only had one tide to swim in, which meant a late start of 1pm. We could have got up at 5am for the end of the last northerly tide but figured for the sake of a few miles we'd get more sleep, which with hindsight didn't matter because I didn't sleep anyway. The crew did though and it was just as important for them to be rested.

We pushed on to Polzeath and then along to Port Isaac, and the going was similar to the day before. I was slowly finding my rhythm. Swim for 90 minutes and then rest for 20 while having a meal. I was tired but making good progress. My muscle memory was slowly starting to form and, now that I didn't have to think as much about what each arm was doing, I could start enjoying the journey.

This part of Cornwall is notoriously busy in the summer. Car parks are full, beaches are overcrowded and traffic is a nightmare. Being at sea meant we didn't see any of it. In fact, because I was only swimming past a few towns each day, most of the time we really did feel like we were completely alone. On my second feed break of the day, I lay on my back in the water balancing a bowl of Lancashire Hot Pot on my belly while trying to eat. I looked up towards the towering cliffs and couldn't help but think we were discovering a new and exotic land. It felt like Jurassic Park and I half expected a pterodactyl to swoop over the cliffs at any moment. Looking to my left and seeing *Friday*, a rickety old wooden yacht, added even more to the sense of early exploration. Somehow, we felt we were discovering things no one else had. Many of the beaches and coves were only accessible from the water and it was likely that some of them hadn't seen people for years. It's very rare to have good enough weather to get ashore even if you wanted to. I started to wonder how long it would take someone to find you if you decided to build a small shelter on one of these secluded beaches.

'Oi, keep swimming!' Jez shouted loudly, bringing me back to reality. He was right. I needed to make the most of each tide if I had any chance of reaching Scotland before the weather started to deteriorate at the end of the summer. Em took my empty bowl and I turned back onto my stomach. I took a few strokes and suddenly something soft and squidgy brushed past my face. I looked up to see a beautiful opaque purple jellyfish calmly floating a few inches below the surface of the water. It looked so graceful and peaceful but I knew what was to come. Pain! It had practically just molested my face. There was no way I had escaped being stung. I braced myself for the pain to start, but it didn't come. Turns out these purple ones don't sting at all, which was a huge relief, because about two metres further along was a bloom of about 100 of them covering an area the size of a small bedroom. If they had been stinging jellyfish, that would have been the end of me, I fear.

The most common stinging jellyfish in Britain is the lion's mane jellyfish. They can grow to the size of a football with tentacles that spread about three metres out in all directions. Luckily, these purples ones were harmless and after making a quick video of me swimming with them, I continued north.

Steve had called to say Arthur's engine was now fixed, at an extra cost of £160. On top of the £220 I had paid before, this was turning out to be an expensive option. Arthur had better be grateful when he gets his practically new engine back, I thought. Our next anchorage was going to be Port Isaac. It had a harbour so I told Steve to meet us there at around 8pm to do the swap. My progress was good and by the end of the tide I had managed to swim a few miles past Port Isaac. Swimming ahead of our anchorage was always good because it meant we could then use the southerly tide to get back. If we had to anchor north of my last swim spot then *Friday* was usually fighting the tide to get there. All these logistics took a lot of planning and decision making. Jez was doing a great job ensuring we made the most of the tides.

After my session we turned around and went to Port Isaac. On arriving we discovered that Port Isaac did indeed have a harbour but it was a drying one. Jez's app didn't show this so he opened the chart which confirmed it. This means that at low tide all the water drains out and boats are left on the mud. Unlike boats that are designed for harbours like this, *Friday* had one long fin keel which meant we couldn't ground her. We could anchor just outside the harbour but she wouldn't be sheltered from the waves. It was quite choppy, which would make it pretty uncomfortable on board, but we didn't have much other choice.

We anchored up and went ashore to meet Steve and get Arthur's engine. We offered him a meal and a pint but he said he needed to get back to Newquay. I was still blown away by Steve and Kate's kindness.

We fitted Arthur's engine and looked back to *Friday* to see her mast sticking up behind the harbour wall. The top of it was moving a good three or four metres from side to side. I knew it was going to be another rough night's sleep. We started to get back into the RIB when Owain's phone rang.

'Really? Thank you so, so much. That's very kind of you. We'll be up shortly.' And he put his phone down with a huge smile on his face.

He said, 'While you were swimming, I tried to get us a B&B and one of them said yes, so we all have a land-bed tonight.'

'No way! That's awesome!' shouted Em. She too was having trouble sleeping in the front bunks with no sides.

'Thanks Owain but I'm going to stay on the yacht again,' Jez said.

'Really?' I asked.

'Yeah, I wouldn't sleep well anyway being away from her. I don't think we can leave *Friday* unattended all night in these conditions. The anchor could drag or even worse the chain could break. It can happen. Also, I'm starting to kinda like *Friday*.'

Jez liked his own space and enjoyed tinkering with things by himself. Owain, on the other hand, was fairly social and always keen to help out. They were very different individuals but it was too early to tell whether they were getting along on the boat while Em and I were out swimming. All seemed good so far.

I also felt slightly bad that I wasn't really getting to know Owain. He was the person I was spending the least amount of time with and also the crew member who was the best at going off on his own and sourcing media and logistical things, not to mention free land-beds.

'Are you sure, mate?' I asked feeling really guilty that Jez was still yet to have a land-bed.

'Yeah. Don't worry, but if you feel that guilty give me a tenner for an ale before bed. That'll help me sleep!' Jez laughed.

It was the least I could do. I had budgeted for beer and pub food for the crew and Jez certainly deserved a few beers tonight.

5

HIGH PRESSURE HEAVEN

The alarm went at 3.45am as I wanted to catch the last few hours of the morning tide. Unfortunately I hadn't slept well at all because the room didn't have much ventilation and was extremely hot. Still bleary eyed, we stumbled in the dark down to the harbour. Jez was there waiting for us in the RIB looking quite tired too.

'Sleep well?' I asked.

'Not bad, not bad,' is all he said. Which probably meant it wasn't that good but Jez wasn't one for complaining.

We motored back to *Friday* and then did the half-hour journey to my last swim point marked on Jez's navigation app on his iPad. At the end of each session he'd drop a pin and write down the co-ordinates as a backup. These co-ordinates could be logged into *Friday*'s GPS, which would tell us where to go. Our third backup was actual charts just in case all else failed. We had two batteries on *Friday*, one for charging phones, laptops and VHF radios, and the other used solely for starting the engine. You never knew when these might fail so having paper backups was really important.

This was the first time I was getting in the water before the sun had risen. Although the water was a constant 14 degrees it somehow felt a lot colder. It's strange how your mind can play such a big role in how you feel.

There is even a general open-water swimming rule that is 'never mention the C word'. That C word is cold. If you don't mention it, it won't affect you, so the thinking goes. I'm not sure I believed it because I was still really chilly. That first minute in the water was always the worst as my outer layer of skin would acclimatise to the sudden change in temperature. Ideally, you'd try do some running and jumping to get warmed up before you got in the water, but *Friday* was way too small for that. The best I could do were some fast squats on deck while holding on to the mast to stop me falling overboard. Once in the water I'd swim as fast as I could to get my heart rate up. I'd also often turn upside down and do some dolphin style kicks underwater for as far as I could go before coming to the surface.

I only had two hours of tide and hoped to get to the next possible safe anchorage four miles away. I put my head down and switched off my brain and churned out the miles. People often ask me what I think about, but the truth is I try and think about nothing. I learned to do this on the round the world cycle when I had to push 16 hours a day on the bike. If your brain is not telling you how tired, cold and fatigued you are then you tend to keep going.

Anything to minimise negative thoughts is always a good thing. Doing this while cycling was, however, a lot easier as I had things to look at to keep me busy. With swimming all you see is sky, water, sky, water, for hours on end so it's a lot harder to switch off.

Left arm, right arm, breathe in, breathe out, repeat. While I was swimming, Em was taking in the sun, Jez was practising his tacking and Owain was doing a spot of fishing for lunch.

I just managed the four miles before the tide started to change direction. I had made it to Tintagel bay, which was by far the best anchorage we had been in. The bay was sunk into the Cornish cliffs and flanked by ancient ruins: crumbling stone walls and right at the very top a breathtakingly old castle overlooking the ocean. This wasn't just any old castle, it was in fact the castle where King Arthur was said to have been born. As picnic spots go, this was certainly one of the best. Just when I thought it couldn't be a better place for lunch Owain showed me a bucket containing four large mackerel he had caught. We had six hours in this anchorage before the next tide so there was no rush to do anything except relax, eat and potentially go ashore for some exploring. I gutted the mackerel, as Owain wasn't too keen, and we fried them as a starter. They were one of the most delicious fish I had ever eaten. There is something special about eating fresh fish you have just caught.

Jez and Em decided to have naps while Owain put on his wetsuit and went for a quick swim.

'Is it cold?' I shouted, as soon as he'd jumped in, knowing full well it was freezing.

'Not ... too ... bad!' he replied, trying to catch his breath.

'Whatever mate, admit it, it's cold!'

'Yeah OK, bloody freezing!'

A small part of me was glad he was freezing. He now knew what I had to deal with all day, every day. Owain lasted 15 minutes before throwing in the towel and coming back on board.

It was a busy day on the coast with loads of tourists walking along the cliffs, a few of them shouting and waving at us. *Friday* had a huge banner and stickers on her side which said 'Swimming Britain'. I wondered if they were waving at us because they'd heard about us, or just because *Friday* must have looked pretty special anchored up in this idyllic bay on such a sunny day.

After lunch we did some *Friday* DIY. Up till now we had 120 litres of water in a bladder under the floorboards, but had no way of getting it because the foot pump had broken off the floor. We'd been using a spare 20-litre jerrycan but that was running out quickly. Eventually we managed to screw the foot pump back onto the floor again but it was a pretty slapdash effort.

We spent the last hour of downtide exploring the shore and getting some land time to keep us sane. Four of us living in such close proximity, where even standing up straight was nearly impossible, certainly pushed us to our limits. Maximising land time was important to fend off the ever-encroaching cabin fever; an illness that I'm sure can make you clinically insane. It's actually well known that your decision-making ability is vastly reduced when you are confined to small spaces.

Within 15 minutes of getting back into the water the waves started to pick up again. The wind had changed direction and was now coming from the north. This meant the wind and the tide were running against each other. When this happens the sea becomes extremely choppy. The waves were only about one and a half metres in height but were very close together and steep. They were coming at me with such speed that I'd swim up one side of the wave and almost get thrust off the top and right into the front of the next wave. I'd then spend a few strokes almost completely submerged before coming to the surface close to the top of the wave and becoming almost airborne again into the next wave. It was relentless, wave after wave hitting me in the face, sending me underwater. All attempts to have any sort of style were hopeless and it became a fight to just keep afloat. It was hard to believe I was making any sort of progress but Jez assured me it was worth continuing.

We had made the decision that if my pace ever dropped below one mile per hour then it would be more beneficial to stop swimming and rest than to try and fight bad conditions while becoming more fatigued. On endurance events that last more than three weeks it's important to manage your energy efficiently as you can easily fall into deep fatigue, which takes weeks to recover from. With shorter races of less than three weeks you can almost operate on adrenalin and body reserves, and you don't need to worry about long-term fatigue. As I was expecting this swim to take between eight and ten weeks, I always needed to factor in proper recovery time and make the most of the good conditions. It was pointless spending two hours trying to swim two miles in bad weather when I could do that in 45 minutes the next day when things looked better. This was all good in theory but if we were hit with a week of bad weather then I may not have much option but to sluggishly move forward. However, for now, the weather was good and, although it was hard fighting the headwind and waves, I was still making progress, so pushed on.

It was 9pm and just getting dark by the time the tide turned. I was surprised to find I had swum over seven miles, which was a lot more than I had expected considering the waves were probably the hardest to swim in so far. My confidence was slowly growing as I was getting stronger. The first week had been a fast learning experience but I was gradually getting into the swing of things, as were the crew.

We had reached Crackington Haven and decided because I had an early start again to get the morning tide, we would skip a shore visit and just go to bed. For dinner, we had sausage casserole and I opened a bottle of wine for the crew.

After a good feed we all went to bed. It was fairly calm, which meant we should have a good night's sleep. As I was drifting off I felt my stomach rumbling again. I knew what was about to come and immediately felt embarrassed as I was only a few feet away from Em. Most athletes will know what I'm talking about when I say 'protein farts'.

I needed to eat probably twice as much protein as I normally would and I got most of this extra protein in the form of powder which I would have after every session. This noticeably helped me recover for the next day. The downside is that your body then produces farts that can end marriages. They really are bad. I had been supplementing my protein for a week now and it was only a matter of time before they'd arrive. I lay there and sneakily looked over to Em. She was facing the other direction. I got my sleeping bag and tightened the neck hole. I then let out a silent one. Within seconds I could smell it. I turned to see if Em had noticed and in doing so loosened the hole a little and a rush of fumes came up my neck. I started to cough. Em turned around.

'Are you … ahhhhhhhhh dude! What the hell?' she barely had time to finish her sentence and was gagging while covering her nose.

'I know right. Damn protein farts,' I was quick to try shift the blame.

'Ahhhhh! Come on!'

With all the commotion, Owain who hadn't gone to bed yet, opened our door and nearly fell over.

'Jeez, dude! What did you eat?' he said with horror, and quickly closed the door again. I could hear him chuckling on the other side.

'Owain! Open the door, you're hot-boxing me in. I think I might die,' Em shouted.

'No way are we letting that into our room!' he called back.

'Well it was nice knowing you all. Tell my parents I love them.'

I was lost for words. It seemed to linger for about ten minutes and just when it seemed safe to breathe normally, I let out another ripper. It's safe to say Em was not impressed but what was I to do. Better out than in right?

Another 5am start and we were greeted with by far the best sea state I think I've ever seen in my life. It was glass smooth; even flatter than the pool I trained in. I could finally start working on my style again. There was no wind for Jez to sail, so they just floated a few hundred metres away. If only the entire swim would stay like this, I kept thinking to myself. It made life so much easier.

Em and I carried on while I basked in the glory of not drinking any sea water, not having to roll my head so high to breathe and not being dunked by huge waves. I was just falling into a trance when I heard the distinctive sound of a full throttle outboard engine. I looked up expecting to see a fishing boat but instead saw Jez bombing along at around 20mph in the RIB, Arthur's engine finally working to its full potential. Jez was sitting near the front of the RIB to get the nose down onto the plane. With his hair blowing in the wind and his neck stretched out, he looked like an excited spaniel with his head out of a car window. I've never seen Jez so happy.

'Mate, you got to give this a go,' he said as he rushed up next to me. It did look fun. I'd probably never get conditions like this again but didn't want to waste swimming time.

'OK. Tell Owain to get some food ready and I'll have a go in 20 minutes and eat at the same time.'

'Cool,' replied Jez, as he opened full throttle and bombed away again.

I was really excited to have a go in our improved RIB and for the next 20 minutes I had an extra spring in my stroke. Jez then came round with *Friday*, and Em and I jumped in the RIB and proceeded to act like rebellious teenagers, doing circles and bombing up and down the coast as fast as possible. I'm not a speed freak by any means, I drive a 20-year-old Land Rover called Mana that only does 60mph, but I have to admit I enjoyed ripping it up, as they say, in the RIB that morning.

Getting into the water seemed a lot easier this time. It's amazing how much your mind plays a role in how you feel in the water. Normally those first few minutes were freezing cold, but the combination of high spirits, some adrenalin and glass-smooth water meant I was actually, for the first time, looking forward to getting swimming again.

I carried on swimming along across the bay towards Bude, and by the end of the tide had done six miles. I got out and we headed for Bude. It was 10am and we had a good six hours of downtide again to do some exploring and get some food. Also, going to land meant we could have a bit of our own space to avoid the ever-threatening case of cabin fever in *Friday*'s confined spaces.

Bude was bustling with people as we ribbed into shore. We found a spot to leave the RIB and went into town for my third breakfast, and then, for a spot of team morale, we decided to start a series of games. First on the list was crazy golf, for no other reason than we saw a course right next to breakfast and decided to add it to the list. We played one round and it's safe to say Tiger Woods has nothing to worry about just yet. I was so bad I gave up counting. Owain took a close win over Jez by two shots.

We then did some errands, a food shop and got the obligatory 99 ice cream, then settled into a pub to write the blog and do a quick radio interview with BBC Gloucestershire, before heading back to *Friday*. We got back to the RIB to discover that it was now low water and the RIB was a good 200 metres up on the sand. Jez managed to find a RIB trailer to borrow, which made getting back to the sea a lot easier. The RIB, with engine and other crap now collected in it, weighed well over 150kg. All four of us could just about push it along the sand for 20 metres before needing to rest.

Just like yesterday, the afternoon headwind picked up and the glassy flat sea had turned into huge waves intent on smashing me in the face. One wave slapped the side of my head so hard that my ears started to ring, slightly disorienting me and sending me swimming off to the left. Em too was taking loads of water into the kayak because she had got rid of the spray deck so that she could keep my water bottles by her feet as the netting wasn't holding them. We'd cut a water bottle in half that she used as a scoop to get the water out when it got too full. She seemed to be scooping more than paddling at the moment.

For the entire afternoon, wave after wave battered my head and shoulders. I swam till early evening before I started to get cold and tired so gave up for the day. I could have gone on for another half hour but my progress was slowing as the tide started to turn. I clambered on board and Jez and Owain had huge smiles on their faces. Something was up?

'Mate! You did your biggest day – 14 miles in total. Well done,' said Jez, patting me on the back. I was knackered but felt good for it.

Owain shouted 'dinner!', while holding a huge pollock right in front of my face, and then spent a few seconds pretending the fish was a puppet while saying, 'Eat me, eat me.' I couldn't help but laugh. I was glad they were having a good time on the boat, because following a swimmer with his face in the water for six or more hours a day can be very boring.

From *Friday*'s deck we could see an amazing beach with a waterfall running down the cliffs, falling onto a flock of seagulls all taking their evening shower. It was idyllic and deserved some exploration. We got some Stowaways and everything needed to make a fire and cook the pollock, and ribbed ashore. Within seconds of getting to the beach Jez had wandered off. Em and Owain collected driftwood for the fire while I gutted the fish. Twenty minutes later the fire was ablaze and Jez came back carrying, and wearing, an array of things he had found on the beach. He wore one odd boot, one small flipper and a diving mask with one screen missing. He was also carrying two different wellies and some rope. This was nothing compared to what he was dragging behind him. He had found a huge fender used to stop ships hitting the side of the harbour wall. It was teardrop shaped and about a metre tall.

'You look ridiculous Jez,' laughed Em.

'I know, I know,' he admitted. 'Most of it is rubbish but we're keeping the buoy, the rope and the wellies.'

Jez had mentioned his hoarding tendencies but this was the first time we saw him in action.

We sat around the fire, cooking the pollock and boiling up a pot of chicken and bacon pasta, our favourite of the Stowaway meals. Dessert was some more marshmallows and some leftover wine from the night before. As I sat there staring onto the dancing flames of the fire, I couldn't help but feel incredibly happy. I had really hoped that this swim would not only be a huge physical challenge, but also a chance to explore places we would never have otherwise seen. The last few days had proved to be exactly that. I was managing to swim hard when the conditions and tides were right, and then spend the rest of the time seeing the Great British coastline. After a tough first week at sea, I finally felt that everything was coming together, and that we were now having what would surely be the adventure of a lifetime.

Clank! Clank! Clank! The jib – the front sail – on the deck flapped around just inches from my and Em's heads all night as the wind rattled. I got up three times to try to secure it but there was also a scraping metal sound which I couldn't identify. The next morning Jez told us it was the anchor dragging along the seabed as the wind and tide pushed us. Jez said he had been keeping an eye on things to make sure we weren't pushed too far off our position and onto rocks. We definitely needed to make a plan with the jib though as neither Em nor I could handle too many more nights like that.

I got up slowly and felt the worst I had all swim. I had been swimming for ten days now and the last two afternoons of fighting head-waves, and a few nights of not much sleep, was starting to take its toll on my now fairly thin body. I started the swim at a reasonable 67kg and in ten days I had dropped down to 63kg. Considering I didn't have much fat to lose I was starting to eat into my muscle reserves. Once that starts happening you risk falling into long-term fatigue, which I really needed to avoid.

Today was the last day along the Cornish coast before cutting north, across the Bristol Channel, and towards Wales. It was going to be a big crossing so I had originally planned to take a day or two off before it to recover. I wanted to be fit as possible. However, while the weather was good I was thinking that maybe I should just go for it. I was also now a few days behind schedule, which added extra pressure. Luckily I hadn't yet told the crew I was hoping to be able to push on as I didn't want to promise anything. I would see how I felt at the end of today's session.

My last GPS point was two miles further south from our overnight anchorage so Jez said he would RIB us there. He also admitted it was because he saw some stuff on the beach he wanted to forage. Brilliant, more crap for *Friday*! We motored back to the start while dragging the kayak and I was in the water by 8am. Jez then went to shore and I carried on swimming back north towards *Friday*. I was feeling very tired and there also seemed to be a weird tide as we approached Hartland Quay. The going was so slow that I was making the least progress all swim: it took me well over two hours to do the two miles to *Friday*.

Eventually, by the end of the tide, I had only done three miles. I felt quite depressed and sat in silence drinking my shake. Em could sense my distress and was trying to comfort me.

'You've been swimming for nearly two weeks solid, Ginge. Of course you are tired.'

'I think I might take the weekend off.' That was in two days' time.

'This weekend, mate?' Jez butted in.

'Yeah, I think I need to rest before the crossing.'

'Well if you do, and tell me if you're not happy with it, but my local pub have a cart entered into the Red Bull soap box derby in London and I'd love to be there.'

I remembered Jez talking about this. They built a cart out of a coffin and called themselves the Coffin Dodgers. It was genius. It certainly added pressure to my decision.

Em then added, 'Also, if you do decide to take the weekend off, my boyfriend and all my friends have booked a cottage in Devon for the weekend.' That was just the excuse I was looking for. If I was going to have a weekend off and not feel guilty then this was probably going to be the best one.

'Awesome, I'll get the wife down too,' said Owain.

'Great! Well then, let's try and push as far as we can for the next two days and take the weekend off.'

'Perfect. There is an amazing village called Clovelly just along a bit. It has a harbour and a good place to leave the boat for the weekend.' Jez said, while looking on Google Maps for safe anchorages. Although tired I was ready to jump back in the water and make the most of the next few days.

'Come on. Let's do this.' I shouted enthusiastically, stood up, hit my head on the roof, sat back down again, and then realised I couldn't swim for the next six hours because we were against tide.

The sun was out and we were once again anchored up right next to an incredible beach. Jez managed to find a shipwreck that was so old you could barely make it out from the rocks except for some quite obvious water or fuel tanks and one huge propeller protruding from the sand. We really did feel like we were following in the footsteps of ancient explorers led by a crazy hoarding skipper. All Jez needed was a silly parrot to complete the look. Even his clothes were starting to tatter.

The afternoon session was a lot more productive than the morning one. I did five miles in the first three hours with a break and still had 90 minutes of tide left, which was very much needed to make up for the disastrous morning session. We could finally see Lundy Island through the low-lying haze across the ocean. Lundy is ten miles offshore or a third of the way into the Bristol Channel towards Wales. It's a small island, about three or four miles in length, and was once occupied by pirates who would commandeer all the cargo ships heading into Bristol. It now has 23 inhabitants who look after the farmlands, small cottages you can rent and the amazing sea life, including seals and puffins. I was really looking forward to exploring it.

Our plan was to use Lundy as an anchorage base for a few days as I crossed the daunting Bristol Channel to Pembrokeshire. We were now at Hartland Quay, which was two miles south of Hartland Point, where I'd start swimming towards Lundy. I was quite nervous about this next section because the Bristol Channel is not only notoriously rough but is also one of the busiest shipping channels in the UK. The plan was to get to Hartland Point tonight and then try and get as far across to Lundy in tomorrow's morning session before the weekend off. I stopped for my last feed before pushing on for the final hour to Hartland Point when two kayakers came up to us.

'Are you the swimmer?' one of them asked.

'Yes, that's me.'

'Ah brill. Where you heading from here?'

'We're heading to Hartland Point and then start the crossing to Wales via Lundy.'

'Lundy? You should have been starting your crossing much further south. The tide is really strong. Even if you start here you will probably miss Lundy.'

We knew the tide was going to be strong but not that strong. In order to hit Lundy the kayakers were saying that I'd have had to start making my way out to sea ten miles back. Ideally by Hartland Quay, where I was now, I should have already been five miles offshore getting pushed towards Lundy. At this rate it was likely I'd pass a few miles south of Lundy with the strong tide.

'So what are the options?' I asked nervously.

'Well, I'd start from here at the end of the southerly tide and head out to sea. You'll get pushed a little further south but will make progress out from the coast. Then when the tide turns north you will hopefully get swept closer towards Lundy. If you go now you'll still get swept under it I reckon. That's just my opinion. I've kayaked these waters loads and that's the strategy I'd take if I was kayaking there.'

That was the last thing I wanted to hear. I had only done eight miles or thereabout so far today. By the sounds of things the next possible time for me to start the crossing would be at 6am tomorrow morning.

'So you wouldn't go now?' I asked, to confirm I understood.

'No, pal. Tomorrow at the end of southerly tide would be my choice.'

Cycling around the world had taught me who to take advice from. The overweight drunk guy in the pub telling you that you can't cycle up that hill was probably talking nonsense. A fit looking kayaker who was actually kayaking where I wanted to swim probably did know what he was talking about. So after more debate about logistics I eventually decided to trust the kayaker and go tomorrow morning.

I said thank you, got out the water and slowly unzipped my wetsuit feeling a little deflated about my short day.

'Well there's only one thing to do then,' joked Owain while pointing towards a pub on the cliffs. It did look bloody inviting, I admitted.

'We'll have a quick one then let's cook dinner on the beach before an early night for the morning.'

Owain had caught another pollock and a few mackerel, which I was keen to fry up again. My body was craving oils and protein.

We went to shore but I just wanted some time alone so sat outside for a while. I was still annoyed that I had done a sub-ten mile day. Up till now I was enjoying the forced exploration time due to downtides but this time it angered me. There were just so many things to consider outside swimming. I guess this is why most big swims in history have been river swims where you don't have to worry about tides.

We had a pint and looked at ye olde maps of all the shipwrecks along the north Cornish coast that were hung around the pub's walls. There were hundreds dating back a century and more. Looking at these maps was a good reminder of how treacherous these waters can be. I'd been extremely lucky so far with the weather. But I was worried that my luck was going to run out sometime. I hope it's not halfway across the Bristol Channel, I thought.

After the pub we went back to *Friday* to collect everything for a beach fire dinner, and jumped back in the

RIB and started the 200 metre trip to shore. I looked up into the cloudless sky, millions of stars winking at me in a gentle and motivating way as if to say, 'You're going to do this.' I wanted to be able to look at them all night.

'Guys, should we sleep on the beach?' I asked.

'We need to get our sleeping bags then,' said Jez, immediately turning the boat around and heading back to *Friday*.

Just then I changed my mind as it would add another half an hour of work getting back to the boat in the morning and the rocks were so uncomfortable I'd never get a good sleep.

'No, actually, let's sleep in the boat,' I said.

'Are you sure mate? Make up your mind now!' Jez said, as we were almost back at *Friday*.

'Nah, let's just get to the beach and make a fire,' I said, although I was disappointed in my choice. Normally I'd have jumped at the idea to sleep on the beach but I really needed a good night's sleep before crossing to Lundy.

Jez turned around again and we headed for land.

We all fell into the same routine. I gutted the fish. Owain and Em sourced wood and built a fire, and we lost Jez to all the flotsam and jetsam scattered along the beach. Within half an hour we were all huddled around the fire eating fish for starters served on flat rocks, Stowaways for mains and a cheeky Rattler cider for dessert. Most people think alcohol is bad for you when doing endurance events but actually, as long as you stay hydrated and don't get absolutely bladdered, it can be a good source of calories. A couple each night were the same calories as a meal and also helped keep the team morale up. However, the Rattlers were pretty strong and I gave the last bit of mine to the Hoarder, as we now called him.

We all sat in silence, now comfortable enough with each other not to feel the need to make small talk, and instead just soak up the environment and fall into a trance watching the flames.

Jez then calmly said, with a slight ironic laugh, 'Guys, um, we have a problem. Look at the tide.'

We all looked out to sea trying to adjust our eyes to the darkness. Then, slowly but surely, we all started to see what the problem was.

'Shit! How did that happen?' gasped Em.

We had come to shore at high water and since then the tide had gone out revealing 100 metres of huge jagged rocks protruding from the ocean floor creating what was almost certainly an impassable barrier between us and *Friday*. We took our torches to see if we could find a way out. Between us and *Friday* – whose anchor light was just barely visible in the distance – was a mini Mordor for us to cross. We looked for a way of getting the RIB over the rocks but not only would we probably damage the RIB, if there was a time when one of us would get injured then this was it.

'Well, what now then?' I asked Jez, finally giving in that we couldn't all get back to the boat.

'I guess we'll have to sleep here till the tide comes in.'

'When will that be?'

'At around 6am,' Jez laughed.

'6am. So basically we have to sleep here.'

'Yup!' said Jez in an annoyingly matter-of-fact way.

It was obvious that the tide would go out but we figured we'd just have to drag the RIB over the sand. Admittedly we had been slightly caught up in the moment, hypnotised by the dancing camp fire, and slightly mellow from a few too many ciders, and hadn't quite kept an eye on things.

After walking slowly back to the fire, we sat down in silence and tried to come to terms with the fact that we were actually going to have to sleep on the cold stones with no sleeping bags or camping mats.

'And we so nearly got our sleeping bags,' said Em.

I felt extremely guilty that I had made the call not to get them.

'Well I guess we need more wood and anything to try and sleep on,' said Owain, being the most proactive of us all. We spent the next half an hour collecting every bit of wood we could find and each found a spot next to the fire. There was a bit of a wind so the only place to get warmth was downwind, but every time the wind picked up the flames and sparks would get worryingly close.

We also scoured the beach for any form of mattress – seaweed, plastic bags, anything to stop the cold – but the only thing we could find was a two square metre pile of tangled up old rope covered in tar in places. We brought it near the fire but figured tar and flames would not be a good combination. Instead we used it as a windbreak to shelter from the now fairly cold wind coming in off the sea.

It was near impossible to find a comfortable position amongst the tennis ball-sized rocks, but after a lot of shuffling I managed to find a gap for my hips which only hurt a little and was bearable. I found two larger rocks and balanced them on top of each other for a pillow and tried to fall asleep.

'Good night chaps, and good luck,' I joked but no one responded. The reality was that it was going to be long cold night for us all.

The only person to fall asleep instantly was obviously Jez and he was happily snoring away, which was as irritating as you can imagine. Owain, Em and I kept moving places, shuffling on the rocks and restocking the fire to keep warm. Although summer, I guess it was still around 14 degrees at night, with the cold stones and wind chill making it feel a lot colder. Eventually, after half an hour, I decided to change location and try the pile of netting as a mattress. It kind of worked and Em decided to try it too. I soon found a fairly comfortable position in the net and even managed to use a section as a duvet. It was more psychological because the holes in the net were the size of grapefruit. I did, however, manage to sleep before I was awoken by a jumping ember from the fire burning my leg. The fire was dying out so I got up to stoke it. I looked over to Owain, who I could tell was awake. I then noticed the bottom of his shoes, which were too close to the fire, had started to melt.

'Owain,' I whispered, 'your shoes, mate.' He sat up looked at his shoes and kind of shrugged and rolled over. He was too tired to care. So was I.

I had managed to find a comfortable place to sleep but was now being kept awake by the cold wind blowing through camp. I decided I needed to make a shelter and the only thing I could find was a small wooden pallet we were going to use as firewood. I took the pallet and a stick and created a shelter from the wind. It wasn't ideal as pallets have huge gaps between each strut but it did help bounce some of the heat back onto me. I curled up again and managed some broken sleep here and there, in-between stoking the fire and checking to see if Mordor had been covered up again, getting progressively more annoyed each time with the minefield of razor sharp rocks preventing me from a good night's sleep.

It was light by 4.30am and with not much more than an hour's sleep I got up to see if we could get back to *Friday*. I was shattered and my heart rate was very high, quite a common side effect from sleep deprivation. Most of Mordor was now covered up but we still needed to wait a good hour or so before the sharp rocks were sufficiently below the water level for us to get back safely. We didn't want to break Arthur's engine or, worse, tear the side walls of the RIB. I looked over to Em who was curled up in the pile of fishing net shivering so I added more wood to the fire.

By 5.30am we all got up and just sat in a daze staring blankly into a pile a smouldering logs that had kept us from freezing to death in the night. We had battle wounds to show for it too. Owain's melted shoes, small burn marks on my legs and all of us with various holes in our jumpers from sparks. No one had slept much and we all felt like death. I also had a slightly tight chest from being cold all night. Looking at the state of us all I knew that doing a session this morning was not going to happen, besides I had also now missed the tide I needed to get to Lundy. It was so frustrating because what was meant to be two days of big miles turned into just one half day. I was hoping to have made it at least to Lundy by now but instead was still on mainland and now had three days of no swimming.

I had swam just shy of 90 miles in 12 days which was about 10% of my total distance but it had taken me twice as long as I had expected with my daily average being a miserable seven and a half miles per day. I really needed to step up my game. Chasing the miles so early on was playing on my mind as the knock-on effect could be catastrophic if I got to Scotland too late in the season. I had a window of about three and a half months and was already nearly a week behind, even before my weekend off.

I had a pretty productive weekend in Clovelly, a village on the north coast of Devon tucked into the forested cliffs. There are no cars and the only way to get into the village is down a pretty steep cobbled path. The entire village is privately owned and has been that way for 800 years with only three families ever owning it. The current family have owned it for nearly 300 years. This means that all 80 properties, every hotel, restaurant and pub are all owned by the one family and you have to lease or rent from them. Not everyone can just rent though. You have to be interviewed to see if you will fit into the village. It was an interesting social dynamic but it seemed to work.

It was strange being there alone without the crew but I made the most of it by meeting the locals, eating as much as my shrivelled stomach could handle, getting a much needed shoulder massage from Emma, the village masseuse who also moonlights as the hotel receptionist, and updating my blog. Stuart the Scab had been getting increasingly big and deep. He went about three millimetres into my foot and I could now see flesh. Being in the water each day meant he wasn't having much time to heal. Spending the weekend out of the water at least meant he had the chance to dry out a bit.

The only thing that was slightly annoying was that I seemed to have pulled my shoulder muscle while trying to start Arthur's RIB engine, which was playing up again. It was however a much-needed weekend's rest.

The crew returned on Sunday looking as fresh as ever too. Jez's Coffin Dodgers had come a close second in the race, Em had seen her mates and Owain had entertained his family in Devon for the weekend. We were all as ready as ever for the next leg – the Bristol Channel. We'd head off in the morning to start the next session.

6
THE BRISTOL CHANNEL

Da! Da! Da! Da! Da! The vibrations from *Friday*'s single cylinder engine were sending shock waves through my skull and down my spine. It was 2.30am and I hadn't slept much because, if I'm honest, I was bricking it for my next section, finally crossing the Bristol Channel. Jez and Owain got up and started the long journey from Clovelly, back to Hartland Quay. It was going to take us at least four or five hours and I was hoping to be in the water by 8am to make the most of the tides. This was by far the longest commute so far and lying in the front bunk for four hours not being able to sleep was increasingly frustrating. Although tired and nursing the niggle in my right shoulder, I was feeling a lot stronger and was glad I had taken the weekend off.

I was nervous getting in the water again but was surprised that I didn't feel nearly as cold as I had done before the weekend. It's amazing how just a little bit of extra body fat can make all the difference. I had purposefully made an effort to eat plenty of carbs and fat over the weekend. A high mixture of both is the best way to gain weight.

To try to play the tides correctly, I swam directly away from Hartland Quay heading in a westerly direction. When the tide turned I'd eventually get swept north-east towards Lundy. The chap in the kayak wasn't lying about the strength of the tide as I was pushed sideways at nearly 4mph. For every 100 metres I swam west, I'd get pushed 400 metres north-east. No matter how fast I swam it soon became clear that I'd get swept quite far south of Lundy and therefore have to swim the slightly further route along the east side of the island instead of the west side as originally planned. At least the weather was good. I'd have been pretty annoyed if I was faced with huge waves after a weekend of glass smooth water sitting in Clovelly, not swimming.

It was a lot harder to work out where I was going because I no longer had land to look at. Instead I had to rely on Em next to me who, at times, looked like she might actually be asleep in the kayak. My right shoulder was still a little fragile but the cold water helped numb the niggle as I pushed on, resting for a few minutes every hour and a half and having a Stowaways meal with nearly half a tub of butter to add more calories and fat. It had to be butter from grass-fed cows (as opposed to grain-fed) because Steve, my nutritionist, told me that was best. Trying to find grass-fed butter is a lot harder than you think. It's not often on the packaging. In fact, the only butter I'd been told for certain was grass-fed was Kerrygold so we had stocked up on ten blocks of it that was now in the wet bilge-fridge. I really needed to get some more weight back on. I carried on right through to the next southerly tide, hoping it would sweep me west and on to Lundy but it started pushing me back towards Cornwall, so I called it a day. I had made it about two miles south-east of Lundy, which wasn't as bad as feared. With a little tidal planning I should make it past the north end of the island by the end of the next tide.

We now had our six hour break so we decided to go on to Lundy to do some exploring. We anchored in the main bay and ribbed ashore and started the long walk up to the top of the island to pay the £5 anchoring fee. We also needed some diesel for *Friday* so took the jerrycan to see if we could buy some.

Lundy was beautiful. It was three miles long and comprised of mostly grassland, one church and a lighthouse. Jez walked up the hill with a strange sense of built-in navigation, straight for the pub, naturally.

In the pub, Jez managed to ask about diesel. Five minutes later the warden of the island, a chap called Derek, came over and chatted to us for a while, telling us all about Lundy. On hearing about my swim he then gave us a free round at the bar and said he'd happily donate us a jerrycan of diesel for *Friday*. What an amazing guy.

Butterflies started dancing in my stomach as we headed back down the hill. The tide times, which move forward each day, were now going well into the evening. Tonight would be my first session where I might have to swim in the dark. I had just about managed to not think about all the scary monsters lurking in the depths below me while it was light, but night-time swimming was going to be a real test for me.

We arrived back at the RIB to find it was full of water and the two oars were washed up the beach 100 metres away. From where we tied it up, we thought it would have just risen with the tide slowly and landed up a bit higher on the beach. It was a wonder that the oars were still around. The RIB was too heavy to lift so we all spent ten minutes bailing enough water out with bits of driftwood and the oars before it was light enough to lift and empty out. At least it got a thorough cleaning.

It was a good hour to get back to my last swim point and I took the time to have a meal and prepare for my first night session. Jez would give the ten minute countdown and then five minutes before we reached our spot, Em and I would clamber over the back of *Friday* and into the RIB where I'd put on my goggles and cap. Em would do the acrobatic task of getting from the RIB into the kayak. She was surprisingly good at this, which was baffling to me. She was still unable to paddle ashore in one-foot waves, but balancing between RIB and kayak in five-foot waves didn't seem to be a problem. Jez would then circle around the GPS pinpoint and when he was eventually on top of the exact spot he'd shout, 'Go!', and I'd fall backward into the freezing water. Once or twice, I took too long and we'd drift past the pinpoint by 10 or 20 metres. If that was further back from where I finished that was fine, but if we had drifted ahead Jez would then shout 'hold on', shake his head and have to turn around and go back again. I have to admit I secretly missed a few on purpose just to get another minute of warmth. Those first few minutes in the water weren't getting easier.

Today was the same as any other day, but as the sun started to set over the horizon so began the noticeable increase in heartbeats. I'm not normally a nervous person but today felt like the time I had to do a duet with my little sister at primary school in front of everyone. I tried not to think about it and decided to keep my eyes closed while face-down and only briefly open them when I breathed to see I was still swimming in the right direction. This seemed to work – out of sight, out of mind.

At least it was dead calm, which made things a lot less trouble. I pushed on, trying my very best to not think about a huge whale coming up from the depths and swallowing me whole. I don't know why I was constantly thinking about the extremely unlikely event of deep-sea creatures lurking in the darkness below when in fact there were far more real and present risks for swimming at night like tides, waves, getting run over by a ship, drifting away from the boat or even getting run over by *Friday* if I swam off to the left too sharply. I think I was subconsciously stressing over the *unlikely*, which somehow seemed to make the *very likely* less daunting. If I actually thought about it properly I may very well have chickened out. Swimming across the Bristol Channel at night was certainly the most brave/stupid thing I'd ever done in my entire life.

Just then, as I took a stroke with my left arm, my hand went straight into something. In a moment of panic I pictured a shark biting off my hand and with lightning reflexes I pulled my arm away and felt a sharp pain in my left tricep. I came up for a breath and looked ahead. Thankfully it was only one of the purple jellyfish but because my nerves were on edge, the knee-jerk reaction had caused me to pull the muscle in my left arm. I rubbed it for a minute or two trying to get blood flow, hoping it wasn't a pulled muscle and just a bit of cramp but it was no use. I had suffered my first swimming injury and all because of a stupid little harmless jellyfish.

I tried to carry on swimming but had no power in my left arm at all. This was adding extra strain to my right shoulder, which was still a bit sore from Arthur's engine. I didn't know what to do. I needed to push on but didn't want to worsen the injury. I hadn't done much more than a mile but after a lot of failed attempts to try and swim I decided to call it quits for the day. The one positive was I didn't have to do a night session. If I'm really honest with myself I think I was probably using the injury as a bit of an excuse to delay the inevitable. Had it been a warm sunny day I may very well have continued, slowly. But for now I wasn't feeling very confident and could put it out of mind as that would be tomorrow's task, which was now even more daunting with an injury. As soon as I was out the water I felt extremely guilty for not carrying on considering I should have been fighting to make the most of every tide. Luckily for my psyche, my arm got progressively worse in the night as the adrenalin wore off, which somewhat helped me cope with the decision to end the session early.

The fact that the second northerly tide was in the evening meant the morning tide wasn't at stupid o'clock and we could all have a relative lie in till 7am. I had a surprisingly good sleep, considering my sore shoulder and arm. I tentatively flexed the sore muscles. My left tricep was still quite painful but nothing a bit of cold water and painkillers couldn't numb.

We were still south-east of Lundy and the plan was to hopefully do about eight miles in the tide and get a good chunk north by the end of the session. I worked out that if I changed my style slightly I didn't have to use my tricep as much, and, although not nearly as efficient, I was still able to make relatively pain-free progress north. We had another calm and sunny day at sea and I managed the eight miles I'd planned.

After my session, we went back and anchored in a bay right in the north of Lundy. Owain then ribbed to the southerly bay to collect the diesel that Derek said he'd leave for us while Em, Jez and I clambered ashore and walked the full length of the island and back to the tavern in the glorious early afternoon sun. From the cliffs we could see hundreds of puffins and even spotted a few seals swimming in the clear blue sea below. From up here the ocean looked so incredibly tropical and inviting, a stark contrast from its finger-and-toe-numbing reality. The water in the UK reaches its warmest temperatures in August/September, which was at least something I was looking forward to. I'd definitely be done by the end of September at the latest just when it would start getting cold again.

We spent the afternoon in the tavern chatting to people and telling them all about the adventure so far. There were four types of reactions from the public. First there was the 'dumbfounded'. This is when people just looked at you blankly, with their mouths slightly open and would often just say one phrase like, 'You're mad,' or, 'Did your parents drop you as a kid?' and then walk off shaking their heads. The second type were the 'questioners'. They would bombard me and the crew with a million questions like, 'How many miles each day?' or, 'How many calories do you eat?' or, 'Do you pee in your wetsuit?' They were really friendly and were most likely to donate a bit to charity. Third were the 'critics'. They were generally people who thought they had some sea experience because they'd gone on a fishing holiday once or took a ferry during a storm. They would concentrate on all the issues that lay ahead of me like, 'The Bristol Channel has the strongest tide in the UK and is a big shipping lane,' or they 'spotted killer whales in Scotland last week you know'. To start with I'd try and defend my decision but eventually gave up and came up with a few stock answers like, 'I'll cross that bridge when it comes', or, 'Jez has that covered.' Fourth were the people who were generally not interested at all but in a typically British way wanted to be polite so would just say 'fair play' give a half-hearted nod and walk off. Luckily we sat next to a family who were 'questioners' and they gave us £40 for War Child, which was incredibly kind – £10 of which came from the young daughters who donated some of their pocket money. Moments like that certainly gave me a boost to get up and go.

At 7.00pm it was time to get back in the water. It was a lovely evening with the setting sun bouncing a rainbow of colour over the smooth water. The colour slowly turned from rich yellows and oranges to deep purples and blues as soon as the sun slowly set. Being midsummer meant it would only get completely dark at around 10pm. This hopefully gave me time to slowly build up the courage for night-time swimming. I'm not sure I'd have been able to start my session in complete darkness. As the session continued my left tricep was becoming more and more painful with each stroke. I think my eight miles morning session had taken its toll. It was so frustrating because this evening had perfect conditions and not making the most of them could have a huge knock-on effect towards the end of the swim when the weather would get worse. If I dropped two miles a day it would add nearly ten days to the swim. That could mean bad weather in Scotland.

At 9.30pm, and just before it was completely dark, I decided to call it a day and rest my arm, which was still painful enough to hinder performance. Not only had it been a short session, which again made me feel pretty depressed, but I was still putting off my first proper night session. No matter what happened, I'd definitely have to do a night session tomorrow. There was no way of getting around it. I needed to make up some miles. It was now 18

July and I had been swimming for nearly three weeks and had only covered 110 miles.

It was so calm in the night you could forget you were even on a boat at all. The windless night, however, meant it was boiling hot. I had borrowed my friend's minus-15 degree sleeping bag too, which didn't help, and I landed up in a pool of my own sweat on the slippery faux leather bunk mattresses.

Three things were certain for today's session, which were making me incredibly nervous. One, I was most definitely going to swim at night. Two, we had no idea where we were going to anchor at all. I'd most likely swim to the exact halfway point between Lundy and Wales, which would be way too far for us to get back to land, so either I'd need to cut my day short so we could get back to Lundy or swim harder to try get closer to Wales. Three, we had to cross a pretty busy shipping lane.

'Am I allowed to just swim across the Bristol Channel. Who owns it?' I asked Jez.

It sounded ridiculous but surely there are rules for this? Who does own the Bristol Channel? The Queen, I guess.

'The sea is free, mate,' Jez replied with a rebellious grin on his face. Turns out, no one, not even the coastguard can stop you. We did however make sure we radioed in our intention so that all tankers knew what they were looking at when they saw a tiny yacht trailed by a red kayak and a swimmer who looked like he was drowning due to the new style he'd adopted to avoid injury.

I started my morning session at around 9am and put in a steady pace. Within a few hours we lost Lundy to the haze behind us and couldn't see Wales ahead of us either. This was the first time that I couldn't see land at all and I started to feel quite alone. With no fixed marker on the shore it was also now near-impossible to swim in the right direction and at times Em and I veered off at nearly 90 degrees until Jez and Owain would shout from *Friday* and point us back on track. It was so disorienting. Eventually, after the fifth time, Jez found a compass and gave it to Em and told her which direction to aim for. There was a bit of science in this because I was now getting pushed sideways so needed to aim slightly off our true direction in order to avoid landing up too far east. This should have worked but only caused more confusion as it was a pretty cheap compass. The combination of me swimming like a drowning sloth and Em trying to use a compass as if firing a gun would certainly have been fit for any Laurel and Hardy sketch. That thought did cause me to chuckle involuntarily a few times, which, when face-down in the water, was the closest I'd come to actually drowning all swim. The irony.

There was a huge shipping lane ahead of us too and for most of the morning we could see enormous tankers bombing up and down. Luckily none of them were ever close enough to be an actual threat, but nevertheless I felt incredibly insignificant and unimportant in comparison.

I did my eight miles in the morning session as per usual. This seemed to be my optimal pace for conserving energy and not burning out. Ideally, I was hoping it would have been closer to ten miles but considering I was fighting a strong side current I was fairly happy with the progress. We had nowhere to anchor for lunch so just turned the engine off and let the tide take us where it wanted to. Jez would monitor things and start to head back to the GPS pinpoint depending on how far we drifted. We all kept to ourselves that afternoon. I lay on deck listening to music and trying to warm up like a seal on a rock. Owain did some fishing. Jez did sailing stuff and tinkered with *Friday* and Em went for a nap.

By 8.30pm it was time to get back in the water. Unless I did in fact get swallowed by a whale before sunset, I would be swimming right through till midnight. The reality of this suddenly brought on the question of whether or not this was actually a safe thing to do and also whether the crew were actually happy with it considering the swim priorities. We hadn't really talked about it. I had just kind of figured we needed to do this. I called a crew meeting.

'Guys. We haven't really talked about this but I wanted to ask whether you are happy to do this night session? Jez, what's the real risk here?' I asked.

'As long as Em has a head torch, you wear your wrist reflector and Owain stays on deck to keep a look-out, we should be fine.'

'What about ships?' asked Owain, being the most sensible of us all.

'We'll see them from miles off. It's a pretty clear night.'

'Em. You happy to kayak at night?' I asked.

'Yes, Ginge. As long as you bloody swim straight,' she joked. It was hard to tell her real feelings as she was always extremely upbeat but I detected a hint of worry.

'Sure, Em?'

'Yes, we have to. We can't fall any further behind.'

'Come on, mate. Get your kit on. We got some mileage to make up,' said Jez.

In a weird way hearing the crew say they were happy to take this risk really helped me. We were after all, all in the same boat. Every pun intended.

'One stroke at a time. One stroke at a time.' I kept repeating to myself. At least it was flat again.

Stroke, stroke, breath. Stroke, stroke, breath. Each hundred metres gained was further into the heart of the busy shipping lanes of the Bristol Channel, and getting darker and darker at the same time. It wasn't long before the orange and reds turned to blues and purples, and then I heard Em shout.

'I need a torch and can you bring his reflectors?'

This was it. There was no getting out of it. I had bought some reflective armbands so that the crew could see me in the water. Em had a head torch on, both so that she could see me and also for me to be able to see her next to me so that I carried on swimming in the right direction. *Friday* was also just on the other side of Em so that she knew where to go.

'I am bricking it,' I confided in Em, as she brought me my reflectors.

'Me too, but you'll get eaten first so I'm OK,' Em said.

'Ah thanks.'

By 10pm, it was completely dark. Suddenly the rest of my senses became far more alert. I could hear Em's paddles going into the water next to me, and *Friday*'s single cylinder engine tutting away off to my right sending small vibrations through the water. Are sharks scared of these vibrations or, like dolphins, attracted to them? I decided it was best not to think about it. Along with extra audio sensitivity I was feeling everything in the water. I could feel the water rushing over my cheeks and across my lips. I could feel all the bubbles from my breath running over my wetsuit. It was a whole new experience and took some time to get used to.

Time seemed to stand still and what felt like an hour in the water would turn out to be 15 minutes. I knew I had to push it to at least try and get nearer to Wales, so I decided to skip a proper meal and just have a recovery shake in the water with extra carb powder. By 11pm I was still not even halfway and knew I had to dig deep and try get within 10–12 miles of Wales. Any further and we'd be stuck in the middle of the channel all night and unable to get to shore and back again in time for the next tide.

I put my face back down and started to pick up my pace. I couldn't have gone further than 10 metres when all of a sudden I felt an electrifying shock across my nose and cheeks, followed by a rush of warmth and then a burning sensation as if I'd fallen flat on a bed of red-hot coals. I let out a yell and turned onto my back. My scream nearly toppled Em over. I knew immediately what had happened. I had been warned about lion's mane jellyfish but was hoping I'd meet them a lot further north, and not on my first night swim, in the middle of busy shipping lane.

'Ginge! Don't move. There are tentacles all over your face.' Em said as she shone her head torch on me. I could see them stretching from my cap and down my cheeks, glistening in the light. Em came over and with her gloves on tried to take the tentacles off me but in doing so let more of the burning toxins onto other parts of my cheeks. I felt like I was on fire.

'Where is it?' I frantically asked in case it was right near me.

'Don't worry it's over there.' Em shone her torch about a metre away from me. There it was, a jellyfish about the size of a football with tentacles reaching well over a metre in all directions. It was just floating there as if nothing had happened, the bastard!

'Can I pee on you?' shouted Owain from *Friday*. I didn't know if he was serious or just trying to lighten the mood, but either way that definitely wasn't going to happen. If anything I'd try and pee on myself, a sentence I never thought I'd say. I'm not entirely certain how you'd even do that. I'd pee in a bottle, I guess, and then pour it all over my face. The thought of that nearly made me vomit. I was ready to try anything though.

'Sorry to put a damper on things mate, but we've only got 45 more minutes of tide and we need to push on,' suggested Jez. He was right. If anything the stinging face was now the most painful thing in my body making my shoulder and tricep secondary concerns. I nervously turned around and put my face back in the water to find the cold surprisingly soothing. This was the one and only time I was grateful for cold water. I carried on until midnight with my face burning with every breath as my face came out of the soothing cold water.

Em was now on jellyfish watch. Whenever she saw one she had to stop me swimming and try and move them out the way with her paddle. There seemed to be hundreds of them and they were all on the surface of the water which was typical for jellyfish when the water was calm. When the waves pick up they tend to go a few metres down. At this moment I'd take bad waves any day over captain fire-face. I had to change my style to look slightly ahead for jellyfish that Em might not see a foot below the surface. This was adding extra strain to my neck but it was worth not getting stung again.

By midnight I had made it to the exact place we didn't want to be – slap bang in the middle of the Bristol Channel. We were pretty much equidistant from both Lundy and Wales. It would be a five-hour sail just to get to a safe anchorage. We had no option but to just stay in the channel all night, much like we did during the lunch break, and drift with the tide.

'Right guys, we need to do shifts to look out for ships, etc.,' explained Jez. I'm not sure what 'etc.' was but was too scared to ask.

'Em, you do now till 2am – a two-hour shift as you need some rest. Owain, you do 2am to 6am and then I'll do the rest until we get back in the water at around 10am.'

Jez then went on to explain what navigation lights to look out for. Red light means you are looking at the port side of the boat. Green means it's the starboard side. Either of those meant the ship was probably passing parallel to us. If however they saw red and green side by side, that meant the ship would be coming straight for us. If that happened they'd need to wake Jez up and we'd move out the way or radio it in. Ships can travel at up to 20 knots, which meant we'd have about ten minutes to move out the way if one was coming directly for us. We knew where we were on the chart and knew where the ships were likely to pass but, even so, going to bed was quite worrying. To make things worse, my face carried on pulsating for a few hours. That, mixed with Stuart the Scab, who was still getting progressively deeper and not healing at all, throbbing away, made sleeping near impossible. I was resigned to the fact I'd have a gaping hole in my foot for the entire swim, all because of a small scratch on the first day. At least the cold water made my foot numb so that I didn't feel the pain while swimming.

After some broken sleep, I saw the sun rise over the glistening ocean at 5am. I knew we didn't risk getting run over in the light, as much anyway, although we were still a tiny speck in the sea from the point of view of these huge container ships. I nevertheless managed a few more hours' sleep till 8.30am. Being in the middle of the Bristol Channel meant that the tide was coming directly from each side. From my left all morning until high water and then from my right all the way back down to low water. The downside was I had no tide to help me along, but the plus side was that I could now swim on both tides. I'd land up swimming a big 'S' shape as the tide pushed me towards Bristol until around 2pm and then back out towards, well, America till around 8pm. This meant that today I had to change my strategy. I needed to slow my pace so that I could swim for longer. I'd also need to eat a lot more as I'd most likely be in the water most of the day burning around 800kcal per hour.

I started my session at 10am and asked Em to make sure I drank every 20 minutes. I'd then stop every 90 minutes for some food and rest up. There wasn't as much of a rush to get going each time I had a break as I had all day to swim but, nevertheless, I really wanted to get across to Wales by the end of the day.

At 3pm *Friday* came alongside me, which was unusual. Jez usually stayed a few hundred metres away. I stopped swimming.

'Sean, look up!' Owain excitedly shouted and pointed ahead while standing on the front of *Friday*. From down here he looked like Leonardo DiCaprio in *Titanic*, only a lot scruffier. I looked ahead of me and in the distance, if I squinted my eyes, through all the haze I could just make out some land. It was Wales. I could see my destination.

'Woohoo!' I let out a worryingly girly scream and everyone cheered. Seeing land gave me a new boost of energy. I now had something to aim towards. It was still ten miles away but I almost felt like I could touch it.

For the next few hours Wales didn't get any closer and my pace started to get slower and slower. I was convinced I was swimming in one spot and the crew were playing a cruel game on me. By 6pm I decided I had had enough. We were about five miles offshore and close enough to get to land and find a pub. Crossing the Bristol Channel was as good as in the bag and we needed to celebrate.

We found a safe anchorage in a calm bay and ribbed ashore. The nearest pub we could find was a good hour's walk but we were willing to do it. We also urgently needed to fill up *Friday*'s water bladder so we all took it in turns carrying the 20-litre empty jerrycan up the green lanes to a small town called Stackpole where we found the inn. It was a quaint pub and I had a dark ale as I felt it was better for me than a lager. We then all sat down in the beer garden with a sense of achievement. It had been a tough few days with torn muscles, not much sleep and jellyfish stings, and it was good to be on dry land again. Although pretty excited to have made the crossing I think we were all too exhausted to really show it. For me it felt like when you're at university, have a few too many pints and then decide to do something stupid like climb up a high tree or try and tightrope walk a sharp metal fence. You wake up in the morning, with the world's worst hangover, and although you haven't impaled yourself you shiver at the thought of what could have happened. I felt like I was in a post-Bristol Channel hangover.

On our second round, Jez got out his iPad to look at the week ahead. Being so far behind schedule meant

I now had no idea when I'd likely hit Scotland. From my last point I'd start swimming slightly west towards St David's Head and then north along the Welsh Coast towards Anglesey. The next big crossing would be in a few weeks' time from north Wales to the Isle of Man and then again a few days later to Scotland. They would be much tougher crossings but hopefully I'd be stronger then. Jez was then scrolling across when I caught some land in the top left corner of his screen, just off to the north-west of St David's Head.

'What's that? Is there an island out in the Irish Sea like Lundy?'

'I dunno,' Jez admitted and started to zoom out slowly. It was an island – Ireland! It looked a lot closer than I remembered when planning my route.

'I had no idea it was that close. How far is it?' I asked.

Jez did his calculations.

'41 nautical miles.'

'How far is it from Wales to Isle of Man?'

'40 nautical miles, only 1 mile shorter.'

My brain immediately jumped to one amazing, scary, adventurous idea.

'How cool would it be if I swam to Ireland?' I said, with a sudden surge of excitement again.

'Yes Ginge. I have never been to Ireland!' said Em, with a huge smile on her face. How had a 28-year-old never been to Ireland?

'I can't see why not,' said Jez in his usual matter-of-fact way. 'It's definitely doable.'

'Right. Let's get another round and think about it.' I got up and went to the bar feeling the most excited I had been since thinking of the idea to swim the length of Britain, before all the detractors started to ruin my excitement. I came back with a tray of beer expecting to celebrate but the mood was very different on my return.

'What's up?' I asked. Jez and Em looked sheepishly at Owain.

'You all right, Owain?'

'I've planned loads of media and stuff in Wales and changing it now means I've wasted my time. I have no contacts in Ireland and if we go there then I think I might go home instead. You'll have no use for me.'

I was shocked. Jez and Em just looked down at the table trying to stay out of it. I thought the crew would jump at the idea to do something adventurous at the spur of the moment.

I thought for a moment.

'I'll tell you what. We still need to get to St David's before we decide so let's think about the pros and cons for the next few days. Right now let's enjoy Wales while we are here.'

I then swiftly tried to change the subject. The mood was very sombre for the rest of the evening and at around 9pm we all took it in turns to carry the now full, and very heavy, water can back down the hill.

I hadn't slept well at all. Em and I stayed up late weighing up the case for swimming to Ireland. The pros were: we'd get the big crossing out of the way early while the weather was good. It also meant we didn't have to do three very big crossings later, instead just one short crossing back to Scotland from Northern Ireland. It was slightly shorter and would save me about 50 miles in total. There were more anchorages in Ireland and, most of all, I just really wanted to go. It excited me.

My family, on my dad's side, left Ireland to move to 'the colonies' 100 years ago and swimming there would be none other than just very cool. That was all. It was the kind of bonkers idea that makes me excited and I hated that Owain's ultimatum was affecting my decisions. We only found one downside to going to Ireland, other than losing Owain who was a great crew member, and that was the issue that my adventure, the website and the huge stickers on the boat all said 'Swimming Britain'. Ireland was not Britain. I didn't know how this would go down. At the end of the day I was still swimming the length of Britain but going via Ireland. At least all the stickers were on the right side of *Friday* for going up the west coast of the UK. They would be facing out to sea if we went up the inside of Ireland so hopefully no one would get offended.

By morning, I had made up my mind. I was going to swim to Ireland. It made the most sense almost to the point that not swimming to Ireland would jeopardise the swim because we'd need to do three big crossings later on when the weather might not be as good. I got out of bed ready to tell Owain my decision. I was really nervous. I didn't want to lose him. He had done so much work getting media connections, taken loads of photos and really knew what the trip was all about, but I knew what I had to do. I walked through to the main saloon, my heart racing. But even before I could open my mouth, Owain started talking.

'Sean. Sorry for last night. I was just dead keen on Wales and was looking forward to it. I've been thinking about it and, you know what, I've never been to Ireland either and arriving by yacht would be kinda cool. I'm in.'

What a huge relief. That was the best news I could have hoped for as trying to find another crew member would have been quite stressful. Plus Owain was awesome at fishing.

We all cheered. Ireland, here we come.

Because I had a potentially four or five-day crossing ahead of me, and now knowing just how difficult they were, I figured we needed to stock up on some supplies and potentially take a day off so that I was in peak shape. The weather was looking good for the next week or so, which was a relief. Besides those few choppy headwind days, we'd had amazing weather since Newquay. My luck was going to run out sooner or later but as long as I wasn't stuck in the middle of the Irish Sea when those big Atlantic rollers came in, I was happy.

I was quite tired from pushing it all day yesterday, as were the crew, so we skipped the morning session to do expedition work. We all went ashore. Jez went to find diesel. Owain went to call various media and sponsors to tell them of our change of plan, and Em and I walked up the green lane and hitched a ride from a lovely old lady called Pam to Pembroke to stock up on various supplies, including another thermal layer as I was still getting cold in the water.

The afternoon swim session went by really quickly. I was now back with some pretty strong tides and swam right up till it was almost dark. Having a new and exciting goal made me completely forget about my sore arm, shoulder, jellyfish and anything else that was playing on my mind before.

My session ended just outside Milford Haven and we anchored up in a quiet bay. Even though I had only done the evening session I had somehow managed to swim 12 miles. The tide certainly helped but also it's amazing what a new sense of excitement can do to your body. I was flying through the water and ready for the next big crossing.

Jez and Owain got up at 4am to get me back to my start point. The engine starting always woke me up but I waited in the front bunk trying to rest until I heard the 45-minute warning. I could tell it was quite wavy out as I rocked up and down listening to the bow crashing through the waves just centimetres from my head. About half an hour later I was amazed that it had calmed right down but then I heard the engine turn off. The door opened and Owain came through.

'We can't make any progress to the last GPS point. Headwinds are too strong. We're going to try a bit later again.'

This was the problem with such a small yacht. It was just way too slow. If there was a headwind, any sort of waves or we were against tide, we were going nowhere. It was so frustrating but there was nothing we could do.

A few hours later Jez tried again and luckily the wind had died down and we were able to get me to my start point.

The most noticeable thing about the day's swim was the sudden increase in wildlife. A lone dolphin came and swam with me again. It didn't get too close and I missed seeing it most of the time but Em saw it frolicking just behind us. There were also hundreds of little black birds bombing past only a few feet from my head. It looked exactly like they were initiating an air strike. They'd start a good 10 foot in the air, about 50 metres away, and then fly directly down towards me and pass a foot over my head before zooming up and circling round again. There was no squawking or any sounds coming from them so I knew they weren't actually feeling threatened by me. I think they generally search for scraps of food from animals like seals in the water. I looked like a seal, I guess. That thought sent sudden shivers down my spine because sharks eat seals. I really needed to stop this 'getting bitten by a shark' fantasy as there has never been a reported fatal shark attack in the UK.

It was coming towards the end of my session when I had the final mini crossing to do – the Milford Haven Waterway. It was by far the busiest port I had crossed all swim, and in the past hour we had seen about five very fast ferries and ships going in and out of it. Unlike the Bristol Channel where the shipping lanes were ten miles wide, here they were condensed down to around one mile. I was quite tired and knew that would take me around 40 minutes but once in the shipping lane we couldn't stop, we just had to keep going. Hanging around the busy shipping lane can result in an angry call from the coastguard who we could see on the top of the cliffs.

I had one last bit of Stowaways food with extra butter and then put my head down. My pace was slow and my arms were sore but I just had to get across to the other side. Jez went ahead as he too couldn't be seen to be hanging around. Eventually I popped out the other side of the shipping lane, exhausted and completely out of energy. Em waved her paddle in the air, the sign that we needed help and *Friday* came back and I called it a day. It had been two good days and although absolutely knackered, I felt good.

We found a typically picturesque Welsh cove to anchor in and all fell asleep pretty early.

The next morning I awoke to Owain chattering loudly. He then came into the front cabin and shoved his phone in my face.

'Hey! Check what they found off Milford Haven yesterday!'

I read the article on the BBC News website. The headline read, 'The fastest shark in the ocean – and a cousin of the Great White – has been caught by a crew fishing off the Pembrokeshire coast.'

'You cannot be serious!' I looked up at Owain. He looked worried. The article went on to say it was a mako shark, aggressive and fast, and has been known to jump into boats. They have attacked over 40 people since the

1980s, killing three of them, and have attacked 20 boats. This was the first time a mako shark had been caught in British waters for 42 years. The worst part is they then released it! To be fair they are pretty endangered but still, I now had a deadly, and probably rather angry, shark in the water somewhere just offshore from where we were.

You couldn't make this up. The first time a shark had been caught, not only happened to be a killer shark, and a cousin to the great white, but it was also caught right where I happened to be swimming on the very same day. My heart began to race. And it was just yesterday that I was thinking about looking like a seal. I couldn't believe it! I gave Owain his phone back.

'Well, now what?'

'Well the figures are still in your favour, no one has been attacked by a shark in the UK,' said Owain

'Yeah, but no one has swum the length of it either.'

Part of me wished he hadn't told me, but just then my phone beeped and it was a few Tweets from people sending me the article, so I would have found out anyway.

I slowly got ready trying not to think about sharks, because I knew it was ridiculous. There was nothing I could do anyway. If it was my time, it was my time. It was out of my control.

Our anchorage was only a few miles from my swim start so Jez ribbed me there for a change. It was a very calm and misty morning as I followed Jez up to coast towards Jack Sound, a notoriously dangerous narrow that is only passable at slack water and the place where I'd start heading towards Ireland.

Unfortunately I didn't swim fast enough and we missed the optimal time to get through the sound by about 20 minutes. We could see the rush of water flowing through at a worryingly fast rate. It looked like a river in full flood. The next time to swim through it would be in six hours' time and considering we were at the point where we would start heading to Ireland I decided now would be the time to take a few days off, rest my tired muscles, restock the boat properly, and most of all let the crew relax a bit.

Jack Sound was even too strong for *Friday* to go through so we went all the way around it, and made our way across towards St David's and anchored up in the bay.

We spent the next few days doing multiple trips from *Friday* to St David's, which involved a 30-minute walk. We couldn't carry everything we needed in one go so all had various tasks. Jez got the raw end of the deal and had to do three trips to get two tanks of diesel and some water, but he said he was happy to do so and became a master at balancing the heavy jerrycans on his shoulders with his head bent forward. I had also arranged for some supplies to be sent to a local tour operator who were happy to accept the delivery. It included a few more goggles from Speedo, more recovery powder and some much-needed suncream for me and the crew. My hands and right cheek were getting really burned. The only suncream that seemed to work was P20 and we were going through it fast.

It was also a time to update the blog and we even had the guys from Simply Swim, one of my kit sponsors, come out to Wales to film an interview.

It was a good and well-earned break for all of us.

7
SWIMMING TO IRELAND

Recovered and rested, we left the comfort of the bay near St David's and went back towards Jack Sound to start what would surely be the hardest section of my swim. Our successful Bristol Channel crossing certainly gave us all a lot more confidence but we had no idea what the tides would be like, how busy the traffic would be, or how big and strong the waves and the currents would be. They were all things we were just going to have to work out as we went along. Out there we'd have no shelter from the elements. If a storm came out of nowhere we'd almost certainly need to call a mayday. *Friday*'s maximum speed when conditions were good was 6mph, but she generally chugged along at around 3mph. If we got into trouble in the middle of the Irish Sea and needed to get to land it would take well over ten hours to get to shore. A very daunting reality but with the weather as good as it had been, it would take something seriously out of the ordinary to happen for us to call for backup.

We arrived at Jack Sound at slack water and I jumped in to swim through it. Because there was no tide it was just like any other swim. I popped out the other side and just before heading off towards Ireland Jez suggested I swim to land so that I can at least say I officially swam across the Bristol Channel. I wasn't that bothered about the 'official' but Jez convinced me to do it and I am glad he did because I think I would have regretted not doing it. I clambered onto the rocks, did a little dance, had my photo taken and then jumped back in the water and started heading north-west into nothingness.

I was feeling strong and together with the tide I managed to swim 18 miles. The waves were quite big too but I was powering through them gaining confidence with every stroke as Wales disappeared behind me. Em and Owain, however, were starting to get seasick again. I seemed to have got my sea legs from being in the water but after a week of flat conditions and a few days on land the others were suffering once again.

That night Em, Jez and Owain took it in turns to watch ship as I tried to get some sleep.

The Irish Sea was a lot rougher than the Bristol Channel. Long high rollers started to run through us lifting me ten foot in the air. By midday on the second day of our crossing I had done a further five miles into the Irish sea and was almost halfway. It was difficult for us to work out a strategy for swimming. Technically the tide, which runs diagonally from south-west to north-east and then in reverse, wasn't ideal. The northerly tide would take me nearer John O'Groats but further from Ireland. The southerly tide would take me further from John O'Groats but closer to Ireland. This meant I was swimming in big 'S' shapes which would add at least 10–20 miles to the crossing, which was already 41 miles long as the crow flies. Even with the extra distance it still seemed to be the correct decision.

By early afternoon the wind and rain started to pick up again. The dark clouds created a dramatic backdrop to an increasingly difficult sea to swim in. Waves were sometimes so big that they would roll me over sideways. Em too was struggling to keep with me, the side-winds often pushing her a hundred metres away from me. I pushed on for hours and hours, stopping every now and then to look up into the heavens as buckets of rain poured down. By 6pm I had had enough and decided to have rest as the southerly tide was pushing me too far in the wrong direction. I really needed to get more mileage west and the best time to do that would be at slack water at around 11pm. I decided to do a two-hour session in the dark to gain some much-needed ground closer to Ireland.

As we approached the mark that night I was even more terrified about swimming in the dark than I had been before. I wasn't sure why but I guess the last few night sessions I started when it was light and it gradually got darker. I couldn't shake the weird dread in my subconscious that as soon as I jumped in I'd go right into the mouth of a shark, even though I knew it was a stupid thought to have. Shivers went down my spine.

'Three ... Two ... One ... Go!' Jez shouted as we drifted over my swim start GPS point.

I jumped in and the first thing I noticed as how the lights from *Friday* were reflecting off the bubbles I created from jumping in. It looked magical. I started swimming and the bubbles kept glistening. I then looked up to ask Jez if we were going in the right direction only to discover he wasn't near me. What was lighting up the bubbles then? Em's head torch wasn't bright enough. I put my face back in the water and kicked my legs about. An explosion of light erupted from my legs. I then put my hands in the water and waved them around. A similar explosion of glistening lights engulfed my hands. It couldn't be? Were these phosphorescence?

'Em, look at this.'

Em came close and shone her head torch into the water but couldn't see anything.

'Turn off your torch.'

'Really? Why?' she asked nervously.

'Trust me.'

She did and I thrashed around in the water creating a cloud of light around me.

'No way. That's amazing!' Em shouted and proceeded to move her paddle around the water, creating even more lights. It was incredible and looked exactly like when Pi Patel was lost at sea in *Life of Pi* and the whale jumped out the water creating an underwater fireworks display.

For the next two hours I swam in a magical world of fantasy as trails of fairy lights followed my fingertips with every stroke. The light in the water created optical illusions and at times I didn't know which was real, as clumps of phosphorescence crowded so close together they created the illusion of larger sea creatures.

I could have swum all night but at 1am it was time to end my session. I got out of the water completely buzzing from the excitement of the night's session. I tried to describe it to Owain and Jez but it was near impossible to explain the experience. You really had to have been there. Those two hours were some of the best of my life and I'll take that experience to the grave.

The next morning we were getting pushed quite far north with the northerly tide and it looked like I'd hit Ireland halfway up towards Dublin at this rate. That would add an extra day at sea but once ten miles offshore we could logistically go to land each night. Today's big problem again was a 20-mile wide shipping lane we had to cross. The waves were picking up, which made swimming increasingly difficult. By early afternoon Jez came near us and shouted.

'Sean, we need to stop now and make for Rosslare. There's a tornado warning.'

'Funny, mate. Nice joke.' Surely there was no way there was a tornado coming. I'd never heard of an actual tornado ever touching down in the UK.

'I'm serious. Get out now. We are seven hours from shore and need to make a run for it. We can't stay at sea tonight.'

Jez had an uncharacteristically stern look on his face. Now I knew he was serious. I got out the water and we listened to the shipping forecast, and true to his word they mentioned a gale force eight or nine with tornado warning for southern Ireland.

The first shark in 40 years just where I was swimming and now surely the first tornado in Ireland for years just where I was swimming.

We chugged along towards Ireland, the waves getting bigger and bigger as we got closer. We had the sail out at full reach and were making good progress. Luckily we were heeled over towards the side of the boat my bunk was on so I could sleep lying almost on the side of the hull. It was surprisingly comfortable with *Friday*'s ribs digging into my back giving me some sort of massage. I was just dosing off when I heard Jez call from the cabin.

'Sean, I need your help.' He sounded quite calm so I got up slowly and went through to the main cabin. Still bleary eyed, I felt my foot go into some water. I looked down to see the floor completely underwater.

Shit! We were sinking! How was this possible? We hadn't hit a rock or anything. My mind suddenly went to thoughts of us all having to abandon *Friday* and get in the RIB, which certainly didn't have enough fuel to get to shore. Tornado versus RIB was a fight I didn't want to have. Everything went into slow motion. Jez was saying something but I didn't hear it. Eventually I snapped out of it.

'Sorry. What was that?' I asked Jez, preparing for the worst.

'We've got a leak.'

'No shit, mate. I can see we have a leak. How bad is it?'

Jez pointed to the side of the hull just above his bunk where water was pouring in. Just then we hit a huge wave and the foldaway table unhooked and came crashing down, completely shattering off its hinges.

'Help me get the floorboards up to see we don't have a more serious hole. Em, can you do the manual bilge pump outside. Owain, can you steer?' Jez jumped into full action mode.

Frantically we lifted the floorboards and felt through the very murky water along the hull to see if there was a bigger issue. There didn't seem to be one and after some frantic pumping from Em on the manual bilge we noticed with huge relief that the water wasn't getting any deeper. It looked like the issue was in fact with the automatic bilge pump, which had short-circuited while we were heeled over. We were at least three hours from Ireland and would have to take it in turns pumping out the water with the hand pump. As if my arms weren't tired enough.

It was 9.30pm when we finally reached Rosslare Harbour. All the fishing boats were rafted up together preparing for a stormy night. I was still sceptical about this tornado malarkey and none of us had any internet so we decided to find a pub with Wi-Fi to see if we would be able to swim tomorrow or not, and hope that the weather was good enough so we could fix the small hole and the bilge pump in time. It was 10.50pm but we might just make it up the hill before the pub closed. We wandered through the deserted harbour port looking for a way out. Owain then mentioned something none of us had even thought of.

'Aren't we in a new country? Shouldn't we have showed someone a passport or something? We could have sailed here from Somalia.'

He had a point. None of us had our passports on us and no one would know where we were from. In fact I had no ID on me whatsoever. From the point of view of anyone who met us wandering the harbour we had just sailed in and looking like a bunch of dirty refugees.

'We'll be fine,' said Jez and just grinned. I wasn't so confident. How did we overlook this?

Just then we saw a security guard waving at us. My heart sank. This was it. I was going to have to swim back to Wales or land up in jail for illegally entering a country. We walked over slowly trying to look as unthreatening as possible by putting Em at the front – although her hair now resembled a rat's nest and did us no favours in the refugee department.

'You must be looking for the pub,' said the security guard before we could even state our case. He had a pretty heavy Irish accent that was quite hard to understand. He continued.

'You better run like feck if you want to get last orders. Through that gate,' he pointed off to the left.

Brilliant. Possibly the worst security guard in the world. See four dirty people wandering around a port at 11pm and instead of ask what they are doing, send them to the pub. Welcome to Ireland. We didn't waste any time in case he started asking questions and immediately started running, shouting our thank yous as we disappeared into the darkness and up the hill towards the town above.

We found the pub just in time. It had Wi-Fi and true to the forecast we saw on an Irish news website that a tornado was due to hit Ireland in the night or early tomorrow. This would be an enforced bad weather rest day, which was slightly annoying because we had a few good weather rest days in Wales preparing for the crossing.

With all the drama of sinking boats and tornados we had neglected to get excited about finally reaching Ireland. We couldn't really celebrate because we technically hadn't made it across the Irish Sea yet as we were still a good 15 miles offshore. Also, Rosslare isn't exactly the most inspiring of places to land either, so all in all it felt a little underwhelming as we sat in the pub drinking Guinness in a corner. A far cry from the huge party I thought we'd have after completing the world's first ever Wales to Ireland swim.

We used the bad weather days to fix *Friday* and restock on supplies. Luckily *Friday*'s hole was above the waterline and only really affected us when we heeled over to the port side. We managed to plug it with a bit of wood and then rewired the automatic bilge pump. *Friday* was growing in character by the day with war wounds to show for her experiences.

Eventually, after three days in Rosslare without ever being asked for passports or any sort of ID whatsoever, we managed to get back to my swim point and I carried on heading north. I was close enough to Ireland now to only swim in the northerly tide and what a tide it was. Even in some pretty big rollers I managed to swim 18 miles in six hours heading towards Arklow, the point at which it was likely Swimming Britain would officially reach land in Ireland.

I was about to get ready to get into the water for the last session of the Irish Sea crossing when I heard a huge shout from Jez in the cockpit. He had a somewhat frantic tone to his voice. I'd never heard him sound distressed like this before, not even when *Friday* was sinking. I jumped out my bunk in a panic and burst into the cabin. I saw Jez bent over doing something on the floor of the cockpit, right above the engine, the stairs shielding what he was doing. It looked serious.

'What's up, mate? Everything all right?' I asked nervously.

'No, it's not all right. I spilt my coffee and I've waited ages for it to get to the right temperature,' he said, genuinely angry.

Making coffee isn't as easy as it sounds on a 50-year-old paraffin stove that takes a good 20 minutes to boil a kettle. I couldn't help but laugh though. The one thing that Jez can't do without is his coffee. *Friday* sinking was fixable. Not having coffee, a disaster.

Not having any land markers to swim towards was starting to be a real drain on morale as it often felt like I was swimming in the same spot. The waves too were pretty choppy, not big, just choppy because of the slight headwind making them shorten and bounce around. Also, because I had become so used to breathing to my right, in order to look at land in Cornwall, that changing to breathe on my left felt really weird. I was also swimming off to my left a lot more than usual. I could compensate for my wonkiness caused by the cheese rolling injury when I had something on shore to aim for, but without any markers within 100 metres I was swimming at 90 degrees to where I should have been going. It was pretty frustrating for the crew who would, every now and then, throw a fish at me to get my attention to swim in a straight line. With my earplugs in I could barely hear anything except my own breathing. This was happening a lot today but at least we were making good progress north.

I was also starting to feel incredibly cold in the water. I thought I was on top of my eating but obviously not. The cold was cutting me deep and I had lost most of my body fat. I decided to email Speedo and ask them for a smaller wetsuit.

Speedo later replied. They would post me two more adult extra small and one child extra large. I would not be impressed if I fit into a child's wetsuit, but anything to stop the cold water pouring down my back.

We got up early to head back to the swim spot. About 20 minutes into the commute we came to a sudden halt as if in a head-on collision. For a moment I thought we had hit a rock. The yacht then suddenly heeled over to the port side at quite a worrying angle. We went outside to have a look. Right off the side of *Friday* was a long rope going down into the depths. We followed it to the hull where we saw a black buoy tangled around the rudder. We had been caught on a lobster pot. This was far from ideal and was taking up precious swimming time.

Jez tried everything to try manoeuvre off the pot but nothing was working. This involved going full throttle back and forth, which inevitably involved us coming to a dead stop, sending most of *Friday*'s contents all over place.

'Someone's going to have to go in?' said Jez looking straight at me. That someone was obviously going to be me as I was already in my wetsuit.

'We need to cut the line unfortunately.'

I put the rest of my kit on and jumped overboard and went under *Friday*. The rope had been caught between the larger rudder and the hull. The only place I could cut the rope safely was about two metres down. I took a deep breath and feeling a little like James Bond swam with the knife in my teeth so that I had my hands free. The rope was at such tension that within a few cuts it snapped free, the recoil of the rope missing my face by a few inches. By the time I got up to the surface again *Friday* was a good 20 metres away, that's how strong the tide was. Jez then circled around and came back and picked me up. We carried on back to my swim point and I continued heading north.

The water was much calmer than it had been since we started the crossing to Ireland. We realised now that we were so close to land we were sheltered from the westerly wind. We hadn't planned this at all but we started to wonder and hope if we might have pretty calm waters all the way up the inside of Ireland. If the wind stayed from the west then surely we would? Of all the reasons to come to Ireland this was probably the best one, even though it hadn't been considered in our decision-making process.

The calm water stayed with us all morning and at around midday a thick blanket of low-lying mist mysteriously engulfed us. It became eerily quiet as I swam into nothingness, not being able to see much further than about 50 metres ahead. *Friday* would sail past and disappear into the mist like a stealthy pirate looking for treasure under the cover of fog. Moments later she'd reappeared and sail back past creating a small ripple, which was the only way we could tell the difference between water and sky. It was very eerie and certainly gave me fuel for my wild imagination, which helped me take my mind off the cold water.

We sat out the southerly tide and went again well into the night on the northerly tide. Again the phosphorescence were breathtaking and I kept asking Em to turn off her head torch so I could see them better. Jez didn't like this as he had no way of seeing where we were in the water. In hindsight this was very irresponsible but it was so calm and I figured they'd never be further than shouting distance from us. Although the sea was calm, the rain started to bucket down again. It didn't bother me but it was seriously miserable for Em and Jez who were out in the cold.

By 11pm we had made it to Arklow and technically finished the Irish crossing. We opened a bottle of champagne and had some cake to celebrate. It was good to be near land again. After one glass (or mug as we didn't have glasses) of champagne, I retired to my bunk as the next northerly tide was in five hours and I had to get up an hour before at 4am.

The wind picked up soon after getting into bed and both Em and I spent all night trying desperately to hold on to our bunks. There was also a very annoying BANG! whenever the front of *Friday* rose and dropped suddenly, making the anchor chain tighten suddenly. It was barely noticeable on deck but when our faces were 10 centimetres from where the anchor chain was, it would make the sound a million times worse. Slight vibration, BANG! Slight vibration, BANG! Every five seconds or so. It was torture.

When the alarm went at 3.45am, Em and I just laughed, in that overtired, 'I've given up' type of way. To make things worse, a headwind had picked up and the water seemed to be a lot colder but that was possibly because I had had no sleep and felt low. I swam past Arklow and did a good ten miles before nearly falling asleep in the water so called it a day and headed back to Arklow to stay in the marina and stock up on food.

I also had one of my best friends from South Africa coming to swim with me for a few days. It had all been a bit last-minute but he was waiting in Arklow to meet us. Although I knew it was going to be nice having a familiar face join the swim I was worried that we'd all get on each other's nerves on *Friday*, where things were already pretty cramped.

*

'Seano! My man. Bloody long time, bro,' said Kenton, as he swaggered through the pub to meet us.

Kenton is a 6 foot, 3 inch swimming machine. He has represented South Africa and even as a kid I remember him getting up at stupid o'clock to go training. When he heard I was doing this swim he decided he wanted to come all the way from South Africa to swim with me for a few days. Although I liked the idea I was concerned about how we'd all fit on *Friday*. Kent would have to sleep on the cold wet floor in between the two bunks in the main cabin, with his head slightly in the toilet because he is too tall. He's a proper bushman though so luckily that didn't bother him.

It was amazing having an outsider come and join us. Kent was so excited to be there it lifted all our spirits. He told us just how many people were following the swim in South Africa. My school was having weekly updates in assembly. It was nice to know that people were getting something from the swim. It definitely made me want to push harder.

That evening we had burgers on the boat and I got a visit from another close family friend who moved from Zimbabwe to Ireland. I felt like I was back home for a moment and the crew mocked me for slipping into a South African accent.

We woke up to perfectly calm and flat water. I was slightly annoyed as I wanted Kent to experience what we had experienced for the last week but welcomed the easy session. Having Kent there certainly made me step up my game. He was fresh-armed and a fast swimmer and at times I couldn't keep up with him. The one thing I had on him was he was not used to the cold, being African and all. He was constantly shivering, which made me laugh because the water was 16 degrees, the warmest it had been all swim. The tide was good and apart from a few jellyfish stings on our hands gained mostly from brushing them out the way, we swam a whopping 22 miles, my biggest day yet. We made it halfway across Dublin Bay. Kenton was like an excitable child and Em was enjoying the challenge of looking after two children at sea.

'Come now boys, swim together. Kenton! Stop swimming off like that. You're going to get lost,' she called to us. The mood of the crew was the highest it had been all swim and even though Kenton had to sleep on the manky floor he remained keen the entire time.

That evening we had yet another calm anchorage in Dublin Port. Kenton then took us out for dinner and a few pints before retiring for the night.

The next day, the wind finally picked up and Kenton got to experience what it was like to do some big wave swimming, as we headed across the rest of Dublin Bay and around the dramatic cliff-lined peninsula towards Howth. Kent loved it, and so did I for that matter, as we surfed down each wave below a lighthouse on the cliffs with a dark and stormy sky above. This was open-water swimming at its most extreme and what better way to share it than with a good mate.

We reached Howth in the early evening, still buzzing, and I was surprised to see Duane, Kenton's brother there.

He had flown over from London to visit us for the night. What a reunion, and a great end to a fantastic swim, the best so far. As we cracked into the beers we realised we had an email from the BBC to say that they were sending a cameraman down to film us for *The One Show* tomorrow. This would be great for the expedition and for War Child. It did however mean we weren't going to swim tomorrow, and I was disappointed for Kenton as I knew how keen he was to swim and he had to fly back to London tomorrow evening. Nevertheless, the few days he was with us were some of the best days of the swim so far.

Predictably, a few beers with Kenton and Duane turned out to be a few too many and I woke up with a pretty heavy head. *The One Show* presenter and crew had already arrived by the time we all frailly arose from the depths of *Friday*. The morning was spent filming on the boat, introducing everyone, including *Friday* and Stuart the Scab (who was now officially part of the crew) to the seven million-odd viewers who would watch it the following day. Everyone was enjoying getting creative with camera angles and telling their side of the story, except Jez, who has some sort of phobia of being photographed and spent most of the morning hiding behind one or all of us.

That afternoon we said our goodbyes to *The One Show* and sadly said goodbye to Kenton. Having him along for a few days was a much-needed boost to team morale and it was sad to see him walk down the pontoon with his bag over his shoulder like a sailor heading home.

That evening we headed off from Howth to make the most of the evening tide. As we left the harbour, Jez asked if I wanted to swim across the next bay or follow the coast, which was an extra 12 miles. The bay was 25 miles wide and I had been doing around 18 miles per day so decided we should cut across. I really needed to make up some mileage. Today was Day 41, which was a little over halfway in time but I had only covered just over a third of the distance.

8
SLACK BAY

We weren't quite at the start of the bay just yet, so the plan was to get as close as possible to it so that I could do most of the crossing the following day. Northern Ireland was on the other side of the bay and a definite psychological milestone to look forward to.

Another incredible evening of swimming with phosphorescence was slightly dampened by the sudden increase in jellyfish stings to the face. Normally, whenever I got stung I'd roll over onto my back and try to rub some of the stings off. This time I didn't bother and just pushed through. When you get stung once all over your face you stop caring about the next sting. The one thing I did notice was that where my beard was coming through I wasn't getting stung as badly. This must have been due to the fact my facial hair was stopping the tentacles from actually hitting my face. I had a hard decision to make. I could either shave and be more streamlined but get stung in the face, which would slow me down, or start growing a beard to protect me and hopefully not get stung so much. I'd see how the next week panned out before deciding.

I got stung so many times during the rest of the evening session that by the end I had already made up my mind. I'd happily sacrifice being streamlined for a facial-hair-jellyfish-protection-shield. They really were that bad. The beard not only needed to stay, it needed to get bigger.

Off in the distance I could see the other side of the bay. It looked a lot closer than 25 miles away. We needed to make this shortcut. We were a few weeks behind schedule now and I had to make it up some time somehow. And yet by the end of the day I had only covered ten miles in two sessions in the water. It dawned on me that the further and further I got into the bay the slower I was swimming. I was now only just over a third of the way across the bay, which also meant we were now too far into the heart of the bay to turn back for an anchorage, so we'd most likely need to spend the night at sea.

I looked at the tidal charts to see what we were dealing with. There in big letters it read 'slack' for most of the day. I asked Jez what this was all about.

'Basically, as the Atlantic fills up, the water rushes around the top and the bottom of Ireland and meets in the middle here. This means there is no tide. Instead, the water just rises up and down in one spot, and more often than not just swirls around in all directions.'

'Really? So basically I have no tide to help me get across the bay.'

'Probably not,' said Jez in his nonchalant way.

'Shit, man. I wish I had known this,' I said, bothered that it looked like we had inadvertently taken on another surprise crossing thrown at us without notice. At this rate it would take three days to cross 'Slack Bay'. That was as much time as it took us to cross from Wales to Ireland.

'We'll be fine, it's much quicker than going along the edge and you said you needed to make up some mileage,' replied Jez still looking at the charts. He had a point. Even if I had known I probably would have stubbornly said, 'Yes, let's do it.' I had become so used to doing proper mileage in the last week I couldn't have predicted just how hard and slow Slack Bay would be.

Annoyed, I retired to my bunk and tried to get into a positive mental attitude to smash out the miles tomorrow and get across the bay. There was no point in dwelling on it. We were too far into the bay to change anything. We just had to get on with it. The only thing slightly different to a normal crossing was that we could drop anchor, which meant the crew didn't need to do night shifts as we floated aimlessly. Incredibly, *Friday* had a 60-metre chain and we were in 33 metres of water, which meant, although not recommended, we could drop anchor. The general rule is you need three times as much anchor chain to allow the anchor to go out at an angle and take grip. An anchor going straight down from a boat is not effective. Technically, *Friday* could only anchor safely in 20 metres of water so 33m was a bit risky and we were likely to drift. Jez said he'd keep an eye on the GPS. In any case you could hear the anchor dragging along the bottom, which usually woke you up anyway.

As much as I tried to sleep, I just couldn't. This was the second night in a row that the rocking and the vibration BANG! of the anchor chain tightening prevented us from sleeping, pushing Em and I to the verge of sure madness. Four times in the night I went out the front hatch on deck and tried to put something under the chain to stop the banging. Nothing worked. Eventually the sun came up and it was time to get in the water again. My chest was tight and I was shivering even before I got in. This was the weakest I had felt all swim, which wasn't surprising considering I'd only had two to three hours' sleep in the past 48 hours.

We all got up slowly preparing for the next session. The mood on the boat was not good, a stark contrast to where we were only a few days earlier. I'd tried hard to get in a positive mindset, but no matter how good an attitude you have, sleep deprivation takes everything out of you. There wasn't much talking as we all did our various chores for the morning session.

The day was long and slow, my immune system was low and the cold was cutting right to my core. I vomited a few times too, which I hadn't done in a while, the slightest taste of salt water making me heave and retch. It was so demoralising swimming in water that didn't really know what it was doing. It was swirling all over the place, and in some patches I'd be against tide and other the tide would push me sideways. Progress was still slow and every time

I asked for a progress report it was usually around 1mph. As the hours went by, the colder I got, and I started to feel the swim slipping away from me. It seemed that every few days we'd somehow drop a day and fall further behind schedule, which was putting me under a lot of pressure. I was constantly thinking about the bad weather closing in or the crew deciding they had had enough. I really needed to be doing 15-20 miles a day to get to Scotland in time. I was very behind schedule already and if I carried on at this rate the swim would take another three months, taking us well into winter. Trying to swim in winter in Scotland would surely be impossible.

I began to sob quietly in the water while still swimming, my tears filling up the inside of my goggles. I didn't want the crew to know I was crying so started to breathe on the other side, away from Em. I knew the sleep deprivation was causing most of my negativity but that didn't help. For the next hour I increased the salt content in the Irish Sea as I let out tears from my goggles while pretending to cough and stretch my shoulder. By the end of the session we were still a good ten miles from the end of the bay and would again have to drop anchor in the middle of the bay, this time at a depth of 44 metres.

Just as we were going to bed Owain got another email from *The One Show* saying they wanted to do a live feed with us from Newcastle in Northern Island tomorrow evening as they had David Walliams, who has swum the English Channel as well as the length of the River Thames, on the show. That was about 15 miles ahead of where we were. There was no way I'd be able to swim there so we'd have to start making progress at around 10am in order to get there in time. This meant I could just about get four hours during the morning's session.

Again, I only managed about an hour's sleep. This surprise crossing was turning out to be the worst decision I had made all swim. I had now only had around three to four hours' sleep in the last 72 hours. That's four hours' sleep away from clinical insanity. Jez had let out all 60 metres of chain for our 44 metres' anchorage and it took him and Owain over an hour to ratchet the chain up using the mast winch, swapping from the left winch to the right winch as they pulled up 50 centimetres at a time. The chain weighed well over 100kg and was impossible to pull up by hand.

We had anchored on my swim point so Em and I left Jez and Owain hauling the anchor and began my session. Within seconds of being in the water I could feel my body seizing up. I had no energy and was shivering so profusely I could barely move my arms. I checked the water temp on my watch and it showed 12 degrees, four degrees colder than it had been. Although it didn't sound like much it really was making a difference. I could barely swim 1mph. My body was just too tired and cold.

Em sensed something wasn't right.

'Ginge, I think you need to stop, this is ridiculous.'

'I know, but I can't, we need to …' I stopped mid-sentence. I felt like crying as the fear of this swim not being possible crept into my thoughts again.

'Come on, Ginge, let's go to Newcastle and have a few days' rest and carry on faster. There is no point in doing 1mph.'

By now Jez and Owain had pulled up the anchor and were heading over to us.

'We're done,' Em shouted to them.

'OK, fair enough,' said Jez as he looped round bringing the RIB near me so I could get out the water. I felt like a failure. I only managed one mile and barely so. If I had known I was only going to swim one mile I would have asked Jez to take us to Newcastle last night and avoid a pretty horrendous anchorage. We were all feeling like shit and it was all my fault because I had said we should swim across the bay. Everything was on me now and the one thing I was meant to be doing, swimming, wasn't even happening. I lay down on my bunk and began to cry again and fell asleep for the first time in days as Jez did the six-hour journey to Newcastle fuelled by lots and lots of coffee.

We reached Newcastle by early evening and went straight to the hotel where they were going to film me. I was really nervous about being on the show again, so soon after the first time, when things really weren't going to plan and the likelihood of me actually completing this swim was growing ever more distant. I tried not to think about it and needed to stay positive, both for my own mindset and so as not to dissuade people from donating money to War Child. If it seemed that I might not make it then people surely wouldn't donate. I needed to be upbeat about the situation, even though I didn't feel remotely confident.

The hotel had kindly given us a free room and then on top of that the producer for *The One Show* had paid out of his own pocket to upgrade us to the suites. An actual bed for each of us. The last proper bed any of us had slept in was that weekend in Clovelly, which was nearly a month ago. At least something was looking up.

We did the live feed to *The One Show* where presenters Matt Baker and Alex Jones seemed genuinely interested in the swim. I had met Matt before when he did his rickshaw ride to London, but I was sure there was no way he would remember so kept quiet! They showed the footage of us that they filmed in Howth, which really did look incredible. They even somehow made me seem quite cool! David Walliams was on the show and he called me annoying for doing a harder swim than his, which I quite enjoyed. It was obviously tongue in cheek, but it cheered us up to be able to talk positively about the swim, and know people were interested. It took our minds off the fact that we still hadn't crossed Slack Bay, and we all ignored the fact that we needed to go back out there sooner or later.

After all the excitement of the TV activities, we went for an amazing Indian dinner, a few pints, the world's longest bath (the first proper bath for me) and then passed out. Beds, and dry ones at that, are seriously underrated and I vowed never to take my bed for granted ever again. Even Jez opted for a land-bed instead of going back to *Friday*.

I slept for 12 hours straight, but still had a tight chest so bought some chest medicine. We spent the day stocking up the boat and I tried to eat as much fatty foods as possible to put some weight on. I needed to do something about my increasing weight loss. The block of butter every couple of days wasn't working. I also bought some more iodine for Stuart the Scab. He hadn't grown over the last week or so and seemed to be settling down, but he was still revealing the red flesh inside my foot.

Arthur's RIB engine was playing up again. It took ages to start and would cut out sometimes. I hated RIB engines, especially this one, as I had spent nearly as much as buying one in getting it fixed and it still wasn't working well.

Technically I had had two full days of not swimming but I didn't feel rested at all. We were 15 miles from my swim point so we got up early to head back. I'd hopefully be able to do a night session.

In the end, it took us over two days to get back to my swim point. As soon as we left the comfort of Newcastle bay we were faced with strong headwinds and waves. *Friday*'s pace dropped down to 1mph as we nearly came to a standstill every time we hit an oncoming wave. Jez was doing all he could but by early afternoon, after being battered for 8 hours, we had only done just over eight miles. It was pointless trying to fight the waves so we headed to the nearest shore and anchored up for the night.

The following day was exactly the same as we were thrown around *Friday* all day as Jez heroically manned the fort for hour upon hour to get us back to my swim point. By the end of the day we were still two miles from the point. Instead of doing a 44 metre anchor in the middle of the bay like before, Jez decided to head another two hours towards the coast for a better anchorage, which was a much better plan. It was a lot calmer nearer the shore, which was incredibly annoying as if I had decided to follow the shore we'd have had good anchorages, calm water and better sleep. We were obviously falling further and further behind schedule, but after four full rest days I felt a whole lot better for it.

The weather took a turn for the better too and I had an easy morning session of flat water as I made my way towards Kilkeel. We had decided to start heading slightly in towards land so that we'd be closer to shore for calm anchoring. Even if it added another 20 miles we weren't going to drop anchor in 40 metres of water ever again. By the end of the session just as I was feeling good again, Jez announced that there was a gale warning and we needed to head to Kilkeel harbour for shelter. This was incredibly frustrating as I really did not need any more non-swimming days.

Kilkeel was a huge fishing port and *Friday* looked ever so dwarfed next to the huge trawlers all rafted up waiting out the imminent storm. Although old and rickety she really had done us well so far. What she lacked in amenities she made up for in pure guts and determination. Jez definitely had a soft spot for her. We all did. She was the fifth crew member and probably the most important.

We rafted alongside two trawlers that weren't going out due to engine problems and settled in for the night. It was likely that we would have to stay in the harbour for a few days due to bad weather.

'Ginge, I'm so sorry!' Em came into the front cabin. I was still half asleep.

'I've dropped your wallet and it's fallen in the water between the wall and a ship. It fell out my pocket when I was climbing up the ladder.'

Em, being crew captain, had been in charge of food shopping and general logistics and had my wallet to go and buy some supplies.

She looked so upset that I tried to make light of the situation. 'Don't worry, dude. It only had a hundred pounds in it. You'll just have to forfeit a few beers over the next few weeks.'

There wasn't anything in the wallet that I really needed and could easily get a new card sent out in a day or two. It wasn't worth stressing over. I had other issucs to deal with, mainly in my mind and the number of non-swimming days I had had in the last week. Em, however, felt really guilty and left the cabin sheepishly apologising.

I got dressed and went out on deck to find a group of people gathering round the ladder trying to look down the one-foot wide gap between one of the fishing boats and the harbour wall. The next thing I saw was a guy called Steve dressing in full drysuit diving gear on the boat.

'What's going on?' I asked.

'This is Steve, he's going to dive for the wallet,' replied Em.

How on earth had this all happened so quickly? I was asleep ten minutes ago! Turns out the fisherman who we were rafted to, Joe, knew Steve and called him to come and help us. He didn't even question it and was there in a jiffy. How kind. Moments later, before I even had time to give my thanks, he was overboard and disappeared between the wall and the boat with a torch. We all waited anxiously, mostly for Steve's safety, as getting pinned between a 30-ton boat and a harbour wall would be fatal.

Steve tried for a good half an hour before giving up. The wallet probably floated away at an angle and with a slight tide could be 50 metres away in any direction. Steve was incredibly apologetic for not being able to find it, which made Em feel even more guilty. I too felt bad that he had gone out of his way to help some random strangers he hadn't even met before. What a true gentleman.

For some reason, Joe the fisherman also felt guilty and somehow managed to find us two huge fish and some seaweed-grown potatoes for dinner. I didn't know what fish they were but frying them in butter and lemon juice moments after gutting them made them taste heavenly.

That night I went to bed feeling a lot better for experiencing some real kindness from Joe and Steve. When people helped me, I felt I should repay their kindness by swimming harder and faster and completing the swim. That inspired me to stop messing around and feeling sorry for myself and just keep going.

The weather improved and we headed back out into the bay to hopefully do the last session before leaving the curse of Slack Bay behind us for good. Although feeling more positive there was nothing I could do to improve my pace, which was just over 1mph. I had been swimming now for 50 days and I guess my body had reached a state of fatigue that would take weeks to recover from. I didn't have weeks and just had to carry on as best I could. I only managed five and a half miles in the session and we headed to shore to sit out the tide. Just as we anchored up, a ray of sunshine broke below the dark and stormy sky creating the most glorious and wonderful full double rainbow any of us had ever seen. We all just stood there staring at the vivid colours contrasting against the dark grey clouds. Then, as quickly as it appeared, it disappeared again returning the momentarily magical oil painting back to a dull and murky seascape. We had four hours at this anchorage so Jez and Em decided to go ashore and do some exploring. I needed to get some sleep and fatten up. Owain, inspired by last night's fish, decided to catch some mackerel for dinner.

Owain caught five fish that we fried for dinner just before my night session, which started at 11pm. Fish have essential fats which are good for recovery and I really needed to make an effort to eat more. Luckily Owain loved fishing otherwise the only other option was to tie a line around my waist and try to catch some while I swam. I was actually intrigued to try this but didn't want to mess up my new extra small wetsuit that Speedo had sent me. (Happily I had retained my manliness: the child's wetsuit didn't fit me.)

Pace dropped even further and further as I pulled my way through millions of phosphorescence well into the night. I got out of the water at 2.45am, just five miles from the end of Slack Bay. Even if I did doggy paddle, I was determined to get out of this hellhole tomorrow and back into some tidal water again.

We were at the time of the month when most of the second tide was from midnight till 6am, so I decided to just make the most of the one daytime tide in the next few days. Although swimming at night was doable, it was putting a noticeable strain on the crew and at this point in time I was concerned that they'd stop enjoying the expedition and leave. I really didn't know how we would cope in that situation. None of them had hinted they weren't enjoying it but I didn't want to risk forcing the issue. They were, after all, volunteering their time. I needed to make sure it wasn't becoming a chore for them. Having a crew was very different from when I cycled around the world. Then I was on my own and didn't have anyone to look after me, or for me to think about. I really needed to keep the crew's experience in mind as I wanted them to have an adventure too.

9
THE DEPARTURE OF JEZ

'Sean, I've got some bad news,' said Jez sheepishly.

Still half asleep, I sat up and bumped my head on the ceiling above me. It hurt like hell.

'Really?' I asked nervously, rubbing my head. He looked more worried than the time he spilt his coffee.

'I've just been offered a job back in London and I think I'm going to take it ...'

Jez carried on talking but I didn't hear any of it. My first thought was that I bloody jinxed it last night by thinking about the crew leaving. Without a skipper I couldn't carry on the swim. My heart sank. I had no luck whatsoever trying to find a skipper at the beginning. How was I going to find another one now? I then immediately started to think about all the times I didn't swim fast enough, for taking those four days off in Clovelly and another four days in Newcastle. A hundred 'if onlys' that could have put me closer to the end by now.

'When do you need to leave?' I eventually managed to open my mouth and speak coherently.

'I need to leave for London a week tomorrow.'

So I had a week to find a skipper. Not only did I need someone who could sail a yacht, I needed someone young and enthusiastic enough to deal with the pretty cramped and now very damp conditions on *Friday*.

'OK. You gotta do what you gotta do. Can you try and see if you can find someone though from your boat connections?'

'Yes, mate. I'll ask for sure. If we push it I can get you across to Scotland again and you and Em might be able to continue with land support in the worst case scenario,' Jez suggested.

It wasn't ideal, those first few days in Cornwall when it was just Em and me were a real struggle, but he did have a point. I could always ask my mum to drive my car up and get Owain to drive it along the coast. This was providing we got across to Scotland before Jez had to leave.

I got in the water feeling pretty helpless. There were just so many hurdles in this challenge that had nothing to do with my swimming ability that were hindering its success. Not having a skipper was potentially a deal-breaker, right up there with *Friday* sinking. Just when I thought things would get better once we left Slack Bay.

For the next two days my mind was consumed with ways to try and find a new skipper. I was swimming as much as possible trying to make as much progress as I could to get across to Scotland while using every break to

Tweet, Facebook, put posts on yachting forums and blog to find someone who might be interested.

At the end of the second day, we were hit with another blow. We anchored up to sit out the southerly tide and when we went to start the engine nothing worked. Click! Click! Click! There was a strong sulphur smell coming from the starter battery.

'Smells like battery problems,' said Owain straight away. I knew his engine knowledge would come in useful.

'I think we've fried them,' added Jez who also knew exactly what had happened.

Friday had two batteries, a starter one to get the engine going and a leisure one for charging things on the boat. For some reason the starter battery was fried and the leisure battery didn't have enough volts to start the engine. We sat for ages trying to decide what to do. It was 5pm and the nearest town was ten miles away. It was too late to get there tonight, and by the time we got there and back in the morning I'd have missed the tide, putting me yet another day behind schedule, a day I didn't have as it was tight whether I'd get to Scotland before Jez left already. I didn't need any more delays.

Just when we had resigned to the fact we were going to miss a session, a chap on a stand up paddle board and another guy on a blow-up kayak suddenly appeared out of nowhere. We had been so focused on the battery we hadn't seen them sneak up on us.

'How yous doin'?' said the guy on the SUP in a friendly Northern Irish accent.

'Not bad, just got a dead battery,' replied Owain.

'Really, what's wrong with it?'

'We fried it, I think.'

'Really? Well you're in luck today because I happen to have a spare battery in my van.'

'Seriously?' we all asked in unison.

'Any chance we could buy it off you?' Owain asked immediately.

'Well, let's see if it works first. Come on. It's just over there. We're Simon by the way. Both of us are Simon.'

Simon and Simon paddled towards the shore and we followed in the RIB, which had now finally given up all life, yet another thing adding to the list of things going wrong. Luckily Jez was good at rowing.

There were a few houses on the cliff tops but no sign of life whatsoever. Simon's black camper van was the only car in the car park. There was also a huge 'E' statue right next to the small harbour. Apparently we were at the most easterly part of Ireland. Em clambered on the statue for a few photos. The mood of the crew always lifted when we had company, mostly because none of us really wanted to admit just how hard things were, as this might open up the inevitable 'you didn't think this through' or 'we told you so' conversation. Instead it was easier to pretend all was well.

We chatted with the Simons for about an hour while charging up the spare battery. Simon not only had a spare battery, but also had jump leads and a voltmeter so we could see how charged it was. It was absolutely incredible.

The first time we see someone at sea since the kayaker at Hartland Point is when we have battery problems and he happens to have the solution for us.

Once the battery was charged Jez rowed it back to *Friday* and gave us the thumbs up to say all was well. Simon insisted we have the battery as he wasn't using it. Just when we thought we'd experienced all the kindness we could with Joe and Scuba Steve in Kilkeel, someone else comes to our rescue. We offered to buy Simon a pint but he said he had to get home so we said our goodbyes.

I managed to get almost to the Belfast crossing by the end of my first session. Things were looking up, the tide was strong again and I managed eight miles in four hours, double what I had been swimming in Slack Bay. We rested out the southerly tide and I managed to get some sleep as we prepared to cross the 10-mile Belfast Channel in one go. This would be by far the busiest shipping lane I would have to cross and conditions needed to be perfect. Unfortunately, when it was time to get back in the water a thick layer of fog engulfed most of the eastern coastline reducing visibility to less than 100 metres. There was no way we could cross a busy shipping lane in such dense fog. We'd most certainly get run over. To make things worse the weather forecast suggested tomorrow would be even worse. I seemed to be not swimming more than swimming at the moment. Besides those few glory days with Kenton, this Ireland leg was proving to be a lot harder than any of us had imagined: tornadoes, Slack Bay, broken engines and soon, I'd be skipperless. The mood on the boat was at an all-time low and there was only one way to fix that, I thought.

'Pub. Open bar on me, guys,' I suggested knowing we wouldn't be swimming tomorrow. Nothing a few beers couldn't fix. That was my way of showing my appreciation to the crew. And that was pretty much the last thing I remembered from that night.

'Mate, the forecast was wrong. We gotta go now,' said Jez, looking about as bad as I felt, peeping his head into the front cabin.

For a moment I had completely forgotten where I was and what I was doing as my head felt like it was about to explode.

'Hah?' I asked not sure if I had heard correctly.

'We need to go, the mist has cleared and it's glass,' Jez shouted.

'Shit? Really. OK, I'm up.'

I closed my eyes again. I had the enthusiasm of a sloth and sounded like Johnny Cash. Glimpses of last night started coming back, including Em trying to row us from the pub back to *Friday*, going in circles many, many times, crashing into three other boats and the harbour wall eventually giving up to Jez. I remember laughing so much I nearly fell into the water but recalled that at the time I wouldn't have minded a cold dip. It would have been a different scenario if I had in fact fallen in, although it might have sobered me up. All in all it had been a fun night and

I think was exactly what we all needed. I now, however, needed to pretend to know how to swim, and not any old swim either, swim across the dauntingly terrifying Belfast Channel. 'Right. It's very important you do as I say. If I say swim you swim hard. When I say stop, you stop. OK?' Jez told Em as I jumped in the freezing water, making my head pound even harder, which completely undermined the 'it'll sober you up notion'. It most certainly didn't.

I swam for about an hour before Jez gave the first order to stop. We stopped and let a terrifyingly fast ferry whizz past us creating a washing machine of water turbulence behind it. I then swam hard for 20 minutes to get ahead of the next ferry which went close behind us. We weren't using the sails but had them up anyway just so we'd become more visible to the oncoming ships. It took three hours to cross the Belfast Channel as we played chicken with various ferries and tankers and eventually were in the now even faster moving tide of the north-east coast.

All I remember for the rest of the session was throwing up a few times and getting one seriously bad jellyfish sting to the face, which on top of a pretty bad hangover, was possibly my least favourite life experience to date.

I somehow swam 18 miles that session, and only Hercules knows how, as I was feeling pretty horrendous. I had at least made up some mileage that I had lost and it looked like I would just get over to Scotland in time. The first smidgeon of positivity in a while was very welcome.

Later that evening, anchored up in one of the calmest bays yet, we met up again with Simon (who helped us with the battery). He had offered to collect a parcel of new thermals that I had had sent to Larne a few days earlier. Not only did he collect them but he then took us into Belfast to do some shopping as we were pretty low on food on the boat. He wanted nothing in return either and just really wanted to help us on our way. It was people like Simon who made me want to complete the swim more than ever and I went to bed that night with a new determination to find another skipper.

I was 13 miles away from the North Channel crossing and 24 or so miles away from reaching the Mull of Kintyre in Scotland, at which point I could potentially carry on with land support. I still hadn't had one reply from anyone even interested in being a skipper. I had two days to do this before Jez had to leave. A fairly tall order but after my 18-mile day yesterday, I was feeling confident.

The afternoon tide only started at 2pm and we were ready and in place, a few hundred metres offshore, a few hours before I needed to get in. *Friday* was pointing north facing the oncoming tide while anchored. As soon as her bow swung round to the south it meant the tide had changed and it was time to get in. The conditions started out calm but, typically, as I jumped in, the wind changed to headwind and the sea became very bouncy. Jez decided it would be best to start the crossing early on so that by the time we got to the narrow, and possibly dangerous, North Channel crossing, I'd be most of the way across already. I pushed hard all session but only managed eight miles as we started to make our way towards the Mull (of Kintyre) which was directly north of us, a disappointing distance, as this now meant I had to swim 16 miles tomorrow.

Here it was. My final day with Jez as my skipper. I was obviously gutted because I needed a skipper to continue but having someone leave the expedition halfway through was really sad. We had become a family and it was awful to see him go and not experience sailing through Scotland, which could arguably be the best section of all. Jez had put in some seriously long hours in the cold and rain getting me to and from each swim point and never once complained. So long as his coffee thermos was full, he was happy. It definitely wouldn't be the same without him.

I needed to give it everything in today's session. If I didn't make Scotland I'd be stuck in Northern Ireland and therefore need a skipper to get me over to the Mull. This is one of the most treacherous stretches of water in the UK, and only one person in history has ever swam it. Wayne Soutter swam it but started in Scotland and swam to Northern Ireland. He said he chose that direction because the tide was so strong he feared he'd miss Scotland if he started in NI. No one has ever swum it from Northern Ireland. I was finding it impossible to get a skipper for normal sailing so finding one that was happy to take the responsibility for me in that stretch of water would, dare I say it, be impossible. I had no option but to get to Scotland today. I jumped in with a new burst of energy.

Scotland would be mine by the end of the day.

10

SHATTERED DREAMS

I lay face-down on my bunk and, for the second time, began to weep uncontrollably. We'd been forced to abandon the crossing at the end of the last tide just four miles short from Scottish soil. We had no choice but to find the best anchorage to leave *Friday* and go ashore. This was a small harbour in Northern Ireland called Glenarm. That was two days ago and the sight of Jez walking down the pontoon and away from the expedition was haunting me. For the past two nights I'd dreamt that he got to the end of the pontoon and then turned around and said, 'Actually. I'm staying now.' I'd wake up and go through to his bunk to see an empty space and realise it was just a dream.

I sent the crew home to see their families and was now all alone in Northern Ireland in a last bid to see if I could find a new skipper, but I knew that the odds were against me.

Friday was an eerily weird place to be all alone. Some important things, like Owain's laptop, Jez's sleeping bag and Em's rucksack, all things that symbolised the adventure was still happening, were gone, and without them there was an overwhelming sense that this adventure was over. *Friday* felt old and dishevelled and her flaws that were once a sign of character and perseverance, now seemed unfixable faults resulting in her being unable to continue.

She was finally broken.

I was finally broken, physically and mentally.

Together we lay there engulfed by the reality that neither of us might ever go back out to sea again.

In all my searching, both before the swim and in the past week, I hadn't even got an, 'I'm interested, tell me more,' email or Tweet. Nothing! Deep down I knew that this was the end of the swim. I didn't get out of bed for two days except to go to the toilet. Nothing mattered any more. All I could think about was packing up everything on *Friday*, who I'd have to sell here in Northern Ireland, and heading home, no doubt to a bombardment of 'I told you so' emails from all the negative voices. Every time I thought of that an overwhelming sense of panic engulfed me. I closed my eyes again and fell asleep.

After three days, I decided to actually do something about it instead of sitting and crying and staring blankly at the last marked day on the toilet door map – Scotland still blank, daunting and worryingly large. I was convinced the map people had got the proportions wrong and expanded Scotland due to widening of the latitude lines when printing a flat map.

I had also run out of food and needed to get up anyway so I went to the local pub to enquire about skippers. I got a few contacts for fishermen and some elderly retired boat owners who might like to help. I sent a few emails and left a few voice messages. I then made the 45-minute walk to the nearest town with a supermarket and bought some food to take back to *Friday*.

The next day I did the same thing in a different town a bit further north. I enquired in pubs, coffee shops, the post office … anywhere that might be able to help. I sent more emails, made more calls and carried on Tweeting.

I did this for eight days until I was forced to admit to myself that I had run out of options. The closest I got was a guy who charted RIB tours along the coast. He initially said he could do it for £1,000 (£500 for each return leg to the Mull to follow me and then take all our kit to the other side) but he then changed his mind as he wasn't sure about insurance and liability.

With each failed day, the more I came to terms with the fact the swim was over. Em had come back to help me but also to collect her stuff to go home. This was it, my dreams of becoming the first person to swim the length of Britain was all but over, and the most annoying thing was that it was something that was out of my control and not due to my swimming ability. There was no more crying, no more panic attacks, as I pushed everything out my mind to prepare with the inevitable emails I was about to get for not completing the challenge.

My parents were feeling pretty sorry for me and Dad had said he'd buy me a flight back to South Africa to rest up, get away from it all, decide what to do in life and recover from yet another failed attempt at an adventurous challenge.

Em was in the pub already when I went up to join her and get Wi-Fi to email my sponsors to say it was all over. I walked in and she greeted me with a huge smile. Before I could ask her what was going on I received a message on my phone. It was from Jez. It read:

'Mate. I can take this Monday off work and come up and get you to Scotland if you want. Let me know.'

Em started shouting. 'Did you get his message? That's good news Ginge! We can get across the channel!'

She was brimming with excitement. But I wasn't so sure. I had already accepted the swim was over and getting across the channel would just be delaying what seemed to be inevitable failure of Swimming Britain. Land support was a nice idea and doable up the Mull and maybe a bit further on, but once out in the Hebrides it wasn't really a feasible option because of the huge cliffs and lack of roads.

'Yeah, I'm not sure.'

'Come on, Ginge! We can get there and look for a skipper in Scotland when we don't have to make the crossing.'

Em's enthusiasm did help but it was still hard to be positive. I then felt guilty for putting her under the pressure to make me happy. Trying to make a depressed person happy can be very frustrating and I didn't want to be 'that guy'. She had a point though. The crossing seemed to be the one thing deterring skippers and with that out the way we'd possibly have more chance. I knew I had to do everything I could for fear of future regret. I replied to Jez accepting his offer and told Owain to come back too. Opening up my emails, I read a few messages from various people mainly asking about what kit I was swimming in. I worked my way through them until one in particular caught my attention. It was from Lou, from Nomad Sailing, who had helped Jez get *Friday* to Land's End. I hadn't heard from her in a while. I opened it.

Hey Sean

Twitter tells me you need a skipper. I'm in Turkey at the moment but am flying back in four days and can give you ten days of my time if you can cover the cost for me to hire another skipper to run my theory classes while I am away. Should be around £200. If you can do that then I'm yours for ten days.

Hope everything else is well. Hear from you soon.

Lou

xxx

I couldn't believe it. Two days with Jez and then ten days with Lou would not only get me quite far up Scotland but give me more time to find another skipper. Just when all hope was gone, like jump leads to the heart I felt alive again. I also noticed for the first time that Stuart the Scab had almost entirely healed. It's amazing how positivity leads to more positivity. Swimming Britain was on, at least for another 12 days.

*

Jez returned on Friday night but annoyingly we couldn't swim on the Saturday due to gale-force winds. Typical. It had been calm for the past few days. This meant we only had Sunday with Jez and he'd have to leave on the Monday, which was the day Lou was coming. We had to make it over to Scotland by then as that's where Lou was meeting us.

I had mixed emotions leaving Glenarm Harbour, my lonely home for the past 12 days. I was on the one hand happy to see it disappear behind me, as it was associated with so much negativity and broken dreams as I tried to find a new skipper. On the other hand, I was leaving the safety of a harbour to be placed right in the middle of one of Britain's most notoriously dangerous stretches of water, the North Channel. If conditions turned for the worse, neither *Friday* nor myself would be able to cope with the strong currents and potentially huge waves. Luckily, for now, the conditions were near perfect and 12 days' rest had helped me put on some much-needed weight and heal some seriously weak shoulder muscles. Although still not completely recovered I was in a much better position to tackle this stretch of water than I had been two weeks ago.

It was now the 8 September, five days from when I should have finished the swim. If things had gone to plan I should have been along the north coast of Scotland by now. Instead I was yet to even reach Scottish soil. The water temperature wouldn't drop for another few weeks but the weather was going to get progressively worse the further north I went and the closer to October I got.

I figured I'd take another month to finish the swim, if all things went to plan, hoping to finish around the 10 October.

It was exhilarating getting back in the water just south of the Mull of Kintyre.

'You're just at the end of the penis, mate,' Owain laughed and pointed to his groin, which was a little out of character but great to see him in a good mood. He was referring to the Mull of Kintyre Rule, which is an unofficial guideline used by the British Board of Film Classification as the benchmark to decide whether a man's penis could be shown on TV. If the 'angle of dangle' as it is known, is greater than that of the Mull of Kintyre, which, with the Isle of Arran off to the east, looks very much like male genitalia, then the penis could not be shown on TV. It had made us all laugh when we found out about it, and it was nice to see the crew banter back again. What better way to kick off than with some pretty offensive penis jokes, as I swam towards the tip, no pun intended.

The current was so strong I had to swim in a north-easterly direction in order to make any progress into the Mull as the tide whipped me round the south-west corner. If I didn't swim fast enough I wouldn't make the current that goes into the Mull and instead be caught in the current that splits off to America, which would be far from ideal. The tide was the fastest I had ever swam in and at times was pushing seven knots. Not only would I not be able to fight the tide, but *Friday* wasn't powerful enough either. If we did get flung towards America we'd have to just point

Friday north and we'd hopefully find shelter somewhere on Islay, which is west of Kintyre.

Thankfully I made it, and by the end of the session I was firmly inside the Mull of Kintyre's northerly current, so we went ahead and found a safe anchorage to do the skipper swap in the morning. Reaching Scotland felt very different to reaching Ireland. It was more of a sense of relief rather than the celebration we'd previously experienced. I had been staring at Kintyre from Glenarm for weeks and it was nice to know I could finally put it behind me. I was now in Scotland and on my final leg. If I averaged 15 miles per day, nine miles in the first tide and six in the second, in the ten days I had Lou with me, I'd get near Skye and a good way up towards Cape Wrath. From there surely I'd be close enough to the end for a potential skipper to say 'well you've come this far and haven't drowned, so I'll help you'? For now though, it was just good to be making progress again, and a small light of hope started to glow in my heart again.

'It's Lou!' Em shouted as we saw a figure a few hundred metres away, walking along the beach towards where we had come ashore.

Lou was in her late forties and petite in stature. Even though she was small she had a confident swagger, the type that you want from a skipper. She looked ever so cool walking along with her duffel bag and sporty sunglasses casually balanced on top of her short silver hair. We, on the other hand, weren't so cool, and downed our game of cricket and ran around in circles like overexcited puppies, led mainly by Em, whose bounding enthusiasm seemed to be at a whole new level. I think she was just glad to have another girl on the expedition. Living on a 26-foot yacht for the past 70 days with three smelly boys probably wasn't much fun, although she never once complained.

We said our goodbyes to Jez and welcomed Lou to Swimming Britain. It was sad to see Jez walk off down the beach.

We packed everything into the RIB and got the oars out. I offered to row but Em insisted I rest my shoulders and she would do it. Lou looked confused.

'Guys, you have an outboard,' she said.

'Yeah, it broke a long time ago and it's now more of a decoration.' If it was my engine I would have happily left it somewhere in a marina but seeing as it was Arthur's engine, I figured I should keep it.

We hadn't made it more than 10 metres when the first wave crashed over all of us soaking Lou through to the bone. Em continued to struggle on doing a few circles on route.

'I can row quite well. Let me do it,' Lou kept laughingly suggesting as we went in circles with Em's alternate-arm rowing technique, as opposed to both arms together.

It's fair to say that we didn't make a good impression on Lou and the slapstick Swimming Britain Comedy Show was at its peak as we made our way back to *Friday*. Lou sat there quietly in the front of the RIB and I knew exactly what she was thinking: 'What have I got myself into? I could be sunning myself on a beach in Turkey right now.'

We didn't waste any time as Lou and Owain, who seemed a lot chirpier than normal and was really going overly out of his way to help on deck, started the commute back to my swim point. We had missed the morning session to do the swap over and I really needed to make the most of the next ten days.

Luckily, Lou knew how *Friday* worked and within minutes we had her sails out, something that we hadn't done in a while as conditions hadn't been in our favour. Lou just hated the sound of engines and I have to say it brought a calmness to the adventure reaching our start point without the mind-numbing monotone throb of the engine.

That calmness was soon shattered as I got in the water; the waves picked up and were coming in short and sharp from the west. Em was struggling to stay with me and kept getting blown away. I could see she nearly capsized a few times. Progress wasn't bad though and I did seven miles before Lou said we needed to stop the session an hour early. Our only anchorage was seven miles north and once the southerly strong tide started we'd not be able to fight it.

Lou was right and we were still one mile from the safety of a mooring buoy when the tide started to push us backwards. We had no option but to anchor where we were, slightly sheltered by Cara Island, a small privately owned uninhabited island south of Gigha.

At two in the morning, the anchor was dragging so much Lou decided to move us further north again. This meant some disrupted sleep but once in the calmness of Gigha bay I fell into deep sleep.

The following day I was again plagued by nasty side-waves. I soon found myself in a deep mindless wander, the first time I'd let my thoughts go in a while. Normally when I swim or cycle for hours on end I can relax my thoughts and often don't think about anything. It's kind of like driving on the motorway for hours. If someone asks you what you saw or thought about, it's hard to answer. Being able to do this helps pass the time and means you aren't worrying. Too much worry creates stress hormones and therefore you don't operate at your full potential.

During the last few weeks I had most definitely forgotten to live in the moment and enjoy the adventure. I had been overwhelmed by all the things that had gone wrong and wasn't allowing myself to enjoy the scenery and the amazing people I had met along the way. I was also noticing that if I was in a bad mood then the crew seemed to get stressed too. I really needed to be more positive, both for my own sanity and enjoyment, and for the crew's sake. They had done a sterling job so far.

A lone seagull hovered within touching distance of my head, staring down at me in wonderment. I wanted Em to take a picture so stopped swimming and looked back where I thought she was but she wasn't there. *Friday* was a good 50 metres away heading back south and away from me. I looked all around but couldn't see Em. How had she disappeared? I then looked back at *Friday* and noticed

Owain standing on deck, with his life jacket on pointing and shouting. Something was wrong.

I looked to where he was pointing – my heart jumped. There was the bottom of an upturned kayak, and no Em. I started swimming towards the kayak as quickly as I could. I looked up every few breaths but couldn't see her. Eventually I saw her head bobbing on the other side of the kayak. By the time I got there she was very out of breath and shivering.

'You OK, Em?'

'Yeah, fine,' was all she said, holding on to the upturned kayak, which was completely filled with water and extremely heavy. She looked petrified.

'Right, Em, get in the RIB!' said Owain from *Friday*, as they circled around bringing the RIB near Em.

'No, I'm fine. Carry on swimming, we need to make progress, I'll catch up.'

'Em, don't be silly. Get in the RIB, you can't swim with all your winter kit on.' Although she had a life jacket on, all her clothes were now wet and heavy, making swimming virtually impossible.

It was the first time I felt annoyed with Em. She had an amazing can-do attitude and a stubborn streak, which was often good, but this time she needed help. Eventually she listened and climbed into the RIB. I then threw her the rope attached to the kayak and climbed onto the RIB too. It took us at least ten minutes of hauling to eventually get the kayak onto the RIB and empty it of all the water before collapsing, exhausted.

Hauling the kayak took a lot of energy out of me, which made the session pretty slow but we eventually made it to Gigha.

Just before bed Em decided she wanted to share something with all of us.

'Guys. I've been hiding this but I figured we know each other well enough now to mention it,' she said while ringing out her wet clothes. 'I'm petrified of the water.'

'Whatever, Em,' I laughed. This was surely a joke.

'I'm serious. I've cried like almost every day. Petrified! All the time.'

I knew Em had been worried a few times but she never once let it affect her ability.

'So that time the dolphins came?'

'I thought it was a shark and may have weed a little,' she joked.

'Seriously?'

'Yup! It's fine though. I'm not letting it control me but I'm petrified all the time and today's capsize was literally hell. Hell!'

I couldn't quite believe what she was saying. We'd done some pretty crazy sessions and the fact that she had, day after day, faced her fear and performed incredibly was pretty amazing. I only hoped that she carried on being so brave even though she didn't have to pretend any more.

Feeling fresh after a good night's sleep, we got up early and headed back south. It was glass smooth and I was looking forward to a good day after yesterday's drama. About a mile from the start point, *Friday* all of sudden started to splutter and suddenly the engine cut out. We all looked at each other. If the yacht broke, it would definitely be game over for the swim. We sat there in silence as we carried on drifting slowly south.

'When did we last fill up with diesel?' I asked.

'I haven't ever done it,' Owain said. 'Jez was in charge of that.'

We opened the tank to find it completely empty. We laughed at our stupidity. The good news was that it wasn't the engine, but the bad news was that when air gets into the fuel system it creates a bubble and needs bleeding. This is not an easy task and it took some serious Googling to actually find out how to bleed an old 10hp Yanmar marine engine, all the while we were slowly drifting with the tide, which after half an hour was taking us right towards a large RIB with a 'diver down' flag showing. This meant we had to avoid the area around it as there were fishermen underwater near the boat. We shouted our problem to the skipper on the RIB and he slowly moved out the way as we floated past. On deck we could see bags and bags of freshly caught scallops. All our mouths started to water. Owain, who was more chirpy than ever, took a break from manually cranking the engine to get rid of the airlock to chat to the skipper.

'Hello mate, got any scallops to spare?' He laughed jokingly.

'Howzit guys,' said the guy in a heavy South African accent.

Owain launched straight into what I was doing, hoping he might give us some scallops.

'Ya, I saw you guys on the telly, hey. That's epic, bro. Andre. Nice to meet you,' he said while trying to manoeuvre around us while the tide took us wherever it wanted to.

'Are there four of you?' he asked.

'Yes,' replied Owain, who seemed to have now completely forgotten about *Friday*, and the fact that this guy was having to carefully get out of our way while his colleagues were diving underneath. His newfound happiness was a nice change, even if it meant he forgot priority one – boat and crew safety.

'Here, my boss won't notice anyway.' He handed over a sack of 16 large freshly caught Scottish scallops.

'Dude, you legend,' Owain shouted excitedly.

We chatted a bit more before Andre had to head back to where his boss was diving and Owain suddenly remembering he had a job to do and carried on bleeding the engine. It was strange that the second time we had engine problems at sea something good came from it.

I finished my session back at Gigha, again after only doing six miles due to the time wasted with the engine. We went ashore for a quick pint to officially welcome Lou to the expedition and have our first drink on Scottish soil. Within half an hour Lou was on the whisky.

'Sean, you are having this,' Lou presented me with a glass of whisky. I've never been a fan of whisky but really liked the idea of it. I took my first sip half expecting to spit it out but was surprised to find it quite smooth.

'Not bad, actually.'

'Yeah, I told you he'd like that one, Owain,' Lou said, gloating a little.

'OK, OK, Seano, when you're done, try Highland Park. You'll like that one better,' suggested Owain winking at Lou.

I guess they had a little behind the scenes bet going on that I knew nothing about. I could see a competition starting.

I spent the next few hours trying various different whiskies as we chatted with the locals on Gigha. Lou's excitement to be on the trip was rubbing off on Owain. I'd never seen this side of Owain before.

Stumbling back to *Friday* at midnight, I asked Em about Owain's new-found enthusiasm.

'So Owain's a different person of late, isn't he?'

'I know, right!' Em replied.

'Why is that?'

'Well!' Em paused slightly. 'I didn't want to stress you out at the time but basically it's because Owain and Jez didn't get on at all.'

'Shit! Really?' I was surprised that I hadn't picked up on it.

'Yeah, they are just so different and their personalities clashed. Neither of them were in the wrong, they were just very different.'

Of course I'd noticed that they didn't necessarily have that much in common, but I'd never known it was that bad and immediately felt guilty. I can't imagine it was much fun for either of them sitting on the boat all day with only each other to speak to. Part of me wondered if that's why Jez decided to leave. It was a surprise we had all actually got on this well up till now. There were bound to be some differences of opinion when in high stress situations. I'm just surprised that I hadn't noticed.

It took two days to get past Jura and towards the Sound of Luing when it should have only taken a day and a half. This was because I was falling five miles short of my 15-mile daily target. The tide up here wasn't nearly as strong as we had been told it might be, and commuting to and from the start point was taking longer and longer each time due to limited safe anchorages. Lou hated a rough night's sleep and always manage to find us amazing anchorages, even if it was an an hour longer commute. The better sleep, and the improved mood of the crew was so worth it.

When we reached the bottom of the Sound of Jura there was even more bad news. There was a gale storm coming and we needed to find a harbour to sit out the storm, potentially for four days. We only had Lou for another six days and taking four off would mean I wouldn't even make the Isle of Mull.

There was nothing I could do about it though and by that afternoon we were tucked up in Craobh Haven Marina. Strangely enough, the pub next to the marina was having a cowboys and Indians themed party, which felt pretty out of place for a small Scottish harbour town with what seemed like less than a dozen houses around it. Within a few minutes Lou was at the bar chatting to a lady cowboy and had somehow managed to steal someone's Stetson.

Lou was a great addition to the Swimming Britain team and her excitement was rubbing off on all of us. I had been nervous whether Lou would actually fit in and, more importantly, cope with living in *Friday*'s pretty rustic conditions. The fact that Lou hadn't been cramped up like the rest of us certainly explained a large part of her enthusiasm, I'm sure. We were old hags of the sea. She was fresh blood, keen to explore new horizons, with a rose-tinted outlook that the rest of us had lost after months of laboured crossings and sleepless nights.

'Get on it, Owain!' Lou said coming back to the table where we were huddled up and putting four double whiskies down. With potentially four days off ahead a few whiskies were in order. There was definitely a noticeable change in crew morale after a few drinks. Also, if I were to look at the statistics, I'd done some of my biggest days after a few too many beers. Although, admittedly, I'm pretty sure that was pure coincidence. Or maybe it numbed the pain. I know the early Tour de France cyclists used to have wine stops at the top of climbs to help with the final slog to the finish line. I looked around. I felt in no way similar to a Tour de France elite athlete as I sat in a bar surrounded by 50 cowboys and girls signing along to Dolly Parton. Eventually at around midnight we headed back to *Friday* and Owain, who after a few pints has the agility of a baked potato, tripped on the boat hook and fell over one of the

JAW BLIMEY!

Thrill . . Julian, pals and shark

A FEARSOME shark is held with its jaws agape — the first of its kind to be caught in British waters in 42 years.

Actor Julian Lewis Jones and three pals landed the 6ft mako — which can swim at 46mph and leap 30ft into the air — while fishing off Milford Haven, West Wales.

Julian, 44, said: "It took 40 minutes to get him on the boat — he went ballistic. We were stoked.

"It's something you dream of."

◁

I was not thrilled to find out that this killer shark was caught just a few miles from where I was swimming!

Lunch break in the water with my friend Kenton, who joined us for the day

▽

△

Joking with the team from BBC's *The One Show* on their third trip to find us

◁

The One Show sent former Olympic 400m sprinter Iwan Thomas to swim with me. Having people from 'the outside world' join us, if only for the day, helped to keep us sane

△

Owain proudly displays his catch of the day

▷

Another amazing sunset in Scotland. As we fell further behind schedule I had to swim on as many northerly tides as I could, no matter what time of day or night

◁ Night swimming freaked me out at first, but experiencing incredible phosphorescence is something I'll always remember

Lou and Owain were heroic in putting in long hours to and from anchorages, getting me to my start point each day ▽

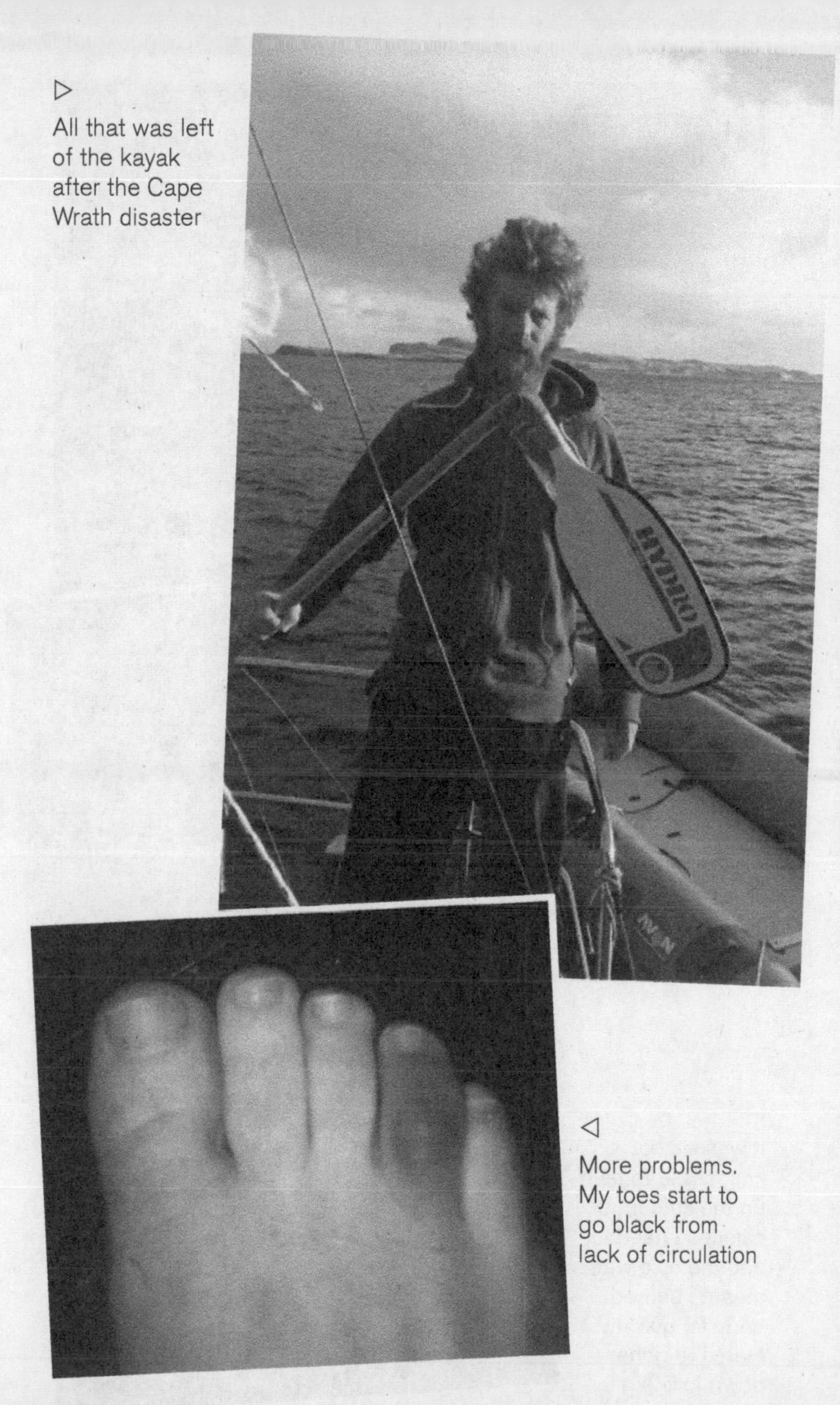

▷ All that was left of the kayak after the Cape Wrath disaster

◁ More problems. My toes start to go black from lack of circulation

△

The very beautiful but intimidating Hebrides and the choppy water we dealt with most days

▷

It was almost impossible to take on the amount of calories I needed, and the cold water meant I burned body fat quickly. Here I've gone down to 60kg

△

Wishing I'd kept my goggles on as my very excited welcome committee sprays champagne in my eyes as I finally finish

The crew (and mum) all together at John O' Groats

▽

©James Carnegie

△

Trying to hold it together and say something insightful to the assembled journalists, despite feeling very emotional at the end. Spoiler: I failed

◁

The newspapers that reported on the story the next day, including *The Times* who put my photo on the front page!

stays on *Friday*, thus earning him the new nickname of Twinkle-Toes from Em.

Temperatures plummeted sharply over the next few days and, as we hid from force nine winds, we were happy I wasn't out at sea. *Friday* was becoming unbearably damp and cold so I bought a paraffin heater. It took up most of the floor space in the main cabin but once lit we wondered how we ever survived without it, even if it did cover everything in fine black soot.

Luckily the storm blew over after two days, and not four as the forecast suggested, and I carried on heading up toward Isle of Mull. To make the most of the last few days with Lou, I was swimming at every possible moment, which meant getting in the water at 2am and swimming till sunrise at this time of the month. We were just north of the Sound of Luing and the plan was to head west of a small island.

The night was the darkest it had ever been as I got into the water. I was completely in autopilot mode as I had been over the last few tiring weeks. There were a few lights on the island just ahead of me and the plan was to keep them on my right as we went past. As I approached the island, with Em to my right, and *Friday* to my left and slightly ahead, it started to get really bouncy, waves jumping in all directions. I had reached the rush, the turbulent water often found around headlands as water is redirected or narrowed. This change sends water from the bottom of the ocean upward to the surface creating short sharp waves that have no consistency. I carried on swimming towards the island when I suddenly felt I was being pulled sideways to my right. It was too dark to know for sure but something felt wrong. I then heard a shout and looked up, but I wasn't really able to hear much because of the ear plugs in my ears. I looked to *Friday* who was now quite far away to my left. I turned to Em who was pointing towards me paddling as hard as she could.

'We need to follow *Friday*,' Em shouted with a note of panic in her voice that I'd never heard before. 'She's over there, keep swimming!'

The ferocity of the water was getting worse and even through my ear plugs it sounded like a fast flowing river. Waves crashed into my face and I swallowed an unhealthy amount of seawater, nearly vomiting again. Instantly I became disorientated. The lights on the island were still on my right but it felt like I was swimming against current. Up till now I was looking at *Friday*'s green navigation lights off to my left, but now they were red but still off to my left. This means she was either going backwards or, or … I wasn't actually sure. I was too tired and cold to try and figure out my port from starboard, left from right? I kept repeating, 'Red, port, left. Green, starboard, right.' But it didn't make sense to me. It was too dark to see anything. I felt helpless in this ever-changing ocean and for the first time all swim I actually felt scared.

'Keep swimming,' I heard Em shout and put my head down again.

It seemed fruitless. Did she even know where I was meant to be swimming or were we just swimming for the sake of it? I thought desperately. Moments later I looked up to see *Friday* was now on my right and slightly ahead still with her red navigation light showing. That made no sense at all. Also the island lights were all of a sudden on my left. I was too tired to work out what that meant. With all the disorientation, it honestly felt we were heading back to harbour. Then as quickly as it all started the water went flat again, bringing an eerie sense of calm. Em shouted something. I looked up.

'You're all right, we don't need to push hard now.'

'What happened?' I asked, out of breath and feeling on edge.

'I'm not sure, but I think we got swept east and *Friday*, who got swept west, had to turn around and fight the current to come to us and then we went east after all. We're heading for that island now,' Em pointed to the flickering lights ahead of us.

From the map I seem to remember the only island that big in the area was Easdale. We reached it and there was a nervous silence as Em and I climbed back on board. I think we all knew that it had been a little too close for comfort. The reality was the tide was so strong near that island *Friday* could easily have been swept west and would never have been able to fight the tide. Em and I would have most certainly been on our own in the pitch dark for quite some time as it was fairly unlikely we'd have been able to go ashore due to the sharp rocky cliffs which are characteristic of these parts of the Highlands.

By the time we reached the Sound of Mull it was time to say goodbye to Lou. I still hadn't found another skipper but the Sound of Mull could definitely be swum with land crew as it had a road running all the way down it and was very narrow. In fact we wouldn't even need land support. We could hide the kayak on the shore and hitch a ride to Tobermory as our base each day. From there I'd look for a new skipper.

I woke up after not much sleep during a pretty windy night that required Lou to drop two anchors just in case one slipped. I got up slowly and hit my head on the roof as usual but something was different. I was used to hearing the Da! Da! Da! of *Friday*'s engine, and today especially as Lou was meant to be well underway getting us to Oban, the nearest port for her departure. I entered the main cabin and was surprised to see Lou sitting on the steps eating some cereal.

'Morning, mate,' she said casually, glancing up momentarily before looking back at the charts on the desk.

'Um, morning … aren't we? Why are we?' I was very confused and sounded like Johnny Cash again.

'So, I've spoken to my brother and he's happy to cover the theory course for another two weeks so get your kit on, you've got some swimming to do, boy.'

I couldn't believe it. I felt like crying. In two weeks I'd surely get fairly close to the end.

'Lou, thank you, thank you, thank you.'

'Lou, are you staying?' Em shouted from her bunk.

'Yes!' I replied on her behalf.

There was an eruption of excitement as Em basically fell out of bed to come into the cabin, her sleeping bag still around her ankles. Owain already knew about Lou's decision to stay and had a huge smile on his face.

'Come on!' I shouted, and then felt embarrassed as I'm usually a more of a shout inside type of person rather than public displays of excitement. Now was different. Once in the Sound of Mull we'd be sheltered from most of the bad weather and could really make some good progress, I was sure of it.

11

FRIDAY GOT ILL

As we approached the entrance to the Sound of Mull, the fog set in, reducing visibility to around 100 metres. Ordinarily this is not a problem when going along the coast, but when entering a busy ferry route it's slightly more daunting. Flashbacks of the Belfast crossing coming to mind. Why did the fog come down whenever we were at our highest risk of getting run over?

The tide was good and we were swept into the sound at nearly six knots. It would have been great to carry on in the full rush of the tide, which runs down the middle of the sound, but unfortunately there are a number of ferries which also take the same route. Would a ferry have right of way over a swimmer? There is a sailing rule that states that non-motorised vessels have right of way. I was definitely a non-motorised vessel. I really didn't want to test that theory though and stuck nearer the edge of the sound for peace of mind.

*

After three days of swimming non-stop most of the day and night, we eventually reached Tobermory where we knew we'd have a good night's sleep in the harbour. Tobermory is often used on postcards and in adverts to promote Scotland, and for good reason. The harbour is lined with brightly coloured terraced buildings below picturesque cliffs. When the sun breaks through the clouds, the contrast between the dark sky and the coloured buildings truly is breathtaking. It had been a long few days in the Sound of Mull and nice to finally be on land again for the first time in a while.

BBC Scotland were coming to interview us in the morning, which meant we could all have a much-needed lie-in. The 3am wake-up calls to catch the tide were starting to put a strain on everyone. We also needed to stock up on various essentials like toilet paper. I'd hate to think what we'd do if we ran out of toilet paper. Owain came up with the only plausible solution, which was using socks! Luckily we had always managed to get to land before ever needing to use our socks.

We had a welcome evening in the pub trying yet more whisky before retiring to the flattest night's sleep we'd had in ages. The next morning we got an email from BBC Scotland saying they couldn't come anymore as the panda in Edinburgh Zoo might be pregnant and they needed to go there instead. Trumped by a potentially pregnant panda – brilliant. (It turned out the panda wasn't pregnant after all.)

We did errands before heading out to my start point, parallel with Tobermory. As we approached the GPS point, we noticed a kayaker just hanging around right where I was to start. On arriving he came over to us.

'Are you the swimmer?' he said to Lou.

'Ha ha,' Lou laughed. 'Not me but Sean is the swimmer and he's below.'

I came out and prepared to get in the water.

'Hey Sean. I'm Anthony. I've been following your tracker online so thought I'd come and kayak with you for a few hours, if that is OK?'

'Of course it is, mate. I'm sure Em would love the company.'

The smile on Em's face seemed to confirm that. Following a cold, miserable swimmer for the last 86 days wasn't much fun for her, especially when I couldn't really even talk to her because of the plugs in my ears. She immediately started to chat to Anthony about, well, I have no idea, although I was getting fairly good a lip reading, I still wasn't up to scratch.

I jumped in and carried on as usual while Em and Anthony kayaked next to me. It was nice to know people were following me online. My online audience were like the crowd cheering me on in a marathon. The closer you get to the end the more they cheered and it was nice to get more support the closer and closer I got to John O'Groats, the point on the map I had been staring at for nearly three months now. I had even downloaded a picture of John O'Groats Harbour onto my laptop and would visualise getting out of the water knowing I'd never have to swim in the cold Atlantic ever again. In some ways that picture and that little 'END' mark on the map on the toilet door really did help me. Keep the end in sight but take each day as it comes, I thought. In theory this is good but the constant chasing of the weather was physiologically demanding. Once winter set in then it was all over. Although I had had a good stretch in the last few days it was ever present in the back of my mind that I was still a month behind schedule. The inner whisper of 'it's too late, you're not going to make it' stayed with me. I dared not talk about it with the crew, for verbalising it was realising the reality. Blind naïvety and stubbornness seemed a better approach.

Anthony stayed with us for a few hours and then had to turn around to head back to wherever he came from, a small town on Mull as far as I could make out through my ear plugs.

By late afternoon, I had come out of the Sound of Mull and had just reached Ardnamurchan Point, the most westerly point of UK mainland and an important milestone, from a yachting point of view anyway. Rounding Ardnamurchan Point allows sailors to put a bunch of heather on the front pulpit of their boat, normally for boats heading north showing they were not hostile. Naturally Lou had some heather ready and waiting, and took great pleasure photographing it and sending it to Jim, her brother who was running their sailing school all on his own. Although I was covering freelancers to run their theory courses, it was a small price to pay to have a yacht master instructor with us, and particularly one that dislikes rough anchorages and loves whisky even more.

We finished the session just as it was getting dark and headed further around to the nearest bay. We found the best anchorage possible and set up for the night. As we were dropping anchor (and two anchors again, which now gave Lou the nickname Two-Anchor Lou) three kayakers came up to us.

'Hey guys. Where are you off to?' they asked.

'Just up to John O'Groats,' replied Em. 'We're with the guy swimming.'

'Really?' replied one of them. 'I heard about him a while back, and don't take this the wrong way, but I thought he gave up long ago.'

I was inside listening in to the chat and laughing to myself. Had people really thought I had given up? Giving up due to being tired or cold was not an option at all. If we could make progress we needed to make the most of it. I was yet to actually succeed in any major adventure and right now the risk of failing again was increasing every day the nearer we got to winter and the dreaded Cape Wrath, which was our final obstacle.

'Is he here?' they asked.

Em shouted down to me and I came up to say hi.

'There's the bearded man himself. Is it true about the jellyfish and the beard?'

This seemed to be the main thing most of the media had picked up on after the seasickness and the one thing people seemed to remember. The fact I used a beard for jellyfish protection seemed far more interesting than swimming 900 miles in 12 degree water for months on end.

'Yes, it's true.'

'Fair play. Well done. You're not far now.'

The three of them then disappeared into the night with their head torches on. It was nice that people were coming to find us and today was the day for kayakers.

Dinner was steak, mash and broccoli. The evening was clear so we had dinner on deck and were just retiring when Two-Anchor Lou decided she wanted to move *Friday* about 100 metres further north to get out the waves which had turned bigger with the change in tide direction. She went to switch the engine on but nothing happened. There was just a small clicking sound. We all looked at each other. Owain, being the only one who knew anything about engines now that Jez was gone, took the floorboards up and moved the stairs out of the way get at the engine. Nothing looked out the ordinary and after much more faffing he figured it was probably the starter motor. I hadn't really paid much attention to boat maintenance in all my preparation, which was a huge oversight. If *Friday*'s engine broke then it would definitely be the end of the swim. I would never be able to afford a replacement engine. I suddenly realised that we hadn't even changed the oil on *Friday*. How could I have been so stupid?

Being anchored and not on a mooring buoy without a working engine is apparently good enough of a reason to call a mayday to the coastguard. My heart raced. The word 'mayday' sends shivers down my spine as calling one usually meant your boat was sinking or there was serious concern for a man overboard or something equally dangerous. It was the phrase that I associated with the swim probably being over. The other option is make a call on Channel 16 (the international distress channel that all sailors have their radios tuned to at all times) out to other boats who might be able to help.

Lou was just about to radio for someone when Owain remembered that we could manually crank the engine. He found the crank arm and attached it. There was a little lever which effectively puts the engine in neutral and allowed the engine to turn. You then needed to crank the engine as fast as possible, like you would an old car. When at full speed, you dropped the lever, and pulled it off as quickly as possible. If you didn't then the crank would spin so fast it could break your wrist. The other problem was that the crank arm, when at the upper right section of its rotation, was very close to the side of the galley wall, which meant you inevitably smashed your knuckles every time you went round.

Owain tried a few times but just couldn't get it going fast enough and wore all the skin off his knuckles, which began to bleed. The only time he did get it going he didn't manage to detach the crank and it stayed on the engine spinning around, which was not safe. If it flew off it could break something, or someone.

We had to cut the engine and try again but it seemed Owain had used all his energy on that one good spin. After ten minutes he gave up, too fatigued to carry on. I offered to give it a go but Em and Lou said they'd try first. The last thing I needed was a broken wrist. Also, after a long day swimming, my arms were feeling very tired. Lou and Em didn't have much luck either and eventually there was no option but for me to try. I braced myself and started slowly, increasing my speed gradually with each turn until I thought I was at my fastest.

'Go!' I shouted and pulled the crank off. The timing was perfect and *Friday*'s engine banged and spluttered into action.

'Yes, Sean!' Lou shouted.

I guess after swimming for three months my arms were relatively strong. Now that the engine was working our only option was to head back to Tobermory and see if we could find someone to fix it. If it was in fact a starter motor it could be days before we could get a new one from somewhere, probably eBay!

It was 3am before we finally made it into Tobermory. It had been a good day swimming but we now had the huge task of trying to fix *Friday*'s engine. Cranking it every day was not an option.

'Ah bonjour, monsieur.' A tall Frenchman approached *Friday* pushing a cart full of tools. It was Philippe, the only boat electrician on the island.

'What is zi problem?' he asked still with a heavy French accent, even though he had lived in Scotland for 'many many year' as he put it.

Philippe got to work straight away while we all crowded around, probably making his life worse. I'm sure he'd have preferred to do it alone but we were all on tenterhooks, waiting for good or bad news.

'Ah, I see!' he said.

My heart skipped a beat.

'It is a fuse. Easy fix, no problem.'

We couldn't have got better news. You could instantly feel the relief run through all of us as Lou offered to do a coffee run. Even though Philippe would be done in ten minutes we still had to wait out the tide for another half hour before heading out again. We may have lost a session but at least it wasn't serious. *Friday* really was an incredible boat.

We somehow always manage to miss something for *Friday* and even though we did a big shop the day before, we forgot to restock on butter and nut oil – the two things I needed the most to increase the fat content in my diet. I was now going through half a tub of butter a day and adding around 500kcal extra of various nut oils in with each meal too. We had enough to last a few more days but I felt we needed more so went off and left Philippe to do his work.

By that afternoon, we were back out on the water heading back to Ardnamurchan Point where I stopped the night before.

It was perfectly calm and I was getting into the swing of things when all of a sudden there were loads of jellyfish again. I hadn't seen any in a while but they tend to come to the surface when it is calm. This slowed my pace a lot but still I felt good. Halfway through the session we were also pounced upon by a pod of dolphins that came up right near us. Em gave an uncharacteristic shriek as a fin came out the water next to her. It still made my heart jump whenever I saw a fin in the water. Thoughts about the mako shark they caught while we were in Pembrokeshire were still present. I'm not sure I'll ever be completely comfortable in the water but instead have just learned to deal with it. You may hate it but you just get on with it.

I was consciously eating more during each session and ate two full Stowaways meals in four hours. With the extra fat that was a total of nearly 3000kcal. If I did that again in the second session, plus dinner and breakfast, my daily intake was around 8000kcal, which was about right. I was still somehow losing weight but I literally couldn't fit more in my stomach.

Although it was calm I somehow only managed three miles in three hours as we got the last of the morning tide. I was steadily getting slower and slower each day, which was partly due to the weather and water getting colder, but mainly because I had now been at sea for 88 days and was the most fatigued I have been in my entire life. I had dropped below ten stone and had no body fat left. I couldn't get enough food in me and with every session I was starting to break down vital muscle tissue for energy. This can become a downhill spiral, but no matter how much I ate nothing was working. In an ideal world I would take two to three weeks off and then carry on. I had no such luxury. Winter was fast approaching, which was actually sending both physical and mental shivers down my spine. I should have been finished two weeks ago and I wasn't even past Skye yet.

We went back to Muck to sit out the southerly tide and then headed back for the evening session. The wind picked up and small sharp waves started to slap the side of my face knocking my goggles off every few minutes. I only managed three miles in the evening session, which meant I probably wasn't actually doing much more than floating with the tide. I didn't really know what to do. I had given it my all. The date was the 25 September and if I carried on at this rate I'd only get to John O'Groats by Christmas, but before that the crew would definitely leave me. I suddenly felt, for the first time since losing Jez, that maybe I wouldn't be able to finish the swim and this time it was all my own fault for not being a strong enough swimmer. I finished the session and we went to Isle of Eigg for anchorage. I confided in Em in the cabin.

'I'm not sure I can carry on like this. I'm just too slow.'

'Don't worry, Ginge. You're doing amazing,' Em replied, always positive.

'I'm not and I hate it. At this rate I'll lake another two months or more. You guys won't stay that long.'

'Ginge. Don't worry about us. I'm with you till the end and so is Owain. We'll just tie Lou to *Friday* so she can't leave,' she joked.

I guess knowing for certain I'd have the crew till the end would make a lot of difference. I hadn't really voiced it from fear of hearing the worst. Em and Owain only signed up for a two-and-a-half month adventure. I didn't know what other commitments they had. It just didn't seem fair on them to keep them here when at this point it seemed the most likely I wouldn't finish.

'Also,' Em continued. 'Please, Ginge, can you be more positive? I know it's hard but if you're down then we're all down.'

She was right. I needed to be more upbeat. Things in Scotland hadn't gone at all to plan but I needed to be more positive, even for my own sanity.

'What if we only did one session a day?' Em suggested. 'We can then kill that session and have the rest of the day to recover and explore and it means Owain and Lou won't have to do two long commutes each day. Remember why you wanted to do this swim in the first place? To explore Great Britain.'

She was right. It seemed since Cornwall we were either doing a huge crossings or fighting bad weather. I had forgotten why I wanted to do this swim.

'But it'll take a week longer. Will Owain stay? And what about Lou?'

'Owain will stay. I've chatted to him and he's here till the end. Lou, I don't know. We'll just have to play it by ear.'

'Let's take the day off tomorrow on Eigg and decide.'

'OK,' I agreed, and Em went through to tell Owain and Lou the plan.

'Great,' Said Lou. 'Now I can get some balsamic vinegar for our salad. I bloody love balsamic vinegar.'

'There is no way they have balsamic vinegar on Eigg,' said Owain.

'Of course they do!' replied Lou.

'If they have balsamic vinegar, I'll swim naked,' said Owain, confidently.

'Deal!' said Em and Lou at the same time.

I didn't fancy Owain's chances, if I was honest.

The next day we went ashore at around midday. Eigg was a very small island, at five and a half miles long and just three miles wide. The island was once privately owned but the community got together and bought it from the landlord in 1997. There are now about 100 people on the island, including the lady who has the ice cream shop and B&B who is also the paramedic. There was a large gathering of people all outside the café/bar right by the harbour. Even though it was only midday on a Thursday quite a few of them were already completely smashed. As we walked up the slipway a very friendly lady called Maggie, who wasn't one of the drunk ones, came towards us with huge smile on her face and a pot of money.

'Swimmer! We've been following your tracker online and have been asking people to donate. We raised £80 so far. Here you go.' Maggie gave us the pot. How incredibly kind she, and the rest of Eigg, were.

'Come now. Have a dram!' She dragged us into the bar, where we sat down and were presented with a whisky each. What a reception. Normally we sneak into a pub unannounced. Eigg had different ideas for us.

'Oh well, when on Eigg!' said Owain referencing the few intoxicated people outside the café.

Lou disappeared and came back a few minutes later with the biggest smile on her face looking straight at Owain.

'Guess what, Owain?'

'No?'

'Yes. Owain. Get your kit off!' shouted Em excitedly as Lou waved a bottle of balsamic vinegar in his face.

Owain just put his head in his hands. At least someone would join me in the water to appreciate how cold it was.

The rest of the afternoon was spent in the bar chatting to various people who live on Eigg. One young fellow we met kayaked to Eigg five years previously and never left. His kayak was still there next to the harbour wall, filled with water and overgrown weeds.

After a few too many pints he staggered over to me at one point and said, 'Mate. You've lost your marbles haven't you? Look I found them. They're all shrivelled and small like, from the cold, look!'

He proceeded to take three small metal marbles or ball bearings out his pocket. Who keeps ball bearings in their pocket? Someone who started drinking at 9am I guess? They were all incredibly friendly though and were by far the most interested in the swim to date, asking millions of questions. In the afternoon we walked to the ice cream shop and then back to *Friday* for dinner, and then decided to go back to the bar for one more drink before retiring. The bar was bustling with people and Lou was in her element showing everyone our route north on the new charts we got in Tobermory.

By the time we left, the bar was getting quite rowdy, but in a friendly way. As we left we were promised that someone would pipe us away in the morning. Someone with bagpipes on the harbour wall as I swam away from Eigg. That would be incredible. Also the kayaker had promised to come and kayak with Em and they should carry on round the world. Judging by the state of him, I figured we wouldn't have another kayak buddy tomorrow. I'm sure not everyone on Eigg drinks heavily but the ones hanging around the harbour certainly know how to let their hair down.

There wasn't a soul to be seen when we woke up and, even after waiting an hour just in case they were getting ready, we came to the conclusion that our bagpiper was probably passed out in a bush somewhere and not going to pipe us out. Less surprisingly, the kayaker was nowhere to be seen either.

I had spoken to Lou and Owain who agreed with our 'one tide a day' strategy from now on even if it meant taking a week longer. Em and Owain assured me they were there till the end, which was a great relief, and Lou also hinted that she might be able to stay longer as Jim, who was now pretty much a living legend in my books, was managing to cover everything for her. I could also see Lou was really enjoying the sailing side of things, always looking at navigation points with her binoculars and taking photos of harbour entrances, which was nice to see. It'd kill me if any of the crew were hating it.

I hadn't quite appreciated how much pressure I was putting myself through not knowing if I'd have crew till the end considering I was so far behind. Having Em and Owain's word really was a weight off my shoulders.

I felt a lot better and after one of the flattest days almost all swim, we anchored off a picturesque beach and had some fresh vegetables we'd got from a guy called Chris on Eigg. Fresh fruit and veg was always welcomed as it was something we couldn't keep for long on the boat due to not having a fridge.

I was feeling positive and, besides two sore toes from where I must have bumped them when my feet were numb at the end of each session, I went to bed happy knowing we didn't have to get up early for the first tide and instead would only do the early afternoon one.

I woke up to a strange purring sound followed by a splutter. I knew exactly what it was. The engine again. I went to the saloon to see Owain cranking away, every now and then swearing from banging his knuckles on the galley wall. It really did seem dead this time. I too gave it a go but this time had no luck. *Friday* really was not willing to start.

'Sean, I'll tell you what,' Lou said, now in captain mode. 'We can sail off this spot and get you back to the start point and the wind is good enough to sail with you all day. There is a harbour in Mallaig just further north of where you will get to this eve. At least we're making progress and Owain can sort a mechanic while we're on the move.'

It was a slow commute back and I was eventually back in the water as the tide turned. I set off swimming and soon left *Friday* way behind me, who would periodically come to a near stop when the wind died down. Eventually we reached Mallaig and I got back on board. This plan, however, meant that we would need to sail into the busy harbour and onto the pontoon. Coming into a harbour under sail is very much frowned upon in yachting communities, as you don't have much control, and you risk smashing into other boats.

'Unless you pull it off, then you're a hero,' said Lou, with a smile on her face. We tried calling the harbour master for ages trying to tell him our intentions but no one was answering.

Steadily we made our way into the harbour with not much issue. The next difficulty was to get onto the pontoon. The only way we could slow *Friday* down was to manually drop the sails. If we did this too early we wouldn't make the pontoon and be drifting around the harbour helplessly. Too late and we'd crash right into the pontoon and almost definitely put a hole in *Friday*. Owain was steering. Em was in charge of putting a fender between *Friday* and the pontoon, I was in charge of dropping the sail when Lou told me to, and Lou was ready to jump off and tie us down before we hit the pontoon. I was slightly worried about Owain's steering ability but Twinkle-Toes' lack of agility and knot-tying ability meant Lou had to do that.

As we started to approach the pontoon, a gust of wind picked up right as the harbour narrowed, increasing our speed a little beyond comfort.

'Drop half the sail,' Lou shouted.

I did so but *Friday* didn't seem to slow down much.

'More, more. Drop it more.'

I pulled more of the sail down as quickly as I could and *Friday* slowed down slightly. We were now a good 20 metres from the pontoon and still at quite a speed.

'Go, drop all of it.'

I did so. There was nothing left to do. Lou was ready and we came careering into the space. Lou jumped off and tied off the stern of *Friday* to the pontoon while Em held the fender against the bow. We came to a screeching halt and banged into the front of the pontoon, nearly sending Em overboard. But *Friday* was OK, we were in the harbour, and we breathed a huge sigh of relief.

'Yeah man. That's how it's done!' Lou cheered. 'Well done, Owain!'

Our success momentarily overshadowed the fact that *Friday* was broken, but Owain said a mechanic would come in the morning. We all went to the pub.

The mechanic turned up an hour late and didn't even try to disguise the fact he was late because he had 'the world's biggest hangover'. He must have been on Eigg, I guess.

It took him a good hour looking for the fault and he was just about to say it was the starter motor when he noticed some frayed wires touching the side of the hull. This was causing the short circuit and blowing the fuse. What a simple fix. Thankfully it wasn't serious. Google did say these Yanmar engines were indestructible. We sure had put this one through its paces.

12
WHEN THE GOING GETS TOUGH

Subject: Do NOT swim through Sound of Sleat.

My name is ********* and I see you are planning to swim through the Sound of Sleat. I highly recommend you skip this section and start again after it. I have over 20 years of experience in these waters and in my opinion if you swim that section you will not survive. This is a nasty stretch of water I've seen boats struggle in the sound. There are underwater whirlpools that you will get sucked into and a boat will not be able to save you.

Please seriously consider my advice.

The email had come from a gentleman who had filled in the form on the Swimming Britain website. I was slightly taken aback. I hadn't received a negative email in a while. He was talking about the Sound of Sleat just north of us and would to be the next section of the swim. It is an extremely narrow channel, the narrowest I'd have to swim through, and by quite a margin, connecting Kyle Rhea and Loch Alsh. It's about two miles long and funnels into a passage no more than 500 metres wide. The tide at full rush can reach speeds of ten knots. We knew this would be a tricky section to navigate but we'd decided it was nothing we couldn't deal with as long as we did it at slack water.

Even though I was confident in dealing with Sleat, I now had a huge feeling of doubt, much like when Bob the fisherman at Sennen Cove said he wouldn't take me to Land's End. I was worried.

'Lou, check this out,' I showed her the email.

'Don't listen to him, at slack water we'll be fine. He's just trying to cover himself I think, for his own conscience.'

'Owain, can you email him back to ask advice and just tell him skipping it is not an option for us and what's the best advice he has for us.'

Owain was good at wording emails. An email from me might have been along the lines of, 'Stop stressing us out and bugger off.' Owain was more diplomatic.

I didn't swim the next day due to ever-stronger winds that even made even the harbour rough. The next morning we got a reply from 'The Naysayer' (as we now called him), which went along the lines of, 'I won't give you any advice except do NOT swim.' He even said if he had the power he'd try come and physically stop us but he couldn't. The sea is free after all.

After reading his email a few times, I began to feel genuinely worried for the first time. I wasn't even this worried when swimming across the Irish Sea. Yes, many, many people had told me this swim wasn't possible, but those people generally sent one email and then I never heard from them again. No one had gone so far out their way as to want to come and physically stop me with their boat.

By the afternoon, the wind had died right down and I carried on north towards the Sound of Sleat. Mr Naysayer had put the fear of God in us. By all accounts this time there seemed a real risk of something going horribly wrong.

'Morning mate!' shouted Iwan from a motorboat alongside me.

The One Show had come to film me again and sent none other than sporting royalty Iwan Thomas, the famous 400 metre Olympic runner. By a strange coincidence Owain's wife had met him only the week before at some event too.

The crew were buzzing again, as was I. It was, however, slightly annoying that the day they came to film was one of the flattest days we'd had in weeks. If they had come yesterday they'd have had a true representation of what the swim was really like, with choppy waves and strong winds. Today it looked like I was taking a casual swim up a pond, which was really misrepresentative of what it's actually been like. Maybe Iwan will get stung by a jellyfish. I wouldn't wish that on anyone but it would make good telly. (OK, I'm going to hell.)

'Sean, come aboard,' Iwan shouted.

I climbed up the ladder and nearly fell off as I had no feeling in my feet. We chatted for a while about everything that had happened since we last saw them and what I was to expect in the next few weeks, including the dreaded Sound of Sleat. Iwan was fantastically excitable and every now and then would interrupt me, shout, 'there's a dolphin', and grab the cameraman to film it. It was great to have people from 'the outside world' come and visit us. It momentarily brought us back to normality.

Months on a small, damp 26-foot yacht and our grasp on reality had become warped. For example, if Owain or I needed a pee, it was normal just to piss over the edge of the boat. Even during conversation. They call it adventurer's bladder when you never have to hold your pee so just go whenever you need to. Initially we'd go all the way up the front of *Friday* but now we barely left where we were and just turned around. It took at least a month before we were comfortable enough to do this around the girls but there was literally nothing we didn't know about each other after months at sea. I'm not sure Lou and Em were ever consulted on our new toilet regime, which always sparked some childish banter whenever we did it. This was normal for us, but very much frowned upon if you did it in the real world, I remembered.

'Right, mate. I'm coming to swim with you. Let's go.'

'Hope you're not scared of jellyfish,' I joked.

'Really? Are there any here?'

'I haven't seen any all morning but they are about. Especially when it's flat like this.'

'Ah, I hope not. Bloody hate them jellies.'

Iwan swam with me for as long as he was allowed to before the production team made him to stop as they needed to get back to shore to do the edit. He was genuinely gutted but we had a manly hug in the water – which is not as easy as it sounds – before he clambered back on board and they zoomed off, leaving us all alone in an eerily calm and quiet bay.

'Sean,' Lou shouted. 'You drifted 200 metres while doing the interview on their boat so we need to go back and cover that distance again.'

I got out of the water and we went back 200 metres and I jumped back in and headed for the dreaded Sound of Sleat. We'd get as close as possible to it this evening and then assess the situation before attempting it at slack water in the morning.

Finally we could see it. The closer I got to it the faster I was moving. Even 100 metres before the entrance I was doing five knots and we weren't even at full flood. At around 50 metres before the entrance Lou shouted.

'Get in.'

I swam to the RIB and jumped in. Lou did a sharp U-turn and started to head away but we had pushed it a little too far. I looked up to see that we were going backwards, getting sucked into the sound. I clambered from the RIB and onto *Friday.* Lou was as calm as ever and didn't seem worried at all.

'Lou, I don't know if you've noticed. We're going backward.'

'If you're not going backward you didn't try hard enough,' she joked and put *Friday* into full throttle.

We slowly started to move forward and when I say slowly, I mean slowly. The GPS said our speed was 0.01 knots. *Friday*'s poor engine felt like it was coming through the floorboards. It took a good 15 minutes to get away from the jaws of Sleat. I'm glad Lou was so calm because it sure looked like we'd get sucked in. I could see what The Naysayer was talking about. The flow of water really was strong and we weren't even at full flood. This didn't help our nerves whatsoever as the mist settled in for a damp and cramped night stuck inside *Friday*.

This was it. The sound looked eerily calm as we headed back to the entrance. My heart was racing. Yesterday's close shave and Mr Naysayer's emails were at the forefront of my mind. I jumped in and for the first time in a while didn't feel cold at all, my body was full of adrenalin. I put my face down and made sure Em was right next to me the whole time. If I did get sucked into a whirlpool at least I had the option of hanging on to the kayak, although I could see Em's fear of the ocean fuelling imagined disasters where we both get sucked into the depths, never to return. I decided not to talk about it with her in an effort not to spark panic.

I steadily started to make my way into the sound, putting more effort into each hand movement than I had ever done, my heart still racing. I suddenly heard Em shout something. I looked up expecting to be told to get out or swim to the left to avoid a whirlpool. Instead she pointed to the shore where there was a family of four waving at me. The young kids were shouting, 'Good luck.' I waved back. I put my head down trying not to overanalyse the meaning of a family coming down to see me swim down potentially the most dangerous stretch of water in the UK. If I was at risk of dying then surely you wouldn't bring your kids to see it. Or was this like car crash … I stopped myself from carrying on. My thoughts made no sense. I was in it now and needed to concentrate on my style rather than feed my overactive imagination.

I pushed on for another ten minutes, entirely fuelled by adrenalin, waiting for a huge whirlpool to appear from nowhere but one never came. By the halfway point I stopped swimming and looked at Em. I didn't even have to say anything and she replied.

'I know. This is easy. What was The Naysayer on about?'

It was so easy there was even seals bobbing up and down behind us, following me the whole way. Eventually I popped out the other side and into Loch Alsh and Lou came alongside me. Owain was on deck and looked furious.

'I really want to phone that idiot and tell him what a twat he was. That was pretty much the easiest section we've done.'

Owain was right. I too wanted to phone him to say that he needlessly put us all under a lot of stress for no reason whatsoever. It wasn't worth it though. We were through it and could see the Skye Bridge ahead, the next milestone. It was better to put our energies to good use, like fishing.

'Fish for dinner, Owain?' I shouted.

'OK then,' he said and sat down and let out some line.

We were delighted to have made it through safely but we all knew my biggest hurdle was still 104 miles away in the form of Cape Wrath, arguably Britain's most notorious stretches of coastline. There was a real chance of something going seriously wrong if we didn't plan that section well.

Conditions over the next few days had somewhat eased and my progress was back to around ten miles per day again. Every few days I'd suggest doing double tides but then realised I'd fall back into that long-term fatigue I was desperately trying to avoid. I was just about balancing recovery with progress on one tide a day and we were all in a better state of mind for it.

We were just nearing Applecross when, during one of my feeds in the water, Owain informed me that the cooker had stopped working. He had taken it completely apart to no avail. It was a very old paraffin cooker and it was likely the injectors had been clogged up and without the proper cleaning kit, which we obviously didn't have, there was nothing we could do. I was struggling to get food down anyway and on the one occasion when I had tried cold food I threw it up. Having a working stove was integral. The sea temperature had dropped to around 12 degrees but more importantly the air temperature was around ten degrees in the day and nearly freezing at night. To make matters worse, he had called every shop in Applecross to find a camping stove but no one had any. We had only one option and that was to head all the way back to Skye.

It was 5pm when we turned around and were immediately faced with a mind-numbingly cold headwind and waves to match. Lou and Owain pushed hard well into the night and eventually at around 2am decided to drop anchor as they weren't making much progress. They then got up at 5am to do the final nine miles back to Skye. Long commutes are always stressful but eventually, after 23 hours, we made it back to Skye, exhausted and cold.

'Guess what today is?' Em shouted from her bunk.

'Miserable!' Owain replied, looking pretty tired.

'It's Day 100!'

Shit. It was Day 100 of the swim and I still wasn't anywhere near the end. I had already surpassed the longest swimming-based adventure in history, from a time point of view, which as far as I was aware was held by Ben Lecomte who controversially swam the Atlantic in 73 days but couldn't account for drifting on the boat at night. Even Martin Strel's Amazon swim, although much further in distance, took him 66 days. It was likely I still had another two weeks to go, at the very least, and that was if I had no bad weather days, which let's be honest, in October in Scotland was not going to happen. It was also slightly disappointing that Day 100 was an irrelevant day trying to find a camping stove in Skye as opposed to swimming somewhere noteworthy. Nevertheless, it was Day 100 and seeing as it was a land day I figured I'd treat the crew to a proper pub meal. They certainly deserved it after a 23-hour commute.

We bought two stoves and 15 gas canisters and started the long journey back towards Applecross. We had the wind behind us this time and it took us only six hours. I managed six miles in the evening session before we needed to take cover in Loch Torridon for some potentially bad weather coming.

We spent the best part of two days in a little bay getting bombarded by heavy winds and the occasional hailstorm. Cabin fever was at an all-time high. It was almost impossible to go to shore as we were flanked by huge cliffs and the wind was so strong it made rowing against it fruitless. Eventually at the end of the second day, we had all had enough and decided to try and clamber up the cliffs just to be on land and out of each other's faces.

Owain stayed on *Friday* to do some fishing while Em, Lou and I went foraging for limpets as a starter to our fishcake dinner that Lou was going to make. There is something special about a dinner that you have caught or foraged yourself. You appreciate it more, even though we all agreed afterwards limpets tasted like dirt. Lou was somehow in the party mood and whipped out a bottle of whisky that she had bought. The deal was that I provided everything including beverages for the crew but Lou insisted she wanted to contribute. Within an hour, Lou was dancing on the stairs listening to Pink on loudspeaker and shouting at Owain.

'Get on it, Owain. Come on. Get on it.'

Owain wasn't budging. *Friday* definitely wasn't big enough for Twinkle-Toes to do any dancing, although I would have paid to see that. The whole scenario was hilarious and a much-needed mood lifter. It's amazing how infectious someone in a good mood can be and Lou was certainly helping us all through it, and her fishcakes were out of this world.

Just before bed, I noticed the two toes that were sore a few days previously were starting to swell a little and felt quite warm to touch. The strange thing was that it was the same toe on each foot, one in from my pinkie toe. I couldn't recall bumping them but my feet were so numb most of the time I wasn't surprised it had happened while trying to get in and out of the RIB each session.

Also my wetsuits were really starting to smell of piss. In each session I peed around three litres and it all stayed around my midriff. When I got out the water, I pulled the front of my suit open to let a rush of cold water in to flush out most of the pee but it didn't really work. They really needed a wash.

Over the next four days, my toes got increasingly worse and slowly started to turn black. I decided that I should probably see a doctor, so we went ashore at the nearest possible place that seemed remotely likely to have a doctor. We were in luck. There was one a few miles up the road so we all walked up and sat in the waiting room looking quite tattered and smelly, quite the sight for some of the other patients in the waiting room. I was quite nervous about seeing a doctor because I was worried they'd tell me not to swim for a few weeks. That would be the worst result because I obviously wouldn't listen, or couldn't afford to listen as winter was already fast approaching and I needed to swim at every possible opportunity. I guess I just wanted some peace of mind.

I was called in to see the first doctor. After studying my toes for a while, he said he needed to get another doctor's opinion. Brilliant. That's what happens when something is properly wrong with you. Moments later another doctor came in. He had a strong Scottish accent.

'You're the swimmer aren't you? I noticed from the beard.'

'Yes, that's me, doc. You obviously know then that I need to carry on. I just want to know if this is something serious. I can deal with the pain but some people online have mentioned frost bite, which worries me.'

The doctor examined my toes closer.

'Right, Mr Conway. It's kind of like frost bite but not frost bite. Basically, the lack of blood to your extremities for a long period of time has caused tissue damage and now there's an infection. Now I know that no matter what I say you're going to continue and to be honest, you should be fine. You shouldn't lose the toe. And if you do, you become a real adventurer right? You don't really need that toe anyway,' he said jokingly. I couldn't quite believe it. I was honestly expecting the 'health and safety' part of his brain to give me the answers he should have, but instead he was refreshingly open to my situation.

'Take some antibiotics over the next week to reduce the swelling and if the black starts going further up your leg then come back and see us.'

A black leg! There was no way I'd let it get that far but I said my thank yous and left feeling a lot more positive now that I had advice that I wasn't going to die or lose my leg. As an added bonus I didn't even have to pay for the medicine as prescriptions are free in Scotland.

We got back to the RIB and decided to check on some emails in the pub nearby. We went in and ordered some tea and Em, who still was in charge of money despite dropping the wallet, came back looking perturbed.

'Ginge, can I have a word?' she asked.

'Sure,' I said and we went to another room.

'Your card has failed and we only have £100 left in the wallet.'

'Shit, really? How have we spanked all the money?'

'Dunno, Ginge.' Em replied.

I went to my laptop and logged on to internet banking and sure enough I was £1,523 overdrawn, which was £23 over my overdraft limit. I sat back in complete despair. I had basically taken too long and now completely run out of money. I had been so caught up in the mental and physical daily battle I had completely overlooked the finances. I really thought I had enough. Not only did I need to buy food for the crew for the next two to three weeks, I also need to pay the replacement skipper Lou was hiring to run courses on her behalf. I did some quick sums and worked out I needed about another £4,000 to get me to the end, or £5,500 if I wanted to pay back my overdraft. Considering the swim was looking like it might take twice as long as I thought, I'm surprised we got this far. Thank you Stowaways for giving us meals otherwise I'd have been out a long time ago.

How could I have left it this late? It was a bit like *Friday*'s engine, something I hadn't even thought about. I sat back and started to rack my brain for a solution. I could ask my dad for some more money, which I hated doing as he had already given me some money at the start. I could ask Speedo for some money. It had been so hard to get sponsorship funding in the first place I knew it'd be difficult to ask for more, especially as I was so far behind and the risk of not finishing growing stronger every day. Thirdly, I could do some crowdfunding and pre-sell a book about the swim. The problem with crowdfunding is if you don't reach the amount you asked for then you don't get any of the money. The last option was I could sell *Friday* and ask the buyer if I could borrow her for another two weeks. That was the last resort so I decided to try the first three options and if none of them worked then I'd look to sell *Friday*, which hurt me to even think about. She had done us proud and I didn't want to see her go.

Firstly I emailed Dad and asked for a loan of £1,000. I then emailed Sal at Speedo and offered my time after the swim. I said I'd do free talks for them, go to trade shows, even work in their store, anything really. For this I asked them for £2,500. With this approach I figured the money wouldn't be coming out of their marketing budget, which I already knew was stretched, but rather their entertainment, or staff salary budget or something. I had no idea if it would work but Sal at Speedo had been very supportive so far. Lastly, after doing a lot of research, I found a crowdfunding platform that paid money directly into your account even if you didn't make the final target, which I had set at £4,000, in case nothing else worked. I now needed to sell stuff. Crowdfunding isn't all about just getting handouts. You need to give the 'backers' something. I came up with the following products.

1 of 100 signed copies of the book
when it comes out – £15

1 of 15 goggles that I wore during the swim – £30

1 of 20 signed swim caps that I got given
from Speedo – £25

1 of 2 of the larger wetsuits I wore
at the beginning – £350

1 of 10 talks about my swim – £400

It took me an hour to set up the page and I then Tweeted my plea before heading back to *Friday* for an early night. All I needed was to sell five books a day and I'd be able to buy the crew food. That didn't seem all that hard to do but it relied heavily on people believing I was going to complete the swim otherwise there was no book to write.

I didn't need to start the day's swim until 5pm, so we had all day to do some chores and most importantly head to Wi-Fi in the hotel to see if I indeed had enough money to get food for the next two days. In case we didn't Lou and Owain went foraging for some mussels and limpets they had spotted on the other side of the bay. Limpets tasted like shite but might be the only thing we'd have for lunch.

I took a deep breath and logged in to my email and an influx of emails clogged up my inbox.

> Sarah Jones has backed your project
> Anthony Riches has backed your project

And so on. There must have been nearly 50 emails. I logged in to the crowdfunding page to see a grand total of £2,000 raised overnight. I had basically sold half the caps and goggles, a load of books and a talk. No one bought any of my pissy wetsuits though, which wasn't all that surprising. I couldn't believe it. How was that possible? I only tweeted it late last night. It turned out that the *Independent* and the *Daily Telegraph* had seen my Tweet about it and run it in the paper.

To make things better, Dad said I could have the money as an early Christmas and birthday present. That would look after some of my overdraft so was a huge help. Then there was an email from Sal at Speedo also agreeing to buying days from me after the swim.

Things couldn't have gone any better. Em and I ran back to tell Lou and Owain the news. I had this huge weight off my shoulder, much like when I got that email from Lou saying she would skipper us. There was nothing worse than potentially being told that your dream was over due to something out of your control. That had happened to me when I got run over in America and every time something similar happens I get scared. Scared of failing. Scared of not achieving my dream. It's a horribly lonely place to be when everything hangs in the decisions or actions of other people. Luckily both times on this swim people had pulled through for me, Lou and now the Great British public. Not only was it a huge relief but I also felt incredibly motivated to now finish the swim as a thank you to everyone who helped me out.

'We've got money for food now guys,' Em shouted.

'Well we won't need these then,' said Lou, cheerfully tipping out all the shitty limpets back into the sea. Not only did I have enough money for food and diesel, I now also had enough to keep Lou for the rest of the swim. Now there was just the small task of finishing the swim. No pressure at all.

The day got even better when Lou presented us with a huge bucket of freshly caught mussels. The mood was at an all-time high.

'Owain, haven't you forgotten something?' said Lou while preparing the mussels.

'Um? No!' replied Owain, looking slightly worried.

'Come on! Get your kit off lad!'

The balsamic naked swim bet. I had totally forgotten.

'Not today! I'll do it I promise, but not today,' Owain replied.

'Owain. Look, the sun is out, which it hasn't been in days. This bay is the cleanest bay we've been in and we are far enough from shore not to offend anyone. If I were you I'd get it over and done with now.'

You could see the cogs in Owain's brain working away. There was a moment of silence before he started to give in.

'Right! I'll do it.'

Owain disappeared below and came out a few moments later in his speedos and a towel. We were all sitting in the cockpit as he walked to the middle of *Friday.* I really didn't want to see Owain naked but did want to see him experience the cold water like I had over the last 108 days.

He slowly took off his Speedos, revealing his pasty white buttocks while clutching his man bits with both hands.

'O-wain! O-wain! O-wain!' Em chanted.

'Damn you balsamic vinegar!' he shouted, and launched himself into the air. Then, instead of doing a good old-fashioned British bomb, he did a flip and decided to dive in which meant, without any warning whatsoever, we all got an upside-down full frontal view of Owain in all his glory.

'Oooooowain! Why did you dive? I can't un-see that,' Em shouted covering her eyes.

Owain came up spluttering and swearing.

'Shit it's cold! Shit! Shit!' as he doggy-paddled round to the RIB.

'How do I get in without injuring my johnson?'

He had the task of trying to get out the water and into the RIB, which usually involves pulling yourself up with both hands and balancing your torso on the edge of the RIB. This can be painful with clothes on. Naked was definitely going to hurt. Owain struggled a few times while we all sat there and laughed and in no way offered to help. He was trying to pull himself up with one hand while holding his man bits with the other. After five attempts he eventually flopped into the RIB in the twinkle-toed fashion we'd come to expect, still clutching his jewels. It sure was one of the funniest things we'd all seen in a while and fair play to him for doing it. I only wish he had done a British bomb.

I had arranged for a friend, who happened to be up in Scotland that week, to take Arthur's engine back to London. I had spent well over £500 in fixing it and had only used it for the first few weeks. Since then it had been nothing more than an ornament weighing the RIB down while we rowed to shore each day. It was strangely comforting taking it off the RIB and sending it away. Part of me wanted to give Arthur a piece of my mind lending me an engine that was pretty much broken, but I knew he had his best intentions so just sent a thank you message.

John O'Groats really was in sight now. The last hurdle was Cape Wrath, which seemed to get more daunting the more we mentioned it. Just the word Wrath made it all the worse. If it had been called Cape Sunflower or something equally pleasing I'm sure we wouldn't have been stressing as much, but it wasn't. It was Wrath and certainly needed to be taken seriously.

The reason it was such a difficult section was because it lay open to the full force of the Atlantic Ocean. Up till now we'd been sheltered by the Outer Hebrides but at

Cape Wrath there was no such shelter. Those waves can start hundreds of miles away, slowly building in speed and strength before smashing against the towering 200-foot cliffs with the force of 1,000 oxen. Not only was it a difficult section to swim but *Friday* was certainly in the 'far too small' side of the scale to attempt unless conditions were perfect. An unlikely scenario now that it was nearly November.

It was tide switchover time, which meant I went from doing late-night sessions to early-morning sessions, which was a real shock to the system. Getting in the water at 5am when it's dark and cold seemed way worse that getting in at sunset. The switchover meant I was spending more time swimming at night and again the phosphorescence were out in full force. There weren't as many of them as back in Ireland but they were considerably bigger in size. So big in fact that when I came up they'd be all caught up in my beard. I looked like a Christmas tree, which was entertaining for everyone and sparked a few jokes about us still being on this adventure and all spending Christmas together on *Friday* while still somewhere in the Hebrides. If all things went to plan we were about three or four days from Cape Wrath, and then four or five days from the end. So in the best case scenario I'd be done in a week, or worst case ten days. Only ten more days in the actual water (excluding bad weather days where I couldn't swim) till I never have to put on a stinking cold wetsuit that smelled of pee ever again. That in itself was enough of a motivator to swim faster.

The very next day we had to take cover in Lochinver as some pretty bad weather was fast approaching. This would add two more days to the potential ten, but as usual there was nothing we could do about it. We sat out the storm taking the opportunity to invite BBC Scotland to come and interview us now that they knew the panda definitely wasn't pregnant. I had set myself a £10,000 target for War Child and I was only halfway, so I really wanted to push the fundraising in the last few weeks and publicity helped.

Bad weather days, although welcomed by my fatigued body, were getting more and more frustrating. The one-week forecast on XC Weather was becoming increasingly orange or red, which meant we couldn't go out. We needed blue or green, which were certainly becoming more infrequent as winter crept worryingly fast towards us.

With two days off and access to a shower, I decided to go for my second shower in nearly two months, my fourth shower since the start of the swim 112 days ago. My shower up till now had consisted of Em boiling the kettle after each session and pouring it onto one of my t-shirts I wasn't using. I'd then wipe myself down, mainly to get the piss off me, before drying myself and getting into my tracksuit. It was also the first time I shampooed my hair and my beard, which uncovered all sorts of weird bits of dirt and grime that had been caught in there for the last three and a half months. I had forgotten just how energising a shower can be and came out feeling a new man.

*

After two bad weather days, we got up at 4am to head back out to sea. The waves were big but nicely formed coming in from slightly behind me and from my left, lifting me a few feet in the air. This was my favourite condition to swim in as I almost felt I was surfing down them.

In an effort to keep Lou and Owain entertained while I was in the water I had offered a bottle of whisky to the person who caught the most fish over a period of three days. It was day two and it's fair to say it was a killing spree out there. They both had lines out with five hooks each. There was one point, when we must have gone through a huge shoal, when they both brought up five fish each at the same time. *Friday* veered off to the left as they both were more interested in getting the fish off the line so that they could get the hooks back in the water. It was a race as the person whose line went back in first had much more chance of getting another batch from the shoal. It was good to hear the cheers from the water every time either of them had a fish. With a bottle of Scotland's finest at stake, it was serious business.

By the end of the day, Lou had caught 22 and Owain 19. The cockpit looked like the scene of a massacre with a bucket of the best six in the middle – the rest they had thrown back. I guess dinner was fish then, a nice change from some of the monotony of the Stowaways. We were down to our least favourite flavours. It's a wonder we could even stomach them at all after this long. I guess that is a testament of actually how good they were but anything after nearly four months is going to become tasteless. A few of my Atlantic Rowing friends said they got sick of their meals after a week, so we had done well all things considered.

I finished my session just shy of ten miles and the nearest safe anchor was behind a small island three hours away. It was days like this that reinforced our decision to only do one tide a day. The commutes to and from anchorages were getting longer and longer the closer we got to Cape Wrath, with safe places to moor up few and far between. It was worth pushing the extra hours to a good anchorage as the safety and better sleep far outweighed the journey.

Two days later and we could finally see Cape Wrath in the distance. If all went to plan, I'd reach it tomorrow. It was a huge moment in the swim because once round the corner we really were on the home straight. I felt a mixture of excitement and nerves every time I stopped to look ahead towards those distinctive towering cliffs. A few times while deep in thought I'd get a live fish flying through the air and land next to me.

'Keep swimming,' Owain would shout and then launch another fish he had just caught into the air. You could almost see the fish trying to swim even before it hit the water. A slightly odd sight to be awakened to after daydreaming of biblical wrath that lay ahead of me. Besides its daunting name, Cape Wrath was going to be the trickiest section of the swim. The tide was so strong I had no option but to try and swim the 20-mile section between Kinlochbervie and Kyle of Durness, the first safe anchorage on the north coast, in one go. There was nothing but towering cliffs in-between the two anchorages and not a place we wanted to hang around. Also with the strong tide it made logistics extremely difficult too. If the tide turned before we made anchorage we'd land up getting flung all the way back out to sea in the wrong direction. Conditions needed to be perfect and I needed to give it my all and not hold anything back.

By the end of the day I had reached Kinlochbervie, the final port of call. We went into the harbour to make sure we got a good night's sleep before attempting Cape Wrath. Ideally I would have liked to take a day off to prepare but Lou said we needed to go tomorrow as the weather was looking bad for the few days after. It was a case of take any weather window we could and tomorrow was looking to be that window. I went to bed feeling quite nervous but prepared. We'd had 115 days to prepare for tomorrow's swim and were as ready as we'd ever be. Cape Wrath was ours to be conquered.

13
DISASTER

As the forecast predicted, the weather was ideal as I got in the water just north of Kinlochbervie. This was the closest I had swum to the shore since Cornwall and it certainly added a sense of grandeur as I looked up to the high cliffs above me.

'Ready for this, Em?'

'Yes, Ginge. Once we're there we're practically done! Big day today. Day 116. Come on.'

It was time to give it everything. I put my face down and did what I had been doing for the last 116 days. Stroke, stroke, breath! Stroke, stroke, breath! Only this time with more urgency and determination than ever.

We slowly worked our way towards Cape Wrath, whose cliffs were getting bigger and more *Lord of the Rings*-like the closer we got. My mind was in a new place, a place it hadn't been before. I had been staring at Cape Wrath on the toilet door map for the best part of 4 months and now I was here. In my mind, once I rounded that corner the swim was as good as done. I was mixed with nerves, excitement and relief.

I was lost in my thoughts when suddenly, about 3 feet below me I saw a bird flying, in the water. I stopped swimming wondering if I had in fact gone mad. I stared at the little creature swimming next to me. It then looked over and winked at me. This was surely a dream. The little bird then darted off, swam up to the surface, and took off, flying high into the sky and over the cliffs. Did that just happen?

'Em, did you see the bird?'

'Yeah, it took off and flew away.'

'It was swimming with me and winked at me.'

'I'm sure it did, Ginge. Now come on, keep swimming.'

To this day, I'm not sure if I dreamt it but that little bird winking at me gave me a strange sense of comfort for what lay ahead. I put my face back in the water and continued north.

I must have zoned out because when I next came up, Em wasn't next to me as she normally was and the waves were all of a sudden much, much bigger. Panicking that she might have capsized again, I quickly looked back towards *Friday* to see her next to the RIB. Just then a small side-wave crashed over my head. I looked out to see millions of white horses (the name for the white bit of foam on the top of a cresting wave) all the way out to sea. The weather had changed quite dramatically in a short space of time. I swam back to *Friday*.

'Everything OK, Em?'

'I'm nearly cap ... ' I didn't hear the rest of the sentence as a wave crashed over my head.

'Capsizing!' Em shouted.

The short sharp side-waves were constantly pushing Em to the tipping point. This was less than ideal. If there was ever a time I needed a kayak this was it.

'Are we OK to continue?' I shouted

'Yes, we'll come close, keep going,' Lou shouted as Em clambered aboard. I was now alone at sea. I was about 500 metres from Cape Wrath and could feel the tide pushing me forward. All I needed to do was get past the top and I knew the tide would push me round the corner.

'OK!' I shouted, and carried on swimming. Lou and *Friday* came round the inside of me and we pushed north. It seemed with every stroke the wind and the waves were getting stronger. This was definitely not in the forecast at all.

I was about 100 metres from Cape Wrath when I looked across to *Friday* and noticed the kayak wasn't anywhere to be seen.

'Kayak!' I shouted and pointed.

Em turned around and looked towards the rocks, then bent over to Lou who then looked in the direction she was pointing. In the distance about 30 metres from *Friday* was the kayak, floating upside down and drifting towards the rocks. It had broken free from *Friday*, because of a frayed rope. Shit. It was Jez's kayak. He'd kill me if I lost it. Also, Em had kayaked the entire way from Land's End and needed to complete her adventure. In some small way that kayak had become part of the crew. It needed saving. I started swimming past *Friday* and towards the kayak, which was drifting dangerously close to the cliffs. I was about ten metres from it when I saw the kayak rope in the water. I grabbed it and pulled as hard as I could and started dragging it back to *Friday*. Em had already jumped into the RIB and was waiting for me. Eventually I got there and threw Em the line. I needed to rest a moment as I had no energy to climb into the RIB. The waves were now getting bigger and bigger. When I could I climbed into the RIB and Em and I struggled to pull the kayak on board to empty it. It took the last bit of energy we had.

'Guys. We're getting pushed into the rocks,' Lou shouted.

Friday was facing east and even at full throttle we were still going west, directly towards the towering cliffs.

'I need to get out of here. It's too dangerous.'

'Lou. Can we hold position?' I shouted.

'Only just. Why?'

'I think I need to get back in and swim out of here. The tide will push me north. Let's just get along the top and we can then make for Durness.'

'You sure?' Lou looked worried.

'I think so.'

It seemed the most ridiculous decision ever but the reality was that getting back to this point again tomorrow would be near impossible. With the counter tides and waves I knew I had to finish my swim at least a few miles along the north coast.

'OK. But hurry!'

Em and I tied the kayak down and I put my goggles back on to prepare to get back in the water. Time stood still for a moment and everything went silent. Huge waves were crashing against the wrath-like cliffs about 20 metres to the left. Seagulls were hovering above, gathering in groups, waiting for disaster. The crew were all soaked and getting bashed from left to right. This was it, a moment in life when you're just about to do something and honestly have no idea how it's going to end. I fell backwards into a wave and the serenity turned to immediate chaos as waves crashed over my head and reverberated around my skull. Both *Friday* and I turned north.

'Just swim towards us,' Lou shouted as *Friday* bobbed from side to side and slowly moved away from the dangerous rocks.

I put my head down and faced north, and swam like I have never swum before. Every hand position, every kick, every breath needed to be perfect.

It wasn't long before *Friday* had been swept a few hundred metres from me. I could see *Friday* but judging by Em and Owain looking in all directions they had lost sight of me. I was now truly alone in one of the most inhospitable stretches of the swim. I began to wave. I waved for a good minute but the times when both *Friday* and I were at the crest of a wave at the same time were almost never. It was useless. I began to hyperventilate. What if they never see me? What if they thought I was further ahead? Alone at sea in these waters would most definitely result in my death. I needed to get closer. I started swimming towards them but for every 20 metres I swam the tide and wind was pushing *Friday* 15 metres away from me. Progress was slow. I'd stop swimming every minute and wave but they still couldn't see me. I was knackered. I lay on my back for a moment floating in the sea, letting the now 20 foot waves crash over me. In theory this tide could float me all the way to Durness but it was likely the tide would turn before I reached the Loch and I'd float all the way back to Cape Wrath.

I looked up again and gave another desperate wave. Thankfully this time Em saw me and signalled to Lou and Owain. They turned around and held position as I made my way towards them.

'Seano. That was insane, man. You OK?' Owain shouted as I clambered onto the RIB.

'I'm OK!' was all I could say.

Normally getting back on *Friday* was my safety but the reality was we were still pretty vulnerable. The waves were getting bigger and bigger, and we still needed to do the two-hour journey to Durness. I clambered onto the yacht and we all sat there in silence for moment as we all tried to make sense of what had happened.

'Owain! Steer,' Lou shouted. 'You guys are shit at knots!'

The kayak had fallen off the RIB and was now upside down causing drag. We needed to tie it on better and Lou was certainly the best at knots. Lou and I jumped into the RIB and slowly pulled the kayak back. The waves were too big. The line from the RIB to *Friday* would slacken on the down waves, and then as *Friday* went over the crest of another wave the rope would tighten and like a bucking bronco send me and Lou flying. On the fourth occasion a huge wave crashed over the back of the RIB and Lou's automatically inflatable life jacket blew up in her face knocking her jaw backwards, the line between the RIB and *Friday* then jerked catching underneath her arm.

'Shit, shit,' Lou screamed, before just about managing to get her arm free when the line slackened again. We had just about got the kayak on board and Lou started tying it on properly.

We both then clambered back onto *Friday* and sat down in silence. Everything was wet. Water was pouring through a hole in the side of *Friday* and waves kept crashing over the back of the RIB and into the cockpit. We needed to make Durness as soon as possible and before the tide changed. It was a race against time and the elements and from where we stood, the elements looked like they would win.

Ten minutes later ...

'The RIB!' Owain shouted.

The RIB had completely flipped upside down and was now being dragged with its nose digging deep into the water.

'What about the kayak?'

'Dunno, must be underneath.'

We looked around and then about 20 metres behind us we saw the nose of the kayak slowly floating further and further away. My heart sank.

'We got to leave it Sean, we can't turn around,' Lou said.

I knew she was right. I stood there watching the tip of the kayak rise up and then disappear below the crest of a wave, getting further and further away from us. I felt bad for Em who had done so much in the kayak. She had formed a special bond with it. It had helped me swim in the right direction, provided me with food and most of all was the reason I had Em, whose charisma and enthusiasm had saved me from the brink of giving up many times. The expedition wouldn't be the same without it.

It wasn't long before the kayak had totally disappeared from view and we continued to drag the upside-down RIB towards Durness. Good thing I had sent Arthur's engine back when I did otherwise we'd be dragging that under the water too. Lou radioed the coastguard to inform them that we had lost a red Prijon kayak and if anyone found it they need not to worry about a missing person. An hour later we got a call from the coastguard informing us they found a kayak, but a yellow one. I guess it wasn't just us having issues at sea. Sailing a 26-foot, old wooden yacht in waves nearly as high as she was long was both physically and mentally demanding. *Friday* didn't have a helm wheel and operating a tiller arm was excruciating. Every time a wave hit us from the side it would push the rudder sending the tiller arm shooting left and right. No matter how strong you were you couldn't fight half a ton of water against the rudder. Lou and Owain would take it in turns swapping sides to give each arm a rest as we battled through the waves doing not much more than three miles per hour.

It took almost two hours to reach the safety of Durness and out of the way of the huge Atlantic rollers. The loch was still very choppy but we managed to find a tiny corner to drop two anchors and assess the damage. The first job was to flip the RIB over. We hauled it up on its side and let it fall upright. Everything that was in the RIB was gone, including two oars, an anchor and chain, a jerrycan and spare line. Two of the four bolts on the hull of the RIB used to attach the drag line had completely broken off leaving a gaping hole in the RIB floor, meaning we'd been two bolts away from losing the RIB altogether. The only thing left was Em's paddle. It had somehow bent completely in half, which was a frightening sight that showed just how much force those waves had.

The mood was very tense as we all sat there in silence trying to make sense of what just happened. Cape Wrath had lived up to its name and it's a wonder how we came out the other side without any major injuries. I then thought of the kayak, floating aimlessly around Cape Wrath. It would probably be stuck in tidal limbo for weeks or months, alone with just enough buoyancy to stop it from sinking, putting it out of its misery. I suddenly felt sad again for Em, who now had no kayak to complete her epic adventure. This swim was a challenge for all of us and Em's had come to a premature end. The worst bit was that I could tell Em was disappointed but she never said anything, instead deciding to retire to the front cabin. As tired as I was, I thought I'd give her some space.

The next issue was to see about the leak in the side of *Friday.* Luckily it was just a plug stopper that had come loose and after some hammering we were able to put it back.

Although in the safety of Durness, there was no way we would be able to stay here. It was just way too rough, we couldn't get to shore as we had no oars and, even if we did make it, there was nothing around for miles. If the weather eased up we could head back to Cape Wrath from here, if not then we really needed to get to the safety of Loch Eriboll, a further two or three hours away. One thing was for certain, we weren't going to do either of those today as the idea of going back out to that sea frightened all of us. We had no choice but to try stick it out here for the night and see what tomorrow would bring.

None of us got any sleep at all as we heaved from left to right all night, being thrown around the cabin as we tried to sleep. It was pouring with rain and everything was wet. The weather, although slightly improved, was not good enough for us to attempt Cape Wrath again, so we decided to fight the waves and head to Eriboll. The journey was a lot like yesterday. The RIB flipped over again and, although Owain managed to get it back upright from *Friday*, which to this day defies human power, it was only a matter of time before it was upside down again.

We reached Eriboll three hours later and headed far down the loch towards a mooring buoy that Lou spotted on Google Earth. We arrived at the buoy and all let out a sigh as we hooked up to it, knowing we were finally safe and could actually let go of all the tension built up over the last few days. The weather forecast suggested gale force eight winds for the next four days so it looked like we were here for a while.

Eriboll was a beautiful loch and our mooring buoy was just below an idyllic white stone cottage tucked into some trees. It took us about an hour to spot it but there, below the house and under a tree, was a very old kayak that looked like it hadn't been used for years.

'Lou, look,' Em shouted and pointed. We all knew what she was thinking. 'I wonder if they would let me use it to carry on?'

'I can't see why not. Doesn't look like anyone uses it.'

'Right! I'm going to ask!'

'Hold fire, I'm coming to shore too. I got a serious case of cabin fever.' Owain shouted.

Owain was right. We really needed to get to land for the sake of our sanity.

We all climbed into the RIB and then stopped and looked at each other. We had no way of paddling. I jumped back into *Friday* to get Em's broken paddle and we snapped it completely. The plan was to use it like an Indian canoe paddle, with one person paddling on each side. Owain and Lou took up the task.

In theory this should be easy, but with tired arms and one person inevitably rowing harder than the other we were just going in circles. Em and I were in stitches at the thought of someone watching us. It took about ten minutes to paddle the 50 metre stretch to land and by the time we landed, Owain had given up, Lou was using one paddle in the front of the boat by herself and Em and I were crying with laughter. It was exactly what we needed. A bit of team spirit to make us forget about Cape Wrath.

While we tied up the RIB, Em went off on her own to knock on the cottage door. We figured a girl by herself was far less intimidating than four dirty grubby people might have been.

Moments later, Em waved to us from the porch so we went up to the cottage.

We were greeted at the door by a very friendly woman. I was half expecting an old lady to be living out here but she was young, in her late thirties.

'Helloo there, come in, come in. I'm Fiona. Tea anyone?' She said.

We all sat around the kitchen counter telling her about what had just happened to us while Fiona just kept repeating, 'You're mad, you're all mad, you are,' and then laughing.

Fiona had heard something about the swim but didn't really know much and was very interested in everything we had done.

It couldn't have been five minutes before the phone rang.

'Hello?' Fiona answered. 'Oh no! It wasn't four men. Two guys and two girls. It's that swimmer guy. Remember from the news. And his crew. We just having tea. When are you back? ... OK, see you soon.' And she put the phone down.

'This is what happens up here. A fisherman out in the bay saw the four of you coming up to the cottage and was worried so phoned John, my husband, to tell him so that was him calling in. Word spreads fast around here doesn't it?'

That was hilarious. I kind of liked that they were all looking out for each other though.

Half an hour later, John arrived.

'What's this? Tea? Come one. You folk need a dram.'

And he went to the cupboard and whipped out a bottle of good single malt.

We spent a wonderful afternoon chatting, drinking tea and whisky, and learning all about the clans and landowners in northern Scotland. By the time we had to head back to *Friday* we had already been invited for breakfast. Fiona and John had taken the notion of hospitality to a whole new level. Em didn't think it was the right time to ask for their kayak so decided to leave it for now. They were so accommodating we didn't want to be seen to take advantage of that.

The next morning, with a slightly heavy head after too many whiskies, we rowed in circles to shore and had a delicious scrambled egg breakfast. After an hour, Em hesitantly asked if we could borrow that kayak. Without even a flinch John was up and went to the shed and brought out another kayak.

'This one is better if you want this one instead, but it needs a few holes fixed, which I can do for you.'

'Wow, thanks John but honestly, the one on the beach is fine.'

'Are you sure. It's nay bother.'

'No, honestly John,' Em insisted. 'You've done enough.'

'OK, then. I guess you'll need a paddle too. I seen you guys going in circles this morning,' John laughed. 'What else you need? I have loads of shite here.'

I'd never met such a hospitable and giving family before. They were up there with Steve and Kate from Cornwall. Such generosity. Em now had a kayak and a paddle and could continue her own adventure.

That afternoon, we headed back to Cape Wrath. We wouldn't be able to do it in one go so would stay in Durness for the night and then make our way to my start point tomorrow. John and Fiona and their kids came out to *Friday* with us, which was a nice send-off as we sailed away to their cheers. After a few days where all hope was lost, or broken, John and Fiona had come to the rescue. We owed them a lot.

We found the same little bay in Durness and dropped two anchors again, and had Stowaways and wine for dinner. Tomorrow we'd go back to where it all went horribly wrong. To say we were nervous was an understatement. Our few days in Eriboll with John and Fiona had been good for us, but it had meant we pushed from our minds the reality of the situation, from fear more than anything. Even though conditions we better they still weren't ideal. Tonight the clocks were going back, which meant winter really was just about upon us. I couldn't believe that it had been a month since we were on Eigg. It felt like yesterday.

We were all on edge as we headed out of Durness and back into hell. By the time we reached my GPS point, the waves were way too big for Em to kayak so it looked like I'd be on my own again. Rain started pelting down as each wave crested and crashed, often coming right over the back of the cockpit and into the main cabin. We needed to get on with it. I jumped in and started swimming. The waves were around 30 feet high as the wind pushed *Friday* away from me. It was too windy for them to stay near me so the strategy was to get pushed ahead 100 metres and then turn around, hold position till I arrived and then do the same. Those times when they went ahead were the most nerve-racking. If they had engine failure, or lost my location in the water, they'd get swept away from me and I'd definitely not survive being alone on this section as there was nowhere to go ashore.

I carried on pushing through, almost surfing down the huge waves, my heart racing every time *Friday* got more than 100 metres from me. Sometimes when she went into the trough of a wave even her mast would disappear from sight. When *Friday* was at the crest of a wave and I was in the trough of the wave, I'd be looking right up into the heavens at her silhouette, sharp and dramatic against a dark and moody sky. At times she was heeling over at such an angle I could see most of the one side of her hull out of the water. The first thing I thought was she needed a clean. There was a lot of seaweed growing on her.

I swam for three hours, covering seven miles, and made it just past the entrance to Durness before Lou decided we need to make for shelter. To this day I'll never forget swimming in those monstrous waves, feeling alone and helpless in an ever-changing sea. I had, however, done it and survived. Now at least, even if we were faced with similar waves tomorrow, we knew we could deal with them. In a weird way I wish we had attempted to swim in big waves like this before but, on thinking back, there wasn't a time when they were ever this huge. Did we miss some potential swimming days for no reason? If I managed to swim today then surely I'd have been able to swim in most of the last bad weather days and therefore probably have completed the swim already. But then, although nothing major had gone wrong, I felt both *Friday* and I were operating at the brink of our capabilities in these big waves, pushing ourselves to the very edge. I couldn't help but think that if we kept doing that, sooner or later something was going to break. Either me or *Friday*, either of which would result in the swim coming to a premature and possibly disastrous end.

An hour later we were in a small bay between Eriboll and Durness tucked up ready for what the morning would bring us.

Just before heading out, a fisherman came over to us and said he'd caught too many crabs and lobster and wanted to know if we wanted any. We laughed as that's not a question you get asked often. We were then presented with two lobsters and five crabs.

'I've always wanted crabs from a fisherman,' joked Owain.

Tonight's dinner was going to be amazing and my mouth was watering already. The same fisherman also offered to give us some diesel and he'd drop it off in the morning at our next anchorage, which Lou pointed out a few miles away. People up here took the concept of friendliness to a whole new level.

I managed only four and a half miles in the afternoon session before the waves really were too high and the RIB kept capsizing. John's kayak was now on the deck of *Friday* as we didn't want to risk losing it too. Em really did not want to get back in the water and I think had come to terms with her adventure ending at Cape Wrath, which is still technically the length of Britain, I guess.

That night we spent a good hour trying to download cooking instructions for crab and lobster with only GPRS internet, and then another two hours trying to break and eat crab without the proper tools. Luckily we had a hammer, which was doing a good job even if most of the crab landed up on the manky floor.

When we awoke the next day, there were two cans of diesel on the deck of *Friday*. The fisherman had come early and dropped them off. I felt bad for not being awake to say thanks.

Progress was slow again as huge waves crashed over me and often right over *Friday* too. For some reason Em and Owain were starting to get really seasick again, their bodies just not used to dealing with this level of wave-battering. The coastguard kept calling us too as apparently people along the shore were calling in a boat doing circles in pretty big waves. Good to know there were people out there looking out for us. I really was pushing the line of safety versus determination but had every faith in Lou. If something did however go wrong, people would have every right to say, ‘well, you deserved it for being so stupid’. I’d like to think we were being bold and charting new ground. Nothing worth achieving is ever easy.

That evening we made it to the Kyle of Tongue and the final safe anchorage till Thurso a good 30 miles away. In order to make the next section we’d need three days of good weather. Instead, as fate would have it, Lou informed us that we had four days of gale-force winds. What were the chances of getting three good weather days along the north coast of Scotland? It was the 29 October. Soon it would be November. NOVEMBER!! If, two months ago when Lou joined, I had thought I’d still be swimming in November, would I have continued? It’s impossible to know the answer to that, but I think ignorance certainly helped us all take one day at a time.

Luckily we found a small hotel, the only one still open around there, that had Wi-Fi so decided to make camp there for four days. After the second day, the landlady asked me to sign the visitors book and there, a few spaces above my name, was Usain Bolt’s. God only know what the world’s fastest runner was doing up here in the middle of winter. Now they had the world’s slowest swimmer to add to their list of athletes who’d stayed in the hotel.

It was a tough four days constantly looking out to sea wondering if in fact I could be swimming. My mind was going crazy thinking of all the times I hadn’t swum when I might have been able to. The time I spent looking for a skipper, the times we missed the tide, the times I skipped a session to do errands. All these things meant I was in Scotland in November and had surely missed my weather window. Would I have to come back next year and complete the swim? That would be pointless.

The problem was there were no safe anchorages if the wind was more than force three or four, and it had been five or six for weeks now. The ten-day forecast didn't look any better. I was thinking of every possible option and one even included swimming on my own. There was a beach every seven miles or so along the coast so technically I could do that with land support. I was also feeling guilty for keeping the crew away from their families and businesses. Lou was only meant to stay with us for ten days. She had now been here for over 60 days, not what she was expecting when she tweeted me from sunny Turkey all that time ago.

On day three, while in the hotel, we got a call from a fisherman saying our RIB had sunk. We ran down to the harbour wall where we had tied the RIB up and it was upside down, one of the sides completely deflated and sinking. The waves had picked up and the rope had snapped, and the RIB had been trashed around against the wall for the past few hours. Now I owed Jez a kayak and Arthur a RIB. We sat there wondering what to do as we now had no way of getting back to *Friday*, anchored about 60 metres offshore. Lou went off and came back a few moments later.

'Right guys. I've spoken to my brother and Nomad Sailing is paying for a night in the hotel for us.'

What legends Lou and her brother where. This would give us the night to find another RIB. Maybe there was one on eBay?

There weren't any RIBs on eBay so we racked our brains for ages about what to do and the only option we kept coming back to was to ask John if he had one. I hated that they had done so much for us yet we were still asking for more help, but it really was our only option. John and Fiona were all too welcoming, and later that evening they came round and brought us their small inflatable RIB. It wouldn't fit all four of us but we could take it in turns ferrying back and forth to *Friday*.

14

GETTING TO THE START LINE IS HARD, BUT THE FINISH LINE, EVEN HARDER

It was time to go back out and try to push at least a few miles to get as far past Tongue as possible. The plan was to get about four miles east of Tongue and then come back for safe anchoring. It was unlikely I'd be able to do this in one session so we set our alarms at 4.30am and started the commute. For some reason, I started to feel a strange sense of panic. This was the first time I had felt this way. I really, really, did not want to get back in that water.

At 6am, however, I had to get back in and started making progress east. Because of commute logistics, I only had three hours to do my best. I managed six miles in those three hours before the tide started to turn, so we went to the nearest anchorage, which was a mooring buoy in a little cove off Neave Island. The island was idyllic, although none of us were in the mood to explore. Instead we sat out the tide, keeping to ourselves. I spent most of the time lying on my bunk wondering how on earth I was going to make it to Thurso if I was only managing six miles a day.

We set out for the evening session just to see if we could do some mileage, anything to get us closer to Thurso. It had a safe harbour and was also so close to John O'Groats it certainly gave us the sense that the swim was almost done. Surely nothing could stop us once we were there?

The days were quite short now, which meant it was dark almost as soon as I got in the water. I swam for about an hour, but because of a heavy headwind I was out-swimming *Friday* and the waves were too big for Em to kayak with me. I decided that night swimming with these waves was just not sensible so decided to stop there. Feeling pretty deflated, we headed back to Neave Island to the safety of the mooring buoy. The weather had drastically changed, rain was coming in at right angles. By the time we got back to the buoy it was high water, so the buoy was a foot below the surface, which made hooking up to it impossible. It was pitch black and Lou kept trying to get as close as possible for Owain to grab the buoy with the boat hook, but we kept getting blown off it. Eventually he managed to grab the buoy but a huge wave hit us, ripping the boat hook from Owain's hands.

'Let's drop the anchors,' Lou shouted over the sound of crashing waves and hard rain.

'OK,' Owain replied, jumping into action and dropped both anchors near the buoy. It wasn't by any means ideal but we had no option.

It was 9pm and this was possibly the roughest we had ever anchored. *Friday* kept swirling around in all directions as waves whirlpooled in the small bay. At 2am, after no sleep at all, we heard the anchor dragging quite significantly. This was not a good sign. We really needed to get on the mooring buoy.

'Right guys. The tide is lower, we should be able to get on the buoy,' Lou suggested. Owain and I got up, put on our life jackets and waterproofs, and went outside. Em took the torch to shine on the buoy.

The idea was to try to lasso the buoy with a smaller line, then bring it towards us and attach it to a stronger line. It took Lou about 15 attempts as *Friday* heaved from left to right but she eventually got the rope around it.

'Sean, hold this and try to bring the buoy up a bit so I can get the bigger line under it.'

She gave me the rope and without thinking I did something very stupid. Instead of just holding the rope with my fingers, I wrapped it around my knuckles. About ten seconds later, while pulling as hard as I could, my knuckles white, *Friday* was hit by a huge wave and heaved a few feet away from the buoy. If I had just been holding the rope it would have been pulled from my hands and I'd have suffered rope burn at worst. With the rope around my knuckles I was pulled across the deck and my hand got jammed between the rope and the pulpit. I wanted to scream but kept my nerve so as not to distract Lou from getting the buoy hooked up. I was pinned down and unable to move my hand. I thought my knuckles were going to explode, pop right out the top of my hand. Luckily *Friday* then pitched back towards the buoy, slackening the line a bit and I was able to free myself. Shafts of pain shot up my arm. I couldn't move my fingers. At that moment, Lou was able to attach the line to the buoy and rejoiced.

'Come on boys. We can sleep now. Two anchors and a mooring buoy. We're not going anywhere.'

I got back into bed clutching my hand. I didn't want to tell anyone so just took some painkillers and hoped it would be better in the morning.

None of us had any sleep as the weather got progressively worse all night. My hand seemed to be OK and looked like just a bruise, which was a relief. We didn't have much internet but just managed to get a forecast, which suggested bad weather for another four days. The problem was we were now stuck on Neave Island. It was too rough to leave the bay or go to shore. Instead we were confined to *Friday* all day, bobbing from side to side, slowly going mad.

The next day we decided to attempt to go back to the safety of Tongue. Lou and Owain got up early and prepared to pull anchor. One anchor came up but the second one was truly stuck. After two hours of trying everything, including starting the engine and trying to free it by going back and forth, nothing was working.

'We're gonna have to cut it unfortunately,' Lou said, quite annoyed. 'I've never lost an anchor and was hoping I never would.'

Cutting an anchor is cause for ridicule in the sailing world, mostly friendly banter, but Lou knew her brother would never let this one go.

'Um Lou, we don't have a hacksaw,' Owain said.

'Really! What do we have?'

'Nothing. A steak knife is all I can find.'

I remembered I had a Leatherman, which had a small metal file on it.

'Try this, Owain,' I said handing him the file.

It wasn't ideal but it was our only option.

It took two hours to file down the anchor chain as we all took 20-minute shifts giving it a go. Eventually we got it free and let the chain slip over the edge and disappear into the depths. We now only had one anchor and it wasn't a good one either. We really did need some good weather to get to Thurso as anchoring safely just got a whole lot more difficult.

We limped back to Tongue and settled back into the hotel, where the landlady was surprised to see us again. It was really depressing being back there, not because of the hotel, but because it felt we had been there forever, not able to make any real progress. I had XC Weather on my laptop and kept staring at it, refreshing the page every few minutes but it really looked like we had missed the weather window. I was now pretty low. I put my head in my hands and closed my eyes wondering whether or not I'd ever be able to finish the swim. From here it seemed very unlikely.

'Hey, Bro!' I heard someone say. I recognised that voice. I looked up. There, standing in that little pub in northern Scotland, was my good friend, Dave Cornthwaite.

'Dave!' I got up and gave him a huge hug. I was good to see a friend from the real world.

'What are you doing here?'

'I just thought I'd come and say hi, you know, to show my support.'

'You're kidding!'

'Of course not, mate. Right, first things first, what are you all drinking?' Dave went to the bar and came back with a tray of drinks.

'Mate, how'd you get here?' I asked, still a bit overwhelmed to see him.

'You wouldn't believe it. A train, plane, two more trains and a taxi from Thurso. The taxi driver is waiting for me outside. I have to get a train back in a few hours.'

Dave had literally just wanted to come say hi and tell me how well I was doing. He informed me that loads of people were wishing me luck for the last bit and how I mustn't give up. It was a great boost to team morale and most of all my mental state. Dave stayed for a few hours as we chatted about all things swimming and having a bit of banter as to whose swim was harder. (Dave swam 1,000 miles down the Missouri River the year before and had Em in his crew.) When Dave left, I was feeling a whole lot more positive about completing the swim. He certainly saved me from falling deeper into a depressing downward spiral.

It was time to try and get to Thurso. The weather was just about good enough for us to potentially anchor on the east side of Strathy Point, the halfway point between here and

Thurso. I needed to make it that far, which was ten miles and almost double what I've done in the last few sessions.

We set our alarms for 3am and I was in the water at 6am. I gave it my all for about half an hour then, as luck would have it, I really needed a shit again.

'Just do it in your suit,' Em shouted from *Friday*. Getting out of the water, out of my suit and going to the loo would take at least 20 minutes, which we didn't have time for. Quite honestly, I considered shitting in my wetsuit that day but then decided against it and went aboard. Twenty minutes later, I was back in the water. My arms were burning with my higher stroke rate but I didn't care. I needed to make Strathy. It truly was winter now and with every breath I could see snow-covered mountains in the distance. Not even Scottish people swim on the north coast in November and for good reason.

Somehow I managed 10.3 miles and we made Strathy. It was time to head for anchorage. After an hour trying various spots we had no option but to head for Thurso, which was at least six hours away against tide. It would have been quicker to go back to Tongue with the tide but to get back here in the morning would have meant using all the good tide or fighting the bad tide for hours. And no one really wanted to go back to Tongue again.

We woke up at 3am and started the journey back to Strathy. Halfway there *Friday*'s engine cut out again. My heart sank. This was not the time for engine failure. We took up the floorboards and checked everywhere including the fuse we had changed earlier. Nothing seemed wrong. She was barely turning over. There was a moment of silence as we all just sat there floating aimlessly at sea. Had *Friday*'s engine finally given up this time? She had done us proud. Chugging away for the past four and a half months, she had covered the same distance as sailing from Africa to South America. Not bad for a 52-year-old boat with a 20-year-old engine.

'What now Lou?' I asked.

'Well, we'll have to call a ...' Lou paused and looked towards some line running overboard. She got up and grabbed and tried to pull it but it was stuck. She leant over the side of *Friday*.

'Ah, you bastard,' she said while tugging at the rope. 'Looks like this is the problem. Line caught in the prop.'

This was what sailors call the propeller, and it was potentially a good result as we might be able to free it, or a very bad result if it was too stuck.

I was already in my suit so it made sense for me to dive down and try set it free. The prop was a good one and a half metres down and the rough waves made diving down quite tricky. I examined the prop. The line had been wrapped around the shaft about eight times and deeply imbedded. I tried to tug it but nothing came free. I came up to the surface to breathe again. I was surprisingly bad at holding my breath, I'd have thought my cardio was better by now.

I dived back down and tried counter-turning the prop, which kind of worked. I could do one half-turn before having to come back for a breath. I repeated this around

20 times, with each turn slowly tugging on the rope while trying to avoid the rudder smashing me in the face every time *Friday* moved in the wind.

After what seemed forever down there, the rope came free and I climbed back on board. My right arm was quite tired from holding on to the line for so long. I did, however, feel extremely warm from the exertion and getting back in the water wasn't as daunting as it had been.

The waves had calmed down drastically, which was a nice change from being dunked every few minutes. My route towards Thurso needed to take a detour because of a nuclear power station on the edge of the cliffs that had a two-mile exclusion zone out to sea. I did wonder what water-based deformities I'd get if I swam through some radiation water? Maybe I'd finally grow gills and become Kevin Costner in *Waterworld*. At least then maybe I'd be able to swim faster.

After a few hours, Thurso was finally in sight, I was there. I felt a huge weight off my shoulders and started to feel suddenly emotional. I immediately vomited in the water, my body giving up slightly, much like those who collapse on the finish line of a marathon. What was meant to be five days to get to Thurso from Cape Wrath landed up being nearly two weeks, and the last few days had certainly been taxing on all of us. I ended my session three miles from Thurso and we went back to the harbour to celebrate. Reaching Thurso surely meant the swim was nearly finished. We moored up and went to the local harbour-side café for some food.

As soon we entered the café, a fisherman recognised me.

'Oi, you're the swimmer aren't you?' he said, his mouth still full of food.

'Yes sir, it's pretty much in the bag, just arrived in Thurso this afternoon,' I said quite proudly, my head uncharacteristically high for the first time, ever.

'Amazing mate. Just the Pentland Firth now. Good luck there!'

'Pentland Firth?' I asked.

'Yes, Britain's most notorious stretch of water,' he said grinning, bits of baked beans stuck in his teeth. Luckily I had already vomited everything out my stomach otherwise I might have vomited again.

Not another one? It seems everywhere is Britain's most dangerous stretch of water.

'I'm sure you've thought about it but I've seen tankers go backwards there. The flood can be up to 16 knots.'

'Thanks but we'll do it at slack so should be fine hopefully.'

'I'm sure you will. Sterling effort so far, well done.'

We all went and sat down.

'Lou, is Pentland Firth really that bad?' I asked nervously.

'Yeah, it's bad at the wrong times but it'll be fine, especially after what we dealt with at Cape Wrath. The tidal atlas says only go when there is force three or less and wind with tide. Apparently even a two wind against tide makes the section pretty hairy.'

It's not over till it's over. We hadn't had a force two or three for weeks. There seemed to always be one more major hurdle and, according to some of the quite terrifying YouTube videos we watched about the Pentland Firth, it certainly looked like this could be the worst of the worst if we didn't plan it correctly. They say getting to the start line is the hardest part of any expedition. Yes that was true, but getting to the finish line this time was most certainly even harder.

That evening we took a taxi into Thurso to send some emails to everyone as it looked like my end date, if the Pentland Firth didn't kill us, would be Monday 11 November at midday, which gave us a few days' grace if the weather did pick up. My mum and Em and Owain's family wanted to come up, so needed some warning, as well as Jez who didn't want to miss the end. Speedo also wanted to be there, which was nice as I couldn't have even started the swim without them.

After the emails, we got the same taxi driver, who was really impressed with the swim and didn't charge us for the return trip. We then settled into the harbour-side pub until it was time for bed, anything to minimise time cramped up on *Friday*. Conditions were now only barely liveable on her with everything completely wet, mouldy and pretty disgusting as housekeeping had taken a backseat now that we were so close to the end.

An hour later our friendly taxi driver came back into the pub with a wad of cash in his hand.

'I'm so impressed with your swim I drove round all the pubs and got some donations for the charity. Here's about £100.'

We all stood there in shock. What wonderful generosity. We offered to buy him a pint but he said he needed to head off and with that disappeared, not wanting any form of recognition. It was gestures like this that made those long hard days seem worth it.

I continued to vomit repeatedly in the water all session as I swam past Thurso and around Dunnet Head, the tide getting stronger and stronger the more into the Pentland Firth I swam. At one point I was doing five knots, which was my second fastest pace after the Mull of Kintyre. The plan was to finish with enough tide so that we could get to Stroma three miles away. Lou pulled me out and we started to head for the safety of the small harbour on the island.

'Guess what, Ginge!' Em shouted as I got on board. She looked excited.

'We're only seven miles from John O'Groats. Seven miles, Ginge! Amazing!'

'No way!' I looked ahead but couldn't quite see the harbour. I'd learnt now not to celebrate too early but there were butterflies in my stomach. These last seven miles were potentially the hardest if conditions weren't perfect. If I didn't swim hard enough I'd get swept right past John O'Groats towards Norway.

We got within 500 metres of Stroma when the tide turned and within a few minutes we were going backwards.

'Shit!' Lou said. 'Pushed it too close. We're going to have to go back to Thurso.'

We turned around and all of a sudden were zooming along at six knots. This Pentland Firth really was strong.

We made it back to Thurso. It was *Friday* and I was due to finish on Monday so we decided to take Saturday off so that I could rest up. I'd then do most of the last seven miles to John O'Groats on Sunday and then the final bit on Monday. Sunday was also looking to be the best weather for the notorious Pentland Firth.

It was a strange last rest day as we all felt a little lost. There were no errands to do, no fuel to get, no food to buy, no route to plot, instead we all went off and did our own thing. I wandered the streets of Thurso aimlessly for hours trying to take in the last four and a half months. Part of me felt like it had gone quickly, but the other part of me felt like it was a lifetime ago we were all throwing up on *Friday* in Sennen Cove.

Sunday came and it was time to fight the Firth. We used a lot of the good tide to get to my last swim point and arrived a few hours before slack when the tide wasn't as strong. The weather was as good as it would ever be and I jumped back in and swam as fast as I could, my shoulders burning like they have never burned before. A mile later I could see John O'Groats ahead of me. We all cheered.

'Six miles to go, Ginge,' Em shouted.

I carried on. It was strange swimming in the Firth. The water was swirling in all directions. There were also loads of small whirlpools, only about an inch wide but would funnel down into the depths below me, like small inverted tornadoes.

'Five miles!' the crew shouted.

I pushed on not really thinking about anything other than that photo of John O'Groats Harbour I had on my laptop.

'Sean!' I heard Lou shout. 'We need to change direction!'

Apparently I wasn't swimming fast enough and on our current course I'd miss the harbour and be swept right past it.

'Follow us!' *Friday* changed course by over 90 degrees. It seemed drastic.

'Are you sure?' I asked from the water, and then felt guilty because I had no way of knowing my direction and also for questioning Lou's judgement, which was just plain ridiculous. She was a yacht master instructor.

'Swim, mate. Harder!' Owain shouted.

I was now facing in almost the opposite direction to John O'Groats, which was at my seven o'clock, behind me.

'Harder, mate,' Owain shouted again.

I was already pushing my hardest and not really sure I had much more in me. I closed my eyes for moment and gave ten hard strokes. I somehow felt better with my eyes closed but knew very well my cheese rolling shoulder was sending me off to the left again so opened them. I was right. I needed to head more to the right.

'Four miles!'

'Three miles!'

'Two miles!'

Those last few miles flew by as I reached an all-time record speed of eight knots, swimming in effect, backwards.

'One mile, Ginge. We're out of the main current. You can slow down now. It's in the bag, mate.'

I started to well up inside my goggles a bit. I had pretty much done it. I swam a further few hundred metres as I tried to compose myself before getting out to do the last section in the morning.

It was 11.45am on 11 November 2013 as I put on my cold, piss-smelling, wetsuit for the last time. I walked along the coast to get in alone without *Friday*, who was moored up in John O'Groats Harbour. I didn't need her today. She had done me proud and looked rugged and adventurous tied up along the harbour wall. I asked Em to kayak in with me. She deserved to do the final section after all her hard work.

I got in the water and Em kayaked from the harbour to meet me in the water.

'You've done it, Ginge! You've proved them all wrong,' Em said.

'Thanks Em for everything,' I said, struggling to get the words out. 'I couldn't have done it without you. Honestly!'

I was trying my best to stay strong. I had so many things running through my head. All those emails from people saying it was a publicity stunt. That it wasn't possible. It wasn't a real swim because I wore a wetsuit. That Sennen Cove café blog. All those people who doubted that this swim was possible – in your face!

I had completed the swim. Yes, it had taken 70 days longer than I had expected. Yes, it was much, much harder than I could ever have imagined, but I hadn't given up, none of us had given up.

Without the crew I would never have been able to make it.

Jez's gung-ho approach and anti-establishment philosophy certainly meant I made headway where certain skippers might have not continued.

Owain's level-headedness, mechanical skills, way with words in drumming up support, not to mention his knack for fishing, were huge assets to the swim.

Lou's ability to always find the best anchorages and elite sailing skills when conditions really were against us, and her enthusiasm for a proper adventure gave us all the comfort that we'd be safe in her hands.

And finally Em, my mum on the swim. She never wavered in her hard work or positive attitude as she looked after me for four and a half months, making sure I had food when I needed it, rinsing my pissy wetsuits, kayaking in the freezing cold water, never once complaining all the while being petrified of the water. Having her enthusiasm right by my side, always smiling, helped me when I was at my lowest.

Those last few hundred metres seemed to take forever as I made my way into the harbour to the cheers of a handful of people, most of whom lived nearby. I knew there was going to be some media there; it was live on BBC News and various other broadcasters were there too with their vans with satellite dishes on the roofs, exactly like you see in the movies.

I thought I should probably say something important, something inspiring for other people who want to do something that others say can't be done. I wanted to tell people two things.

One was that you should never let someone else's opinion (and opinion is all it is) of your ability affect the decisions you make in life. They don't know how hard you want it, what you're truly capable of. If I had listened to those opinions I wouldn't ever have got in the water 135 days ago.

I also wanted to tell people that we are all physically and mentally stronger than we think we are.

I wanted to tell people to aim a little higher, push a little harder, because I think they'd surprise themselves.

I had this speech all in my mind as I approached the slipway. And then, as soon as my foot hit land it all became too overwhelming. I burst out crying. Tears filled up my goggles, so I took them off and threw them away. I then felt my eyes burning. Someone had opened a bottle of champagne and sprayed it all over me. I was weeping and could barely talk and now couldn't see, and all I could hear were the voices of journalists shouting questions at me. It was all too much.

I didn't care about anything anymore as a huge sense of relief came over me.

No more jellyfish stings to the face, no more vomiting, no more toes that might fall off, no more cold, wet, sleepless nights and I could finally hang up my wetsuit.

I was done. I had finally achieved what many thought was impossible.

I had just become the first person in history to swim the length of Britain.

I never did manage to tell everyone what I wanted to. Instead I cried like a baby and talked about my beard a lot.

EPILOGUE

Three weeks later ...

I finally made it home. The three weeks after the swim were a whirlwind of rushing around the country doing magazine interviews, TV appearances and giving talks. It was surreal and at times I had to pinch myself to see if I was dreaming, most memorably when I sat next to Jason Donovan on *The One Show* sofa, which resulted a bombardment of Tweets from people saying, 'Wow, Kylie is looking hairy nowadays.'

I've been able to open my emails with confidence, knowing that I wasn't going to get any of the 'I told you it wasn't possible' or 'I'm sorry you didn't make it' messages like I received after my cycle ride. All the blogs, forums and critics have gone quiet, and instead been replaced with emails from people saying things like, 'I was too scared to cycle the length of Britain but seeing as you've swum it has giving me the confidence to get on my bike and do it.'

After sorting through my inbox, one email catches my attention; it's one from Jez. The subject is 'all moored up'. I knew instantly what he was talking about. At the end of the swim Jez had emailed me to ask what I was doing with *Friday*. He wanted to know if I wanted to sell her to him. It was a hard decision as *Friday* had been such a huge part of my adventure, but after much thought I realised that I didn't have the skill or knowledge to get her back to her former glory and if one person did, it was Jez. After my arrival in John O'Groats, Jez then took *Friday* round to Wick to rest up for the winter. He went on to repair everything, sand her down, paint her and then sailed her through the Caledonian Canal. I was really sad to see her go but it's nice to know she is still in the family.

After the swim, Em was offered some great opportunities working for adventure magazines and still emails me to contribute pieces about things I'm up to. That's after she wrote about being the first woman to kayak the length of Britain of course.

Owain now runs his adventure media consultancy business, which he started after the swim. He also arranges the talks I do in schools, so I can hopefully inspire kids to think big and not listen to people who try to tell them what they are capable of.

Lou went back to her business Nomad Sailing to relieve Jim, her brother, after he held the fort for a lot longer than expected! I managed to go out on her amazing yacht for a day when the *Guardian* filmed a feature about my swim. It was a little bit nicer than *Friday* ...

I also finally reached my £10,000 target for War Child, most of it coming in after the swim. It was nice to see the total jumping up every time I did an interview and certainly made the long journeys rushing around worth it.

Swimming the length of Britain was the hardest thing I'll probably ever do, but it certainly has given me the confidence that, if I work really hard, surround myself with the right people and never give up, I can achieve whatever I put my mind to.

ACKNOWLEDGEMENTS

My family. Mum Babette, dad Tony and sister Kerry for always supporting me in my adventures. I've put you through hell over the years but you've always supported my decisions in life. Thank you.

My crew. Jez, Em, Owain and Lou. You guys made this adventure what is was. We had an incredible time together. Thank you for giving me so much of your time.

Sally at Speedo. Out of the 350 companies I approached, you were the only one who believed in the swim as much as I did and were willing to take the risk. It was a pleasure working with you and thank you for replying to all of my many emails.

Crowdfunders. Without all of you I couldn't have finished the swim. I've mentioned you all in the next few pages but

I wanted to single out one person. A huge thank you to Anthony Riches. You know why.

CROWDFUNDERS

A huge thank you to the following people for helping me finish the swim. I couldn't have done it without you.

Denise Adams
Tracey Apperley
Thomas Arbs
Liz Barraclough
Karah Bausch
H J Beales
Christine Bellamy
Rebecca Bennett
Keely Beresford
Ali Berry
Mathew Bevan
David Bickerstaff
Sylvia Boker-Price
Adam Boon
Joe Boyce
Stuart Bradburn
Neil Bridgstock
Jo Bridle
Heather Bright
Adam Bristowe
Poul Brix
Debbie Brown
Malcolm Burns
David Butler
Will Carnegie
Tracy Chapman
Jackie Cobell
Tristan Cochrane

Adam Colburn
Colin Constance
Annie Cooper
John Corvesor
John Coxon
Gabrielle Cross
Amy-Catherine Cunningham
Alan Curr
Sean Curran
H S R Davenport
Sadie Davies
David & Samantha Dewar
Dizmon
Tracy Doyle
Nelson Edwards
Verla Edwards
Mark Everard
Sean Fane
Steven Feeney
Philippe Flamand
Jonathan Ford
Alex Gaskell
Gary Gibbons
Izi Glover
Nicola Goodchild
Simon Griffiths
Georgie Guernsey
Rachel Hall
Robert Hall-McNair
Linus Halton
Monica Hardwick
Lesley Hargrave
Susan Harper
Philip Harris
Mrs A Harrison
Bee Heller
Darren Henwood
F Hickie
Desmond Hodgkiss
Gary Hurr
Tony Ingles
Katherine Irvine
Chris Jackson
Daniel Jarman
D Jones
Michael Jones
David Kay
Rupert Kelton
Leila Ken
Mark Kleanthous
Gwendolen A Lansley
Adam Latcham
Sarah Learoyd
Bruce Loxley
Martin MacGilp
James MacKeddie
Rob Macleod
George Mahood